Ōoku

⬤ THE INNER CHAMBERS

by **Fumi Yoshinaga**

VOL. **12**

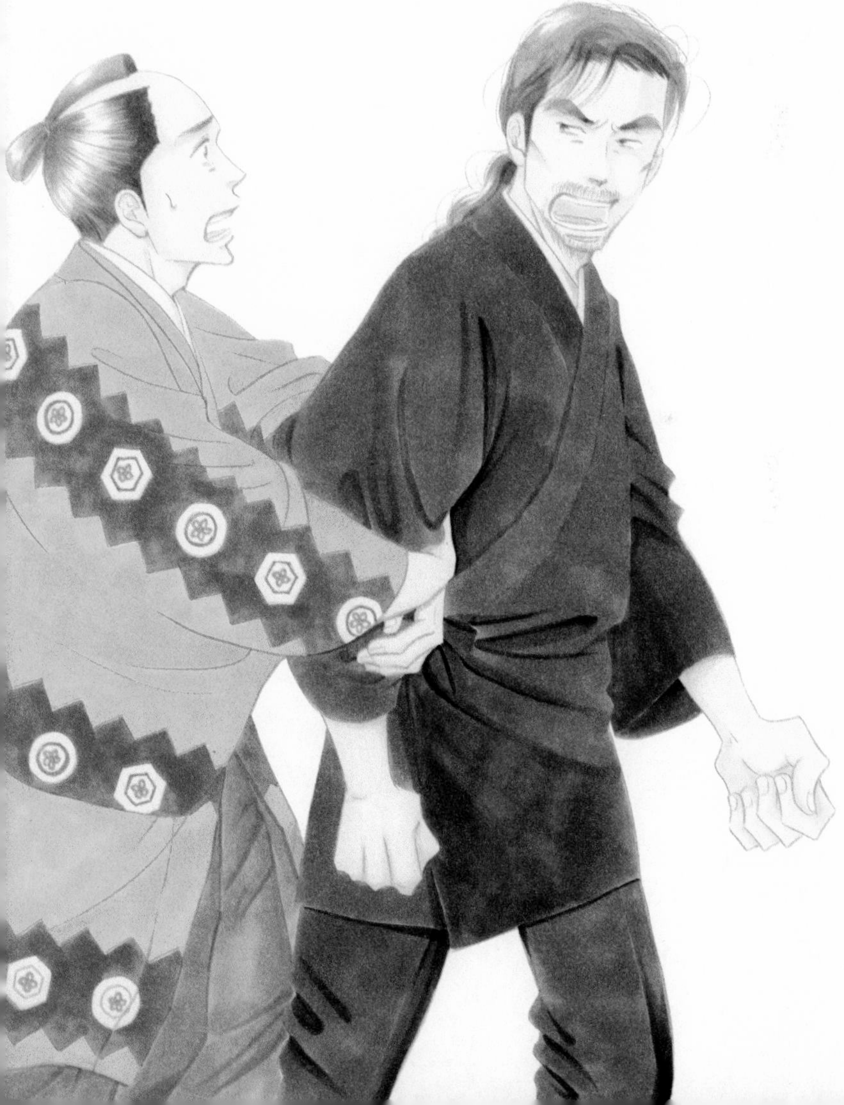

TABLE *of* CONTENTS

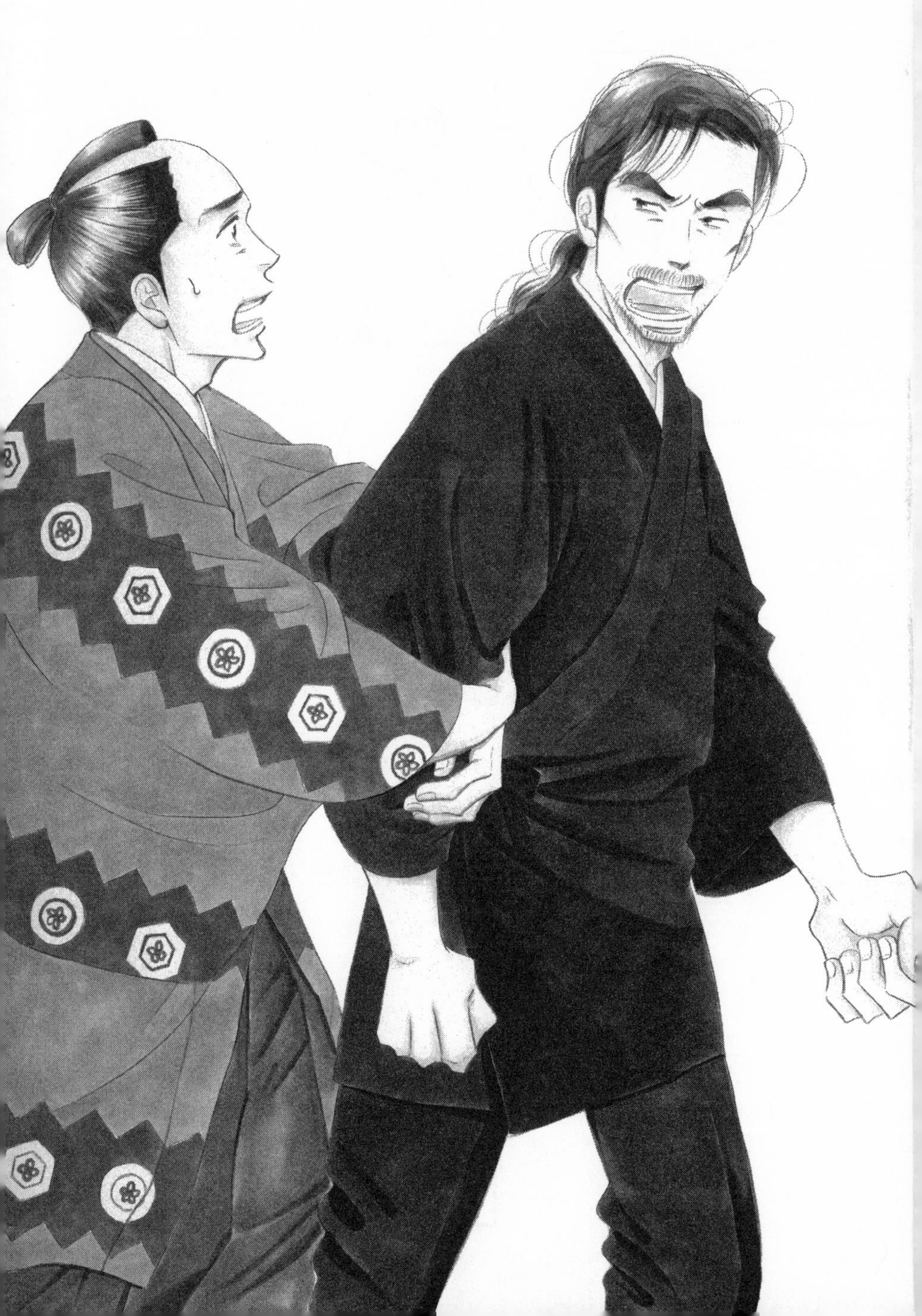

THE INNER CHAMBERS

CAST *of* CHARACTERS

From the birth of the "inverse Inner Chambers" to its zenith, and on to ending the Redface Pox?!

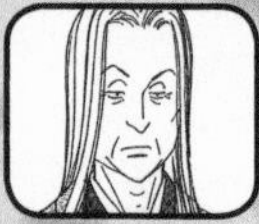

SENIOR CHAMBERLAIN

LADY KASUGA

↓

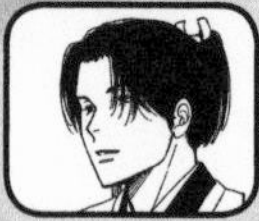

MADE-NOKOJI ARIKOTO

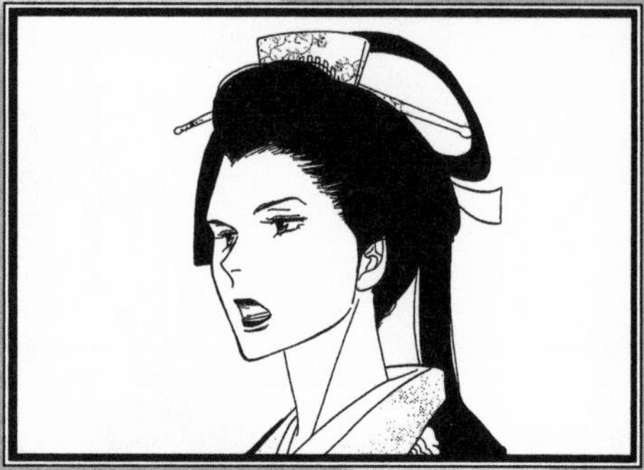

TOKUGAWA IEMITSU (III)

Impersonated her father, Iemitsu, at Lady Kasuga's urging after he died of the Redface Pox. Later became the first female shogun.

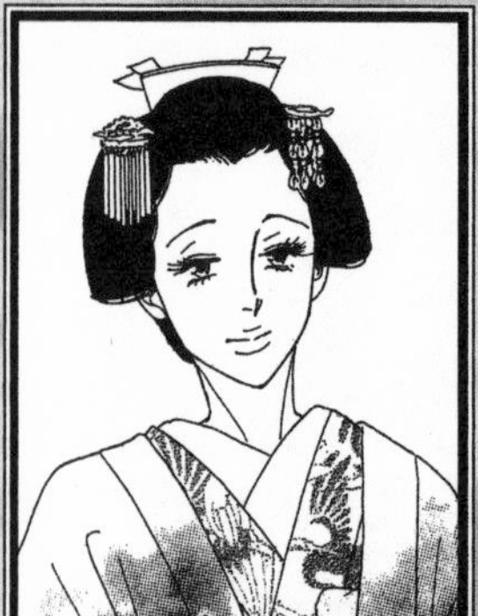

TOKU-GAWA TSUNA-YOSHI (V)

Iemitsu's third daughter. Endowed with both intellect and beauty, she did her best to rule wisely, but became known as "the Dog Shogun" due to unpopular policy mistakes later in her reign. The Ako Ronin incident led to official recognition of female inheritance of domain lord titles.

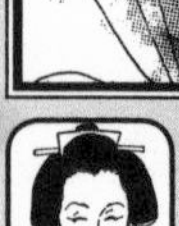

PRIVY COUNCILLOR

ANAGISAWA YOSHIYASU

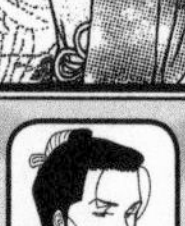

SENIOR CHAMBERLAIN

EMONNOSUKE

↓

AKIMOTO

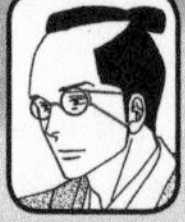

TOKUGAWA TSUNASHIGE

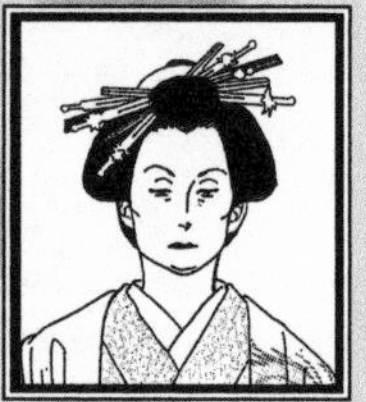

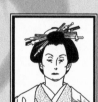

TOKU-GAWA IENOBU (VI)

Iemitsu's granddaughter and Tsunayoshi's niece. A ruler of sterling character but poor health, who died soon after assuming office.

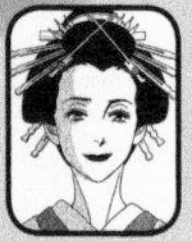

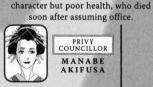

PRIVY COUNCILLOR

MANABE AKIFUSA

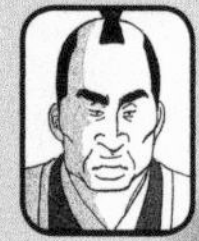

SENIOR CHAMBERLAIN

EJIMA

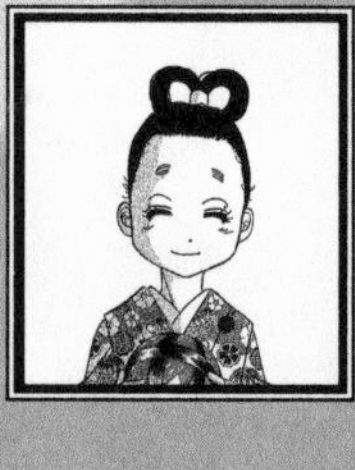

TOKUGAWA IETSUGU (VII)

Ienobu's fourth daughter, she died in childhood.

TOKUGAWA IETSUNA (IV)

Iemitsu's eldest daughter, known as "Lord Aye-do-so."

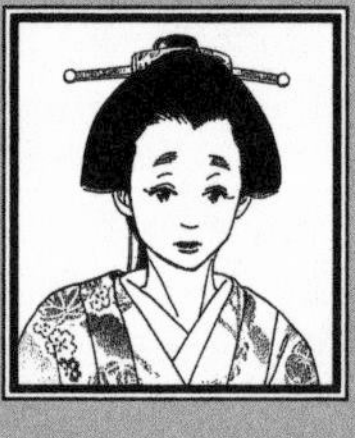

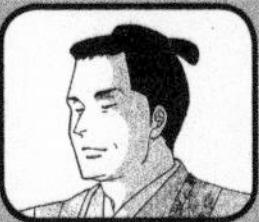

SENIOR CHAMBERLAIN

FUJINAMI

↓

SUGISHITA

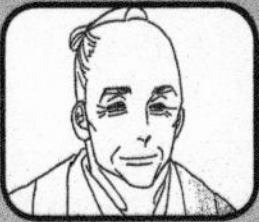

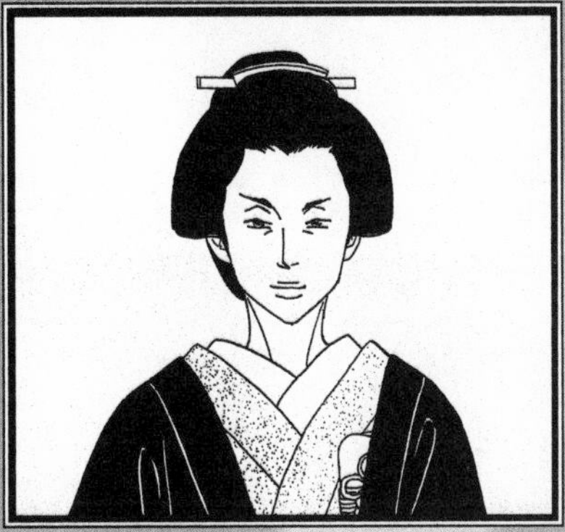

TOKUGAWA YOSHIMUNE (VIII)

Third daughter of Mitsusada, the second head of the Kii branch of the Tokugawa family. Acceded to domain lord and then, upon the death of Ietsugu, to shogun. Imposed and lived by a strict policy of austerity, dismissing large numbers of Inner Chamber courtiers and pursuing policies designed to increase income to the treasury.

PRIVY COUNCILLOR

KANO HISAMICHI

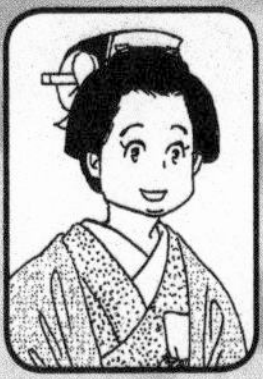

MUNETADA (HITOTSUBASHI BRANCH)

Yoshimune's third daughter

TOKUGAWA HARUSADA

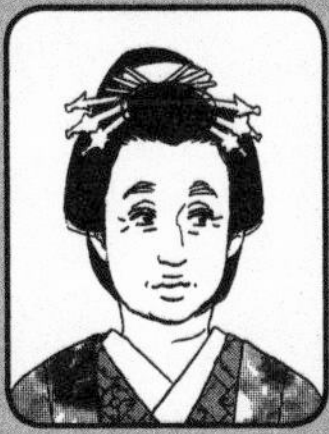

A champion schemer whose machinations have made her son the new shogun.

TOKUGAWA IENARI (XI)

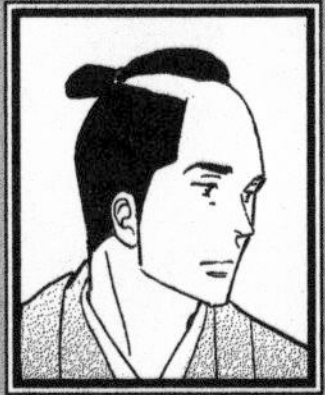

Son of Harusada. Obedient, but slightly weak and timid.

MUNETAKE (TAYASU BRANCH)

Yoshimune's second daughter

MATSUDAIRA SADANOBU

Munetake's daughter, she idolizes Yoshimune. Although she became a Senior Councillor after Tanuma's downfall, she was dismissed from this post after clashing with Harusada.

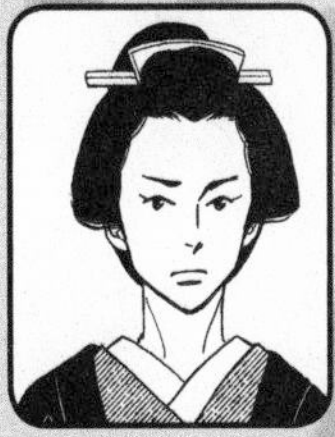

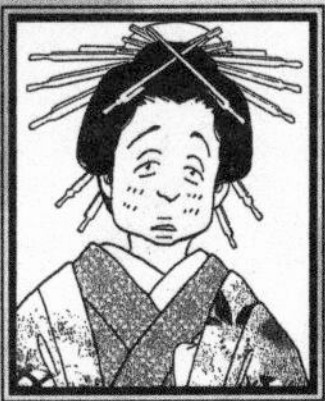

TOKUGAWA IESHIGE (IX)

Yoshimune's eldest daughter. Afflicted with a speech impediment, but not mentally disabled.

CHAMBERLAIN ↓ SENIOR COUNCILLOR

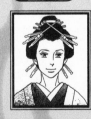

TANUMA OKITSUGU

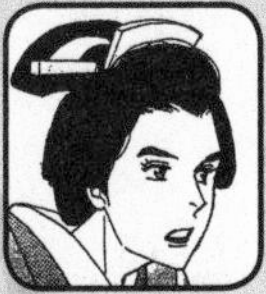

After serving Ieshige, promoted to Senior Councillor by Ieharu. Charged by Yoshimune with finding a cure for the Redface Pox, but fell from grace before achieving this mission.

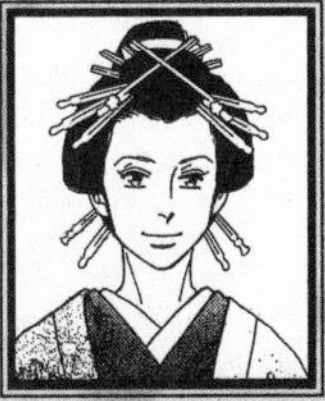

TOKUGAWA IEHARU (X)

Yoshimune's granddaughter. Intelligent and obedient to her mother and grandmother.

TEAM SEEKING A CURE FOR THE REDFACE POX

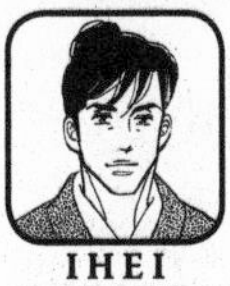

IHEI

Studied under Aonuma with Kuroki.

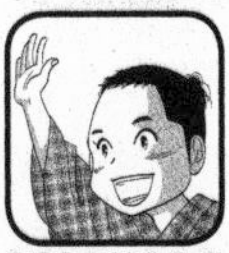

SEISHIRO

Kuroki's son and only child.

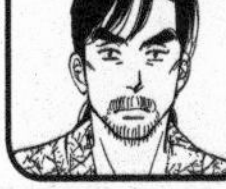

KUROKI RYOJUN

He studied Hollander medicine under Aonuma and became his assistant, but was later banished from the Inner Chambers and opened a medical clinic to serve townspeople.

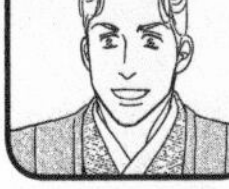

AONUMA

Mixed-race physician of Western medicine from Nagasaki. Called to the Inner Chambers, where he succeeded in vaccinating patients against the Redface Pox, but was sentenced to death following the downfall of Lady Tanuma.

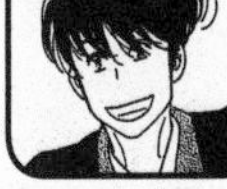

HIRAGA GENNAI

Multitalented genius and deep admirer of Tanuma. Devoted to finding a solution to the Redface Pox. Deceased.

Ōoku

THE INNER CHAMBERS

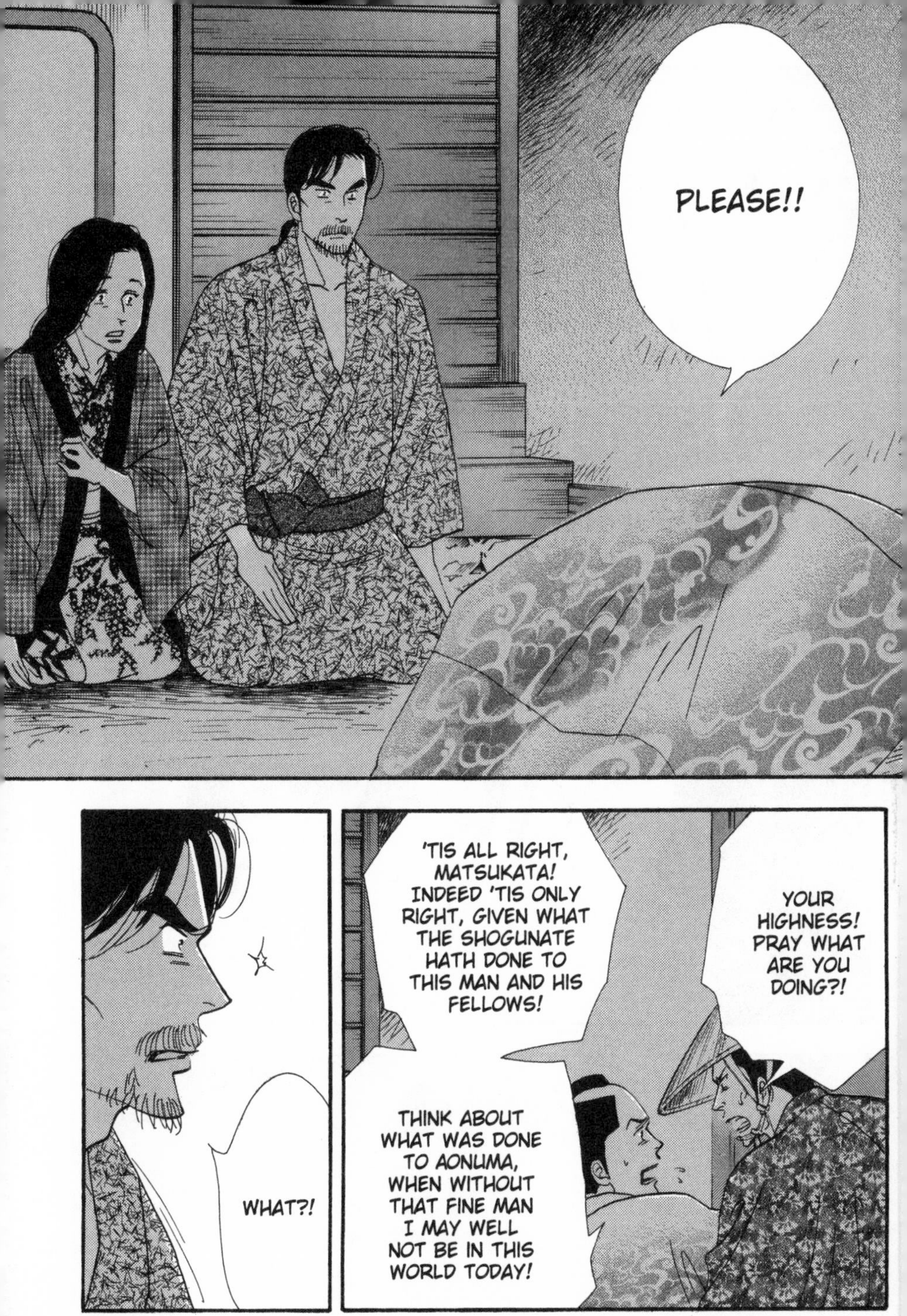
PLEASE!!
YOUR HIGHNESS! PRAY WHAT ARE YOU DOING?!
'TIS ALL RIGHT, MATSUKATA! INDEED 'TIS ONLY RIGHT, GIVEN WHAT THE SHOGUNATE HATH DONE TO THIS MAN AND HIS FELLOWS!
THINK ABOUT WHAT WAS DONE TO AONUMA, WHEN WITHOUT THAT FINE MAN I MAY WELL NOT BE IN THIS WORLD TODAY!
WHAT?!

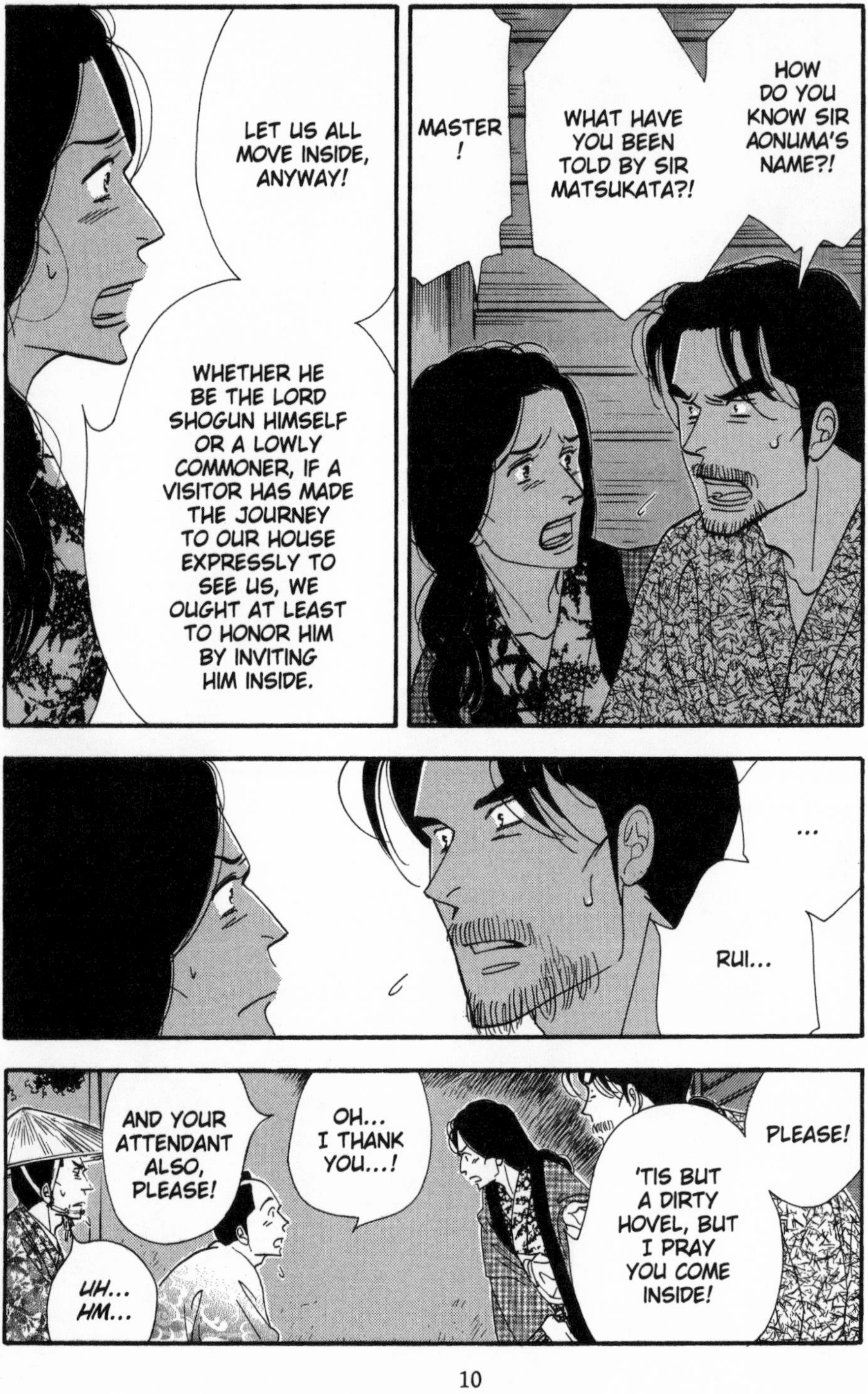
HOW DO YOU KNOW SIR AONUMA'S NAME?!
WHAT HAVE YOU BEEN TOLD BY SIR MATSUKATA?!
MASTER!
LET US ALL MOVE INSIDE, ANYWAY!
WHETHER HE BE THE LORD SHOGUN HIMSELF OR A LOWLY COMMONER, IF A VISITOR HAS MADE THE JOURNEY TO OUR HOUSE EXPRESSLY TO SEE US, WE OUGHT AT LEAST TO HONOR HIM BY INVITING HIM INSIDE.
...
RUI...
PLEASE!
'TIS BUT A DIRTY HOVEL, BUT I PRAY YOU COME INSIDE!
OH... I THANK YOU...!
AND YOUR ATTENDANT ALSO, PLEASE!
UH... HM...

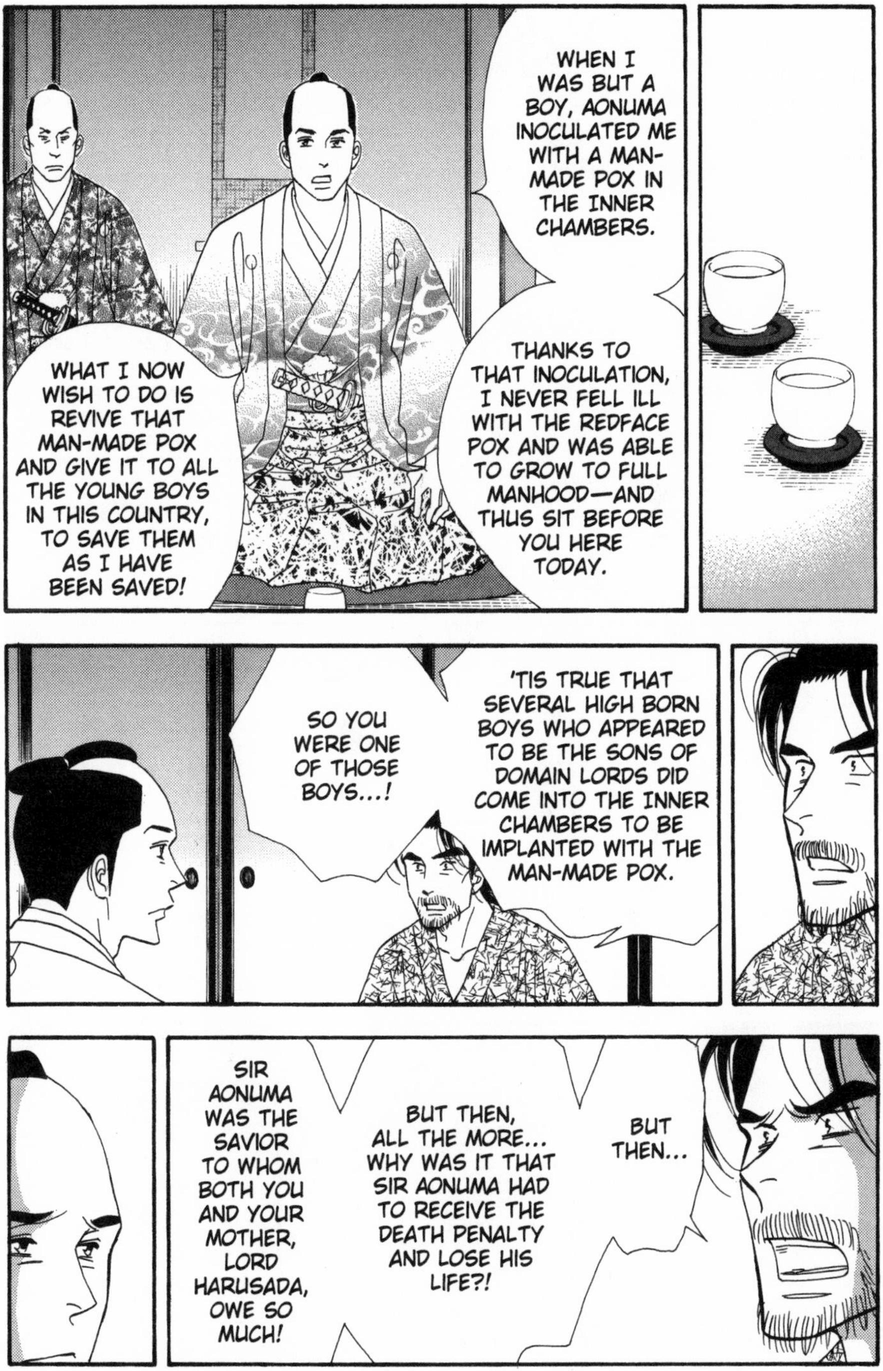
WHEN I WAS BUT A BOY, AONUMA INOCULATED ME WITH A MAN-MADE POX IN THE INNER CHAMBERS.
THANKS TO THAT INOCULATION, I NEVER FELL ILL WITH THE REDFACE POX AND WAS ABLE TO GROW TO FULL MANHOOD—AND THUS SIT BEFORE YOU HERE TODAY.
WHAT I NOW WISH TO DO IS REVIVE THAT MAN-MADE POX AND GIVE IT TO ALL THE YOUNG BOYS IN THIS COUNTRY, TO SAVE THEM AS I HAVE BEEN SAVED!
'TIS TRUE THAT SEVERAL HIGH BORN BOYS WHO APPEARED TO BE THE SONS OF DOMAIN LORDS DID COME INTO THE INNER CHAMBERS TO BE IMPLANTED WITH THE MAN-MADE POX.
SO YOU WERE ONE OF THOSE BOYS...!
BUT THEN...
BUT THEN, ALL THE MORE... WHY WAS IT THAT SIR AONUMA HAD TO RECEIVE THE DEATH PENALTY AND LOSE HIS LIFE?!
SIR AONUMA WAS THE SAVIOR TO WHOM BOTH YOU AND YOUR MOTHER, LORD HARUSADA, OWE SO MUCH!

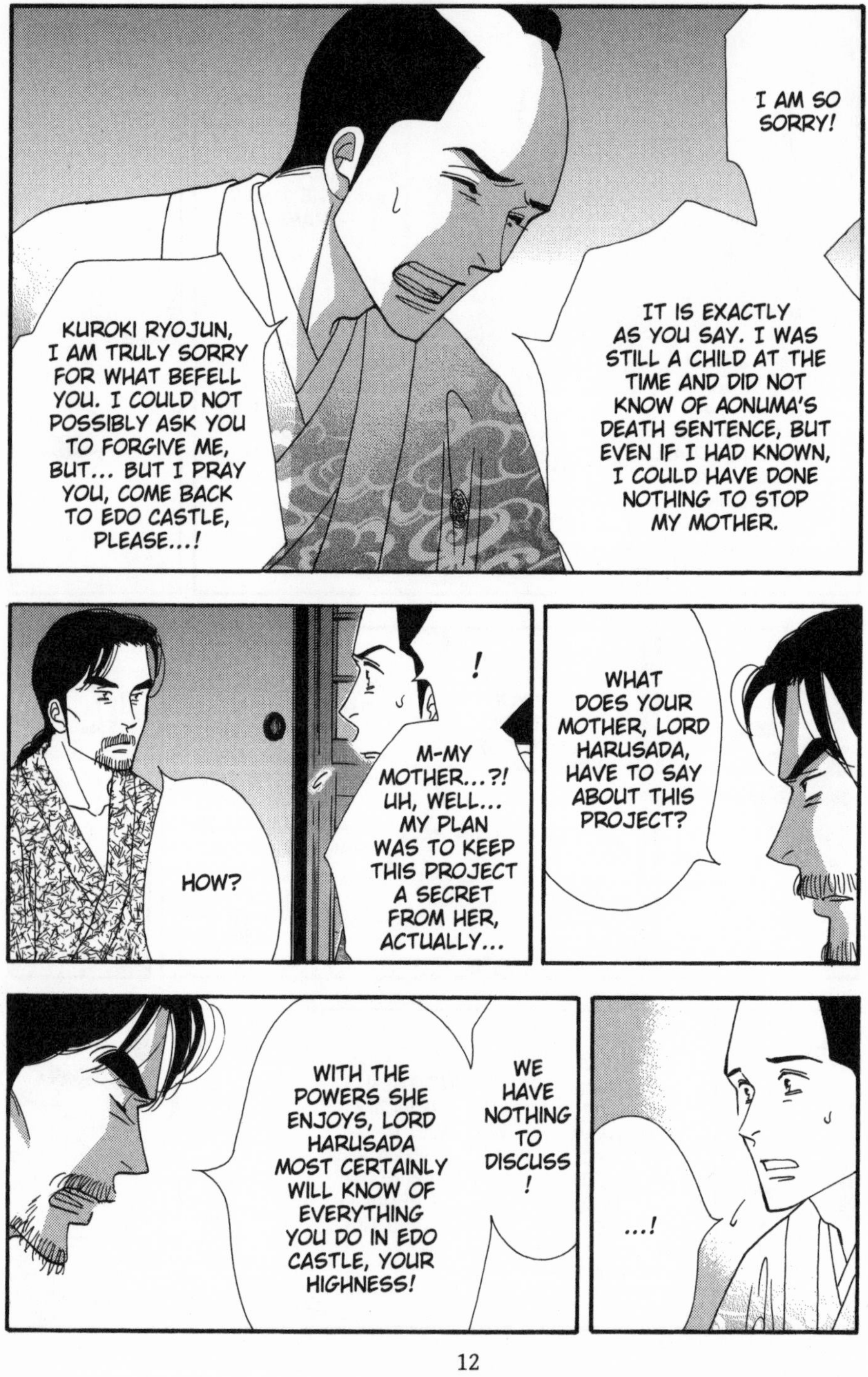
I AM SO SORRY!
IT IS EXACTLY AS YOU SAY. I WAS STILL A CHILD AT THE TIME AND DID NOT KNOW OF AONUMA'S DEATH SENTENCE, BUT EVEN IF I HAD KNOWN, I COULD HAVE DONE NOTHING TO STOP MY MOTHER.
KUROKI RYOJUN, I AM TRULY SORRY FOR WHAT BEFELL YOU. I COULD NOT POSSIBLY ASK YOU TO FORGIVE ME, BUT... BUT I PRAY YOU, COME BACK TO EDO CASTLE, PLEASE...!
WHAT DOES YOUR MOTHER, LORD HARUSADA, HAVE TO SAY ABOUT THIS PROJECT?
!
M-MY MOTHER...?! UH, WELL... MY PLAN WAS TO KEEP THIS PROJECT A SECRET FROM HER, ACTUALLY...
HOW?
...!
WE HAVE NOTHING TO DISCUSS!
WITH THE POWERS SHE ENJOYS, LORD HARUSADA MOST CERTAINLY WILL KNOW OF EVERYTHING YOU DO IN EDO CASTLE, YOUR HIGHNESS!

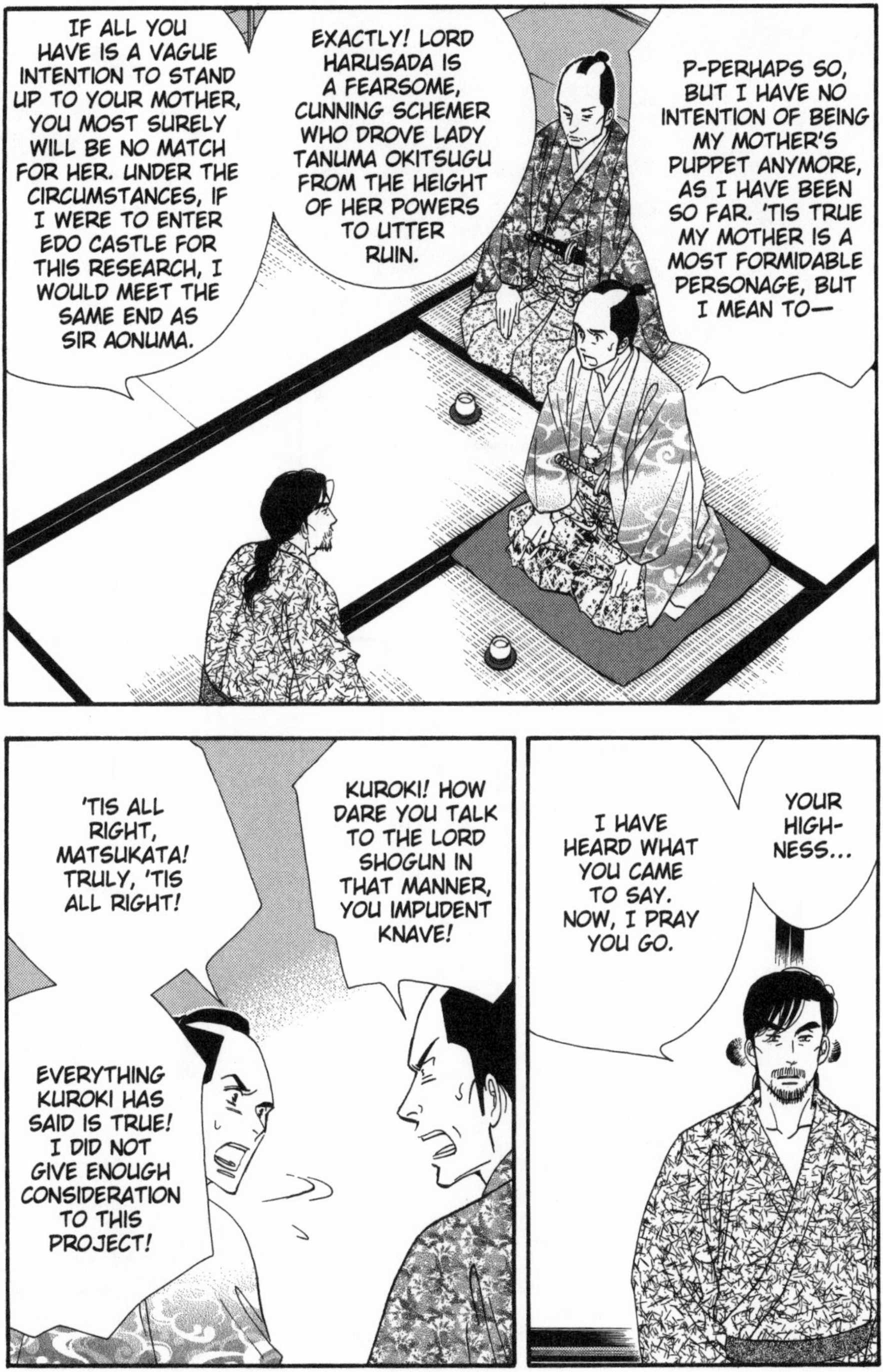
P-PERHAPS SO, BUT I HAVE NO INTENTION OF BEING MY MOTHER'S PUPPET ANYMORE, AS I HAVE BEEN SO FAR. 'TIS TRUE MY MOTHER IS A MOST FORMIDABLE PERSONAGE, BUT I MEAN TO—
EXACTLY! LORD HARUSADA IS A FEARSOME, CUNNING SCHEMER WHO DROVE LADY TANUMA OKITSUGU FROM THE HEIGHT OF HER POWERS TO UTTER RUIN.
IF ALL YOU HAVE IS A VAGUE INTENTION TO STAND UP TO YOUR MOTHER, YOU MOST SURELY WILL BE NO MATCH FOR HER. UNDER THE CIRCUMSTANCES, IF I WERE TO ENTER EDO CASTLE FOR THIS RESEARCH, I WOULD MEET THE SAME END AS SIR AONUMA.
YOUR HIGH-NESS...
I HAVE HEARD WHAT YOU CAME TO SAY. NOW, I PRAY YOU GO.
KUROKI! HOW DARE YOU TALK TO THE LORD SHOGUN IN THAT MANNER, YOU IMPUDENT KNAVE!
'TIS ALL RIGHT, MATSUKATA! TRULY, 'TIS ALL RIGHT!
EVERYTHING KUROKI HAS SAID IS TRUE! I DID NOT GIVE ENOUGH CONSIDERATION TO THIS PROJECT!

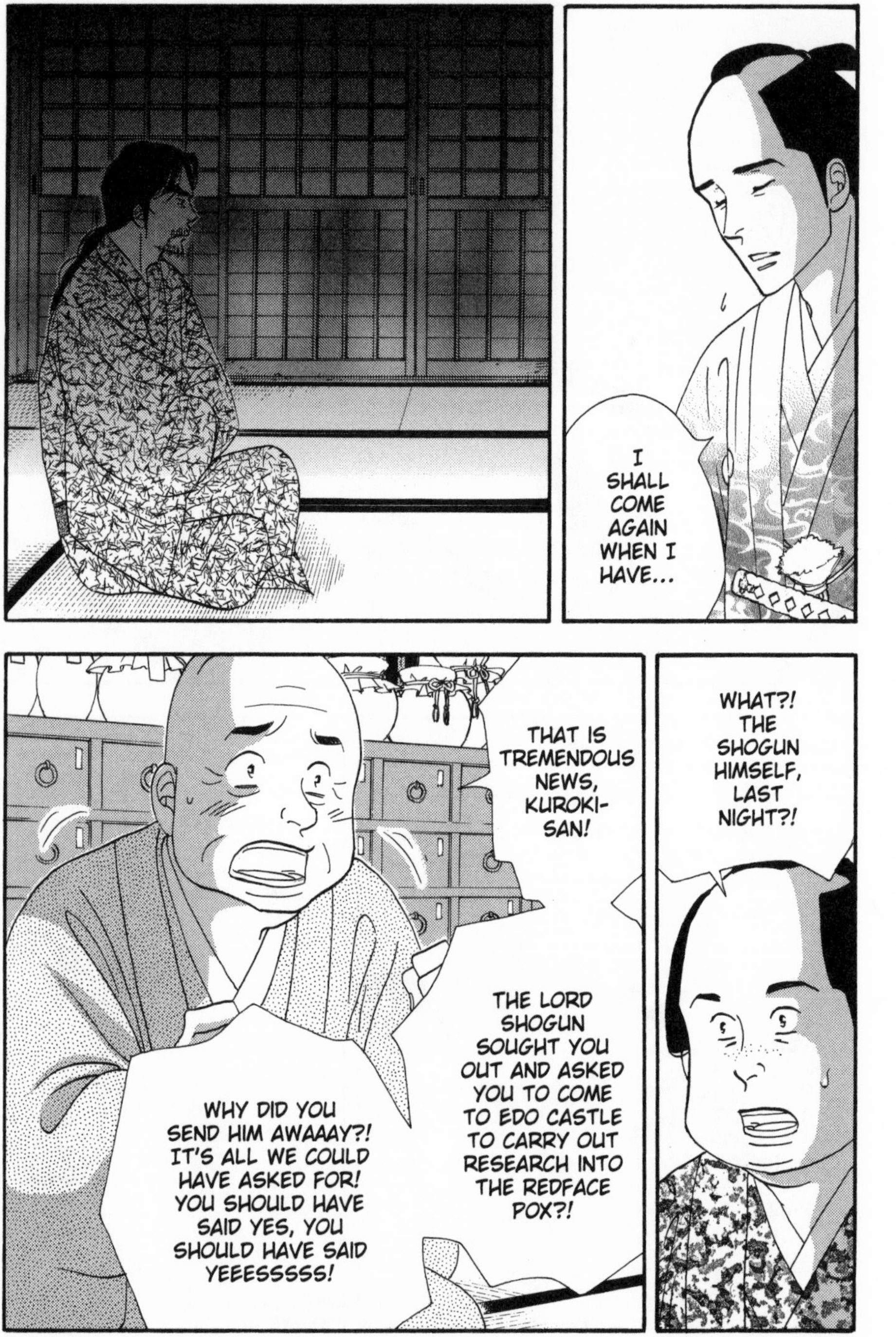
I SHALL COME AGAIN WHEN I HAVE...
WHAT?! THE SHOGUN HIMSELF, LAST NIGHT?!
THAT IS TREMENDOUS NEWS, KUROKI-SAN!
THE LORD SHOGUN SOUGHT YOU OUT AND ASKED YOU TO COME TO EDO CASTLE TO CARRY OUT RESEARCH INTO THE REDFACE POX?!
WHY DID YOU SEND HIM AWAAAY?! IT'S ALL WE COULD HAVE ASKED FOR! YOU SHOULD HAVE SAID YES, YOU SHOULD HAVE SAID YEEESSSSS!

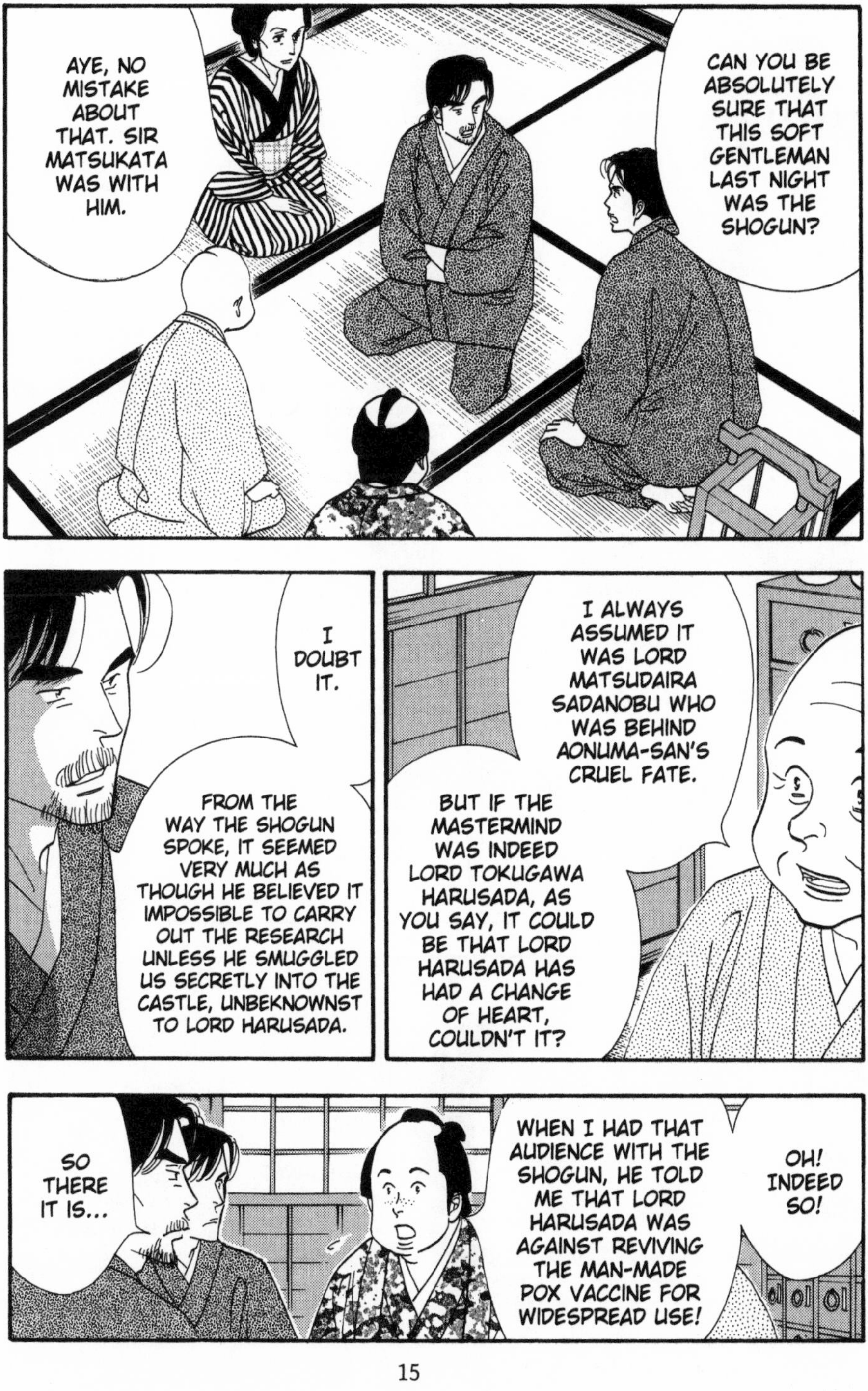
CAN YOU BE ABSOLUTELY SURE THAT THIS SOFT GENTLEMAN LAST NIGHT WAS THE SHOGUN?
AYE, NO MISTAKE ABOUT THAT. SIR MATSUKATA WAS WITH HIM.
I ALWAYS ASSUMED IT WAS LORD MATSUDAIRA SADANOBU WHO WAS BEHIND AONUMA-SAN'S CRUEL FATE.
BUT IF THE MASTERMIND WAS INDEED LORD TOKUGAWA HARUSADA, AS YOU SAY, IT COULD BE THAT LORD HARUSADA HAS HAD A CHANGE OF HEART, COULDN'T IT?
I DOUBT IT.
FROM THE WAY THE SHOGUN SPOKE, IT SEEMED VERY MUCH AS THOUGH HE BELIEVED IT IMPOSSIBLE TO CARRY OUT THE RESEARCH UNLESS HE SMUGGLED US SECRETLY INTO THE CASTLE, UNBEKNOWNST TO LORD HARUSADA.
OH! INDEED SO!
WHEN I HAD THAT AUDIENCE WITH THE SHOGUN, HE TOLD ME THAT LORD HARUSADA WAS AGAINST REVIVING THE MAN-MADE POX VACCINE FOR WIDESPREAD USE!
SO THERE IT IS...

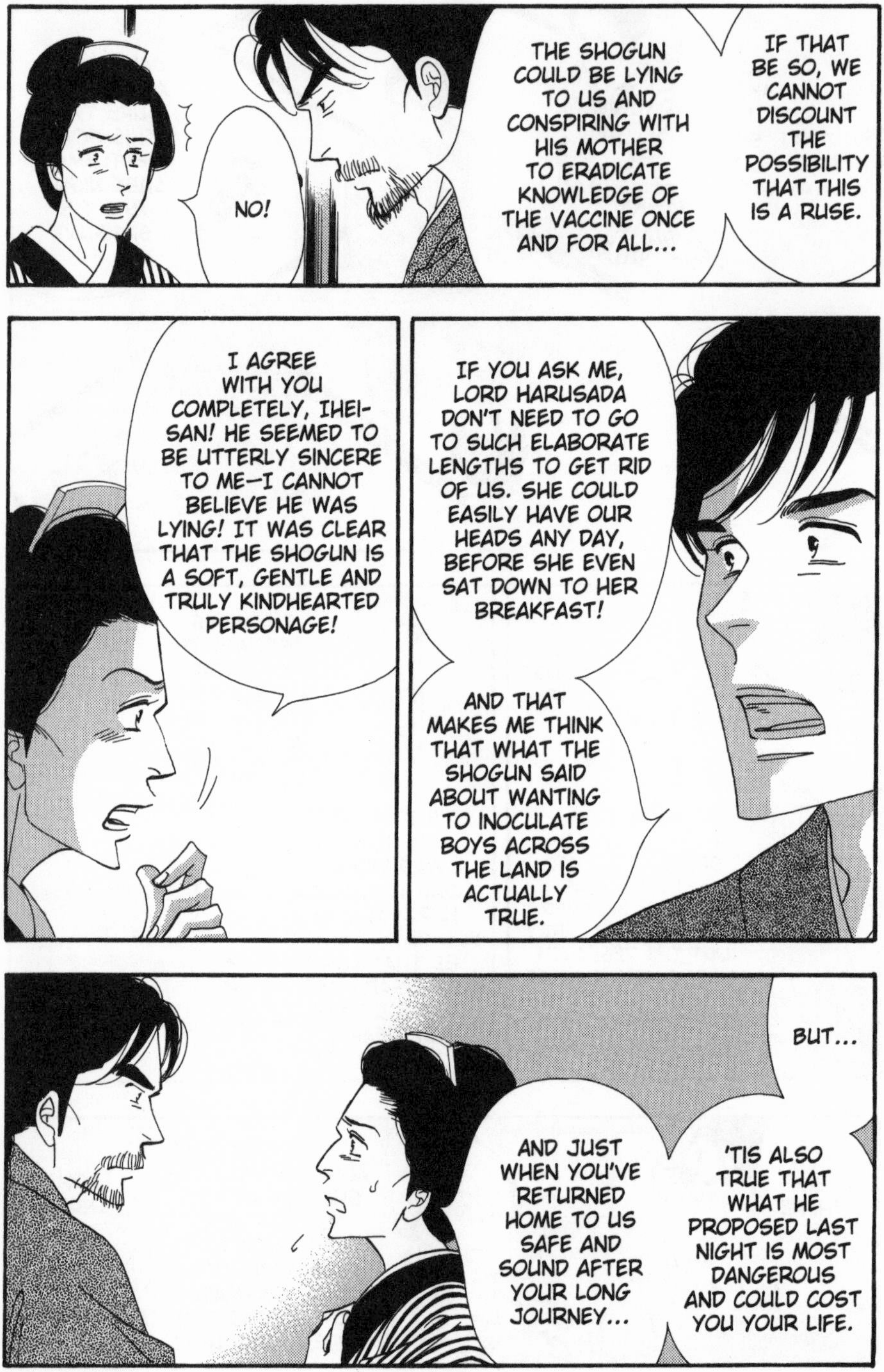
IF THAT BE SO, WE CANNOT DISCOUNT THE POSSIBILITY THAT THIS IS A RUSE.
THE SHOGUN COULD BE LYING TO US AND CONSPIRING WITH HIS MOTHER TO ERADICATE KNOWLEDGE OF THE VACCINE ONCE AND FOR ALL...
NO!
IF YOU ASK ME, LORD HARUSADA DON'T NEED TO GO TO SUCH ELABORATE LENGTHS TO GET RID OF US. SHE COULD EASILY HAVE OUR HEADS ANY DAY, BEFORE SHE EVEN SAT DOWN TO HER BREAKFAST!
AND THAT MAKES ME THINK THAT WHAT THE SHOGUN SAID ABOUT WANTING TO INOCULATE BOYS ACROSS THE LAND IS ACTUALLY TRUE.
I AGREE WITH YOU COMPLETELY, IHEI-SAN! HE SEEMED TO BE UTTERLY SINCERE TO ME—I CANNOT BELIEVE HE WAS LYING! IT WAS CLEAR THAT THE SHOGUN IS A SOFT, GENTLE AND TRULY KINDHEARTED PERSONAGE!
BUT...
'TIS ALSO TRUE THAT WHAT HE PROPOSED LAST NIGHT IS MOST DANGEROUS AND COULD COST YOU YOUR LIFE.
AND JUST WHEN YOU'VE RETURNED HOME TO US SAFE AND SOUND AFTER YOUR LONG JOURNEY...

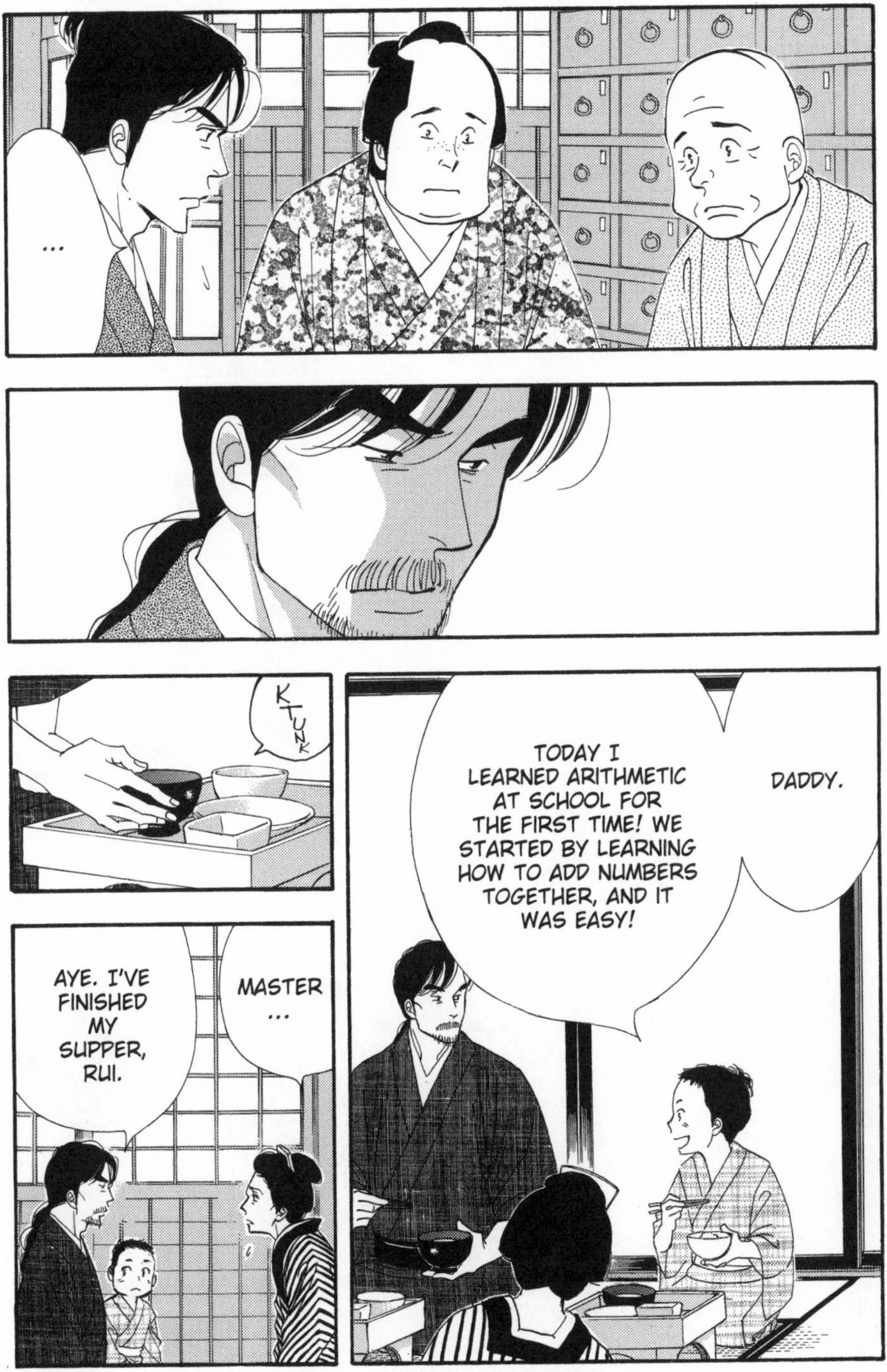
...
DADDY.
TODAY I LEARNED ARITHMETIC AT SCHOOL FOR THE FIRST TIME! WE STARTED BY LEARNING HOW TO ADD NUMBERS TOGETHER, AND IT WAS EASY!
KTUNK
MASTER ...
AYE. I'VE FINISHED MY SUPPER, RUI.

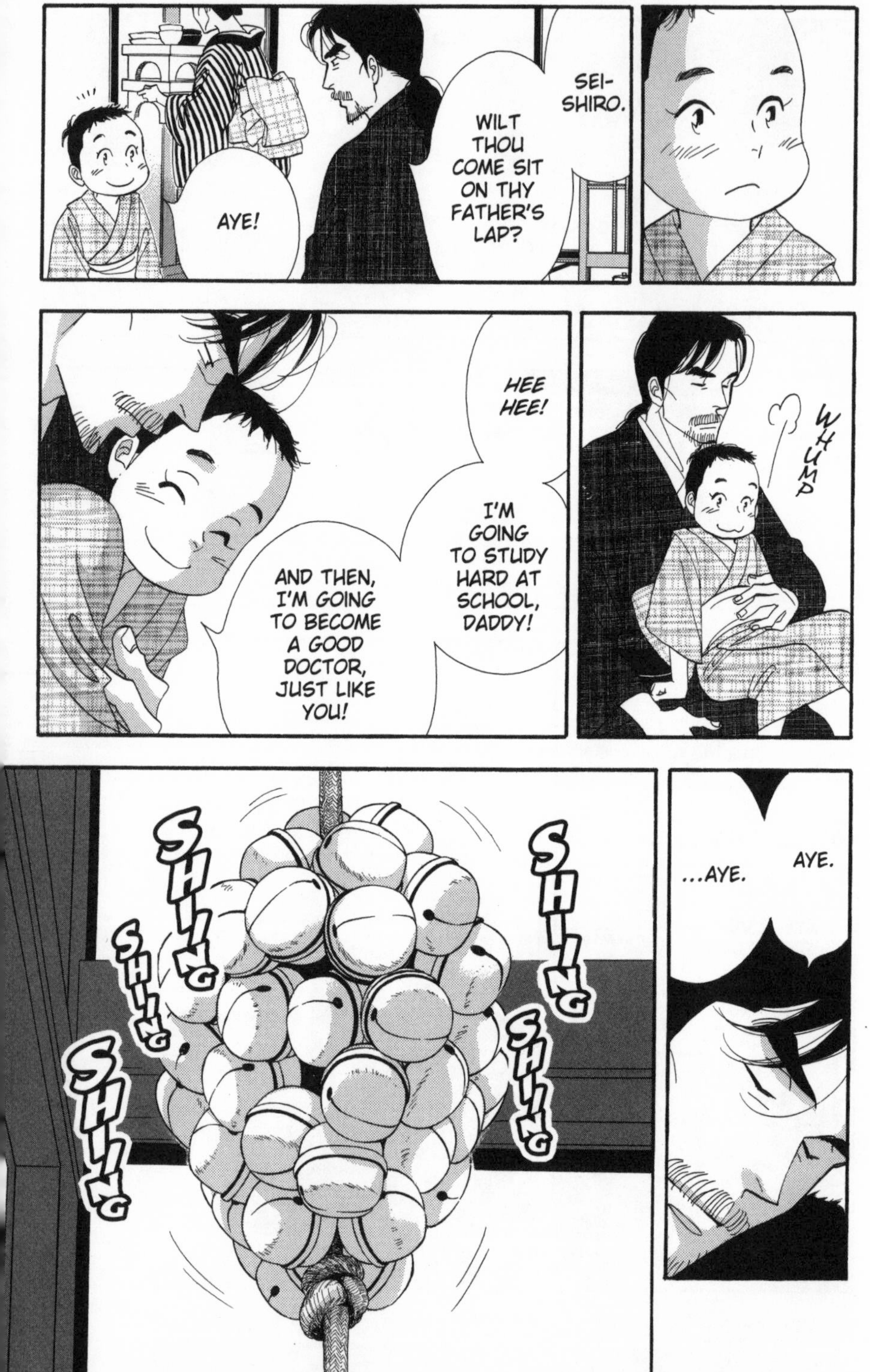
SEI-SHIRO.
WILT THOU COME SIT ON THY FATHER'S LAP?
AYE!
WHUMP
HEE HEE!
I'M GOING TO STUDY HARD AT SCHOOL, DADDY!
AND THEN, I'M GOING TO BECOME A GOOD DOCTOR, JUST LIKE YOU!
AYE.
...AYE.
SHING
SHING
SHING
SHING
SHING

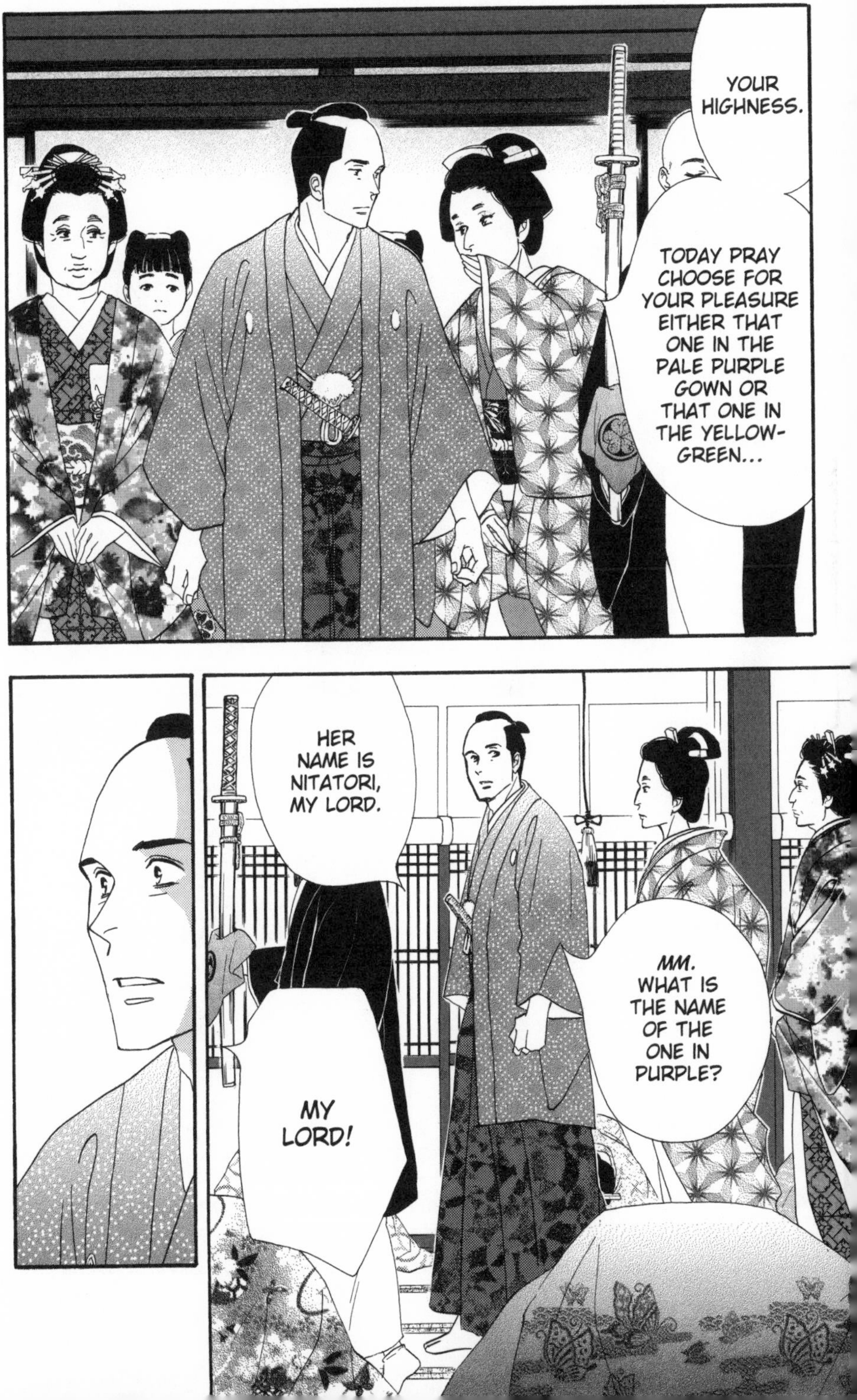
YOUR HIGHNESS.
TODAY PRAY CHOOSE FOR YOUR PLEASURE EITHER THAT ONE IN THE PALE PURPLE GOWN OR THAT ONE IN THE YELLOW-GREEN...
MM. WHAT IS THE NAME OF THE ONE IN PURPLE?
HER NAME IS NITATORI, MY LORD.
MY LORD!

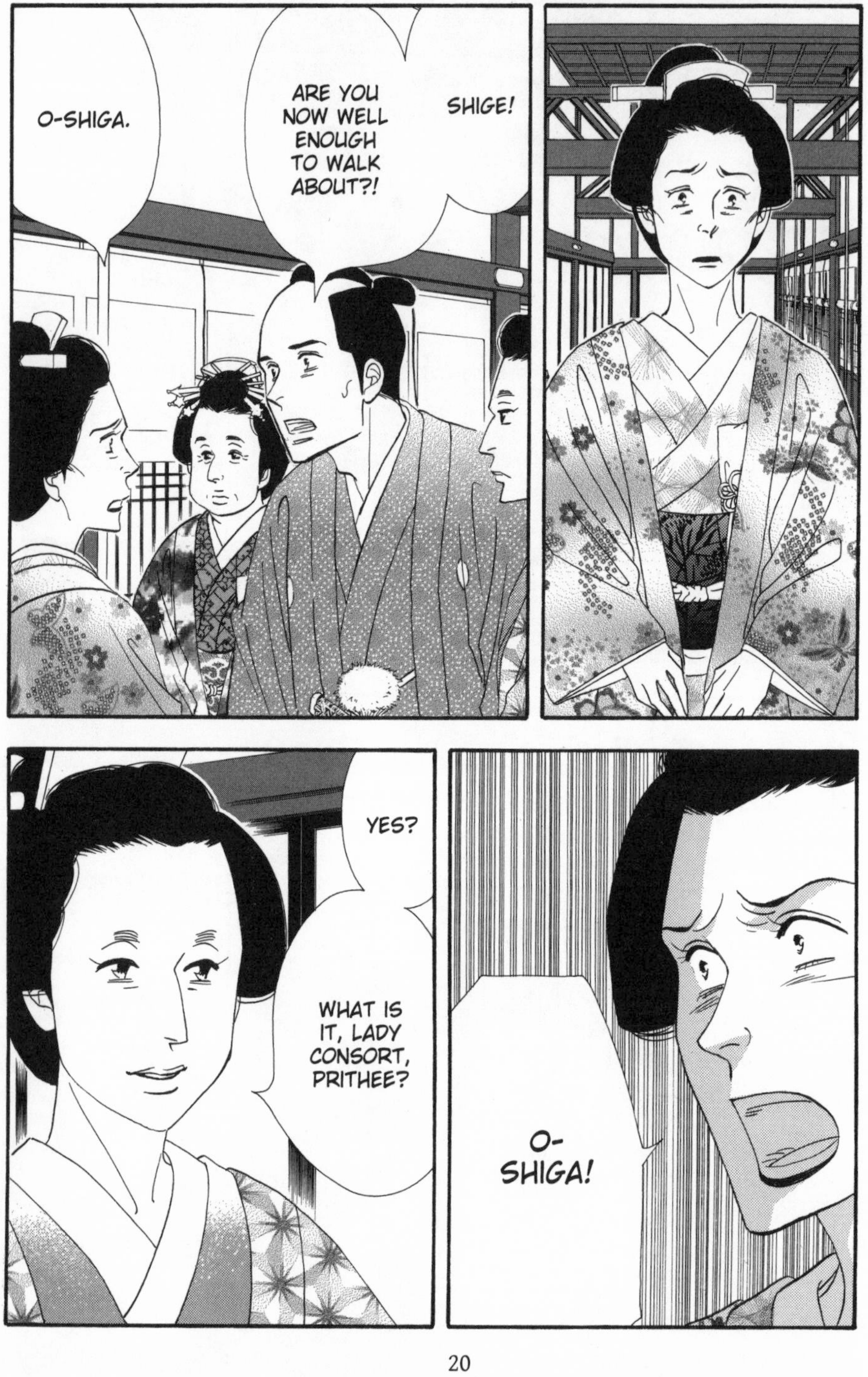
SHIGE!
ARE YOU NOW WELL ENOUGH TO WALK ABOUT?!
O-SHIGA.
O-SHIGA!
YES?
WHAT IS IT, LADY CONSORT, PRITHEE?

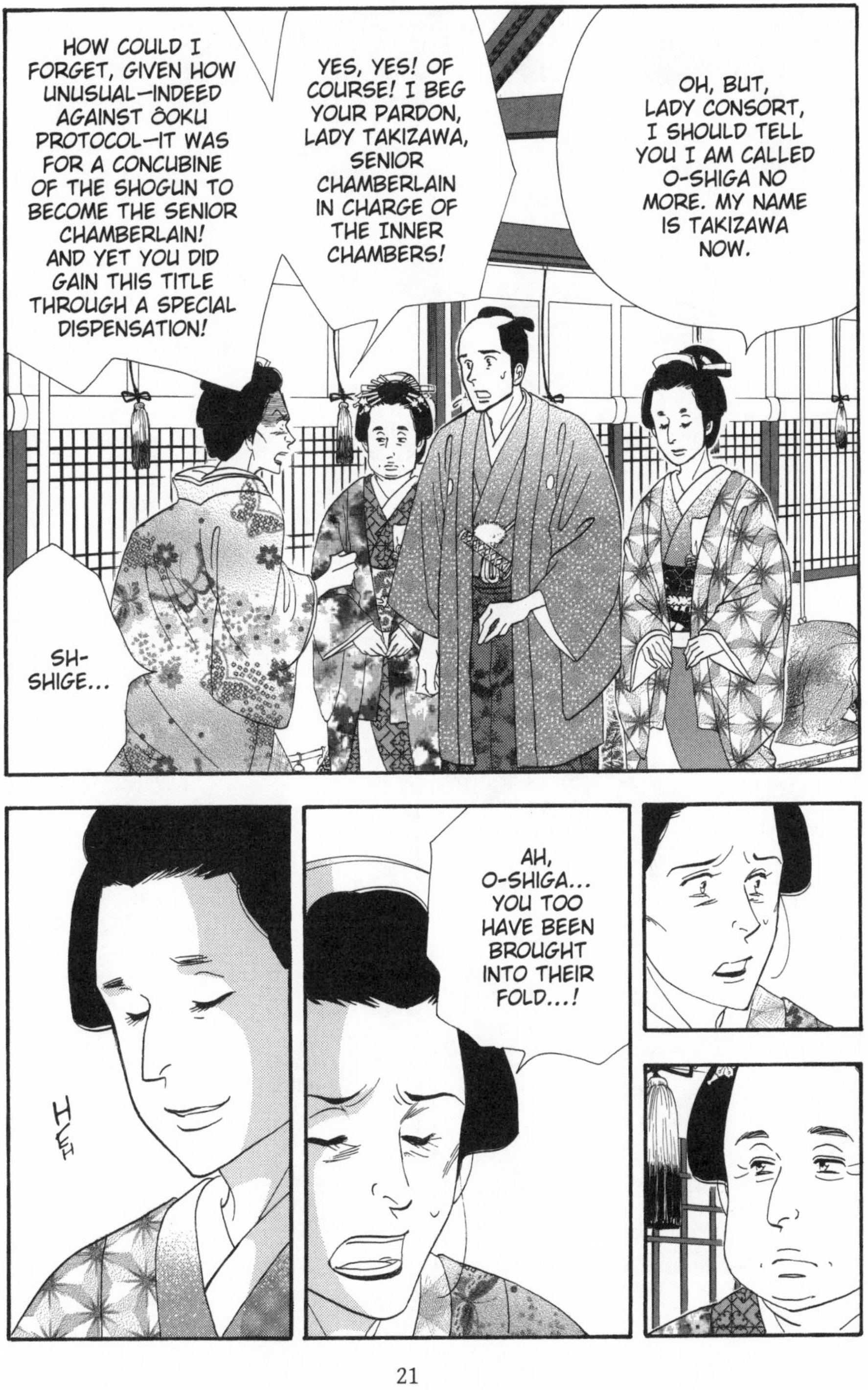
OH, BUT, LADY CONSORT, I SHOULD TELL YOU I AM CALLED O-SHIGA NO MORE. MY NAME IS TAKIZAWA NOW.
YES, YES! OF COURSE! I BEG YOUR PARDON, LADY TAKIZAWA, SENIOR CHAMBERLAIN IN CHARGE OF THE INNER CHAMBERS!
HOW COULD I FORGET, GIVEN HOW UNUSUAL—INDEED AGAINST ÔOKU PROTOCOL—IT WAS FOR A CONCUBINE OF THE SHOGUN TO BECOME THE SENIOR CHAMBERLAIN! AND YET YOU DID GAIN THIS TITLE THROUGH A SPECIAL DISPENSATION!
SH-SHIGE...
AH, O-SHIGA... YOU TOO HAVE BEEN BROUGHT INTO THEIR FOLD...!
HEH

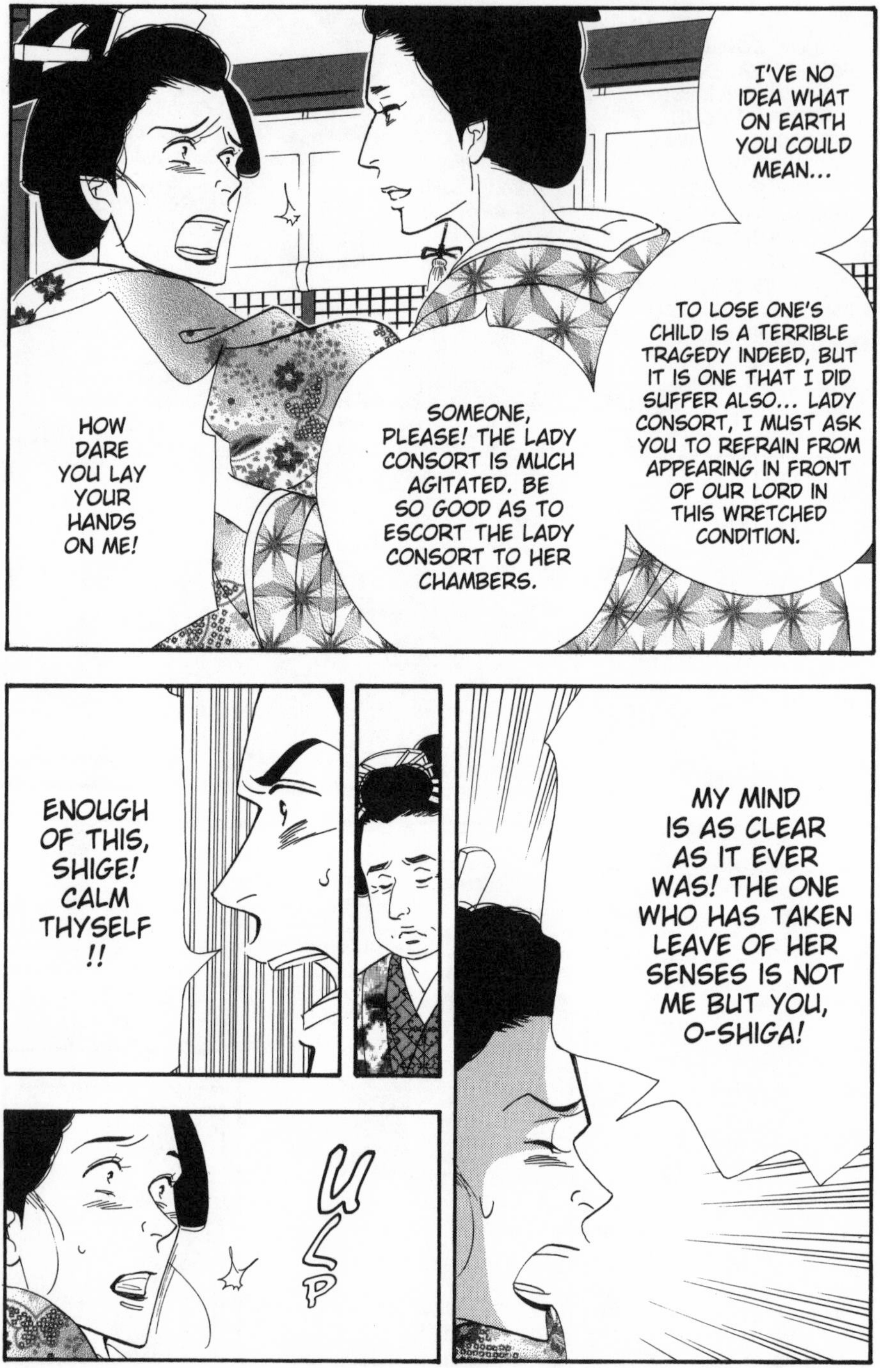
I'VE NO IDEA WHAT ON EARTH YOU COULD MEAN...
TO LOSE ONE'S CHILD IS A TERRIBLE TRAGEDY INDEED, BUT IT IS ONE THAT I DID SUFFER ALSO... LADY CONSORT, I MUST ASK YOU TO REFRAIN FROM APPEARING IN FRONT OF OUR LORD IN THIS WRETCHED CONDITION.
SOMEONE, PLEASE! THE LADY CONSORT IS MUCH AGITATED. BE SO GOOD AS TO ESCORT THE LADY CONSORT TO HER CHAMBERS.
HOW DARE YOU LAY YOUR HANDS ON ME!
MY MIND IS AS CLEAR AS IT EVER WAS! THE ONE WHO HAS TAKEN LEAVE OF HER SENSES IS NOT ME BUT YOU, O-SHIGA!
ENOUGH OF THIS, SHIGE! CALM THYSELF !!
ULP

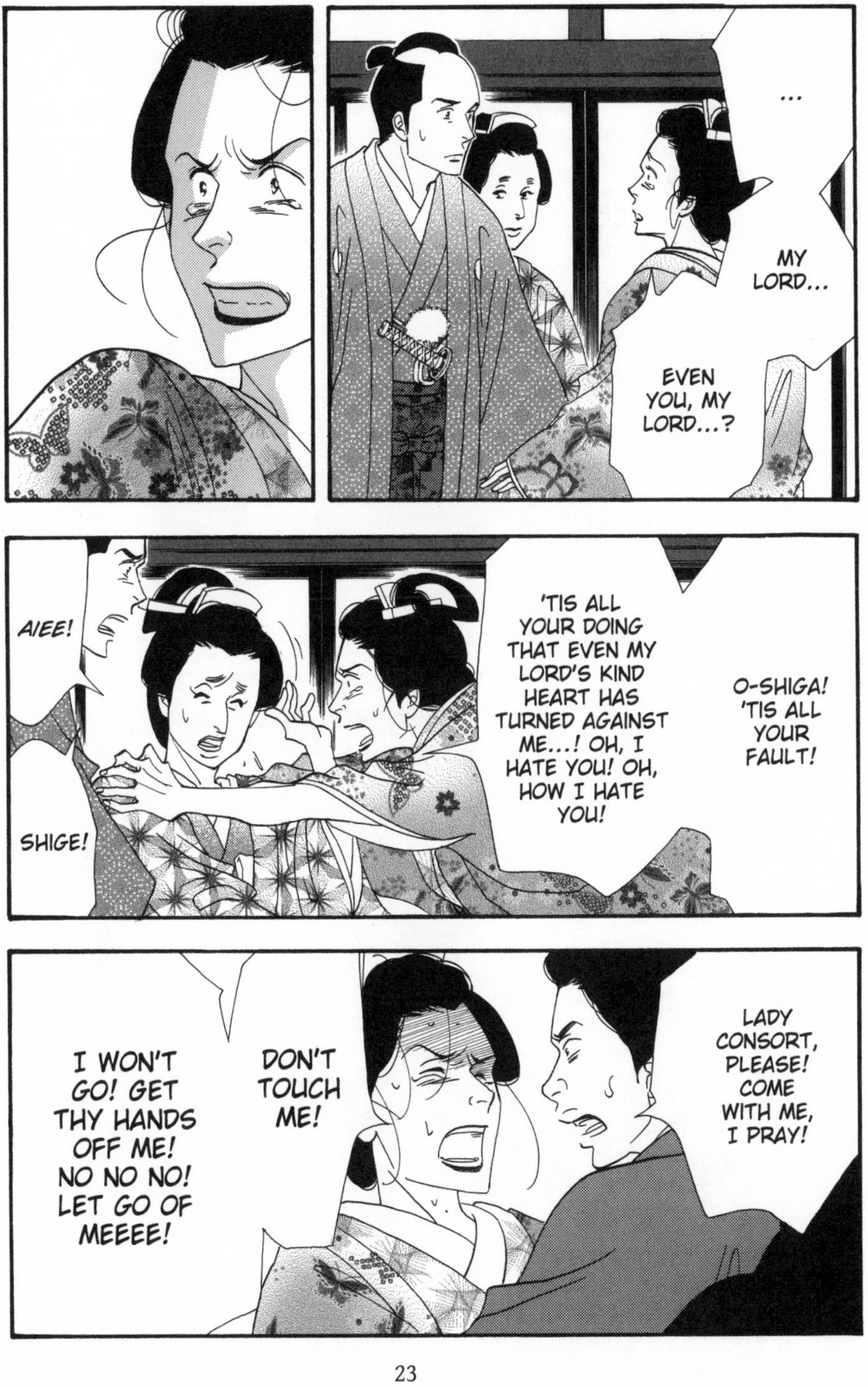
...
MY LORD...
EVEN YOU, MY LORD...?
O-SHIGA! 'TIS ALL YOUR FAULT!
'TIS ALL YOUR DOING THAT EVEN MY LORD'S KIND HEART HAS TURNED AGAINST ME...! OH, I HATE YOU! OH, HOW I HATE YOU!
AIEE!
SHIGE!
LADY CONSORT, PLEASE! COME WITH ME, I PRAY!
DON'T TOUCH ME!
I WON'T GO! GET THY HANDS OFF ME! NO NO NO! LET GO OF MEEEE!

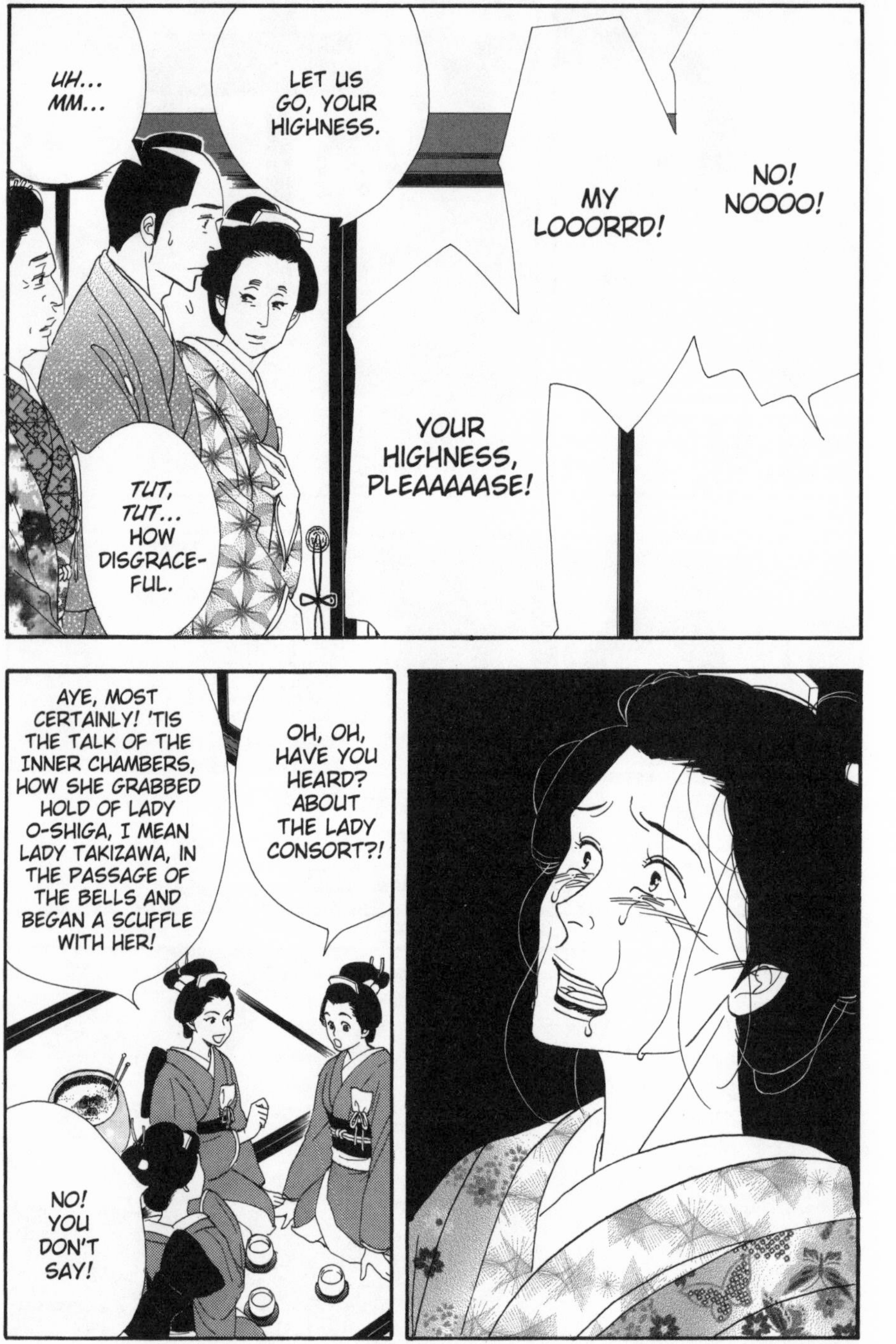
NO! NOOOO!
MY LOOORRD!
LET US GO, YOUR HIGHNESS.
UH... MM...
YOUR HIGHNESS, PLEAAAAAASE!
TUT, TUT... HOW DISGRACE-FUL.
OH, OH, HAVE YOU HEARD? ABOUT THE LADY CONSORT?!
AYE, MOST CERTAINLY! 'TIS THE TALK OF THE INNER CHAMBERS, HOW SHE GRABBED HOLD OF LADY O-SHIGA, I MEAN LADY TAKIZAWA, IN THE PASSAGE OF THE BELLS AND BEGAN A SCUFFLE WITH HER!
NO! YOU DON'T SAY!

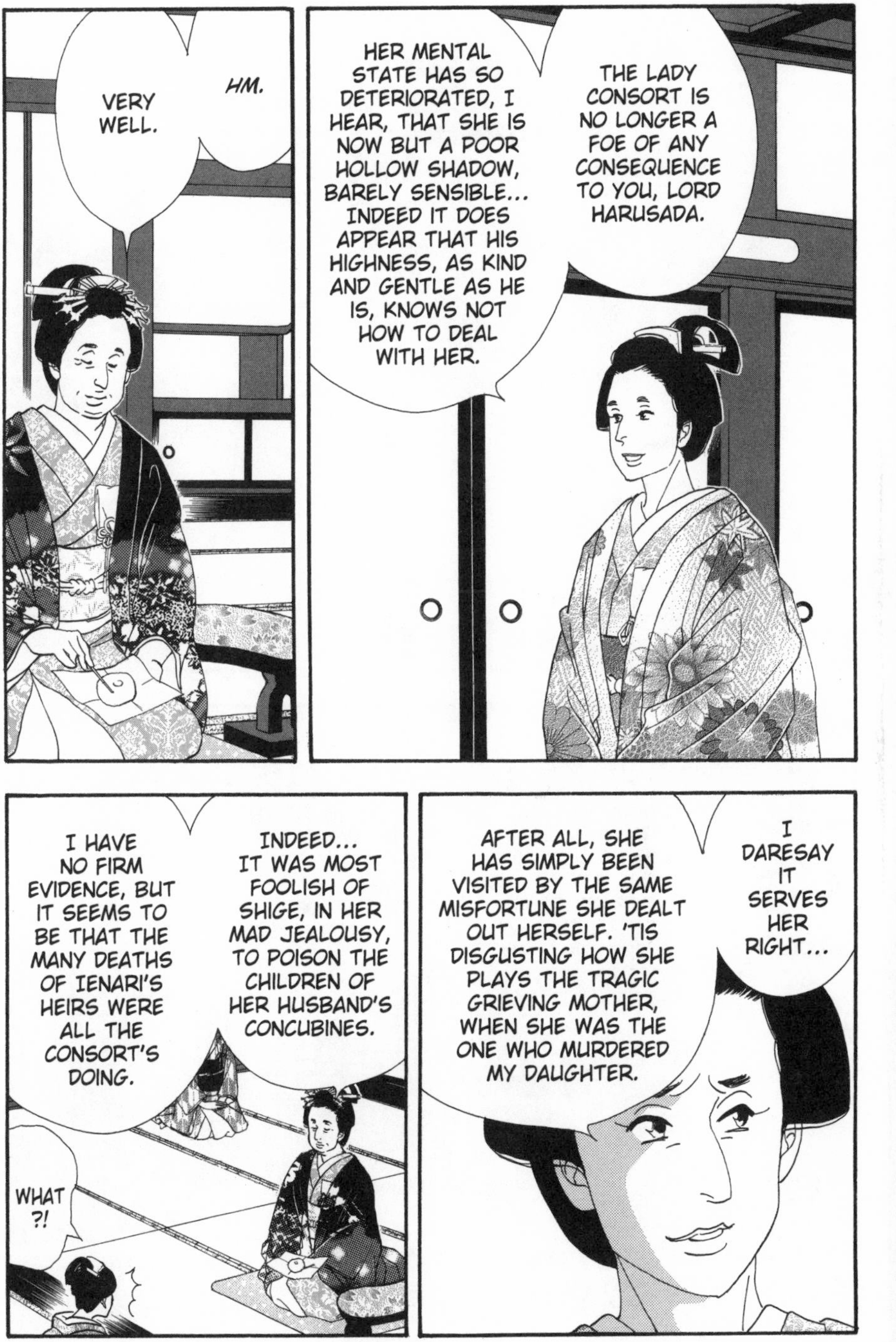
THE LADY CONSORT IS NO LONGER A FOE OF ANY CONSEQUENCE TO YOU, LORD HARUSADA.
HER MENTAL STATE HAS SO DETERIORATED, I HEAR, THAT SHE IS NOW BUT A POOR HOLLOW SHADOW, BARELY SENSIBLE... INDEED IT DOES APPEAR THAT HIS HIGHNESS, AS KIND AND GENTLE AS HE IS, KNOWS NOT HOW TO DEAL WITH HER.
HM.
VERY WELL.
I DARESAY IT SERVES HER RIGHT...
AFTER ALL, SHE HAS SIMPLY BEEN VISITED BY THE SAME MISFORTUNE SHE DEALT OUT HERSELF. 'TIS DISGUSTING HOW SHE PLAYS THE TRAGIC GRIEVING MOTHER, WHEN SHE WAS THE ONE WHO MURDERED MY DAUGHTER.
INDEED... IT WAS MOST FOOLISH OF SHIGE, IN HER MAD JEALOUSY, TO POISON THE CHILDREN OF HER HUSBAND'S CONCUBINES.
I HAVE NO FIRM EVIDENCE, BUT IT SEEMS TO BE THAT THE MANY DEATHS OF IENARI'S HEIRS WERE ALL THE CONSORT'S DOING.
WHAT ?!

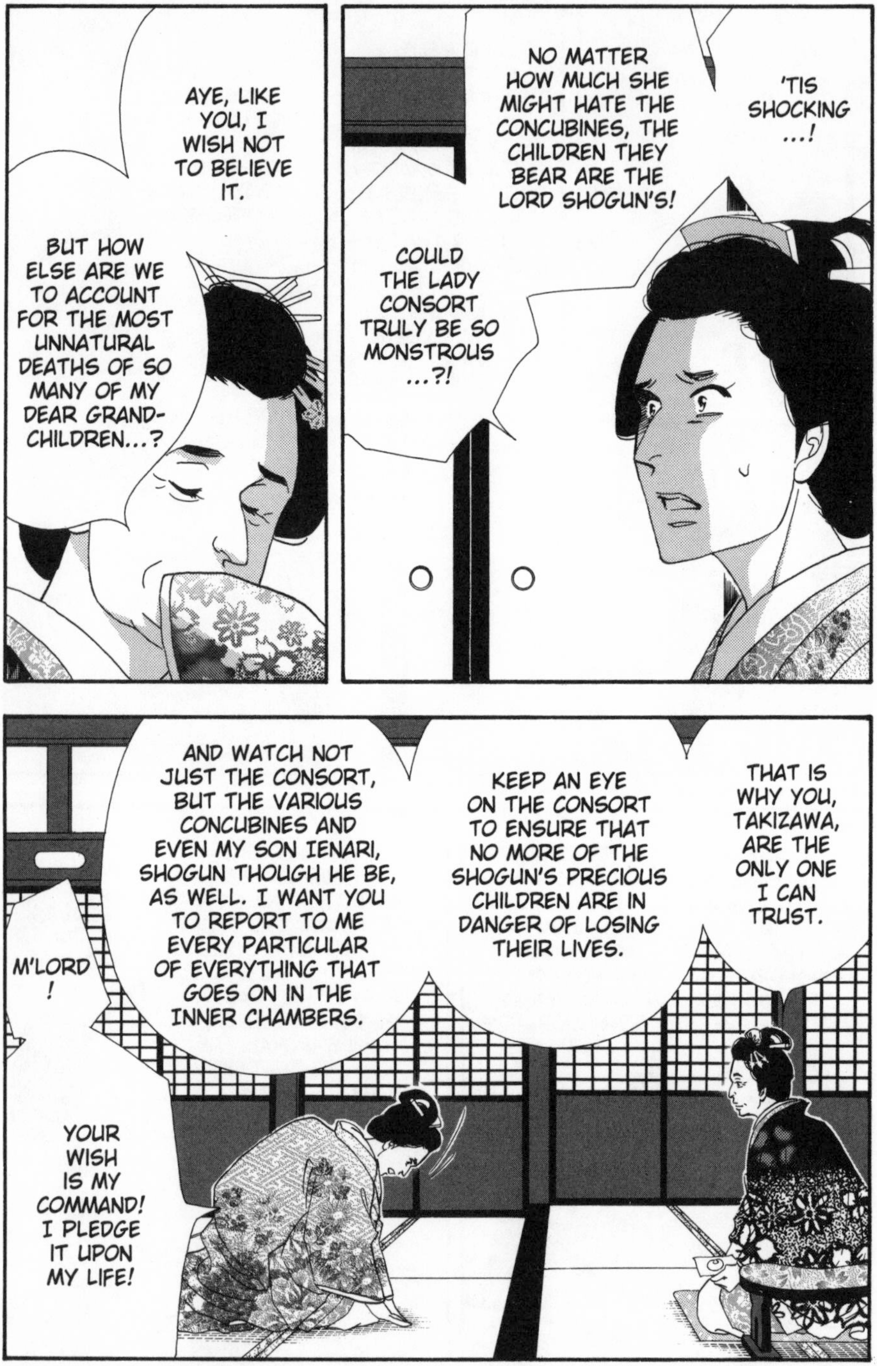
'TIS SHOCKING ...!
NO MATTER HOW MUCH SHE MIGHT HATE THE CONCUBINES, THE CHILDREN THEY BEAR ARE THE LORD SHOGUN'S!
COULD THE LADY CONSORT TRULY BE SO MONSTROUS ...?!
AYE, LIKE YOU, I WISH NOT TO BELIEVE IT.
BUT HOW ELSE ARE WE TO ACCOUNT FOR THE MOST UNNATURAL DEATHS OF SO MANY OF MY DEAR GRAND-CHILDREN...?
THAT IS WHY YOU, TAKIZAWA, ARE THE ONLY ONE I CAN TRUST.
KEEP AN EYE ON THE CONSORT TO ENSURE THAT NO MORE OF THE SHOGUN'S PRECIOUS CHILDREN ARE IN DANGER OF LOSING THEIR LIVES.
AND WATCH NOT JUST THE CONSORT, BUT THE VARIOUS CONCUBINES AND EVEN MY SON IENARI, SHOGUN THOUGH HE BE, AS WELL. I WANT YOU TO REPORT TO ME EVERY PARTICULAR OF EVERYTHING THAT GOES ON IN THE INNER CHAMBERS.
M'LORD!
YOUR WISH IS MY COMMAND! I PLEDGE IT UPON MY LIFE!

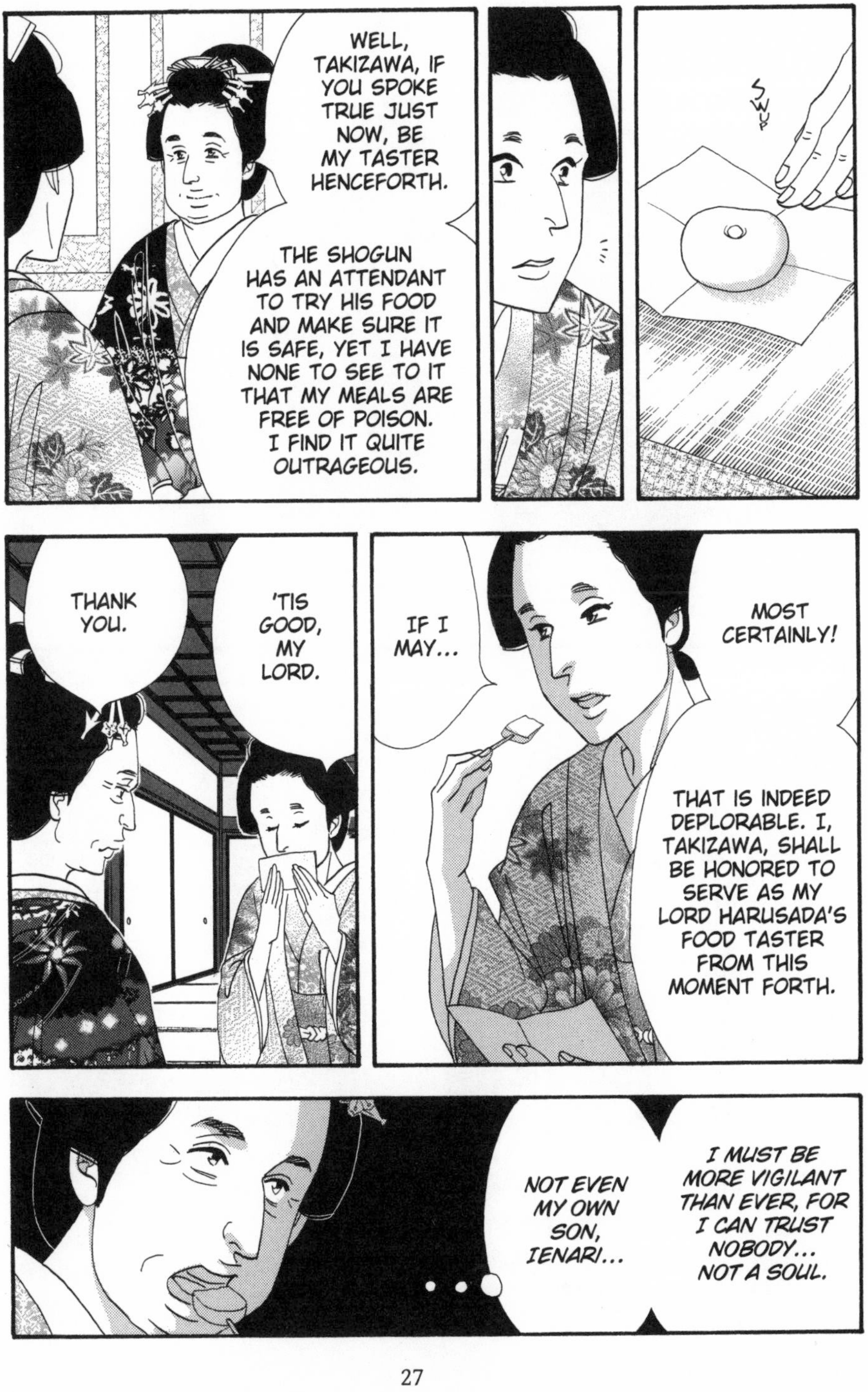
SWUP
WELL, TAKIZAWA, IF YOU SPOKE TRUE JUST NOW, BE MY TASTER HENCEFORTH.
THE SHOGUN HAS AN ATTENDANT TO TRY HIS FOOD AND MAKE SURE IT IS SAFE, YET I HAVE NONE TO SEE TO IT THAT MY MEALS ARE FREE OF POISON. I FIND IT QUITE OUTRAGEOUS.
MOST CERTAINLY!
THAT IS INDEED DEPLORABLE. I, TAKIZAWA, SHALL BE HONORED TO SERVE AS MY LORD HARUSADA'S FOOD TASTER FROM THIS MOMENT FORTH.
IF I MAY...
'TIS GOOD, MY LORD.
THANK YOU.
I MUST BE MORE VIGILANT THAN EVER, FOR I CAN TRUST NOBODY... NOT A SOUL.
NOT EVEN MY OWN SON, IENARI...

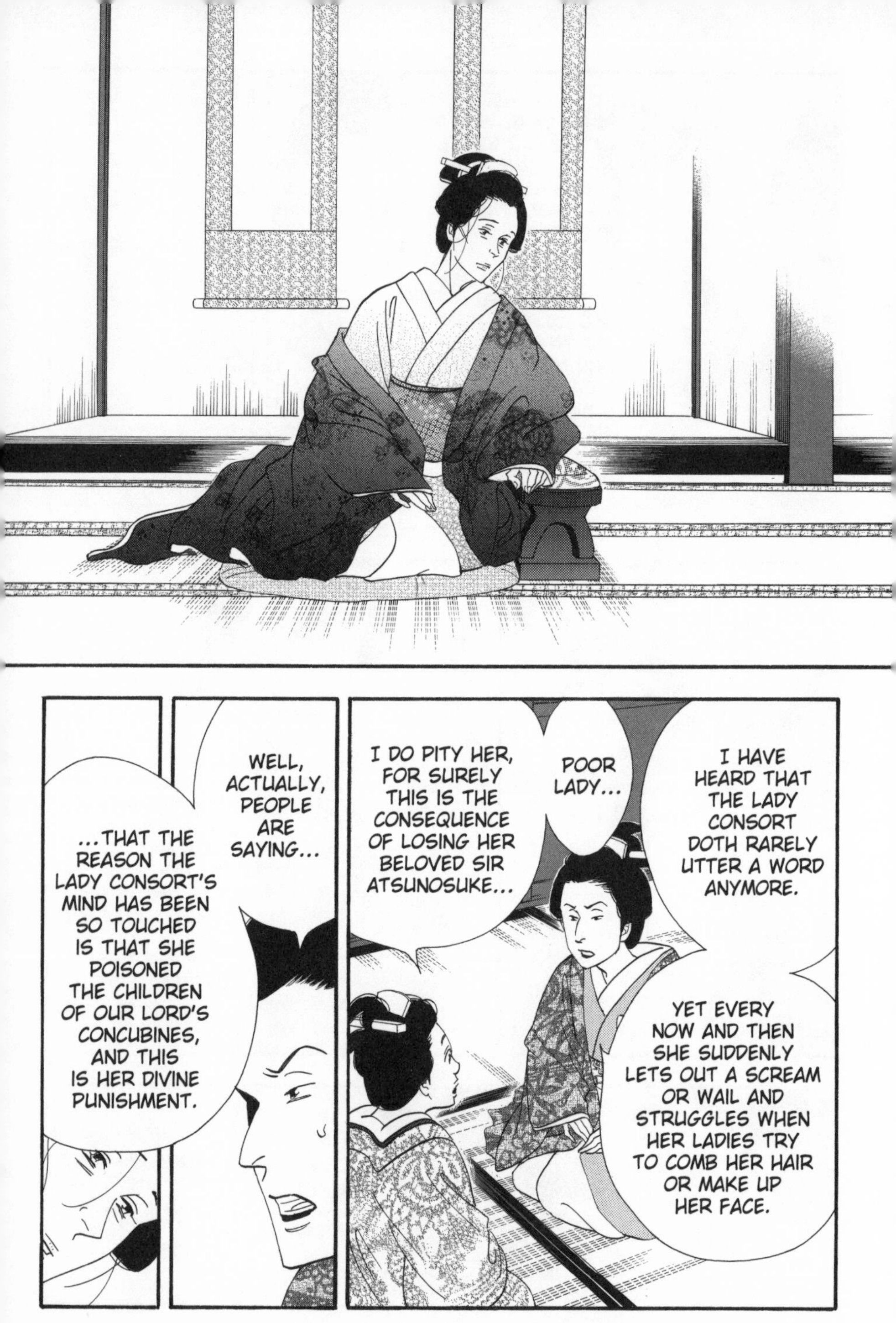
I HAVE HEARD THAT THE LADY CONSORT DOTH RARELY UTTER A WORD ANYMORE.
YET EVERY NOW AND THEN SHE SUDDENLY LETS OUT A SCREAM OR WAIL AND STRUGGLES WHEN HER LADIES TRY TO COMB HER HAIR OR MAKE UP HER FACE.
POOR LADY...
I DO PITY HER, FOR SURELY THIS IS THE CONSEQUENCE OF LOSING HER BELOVED SIR ATSUNOSUKE...
WELL, ACTUALLY, PEOPLE ARE SAYING...
...THAT THE REASON THE LADY CONSORT'S MIND HAS BEEN SO TOUCHED IS THAT SHE POISONED THE CHILDREN OF OUR LORD'S CONCUBINES, AND THIS IS HER DIVINE PUNISHMENT.

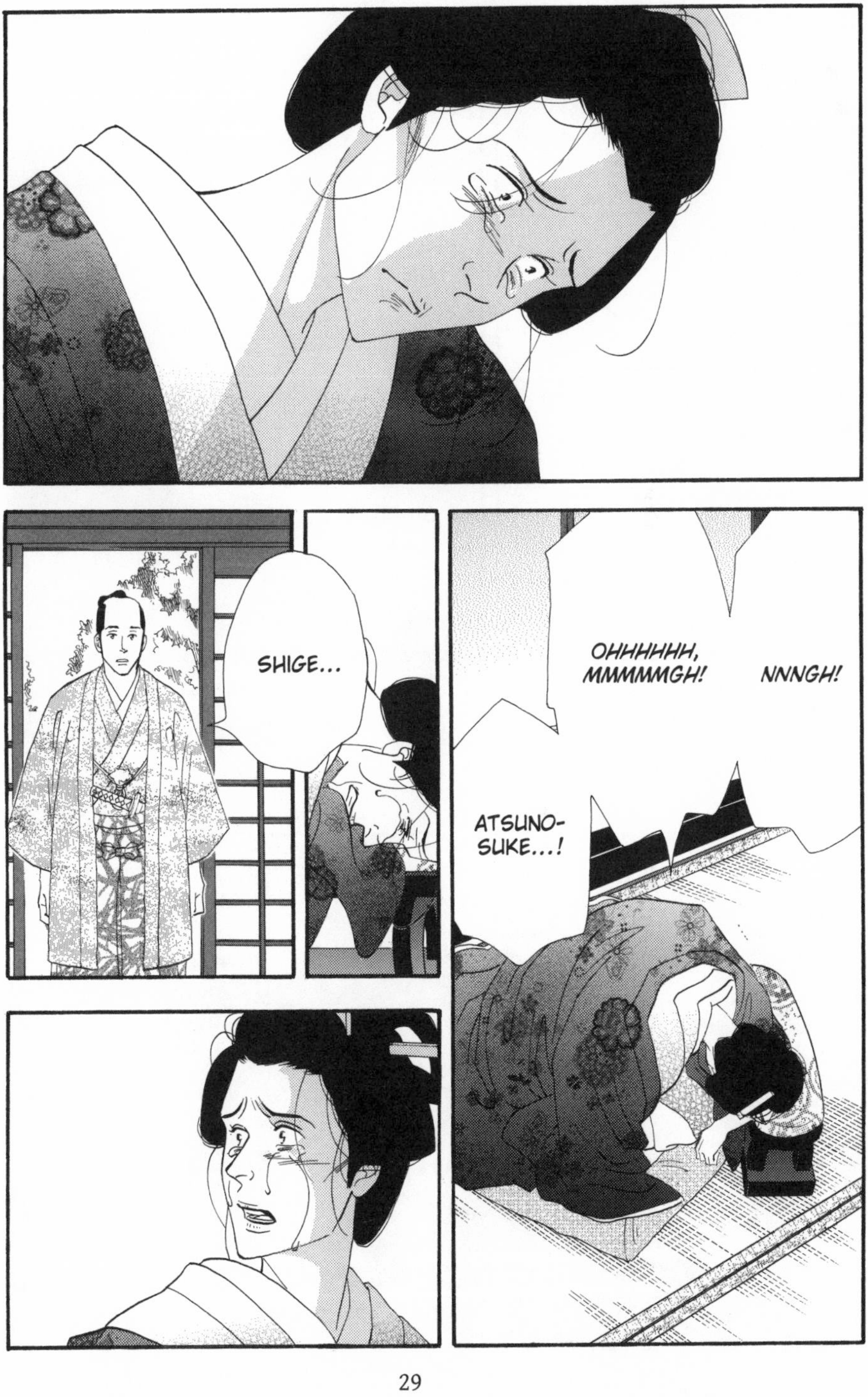
NNNGH!
OHHHHHH, MMMMMGH!
ATSUNO-SUKE...!
SHIGE...

...

WHO
ARE
YOU...?

EVERYONE
...

...

SHIGE
...

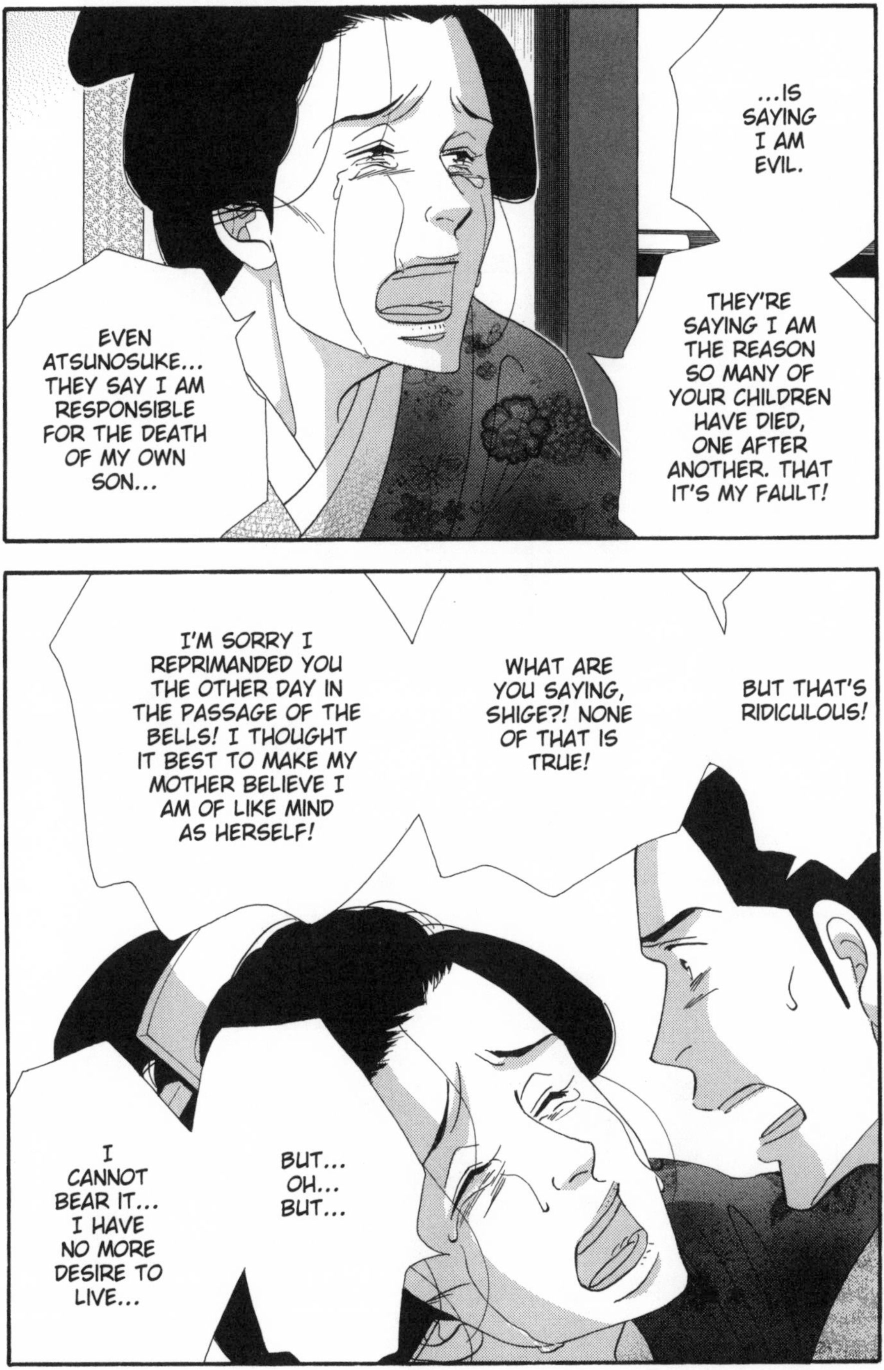
...IS SAYING I AM EVIL.
THEY'RE SAYING I AM THE REASON SO MANY OF YOUR CHILDREN HAVE DIED, ONE AFTER ANOTHER. THAT IT'S MY FAULT!
EVEN ATSUNOSUKE... THEY SAY I AM RESPONSIBLE FOR THE DEATH OF MY OWN SON...
BUT THAT'S RIDICULOUS!
WHAT ARE YOU SAYING, SHIGE?! NONE OF THAT IS TRUE!
I'M SORRY I REPRIMANDED YOU THE OTHER DAY IN THE PASSAGE OF THE BELLS! I THOUGHT IT BEST TO MAKE MY MOTHER BELIEVE I AM OF LIKE MIND AS HERSELF!
BUT... OH... BUT...
I CANNOT BEAR IT... I HAVE NO MORE DESIRE TO LIVE...

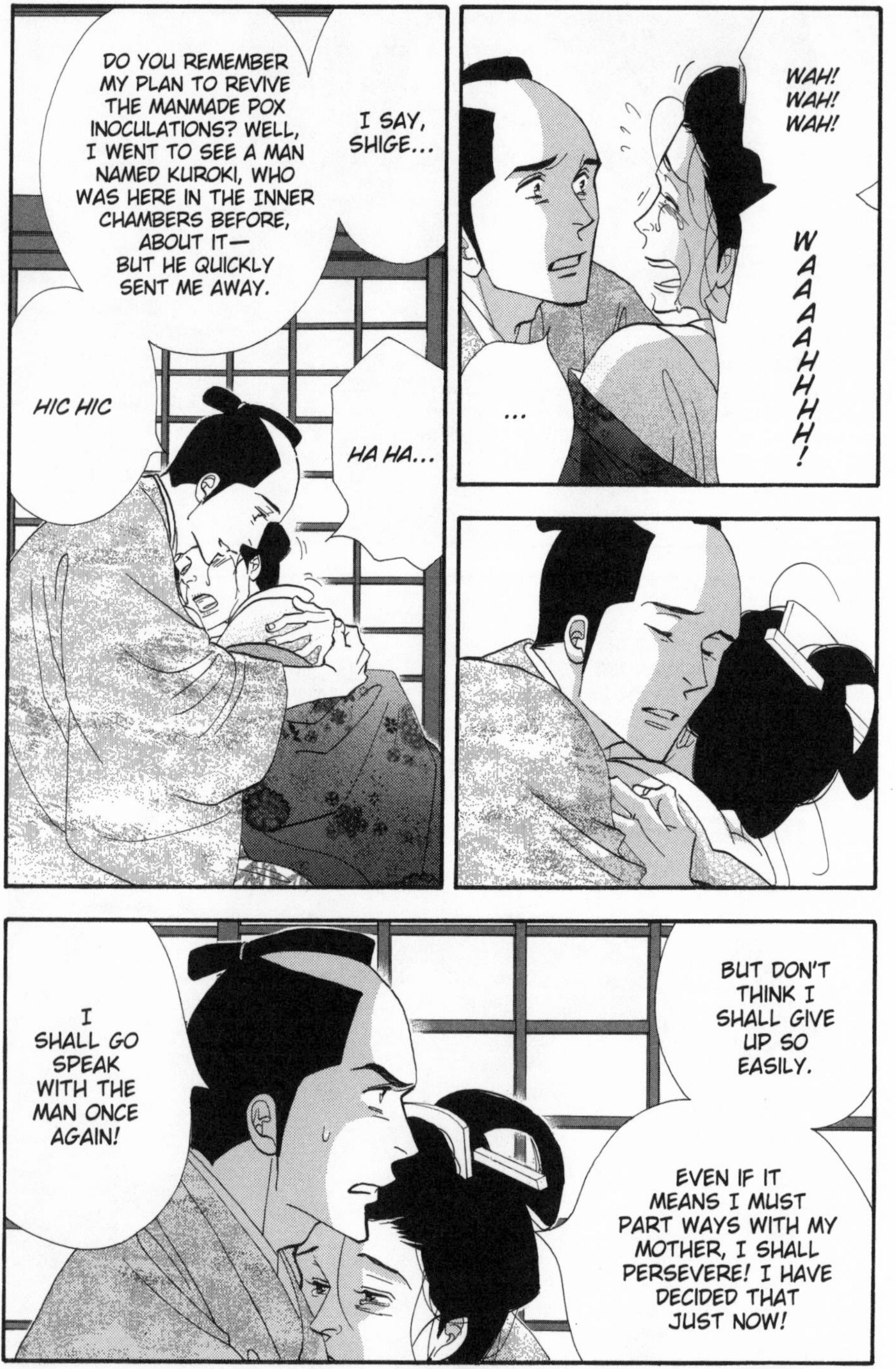
WAH! WAH! WAH!
WAAAAHHHH!
...
I SAY, SHIGE...
DO YOU REMEMBER MY PLAN TO REVIVE THE MANMADE POX INOCULATIONS? WELL, I WENT TO SEE A MAN NAMED KUROKI, WHO WAS HERE IN THE INNER CHAMBERS BEFORE, ABOUT IT— BUT HE QUICKLY SENT ME AWAY.
HA HA...
HIC HIC
BUT DON'T THINK I SHALL GIVE UP SO EASILY.
EVEN IF IT MEANS I MUST PART WAYS WITH MY MOTHER, I SHALL PERSEVERE! I HAVE DECIDED THAT JUST NOW!
I SHALL GO SPEAK WITH THE MAN ONCE AGAIN!

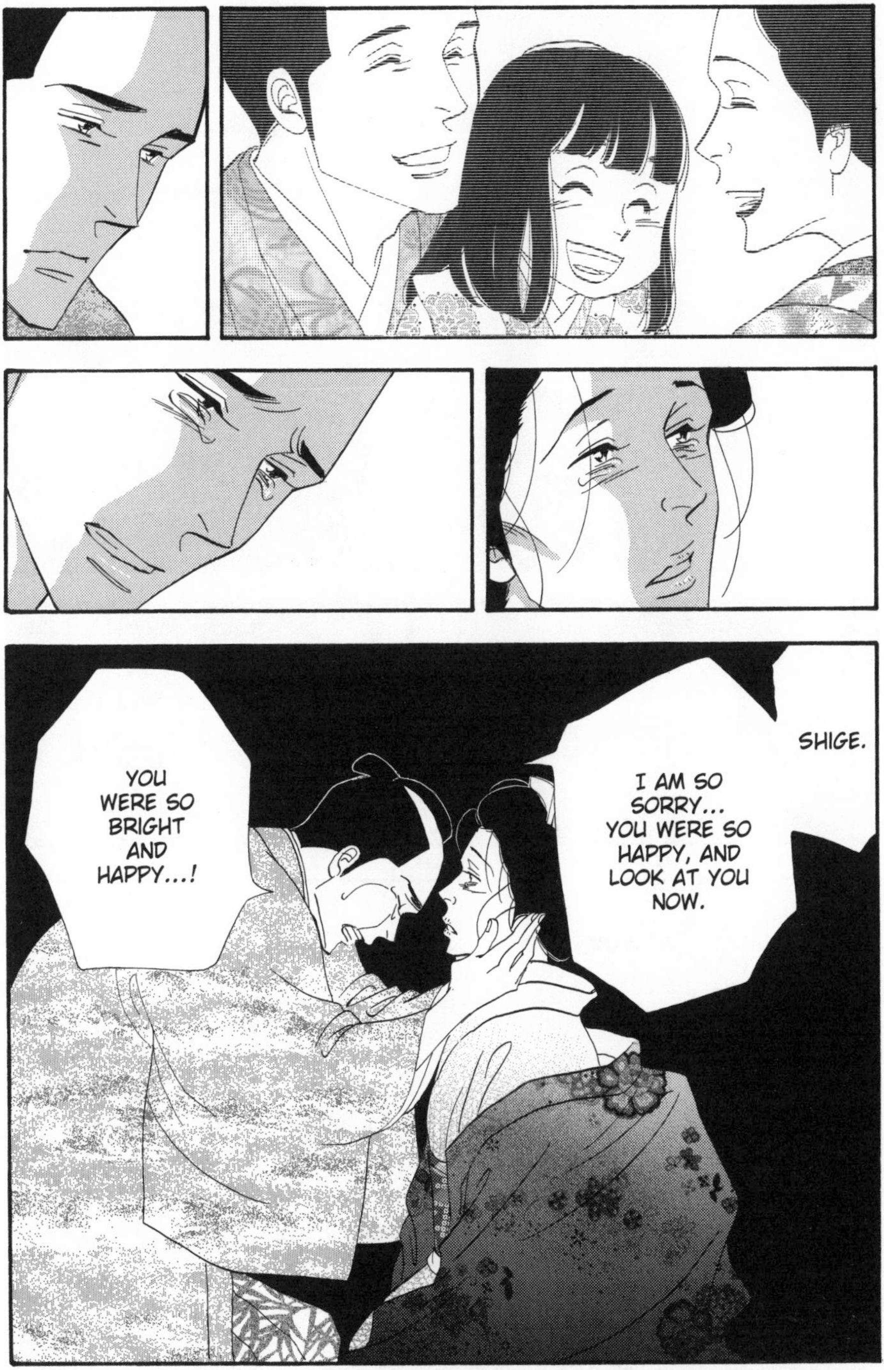
SHIGE.
I AM SO SORRY... YOU WERE SO HAPPY, AND LOOK AT YOU NOW.
YOU WERE SO BRIGHT AND HAPPY...!

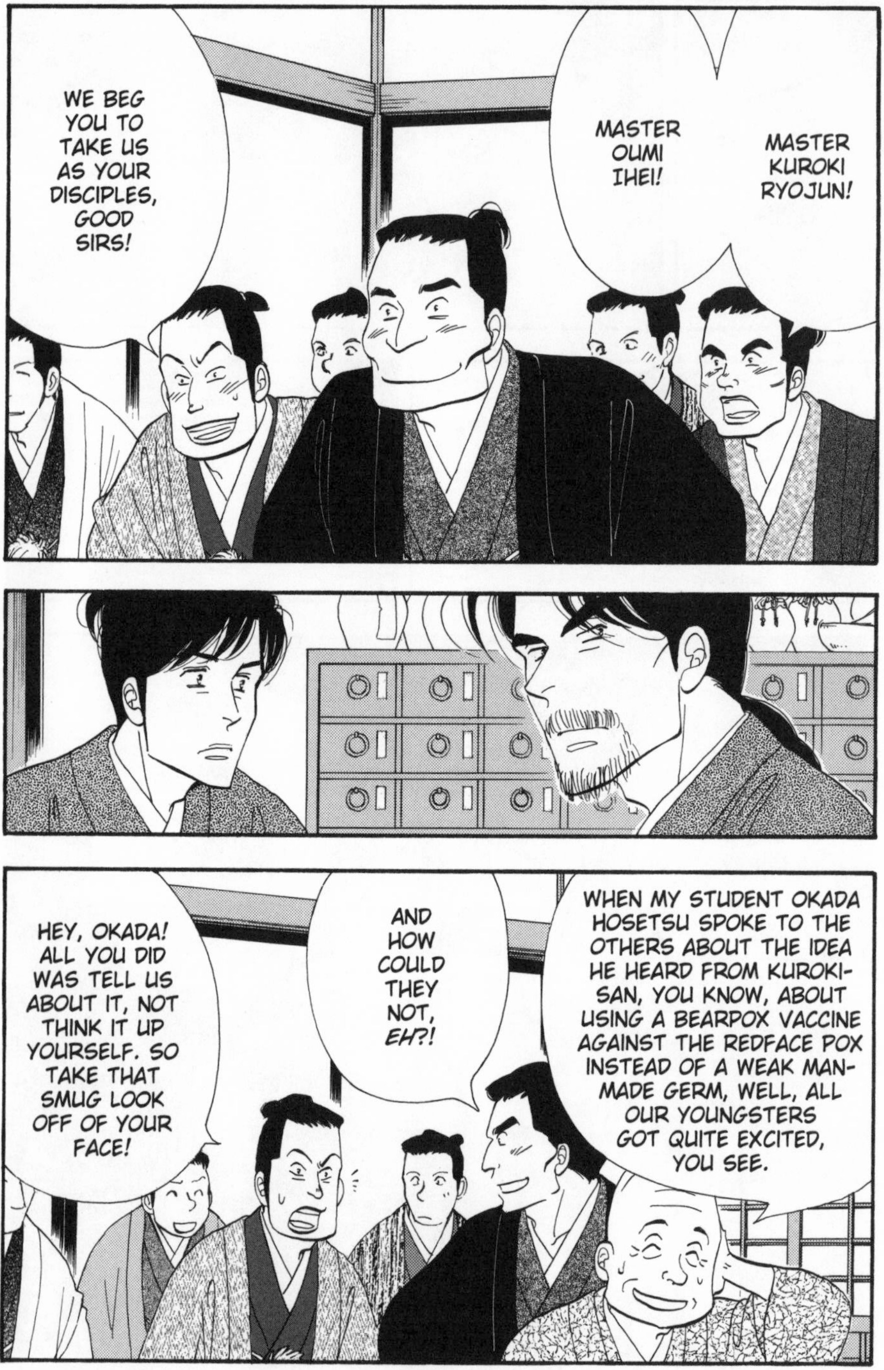
MASTER OUMI IHEI!
MASTER KUROKI RYOJUN!
WE BEG YOU TO TAKE US AS YOUR DISCIPLES, GOOD SIRS!
WHEN MY STUDENT OKADA HOSETSU SPOKE TO THE OTHERS ABOUT THE IDEA HE HEARD FROM KUROKI-SAN, YOU KNOW, ABOUT USING A BEARPOX VACCINE AGAINST THE REDFACE POX INSTEAD OF A WEAK MAN-MADE GERM, WELL, ALL OUR YOUNGSTERS GOT QUITE EXCITED, YOU SEE.
AND HOW COULD THEY NOT, *EH?!*
HEY, OKADA! ALL YOU DID WAS TELL US ABOUT IT, NOT THINK IT UP YOURSELF. SO TAKE THAT SMUG LOOK OFF OF YOUR FACE!

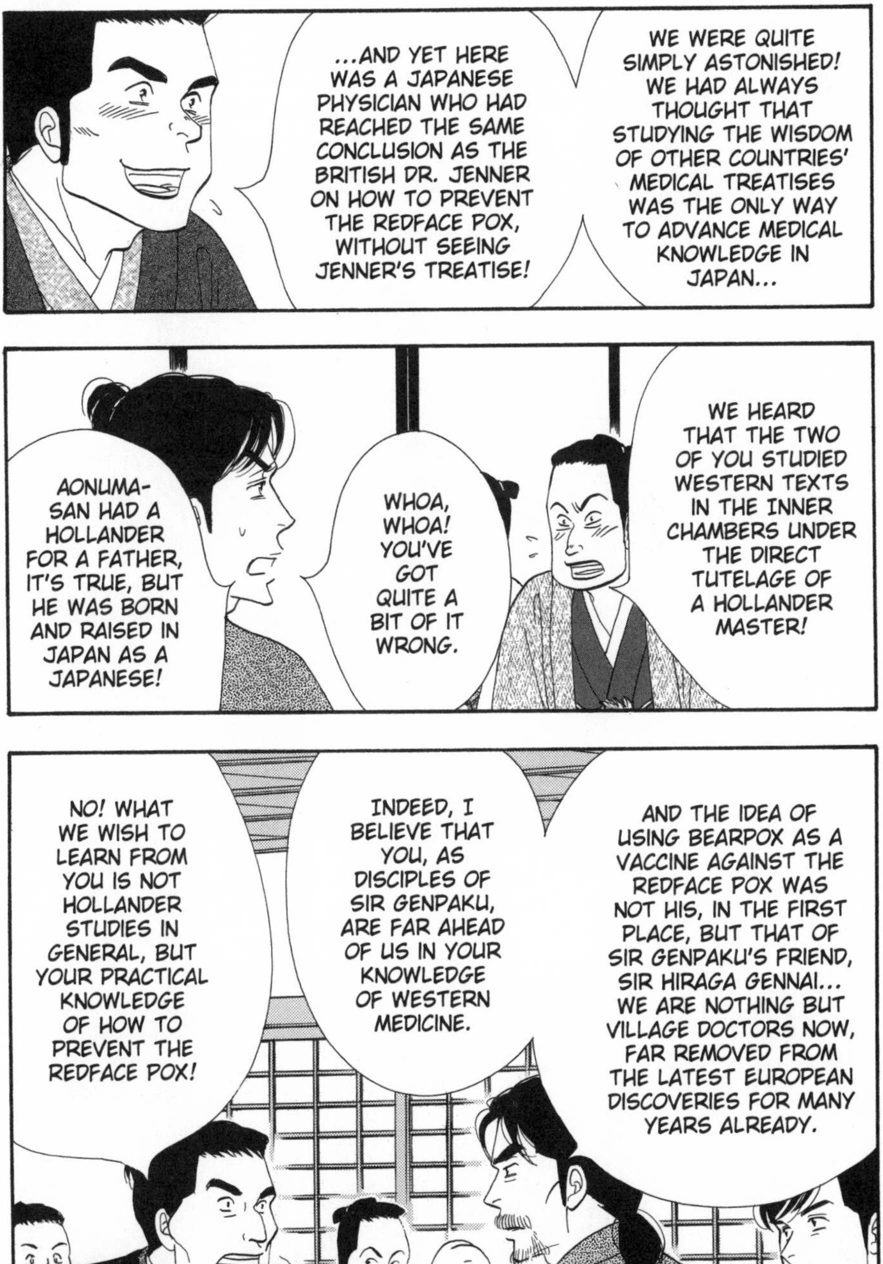
WE WERE QUITE SIMPLY ASTONISHED! WE HAD ALWAYS THOUGHT THAT STUDYING THE WISDOM OF OTHER COUNTRIES' MEDICAL TREATISES WAS THE ONLY WAY TO ADVANCE MEDICAL KNOWLEDGE IN JAPAN...
...AND YET HERE WAS A JAPANESE PHYSICIAN WHO HAD REACHED THE SAME CONCLUSION AS THE BRITISH DR. JENNER ON HOW TO PREVENT THE REDFACE POX, WITHOUT SEEING JENNER'S TREATISE!
WE HEARD THAT THE TWO OF YOU STUDIED WESTERN TEXTS IN THE INNER CHAMBERS UNDER THE DIRECT TUTELAGE OF A HOLLANDER MASTER!
WHOA, WHOA! YOU'VE GOT QUITE A BIT OF IT WRONG.
AONUMA-SAN HAD A HOLLANDER FOR A FATHER, IT'S TRUE, BUT HE WAS BORN AND RAISED IN JAPAN AS A JAPANESE!
AND THE IDEA OF USING BEARPOX AS A VACCINE AGAINST THE REDFACE POX WAS NOT HIS, IN THE FIRST PLACE, BUT THAT OF SIR GENPAKU'S FRIEND, SIR HIRAGA GENNAI... WE ARE NOTHING BUT VILLAGE DOCTORS NOW, FAR REMOVED FROM THE LATEST EUROPEAN DISCOVERIES FOR MANY YEARS ALREADY.
INDEED, I BELIEVE THAT YOU, AS DISCIPLES OF SIR GENPAKU, ARE FAR AHEAD OF US IN YOUR KNOWLEDGE OF WESTERN MEDICINE.
NO! WHAT WE WISH TO LEARN FROM YOU IS NOT HOLLANDER STUDIES IN GENERAL, BUT YOUR PRACTICAL KNOWLEDGE OF HOW TO PREVENT THE REDFACE POX!

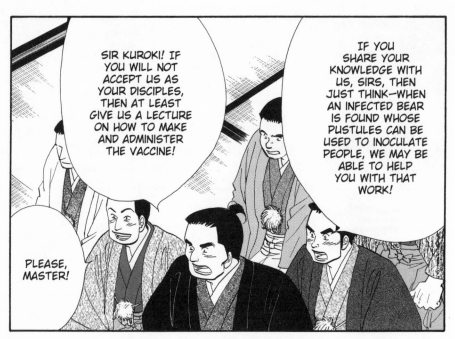

IF YOU SHARE YOUR KNOWLEDGE WITH US, SIRS, THEN JUST THINK—WHEN AN INFECTED BEAR IS FOUND WHOSE PUSTULES CAN BE USED TO INOCULATE PEOPLE, WE MAY BE ABLE TO HELP YOU WITH THAT WORK!
SIR KUROKI! IF YOU WILL NOT ACCEPT US AS YOUR DISCIPLES, THEN AT LEAST GIVE US A LECTURE ON HOW TO MAKE AND ADMINISTER THE VACCINE!
PLEASE, MASTER!
IN OUR WORLD TODAY, WE MEN WHO HAVE GROWN TO ADULTHOOD ARE FEW ENOUGH TO BE PRIZED AS STALLIONS, PAID BY WOMEN TO GET THEM WITH CHILD AND ABLE TO LIVE AN INDOLENT LIFE ON THE PROCEEDS.
BUT WE KNOW TOO WELL HOW HARD OUR MOTHERS AND OUR SISTERS HAVE WORKED TO SUPPORT OUR FAMILIES AND TO GET CHILDREN OF THEIR OWN!
WE MUST CHANGE THIS WORLD OF OURS! THAT IS THE VERY REASON WE ARE STUDYING WESTERN MEDICINE—TO RID OUR COUNTRY OF THIS PLAGUE CALLED THE REDFACE POX, WHICH IS UNKNOWN ANYWHERE ELSE, AND SECURE A BRIGHTER FUTURE!

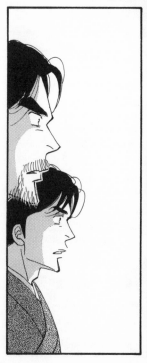

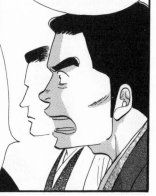

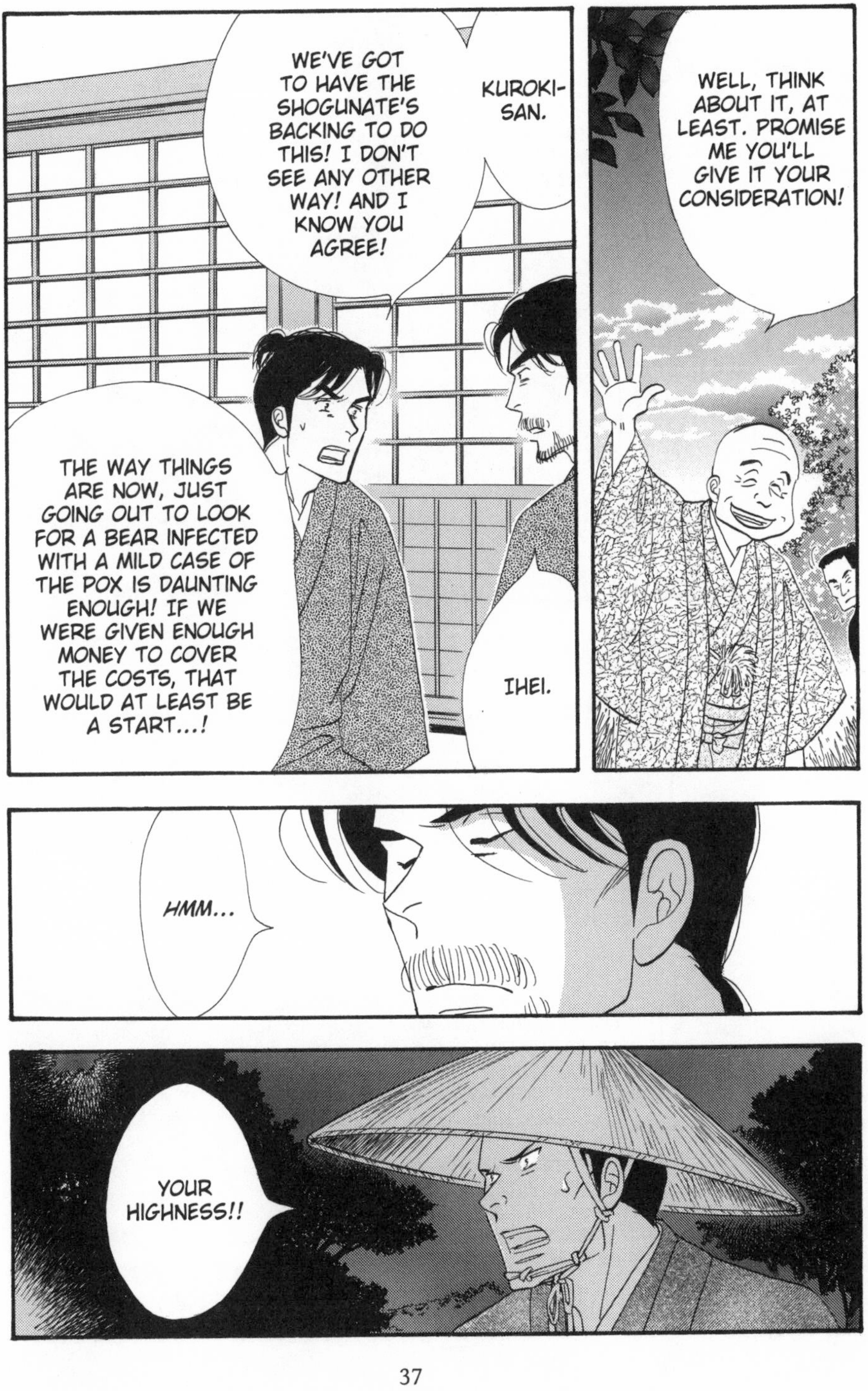
WELL, THINK ABOUT IT, AT LEAST. PROMISE ME YOU'LL GIVE IT YOUR CONSIDERATION!
KUROKI-SAN.
WE'VE GOT TO HAVE THE SHOGUNATE'S BACKING TO DO THIS! I DON'T SEE ANY OTHER WAY! AND I KNOW YOU AGREE!
THE WAY THINGS ARE NOW, JUST GOING OUT TO LOOK FOR A BEAR INFECTED WITH A MILD CASE OF THE POX IS DAUNTING ENOUGH! IF WE WERE GIVEN ENOUGH MONEY TO COVER THE COSTS, THAT WOULD AT LEAST BE A START...!
IHEI.
HMM...
YOUR HIGHNESS!!

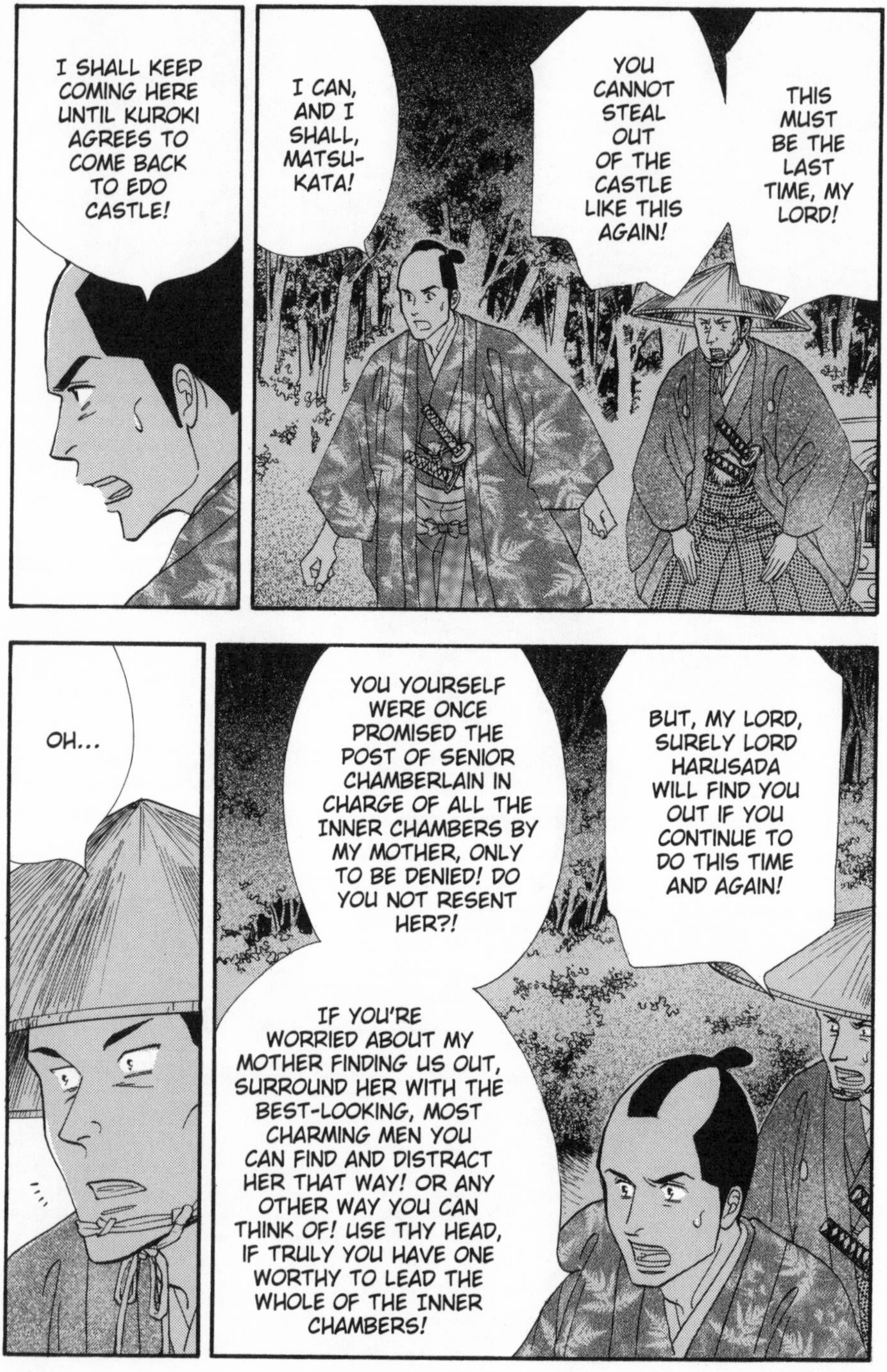

THIS MUST BE THE LAST TIME, MY LORD!
YOU CANNOT STEAL OUT OF THE CASTLE LIKE THIS AGAIN!
I CAN, AND I SHALL, MATSUKATA!
I SHALL KEEP COMING HERE UNTIL KUROKI AGREES TO COME BACK TO EDO CASTLE!
BUT, MY LORD, SURELY LORD HARUSADA WILL FIND YOU OUT IF YOU CONTINUE TO DO THIS TIME AND AGAIN!
YOU YOURSELF WERE ONCE PROMISED THE POST OF SENIOR CHAMBERLAIN IN CHARGE OF ALL THE INNER CHAMBERS BY MY MOTHER, ONLY TO BE DENIED! DO YOU NOT RESENT HER?!
IF YOU'RE WORRIED ABOUT MY MOTHER FINDING US OUT, SURROUND HER WITH THE BEST-LOOKING, MOST CHARMING MEN YOU CAN FIND AND DISTRACT HER THAT WAY! OR ANY OTHER WAY YOU CAN THINK OF! USE THY HEAD, IF TRULY YOU HAVE ONE WORTHY TO LEAD THE WHOLE OF THE INNER CHAMBERS!
OH...

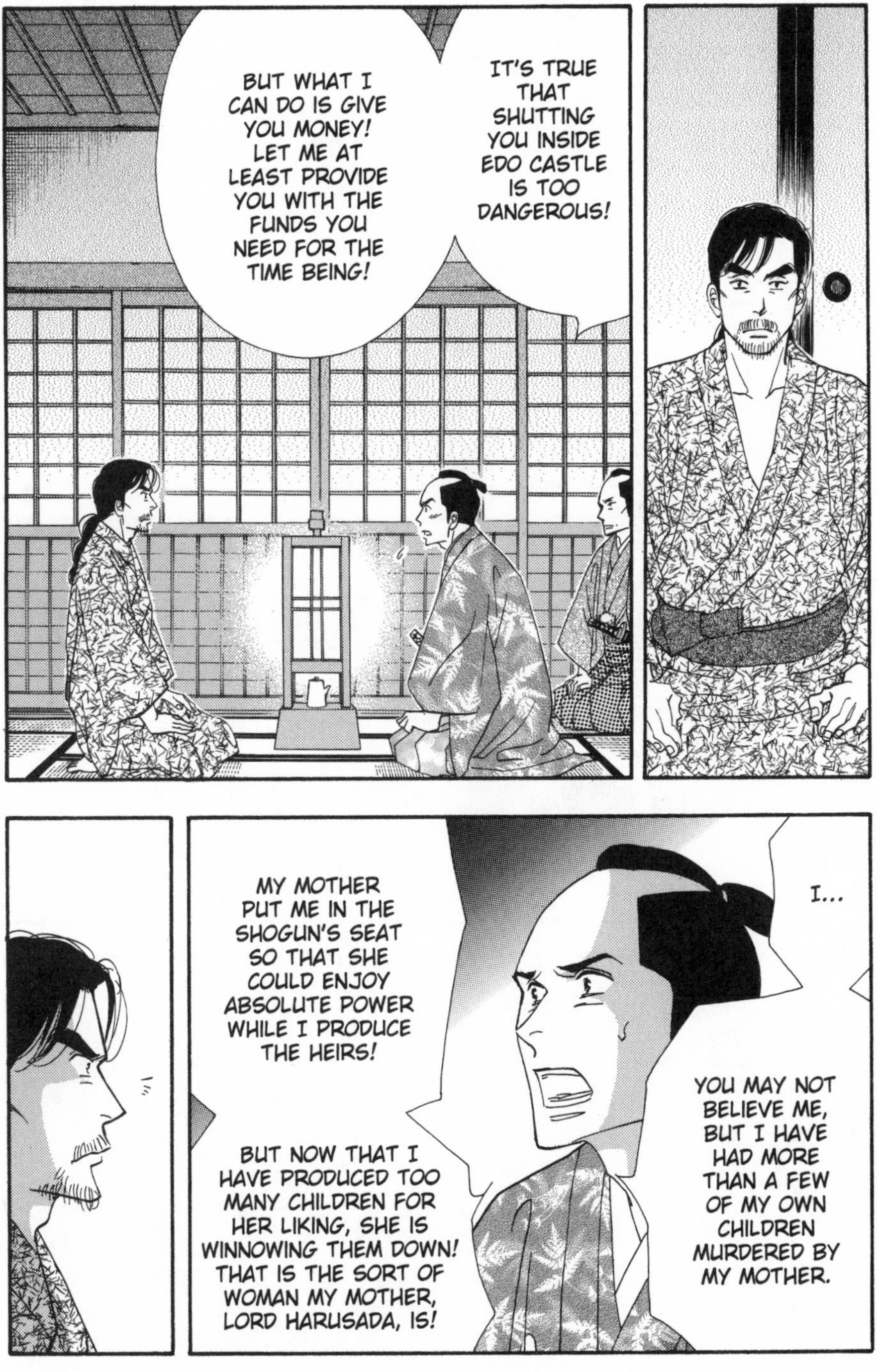
IT'S TRUE THAT SHUTTING YOU INSIDE EDO CASTLE IS TOO DANGEROUS!
BUT WHAT I CAN DO IS GIVE YOU MONEY! LET ME AT LEAST PROVIDE YOU WITH THE FUNDS YOU NEED FOR THE TIME BEING!
I...
YOU MAY NOT BELIEVE ME, BUT I HAVE HAD MORE THAN A FEW OF MY OWN CHILDREN MURDERED BY MY MOTHER.
MY MOTHER PUT ME IN THE SHOGUN'S SEAT SO THAT SHE COULD ENJOY ABSOLUTE POWER WHILE I PRODUCE THE HEIRS!
BUT NOW THAT I HAVE PRODUCED TOO MANY CHILDREN FOR HER LIKING, SHE IS WINNOWING THEM DOWN! THAT IS THE SORT OF WOMAN MY MOTHER, LORD HARUSADA, IS!

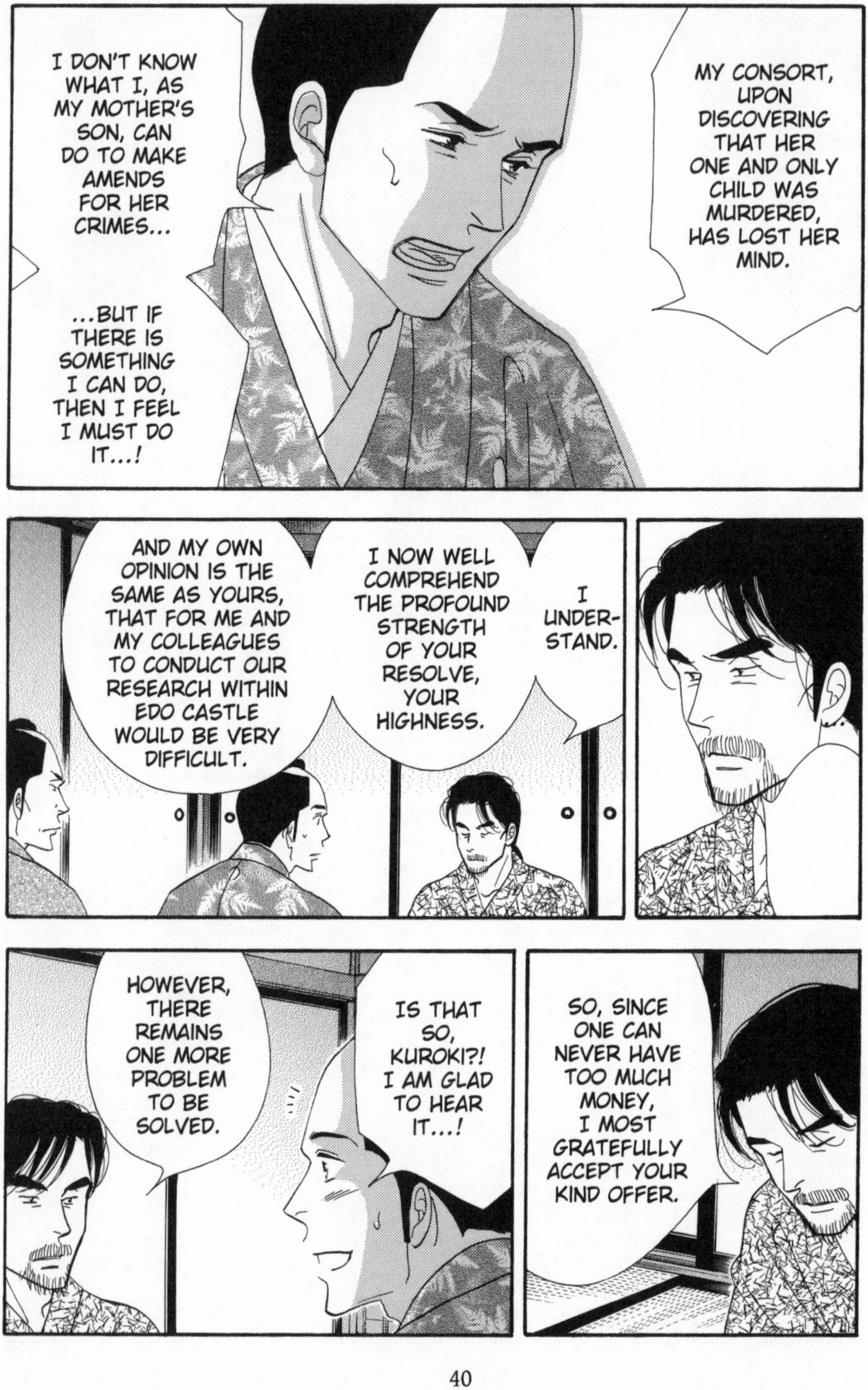
MY CONSORT, UPON DISCOVERING THAT HER ONE AND ONLY CHILD WAS MURDERED, HAS LOST HER MIND.
I DON'T KNOW WHAT I, AS MY MOTHER'S SON, CAN DO TO MAKE AMENDS FOR HER CRIMES...
...BUT IF THERE IS SOMETHING I CAN DO, THEN I FEEL I MUST DO IT...!
I UNDER-STAND.
I NOW WELL COMPREHEND THE PROFOUND STRENGTH OF YOUR RESOLVE, YOUR HIGHNESS.
AND MY OWN OPINION IS THE SAME AS YOURS, THAT FOR ME AND MY COLLEAGUES TO CONDUCT OUR RESEARCH WITHIN EDO CASTLE WOULD BE VERY DIFFICULT.
SO, SINCE ONE CAN NEVER HAVE TOO MUCH MONEY, I MOST GRATEFULLY ACCEPT YOUR KIND OFFER.
IS THAT SO, KUROKI?! I AM GLAD TO HEAR IT...!
HOWEVER, THERE REMAINS ONE MORE PROBLEM TO BE SOLVED.

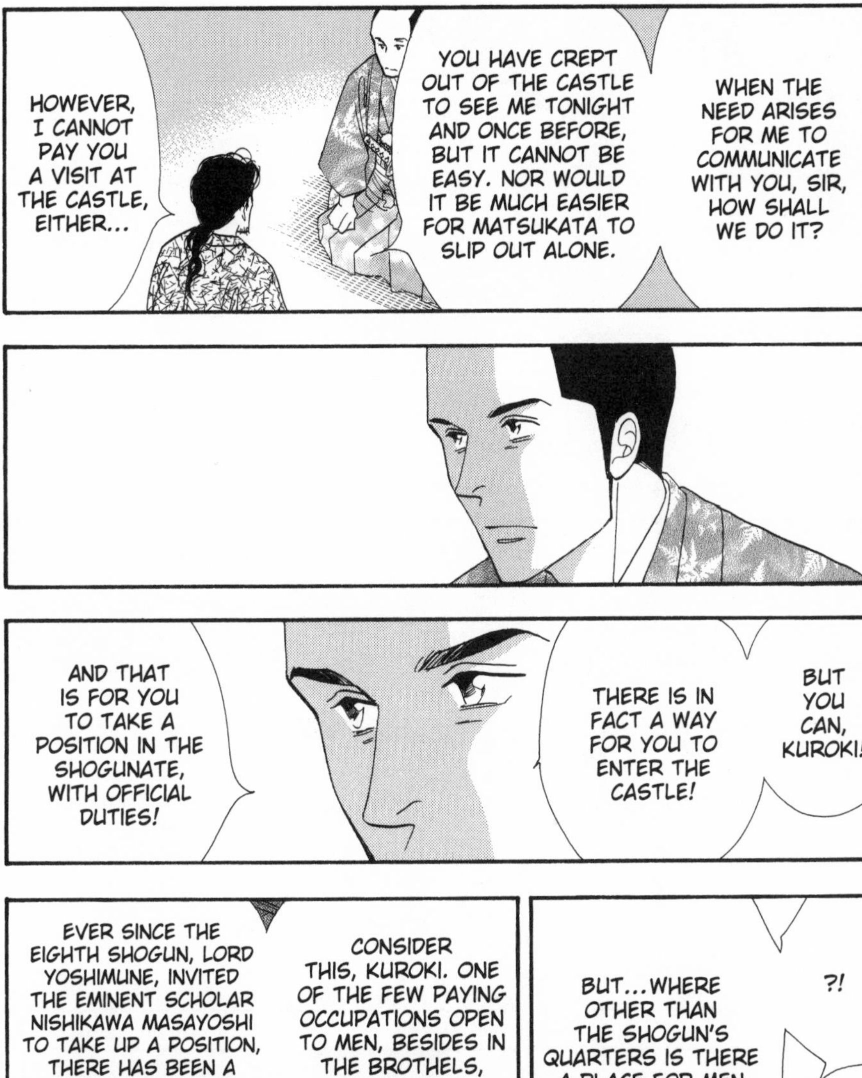
WHEN THE NEED ARISES FOR ME TO COMMUNICATE WITH YOU, SIR, HOW SHALL WE DO IT?
YOU HAVE CREPT OUT OF THE CASTLE TO SEE ME TONIGHT AND ONCE BEFORE, BUT IT CANNOT BE EASY. NOR WOULD IT BE MUCH EASIER FOR MATSUKATA TO SLIP OUT ALONE.
HOWEVER, I CANNOT PAY YOU A VISIT AT THE CASTLE, EITHER...
BUT YOU CAN, KUROKI!
THERE IS IN FACT A WAY FOR YOU TO ENTER THE CASTLE!
AND THAT IS FOR YOU TO TAKE A POSITION IN THE SHOGUNATE, WITH OFFICIAL DUTIES!
?!
BUT...WHERE OTHER THAN THE SHOGUN'S QUARTERS IS THERE A PLACE FOR MEN TO BE EMPLOYED IN EDO CASTLE?
CONSIDER THIS, KUROKI. ONE OF THE FEW PAYING OCCUPATIONS OPEN TO MEN, BESIDES IN THE BROTHELS, IS THAT OF SCHOLAR.
EVER SINCE THE EIGHTH SHOGUN, LORD YOSHIMUNE, INVITED THE EMINENT SCHOLAR NISHIKAWA MASAYOSHI TO TAKE UP A POSITION, THERE HAS BEEN A PLACE WITHIN THE SHOGUNATE THAT EVEN TODAY CONTINUES TO EMPLOY MEN...
THE ASTRONOMY DEPARTMENT!

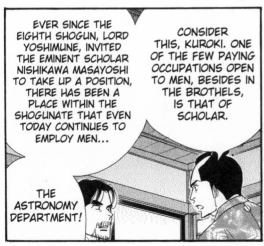

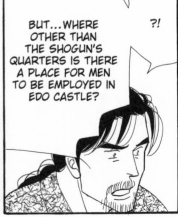

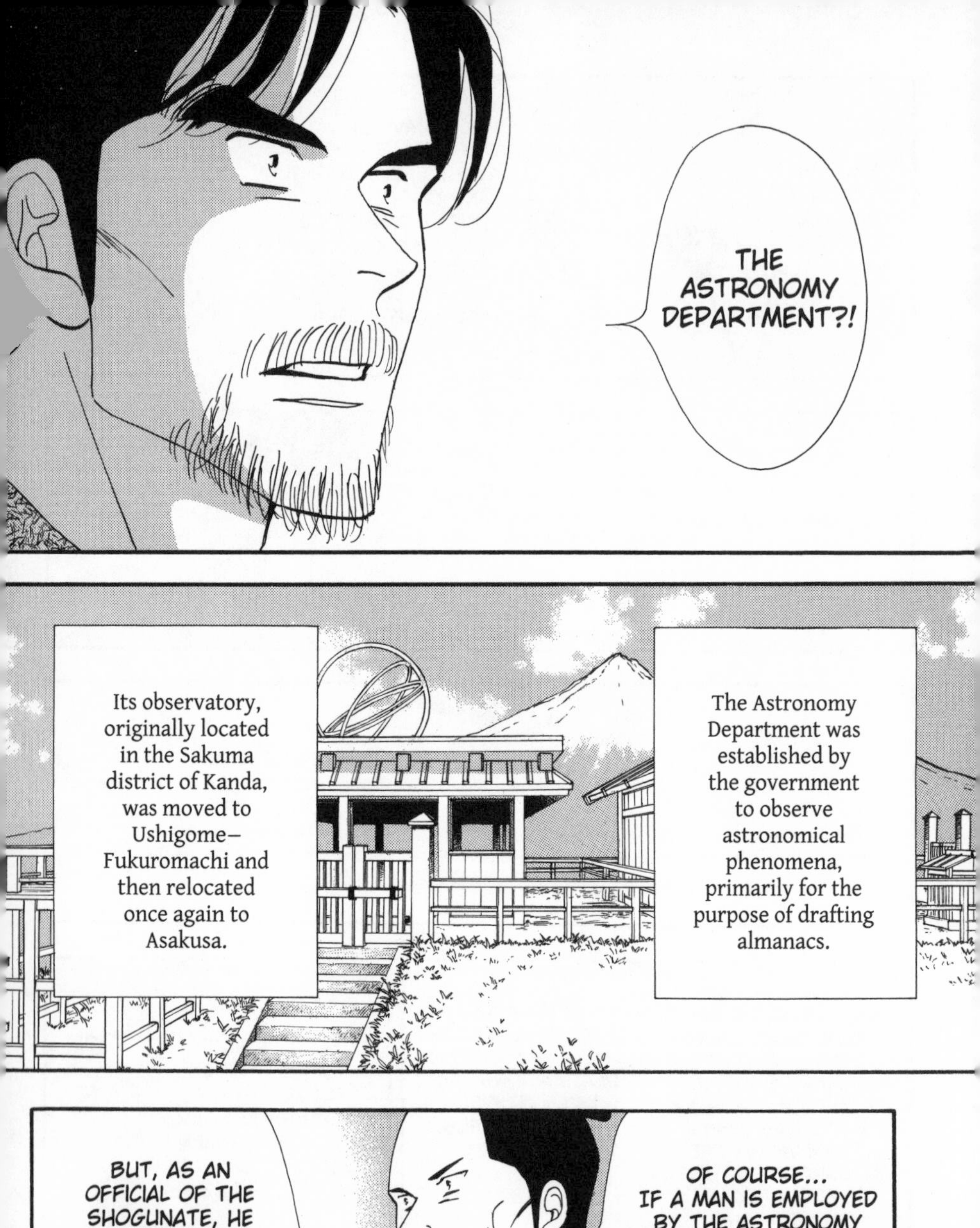
THE ASTRONOMY DEPARTMENT?!
The Astronomy Department was established by the government to observe astronomical phenomena, primarily for the purpose of drafting almanacs.
Its observatory, originally located in the Sakuma district of Kanda, was moved to Ushigome–Fukuromachi and then relocated once again to Asakusa.
OF COURSE... IF A MAN IS EMPLOYED BY THE ASTRONOMY DEPARTMENT, HE WOULD REPORT FOR DUTY TO THE OBSERVATORY IN ASAKUSA EVERY DAY. HE NEEDN'T BE LOCKED UP IN EDO CASTLE!
BUT, AS AN OFFICIAL OF THE SHOGUNATE, HE COULD ENTER EDO CASTLE AS A MAN AMONG ALL THE WOMEN, WITHOUT DRAWING SUSPICION...!

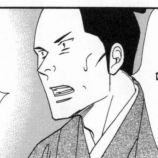

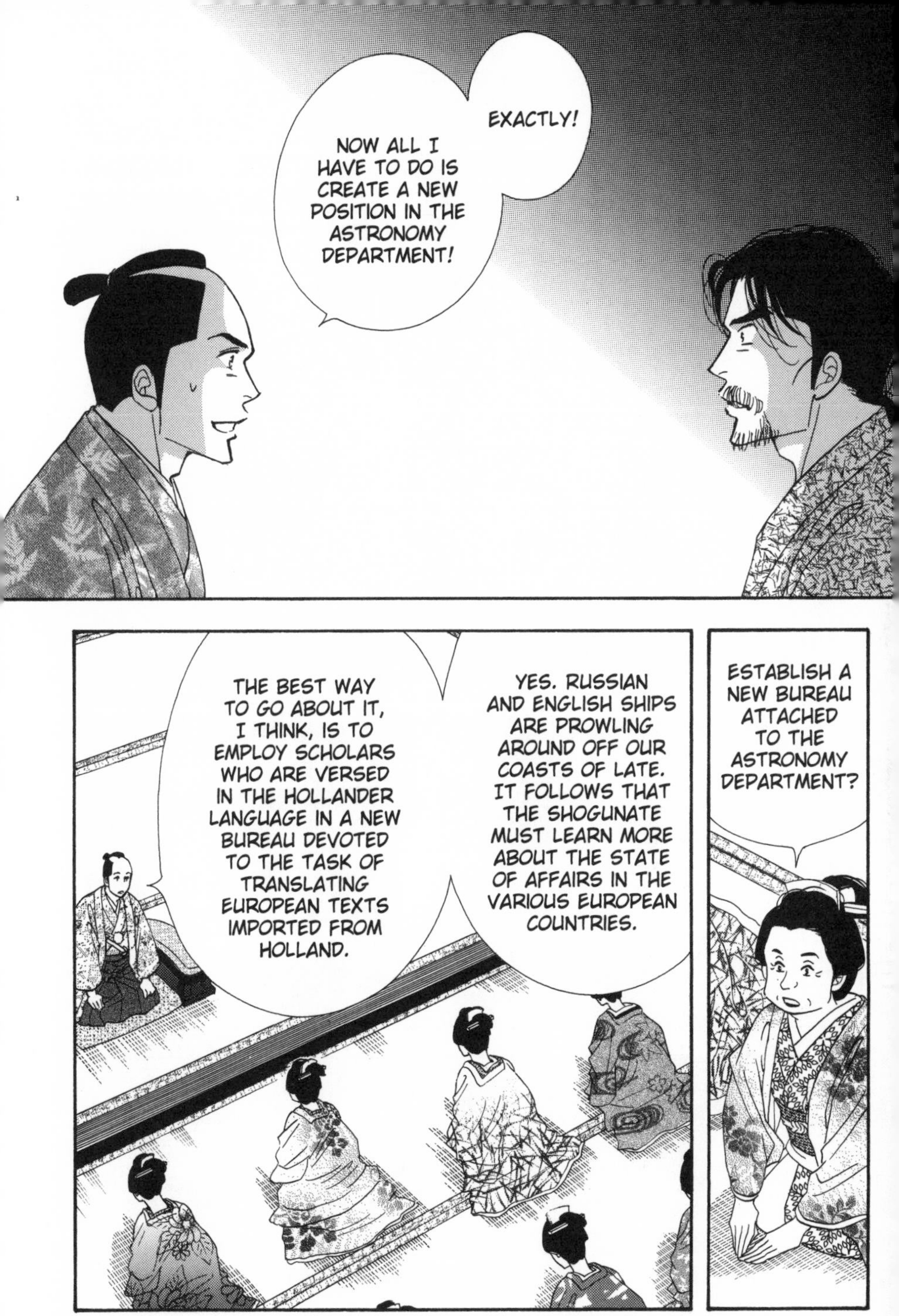
EXACTLY!
NOW ALL I HAVE TO DO IS CREATE A NEW POSITION IN THE ASTRONOMY DEPARTMENT!
ESTABLISH A NEW BUREAU ATTACHED TO THE ASTRONOMY DEPARTMENT?
YES. RUSSIAN AND ENGLISH SHIPS ARE PROWLING AROUND OFF OUR COASTS OF LATE. IT FOLLOWS THAT THE SHOGUNATE MUST LEARN MORE ABOUT THE STATE OF AFFAIRS IN THE VARIOUS EUROPEAN COUNTRIES.
THE BEST WAY TO GO ABOUT IT, I THINK, IS TO EMPLOY SCHOLARS WHO ARE VERSED IN THE HOLLANDER LANGUAGE IN A NEW BUREAU DEVOTED TO THE TASK OF TRANSLATING EUROPEAN TEXTS IMPORTED FROM HOLLAND.

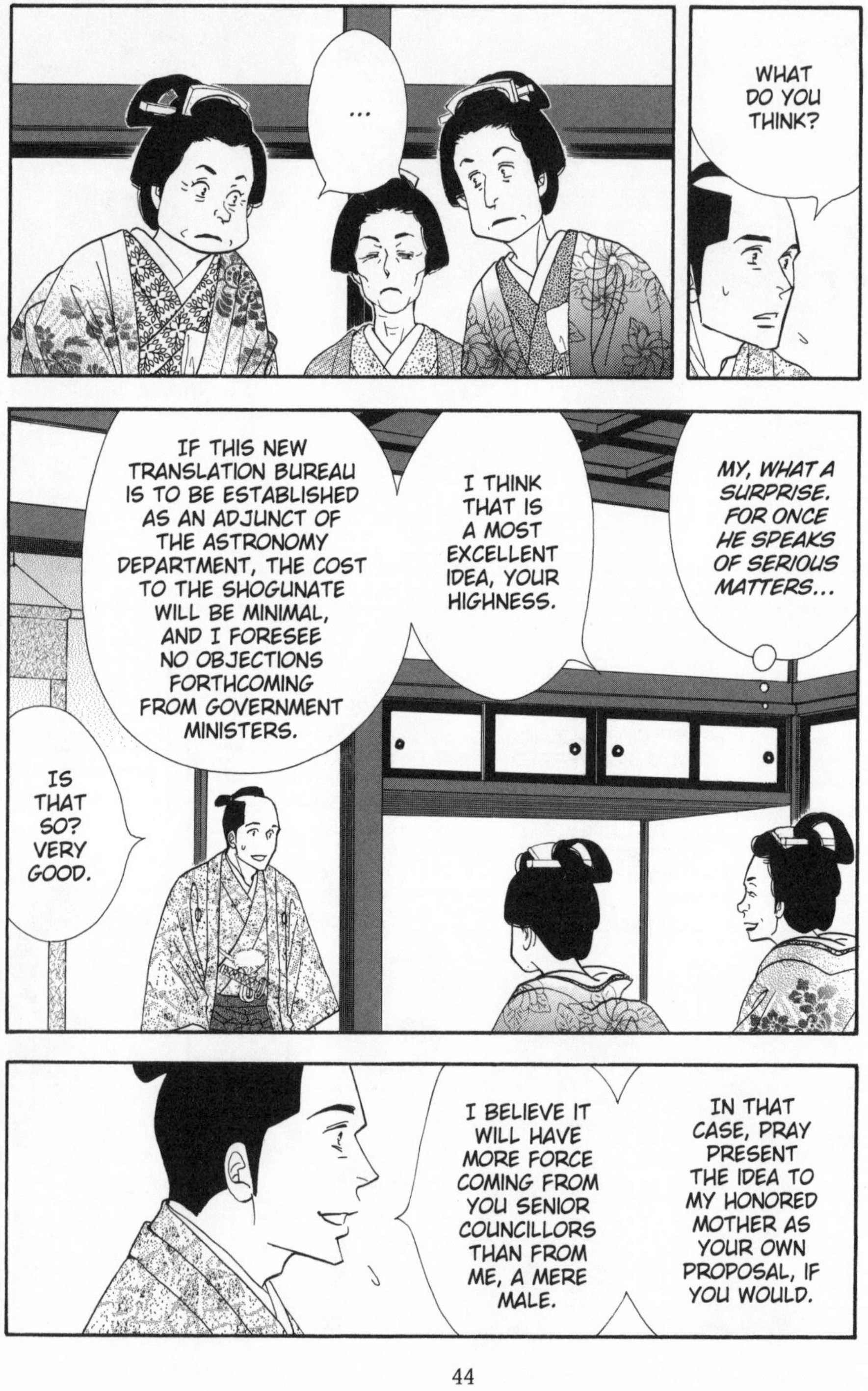
WHAT DO YOU THINK?
...
MY, WHAT A SURPRISE. FOR ONCE HE SPEAKS OF SERIOUS MATTERS...
I THINK THAT IS A MOST EXCELLENT IDEA, YOUR HIGHNESS.
IF THIS NEW TRANSLATION BUREAU IS TO BE ESTABLISHED AS AN ADJUNCT OF THE ASTRONOMY DEPARTMENT, THE COST TO THE SHOGUNATE WILL BE MINIMAL, AND I FORESEE NO OBJECTIONS FORTHCOMING FROM GOVERNMENT MINISTERS.
IS THAT SO? VERY GOOD.
IN THAT CASE, PRAY PRESENT THE IDEA TO MY HONORED MOTHER AS YOUR OWN PROPOSAL, IF YOU WOULD.
I BELIEVE IT WILL HAVE MORE FORCE COMING FROM YOU SENIOR COUNCILLORS THAN FROM ME, A MERE MALE.

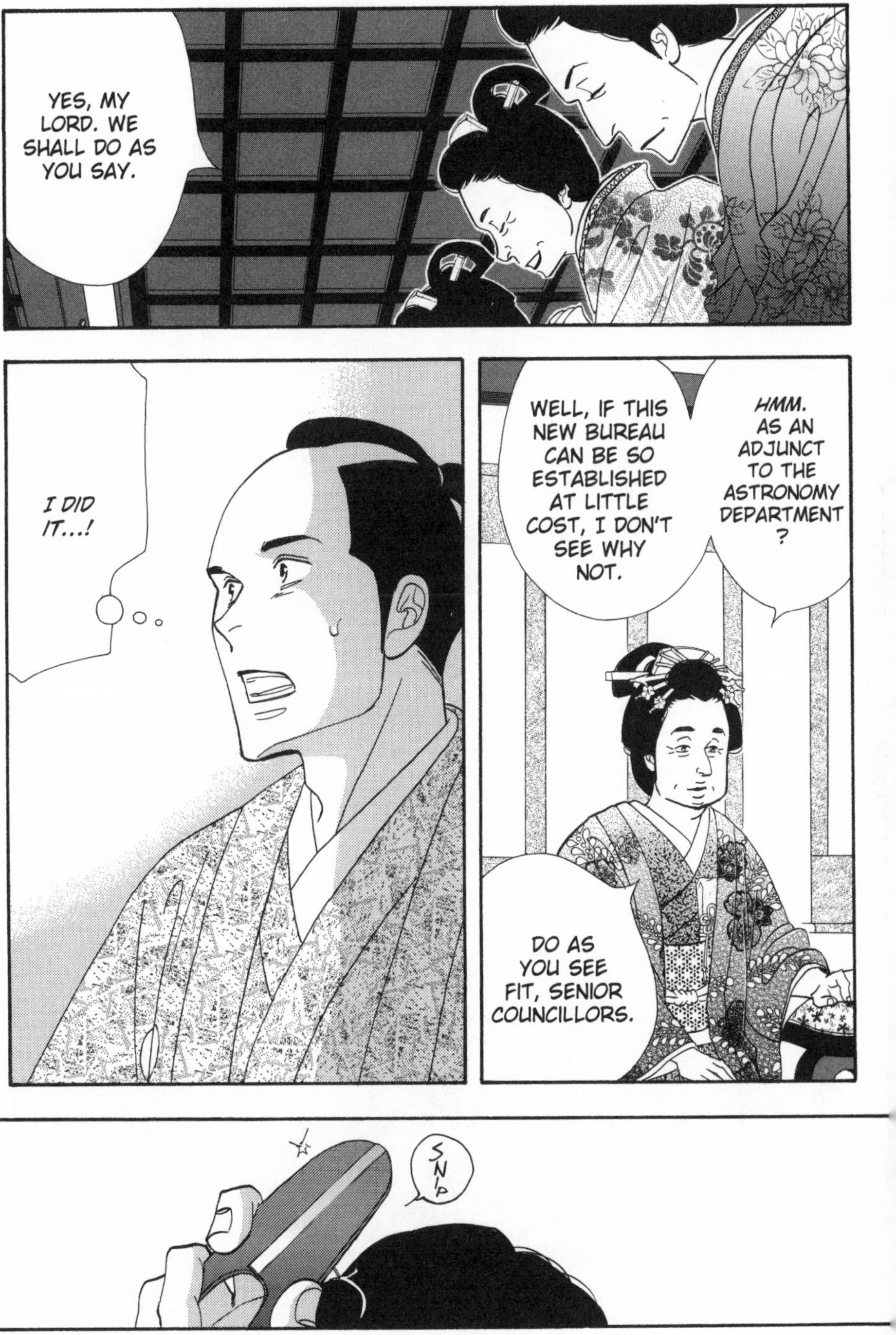
YES, MY LORD. WE SHALL DO AS YOU SAY.
HMM. AS AN ADJUNCT TO THE ASTRONOMY DEPARTMENT?
WELL, IF THIS NEW BUREAU CAN BE SO ESTABLISHED AT LITTLE COST, I DON'T SEE WHY NOT.
DO AS YOU SEE FIT, SENIOR COUNCILLORS.
I DID IT...!
SNIP

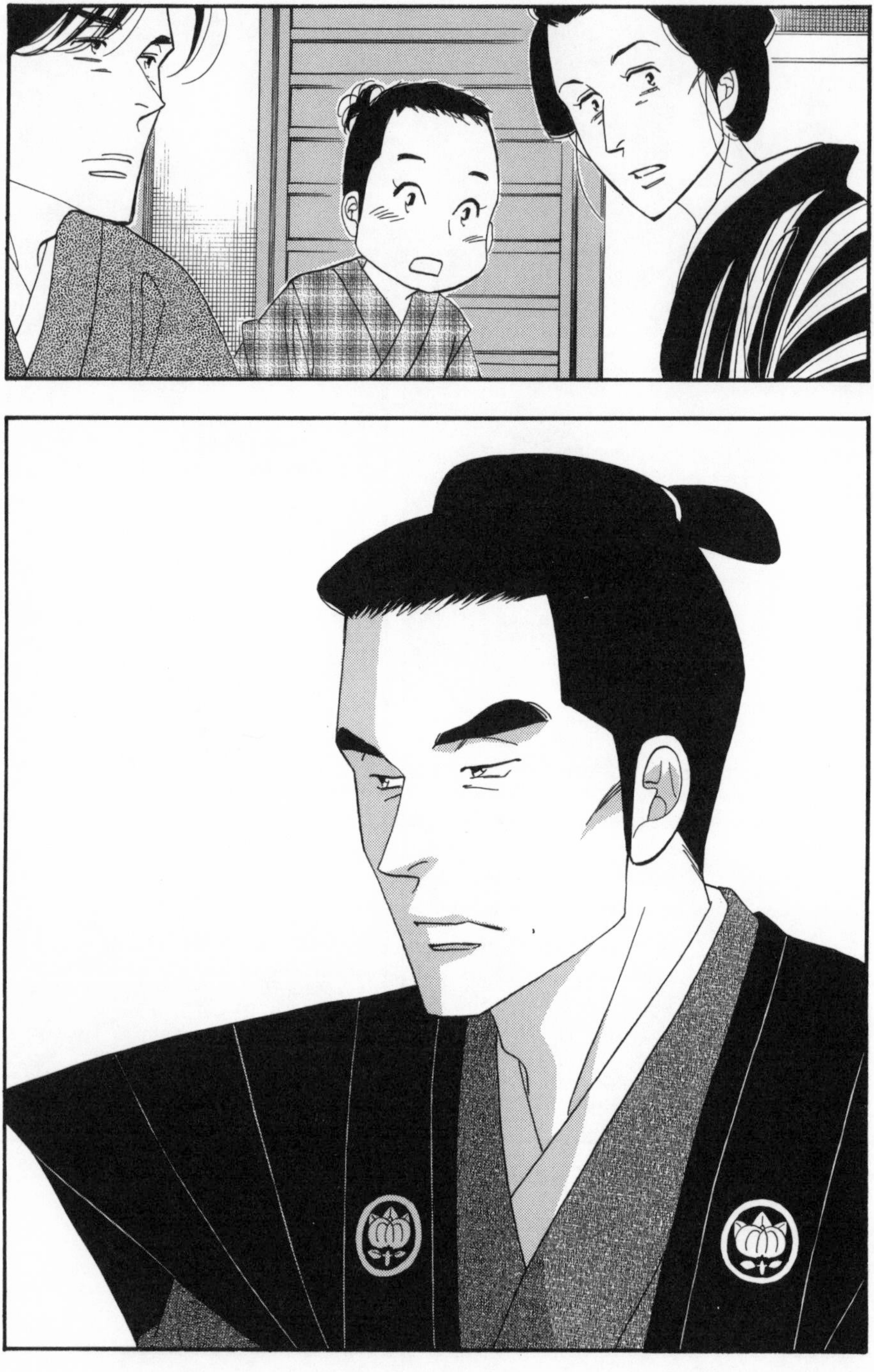

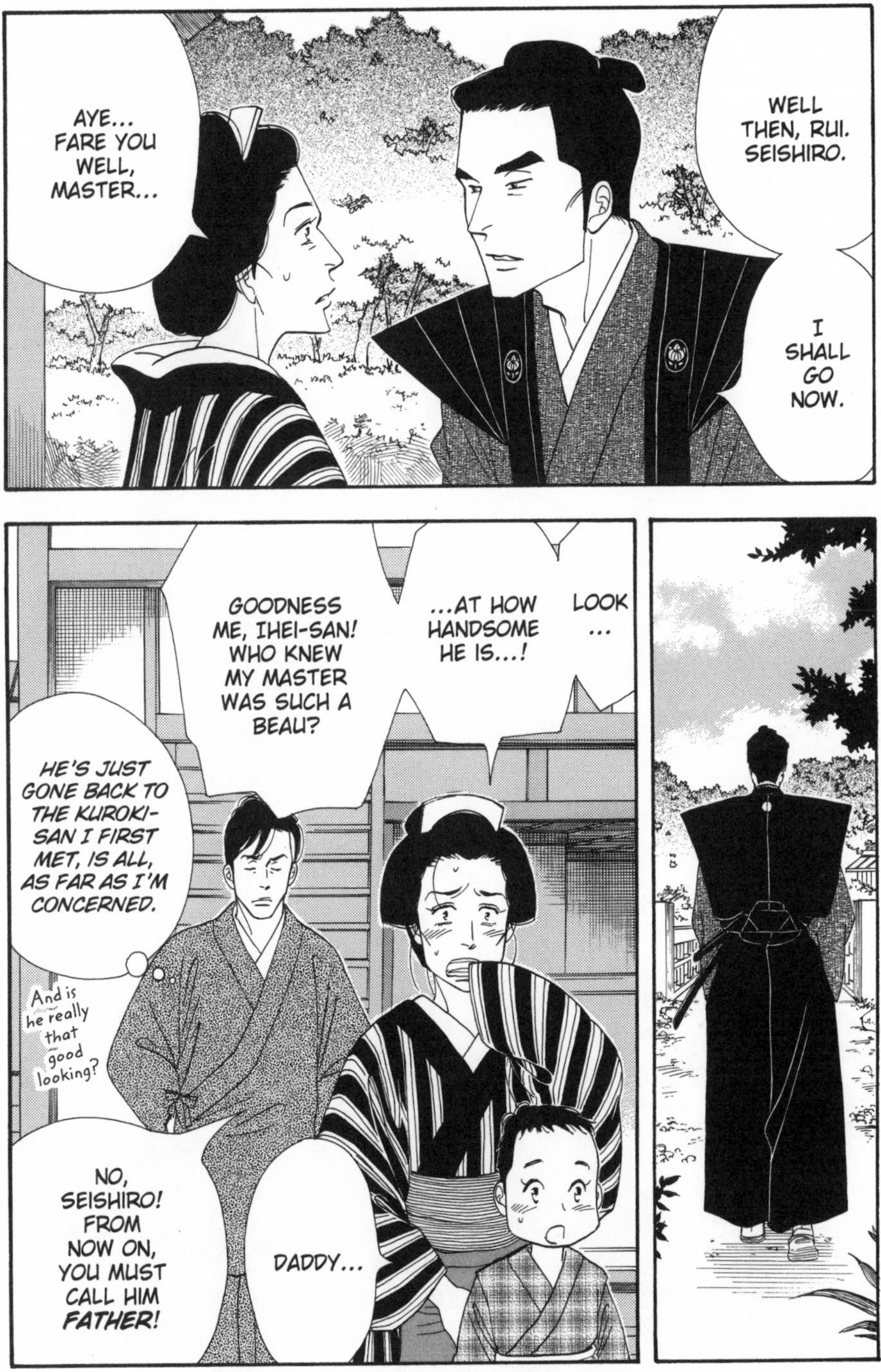
WELL THEN, RUI. SEISHIRO.
I SHALL GO NOW.
AYE... FARE YOU WELL, MASTER...
LOOK...
...AT HOW HANDSOME HE IS...!
GOODNESS ME, IHEI-SAN! WHO KNEW MY MASTER WAS SUCH A BEAU?
HE'S JUST GONE BACK TO THE KUROKI-SAN I FIRST MET, IS ALL, AS FAR AS I'M CONCERNED.
And is he really that good looking?
DADDY...
NO, SEISHIRO! FROM NOW ON, YOU MUST CALL HIM FATHER!

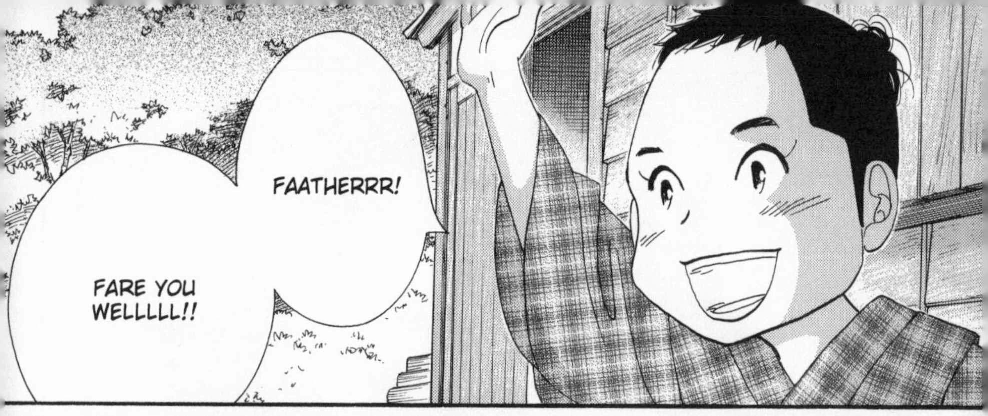
FAATHERRR!
FARE YOU WELLLLL!!
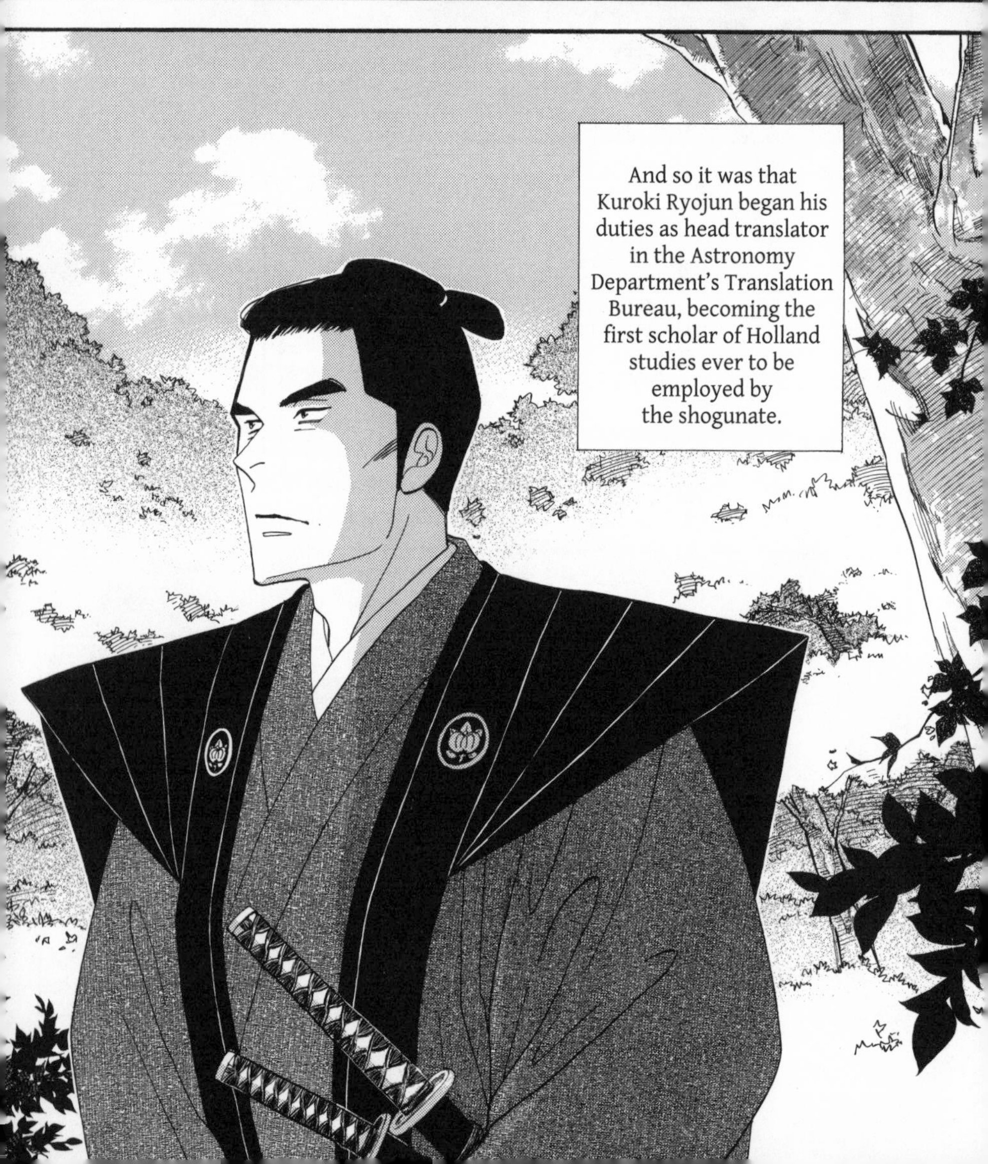
And so it was that Kuroki Ryojun began his duties as head translator in the Astronomy Department's Translation Bureau, becoming the first scholar of Holland studies ever to be employed by the shogunate.

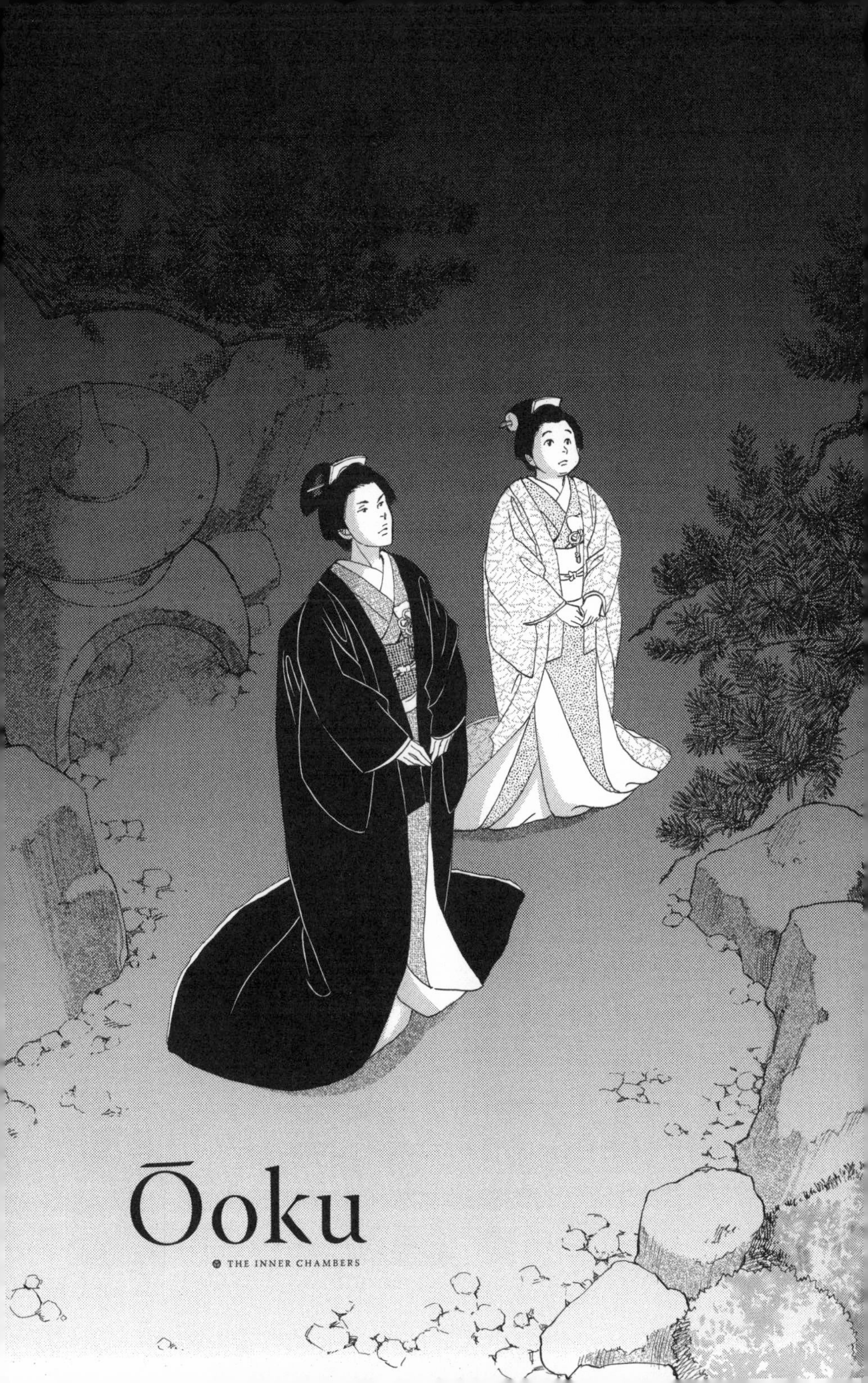
Ōoku
THE INNER CHAMBERS

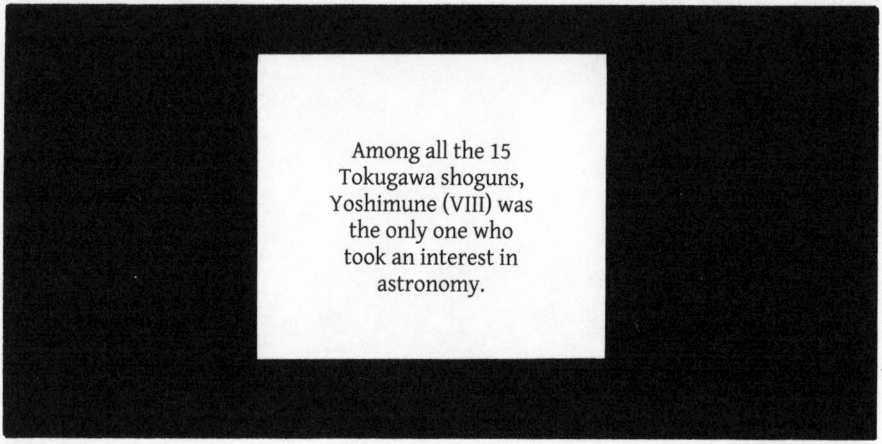
Among all the 15 Tokugawa shoguns, Yoshimune (VIII) was the only one who took an interest in astronomy.

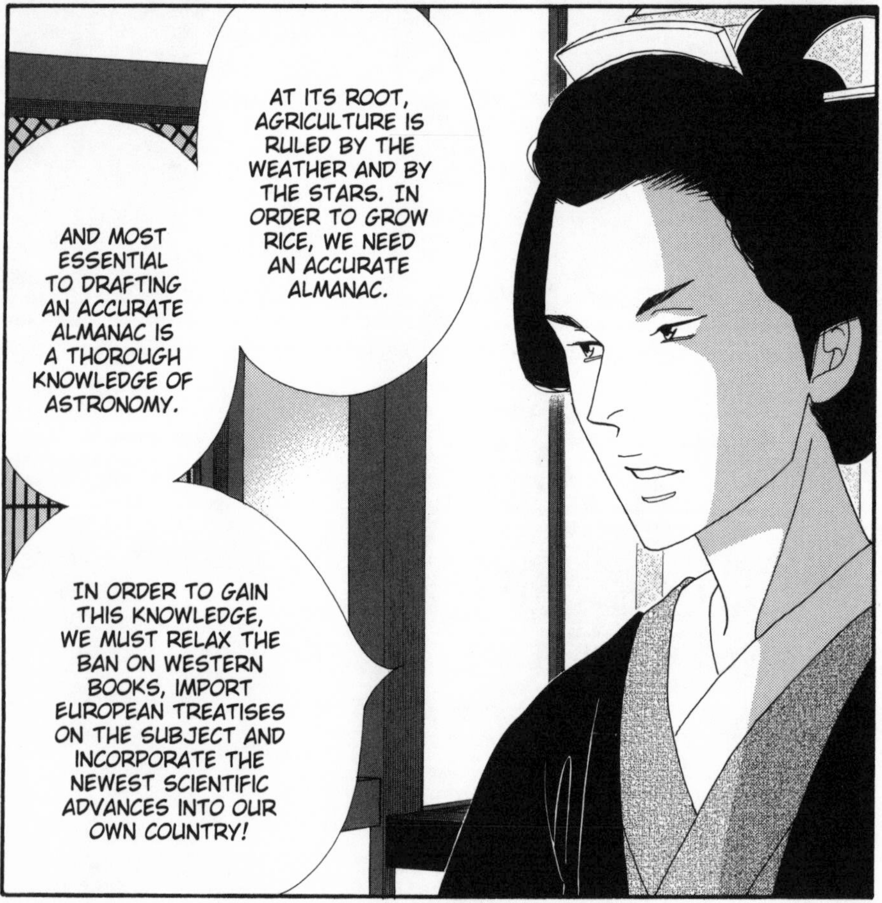
AT ITS ROOT, AGRICULTURE IS RULED BY THE WEATHER AND BY THE STARS. IN ORDER TO GROW RICE, WE NEED AN ACCURATE ALMANAC.
AND MOST ESSENTIAL TO DRAFTING AN ACCURATE ALMANAC IS A THOROUGH KNOWLEDGE OF ASTRONOMY.
IN ORDER TO GAIN THIS KNOWLEDGE, WE MUST RELAX THE BAN ON WESTERN BOOKS, IMPORT EUROPEAN TREATISES ON THE SUBJECT AND INCORPORATE THE NEWEST SCIENTIFIC ADVANCES INTO OUR OWN COUNTRY!

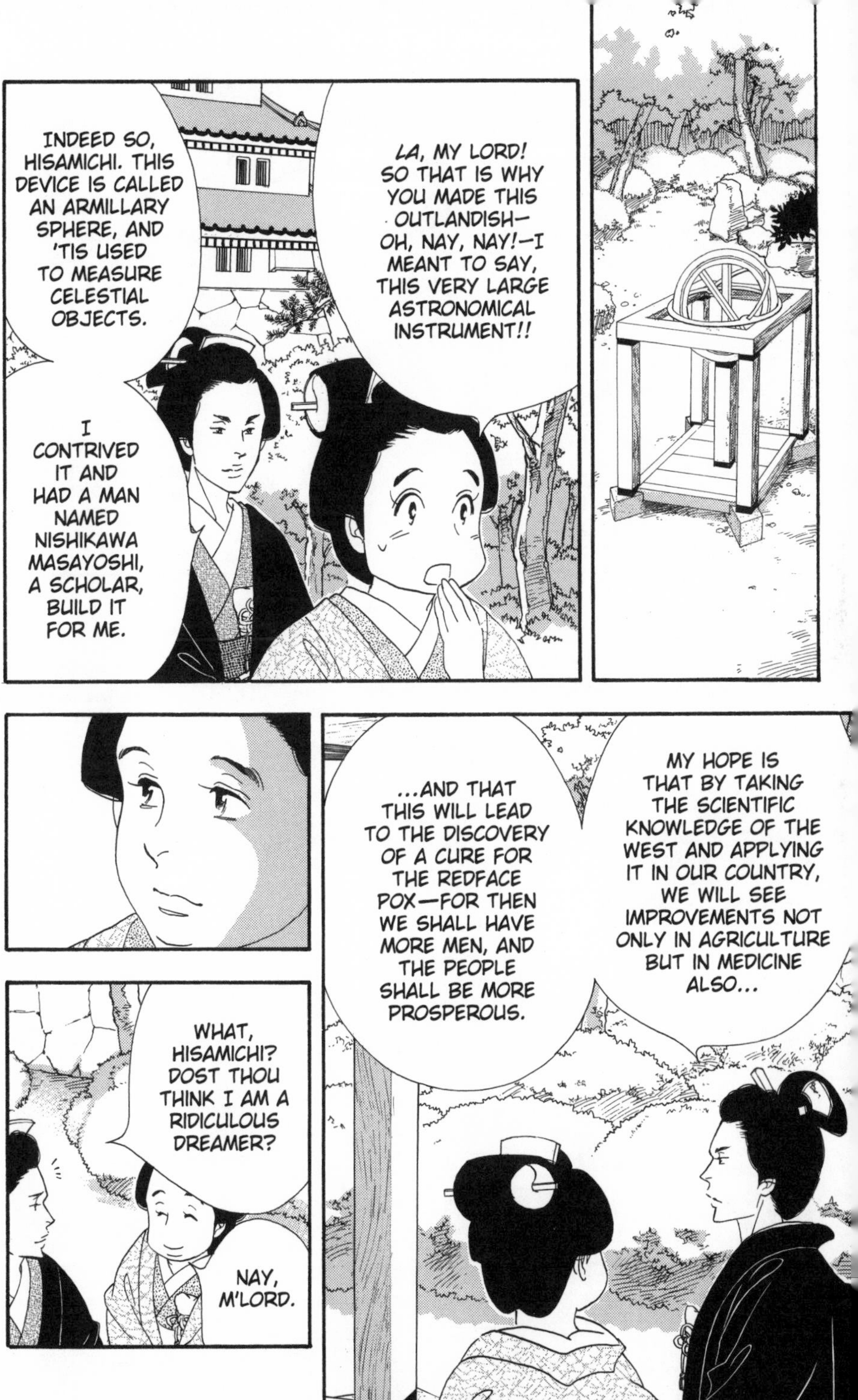
LA, MY LORD! SO THAT IS WHY YOU MADE THIS OUTLANDISH—OH, NAY, NAY!—I MEANT TO SAY, THIS VERY LARGE ASTRONOMICAL INSTRUMENT!!
INDEED SO, HISAMICHI. THIS DEVICE IS CALLED AN ARMILLARY SPHERE, AND 'TIS USED TO MEASURE CELESTIAL OBJECTS.
I CONTRIVED IT AND HAD A MAN NAMED NISHIKAWA MASAYOSHI, A SCHOLAR, BUILD IT FOR ME.
MY HOPE IS THAT BY TAKING THE SCIENTIFIC KNOWLEDGE OF THE WEST AND APPLYING IT IN OUR COUNTRY, WE WILL SEE IMPROVEMENTS NOT ONLY IN AGRICULTURE BUT IN MEDICINE ALSO...
...AND THAT THIS WILL LEAD TO THE DISCOVERY OF A CURE FOR THE REDFACE POX—FOR THEN WE SHALL HAVE MORE MEN, AND THE PEOPLE SHALL BE MORE PROSPEROUS.
WHAT, HISAMICHI? DOST THOU THINK I AM A RIDICULOUS DREAMER?
NAY, M'LORD.

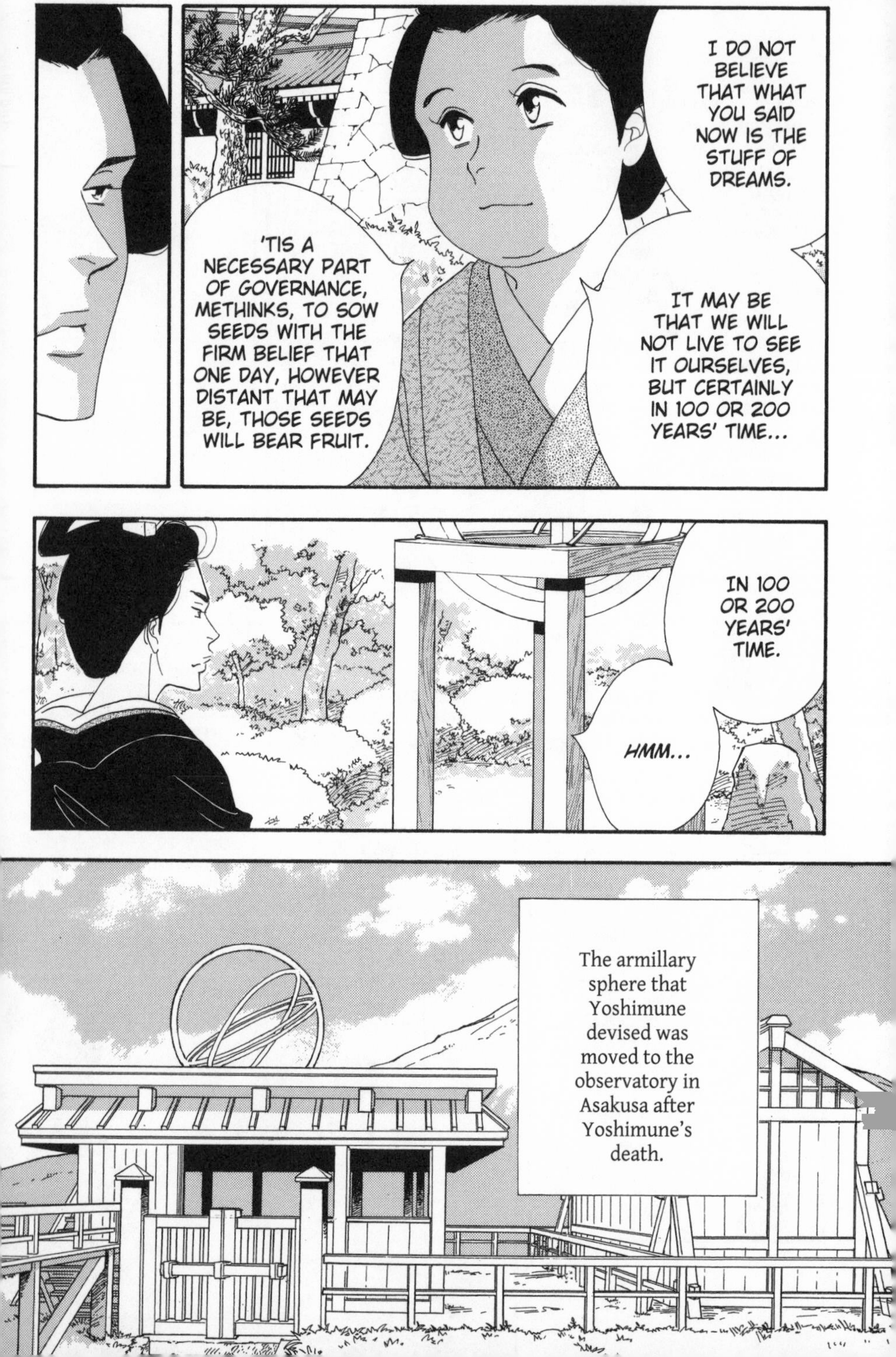
I DO NOT BELIEVE THAT WHAT YOU SAID NOW IS THE STUFF OF DREAMS.
IT MAY BE THAT WE WILL NOT LIVE TO SEE IT OURSELVES, BUT CERTAINLY IN 100 OR 200 YEARS' TIME...
'TIS A NECESSARY PART OF GOVERNANCE, METHINKS, TO SOW SEEDS WITH THE FIRM BELIEF THAT ONE DAY, HOWEVER DISTANT THAT MAY BE, THOSE SEEDS WILL BEAR FRUIT.
IN 100 OR 200 YEARS' TIME.
HMM...
The armillary sphere that Yoshimune devised was moved to the observatory in Asakusa after Yoshimune's death.

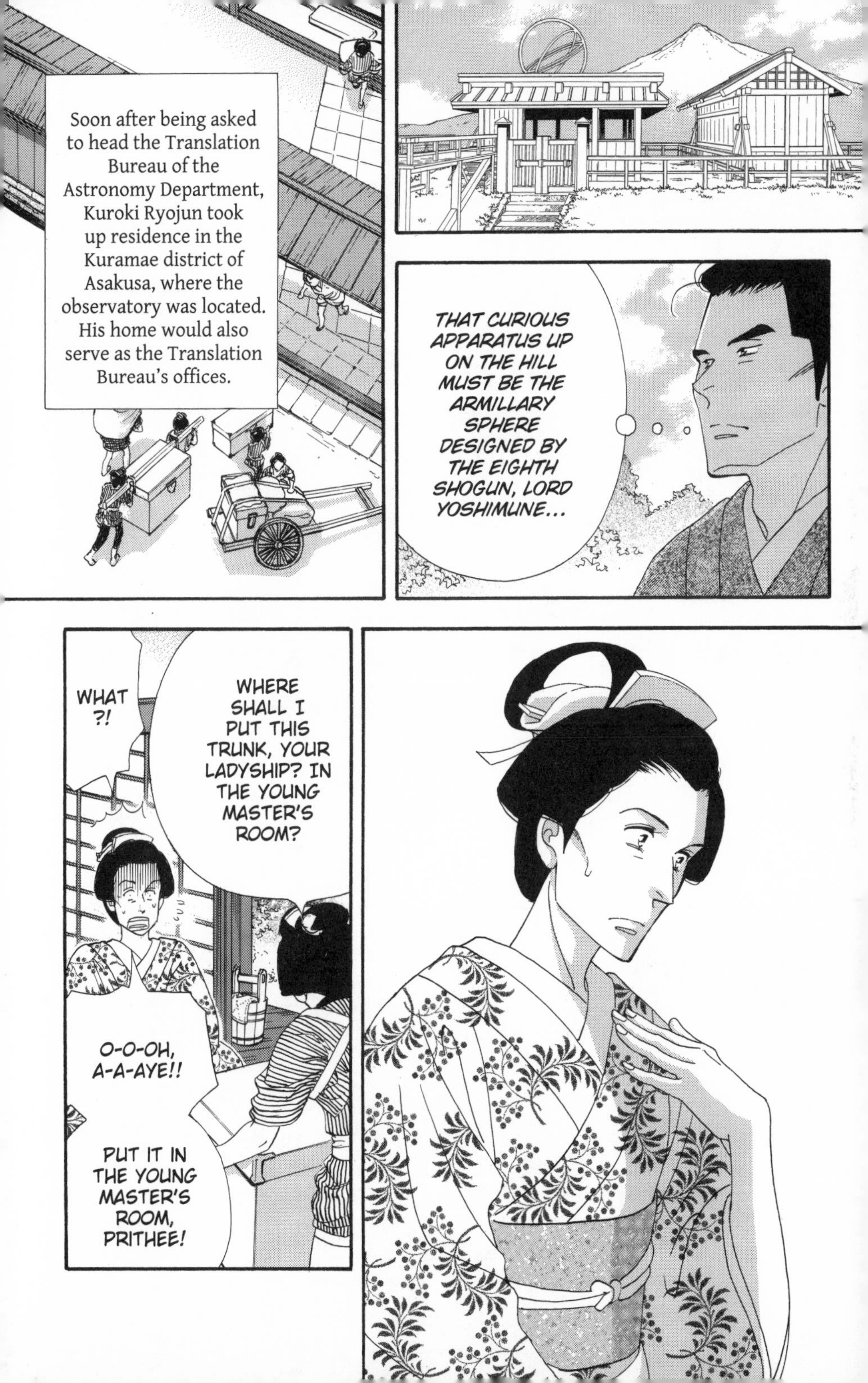
THAT CURIOUS APPARATUS UP ON THE HILL MUST BE THE ARMILLARY SPHERE DESIGNED BY THE EIGHTH SHOGUN, LORD YOSHIMUNE...
Soon after being asked to head the Translation Bureau of the Astronomy Department, Kuroki Ryojun took up residence in the Kuramae district of Asakusa, where the observatory was located. His home would also serve as the Translation Bureau's offices.
WHERE SHALL I PUT THIS TRUNK, YOUR LADYSHIP? IN THE YOUNG MASTER'S ROOM?
WHAT?!
O-O-OH, A-A-AYE!!
PUT IT IN THE YOUNG MASTER'S ROOM, PRITHEE!

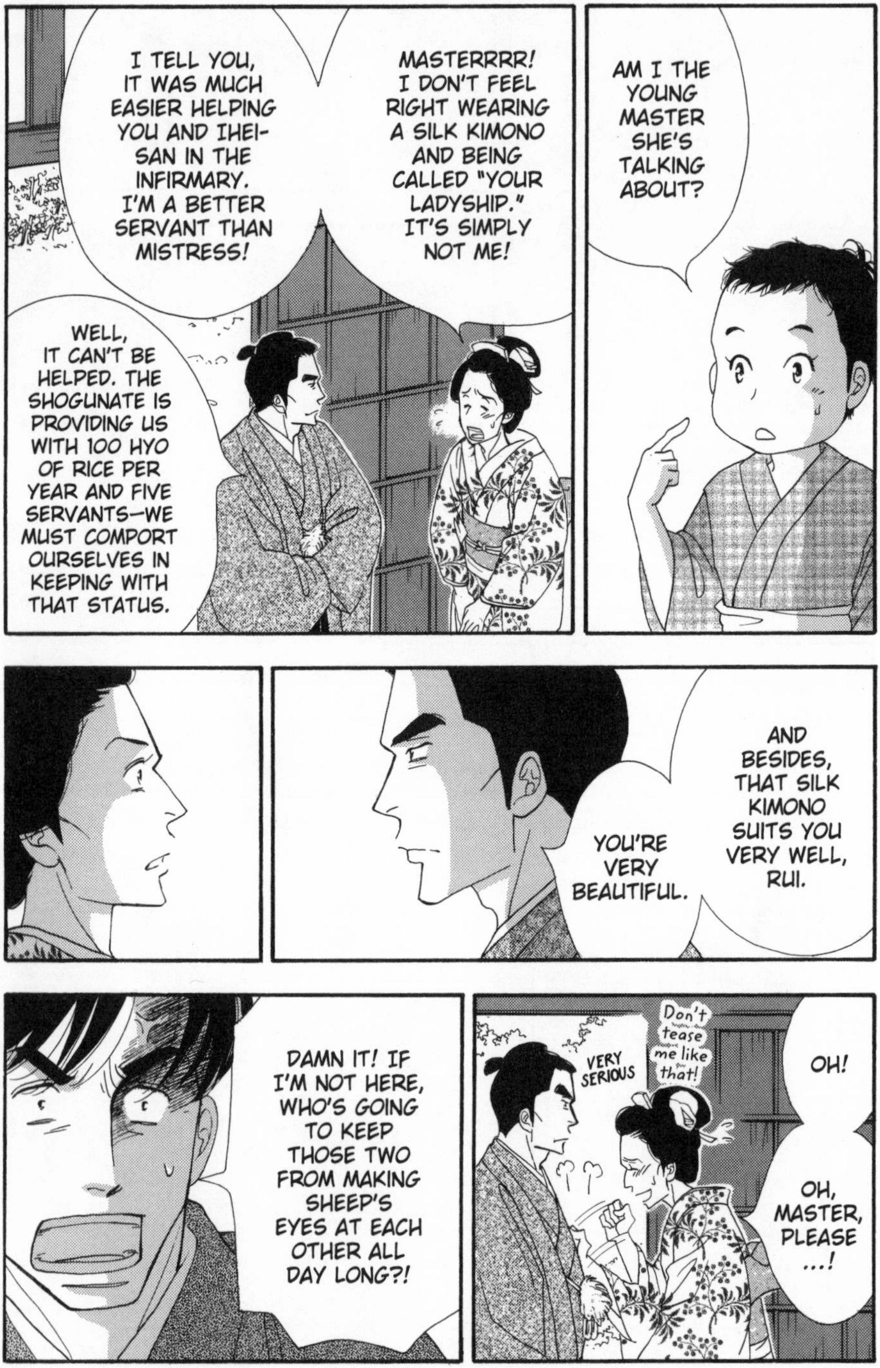
AM I THE YOUNG MASTER SHE'S TALKING ABOUT?
MASTERRRR! I DON'T FEEL RIGHT WEARING A SILK KIMONO AND BEING CALLED "YOUR LADYSHIP." IT'S SIMPLY NOT ME!
I TELL YOU, IT WAS MUCH EASIER HELPING YOU AND IHEI-SAN IN THE INFIRMARY. I'M A BETTER SERVANT THAN MISTRESS!
WELL, IT CAN'T BE HELPED. THE SHOGUNATE IS PROVIDING US WITH 100 HYO OF RICE PER YEAR AND FIVE SERVANTS—WE MUST COMPORT OURSELVES IN KEEPING WITH THAT STATUS.
YOU'RE VERY BEAUTIFUL.
AND BESIDES, THAT SILK KIMONO SUITS YOU VERY WELL, RUI.
OH!
OH, MASTER, PLEASE ...!
Don't tease me like that!
VERY SERIOUS
DAMN IT! IF I'M NOT HERE, WHO'S GOING TO KEEP THOSE TWO FROM MAKING SHEEP'S EYES AT EACH OTHER ALL DAY LONG?!

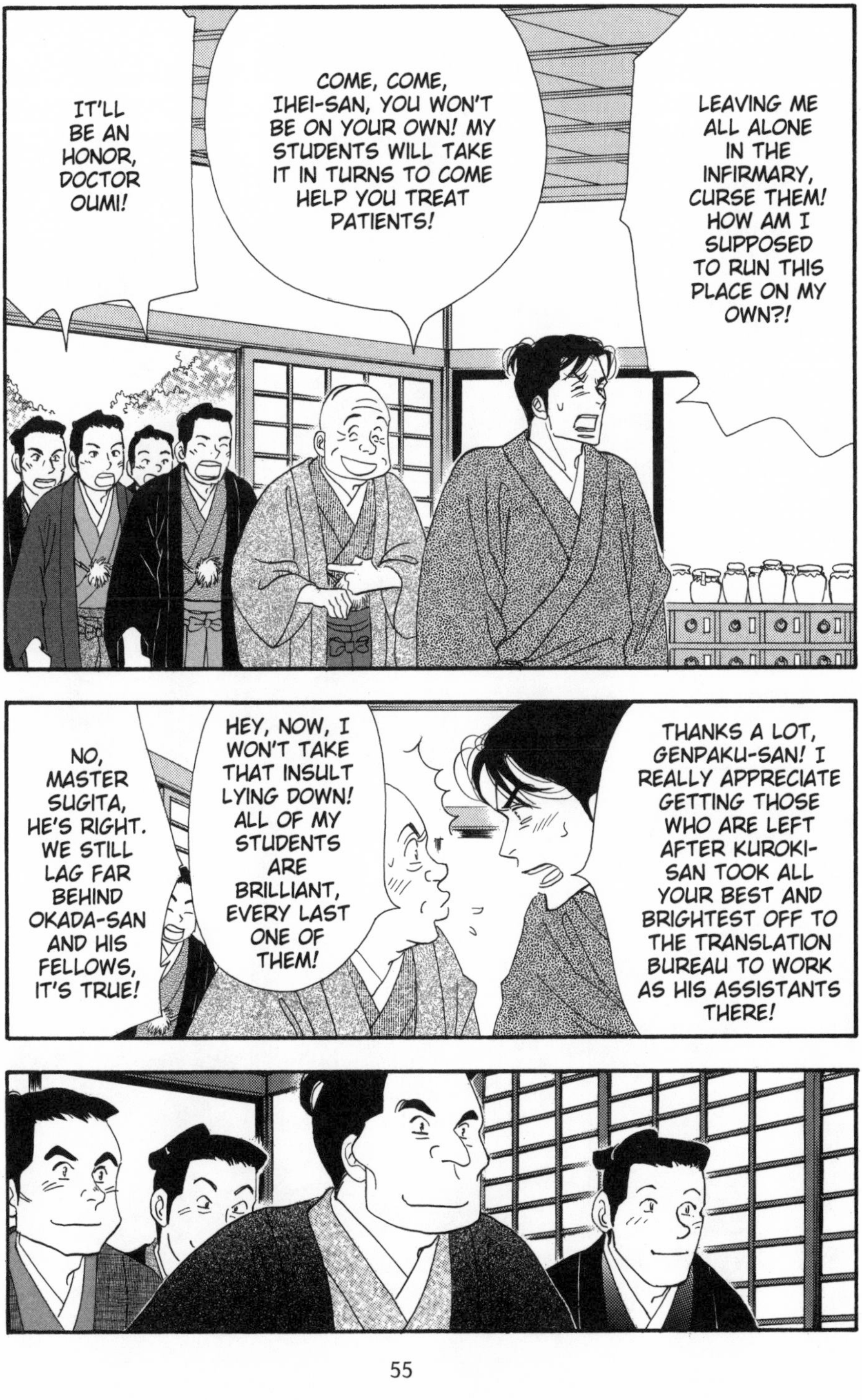
LEAVING ME ALL ALONE IN THE INFIRMARY, CURSE THEM! HOW AM I SUPPOSED TO RUN THIS PLACE ON MY OWN?!
COME, COME, IHEI-SAN, YOU WON'T BE ON YOUR OWN! MY STUDENTS WILL TAKE IT IN TURNS TO COME HELP YOU TREAT PATIENTS!
IT'LL BE AN HONOR, DOCTOR OUMI!
THANKS A LOT, GENPAKU-SAN! I REALLY APPRECIATE GETTING THOSE WHO ARE LEFT AFTER KUROKI-SAN TOOK ALL YOUR BEST AND BRIGHTEST OFF TO THE TRANSLATION BUREAU TO WORK AS HIS ASSISTANTS THERE!
HEY, NOW, I WON'T TAKE THAT INSULT LYING DOWN! ALL OF MY STUDENTS ARE BRILLIANT, EVERY LAST ONE OF THEM!
NO, MASTER SUGITA, HE'S RIGHT. WE STILL LAG FAR BEHIND OKADA-SAN AND HIS FELLOWS, IT'S TRUE!

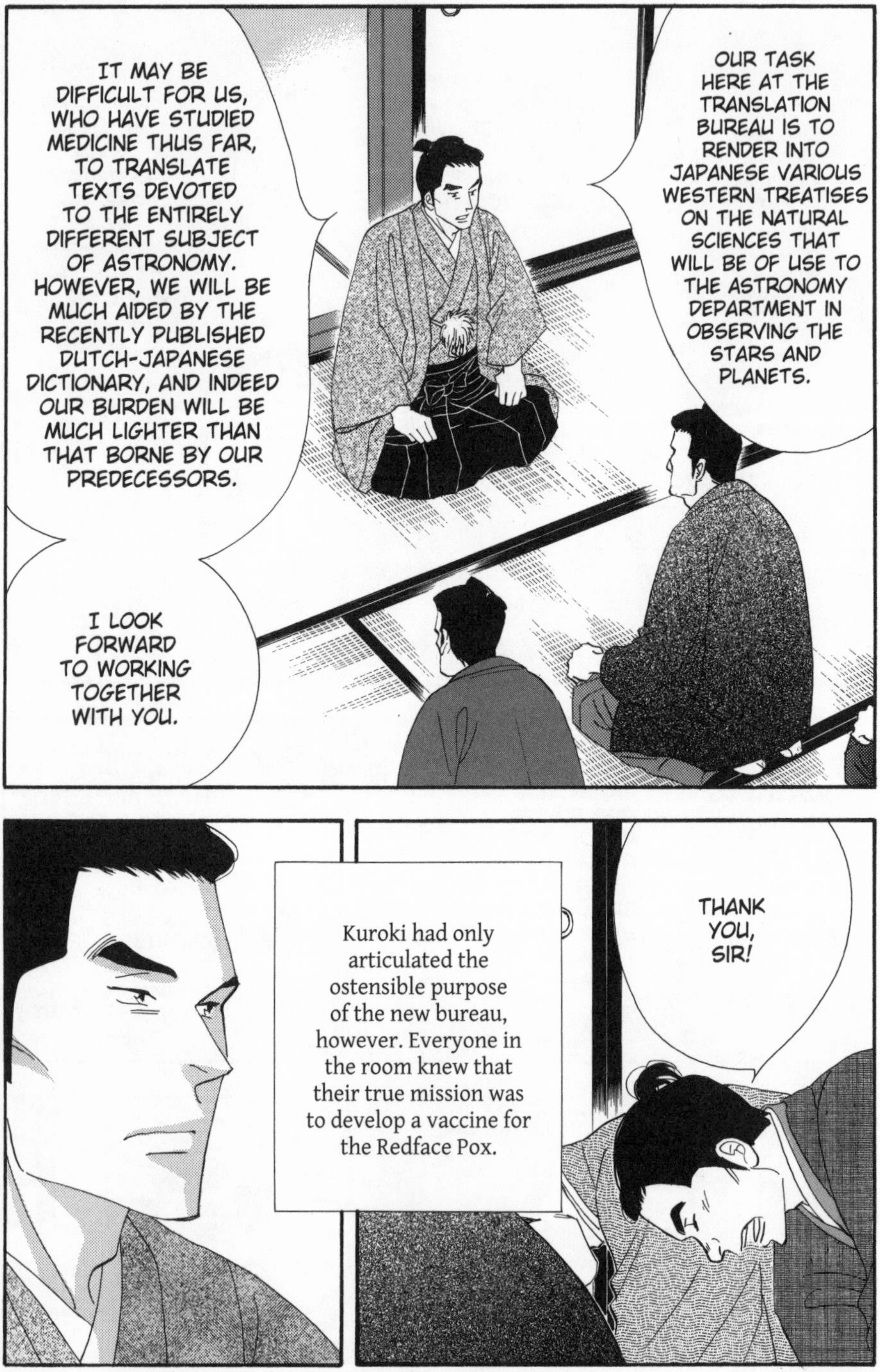
OUR TASK HERE AT THE TRANSLATION BUREAU IS TO RENDER INTO JAPANESE VARIOUS WESTERN TREATISES ON THE NATURAL SCIENCES THAT WILL BE OF USE TO THE ASTRONOMY DEPARTMENT IN OBSERVING THE STARS AND PLANETS.
IT MAY BE DIFFICULT FOR US, WHO HAVE STUDIED MEDICINE THUS FAR, TO TRANSLATE TEXTS DEVOTED TO THE ENTIRELY DIFFERENT SUBJECT OF ASTRONOMY. HOWEVER, WE WILL BE MUCH AIDED BY THE RECENTLY PUBLISHED DUTCH-JAPANESE DICTIONARY, AND INDEED OUR BURDEN WILL BE MUCH LIGHTER THAN THAT BORNE BY OUR PREDECESSORS.
I LOOK FORWARD TO WORKING TOGETHER WITH YOU.
THANK YOU, SIR!
Kuroki had only articulated the ostensible purpose of the new bureau, however. Everyone in the room knew that their true mission was to develop a vaccine for the Redface Pox.

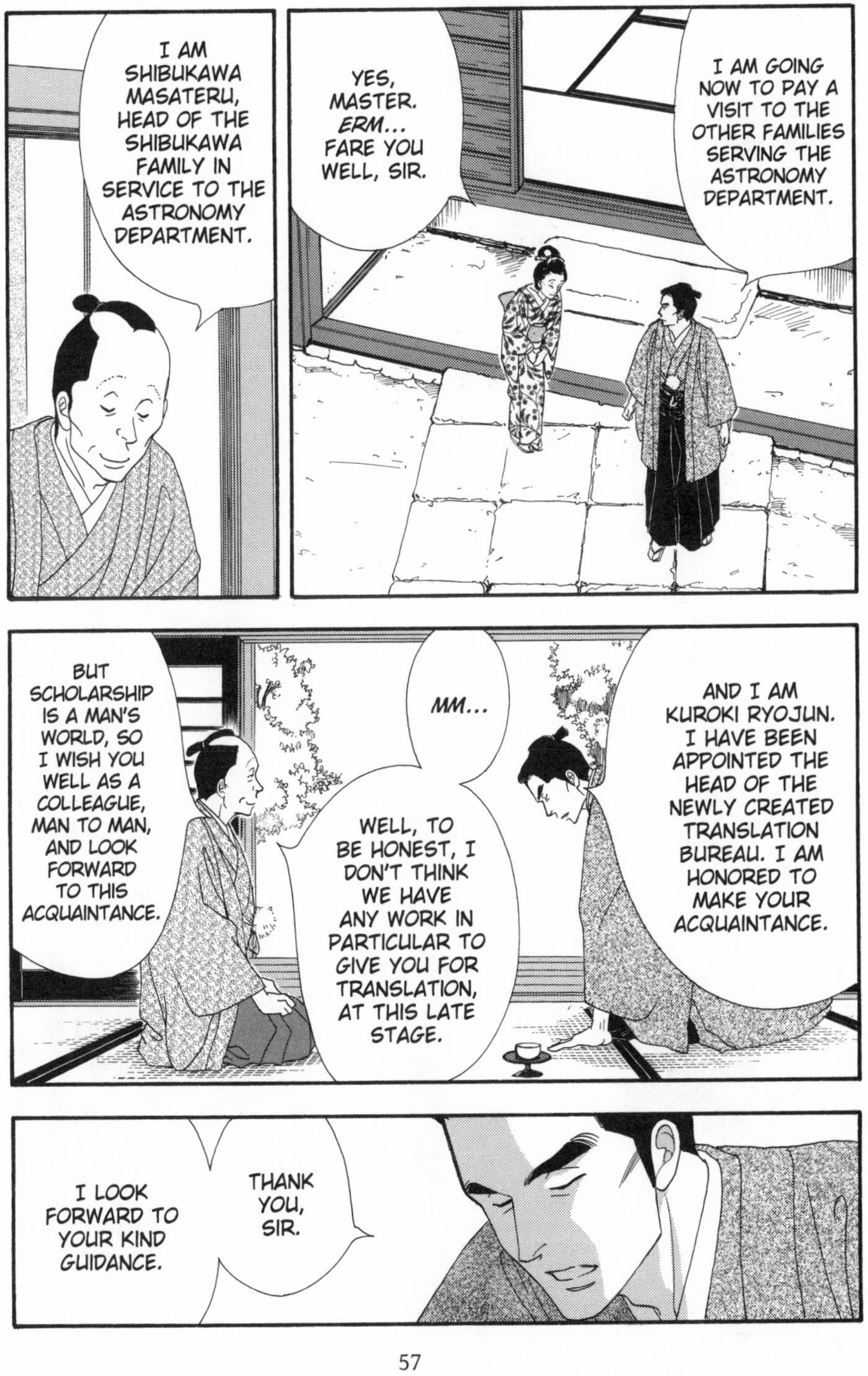
I AM GOING NOW TO PAY A VISIT TO THE OTHER FAMILIES SERVING THE ASTRONOMY DEPARTMENT.
YES, MASTER. *ERM...* FARE YOU WELL, SIR.
I AM SHIBUKAWA MASATERU, HEAD OF THE SHIBUKAWA FAMILY IN SERVICE TO THE ASTRONOMY DEPARTMENT.
AND I AM KUROKI RYOJUN. I HAVE BEEN APPOINTED THE HEAD OF THE NEWLY CREATED TRANSLATION BUREAU. I AM HONORED TO MAKE YOUR ACQUAINTANCE.
MM...
WELL, TO BE HONEST, I DON'T THINK WE HAVE ANY WORK IN PARTICULAR TO GIVE YOU FOR TRANSLATION, AT THIS LATE STAGE.
BUT SCHOLARSHIP IS A MAN'S WORLD, SO I WISH YOU WELL AS A COLLEAGUE, MAN TO MAN, AND LOOK FORWARD TO THIS ACQUAINTANCE.
THANK YOU, SIR.
I LOOK FORWARD TO YOUR KIND GUIDANCE.

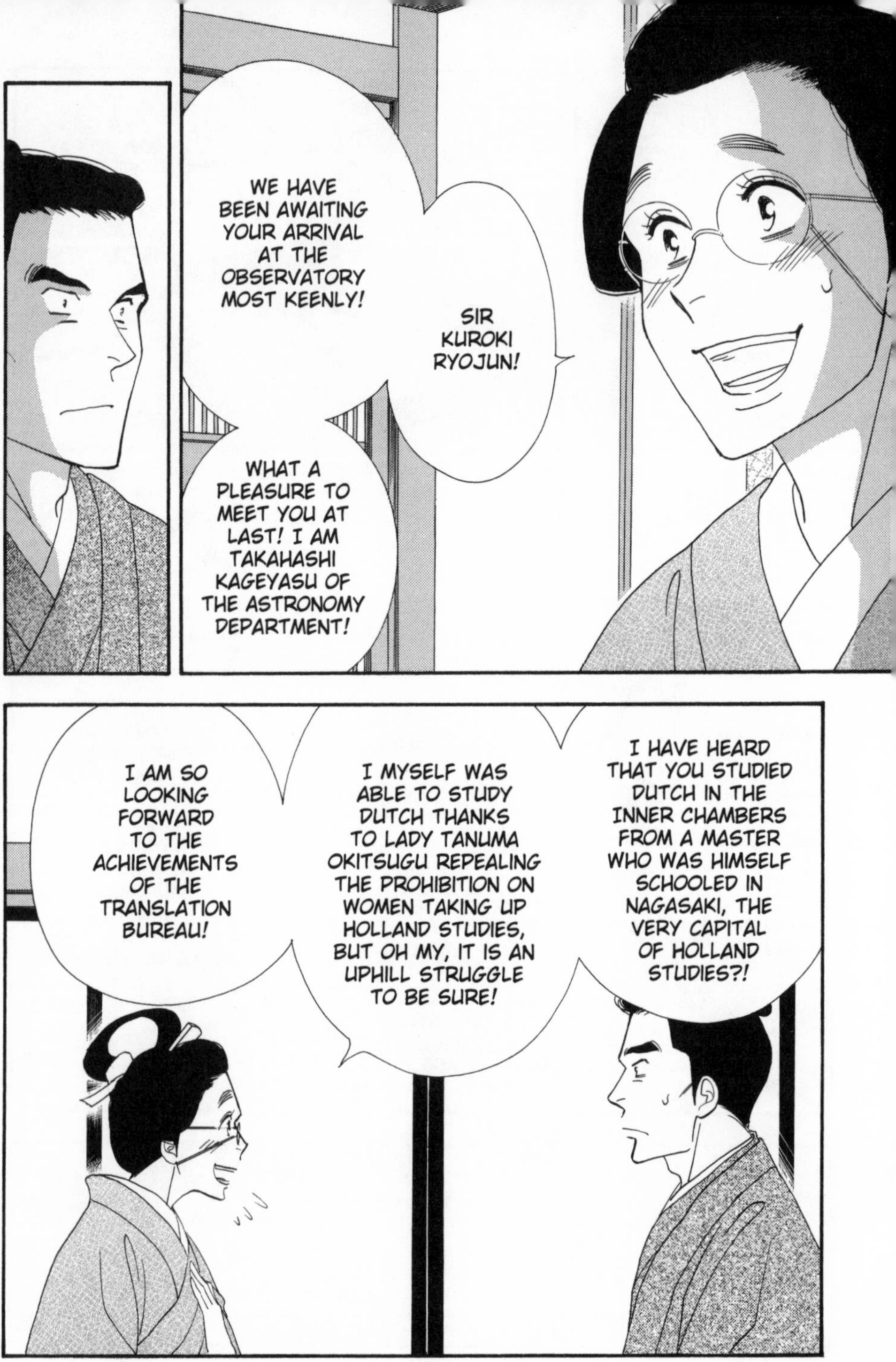
SIR KUROKI RYOJUN!
WE HAVE BEEN AWAITING YOUR ARRIVAL AT THE OBSERVATORY MOST KEENLY!
WHAT A PLEASURE TO MEET YOU AT LAST! I AM TAKAHASHI KAGEYASU OF THE ASTRONOMY DEPARTMENT!
I HAVE HEARD THAT YOU STUDIED DUTCH IN THE INNER CHAMBERS FROM A MASTER WHO WAS HIMSELF SCHOOLED IN NAGASAKI, THE VERY CAPITAL OF HOLLAND STUDIES?!
I MYSELF WAS ABLE TO STUDY DUTCH THANKS TO LADY TANUMA OKITSUGU REPEALING THE PROHIBITION ON WOMEN TAKING UP HOLLAND STUDIES, BUT OH MY, IT IS AN UPHILL STRUGGLE TO BE SURE!
I AM SO LOOKING FORWARD TO THE ACHIEVEMENTS OF THE TRANSLATION BUREAU!

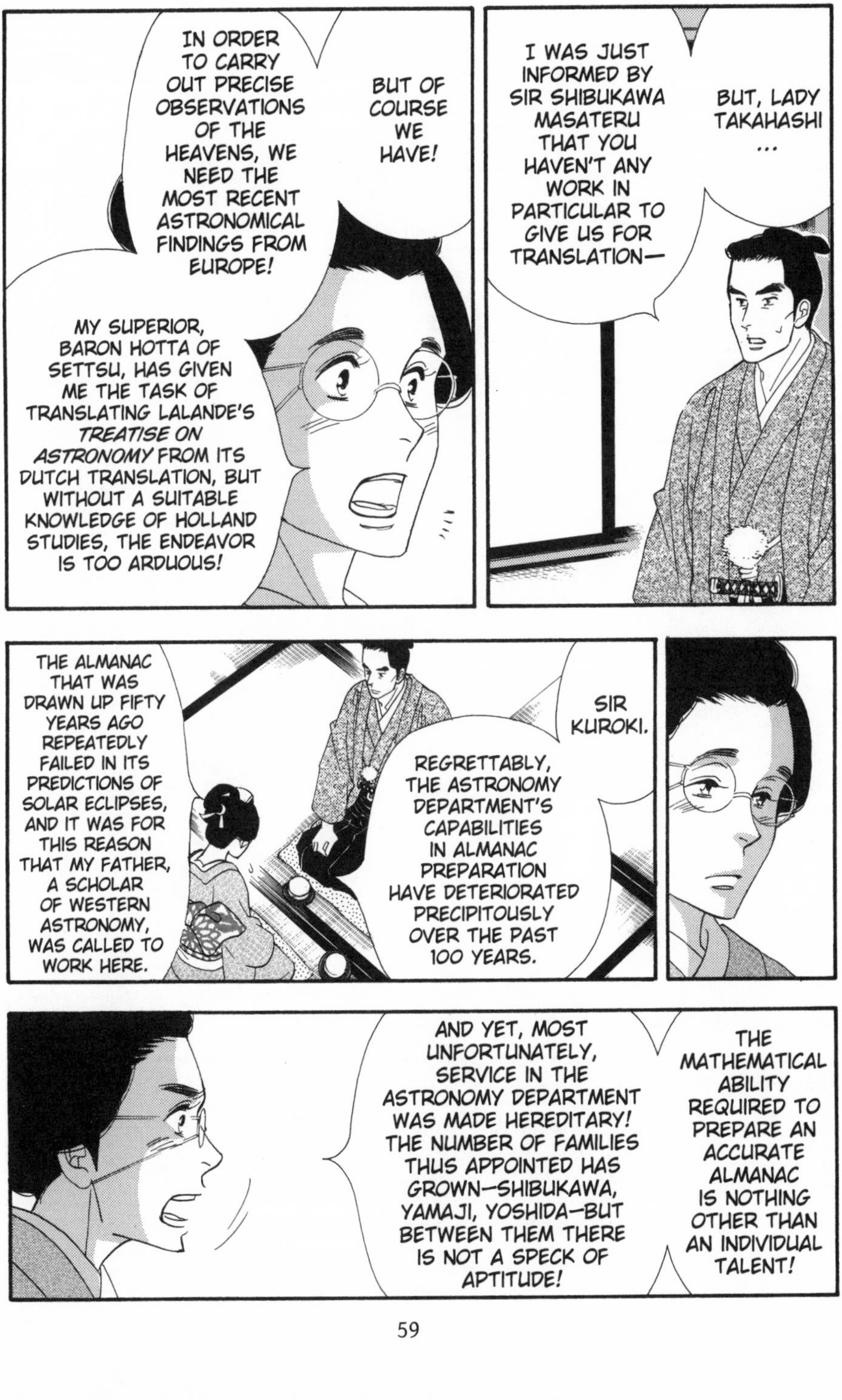
BUT, LADY TAKAHASHI ...
I WAS JUST INFORMED BY SIR SHIBUKAWA MASATERU THAT YOU HAVEN'T ANY WORK IN PARTICULAR TO GIVE US FOR TRANSLATION—
BUT OF COURSE WE HAVE!
IN ORDER TO CARRY OUT PRECISE OBSERVATIONS OF THE HEAVENS, WE NEED THE MOST RECENT ASTRONOMICAL FINDINGS FROM EUROPE!
MY SUPERIOR, BARON HOTTA OF SETTSU, HAS GIVEN ME THE TASK OF TRANSLATING LALANDE'S *TREATISE ON ASTRONOMY* FROM ITS DUTCH TRANSLATION, BUT WITHOUT A SUITABLE KNOWLEDGE OF HOLLAND STUDIES, THE ENDEAVOR IS TOO ARDUOUS!
SIR KUROKI.
REGRETTABLY, THE ASTRONOMY DEPARTMENT'S CAPABILITIES IN ALMANAC PREPARATION HAVE DETERIORATED PRECIPITOUSLY OVER THE PAST 100 YEARS.
THE ALMANAC THAT WAS DRAWN UP FIFTY YEARS AGO REPEATEDLY FAILED IN ITS PREDICTIONS OF SOLAR ECLIPSES, AND IT WAS FOR THIS REASON THAT MY FATHER, A SCHOLAR OF WESTERN ASTRONOMY, WAS CALLED TO WORK HERE.
THE MATHEMATICAL ABILITY REQUIRED TO PREPARE AN ACCURATE ALMANAC IS NOTHING OTHER THAN AN INDIVIDUAL TALENT!
AND YET, MOST UNFORTUNATELY, SERVICE IN THE ASTRONOMY DEPARTMENT WAS MADE HEREDITARY! THE NUMBER OF FAMILIES THUS APPOINTED HAS GROWN—SHIBUKAWA, YAMAJI, YOSHIDA—BUT BETWEEN THEM THERE IS NOT A SPECK OF APTITUDE!

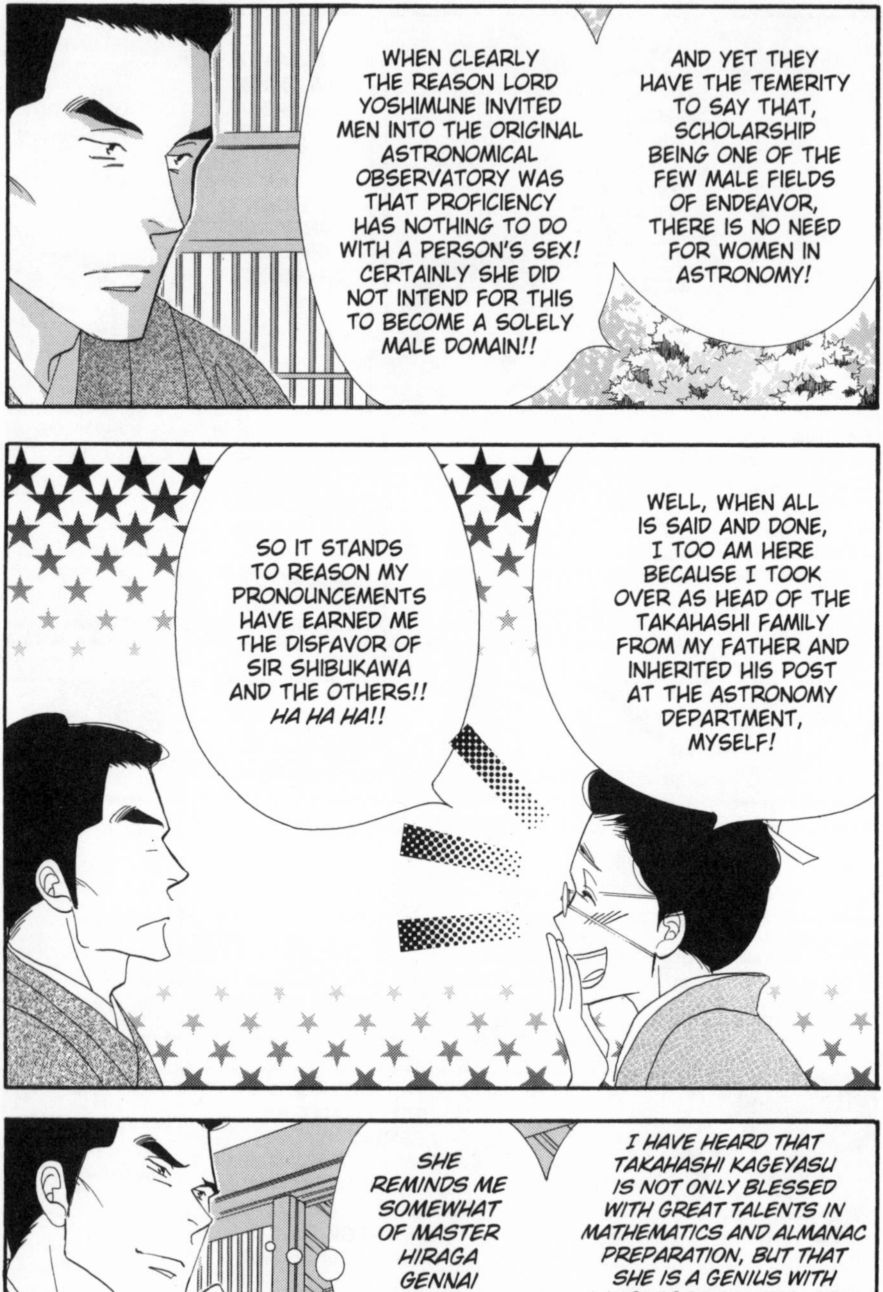
AND YET THEY HAVE THE TEMERITY TO SAY THAT, SCHOLARSHIP BEING ONE OF THE FEW MALE FIELDS OF ENDEAVOR, THERE IS NO NEED FOR WOMEN IN ASTRONOMY!
WHEN CLEARLY THE REASON LORD YOSHIMUNE INVITED MEN INTO THE ORIGINAL ASTRONOMICAL OBSERVATORY WAS THAT PROFICIENCY HAS NOTHING TO DO WITH A PERSON'S SEX! CERTAINLY SHE DID NOT INTEND FOR THIS TO BECOME A SOLELY MALE DOMAIN!!
WELL, WHEN ALL IS SAID AND DONE, I TOO AM HERE BECAUSE I TOOK OVER AS HEAD OF THE TAKAHASHI FAMILY FROM MY FATHER AND INHERITED HIS POST AT THE ASTRONOMY DEPARTMENT, MYSELF!
SO IT STANDS TO REASON MY PRONOUNCEMENTS HAVE EARNED ME THE DISFAVOR OF SIR SHIBUKAWA AND THE OTHERS!! *HA HA HA!!*
I HAVE HEARD THAT TAKAHASHI KAGEYASU IS NOT ONLY BLESSED WITH GREAT TALENTS IN MATHEMATICS AND ALMANAC PREPARATION, BUT THAT SHE IS A GENIUS WITH LANGUAGES AS WELL, ABLE TO UNDERSTAND DUTCH, RUSSIAN AND CHINESE.
SHE REMINDS ME SOMEWHAT OF MASTER HIRAGA GENNAI IN THAT REGARD...

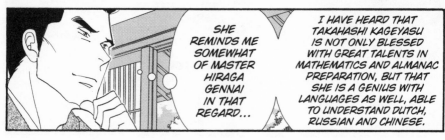

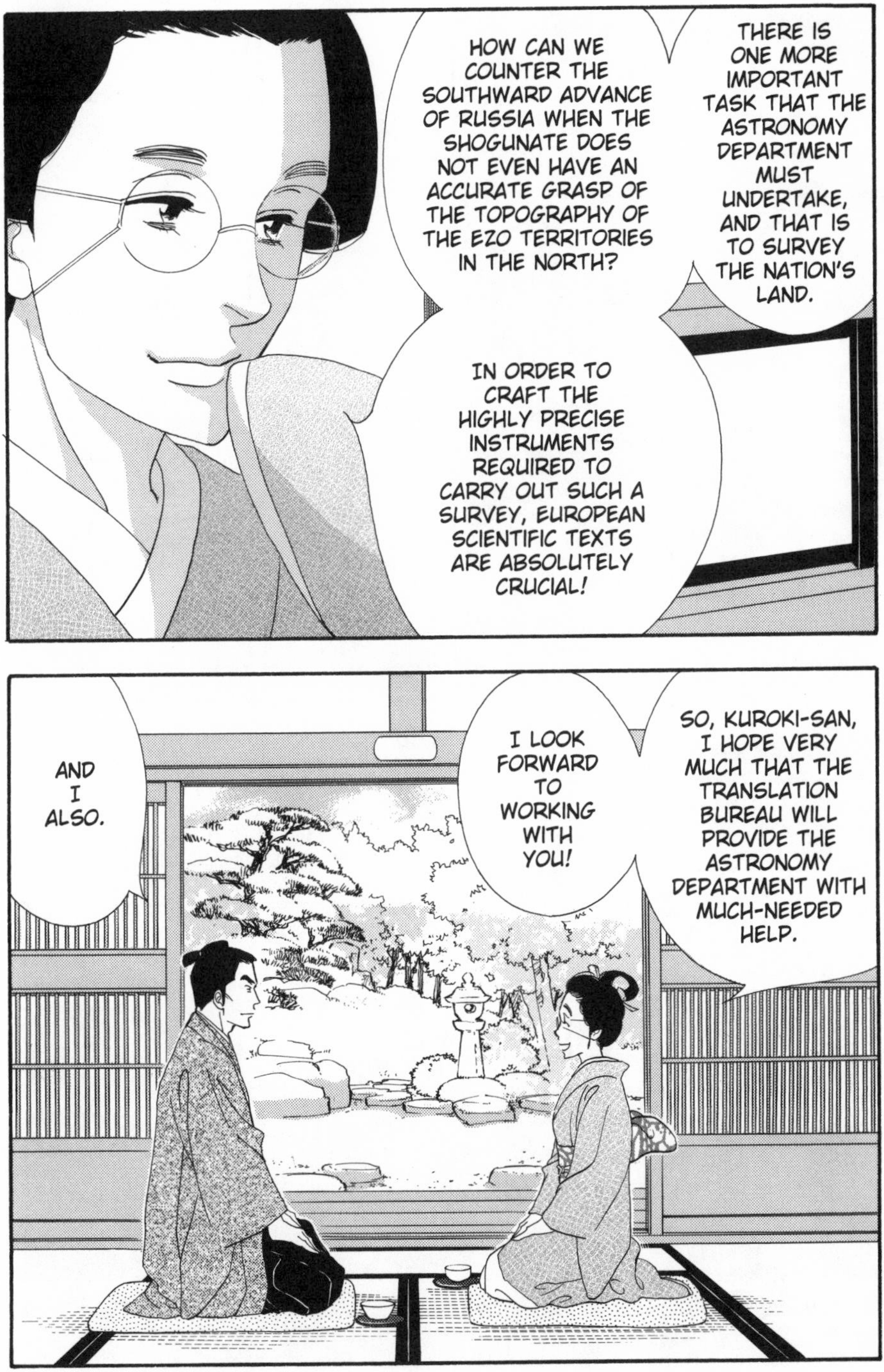
THERE IS ONE MORE IMPORTANT TASK THAT THE ASTRONOMY DEPARTMENT MUST UNDERTAKE, AND THAT IS TO SURVEY THE NATION'S LAND.
HOW CAN WE COUNTER THE SOUTHWARD ADVANCE OF RUSSIA WHEN THE SHOGUNATE DOES NOT EVEN HAVE AN ACCURATE GRASP OF THE TOPOGRAPHY OF THE EZO TERRITORIES IN THE NORTH?
IN ORDER TO CRAFT THE HIGHLY PRECISE INSTRUMENTS REQUIRED TO CARRY OUT SUCH A SURVEY, EUROPEAN SCIENTIFIC TEXTS ARE ABSOLUTELY CRUCIAL!
SO, KUROKI-SAN, I HOPE VERY MUCH THAT THE TRANSLATION BUREAU WILL PROVIDE THE ASTRONOMY DEPARTMENT WITH MUCH-NEEDED HELP.
I LOOK FORWARD TO WORKING WITH YOU!
AND I ALSO.

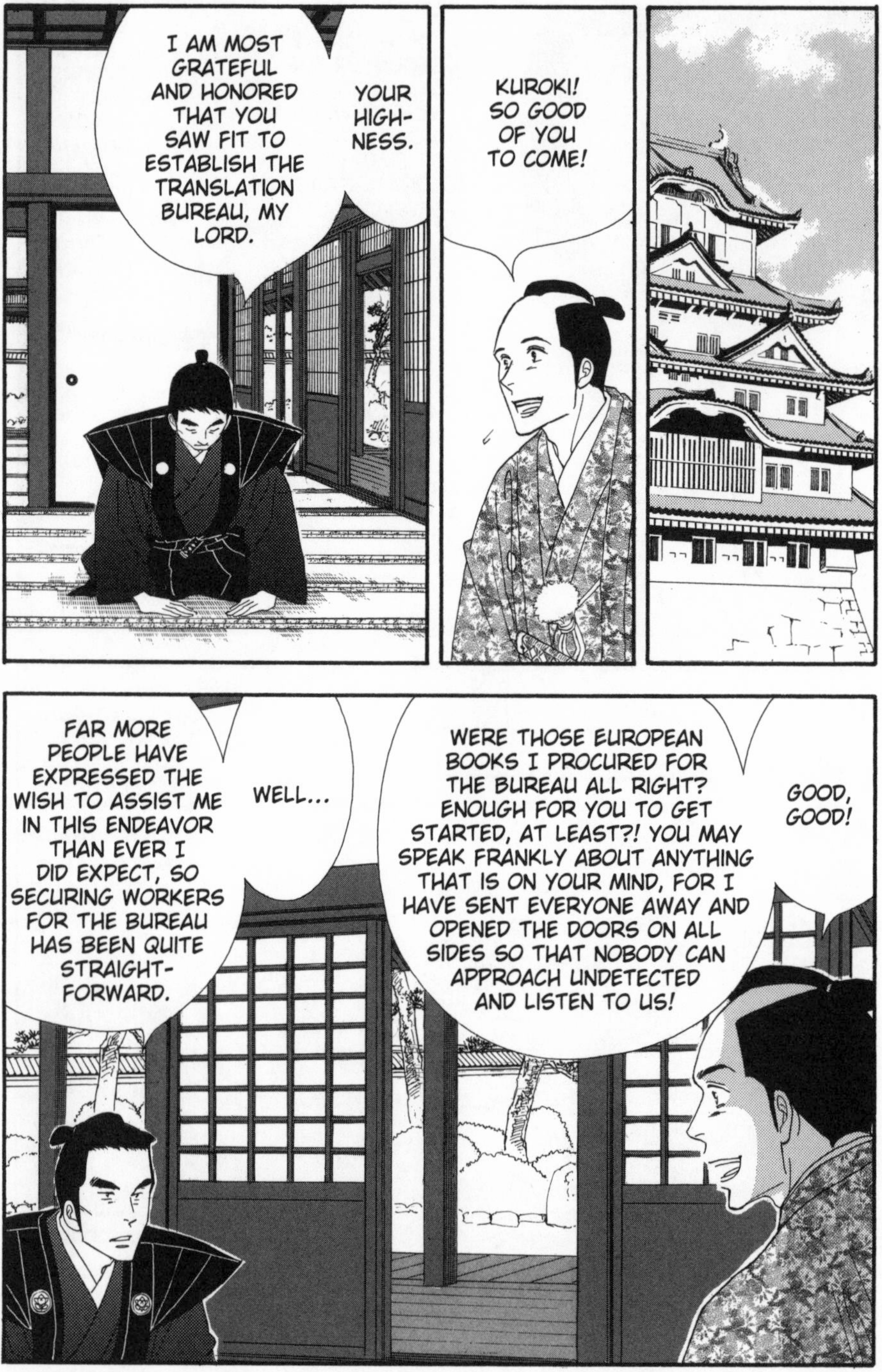
KUROKI! SO GOOD OF YOU TO COME!
YOUR HIGHNESS.
I AM MOST GRATEFUL AND HONORED THAT YOU SAW FIT TO ESTABLISH THE TRANSLATION BUREAU, MY LORD.
GOOD, GOOD!
WERE THOSE EUROPEAN BOOKS I PROCURED FOR THE BUREAU ALL RIGHT? ENOUGH FOR YOU TO GET STARTED, AT LEAST?! YOU MAY SPEAK FRANKLY ABOUT ANYTHING THAT IS ON YOUR MIND, FOR I HAVE SENT EVERYONE AWAY AND OPENED THE DOORS ON ALL SIDES SO THAT NOBODY CAN APPROACH UNDETECTED AND LISTEN TO US!
WELL...
FAR MORE PEOPLE HAVE EXPRESSED THE WISH TO ASSIST ME IN THIS ENDEAVOR THAN EVER I DID EXPECT, SO SECURING WORKERS FOR THE BUREAU HAS BEEN QUITE STRAIGHT-FORWARD.

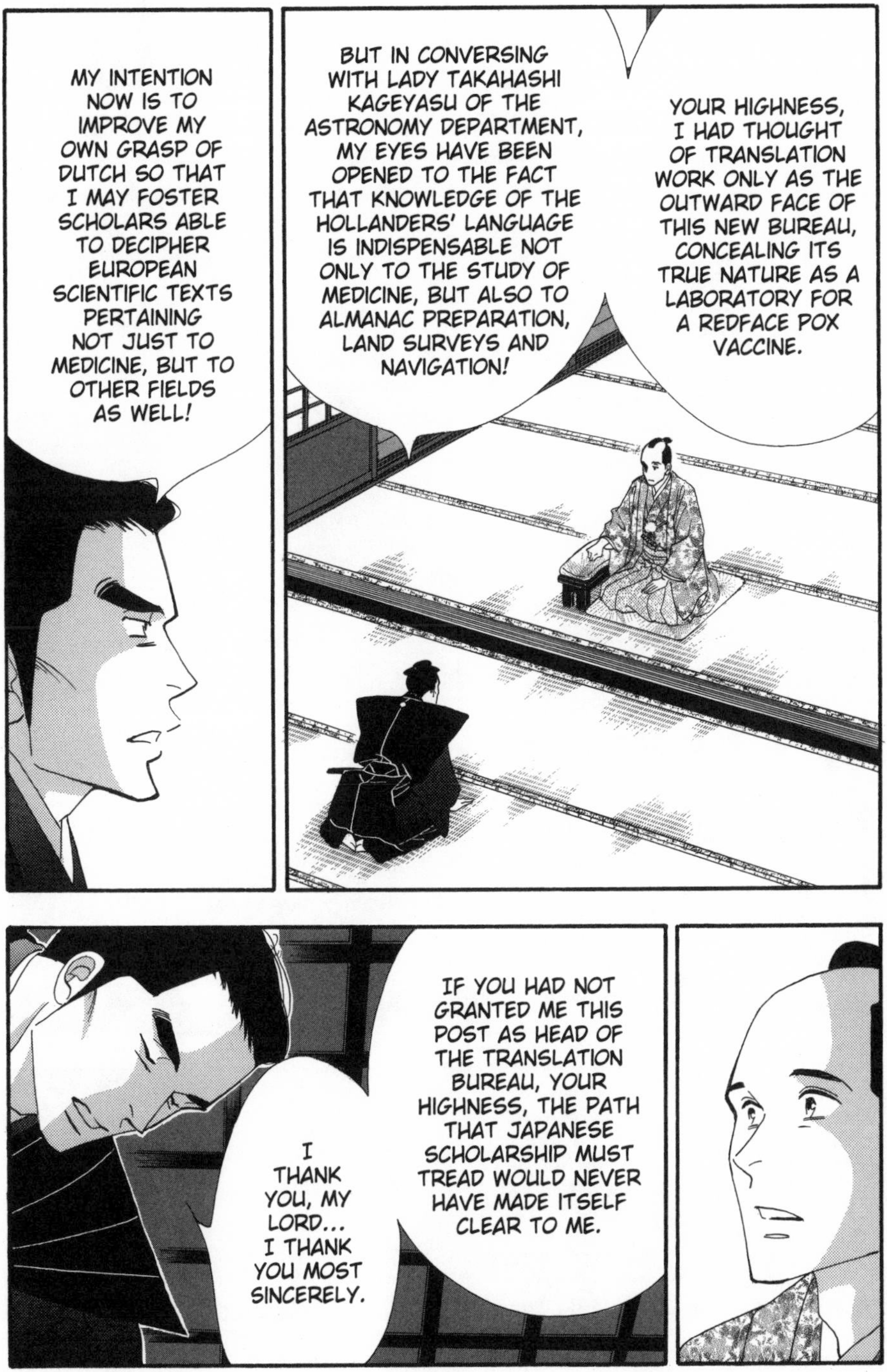
YOUR HIGHNESS, I HAD THOUGHT OF TRANSLATION WORK ONLY AS THE OUTWARD FACE OF THIS NEW BUREAU, CONCEALING ITS TRUE NATURE AS A LABORATORY FOR A REDFACE POX VACCINE.
BUT IN CONVERSING WITH LADY TAKAHASHI KAGEYASU OF THE ASTRONOMY DEPARTMENT, MY EYES HAVE BEEN OPENED TO THE FACT THAT KNOWLEDGE OF THE HOLLANDERS' LANGUAGE IS INDISPENSABLE NOT ONLY TO THE STUDY OF MEDICINE, BUT ALSO TO ALMANAC PREPARATION, LAND SURVEYS AND NAVIGATION!
MY INTENTION NOW IS TO IMPROVE MY OWN GRASP OF DUTCH SO THAT I MAY FOSTER SCHOLARS ABLE TO DECIPHER EUROPEAN SCIENTIFIC TEXTS PERTAINING NOT JUST TO MEDICINE, BUT TO OTHER FIELDS AS WELL!
IF YOU HAD NOT GRANTED ME THIS POST AS HEAD OF THE TRANSLATION BUREAU, YOUR HIGHNESS, THE PATH THAT JAPANESE SCHOLARSHIP MUST TREAD WOULD NEVER HAVE MADE ITSELF CLEAR TO ME.
I THANK YOU, MY LORD... I THANK YOU MOST SINCERELY.

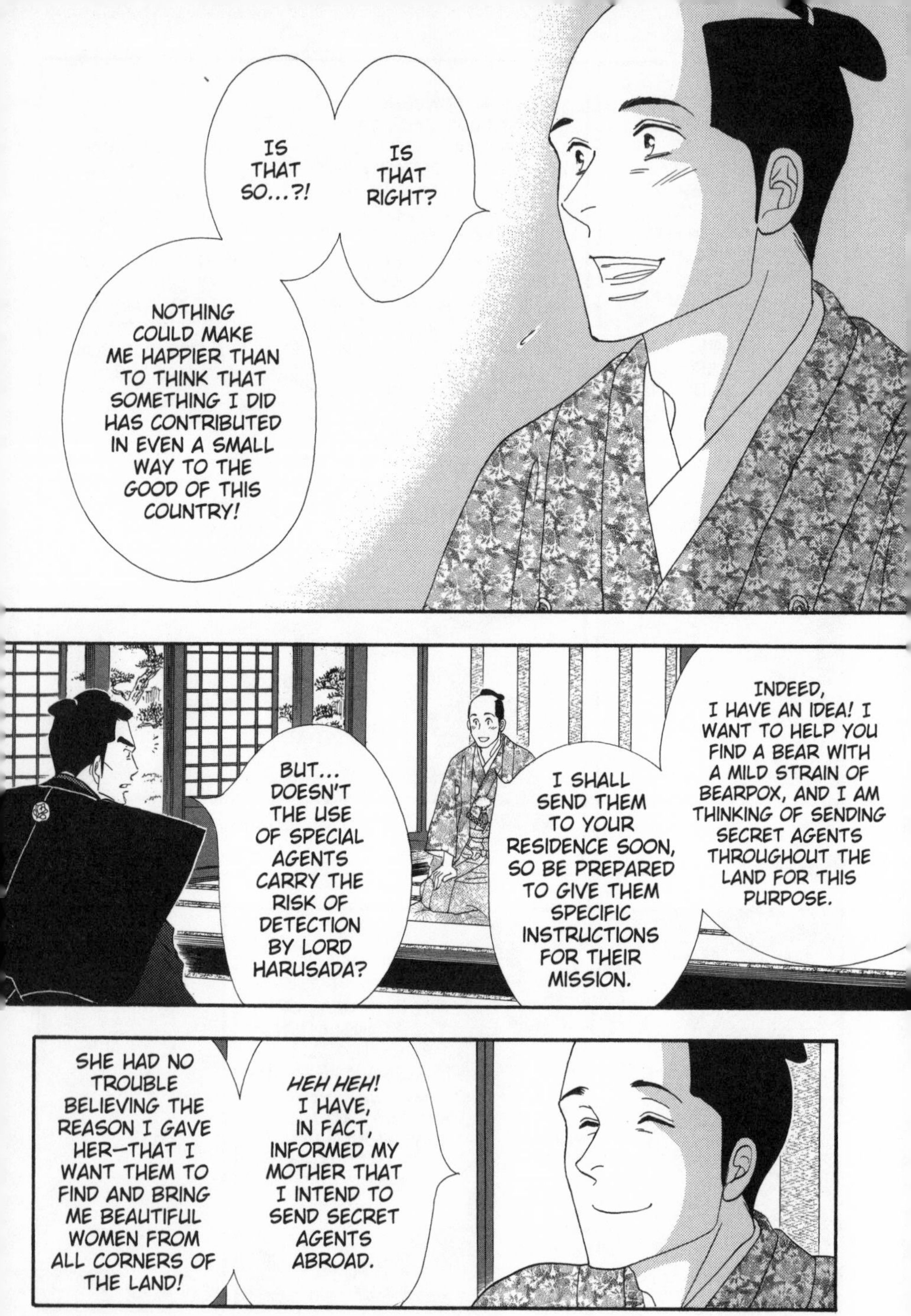
IS THAT RIGHT?
IS THAT SO...?!
NOTHING COULD MAKE ME HAPPIER THAN TO THINK THAT SOMETHING I DID HAS CONTRIBUTED IN EVEN A SMALL WAY TO THE GOOD OF THIS COUNTRY!
INDEED, I HAVE AN IDEA! I WANT TO HELP YOU FIND A BEAR WITH A MILD STRAIN OF BEARPOX, AND I AM THINKING OF SENDING SECRET AGENTS THROUGHOUT THE LAND FOR THIS PURPOSE.
I SHALL SEND THEM TO YOUR RESIDENCE SOON, SO BE PREPARED TO GIVE THEM SPECIFIC INSTRUCTIONS FOR THEIR MISSION.
BUT... DOESN'T THE USE OF SPECIAL AGENTS CARRY THE RISK OF DETECTION BY LORD HARUSADA?
HEH HEH! I HAVE, IN FACT, INFORMED MY MOTHER THAT I INTEND TO SEND SECRET AGENTS ABROAD.
SHE HAD NO TROUBLE BELIEVING THE REASON I GAVE HER—THAT I WANT THEM TO FIND AND BRING ME BEAUTIFUL WOMEN FROM ALL CORNERS OF THE LAND!

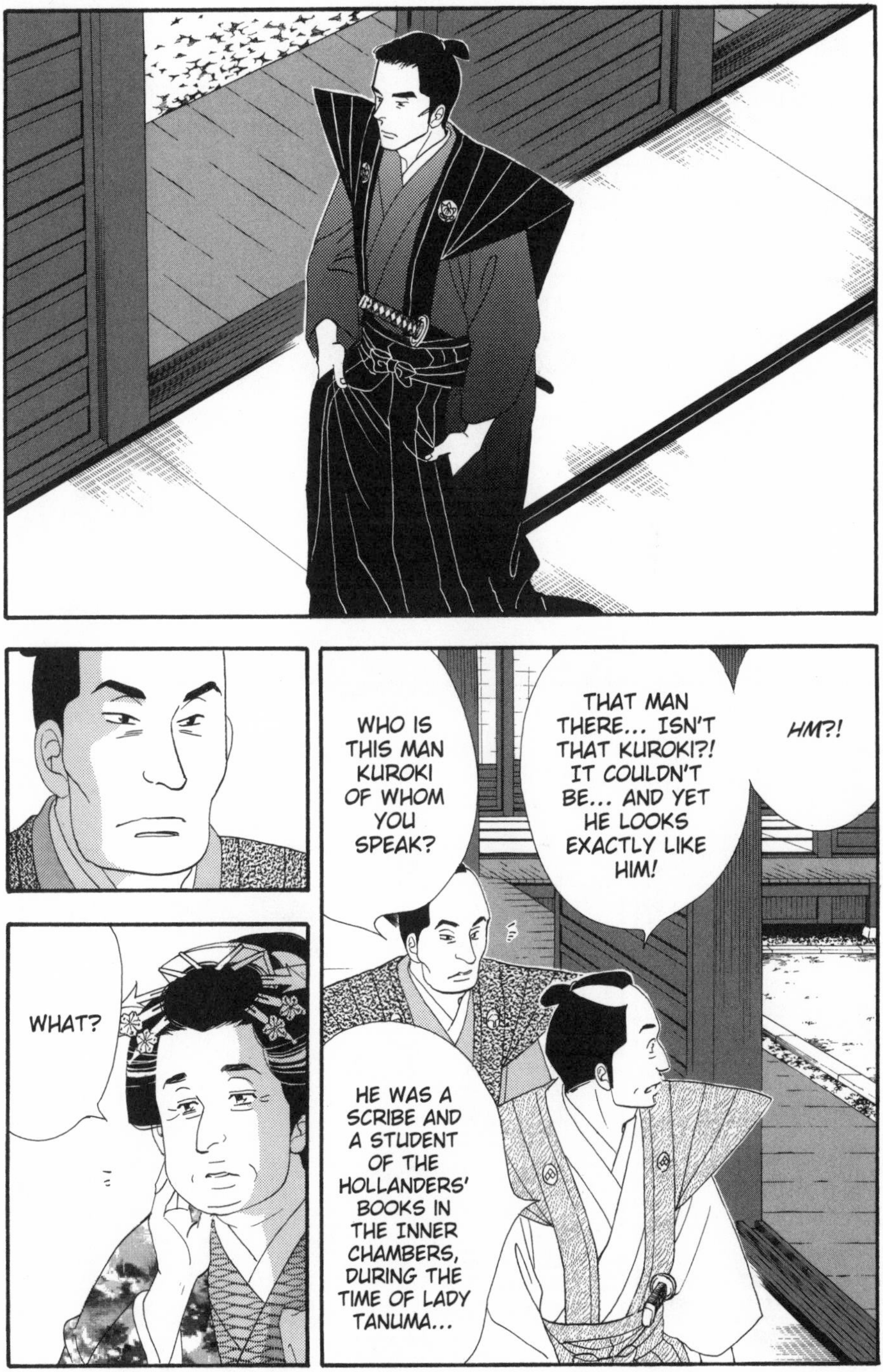
HM?!
THAT MAN THERE... ISN'T THAT KUROKI?! IT COULDN'T BE... AND YET HE LOOKS EXACTLY LIKE HIM!
WHO IS THIS MAN KUROKI OF WHOM YOU SPEAK?
HE WAS A SCRIBE AND A STUDENT OF THE HOLLANDERS' BOOKS IN THE INNER CHAMBERS, DURING THE TIME OF LADY TANUMA...
WHAT?

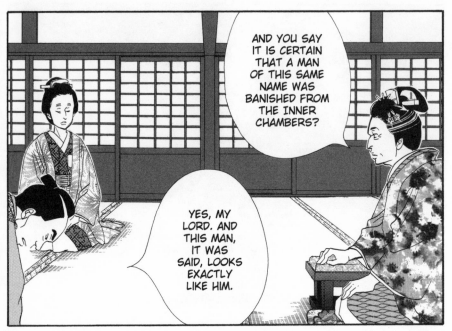

AND YOU SAY IT IS CERTAIN THAT A MAN OF THIS SAME NAME WAS BANISHED FROM THE INNER CHAMBERS?

YES, MY LORD. AND THIS MAN, IT WAS SAID, LOOKS EXACTLY LIKE HIM.

THAT'S RIGHT! AONUMA'S NOTEBOOKS AND PRIVATE LIBRARY! I HAVE THAT LARGE CHEST IN MY QUARTERS, FROM THAT FORMER SCRIBE, SHOJI!

I MEANT TO SEND IT TO KUROKI AND HAD COMPLETELY FORGOTTEN!

OH!

66

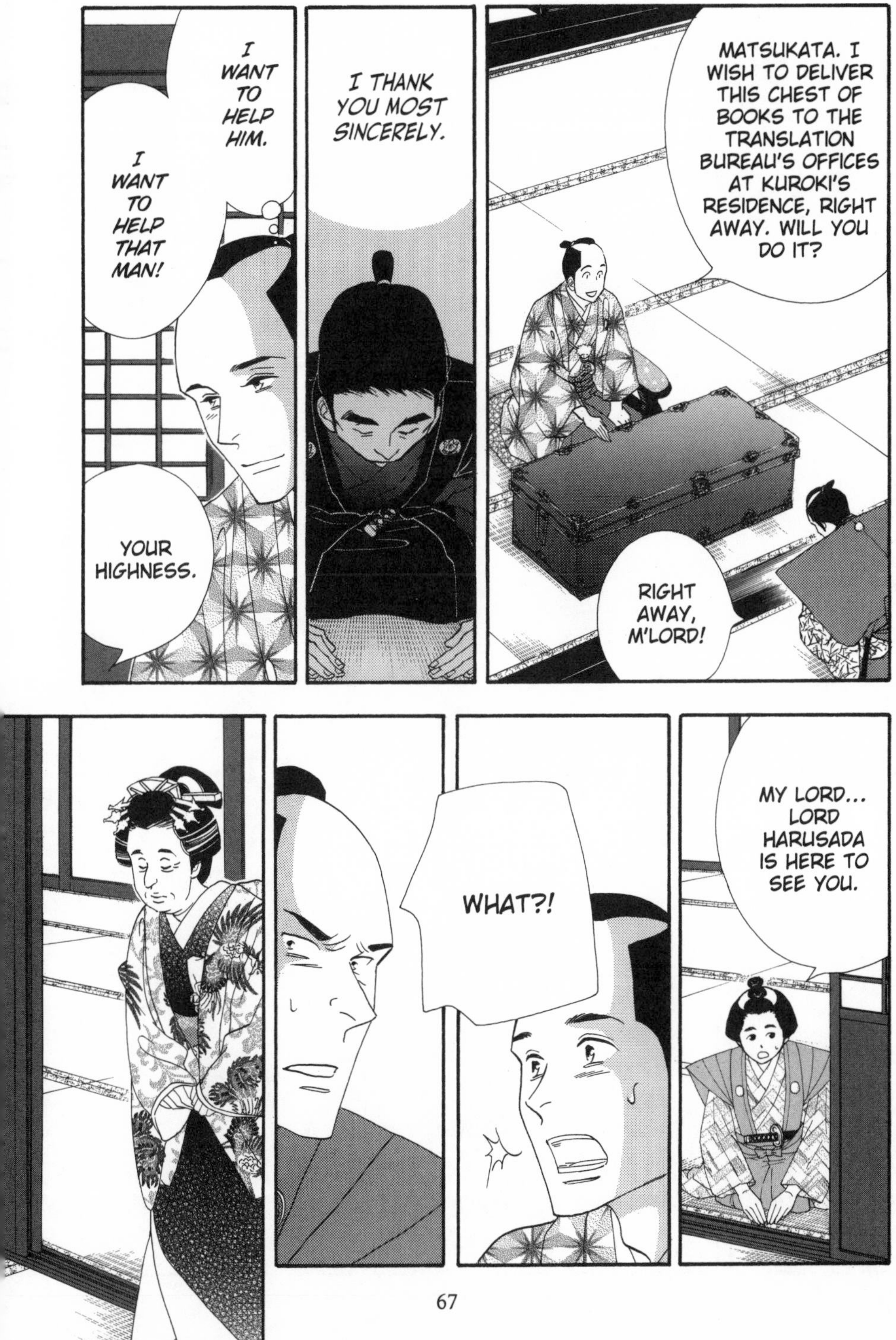
MATSUKATA. I WISH TO DELIVER THIS CHEST OF BOOKS TO THE TRANSLATION BUREAU'S OFFICES AT KUROKI'S RESIDENCE, RIGHT AWAY. WILL YOU DO IT?
RIGHT AWAY, M'LORD!
I THANK YOU MOST SINCERELY.
I WANT TO HELP HIM.
I WANT TO HELP THAT MAN!
YOUR HIGHNESS.
MY LORD... LORD HARUSADA IS HERE TO SEE YOU.
WHAT?!

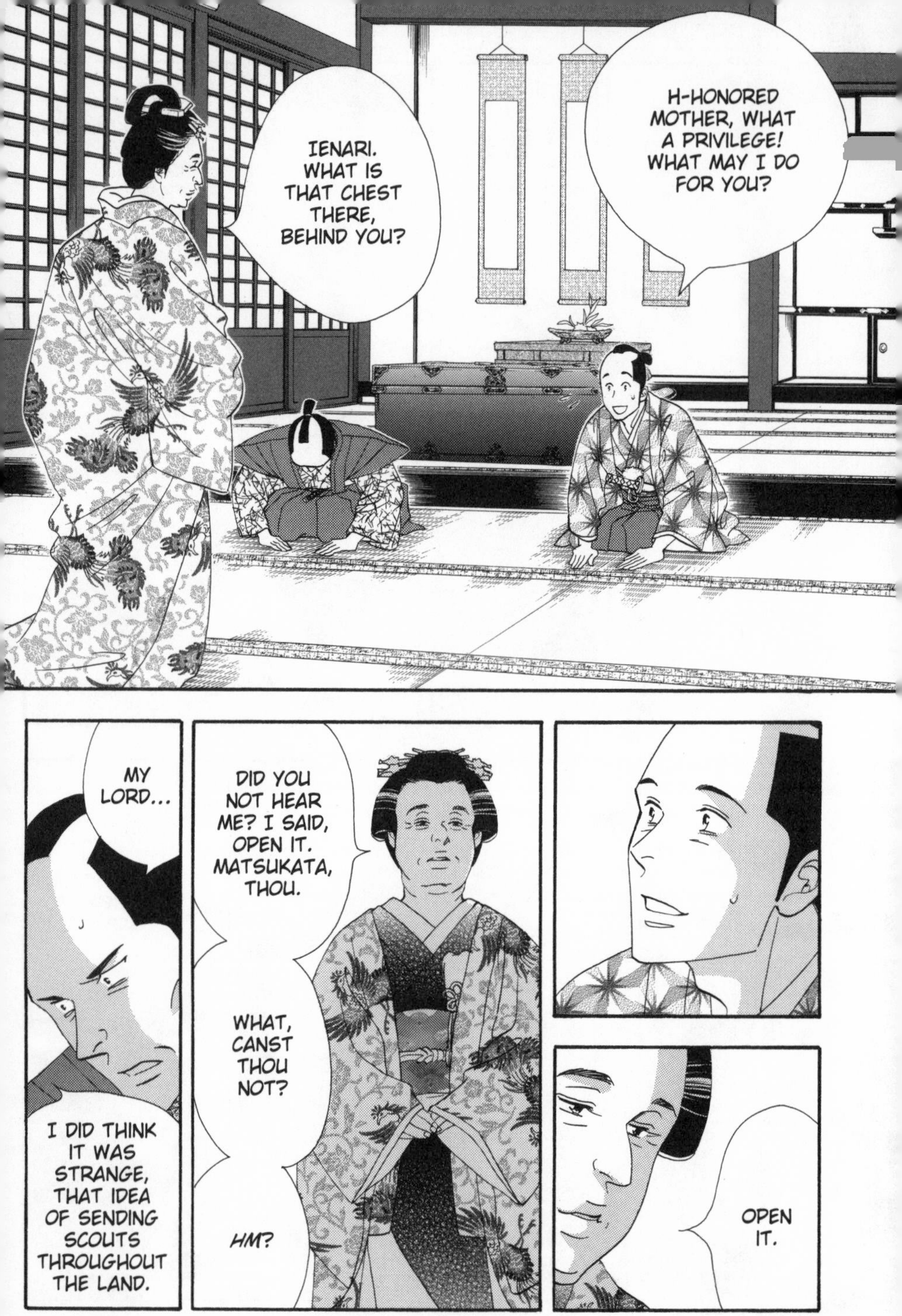
H-HONORED MOTHER, WHAT A PRIVILEGE! WHAT MAY I DO FOR YOU?
IENARI. WHAT IS THAT CHEST THERE, BEHIND YOU?
OPEN IT.
DID YOU NOT HEAR ME? I SAID, OPEN IT. MATSUKATA, THOU.
WHAT, CANST THOU NOT?
HM?
MY LORD...
I DID THINK IT WAS STRANGE, THAT IDEA OF SENDING SCOUTS THROUGHOUT THE LAND.

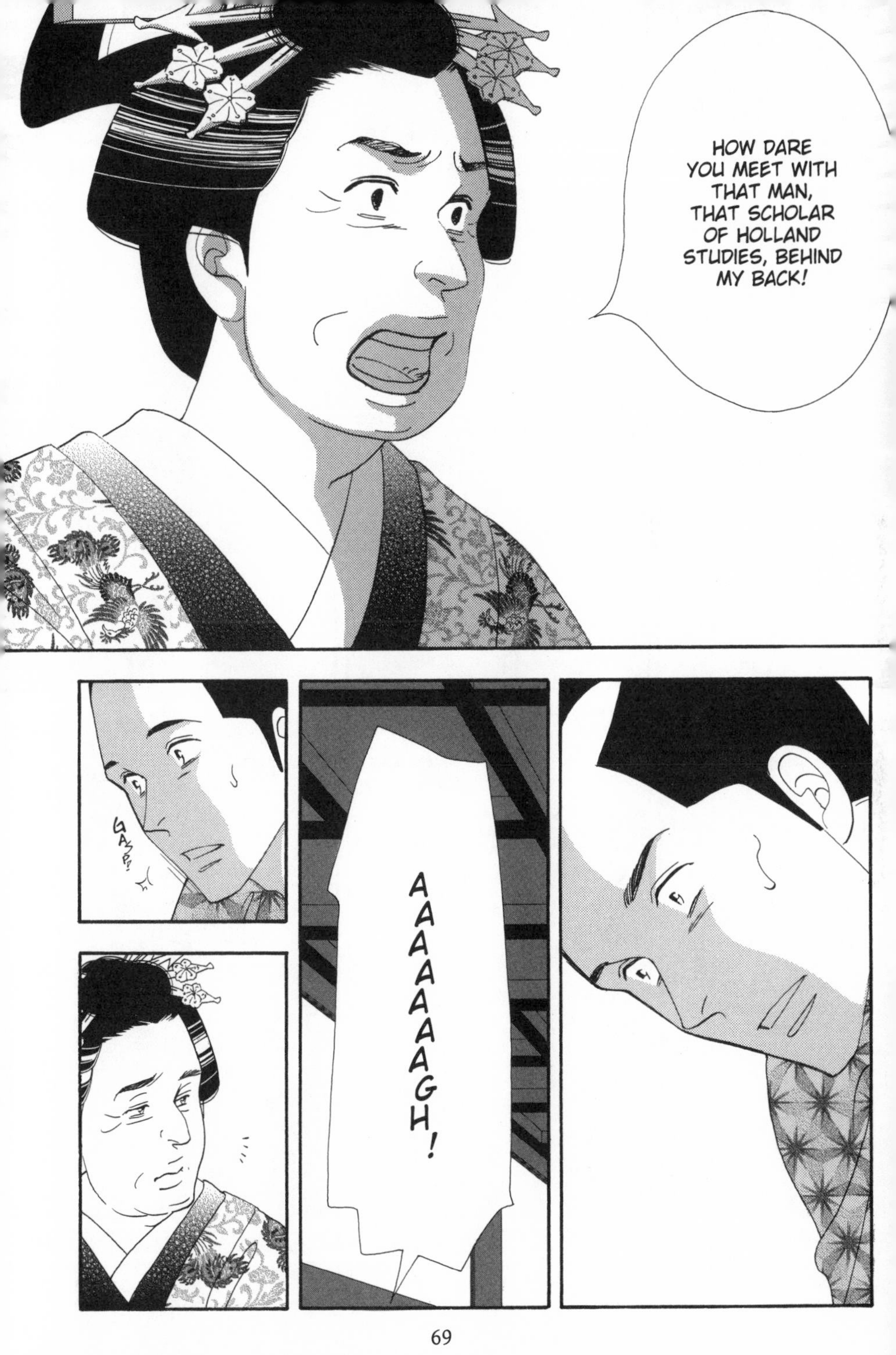
HOW DARE YOU MEET WITH THAT MAN, THAT SCHOLAR OF HOLLAND STUDIES, BEHIND MY BACK!
AAAAAAAGH!
GASP!

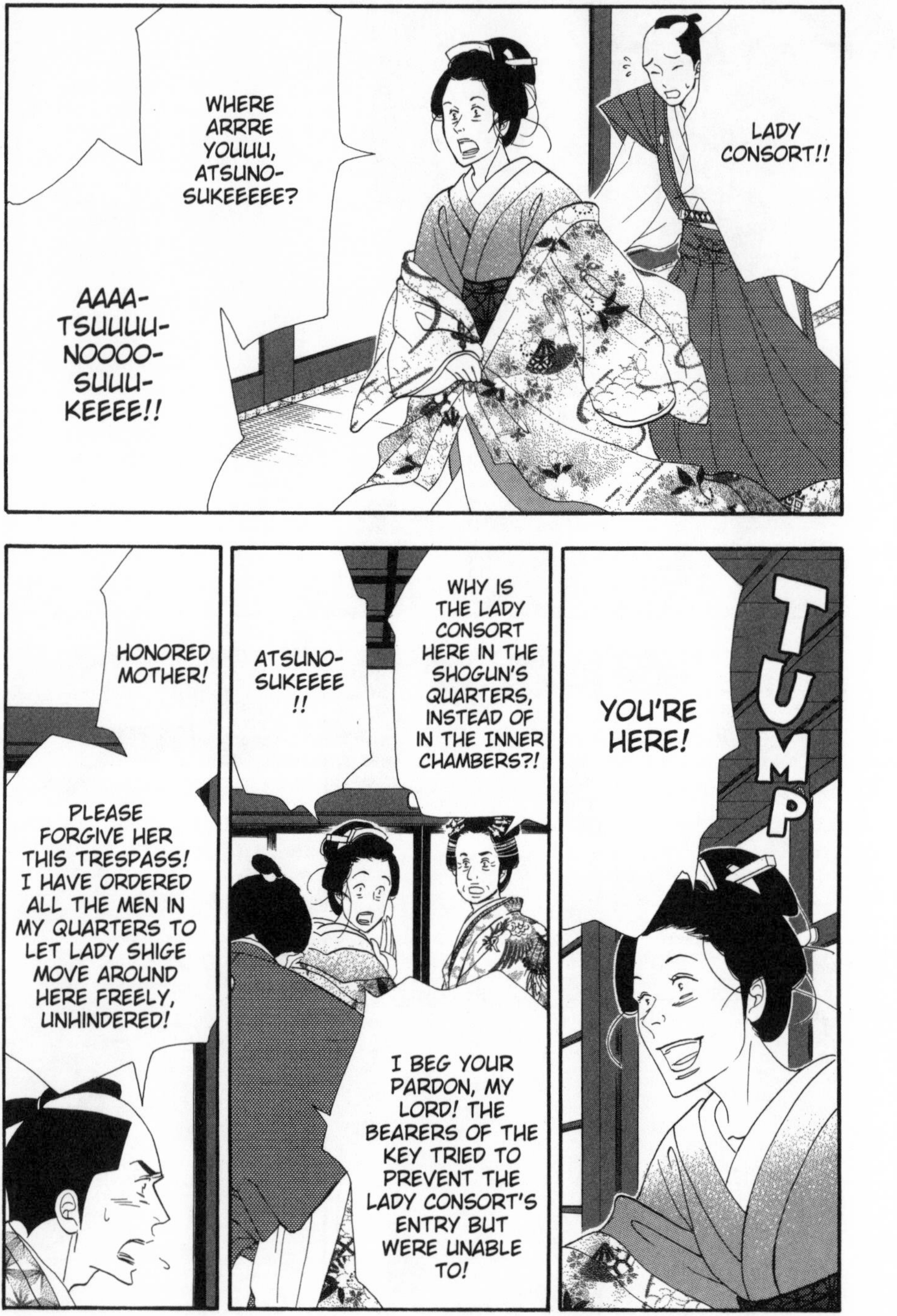
LADY CONSORT!!
WHERE ARRRE YOUUU, ATSUNO-SUKEEEEE?
AAAA-TSUUUU-NOOOO-SUUU-KEEEE!!
TUMP
YOU'RE HERE!
WHY IS THE LADY CONSORT HERE IN THE SHOGUN'S QUARTERS, INSTEAD OF IN THE INNER CHAMBERS?!
ATSUNO-SUKEEEE!!
I BEG YOUR PARDON, MY LORD! THE BEARERS OF THE KEY TRIED TO PREVENT THE LADY CONSORT'S ENTRY BUT WERE UNABLE TO!
HONORED MOTHER!
PLEASE FORGIVE HER THIS TRESPASS! I HAVE ORDERED ALL THE MEN IN MY QUARTERS TO LET LADY SHIGE MOVE AROUND HERE FREELY, UNHINDERED!

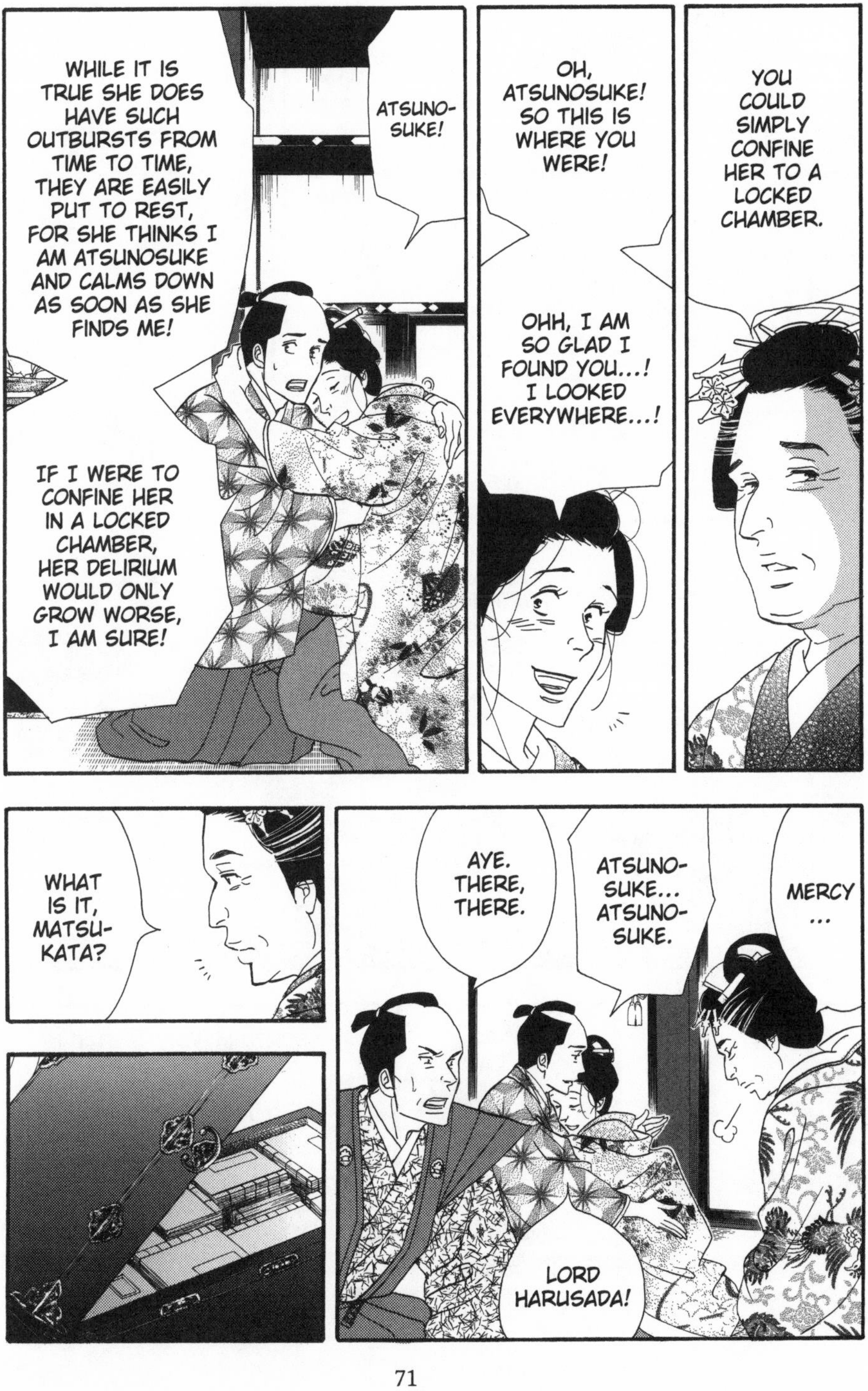
YOU COULD SIMPLY CONFINE HER TO A LOCKED CHAMBER.
OH, ATSUNOSUKE! SO THIS IS WHERE YOU WERE!
OHH, I AM SO GLAD I FOUND YOU...! I LOOKED EVERYWHERE...!
ATSUNO-SUKE!
WHILE IT IS TRUE SHE DOES HAVE SUCH OUTBURSTS FROM TIME TO TIME, THEY ARE EASILY PUT TO REST, FOR SHE THINKS I AM ATSUNOSUKE AND CALMS DOWN AS SOON AS SHE FINDS ME!
IF I WERE TO CONFINE HER IN A LOCKED CHAMBER, HER DELIRIUM WOULD ONLY GROW WORSE, I AM SURE!
MERCY ...
ATSUNO-SUKE... ATSUNO-SUKE.
AYE. THERE, THERE.
LORD HARUSADA!
WHAT IS IT, MATSU-KATA?

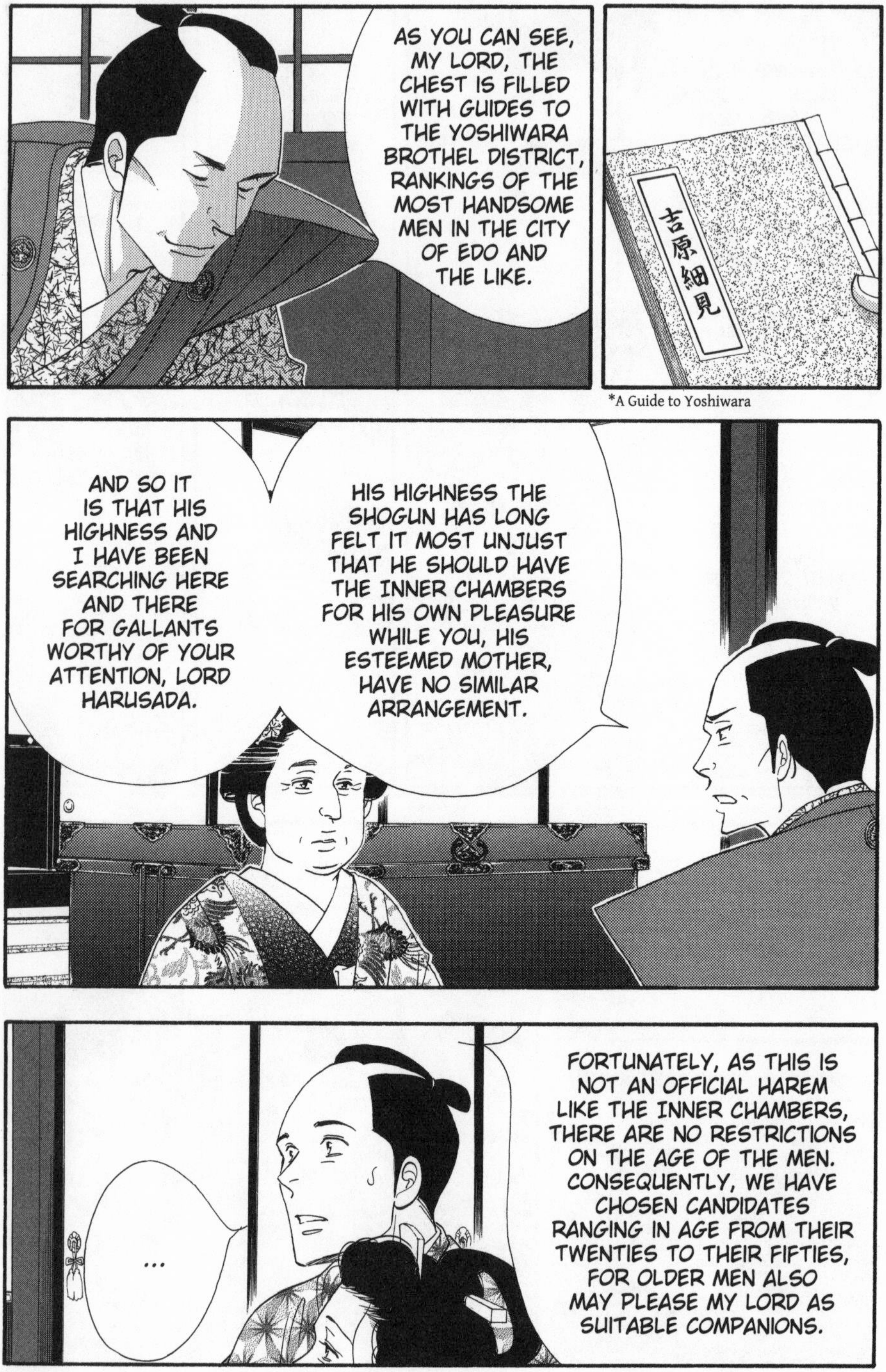
吉原細見
*A Guide to Yoshiwara
AS YOU CAN SEE, MY LORD, THE CHEST IS FILLED WITH GUIDES TO THE YOSHIWARA BROTHEL DISTRICT, RANKINGS OF THE MOST HANDSOME MEN IN THE CITY OF EDO AND THE LIKE.
HIS HIGHNESS THE SHOGUN HAS LONG FELT IT MOST UNJUST THAT HE SHOULD HAVE THE INNER CHAMBERS FOR HIS OWN PLEASURE WHILE YOU, HIS ESTEEMED MOTHER, HAVE NO SIMILAR ARRANGEMENT.
AND SO IT IS THAT HIS HIGHNESS AND I HAVE BEEN SEARCHING HERE AND THERE FOR GALLANTS WORTHY OF YOUR ATTENTION, LORD HARUSADA.
FORTUNATELY, AS THIS IS NOT AN OFFICIAL HAREM LIKE THE INNER CHAMBERS, THERE ARE NO RESTRICTIONS ON THE AGE OF THE MEN. CONSEQUENTLY, WE HAVE CHOSEN CANDIDATES RANGING IN AGE FROM THEIR TWENTIES TO THEIR FIFTIES, FOR OLDER MEN ALSO MAY PLEASE MY LORD AS SUITABLE COMPANIONS.
...

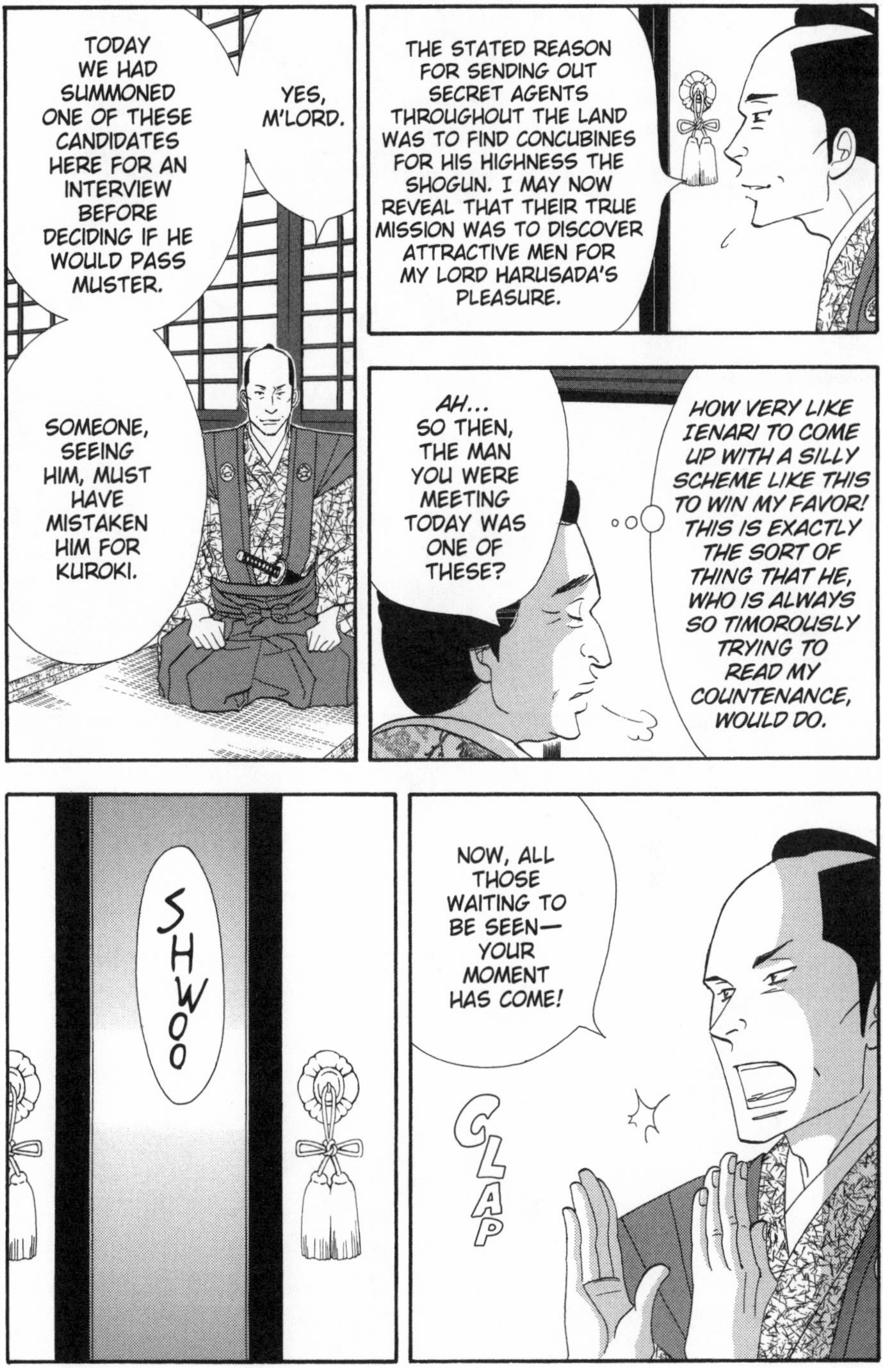
THE STATED REASON FOR SENDING OUT SECRET AGENTS THROUGHOUT THE LAND WAS TO FIND CONCUBINES FOR HIS HIGHNESS THE SHOGUN. I MAY NOW REVEAL THAT THEIR TRUE MISSION WAS TO DISCOVER ATTRACTIVE MEN FOR MY LORD HARUSADA'S PLEASURE.
HOW VERY LIKE IENARI TO COME UP WITH A SILLY SCHEME LIKE THIS TO WIN MY FAVOR! THIS IS EXACTLY THE SORT OF THING THAT HE, WHO IS ALWAYS SO TIMOROUSLY TRYING TO READ MY COUNTENANCE, WOULD DO.
AH... SO THEN, THE MAN YOU WERE MEETING TODAY WAS ONE OF THESE?
YES, M'LORD.
TODAY WE HAD SUMMONED ONE OF THESE CANDIDATES HERE FOR AN INTERVIEW BEFORE DECIDING IF HE WOULD PASS MUSTER.
SOMEONE, SEEING HIM, MUST HAVE MISTAKEN HIM FOR KUROKI.
NOW, ALL THOSE WAITING TO BE SEEN— YOUR MOMENT HAS COME!
CLAP
SHWOO

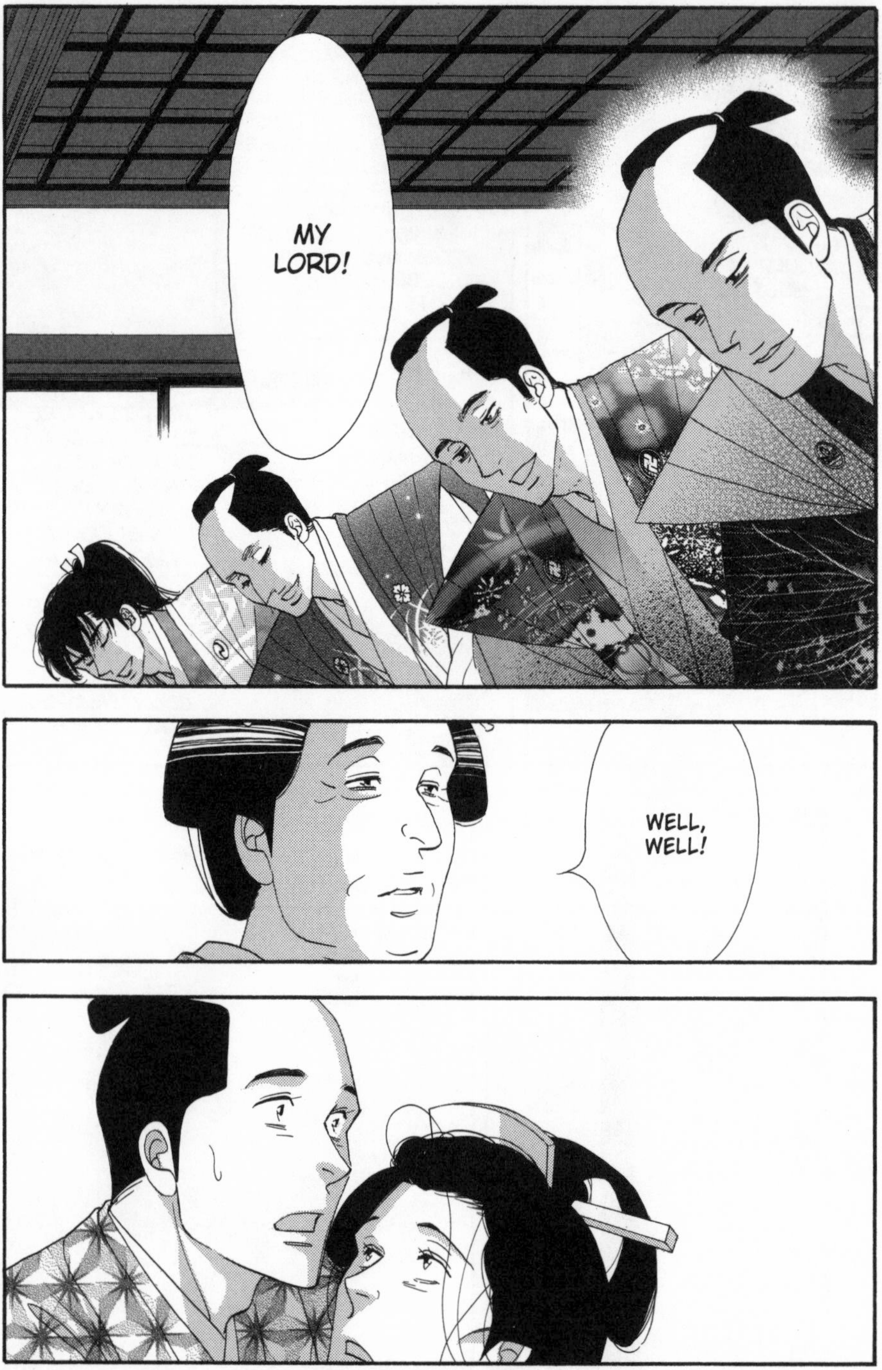
MY LORD!
WELL, WELL!

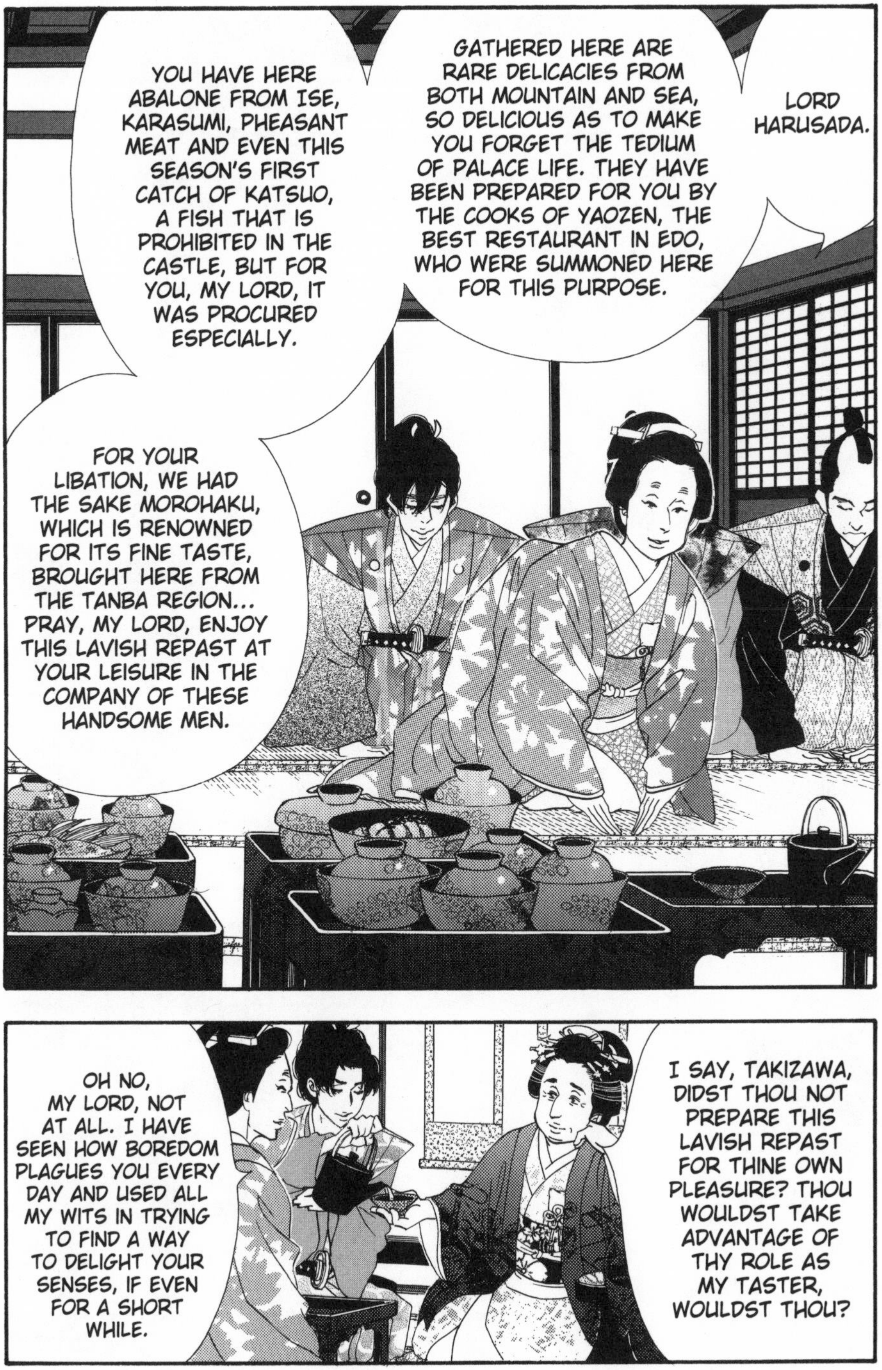
LORD HARUSADA.
GATHERED HERE ARE RARE DELICACIES FROM BOTH MOUNTAIN AND SEA, SO DELICIOUS AS TO MAKE YOU FORGET THE TEDIUM OF PALACE LIFE. THEY HAVE BEEN PREPARED FOR YOU BY THE COOKS OF YAOZEN, THE BEST RESTAURANT IN EDO, WHO WERE SUMMONED HERE FOR THIS PURPOSE.
YOU HAVE HERE ABALONE FROM ISE, KARASUMI, PHEASANT MEAT AND EVEN THIS SEASON'S FIRST CATCH OF KATSUO, A FISH THAT IS PROHIBITED IN THE CASTLE, BUT FOR YOU, MY LORD, IT WAS PROCURED ESPECIALLY.
FOR YOUR LIBATION, WE HAD THE SAKE MOROHAKU, WHICH IS RENOWNED FOR ITS FINE TASTE, BROUGHT HERE FROM THE TANBA REGION... PRAY, MY LORD, ENJOY THIS LAVISH REPAST AT YOUR LEISURE IN THE COMPANY OF THESE HANDSOME MEN.
I SAY, TAKIZAWA, DIDST THOU NOT PREPARE THIS LAVISH REPAST FOR THINE OWN PLEASURE? THOU WOULDST TAKE ADVANTAGE OF THY ROLE AS MY TASTER, WOULDST THOU?
OH NO, MY LORD, NOT AT ALL. I HAVE SEEN HOW BOREDOM PLAGUES YOU EVERY DAY AND USED ALL MY WITS IN TRYING TO FIND A WAY TO DELIGHT YOUR SENSES, IF EVEN FOR A SHORT WHILE.

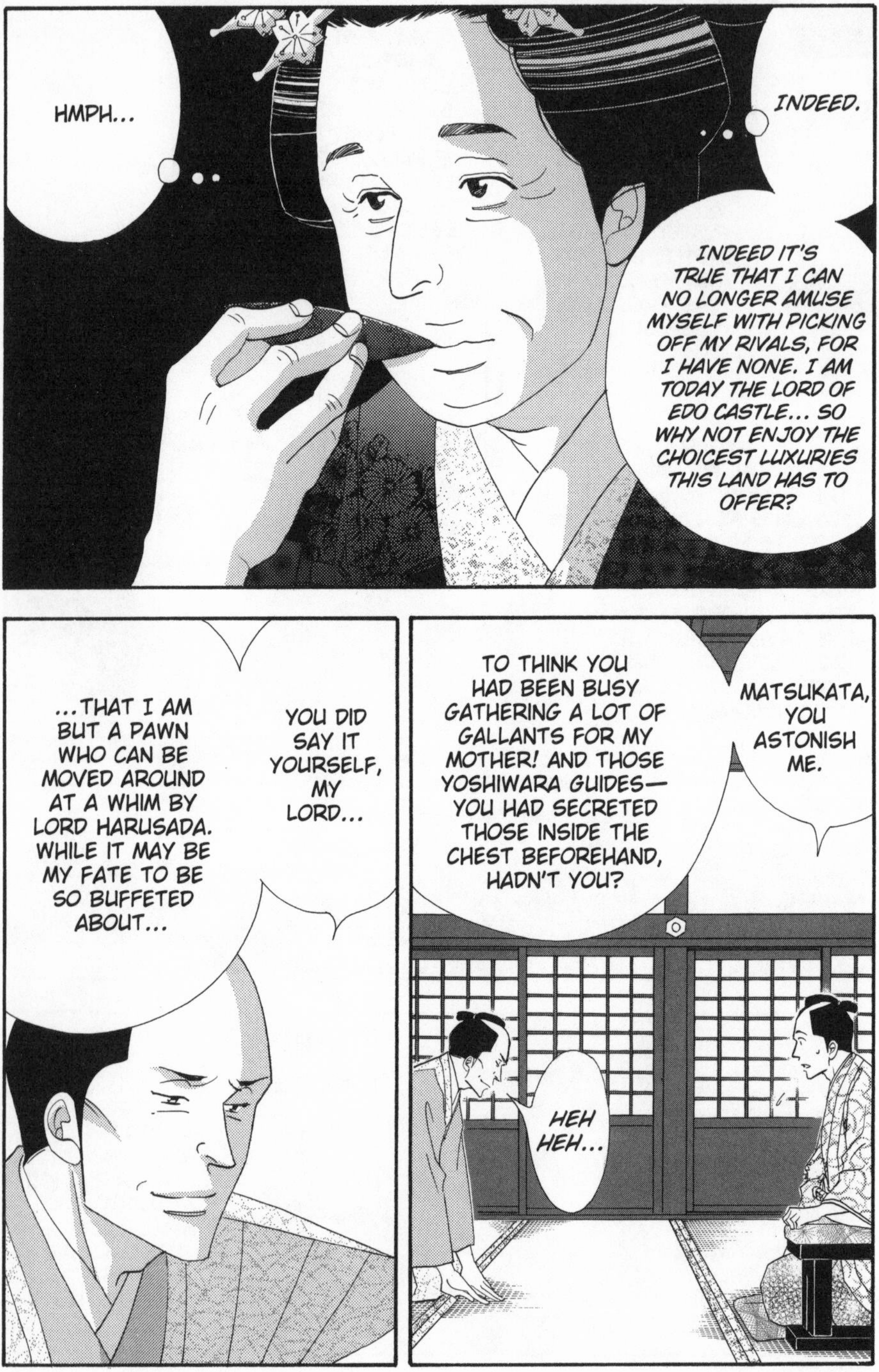
INDEED.
INDEED IT'S TRUE THAT I CAN NO LONGER AMUSE MYSELF WITH PICKING OFF MY RIVALS, FOR I HAVE NONE. I AM TODAY THE LORD OF EDO CASTLE... SO WHY NOT ENJOY THE CHOICEST LUXURIES THIS LAND HAS TO OFFER?
HMPH...
MATSUKATA, YOU ASTONISH ME.
TO THINK YOU HAD BEEN BUSY GATHERING A LOT OF GALLANTS FOR MY MOTHER! AND THOSE YOSHIWARA GUIDES—YOU HAD SECRETED THOSE INSIDE THE CHEST BEFOREHAND, HADN'T YOU?
HEH HEH...
YOU DID SAY IT YOURSELF, MY LORD...
...THAT I AM BUT A PAWN WHO CAN BE MOVED AROUND AT A WHIM BY LORD HARUSADA. WHILE IT MAY BE MY FATE TO BE SO BUFFETED ABOUT...

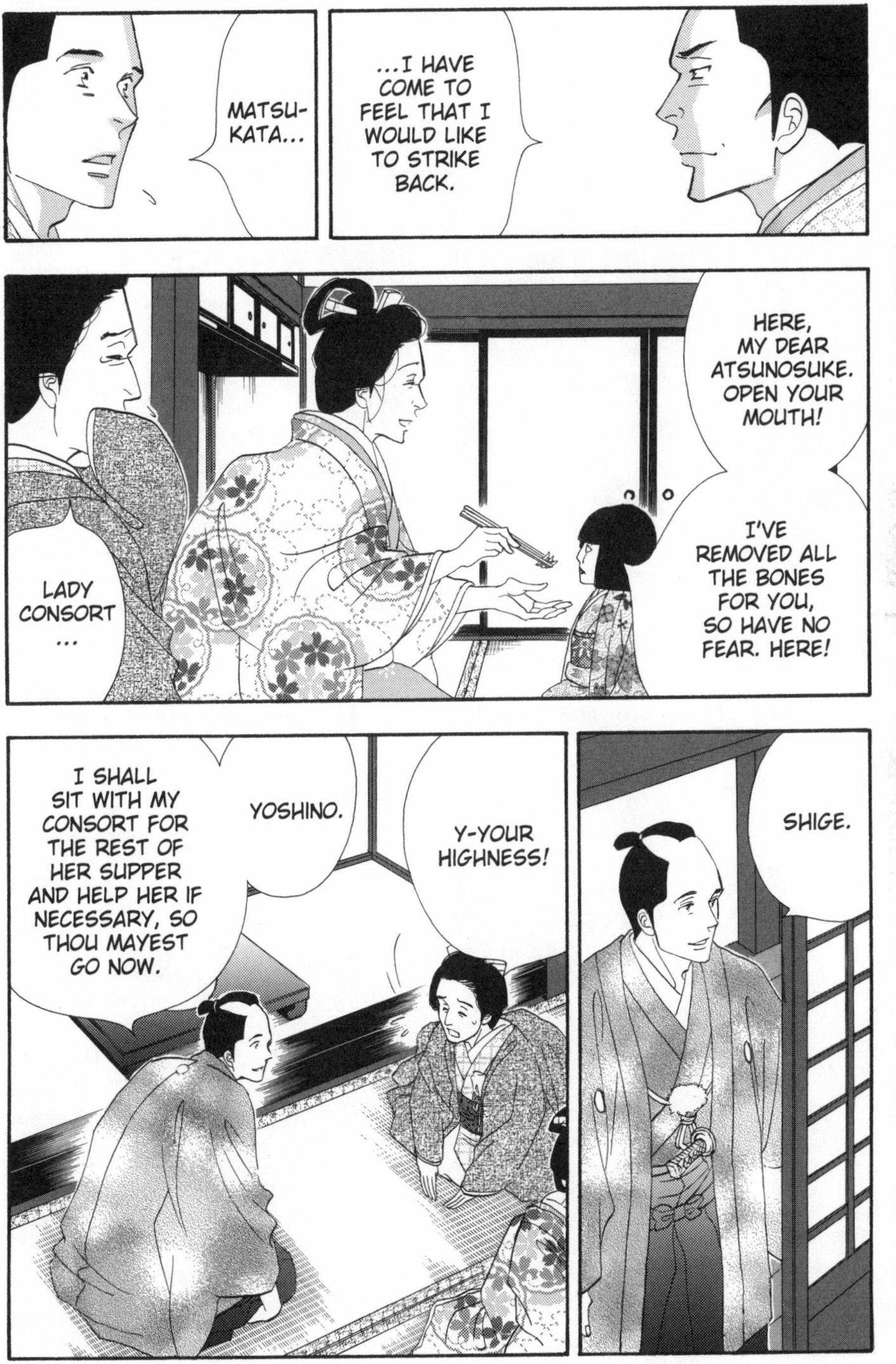
...I HAVE COME TO FEEL THAT I WOULD LIKE TO STRIKE BACK.
MATSU-KATA...
HERE, MY DEAR ATSUNOSUKE. OPEN YOUR MOUTH!
I'VE REMOVED ALL THE BONES FOR YOU, SO HAVE NO FEAR. HERE!
LADY CONSORT ...
SHIGE.
Y-YOUR HIGHNESS!
YOSHINO.
I SHALL SIT WITH MY CONSORT FOR THE REST OF HER SUPPER AND HELP HER IF NECESSARY, SO THOU MAYEST GO NOW.

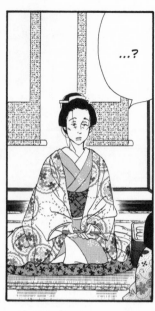

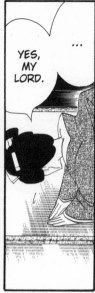

GO, MY LORD? B-BUT...!
I WANT TO BE ALONE WITH HER.
...
YES, MY LORD.
...?
SHIGE.
YOU TRULY SAVED ME TODAY BY ARRIVING AT JUST THE RIGHT MOMENT.
THANK YOU...
ATSUNO-SUKE!
AHH, ATSUNO-SUKE, ATSUNO-SUKE!
OH, GOOD! SO THIS IS WHERE YOU WERE!
AYE, AYE.

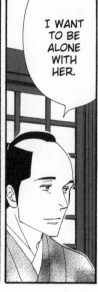

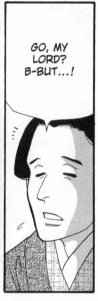

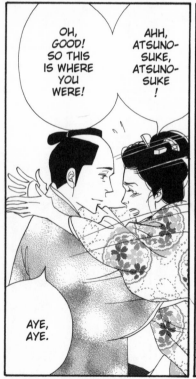

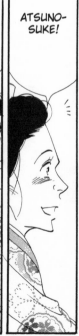

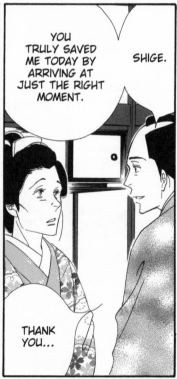

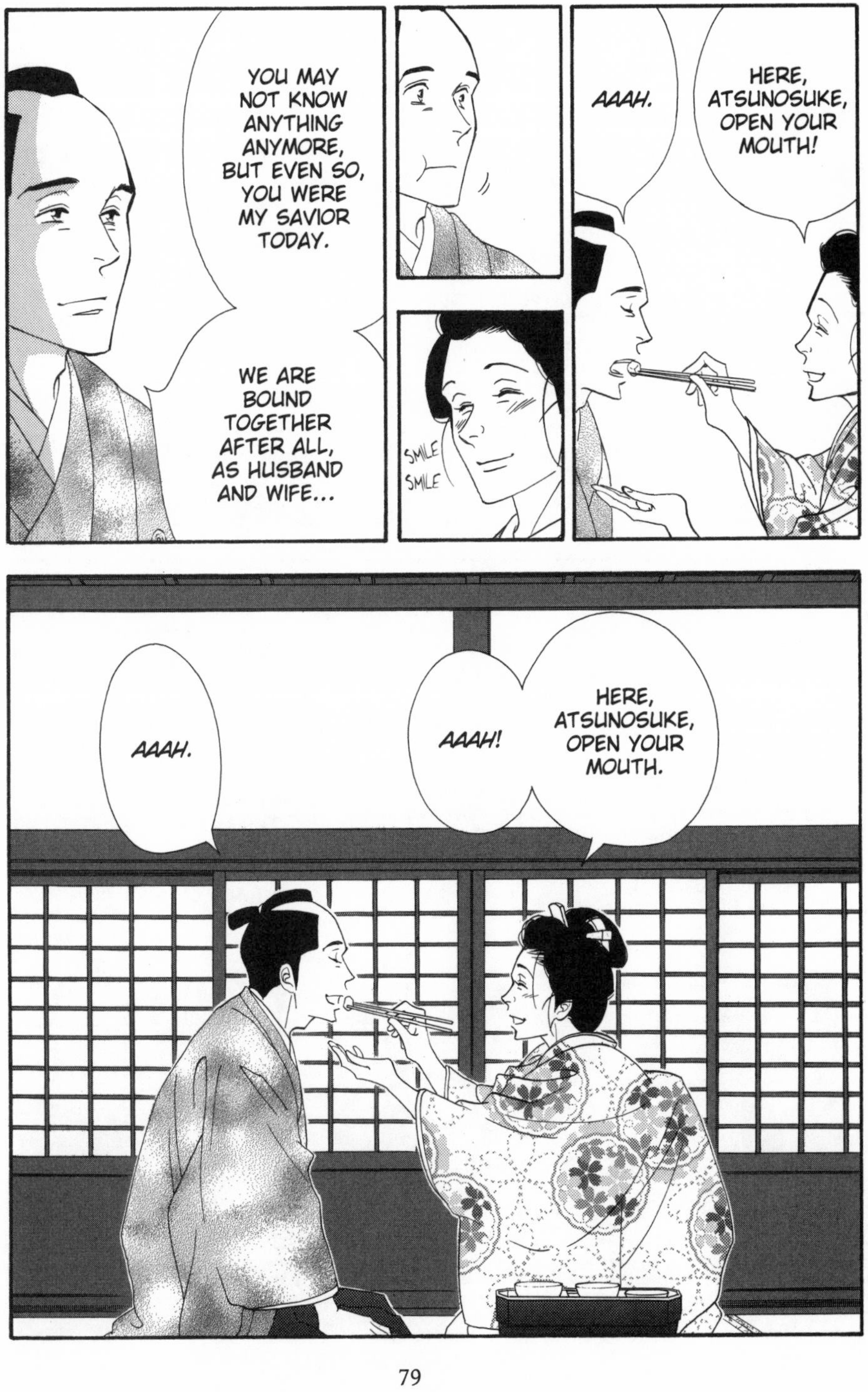
HERE, ATSUNOSUKE, OPEN YOUR MOUTH!
AAAH.
SMILE SMILE
YOU MAY NOT KNOW ANYTHING ANYMORE, BUT EVEN SO, YOU WERE MY SAVIOR TODAY.
WE ARE BOUND TOGETHER AFTER ALL, AS HUSBAND AND WIFE...
HERE, ATSUNOSUKE, OPEN YOUR MOUTH.
AAAH!
AAAH.

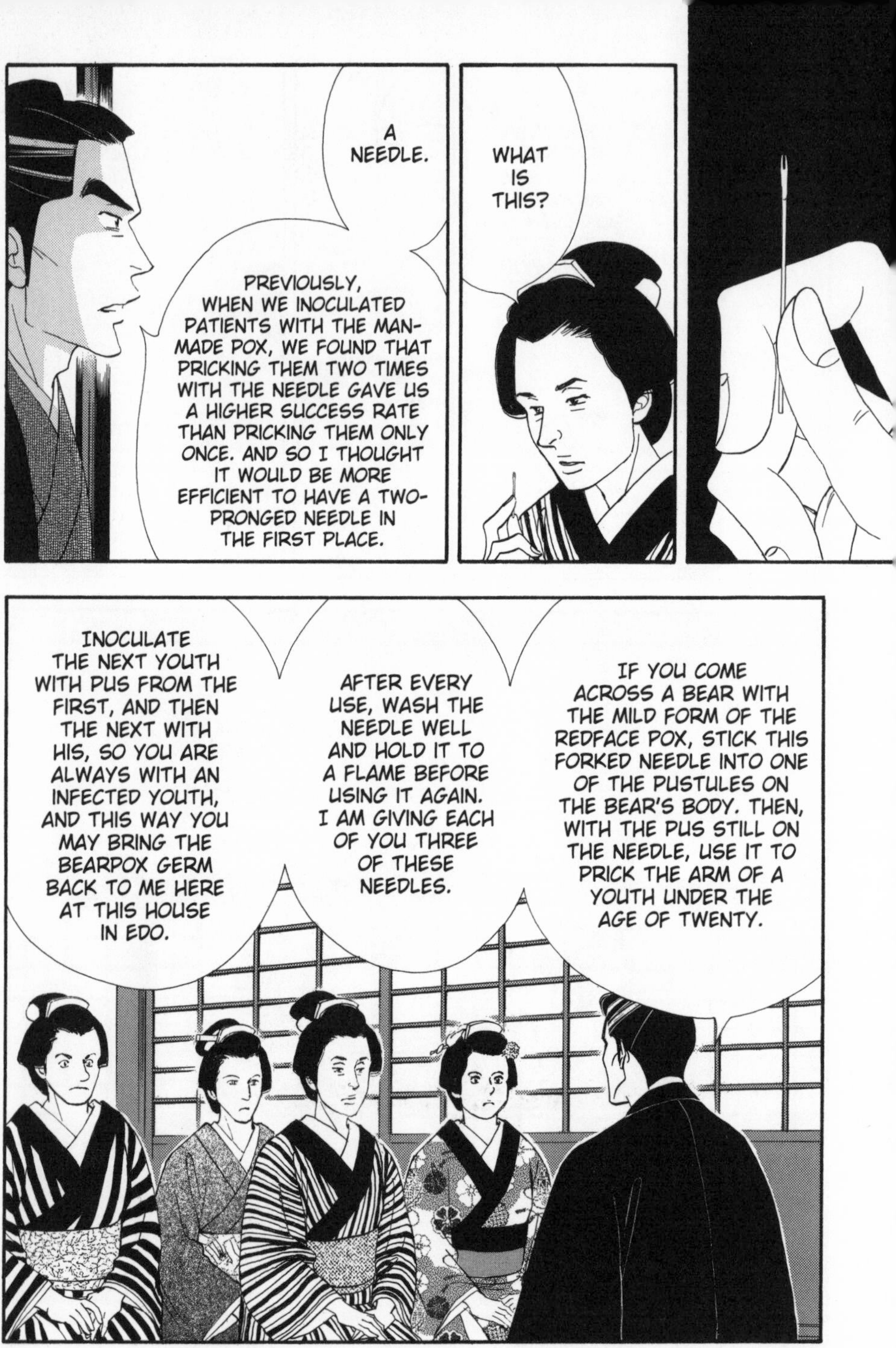
WHAT IS THIS?
A NEEDLE.
PREVIOUSLY, WHEN WE INOCULATED PATIENTS WITH THE MAN-MADE POX, WE FOUND THAT PRICKING THEM TWO TIMES WITH THE NEEDLE GAVE US A HIGHER SUCCESS RATE THAN PRICKING THEM ONLY ONCE. AND SO I THOUGHT IT WOULD BE MORE EFFICIENT TO HAVE A TWO-PRONGED NEEDLE IN THE FIRST PLACE.
IF YOU COME ACROSS A BEAR WITH THE MILD FORM OF THE REDFACE POX, STICK THIS FORKED NEEDLE INTO ONE OF THE PUSTULES ON THE BEAR'S BODY. THEN, WITH THE PUS STILL ON THE NEEDLE, USE IT TO PRICK THE ARM OF A YOUTH UNDER THE AGE OF TWENTY.
AFTER EVERY USE, WASH THE NEEDLE WELL AND HOLD IT TO A FLAME BEFORE USING IT AGAIN. I AM GIVING EACH OF YOU THREE OF THESE NEEDLES.
INOCULATE THE NEXT YOUTH WITH PUS FROM THE FIRST, AND THEN THE NEXT WITH HIS, SO YOU ARE ALWAYS WITH AN INFECTED YOUTH, AND THIS WAY YOU MAY BRING THE BEARPOX GERM BACK TO ME HERE AT THIS HOUSE IN EDO.

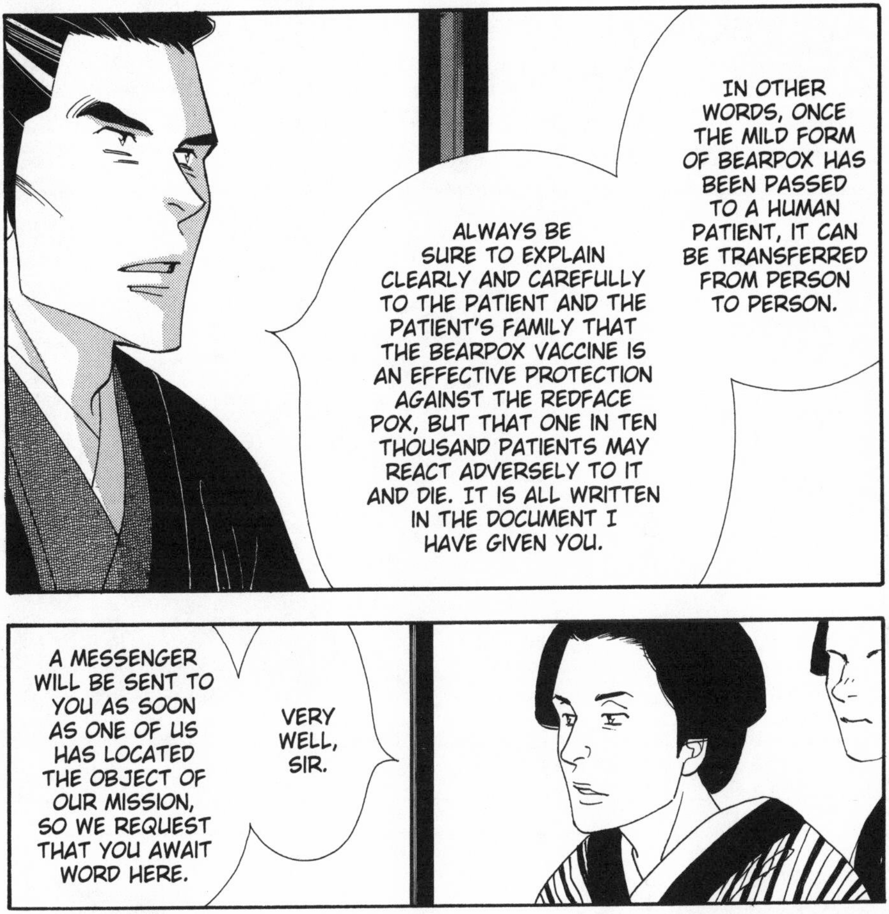
IN OTHER WORDS, ONCE THE MILD FORM OF BEARPOX HAS BEEN PASSED TO A HUMAN PATIENT, IT CAN BE TRANSFERRED FROM PERSON TO PERSON.
ALWAYS BE SURE TO EXPLAIN CLEARLY AND CAREFULLY TO THE PATIENT AND THE PATIENT'S FAMILY THAT THE BEARPOX VACCINE IS AN EFFECTIVE PROTECTION AGAINST THE REDFACE POX, BUT THAT ONE IN TEN THOUSAND PATIENTS MAY REACT ADVERSELY TO IT AND DIE. IT IS ALL WRITTEN IN THE DOCUMENT I HAVE GIVEN YOU.
A MESSENGER WILL BE SENT TO YOU AS SOON AS ONE OF US HAS LOCATED THE OBJECT OF OUR MISSION, SO WE REQUEST THAT YOU AWAIT WORD HERE.
VERY WELL, SIR.
MAY GOOD FORTUNE BE WITH YOU.
THANK YOU, SIR!

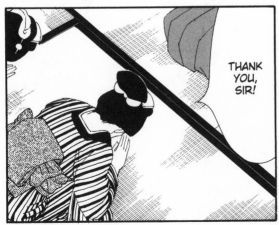

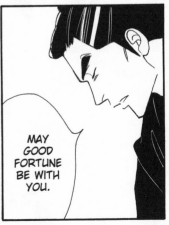

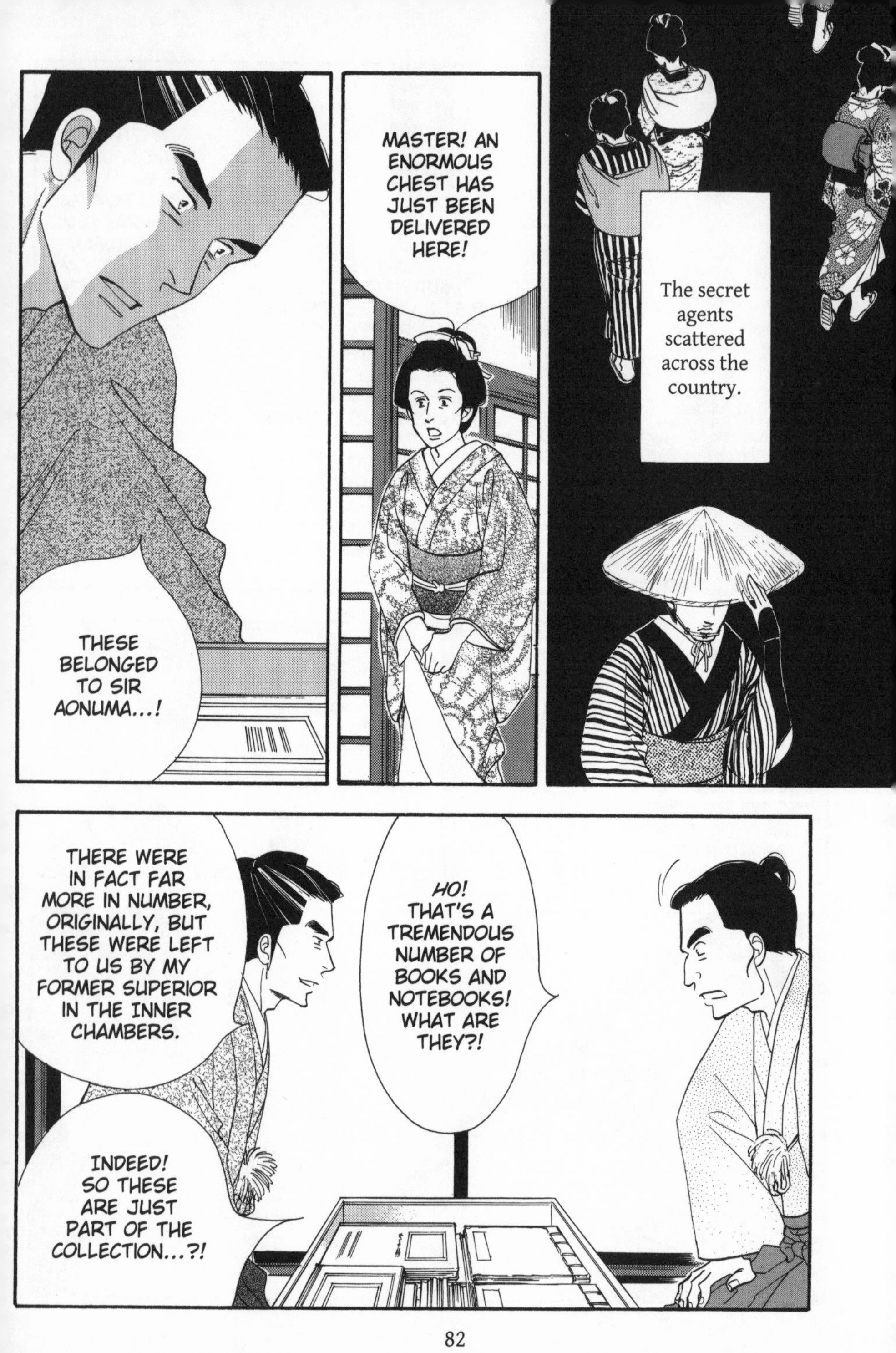
The secret agents scattered across the country.
MASTER! AN ENORMOUS CHEST HAS JUST BEEN DELIVERED HERE!
THESE BELONGED TO SIR AONUMA...!
HO! THAT'S A TREMENDOUS NUMBER OF BOOKS AND NOTEBOOKS! WHAT ARE THEY?!
THERE WERE IN FACT FAR MORE IN NUMBER, ORIGINALLY, BUT THESE WERE LEFT TO US BY MY FORMER SUPERIOR IN THE INNER CHAMBERS.
INDEED! SO THESE ARE JUST PART OF THE COLLECTION...?!

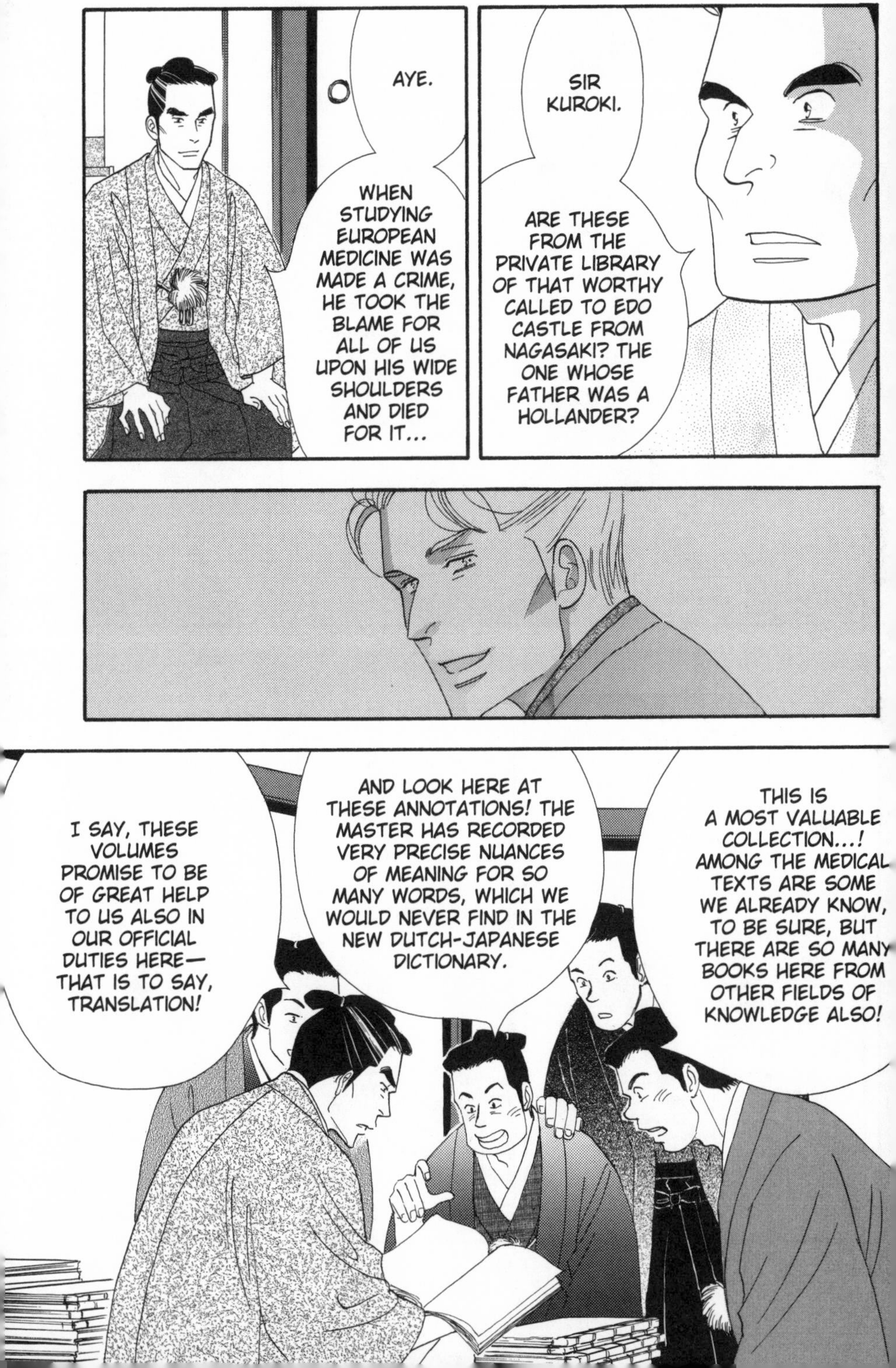
SIR KUROKI.
ARE THESE FROM THE PRIVATE LIBRARY OF THAT WORTHY CALLED TO EDO CASTLE FROM NAGASAKI? THE ONE WHOSE FATHER WAS A HOLLANDER?
AYE.
WHEN STUDYING EUROPEAN MEDICINE WAS MADE A CRIME, HE TOOK THE BLAME FOR ALL OF US UPON HIS WIDE SHOULDERS AND DIED FOR IT...
THIS IS A MOST VALUABLE COLLECTION...! AMONG THE MEDICAL TEXTS ARE SOME WE ALREADY KNOW, TO BE SURE, BUT THERE ARE SO MANY BOOKS HERE FROM OTHER FIELDS OF KNOWLEDGE ALSO!
AND LOOK HERE AT THESE ANNOTATIONS! THE MASTER HAS RECORDED VERY PRECISE NUANCES OF MEANING FOR SO MANY WORDS, WHICH WE WOULD NEVER FIND IN THE NEW DUTCH-JAPANESE DICTIONARY.
I SAY, THESE VOLUMES PROMISE TO BE OF GREAT HELP TO US ALSO IN OUR OFFICIAL DUTIES HERE—THAT IS TO SAY, TRANSLATION!

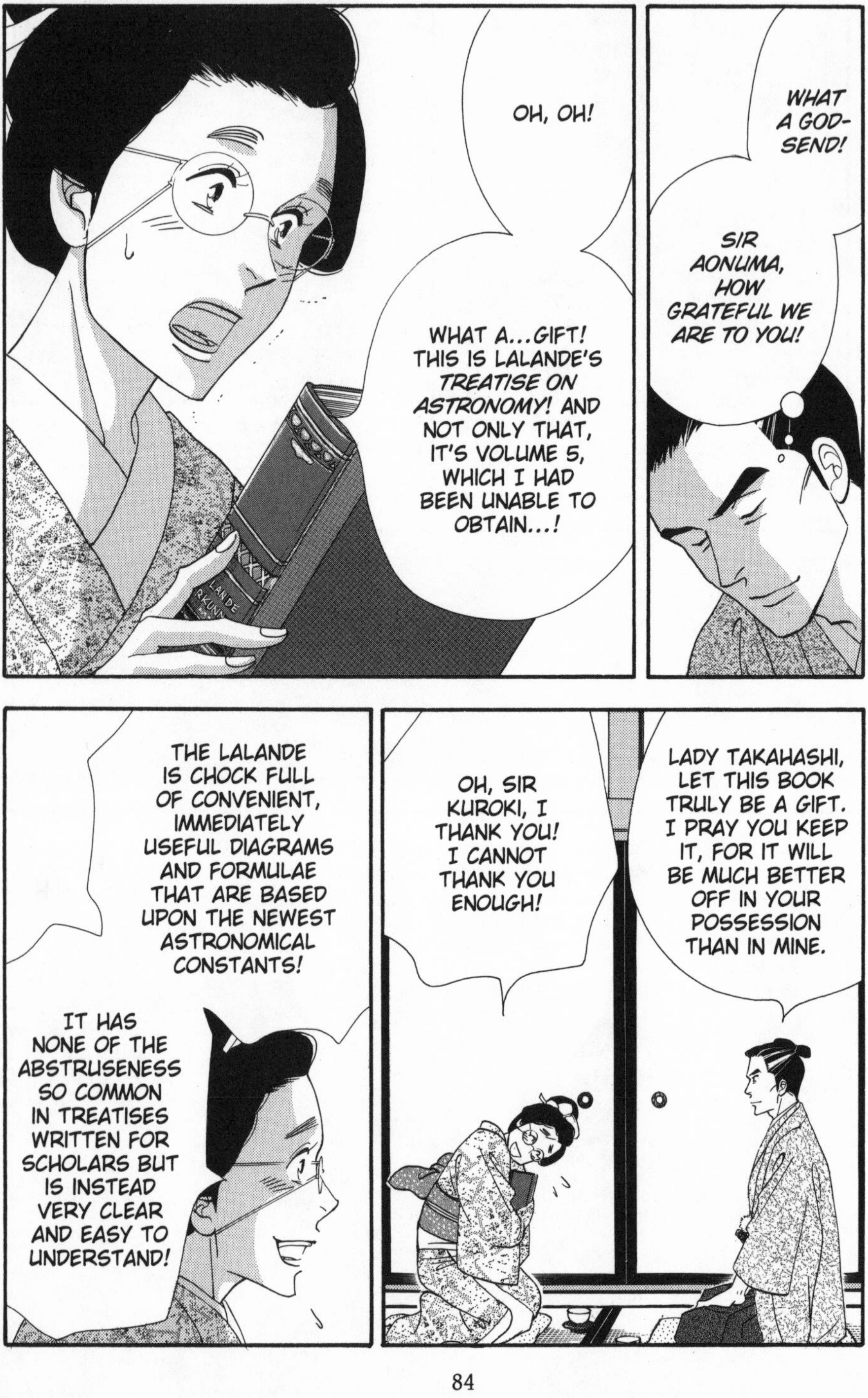
WHAT A GOD-SEND!
SIR AONUMA, HOW GRATEFUL WE ARE TO YOU!
OH, OH!
WHAT A...GIFT! THIS IS LALANDE'S *TREATISE ON ASTRONOMY!* AND NOT ONLY THAT, IT'S VOLUME 5, WHICH I HAD BEEN UNABLE TO OBTAIN...!
LADY TAKAHASHI, LET THIS BOOK TRULY BE A GIFT. I PRAY YOU KEEP IT, FOR IT WILL BE MUCH BETTER OFF IN YOUR POSSESSION THAN IN MINE.
OH, SIR KUROKI, I THANK YOU! I CANNOT THANK YOU ENOUGH!
THE LALANDE IS CHOCK FULL OF CONVENIENT, IMMEDIATELY USEFUL DIAGRAMS AND FORMULAE THAT ARE BASED UPON THE NEWEST ASTRONOMICAL CONSTANTS!
IT HAS NONE OF THE ABSTRUSENESS SO COMMON IN TREATISES WRITTEN FOR SCHOLARS BUT IS INSTEAD VERY CLEAR AND EASY TO UNDERSTAND!

"EASY," YOU SAY...
ALTHOUGH WE DO OUR BEST TO HELP YOU WITH THE TRANSLATIONS, THE PRINCIPLES OF ASTRONOMY ARE FAR TOO DIFFICULT FOR US PHYSICIANS TO GRASP.
FOR EXAMPLE, HOW IS IT THAT ONE STARTS OUT USING ARITHMETIC AND ARRIVES AT THE CONCLUSION THAT THIS EARTH UPON WHICH WE STAND IS ROUND...?
TEE HEE HEE. IT'S SLIGHTLY ELLIPTICAL, ACTUALLY.
BUT ARITHMETIC IS IN ITSELF A MOST PRACTICAL DISCIPLINE INDEED, WOULDN'T YOU AGREE? IT IS BOTH USEFUL AND NECESSARY IN EVERY ASPECT OF DAILY LIFE, FROM BUILDING A HOUSE TO SEWING A GARMENT.
IF ONE CONTINUES FROM THERE, DEVELOPING ONE'S IDEAS IN SEQUENCE, THERE IS NOTHING DIFFICULT TO GRASP AT ALL. COME, LET US DISCUSS ASTRONOMY THE NEXT TIME WE MEET!
OH, THAT REMINDS ME! MY SON RYOTA TELLS ME HE IS IN THE SAME ARITHMETIC CLASS AS YOUR SON AND THAT THE TWO OF THEM HAVE BECOME FRIENDS!
YES, SEISHIRO HAS TOLD ME THE SAME THING.
HE SAID THAT EVEN AFTER THE CLASS IS OVER, HE AND YOUNG MASTER RYOTA STOP AT THE SHRINE AND SOLVE THE PROBLEMS THEY FIND ON THE SANGAKU THERE, FOR FUN.

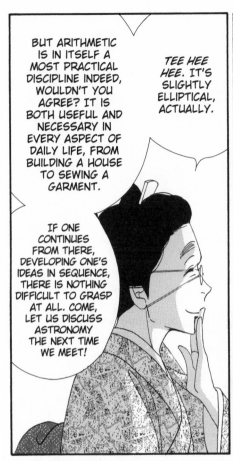

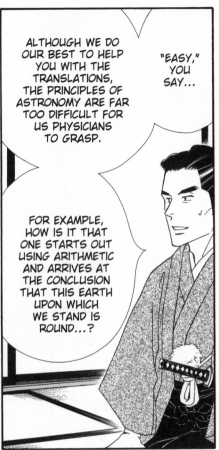

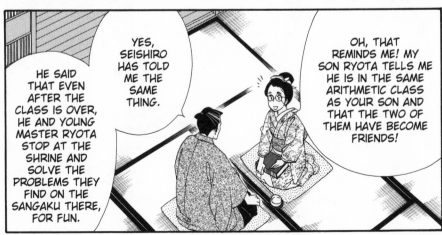

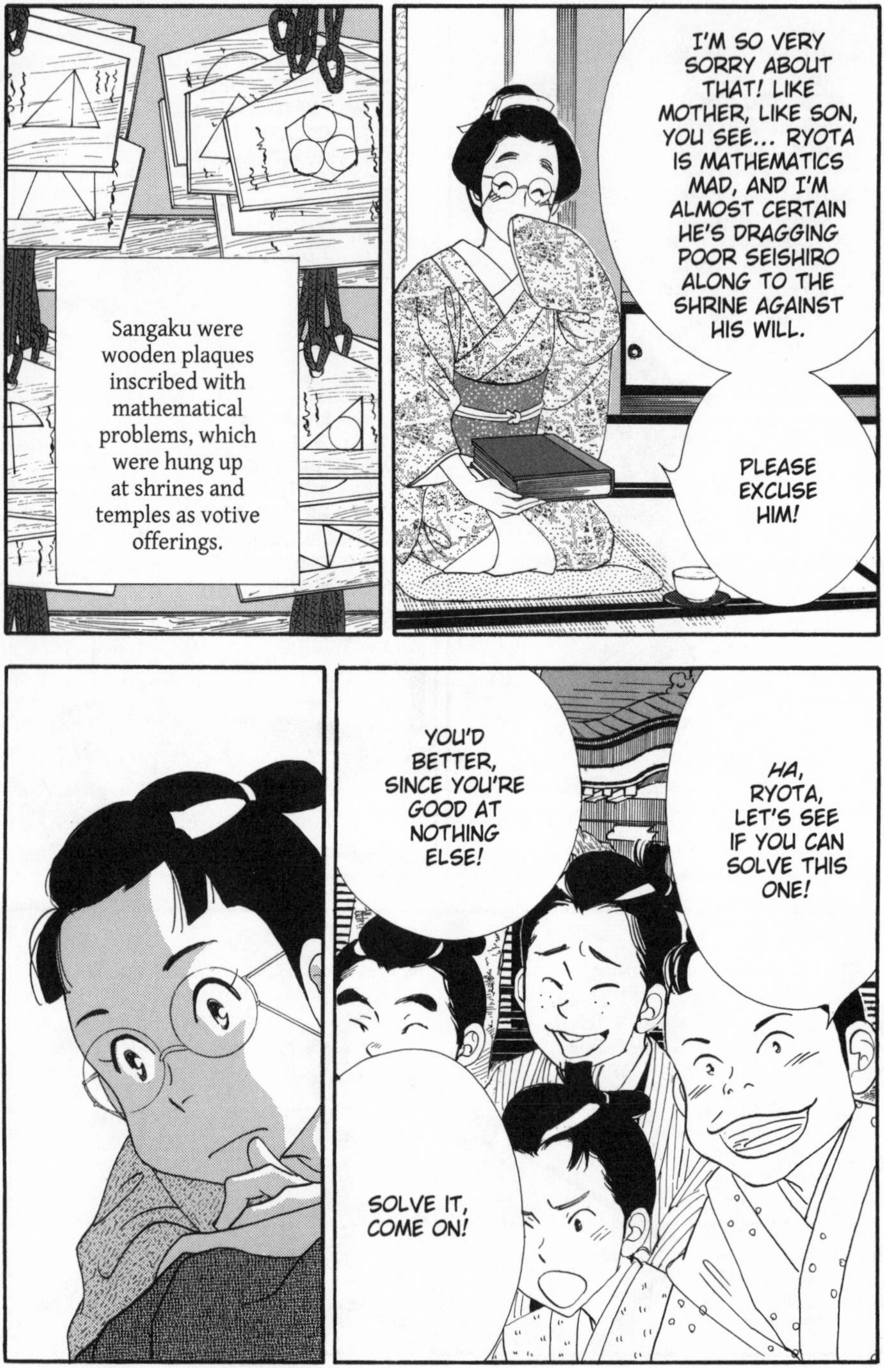
I'M SO VERY SORRY ABOUT THAT! LIKE MOTHER, LIKE SON, YOU SEE... RYOTA IS MATHEMATICS MAD, AND I'M ALMOST CERTAIN HE'S DRAGGING POOR SEISHIRO ALONG TO THE SHRINE AGAINST HIS WILL.
PLEASE EXCUSE HIM!
Sangaku were wooden plaques inscribed with mathematical problems, which were hung up at shrines and temples as votive offerings.
HA, RYOTA, LET'S SEE IF YOU CAN SOLVE THIS ONE!
YOU'D BETTER, SINCE YOU'RE GOOD AT NOTHING ELSE!
SOLVE IT, COME ON!

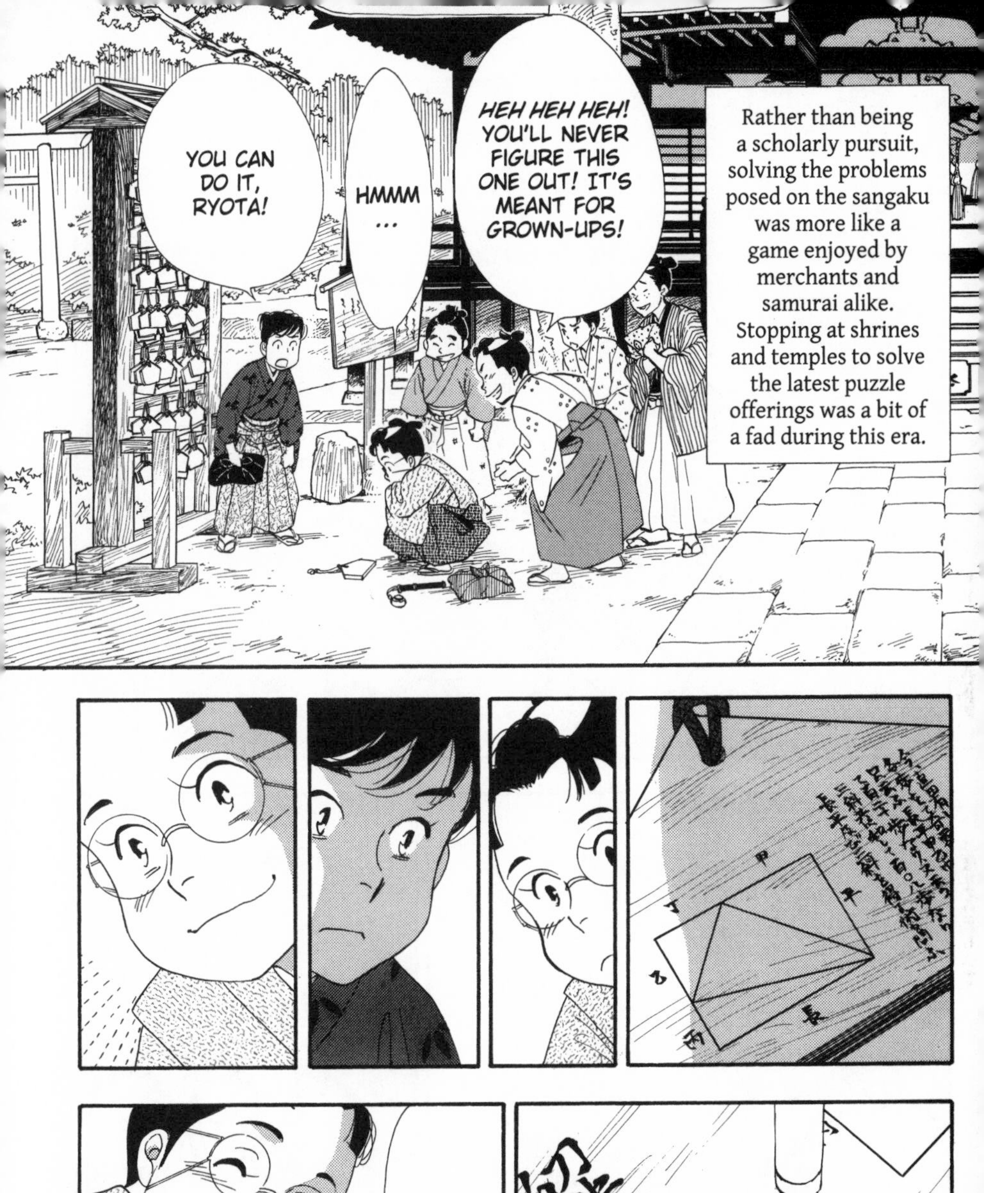

Rather than being a scholarly pursuit, solving the problems posed on the sangaku was more like a game enjoyed by merchants and samurai alike. Stopping at shrines and temples to solve the latest puzzle offerings was a bit of a fad during this era.
HEH HEH HEH! YOU'LL NEVER FIGURE THIS ONE OUT! IT'S MEANT FOR GROWN-UPS!
HMMM ...
YOU CAN DO IT, RYOTA!
解無
DONE!

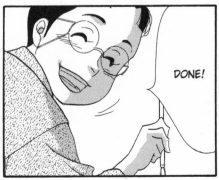

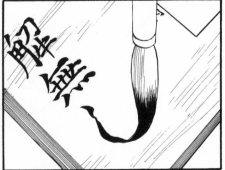

*No Solution

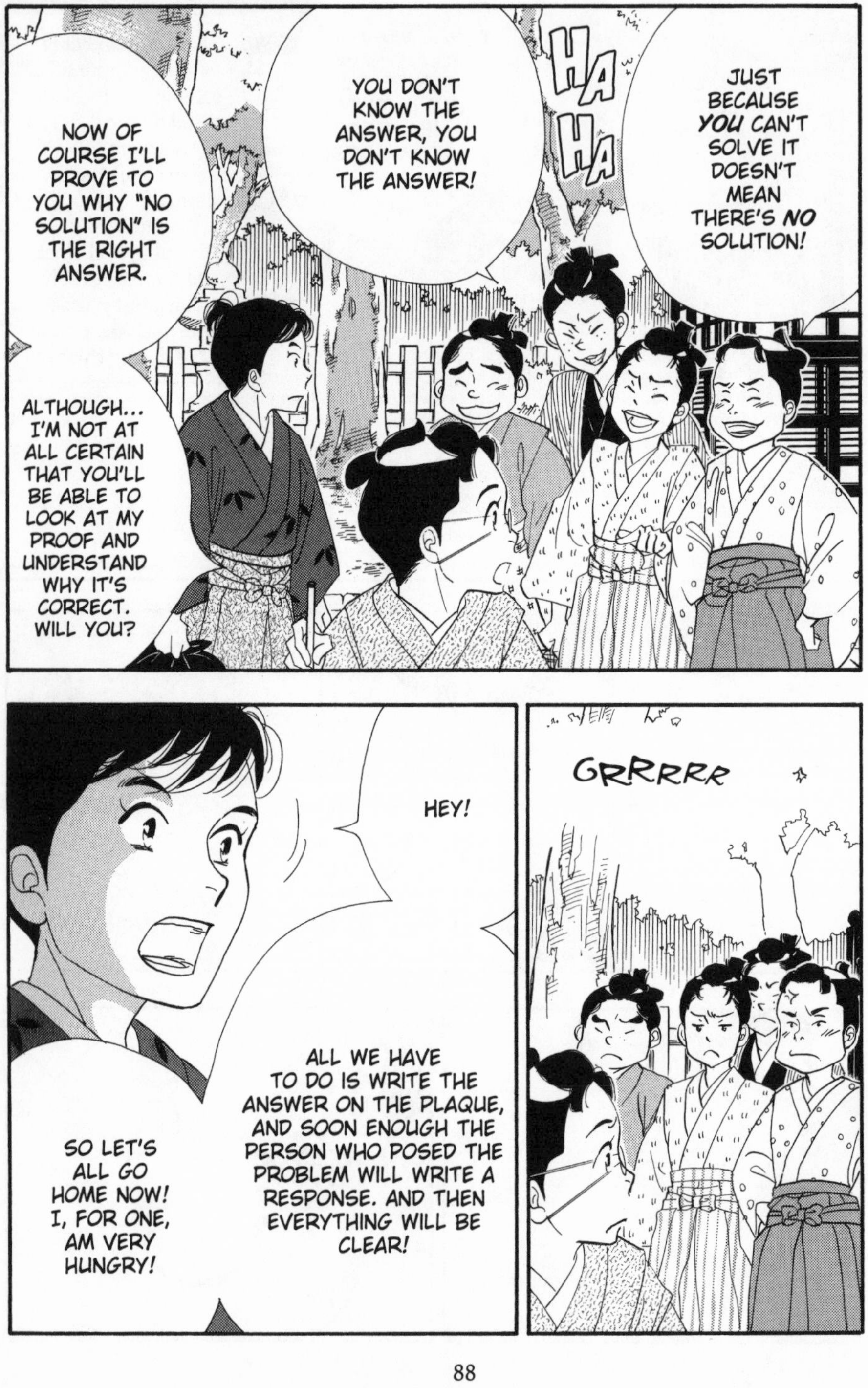
JUST BECAUSE *YOU* CAN'T SOLVE IT DOESN'T MEAN THERE'S *NO* SOLUTION!
HA HA
YOU DON'T KNOW THE ANSWER, YOU DON'T KNOW THE ANSWER!
NOW OF COURSE I'LL PROVE TO YOU WHY "NO SOLUTION" IS THE RIGHT ANSWER.
ALTHOUGH... I'M NOT AT ALL CERTAIN THAT YOU'LL BE ABLE TO LOOK AT MY PROOF AND UNDERSTAND WHY IT'S CORRECT. WILL YOU?
GRRRRR
HEY!
ALL WE HAVE TO DO IS WRITE THE ANSWER ON THE PLAQUE, AND SOON ENOUGH THE PERSON WHO POSED THE PROBLEM WILL WRITE A RESPONSE. AND THEN EVERYTHING WILL BE CLEAR!
SO LET'S ALL GO HOME NOW! I, FOR ONE, AM VERY HUNGRY!

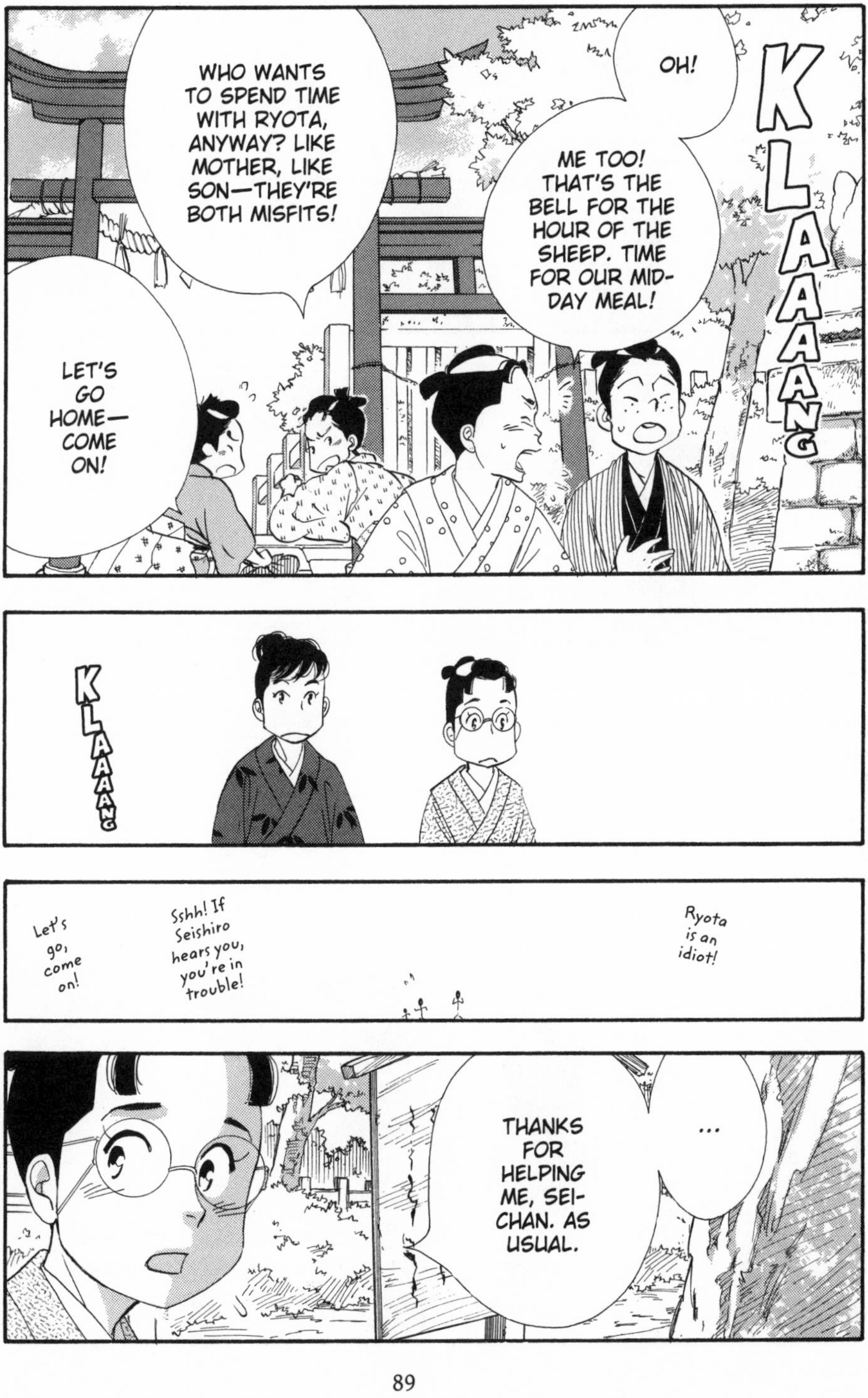
KLAAAAANG
OH!
ME TOO! THAT'S THE BELL FOR THE HOUR OF THE SHEEP. TIME FOR OUR MID-DAY MEAL!
WHO WANTS TO SPEND TIME WITH RYOTA, ANYWAY? LIKE MOTHER, LIKE SON—THEY'RE BOTH MISFITS!
LET'S GO HOME—COME ON!
KLAAAAANG
Ryota is an idiot!
Sshh! If Seishiro hears you, you're in trouble!
Let's go, come on!
...
THANKS FOR HELPING ME, SEI-CHAN. AS USUAL.

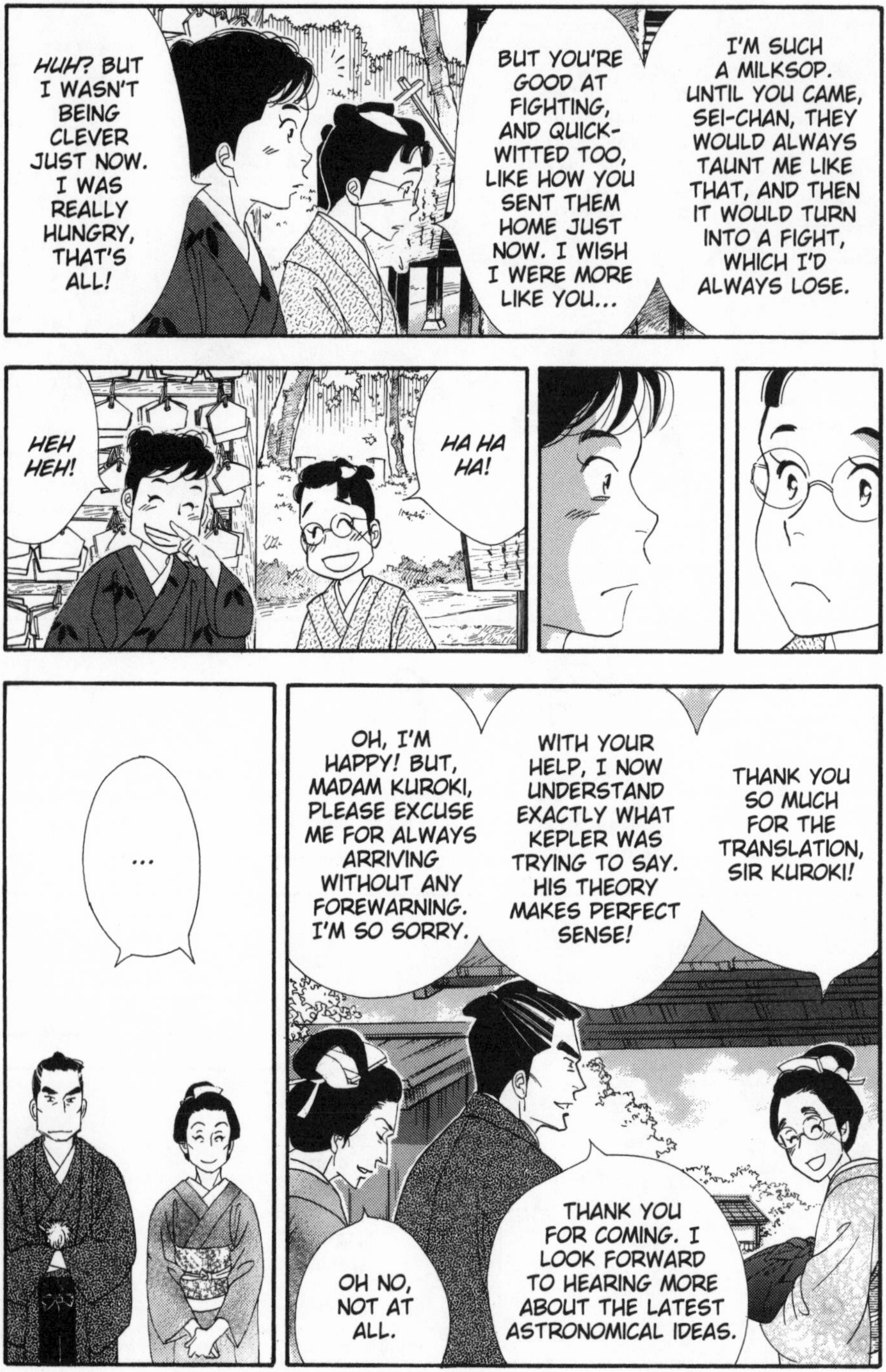
I'M SUCH A MILKSOP. UNTIL YOU CAME, SEI-CHAN, THEY WOULD ALWAYS TAUNT ME LIKE THAT, AND THEN IT WOULD TURN INTO A FIGHT, WHICH I'D ALWAYS LOSE.
BUT YOU'RE GOOD AT FIGHTING, AND QUICK-WITTED TOO, LIKE HOW YOU SENT THEM HOME JUST NOW. I WISH I WERE MORE LIKE YOU...
HUH? BUT I WASN'T BEING CLEVER JUST NOW. I WAS REALLY HUNGRY, THAT'S ALL!
HA HA HA!
HEH HEH!
THANK YOU SO MUCH FOR THE TRANSLATION, SIR KUROKI!
WITH YOUR HELP, I NOW UNDERSTAND EXACTLY WHAT KEPLER WAS TRYING TO SAY. HIS THEORY MAKES PERFECT SENSE!
OH, I'M HAPPY! BUT, MADAM KUROKI, PLEASE EXCUSE ME FOR ALWAYS ARRIVING WITHOUT ANY FOREWARNING. I'M SO SORRY.
THANK YOU FOR COMING. I LOOK FORWARD TO HEARING MORE ABOUT THE LATEST ASTRONOMICAL IDEAS.
OH NO, NOT AT ALL.
...

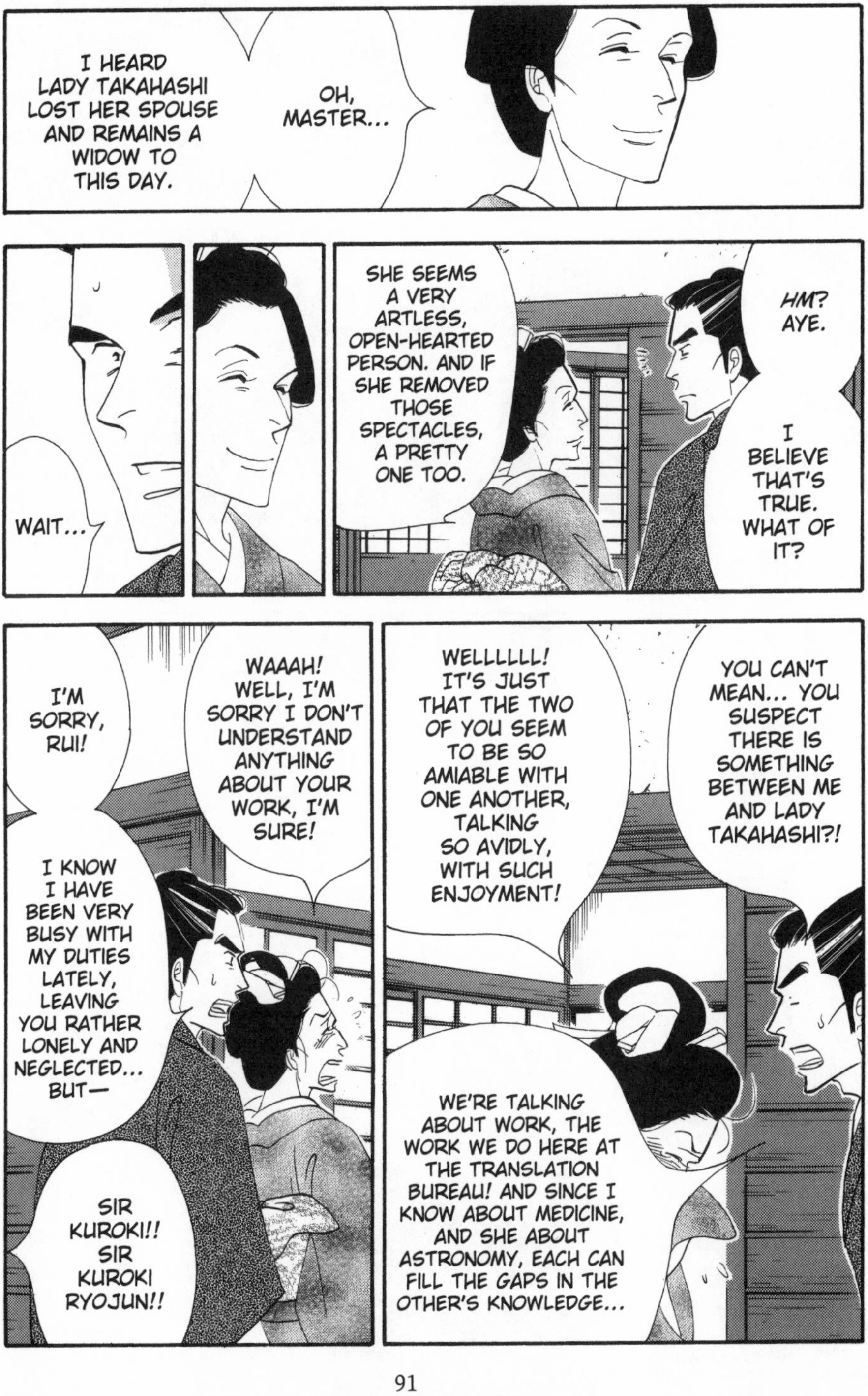
OH, MASTER...
I HEARD LADY TAKAHASHI LOST HER SPOUSE AND REMAINS A WIDOW TO THIS DAY.
SHE SEEMS A VERY ARTLESS, OPEN-HEARTED PERSON. AND IF SHE REMOVED THOSE SPECTACLES, A PRETTY ONE TOO.
HM? AYE.
I BELIEVE THAT'S TRUE. WHAT OF IT?
WAIT...
YOU CAN'T MEAN... YOU SUSPECT THERE IS SOMETHING BETWEEN ME AND LADY TAKAHASHI?!
WELLLLLL! IT'S JUST THAT THE TWO OF YOU SEEM TO BE SO AMIABLE WITH ONE ANOTHER, TALKING SO AVIDLY, WITH SUCH ENJOYMENT!
WE'RE TALKING ABOUT WORK, THE WORK WE DO HERE AT THE TRANSLATION BUREAU! AND SINCE I KNOW ABOUT MEDICINE, AND SHE ABOUT ASTRONOMY, EACH CAN FILL THE GAPS IN THE OTHER'S KNOWLEDGE...
WAAAH! WELL, I'M SORRY I DON'T UNDERSTAND ANYTHING ABOUT YOUR WORK, I'M SURE!
I'M SORRY, RUI!
I KNOW I HAVE BEEN VERY BUSY WITH MY DUTIES LATELY, LEAVING YOU RATHER LONELY AND NEGLECTED... BUT—
SIR KUROKI!! SIR KUROKI RYOJUN!!

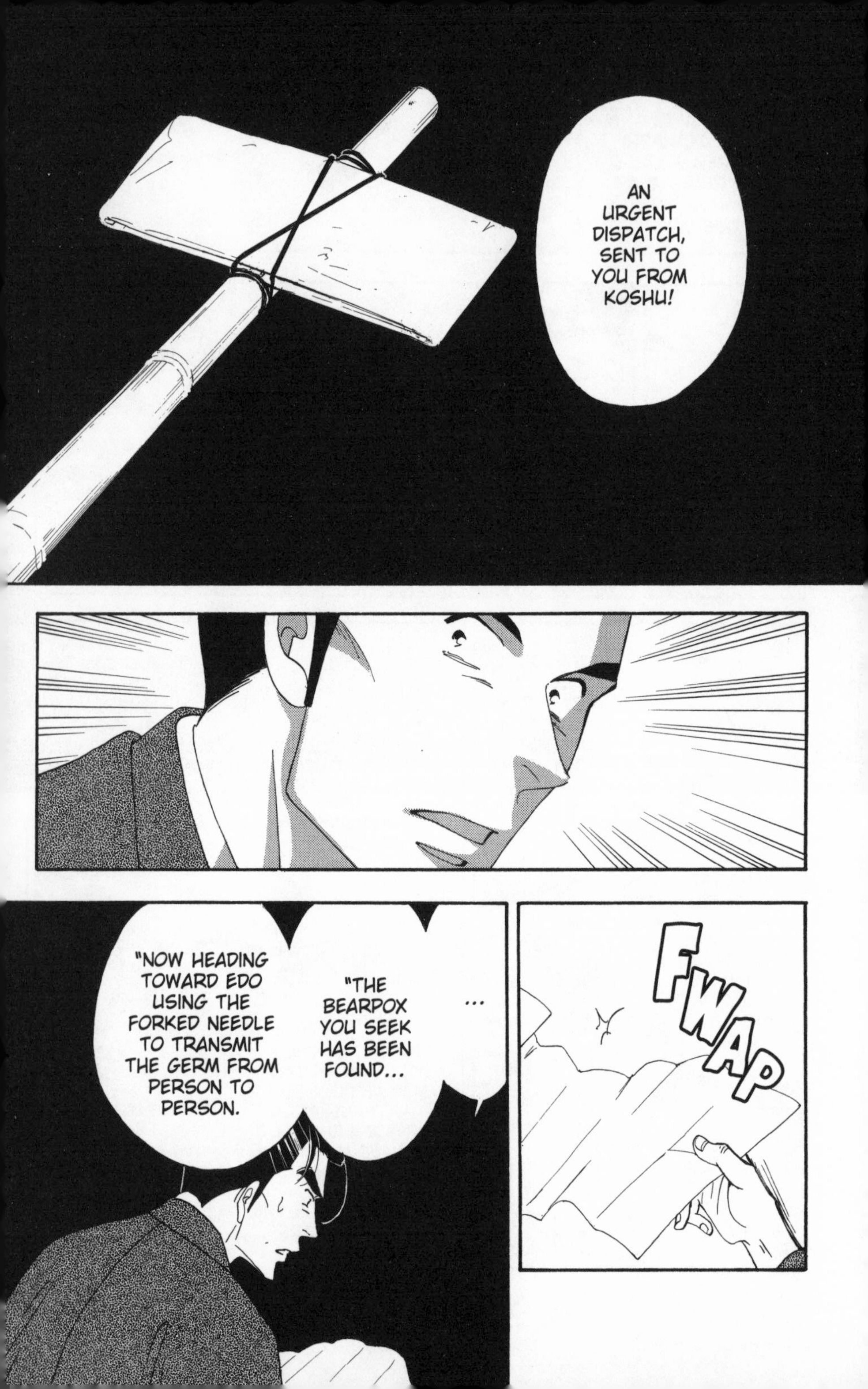
AN URGENT DISPATCH, SENT TO YOU FROM KOSHU!
FWAP
...
"THE BEARPOX YOU SEEK HAS BEEN FOUND...
"NOW HEADING TOWARD EDO USING THE FORKED NEEDLE TO TRANSMIT THE GERM FROM PERSON TO PERSON.

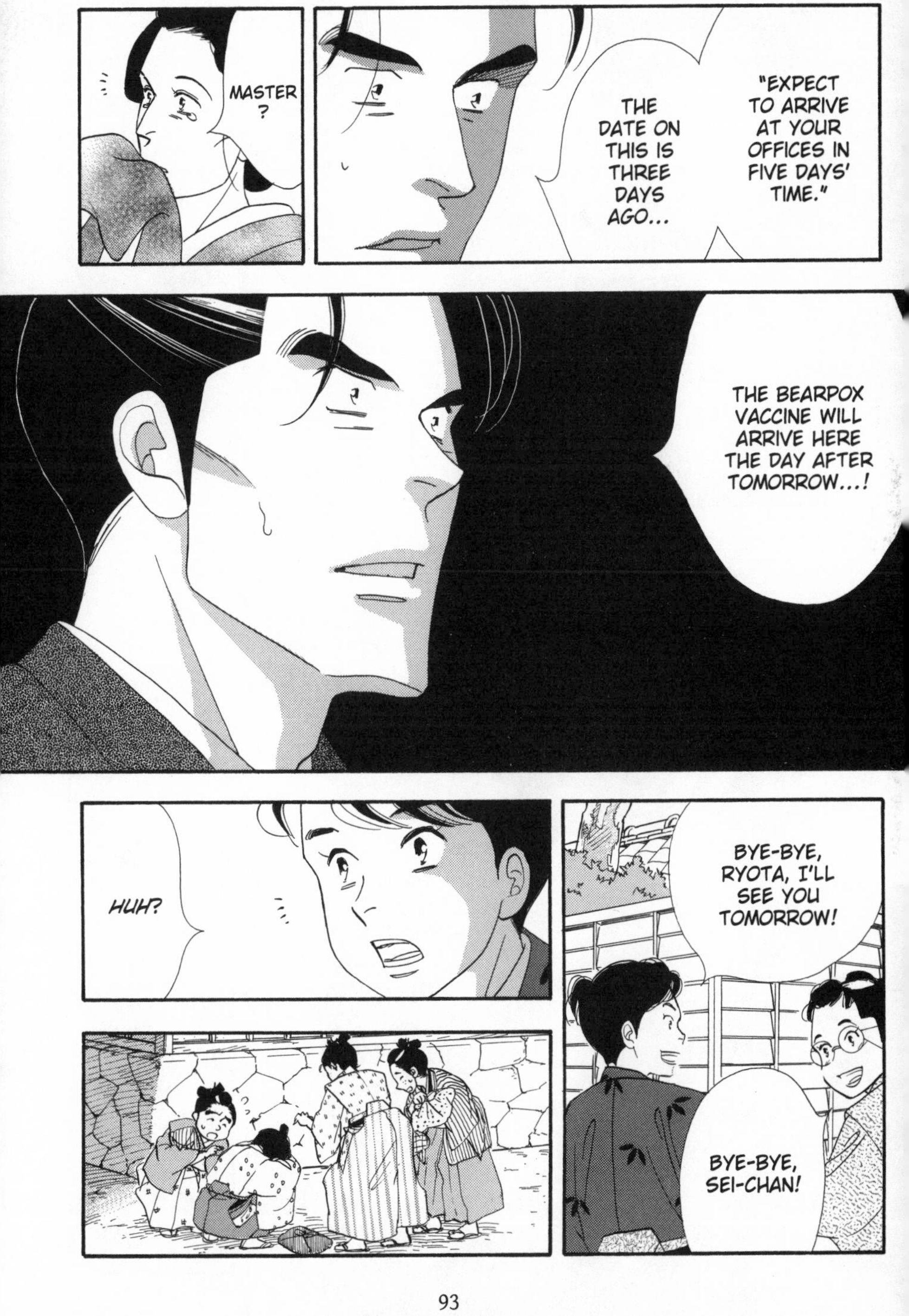
"EXPECT TO ARRIVE AT YOUR OFFICES IN FIVE DAYS' TIME."
THE DATE ON THIS IS THREE DAYS AGO...
MASTER?
THE BEARPOX VACCINE WILL ARRIVE HERE THE DAY AFTER TOMORROW...!
BYE-BYE, RYOTA, I'LL SEE YOU TOMORROW!
BYE-BYE, SEI-CHAN!
HUH?

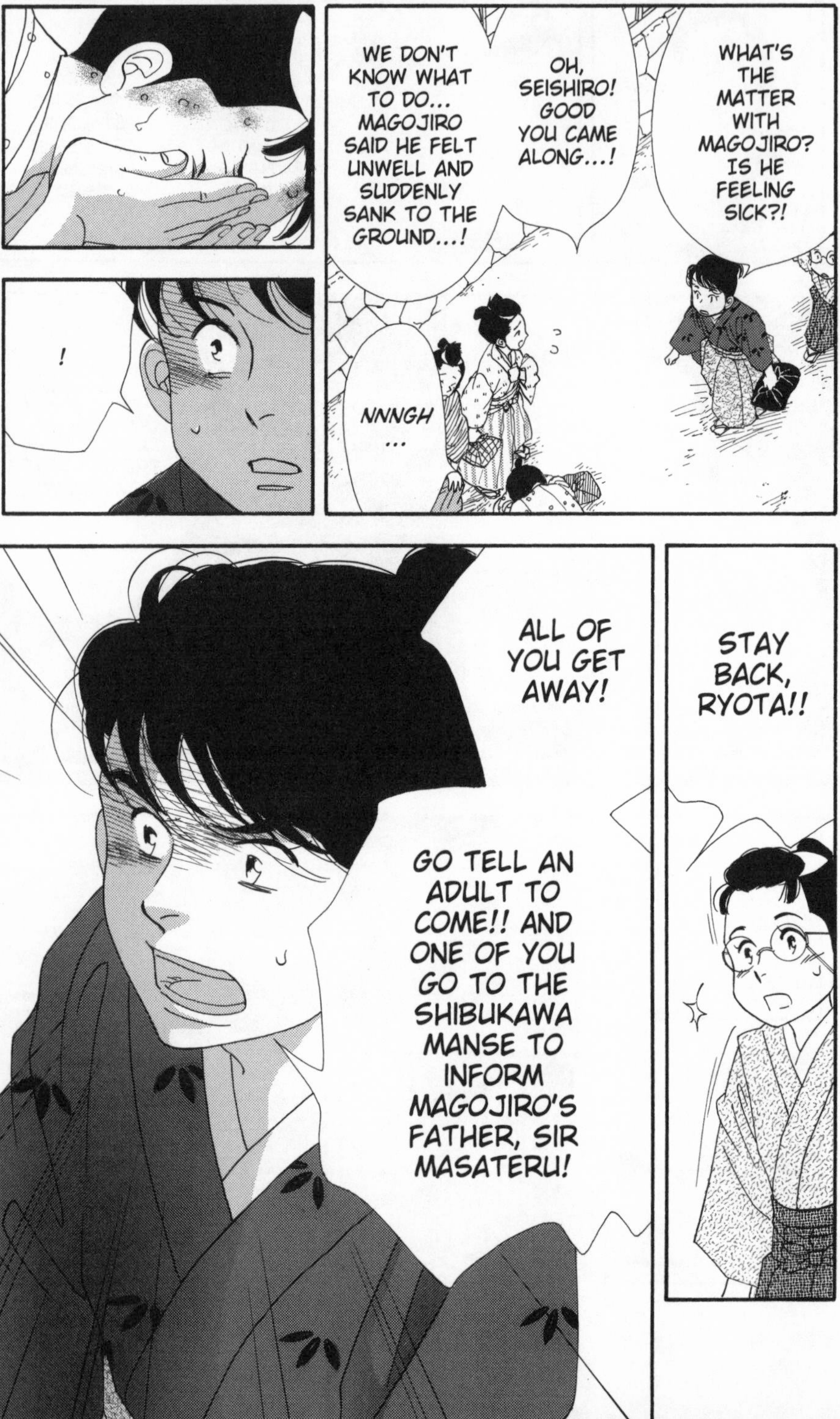
WHAT'S THE MATTER WITH MAGOJIRO? IS HE FEELING SICK?!
OH, SEISHIRO! GOOD YOU CAME ALONG...!
WE DON'T KNOW WHAT TO DO... MAGOJIRO SAID HE FELT UNWELL AND SUDDENLY SANK TO THE GROUND...!
NNNGH...
!
STAY BACK, RYOTA!!
ALL OF YOU GET AWAY!
GO TELL AN ADULT TO COME!! AND ONE OF YOU GO TO THE SHIBUKAWA MANSE TO INFORM MAGOJIRO'S FATHER, SIR MASATERU!

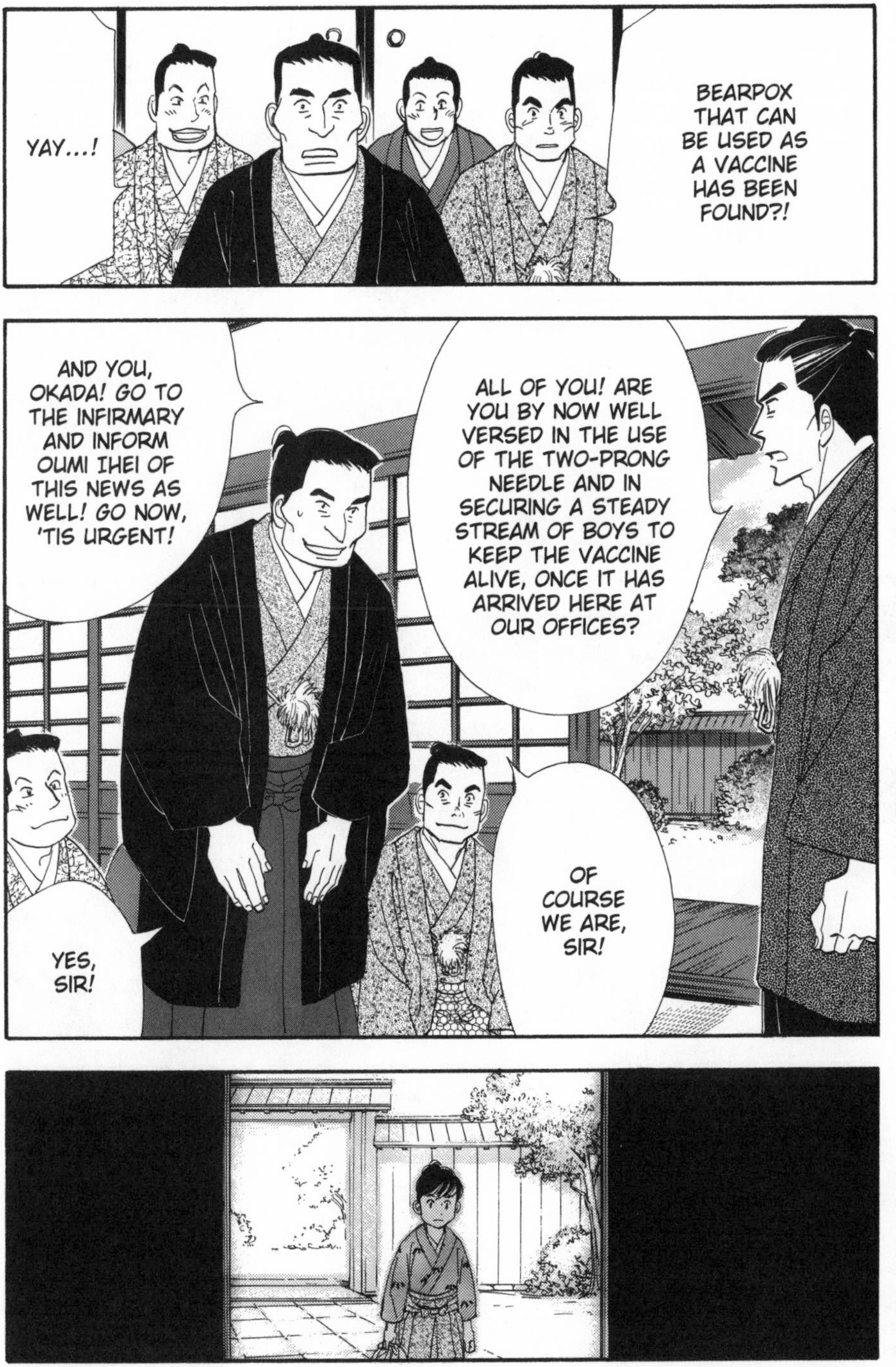
BEARPOX THAT CAN BE USED AS A VACCINE HAS BEEN FOUND?!
YAY...!
ALL OF YOU! ARE YOU BY NOW WELL VERSED IN THE USE OF THE TWO-PRONG NEEDLE AND IN SECURING A STEADY STREAM OF BOYS TO KEEP THE VACCINE ALIVE, ONCE IT HAS ARRIVED HERE AT OUR OFFICES?
AND YOU, OKADA! GO TO THE INFIRMARY AND INFORM OUMI IHEI OF THIS NEWS AS WELL! GO NOW, 'TIS URGENT!
OF COURSE WE ARE, SIR!
YES, SIR!

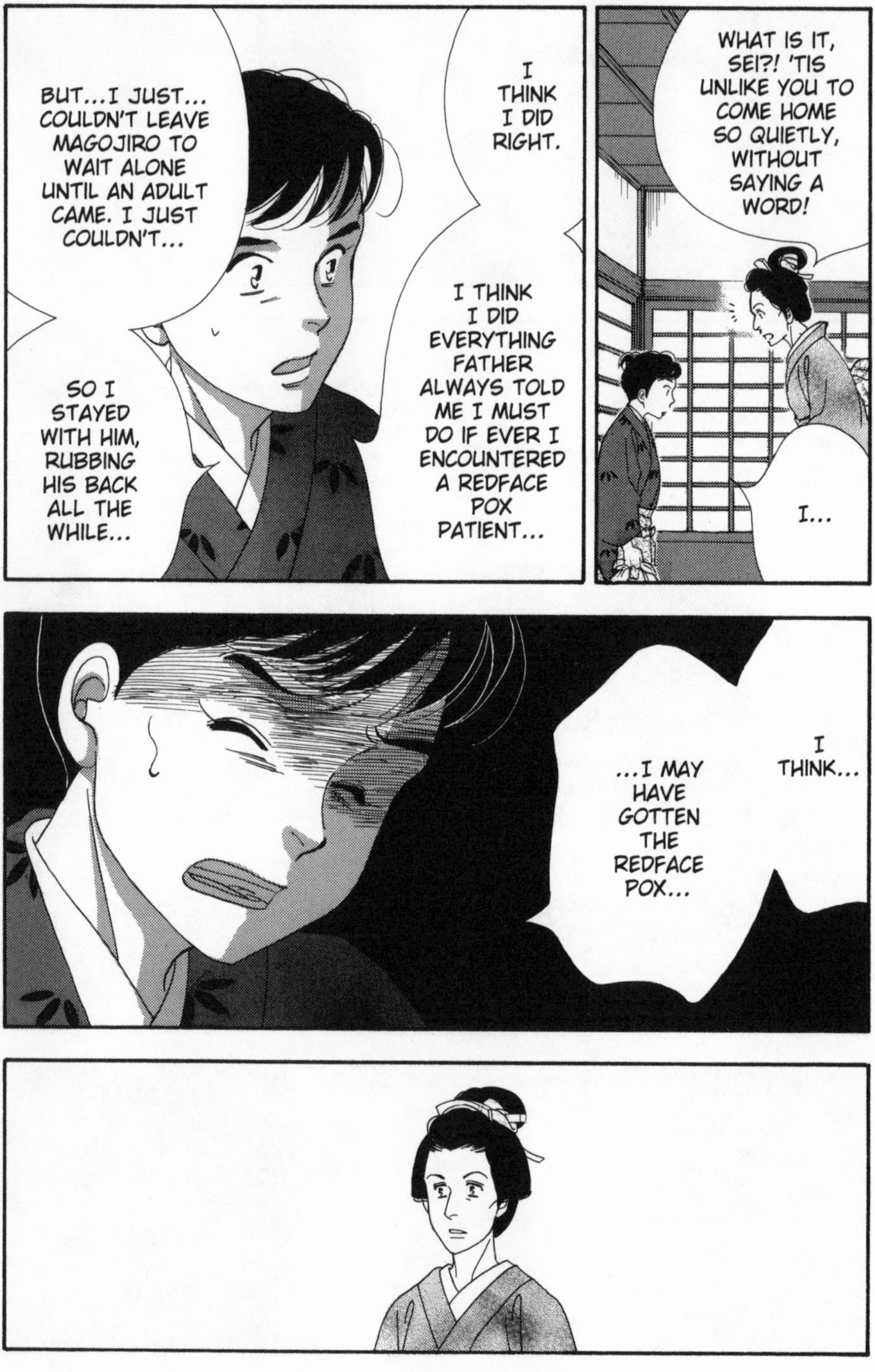
WHAT IS IT, SEI?! 'TIS UNLIKE YOU TO COME HOME SO QUIETLY, WITHOUT SAYING A WORD!
I...
I THINK I DID RIGHT.
I THINK I DID EVERYTHING FATHER ALWAYS TOLD ME I MUST DO IF EVER I ENCOUNTERED A REDFACE POX PATIENT...
BUT...I JUST... COULDN'T LEAVE MAGOJIRO TO WAIT ALONE UNTIL AN ADULT CAME. I JUST COULDN'T...
SO I STAYED WITH HIM, RUBBING HIS BACK ALL THE WHILE...
I THINK...
...I MAY HAVE GOTTEN THE REDFACE POX...

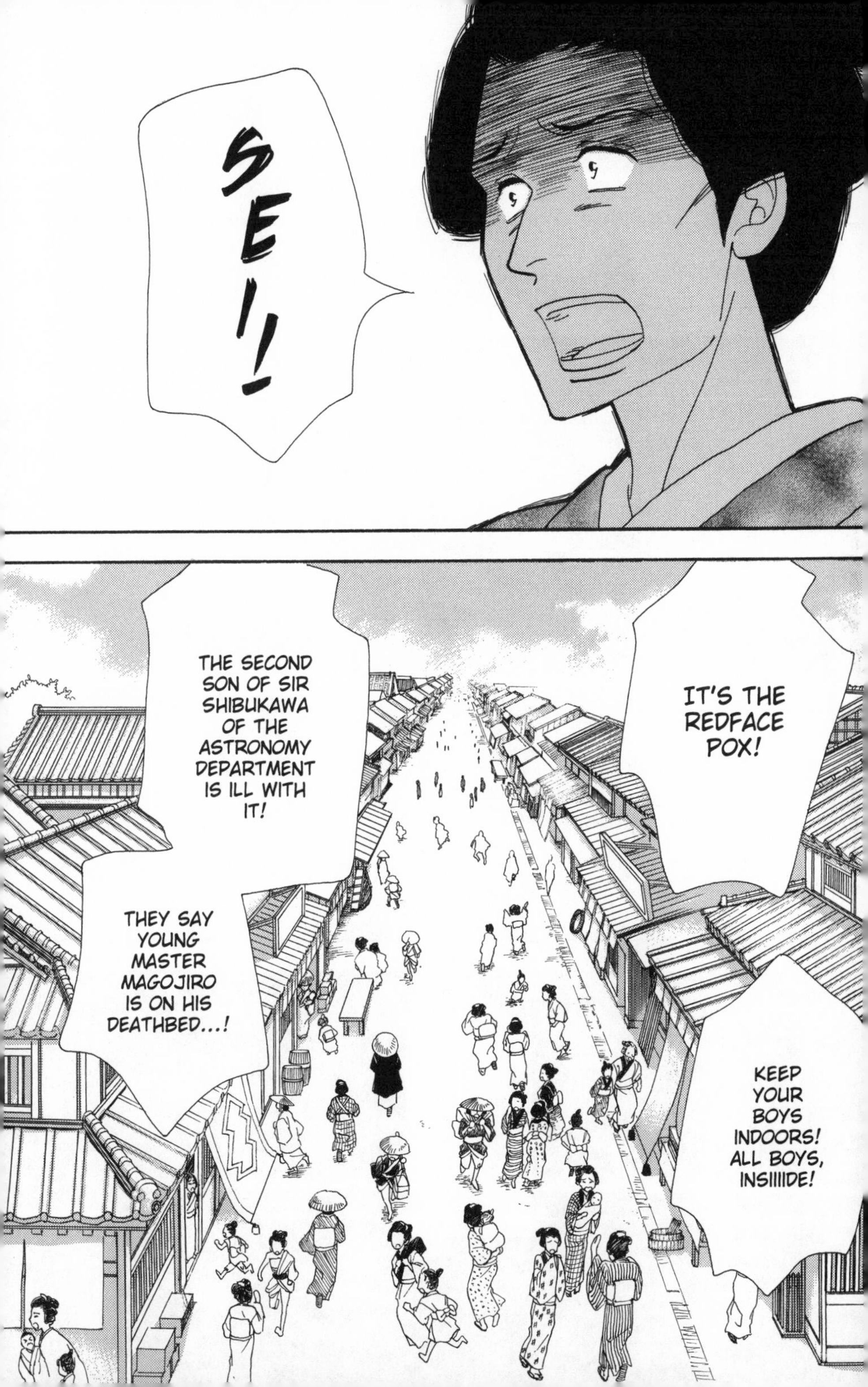
SEI!!
IT'S THE REDFACE POX!
THE SECOND SON OF SIR SHIBUKAWA OF THE ASTRONOMY DEPARTMENT IS ILL WITH IT!
THEY SAY YOUNG MASTER MAGOJIRO IS ON HIS DEATHBED...!
KEEP YOUR BOYS INDOORS! ALL BOYS, INSIIIIDE!

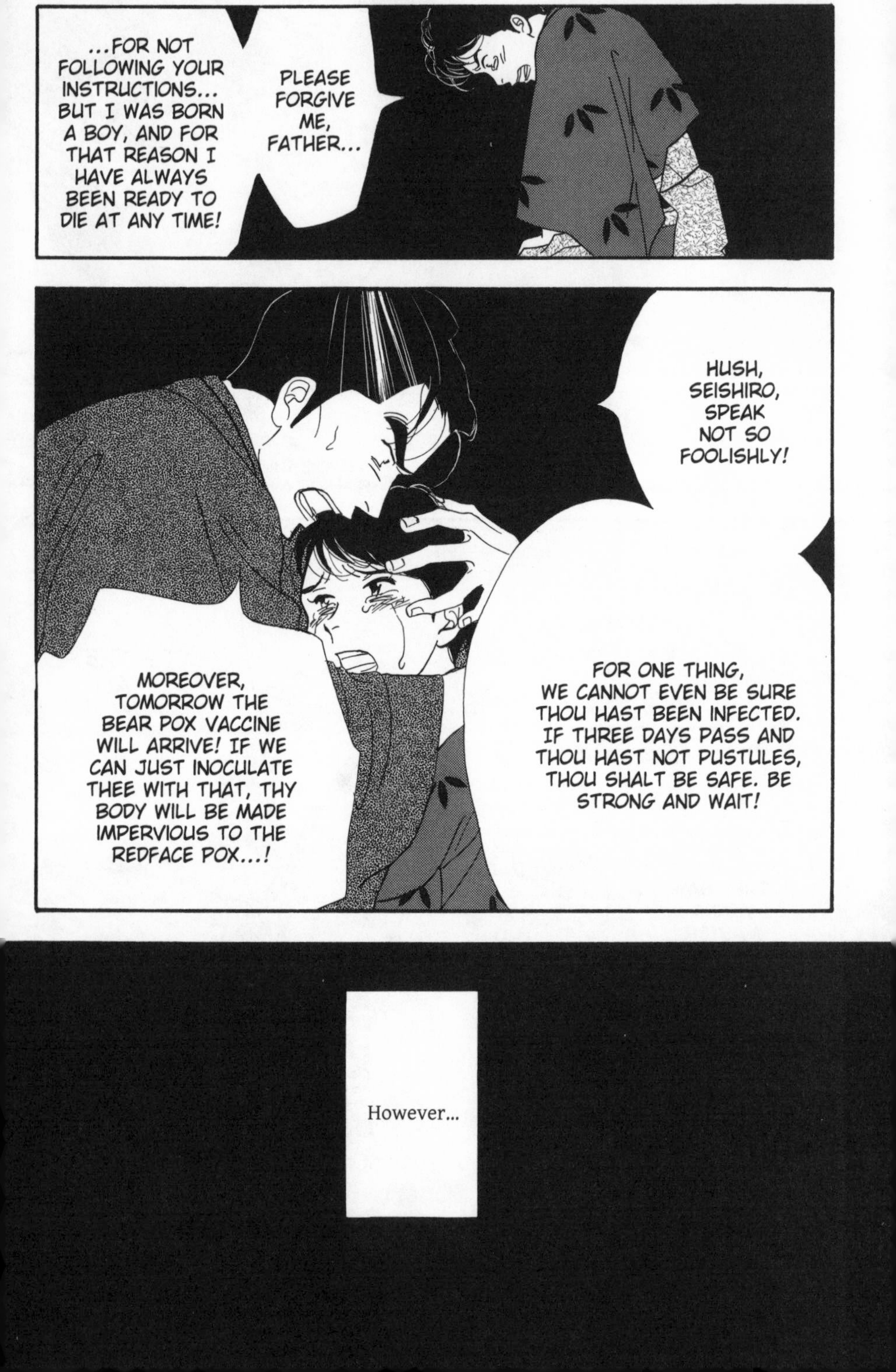
PLEASE FORGIVE ME, FATHER...
...FOR NOT FOLLOWING YOUR INSTRUCTIONS... BUT I WAS BORN A BOY, AND FOR THAT REASON I HAVE ALWAYS BEEN READY TO DIE AT ANY TIME!
HUSH, SEISHIRO, SPEAK NOT SO FOOLISHLY!
FOR ONE THING, WE CANNOT EVEN BE SURE THOU HAST BEEN INFECTED. IF THREE DAYS PASS AND THOU HAST NOT PUSTULES, THOU SHALT BE SAFE. BE STRONG AND WAIT!
MOREOVER, TOMORROW THE BEAR POX VACCINE WILL ARRIVE! IF WE CAN JUST INOCULATE THEE WITH THAT, THY BODY WILL BE MADE IMPERVIOUS TO THE REDFACE POX...!
However...

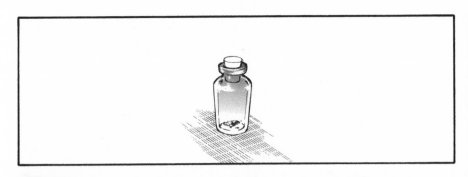

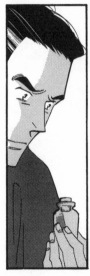

I BEG YOUR PARDON!
THE LAST CHILD'S RECOVERY WAS QUICKER THAN EXPECTED, AND I WAS UNABLE TO BRING BACK THE LIVING FORM OF THE BEARPOX GERM!
AND SO, AS A LAST RESORT, I PULLED THE SCABS OFF HIS PUSTULES BEFORE HE WAS COMPLETELY HEALED AND PLACED THEM IN THIS BOTTLE, WHICH I CARRIED FOR THIS PURPOSE!
AHHH...
TRULY, SIR KUROKI, I HAVE NO EXCUSE FOR THIS FAILURE!
DON'T SAY THAT!
YOU MADE THE RIGHT DECISION IN THE FACE OF THE UNEXPECTED, AND I AM MOST GRATEFUL TO YOU FOR IT!
NOW YOU MUST BE VERY TIRED AFTER YOUR LONG JOURNEY. PRAY STAY AWHILE AND REST.

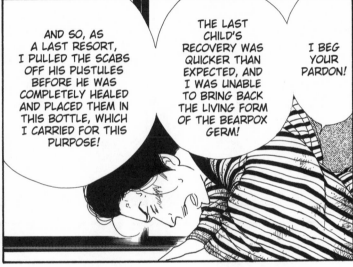

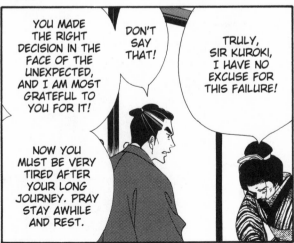

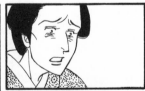

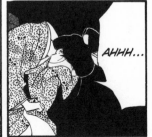

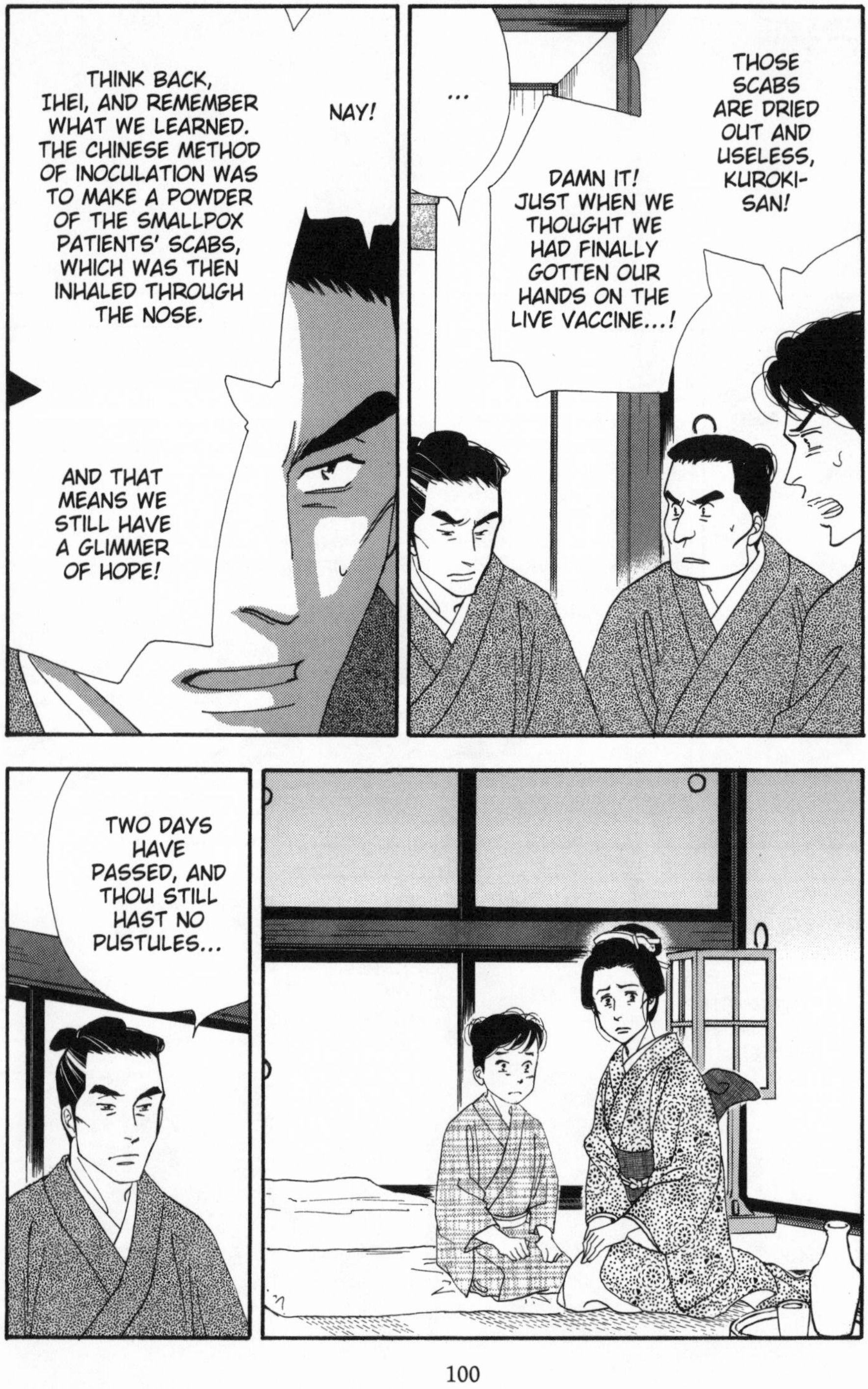

THOSE SCABS ARE DRIED OUT AND USELESS, KUROKI-SAN!
DAMN IT! JUST WHEN WE THOUGHT WE HAD FINALLY GOTTEN OUR HANDS ON THE LIVE VACCINE...!
...
NAY!
THINK BACK, IHEI, AND REMEMBER WHAT WE LEARNED. THE CHINESE METHOD OF INOCULATION WAS TO MAKE A POWDER OF THE SMALLPOX PATIENTS' SCABS, WHICH WAS THEN INHALED THROUGH THE NOSE.
AND THAT MEANS WE STILL HAVE A GLIMMER OF HOPE!
TWO DAYS HAVE PASSED, AND THOU STILL HAST NO PUSTULES...

YES, FATHER.

SEISHIRO.

GIVE ME THINE ARM.

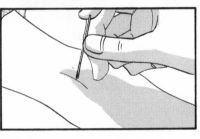

IF ALL OF YOU KEEP ALIGHT THE FIRE OF RESOLVE, AN OPPORTUNITY WILL ARISE ONCE AGAIN, I AM SURE!

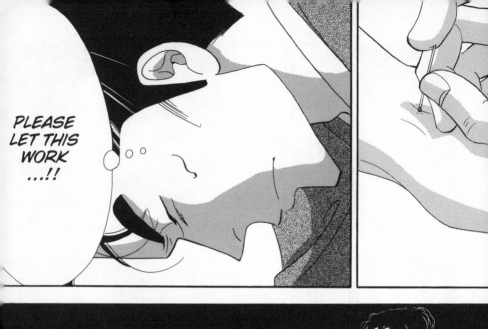

PLEASE
LET THIS
WORK
...!!

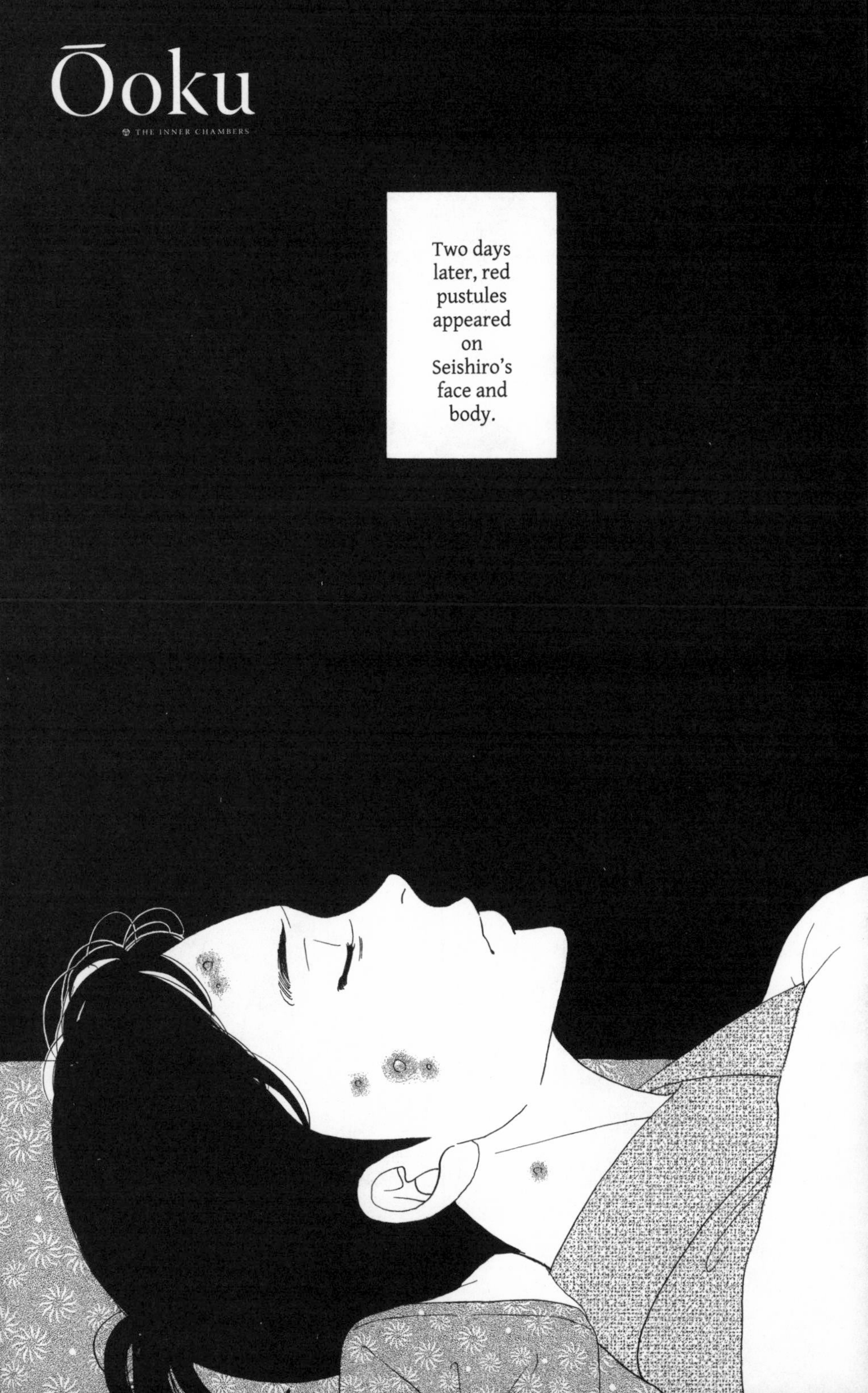
Ōoku
THE INNER CHAMBERS
Two days later, red pustules appeared on Seishiro's face and body.

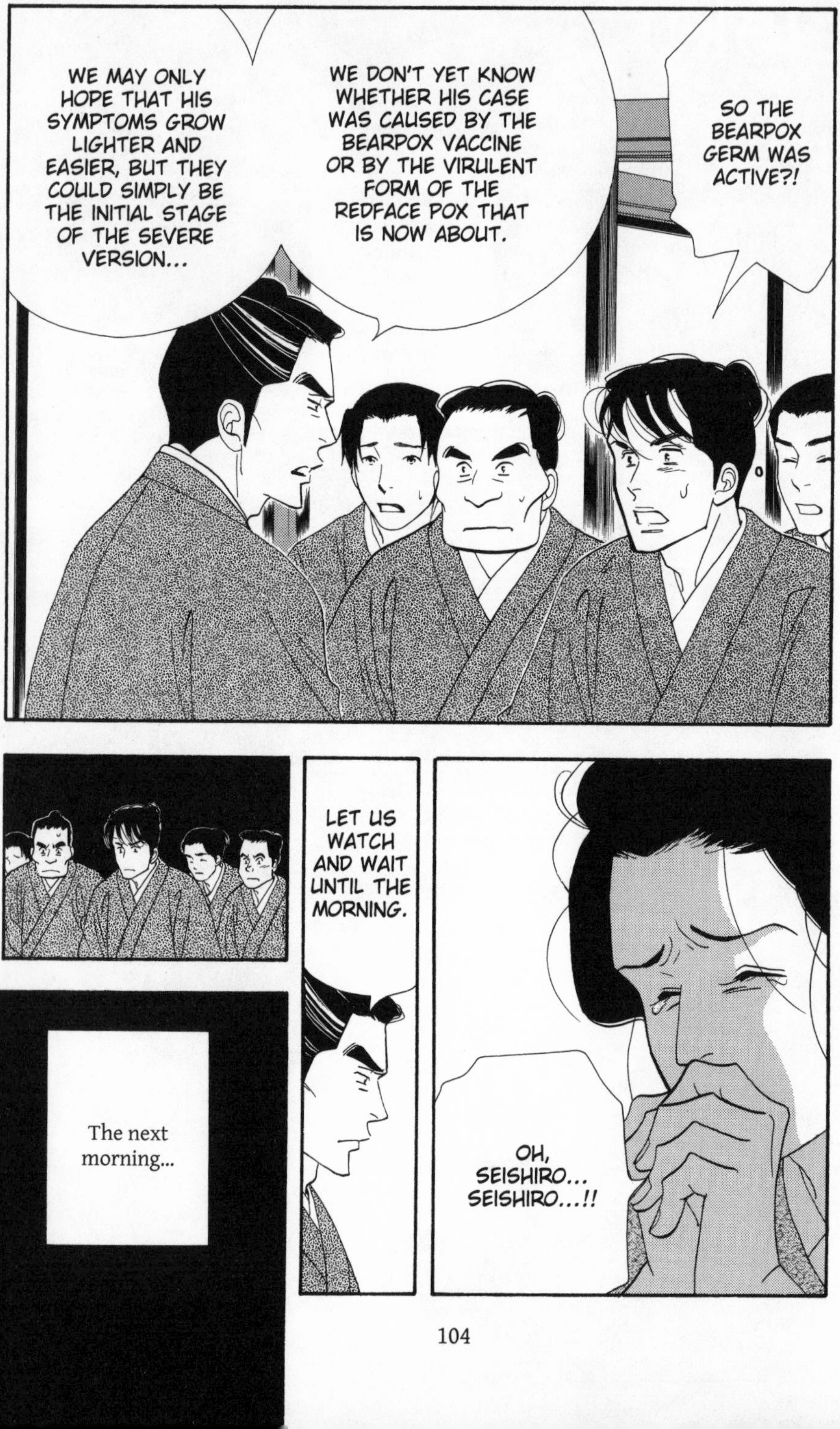
SO THE BEARPOX GERM WAS ACTIVE?!
WE DON'T YET KNOW WHETHER HIS CASE WAS CAUSED BY THE BEARPOX VACCINE OR BY THE VIRULENT FORM OF THE REDFACE POX THAT IS NOW ABOUT.
WE MAY ONLY HOPE THAT HIS SYMPTOMS GROW LIGHTER AND EASIER, BUT THEY COULD SIMPLY BE THE INITIAL STAGE OF THE SEVERE VERSION...
OH, SEISHIRO... SEISHIRO...!!
LET US WATCH AND WAIT UNTIL THE MORNING.
The next morning...

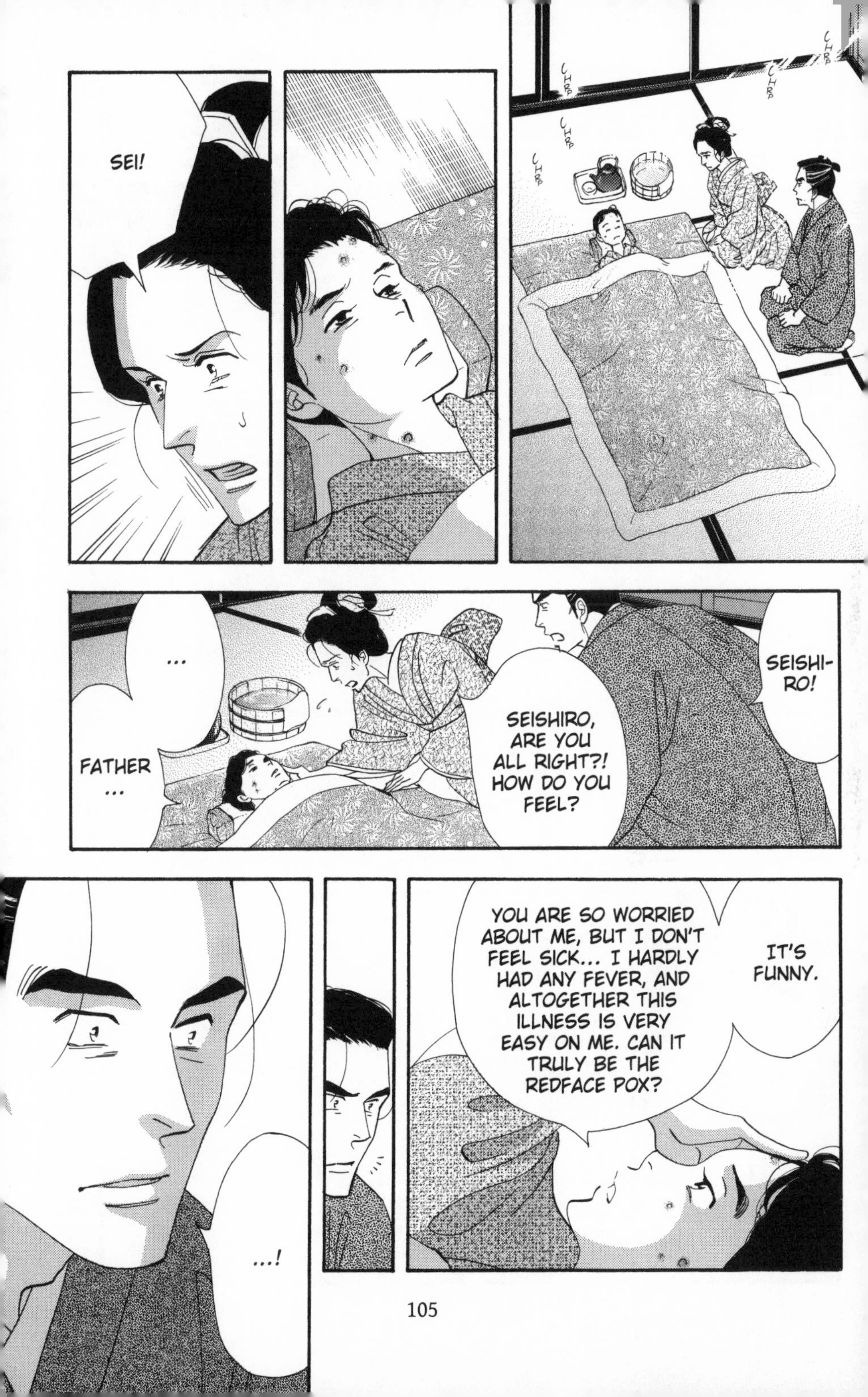
CHRP
CHRP
CHRP
CHRP
CHRP
SEI!
SEISHI-RO!
SEISHIRO, ARE YOU ALL RIGHT?! HOW DO YOU FEEL?
...
FATHER ...
IT'S FUNNY.
YOU ARE SO WORRIED ABOUT ME, BUT I DON'T FEEL SICK... I HARDLY HAD ANY FEVER, AND ALTOGETHER THIS ILLNESS IS VERY EASY ON ME. CAN IT TRULY BE THE REDFACE POX?
...!

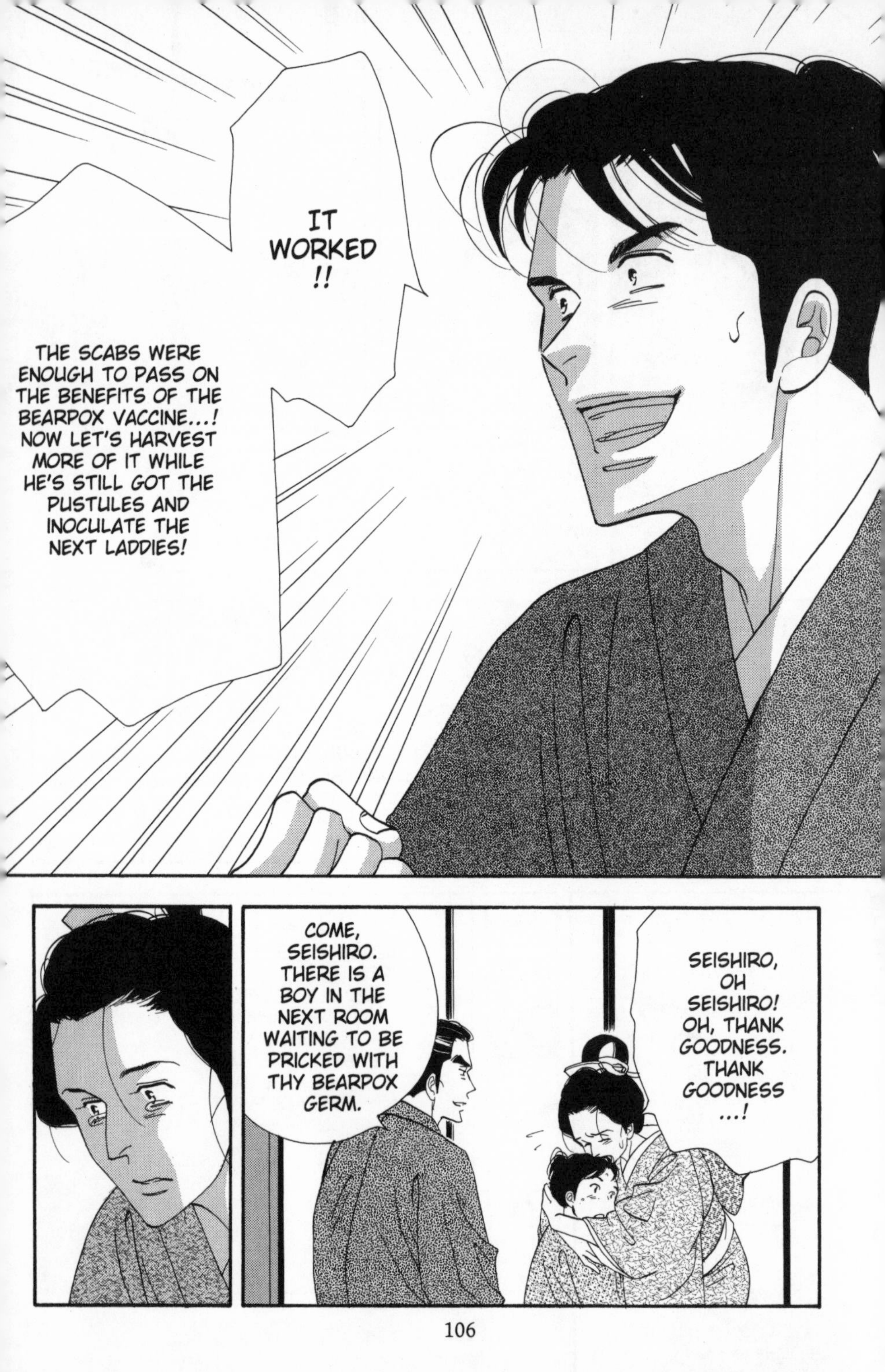
IT WORKED !!
THE SCABS WERE ENOUGH TO PASS ON THE BENEFITS OF THE BEARPOX VACCINE...! NOW LET'S HARVEST MORE OF IT WHILE HE'S STILL GOT THE PUSTULES AND INOCULATE THE NEXT LADDIES!
SEISHIRO, OH SEISHIRO! OH, THANK GOODNESS. THANK GOODNESS ...!
COME, SEISHIRO. THERE IS A BOY IN THE NEXT ROOM WAITING TO BE PRICKED WITH THY BEARPOX GERM.

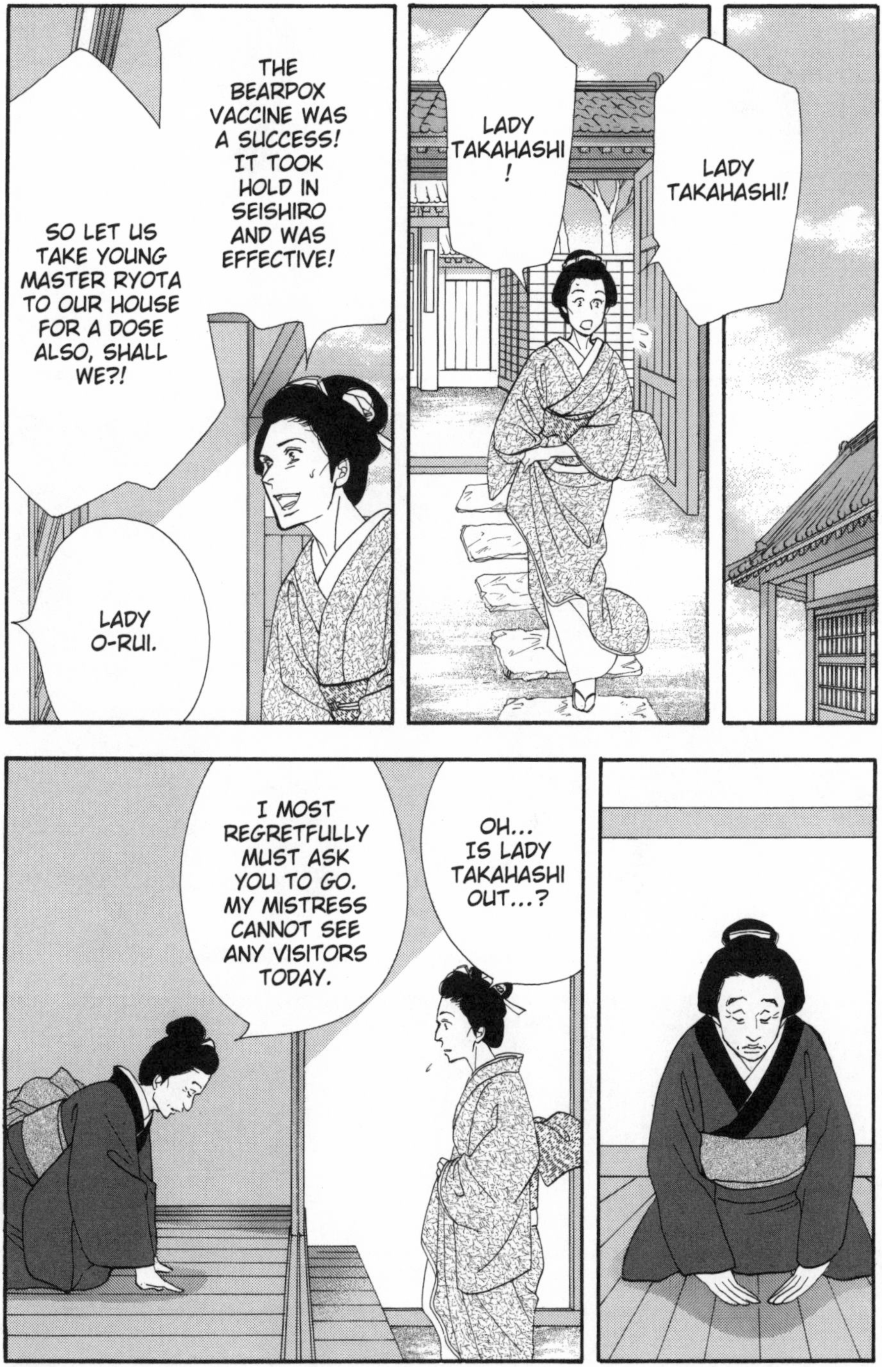
LADY TAKAHASHI!
LADY TAKAHASHI !
THE BEARPOX VACCINE WAS A SUCCESS! IT TOOK HOLD IN SEISHIRO AND WAS EFFECTIVE!
SO LET US TAKE YOUNG MASTER RYOTA TO OUR HOUSE FOR A DOSE ALSO, SHALL WE?!
LADY O-RUI.
OH... IS LADY TAKAHASHI OUT...?
I MOST REGRETFULLY MUST ASK YOU TO GO. MY MISTRESS CANNOT SEE ANY VISITORS TODAY.

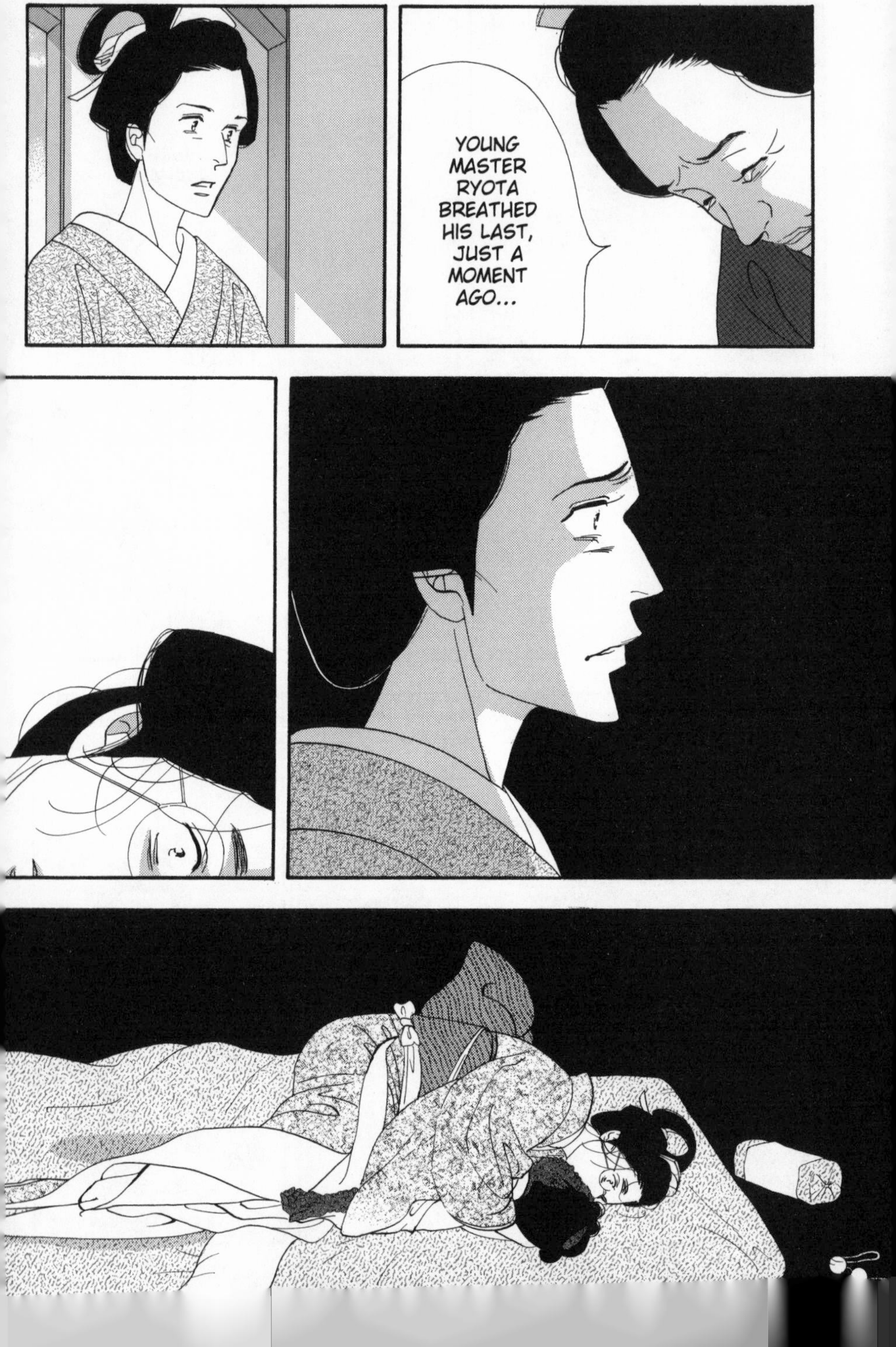
YOUNG MASTER RYOTA BREATHED HIS LAST, JUST A MOMENT AGO...

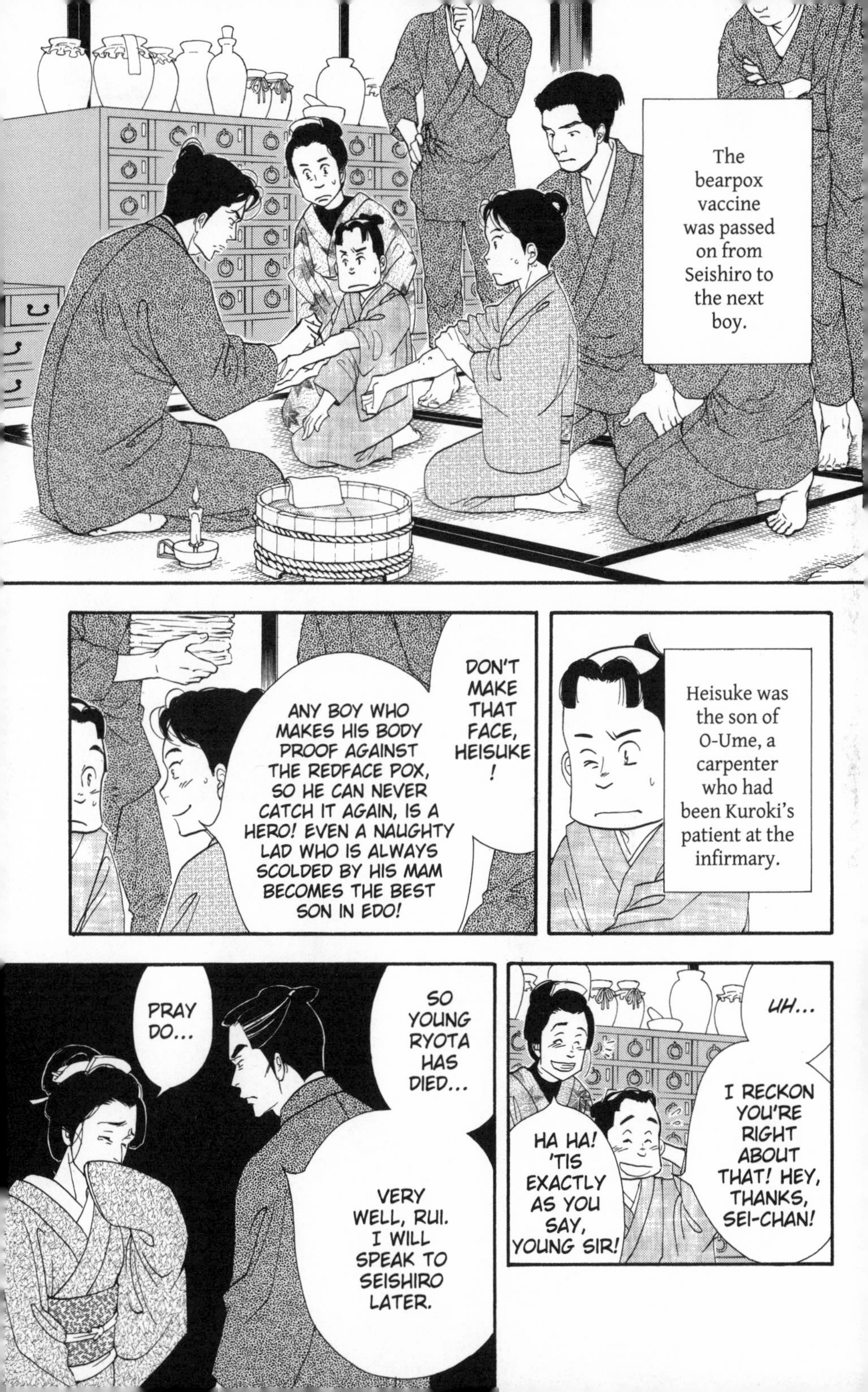
The bearpox vaccine was passed on from Seishiro to the next boy.
Heisuke was the son of O-Ume, a carpenter who had been Kuroki's patient at the infirmary.
DON'T MAKE THAT FACE, HEISUKE!
ANY BOY WHO MAKES HIS BODY PROOF AGAINST THE REDFACE POX, SO HE CAN NEVER CATCH IT AGAIN, IS A HERO! EVEN A NAUGHTY LAD WHO IS ALWAYS SCOLDED BY HIS MAM BECOMES THE BEST SON IN EDO!
UH...
I RECKON YOU'RE RIGHT ABOUT THAT! HEY, THANKS, SEI-CHAN!
HA HA! 'TIS EXACTLY AS YOU SAY, YOUNG SIR!
SO YOUNG RYOTA HAS DIED...
VERY WELL, RUI. I WILL SPEAK TO SEISHIRO LATER.
PRAY DO...

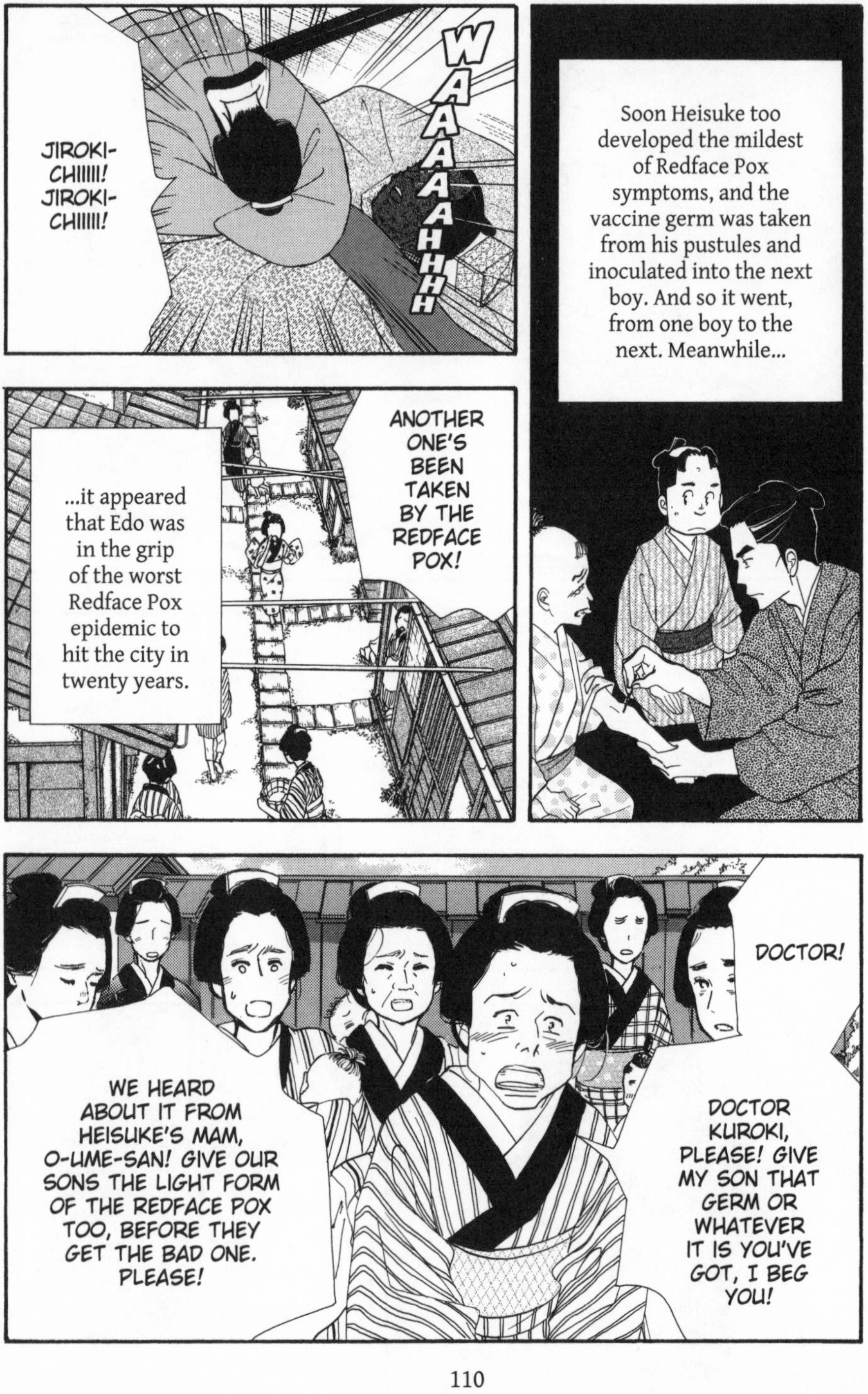
Soon Heisuke too developed the mildest of Redface Pox symptoms, and the vaccine germ was taken from his pustules and inoculated into the next boy. And so it went, from one boy to the next. Meanwhile...
WAAAAAAHHHH
JIROKI-CHIIIII! JIROKI-CHIIIII!
ANOTHER ONE'S BEEN TAKEN BY THE REDFACE POX!
...it appeared that Edo was in the grip of the worst Redface Pox epidemic to hit the city in twenty years.
DOCTOR!
DOCTOR KUROKI, PLEASE! GIVE MY SON THAT GERM OR WHATEVER IT IS YOU'VE GOT, I BEG YOU!
WE HEARD ABOUT IT FROM HEISUKE'S MAM, O-UME-SAN! GIVE OUR SONS THE LIGHT FORM OF THE REDFACE POX TOO, BEFORE THEY GET THE BAD ONE. PLEASE!

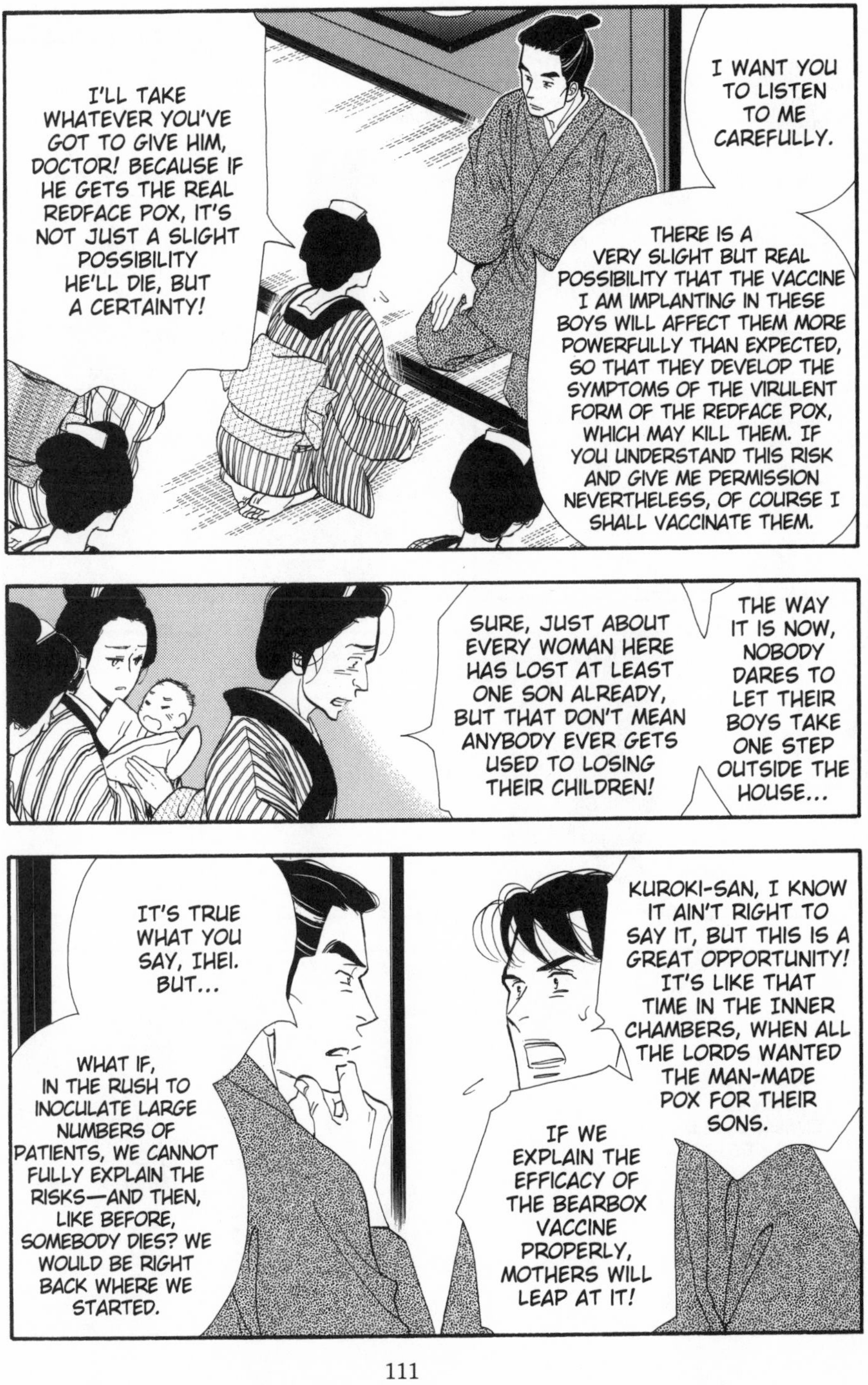
I WANT YOU TO LISTEN TO ME CAREFULLY.
THERE IS A VERY SLIGHT BUT REAL POSSIBILITY THAT THE VACCINE I AM IMPLANTING IN THESE BOYS WILL AFFECT THEM MORE POWERFULLY THAN EXPECTED, SO THAT THEY DEVELOP THE SYMPTOMS OF THE VIRULENT FORM OF THE REDFACE POX, WHICH MAY KILL THEM. IF YOU UNDERSTAND THIS RISK AND GIVE ME PERMISSION NEVERTHELESS, OF COURSE I SHALL VACCINATE THEM.
I'LL TAKE WHATEVER YOU'VE GOT TO GIVE HIM, DOCTOR! BECAUSE IF HE GETS THE REAL REDFACE POX, IT'S NOT JUST A SLIGHT POSSIBILITY HE'LL DIE, BUT A CERTAINTY!
THE WAY IT IS NOW, NOBODY DARES TO LET THEIR BOYS TAKE ONE STEP OUTSIDE THE HOUSE...
SURE, JUST ABOUT EVERY WOMAN HERE HAS LOST AT LEAST ONE SON ALREADY, BUT THAT DON'T MEAN ANYBODY EVER GETS USED TO LOSING THEIR CHILDREN!
KUROKI-SAN, I KNOW IT AIN'T RIGHT TO SAY IT, BUT THIS IS A GREAT OPPORTUNITY! IT'S LIKE THAT TIME IN THE INNER CHAMBERS, WHEN ALL THE LORDS WANTED THE MAN-MADE POX FOR THEIR SONS.
IF WE EXPLAIN THE EFFICACY OF THE BEARBOX VACCINE PROPERLY, MOTHERS WILL LEAP AT IT!
IT'S TRUE WHAT YOU SAY, IHEI. BUT...
WHAT IF, IN THE RUSH TO INOCULATE LARGE NUMBERS OF PATIENTS, WE CANNOT FULLY EXPLAIN THE RISKS—AND THEN, LIKE BEFORE, SOMEBODY DIES? WE WOULD BE RIGHT BACK WHERE WE STARTED.

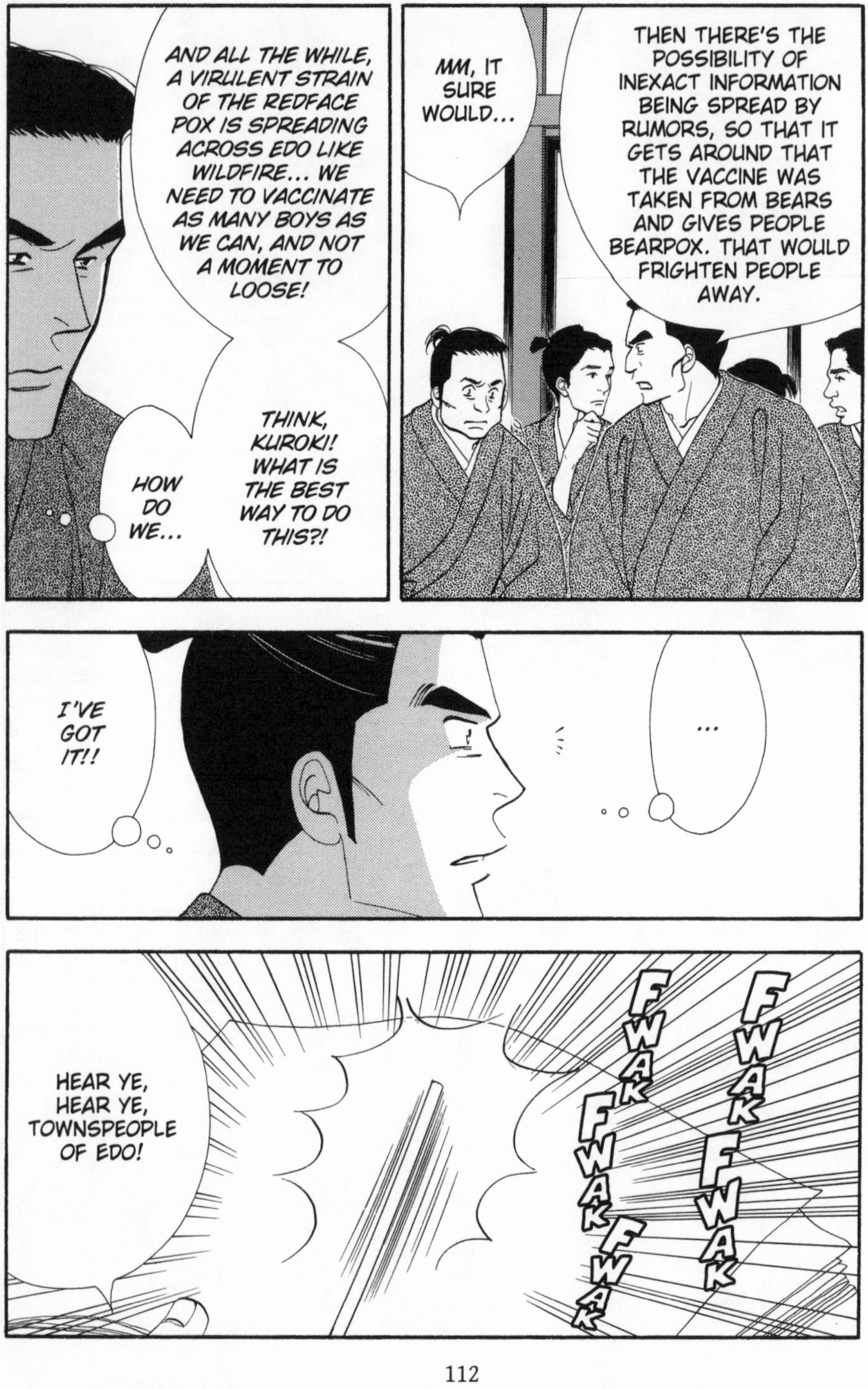
THEN THERE'S THE POSSIBILITY OF INEXACT INFORMATION BEING SPREAD BY RUMORS, SO THAT IT GETS AROUND THAT THE VACCINE WAS TAKEN FROM BEARS AND GIVES PEOPLE BEARPOX. THAT WOULD FRIGHTEN PEOPLE AWAY.
MM, IT SURE WOULD...
AND ALL THE WHILE, A VIRULENT STRAIN OF THE REDFACE POX IS SPREADING ACROSS EDO LIKE WILDFIRE... WE NEED TO VACCINATE AS MANY BOYS AS WE CAN, AND NOT A MOMENT TO LOOSE!
THINK, KUROKI! WHAT IS THE BEST WAY TO DO THIS?!
HOW DO WE...
...
I'VE GOT IT!!
FWAK FWAK
FWAK FWAK
FWAK FWAK
HEAR YE, HEAR YE, TOWNSPEOPLE OF EDO!

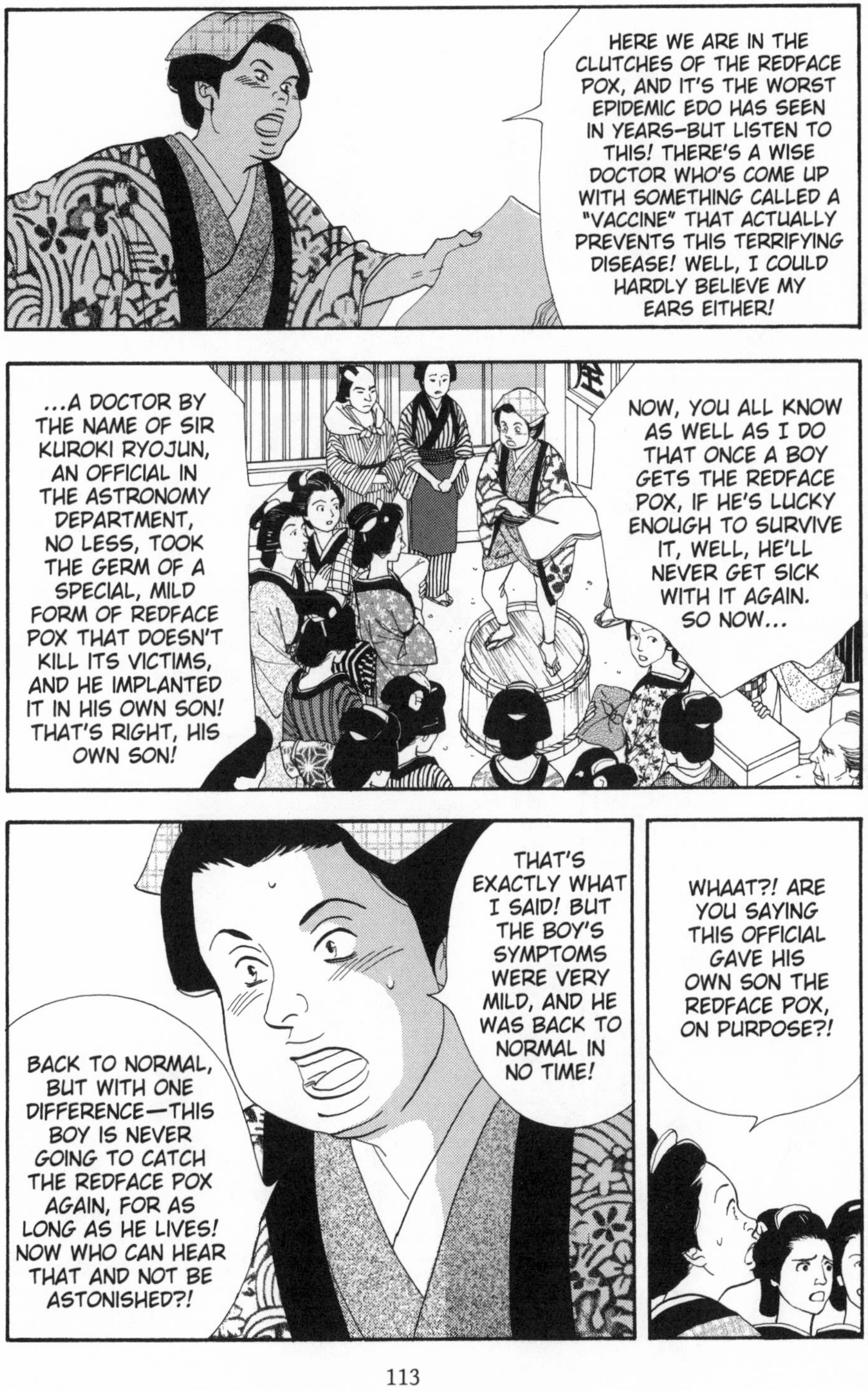
HERE WE ARE IN THE CLUTCHES OF THE REDFACE POX, AND IT'S THE WORST EPIDEMIC EDO HAS SEEN IN YEARS—BUT LISTEN TO THIS! THERE'S A WISE DOCTOR WHO'S COME UP WITH SOMETHING CALLED A "VACCINE" THAT ACTUALLY PREVENTS THIS TERRIFYING DISEASE! WELL, I COULD HARDLY BELIEVE MY EARS EITHER!
NOW, YOU ALL KNOW AS WELL AS I DO THAT ONCE A BOY GETS THE REDFACE POX, IF HE'S LUCKY ENOUGH TO SURVIVE IT, WELL, HE'LL NEVER GET SICK WITH IT AGAIN. SO NOW...
...A DOCTOR BY THE NAME OF SIR KUROKI RYOJUN, AN OFFICIAL IN THE ASTRONOMY DEPARTMENT, NO LESS, TOOK THE GERM OF A SPECIAL, MILD FORM OF REDFACE POX THAT DOESN'T KILL ITS VICTIMS, AND HE IMPLANTED IT IN HIS OWN SON! THAT'S RIGHT, HIS OWN SON!
WHAAT?! ARE YOU SAYING THIS OFFICIAL GAVE HIS OWN SON THE REDFACE POX, ON PURPOSE?!
THAT'S EXACTLY WHAT I SAID! BUT THE BOY'S SYMPTOMS WERE VERY MILD, AND HE WAS BACK TO NORMAL IN NO TIME!
BACK TO NORMAL, BUT WITH ONE DIFFERENCE—THIS BOY IS NEVER GOING TO CATCH THE REDFACE POX AGAIN, FOR AS LONG AS HE LIVES! NOW WHO CAN HEAR THAT AND NOT BE ASTONISHED?!

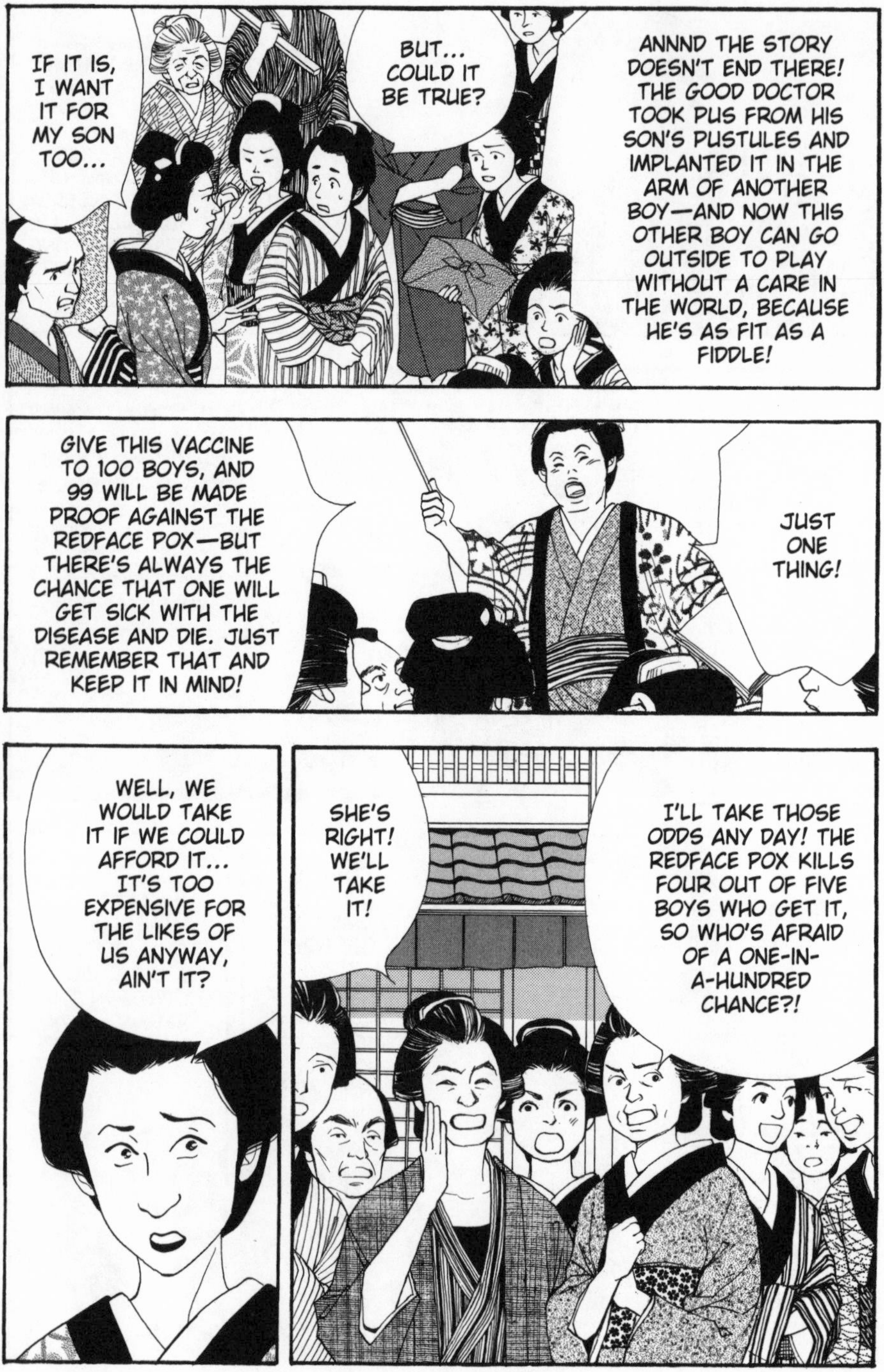
ANNND THE STORY DOESN'T END THERE! THE GOOD DOCTOR TOOK PUS FROM HIS SON'S PUSTULES AND IMPLANTED IT IN THE ARM OF ANOTHER BOY—AND NOW THIS OTHER BOY CAN GO OUTSIDE TO PLAY WITHOUT A CARE IN THE WORLD, BECAUSE HE'S AS FIT AS A FIDDLE!
BUT... COULD IT BE TRUE?
IF IT IS, I WANT IT FOR MY SON TOO...
JUST ONE THING!
GIVE THIS VACCINE TO 100 BOYS, AND 99 WILL BE MADE PROOF AGAINST THE REDFACE POX—BUT THERE'S ALWAYS THE CHANCE THAT ONE WILL GET SICK WITH THE DISEASE AND DIE. JUST REMEMBER THAT AND KEEP IT IN MIND!
I'LL TAKE THOSE ODDS ANY DAY! THE REDFACE POX KILLS FOUR OUT OF FIVE BOYS WHO GET IT, SO WHO'S AFRAID OF A ONE-IN-A-HUNDRED CHANCE?!
SHE'S RIGHT! WE'LL TAKE IT!
WELL, WE WOULD TAKE IT IF WE COULD AFFORD IT... IT'S TOO EXPENSIVE FOR THE LIKES OF US ANYWAY, AIN'T IT?

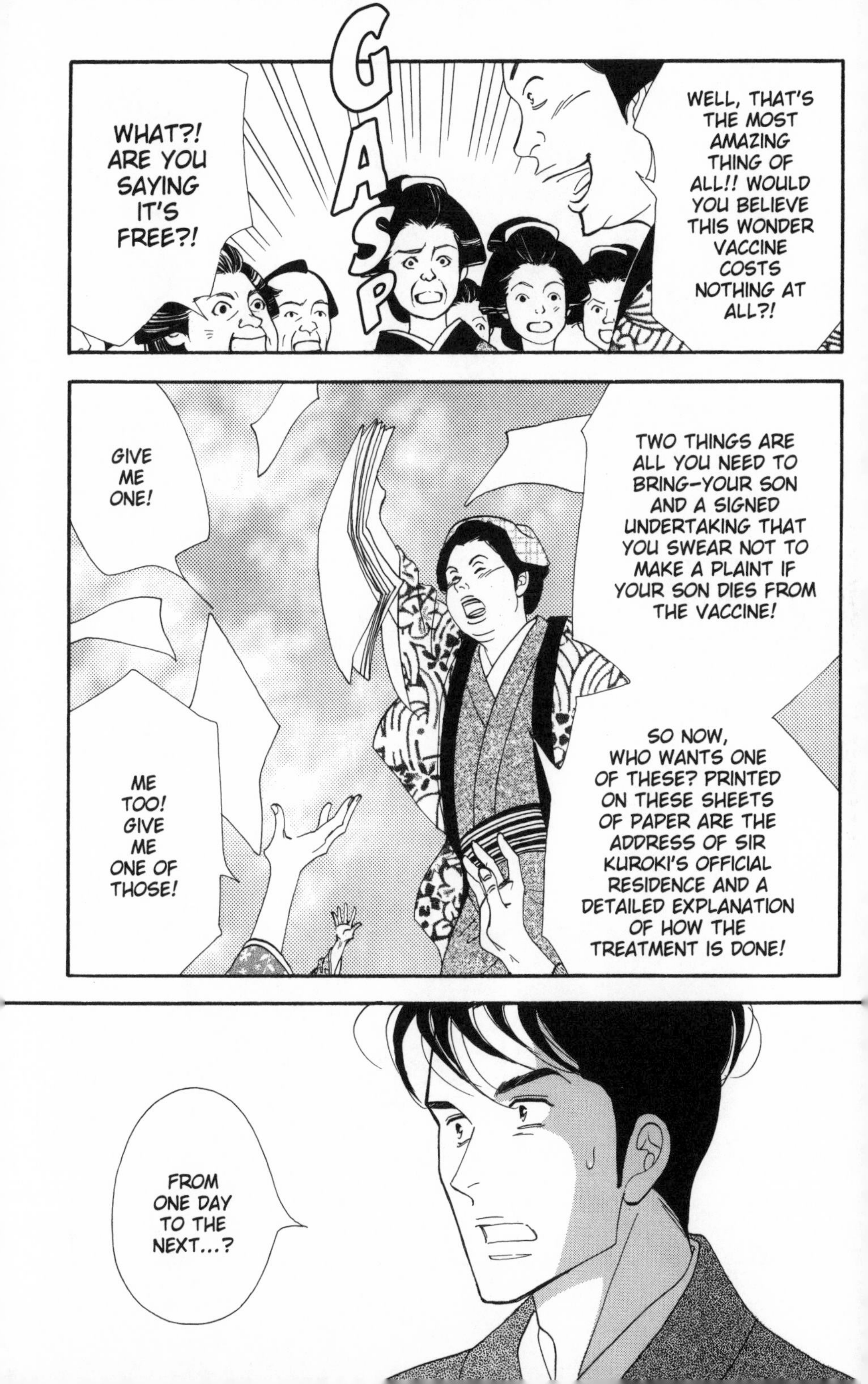
WELL, THAT'S THE MOST AMAZING THING OF ALL!! WOULD YOU BELIEVE THIS WONDER VACCINE COSTS NOTHING AT ALL?!
GASP
WHAT?! ARE YOU SAYING IT'S FREE?!
TWO THINGS ARE ALL YOU NEED TO BRING–YOUR SON AND A SIGNED UNDERTAKING THAT YOU SWEAR NOT TO MAKE A PLAINT IF YOUR SON DIES FROM THE VACCINE!
SO NOW, WHO WANTS ONE OF THESE? PRINTED ON THESE SHEETS OF PAPER ARE THE ADDRESS OF SIR KUROKI'S OFFICIAL RESIDENCE AND A DETAILED EXPLANATION OF HOW THE TREATMENT IS DONE!
GIVE ME ONE!
ME TOO! GIVE ME ONE OF THOSE!
FROM ONE DAY TO THE NEXT...?

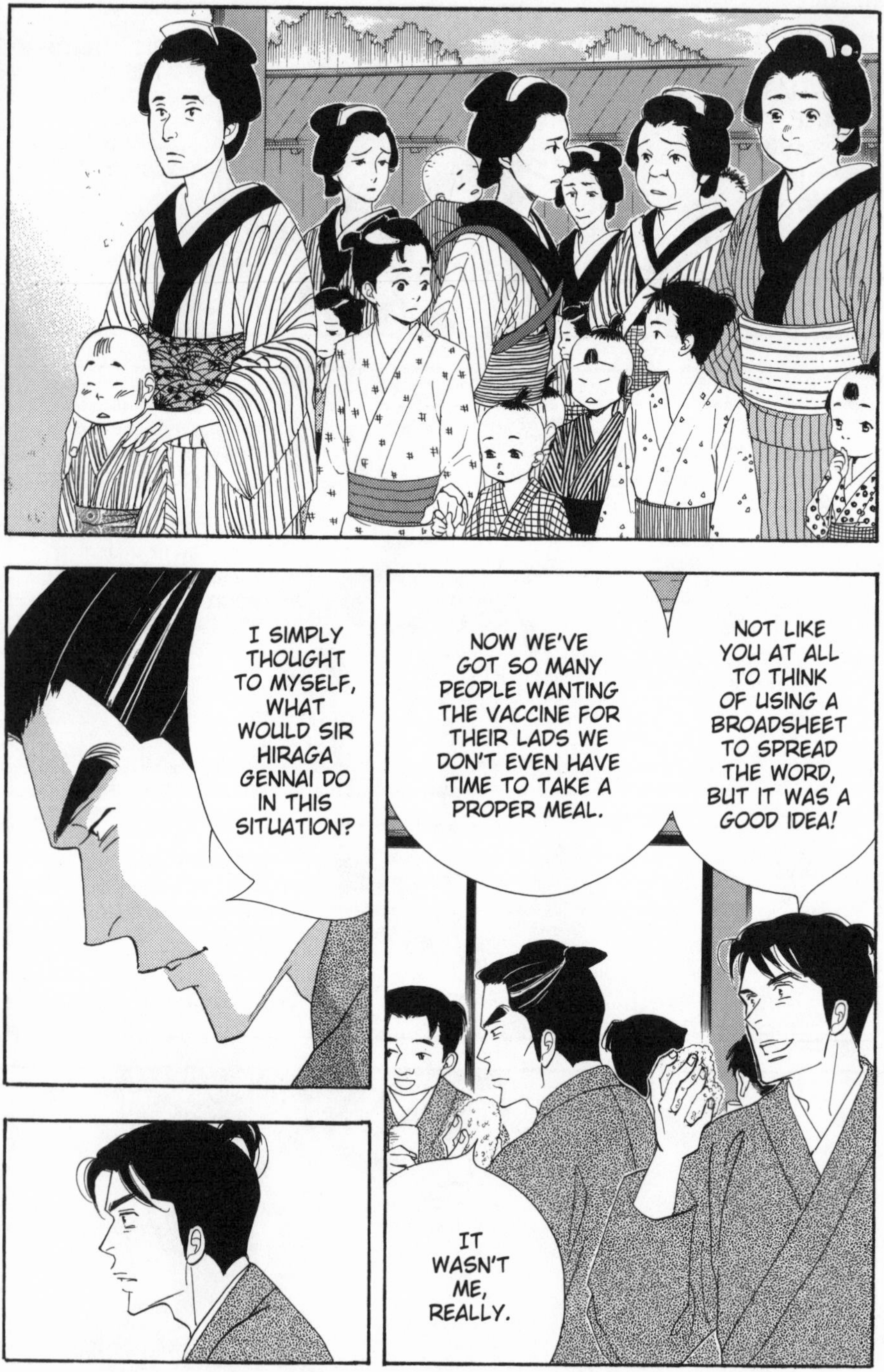
NOT LIKE YOU AT ALL TO THINK OF USING A BROADSHEET TO SPREAD THE WORD, BUT IT WAS A GOOD IDEA!
NOW WE'VE GOT SO MANY PEOPLE WANTING THE VACCINE FOR THEIR LADS WE DON'T EVEN HAVE TIME TO TAKE A PROPER MEAL.
IT WASN'T ME, REALLY.
I SIMPLY THOUGHT TO MYSELF, WHAT WOULD SIR HIRAGA GENNAI DO IN THIS SITUATION?

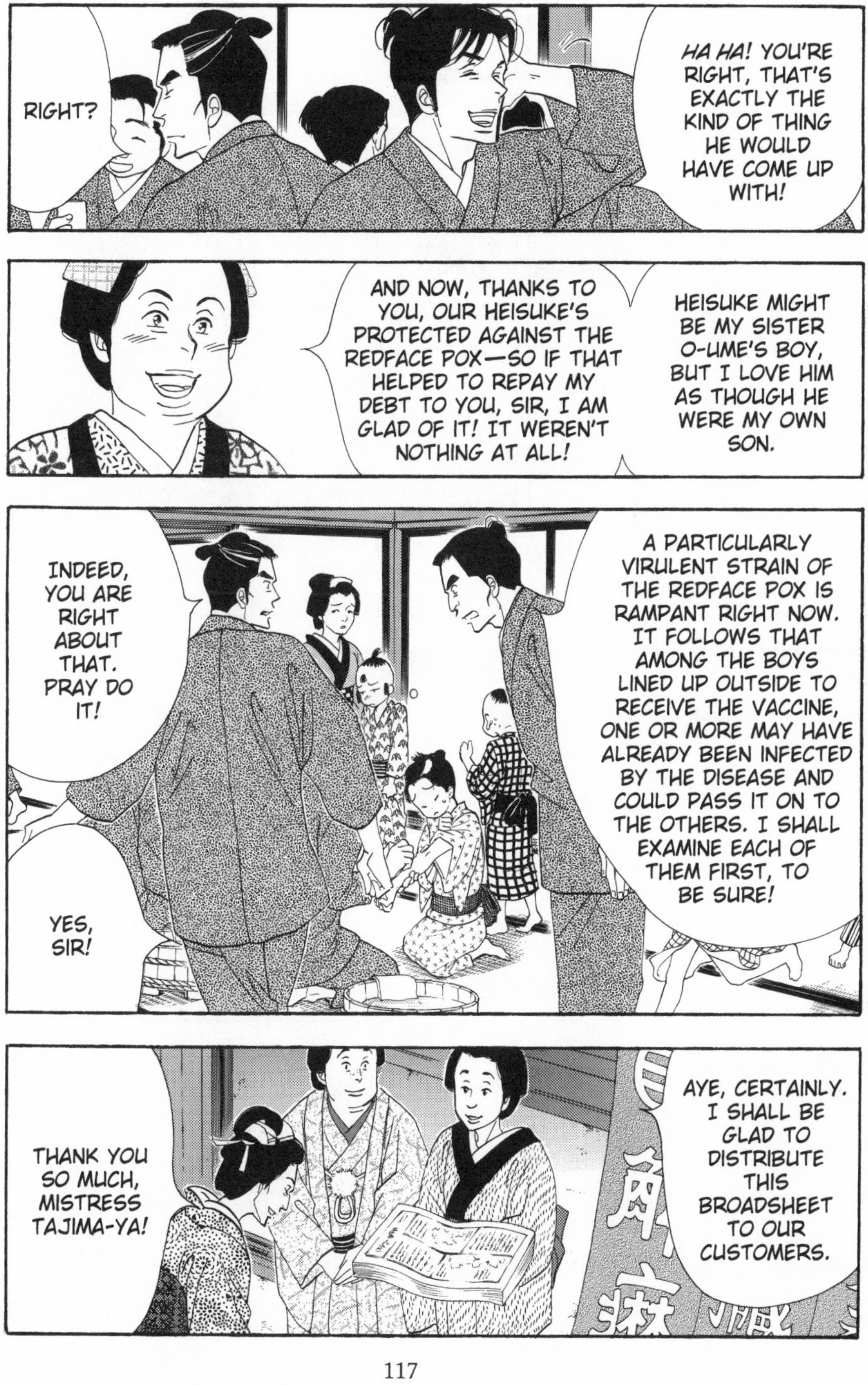
HA HA! YOU'RE RIGHT, THAT'S EXACTLY THE KIND OF THING HE WOULD HAVE COME UP WITH!
RIGHT?
HEISUKE MIGHT BE MY SISTER O-UME'S BOY, BUT I LOVE HIM AS THOUGH HE WERE MY OWN SON.
AND NOW, THANKS TO YOU, OUR HEISUKE'S PROTECTED AGAINST THE REDFACE POX—SO IF THAT HELPED TO REPAY MY DEBT TO YOU, SIR, I AM GLAD OF IT! IT WEREN'T NOTHING AT ALL!
A PARTICULARLY VIRULENT STRAIN OF THE REDFACE POX IS RAMPANT RIGHT NOW. IT FOLLOWS THAT AMONG THE BOYS LINED UP OUTSIDE TO RECEIVE THE VACCINE, ONE OR MORE MAY HAVE ALREADY BEEN INFECTED BY THE DISEASE AND COULD PASS IT ON TO THE OTHERS. I SHALL EXAMINE EACH OF THEM FIRST, TO BE SURE!
INDEED, YOU ARE RIGHT ABOUT THAT. PRAY DO IT!
YES, SIR!
AYE, CERTAINLY. I SHALL BE GLAD TO DISTRIBUTE THIS BROADSHEET TO OUR CUSTOMERS.
THANK YOU SO MUCH, MISTRESS TAJIMA-YA!

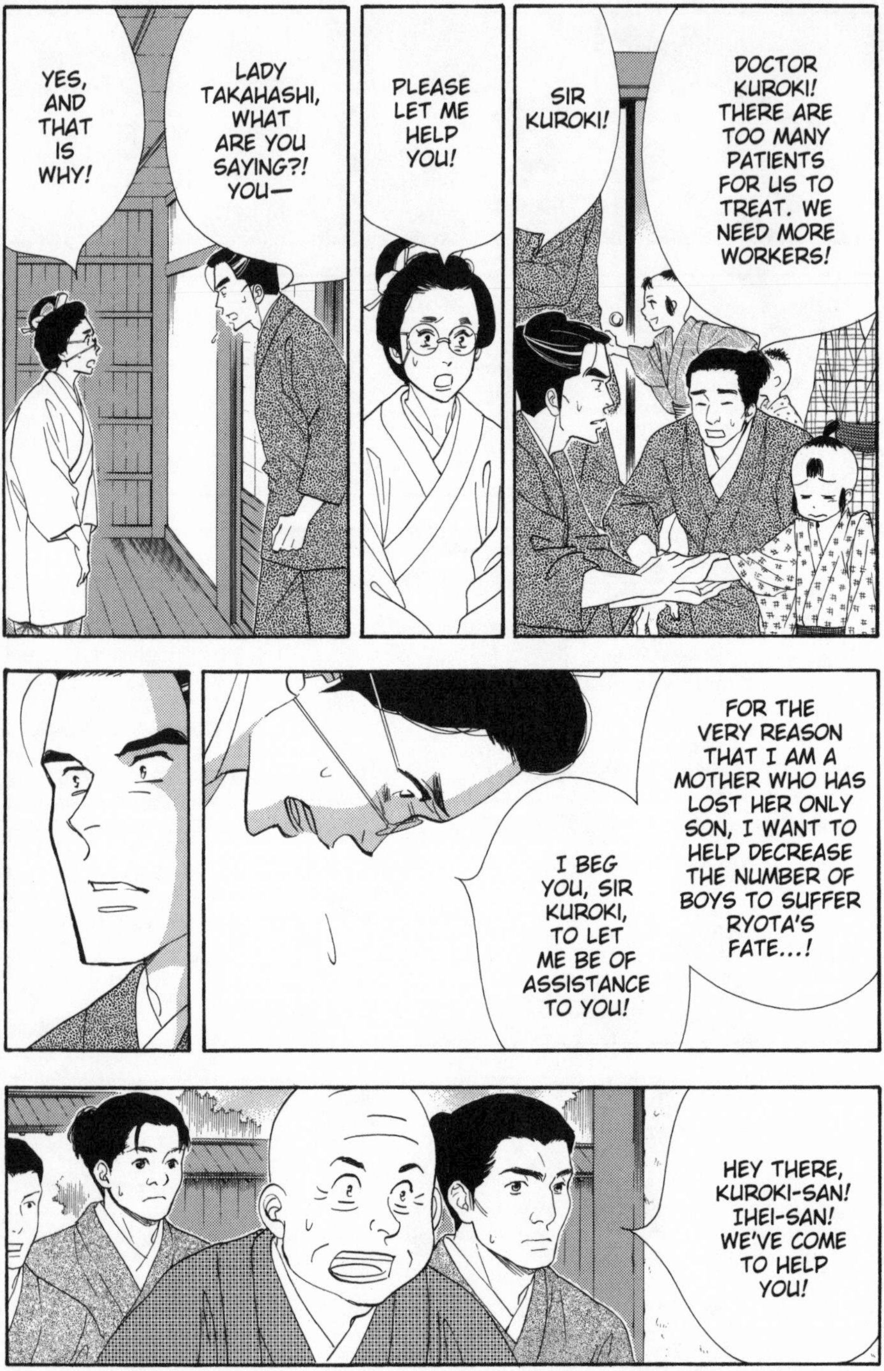
DOCTOR KUROKI! THERE ARE TOO MANY PATIENTS FOR US TO TREAT. WE NEED MORE WORKERS!
SIR KUROKI!
PLEASE LET ME HELP YOU!
LADY TAKAHASHI, WHAT ARE YOU SAYING?! YOU—
YES, AND THAT IS WHY!
FOR THE VERY REASON THAT I AM A MOTHER WHO HAS LOST HER ONLY SON, I WANT TO HELP DECREASE THE NUMBER OF BOYS TO SUFFER RYOTA'S FATE...!
I BEG YOU, SIR KUROKI, TO LET ME BE OF ASSISTANCE TO YOU!
HEY THERE, KUROKI-SAN! IHEI-SAN! WE'VE COME TO HELP YOU!

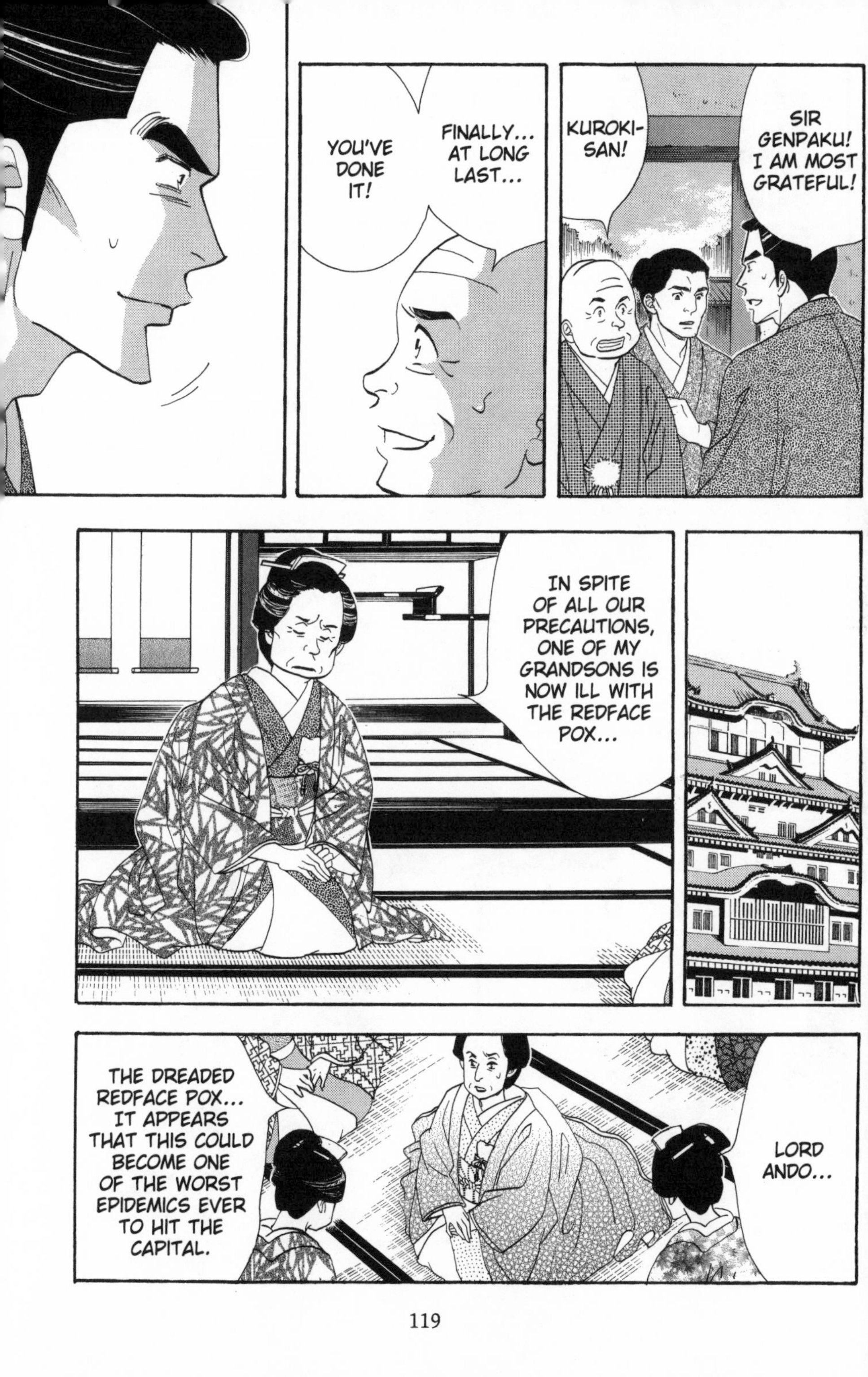
SIR GENPAKU! I AM MOST GRATEFUL!
KUROKI-SAN!
FINALLY... AT LONG LAST...
YOU'VE DONE IT!
IN SPITE OF ALL OUR PRECAUTIONS, ONE OF MY GRANDSONS IS NOW ILL WITH THE REDFACE POX...
LORD ANDO...
THE DREADED REDFACE POX... IT APPEARS THAT THIS COULD BECOME ONE OF THE WORST EPIDEMICS EVER TO HIT THE CAPITAL.

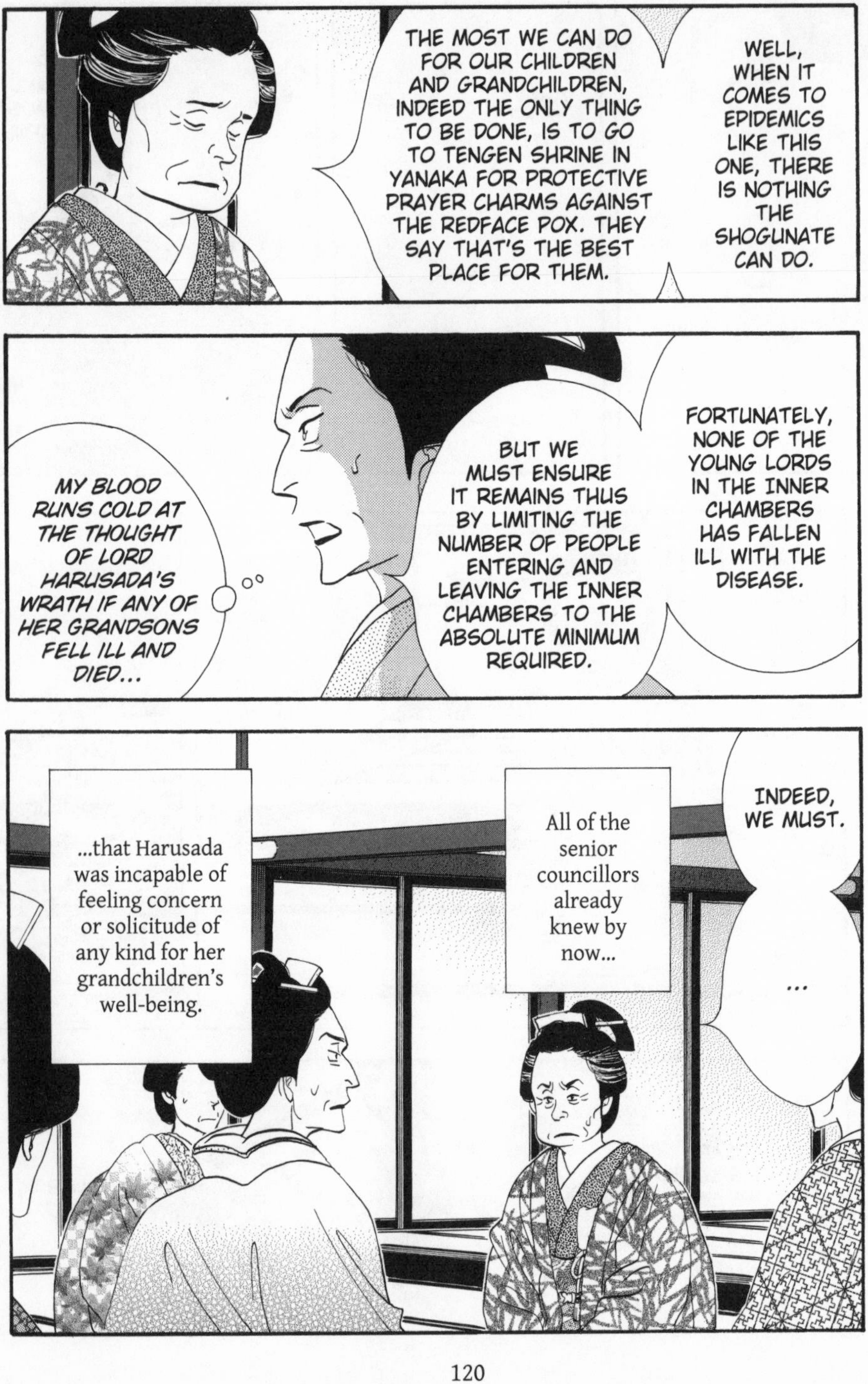
WELL, WHEN IT COMES TO EPIDEMICS LIKE THIS ONE, THERE IS NOTHING THE SHOGUNATE CAN DO.
THE MOST WE CAN DO FOR OUR CHILDREN AND GRANDCHILDREN, INDEED THE ONLY THING TO BE DONE, IS TO GO TO TENGEN SHRINE IN YANAKA FOR PROTECTIVE PRAYER CHARMS AGAINST THE REDFACE POX. THEY SAY THAT'S THE BEST PLACE FOR THEM.
FORTUNATELY, NONE OF THE YOUNG LORDS IN THE INNER CHAMBERS HAS FALLEN ILL WITH THE DISEASE.
BUT WE MUST ENSURE IT REMAINS THUS BY LIMITING THE NUMBER OF PEOPLE ENTERING AND LEAVING THE INNER CHAMBERS TO THE ABSOLUTE MINIMUM REQUIRED.
MY BLOOD RUNS COLD AT THE THOUGHT OF LORD HARUSADA'S WRATH IF ANY OF HER GRANDSONS FELL ILL AND DIED...
INDEED, WE MUST.
...
All of the senior councillors already knew by now...
...that Harusada was incapable of feeling concern or solicitude of any kind for her grandchildren's well-being.

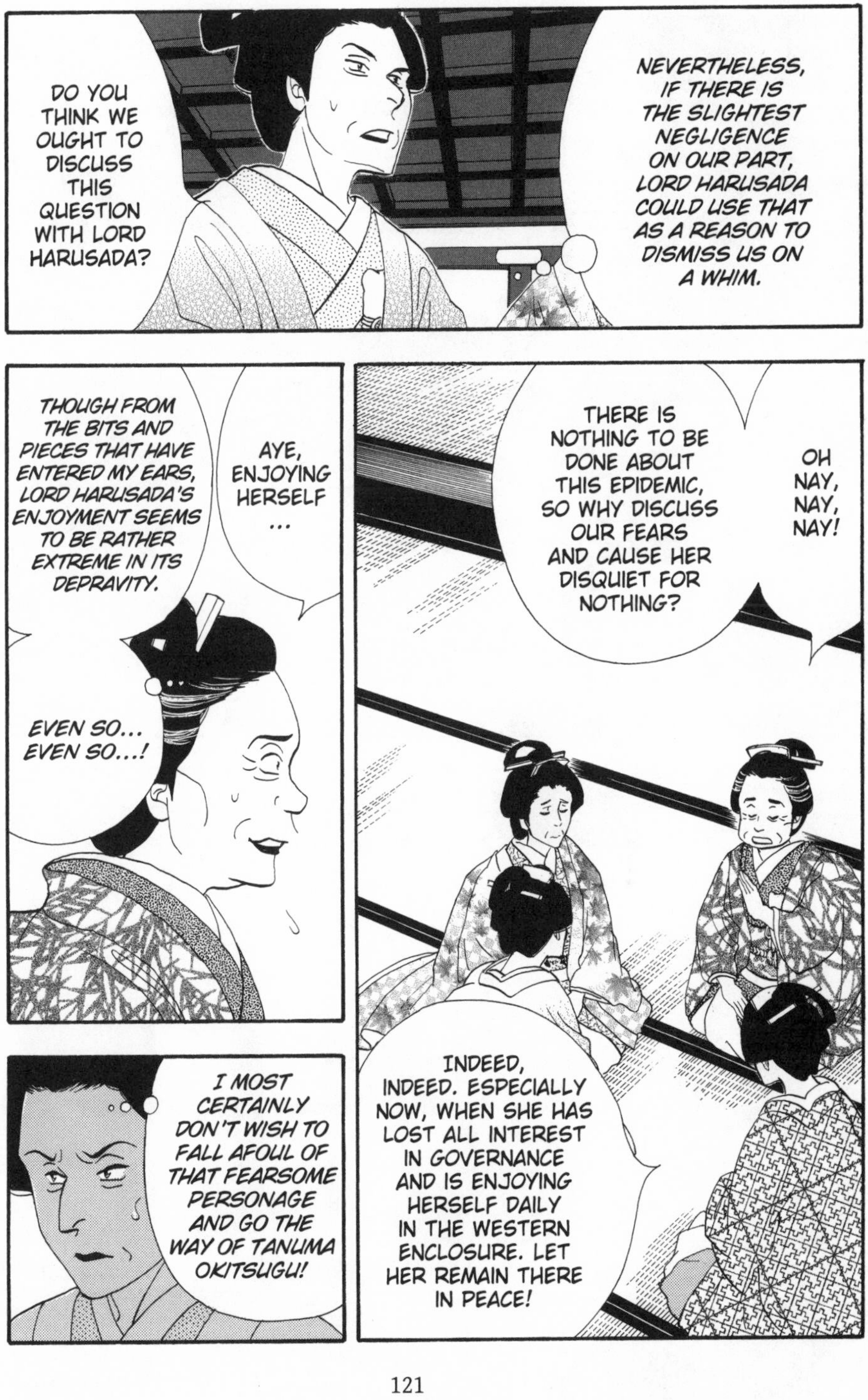
NEVERTHELESS, IF THERE IS THE SLIGHTEST NEGLIGENCE ON OUR PART, LORD HARUSADA COULD USE THAT AS A REASON TO DISMISS US ON A WHIM.
DO YOU THINK WE OUGHT TO DISCUSS THIS QUESTION WITH LORD HARUSADA?
THERE IS NOTHING TO BE DONE ABOUT THIS EPIDEMIC, SO WHY DISCUSS OUR FEARS AND CAUSE HER DISQUIET FOR NOTHING?
OH NAY, NAY, NAY!
INDEED, INDEED. ESPECIALLY NOW, WHEN SHE HAS LOST ALL INTEREST IN GOVERNANCE AND IS ENJOYING HERSELF DAILY IN THE WESTERN ENCLOSURE. LET HER REMAIN THERE IN PEACE!
AYE, ENJOYING HERSELF …
THOUGH FROM THE BITS AND PIECES THAT HAVE ENTERED MY EARS, LORD HARUSADA'S ENJOYMENT SEEMS TO BE RATHER EXTREME IN ITS DEPRAVITY.
EVEN SO… EVEN SO…!
I MOST CERTAINLY DON'T WISH TO FALL AFOUL OF THAT FEARSOME PERSONAGE AND GO THE WAY OF TANUMA OKITSUGU!

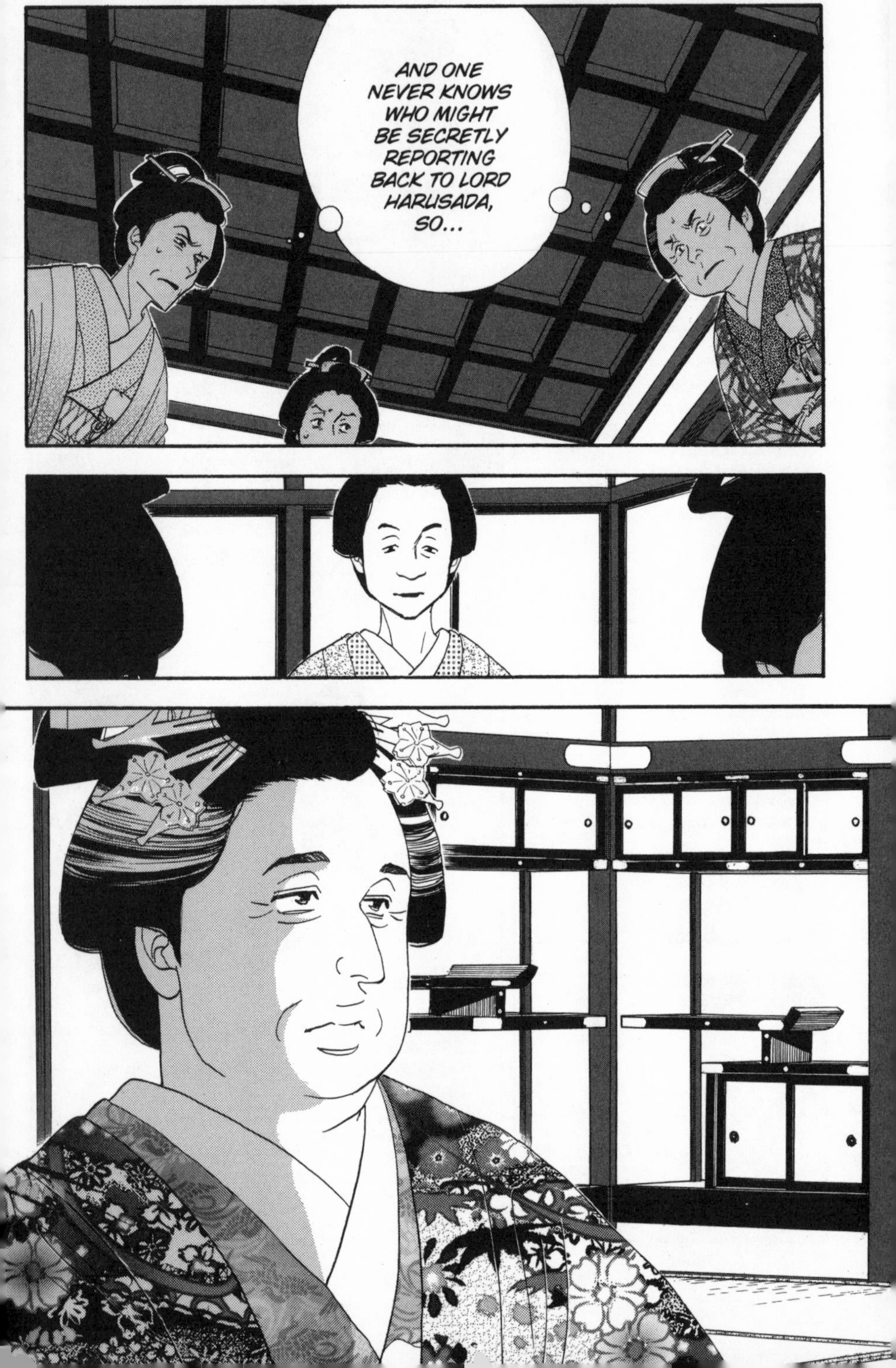
AND ONE NEVER KNOWS WHO MIGHT BE SECRETLY REPORTING BACK TO LORD HARUSADA, SO...

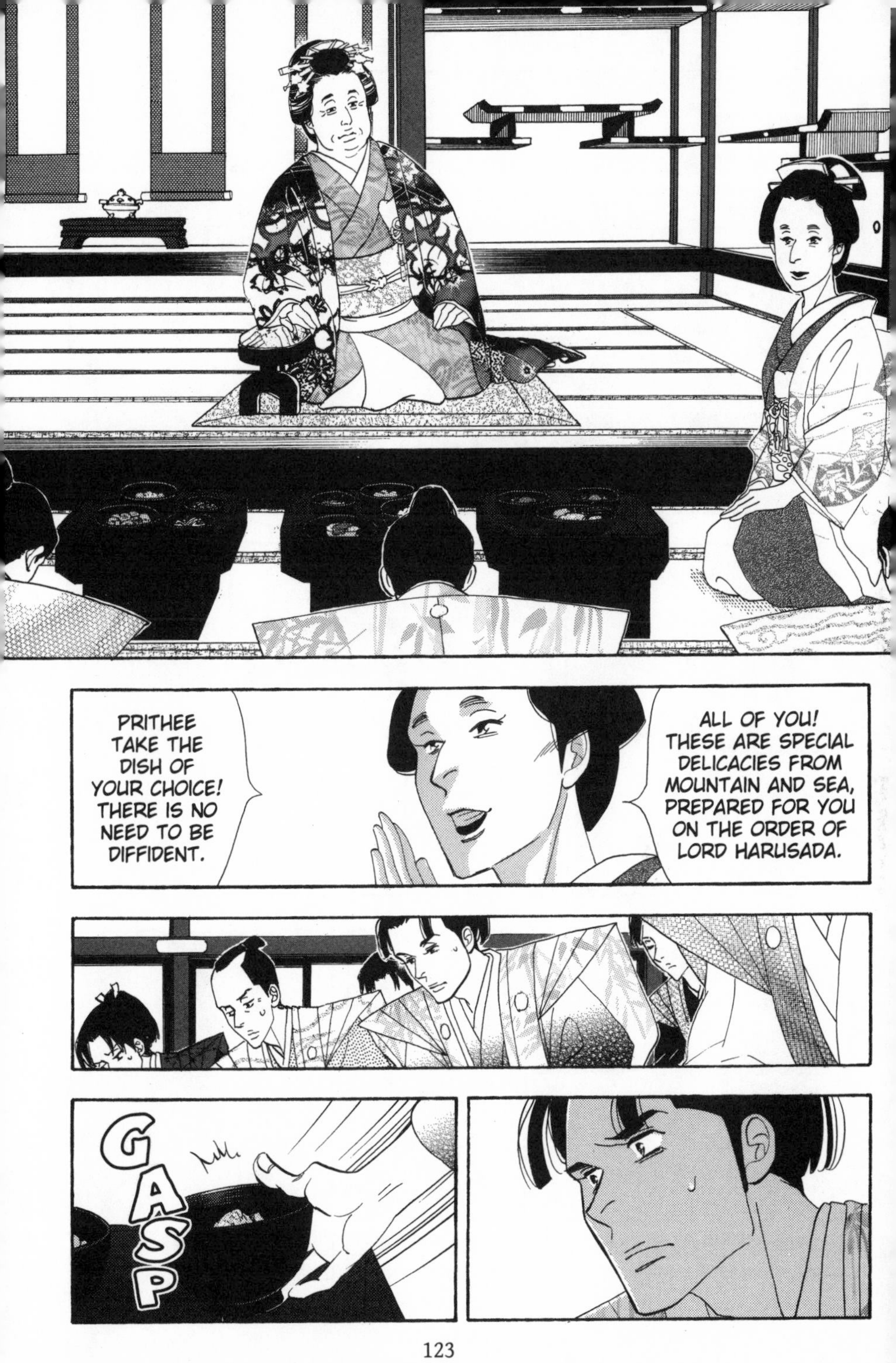
ALL OF YOU! THESE ARE SPECIAL DELICACIES FROM MOUNTAIN AND SEA, PREPARED FOR YOU ON THE ORDER OF LORD HARUSADA.
PRITHEE TAKE THE DISH OF YOUR CHOICE! THERE IS NO NEED TO BE DIFFIDENT.
GASP

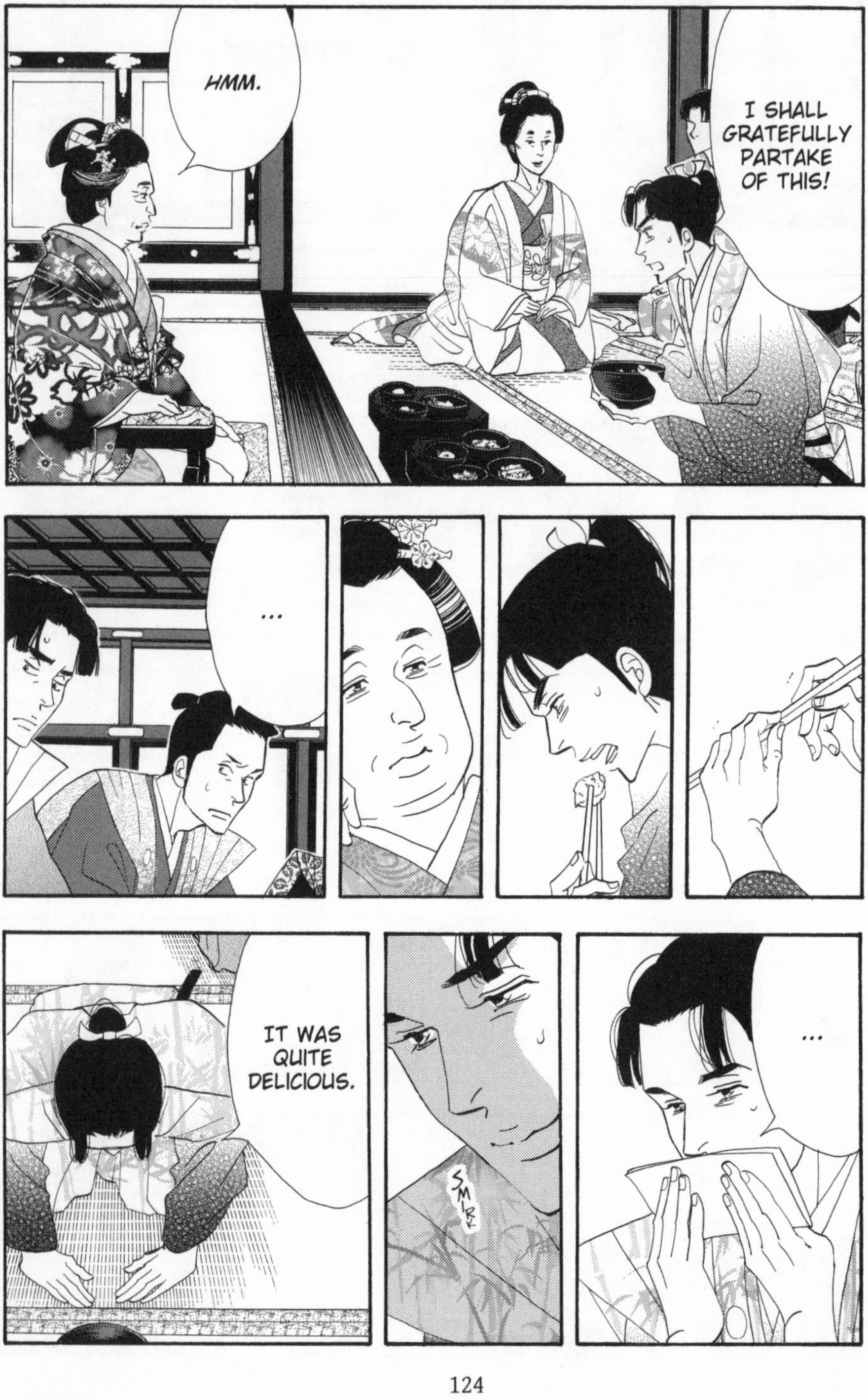
I SHALL GRATEFULLY PARTAKE OF THIS!
HMM.
...
...
SMIRK
IT WAS QUITE DELICIOUS.

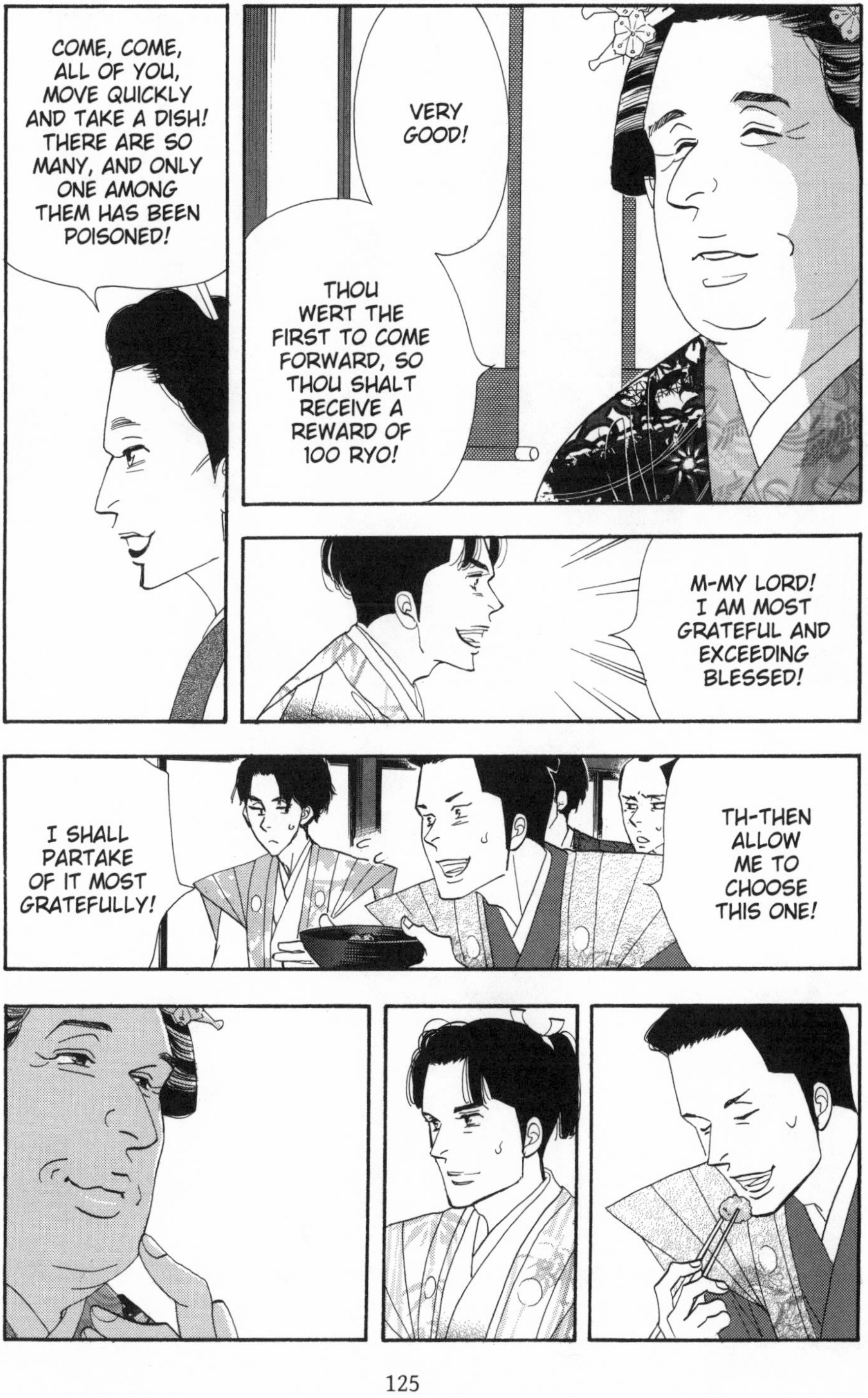
VERY GOOD!
THOU WERT THE FIRST TO COME FORWARD, SO THOU SHALT RECEIVE A REWARD OF 100 RYO!
M-MY LORD! I AM MOST GRATEFUL AND EXCEEDING BLESSED!
COME, COME, ALL OF YOU, MOVE QUICKLY AND TAKE A DISH! THERE ARE SO MANY, AND ONLY ONE AMONG THEM HAS BEEN POISONED!
TH-THEN ALLOW ME TO CHOOSE THIS ONE!
I SHALL PARTAKE OF IT MOST GRATEFULLY!

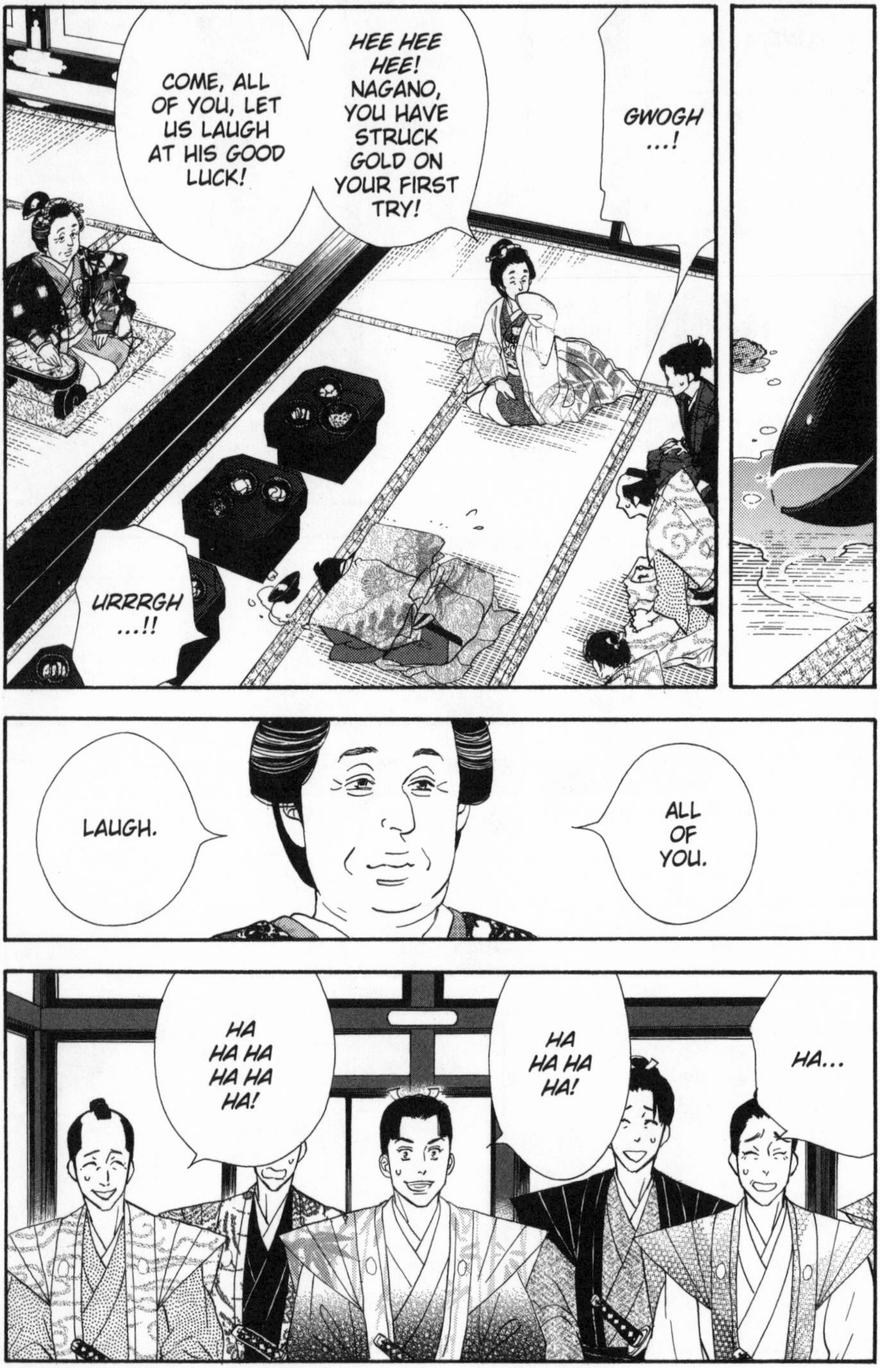
GWOGH ...!
HEE HEE HEE! NAGANO, YOU HAVE STRUCK GOLD ON YOUR FIRST TRY!
COME, ALL OF YOU, LET US LAUGH AT HIS GOOD LUCK!
URRRGH ...!!
ALL OF YOU.
LAUGH.
HA...
HA HA HA HA!
HA HA HA HA HA HA!

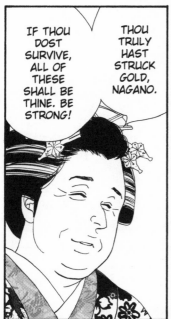

THUNK
KLINK KLANK
THOU TRULY HAST STRUCK GOLD, NAGANO.
IF THOU DOST SURVIVE, ALL OF THESE SHALL BE THINE. BE STRONG!
M—
M'LORD!
GGGH...
I AM MOST GRATEFUL AND EXCEEDING BLESSED. I SHALL STRIVE TO BE STRONG.
KLINK
HA HA HA!
O FORTUNATE NAGANO! HE HAS STRUCK GOLD!
FOR-TUNATE IS HE WHO HAS STRUCK GOLD!

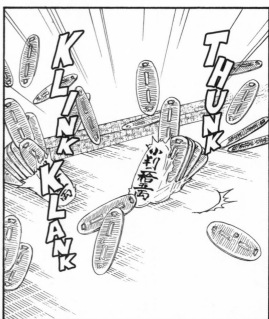

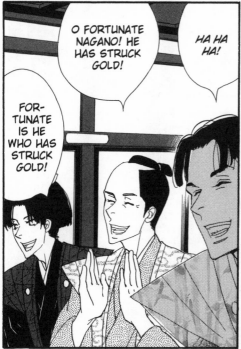

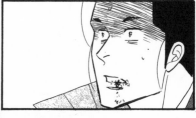

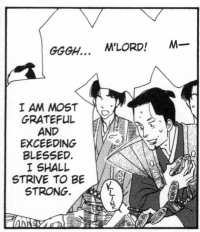

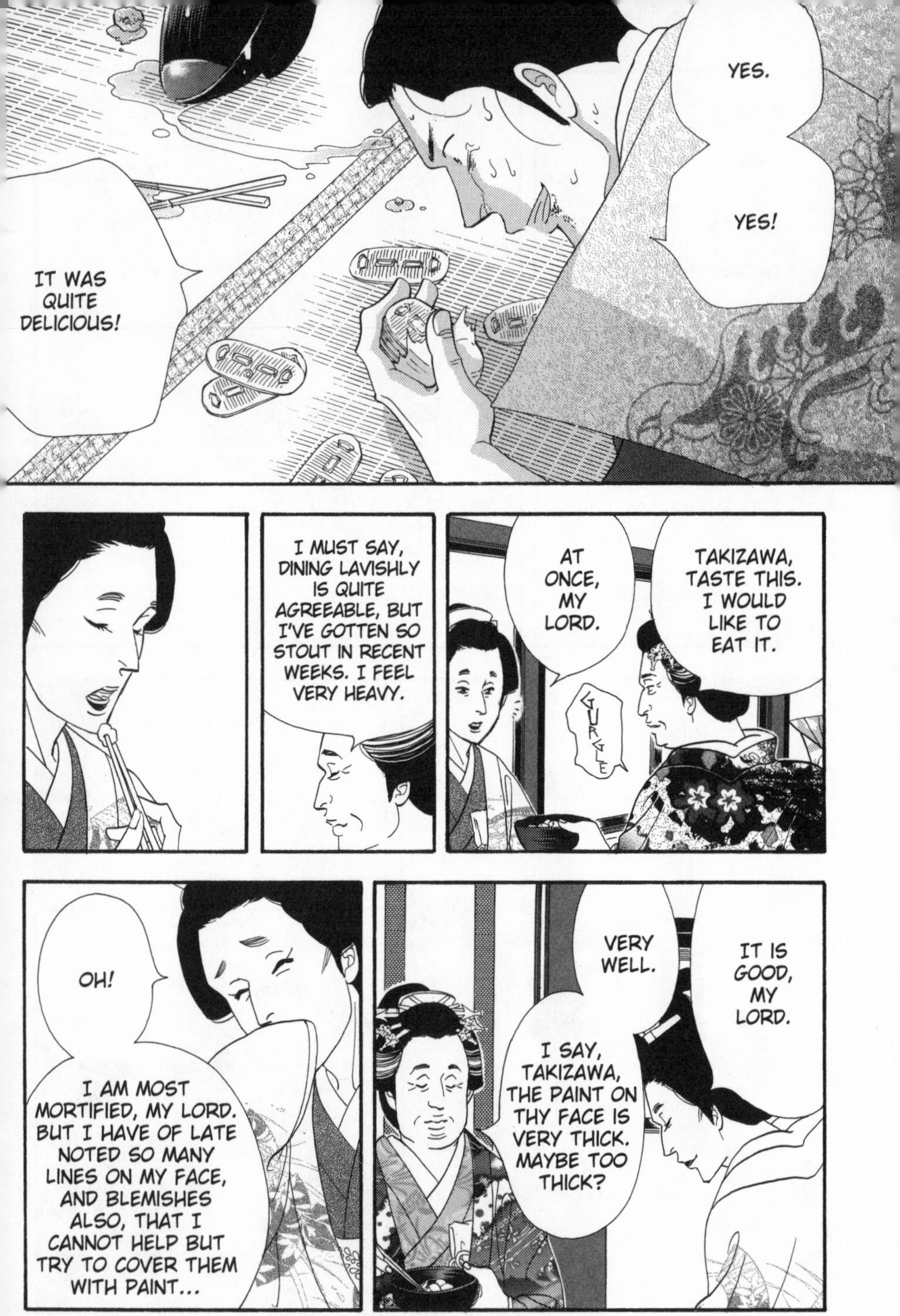
YES.
YES!
IT WAS QUITE DELICIOUS!
TAKIZAWA, TASTE THIS. I WOULD LIKE TO EAT IT.
AT ONCE, MY LORD.
GURGLE
I MUST SAY, DINING LAVISHLY IS QUITE AGREEABLE, BUT I'VE GOTTEN SO STOUT IN RECENT WEEKS. I FEEL VERY HEAVY.
IT IS GOOD, MY LORD.
VERY WELL.
I SAY, TAKIZAWA, THE PAINT ON THY FACE IS VERY THICK. MAYBE TOO THICK?
OH!
I AM MOST MORTIFIED, MY LORD. BUT I HAVE OF LATE NOTED SO MANY LINES ON MY FACE, AND BLEMISHES ALSO, THAT I CANNOT HELP BUT TRY TO COVER THEM WITH PAINT...

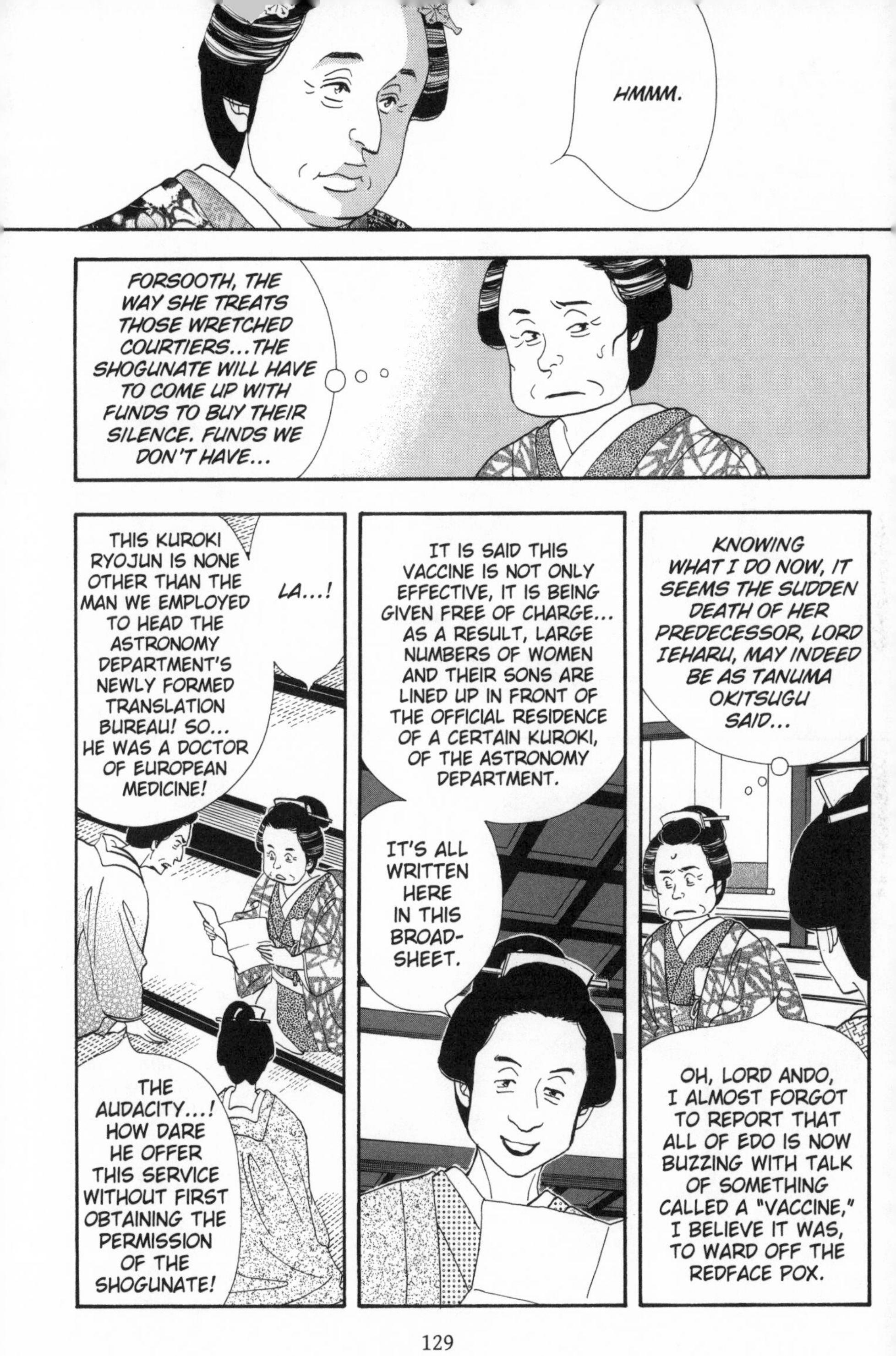
HMMM.
FORSOOTH, THE WAY SHE TREATS THOSE WRETCHED COURTIERS...THE SHOGUNATE WILL HAVE TO COME UP WITH FUNDS TO BUY THEIR SILENCE. FUNDS WE DON'T HAVE...
KNOWING WHAT I DO NOW, IT SEEMS THE SUDDEN DEATH OF HER PREDECESSOR, LORD IEHARU, MAY INDEED BE AS TANUMA OKITSUGU SAID...
OH, LORD ANDO, I ALMOST FORGOT TO REPORT THAT ALL OF EDO IS NOW BUZZING WITH TALK OF SOMETHING CALLED A "VACCINE," I BELIEVE IT WAS, TO WARD OFF THE REDFACE POX.
IT IS SAID THIS VACCINE IS NOT ONLY EFFECTIVE, IT IS BEING GIVEN FREE OF CHARGE... AS A RESULT, LARGE NUMBERS OF WOMEN AND THEIR SONS ARE LINED UP IN FRONT OF THE OFFICIAL RESIDENCE OF A CERTAIN KUROKI, OF THE ASTRONOMY DEPARTMENT.
IT'S ALL WRITTEN HERE IN THIS BROAD-SHEET.
LA...!
THIS KUROKI RYOJUN IS NONE OTHER THAN THE MAN WE EMPLOYED TO HEAD THE ASTRONOMY DEPARTMENT'S NEWLY FORMED TRANSLATION BUREAU! SO... HE WAS A DOCTOR OF EUROPEAN MEDICINE!
THE AUDACITY...! HOW DARE HE OFFER THIS SERVICE WITHOUT FIRST OBTAINING THE PERMISSION OF THE SHOGUNATE!

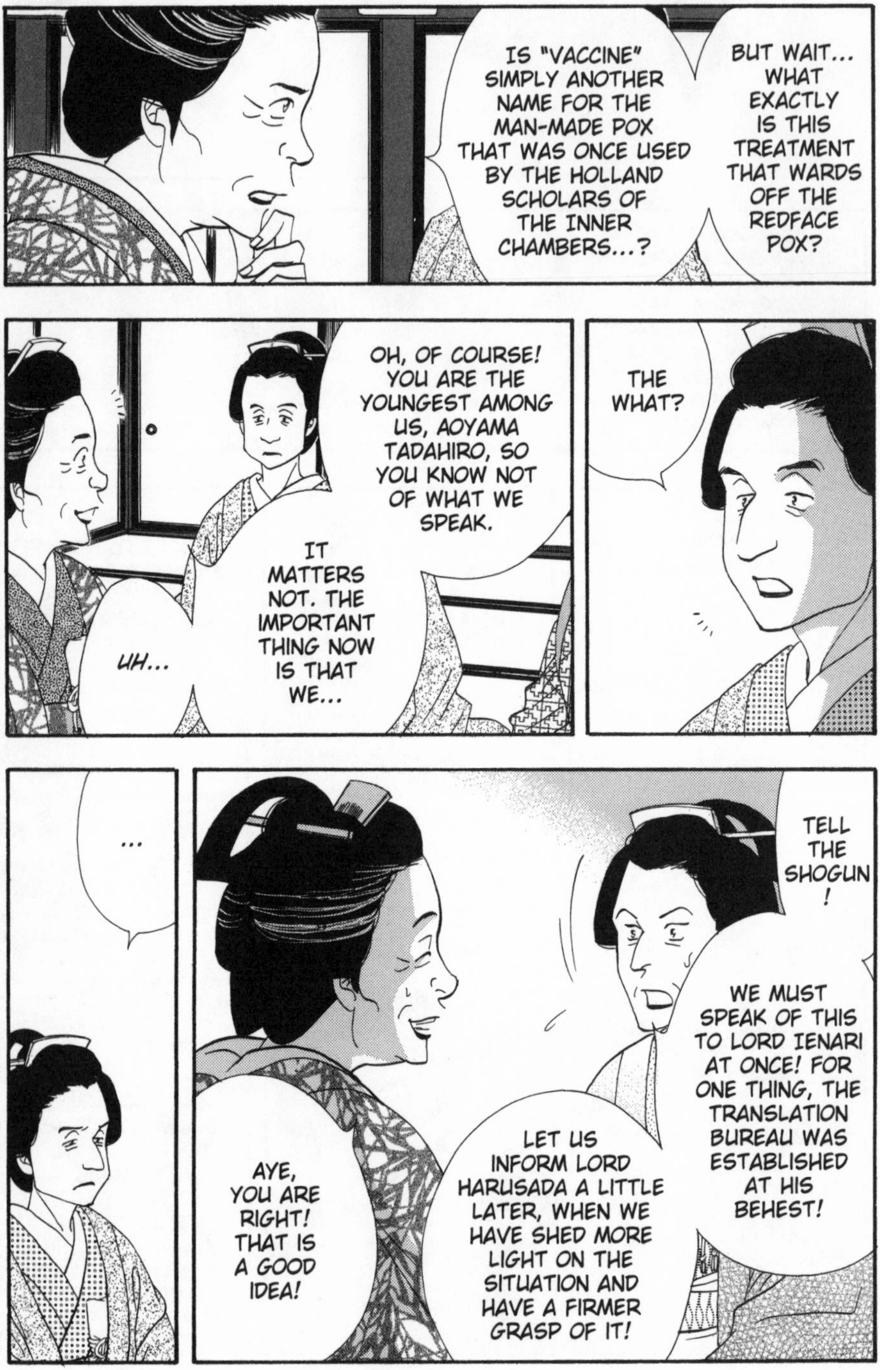
BUT WAIT... WHAT EXACTLY IS THIS TREATMENT THAT WARDS OFF THE REDFACE POX?
IS "VACCINE" SIMPLY ANOTHER NAME FOR THE MAN-MADE POX THAT WAS ONCE USED BY THE HOLLAND SCHOLARS OF THE INNER CHAMBERS...?
THE WHAT?
OH, OF COURSE! YOU ARE THE YOUNGEST AMONG US, AOYAMA TADAHIRO, SO YOU KNOW NOT OF WHAT WE SPEAK.
IT MATTERS NOT. THE IMPORTANT THING NOW IS THAT WE...
UH...
TELL THE SHOGUN!
WE MUST SPEAK OF THIS TO LORD IENARI AT ONCE! FOR ONE THING, THE TRANSLATION BUREAU WAS ESTABLISHED AT HIS BEHEST!
LET US INFORM LORD HARUSADA A LITTLE LATER, WHEN WE HAVE SHED MORE LIGHT ON THE SITUATION AND HAVE A FIRMER GRASP OF IT!
AYE, YOU ARE RIGHT! THAT IS A GOOD IDEA!
...

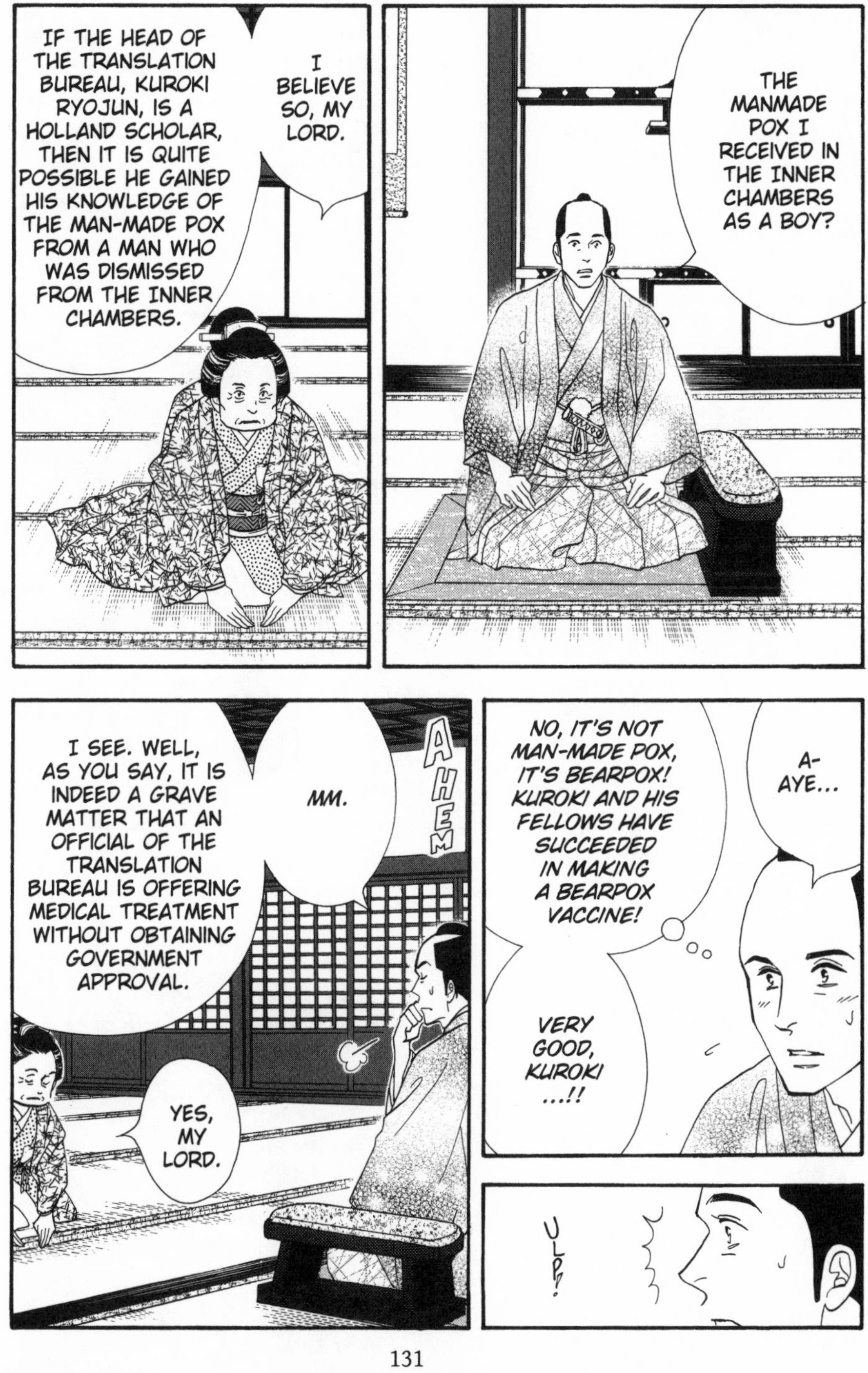
THE MANMADE POX I RECEIVED IN THE INNER CHAMBERS AS A BOY?
I BELIEVE SO, MY LORD.
IF THE HEAD OF THE TRANSLATION BUREAU, KUROKI RYOJUN, IS A HOLLAND SCHOLAR, THEN IT IS QUITE POSSIBLE HE GAINED HIS KNOWLEDGE OF THE MAN-MADE POX FROM A MAN WHO WAS DISMISSED FROM THE INNER CHAMBERS.
A- AYE...
NO, IT'S NOT MAN-MADE POX, IT'S BEARPOX! KUROKI AND HIS FELLOWS HAVE SUCCEEDED IN MAKING A BEARPOX VACCINE!
VERY GOOD, KUROKI ...!!
ULP!
AHEM
MM.
I SEE. WELL, AS YOU SAY, IT IS INDEED A GRAVE MATTER THAT AN OFFICIAL OF THE TRANSLATION BUREAU IS OFFERING MEDICAL TREATMENT WITHOUT OBTAINING GOVERNMENT APPROVAL.
YES, MY LORD.

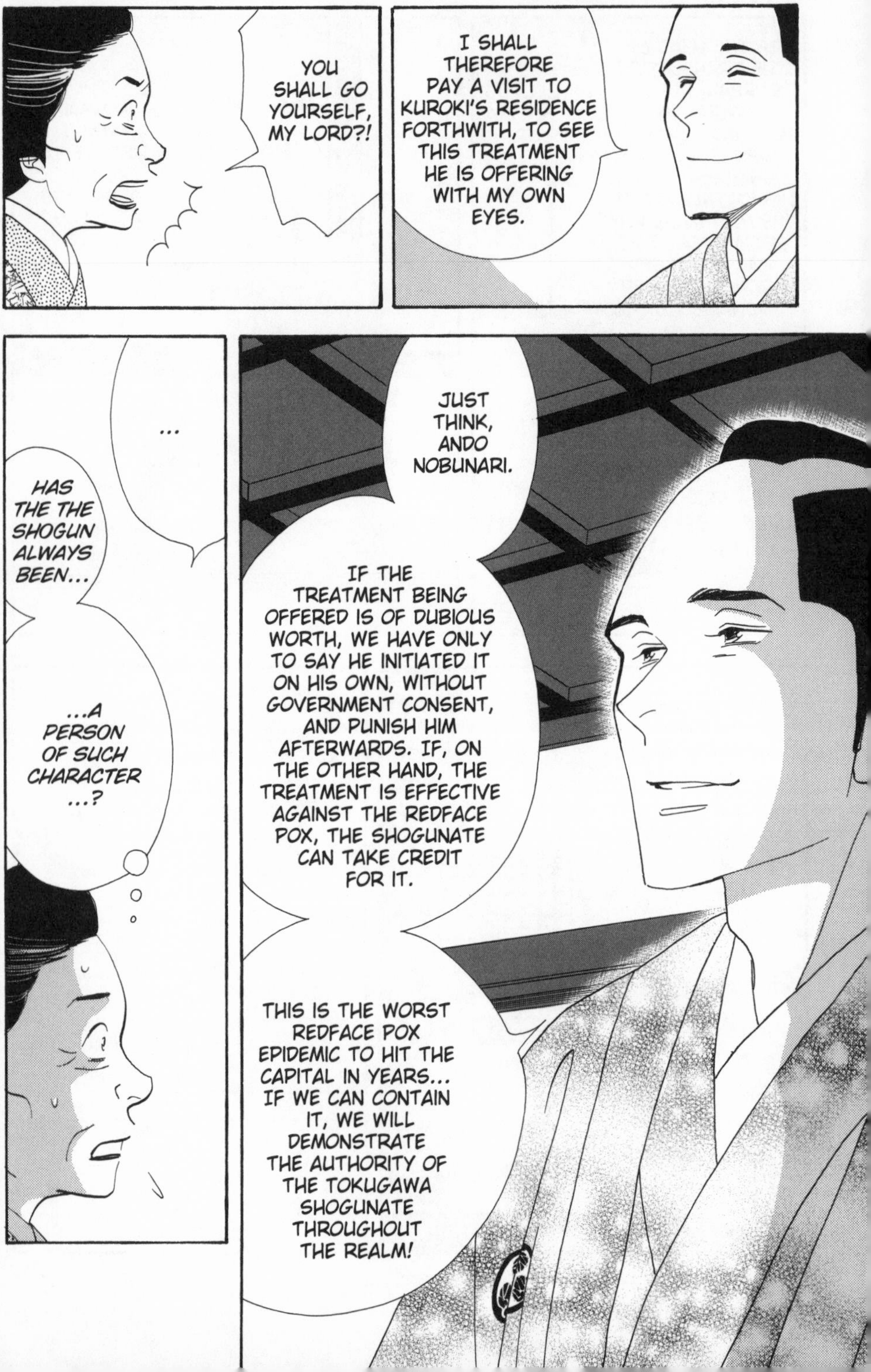
I SHALL THEREFORE PAY A VISIT TO KUROKI'S RESIDENCE FORTHWITH, TO SEE THIS TREATMENT HE IS OFFERING WITH MY OWN EYES.
YOU SHALL GO YOURSELF, MY LORD?!
JUST THINK, ANDO NOBUNARI.
IF THE TREATMENT BEING OFFERED IS OF DUBIOUS WORTH, WE HAVE ONLY TO SAY HE INITIATED IT ON HIS OWN, WITHOUT GOVERNMENT CONSENT, AND PUNISH HIM AFTERWARDS. IF, ON THE OTHER HAND, THE TREATMENT IS EFFECTIVE AGAINST THE REDFACE POX, THE SHOGUNATE CAN TAKE CREDIT FOR IT.
THIS IS THE WORST REDFACE POX EPIDEMIC TO HIT THE CAPITAL IN YEARS... IF WE CAN CONTAIN IT, WE WILL DEMONSTRATE THE AUTHORITY OF THE TOKUGAWA SHOGUNATE THROUGHOUT THE REALM!
...
HAS THE THE SHOGUN ALWAYS BEEN...
...A PERSON OF SUCH CHARACTER...?

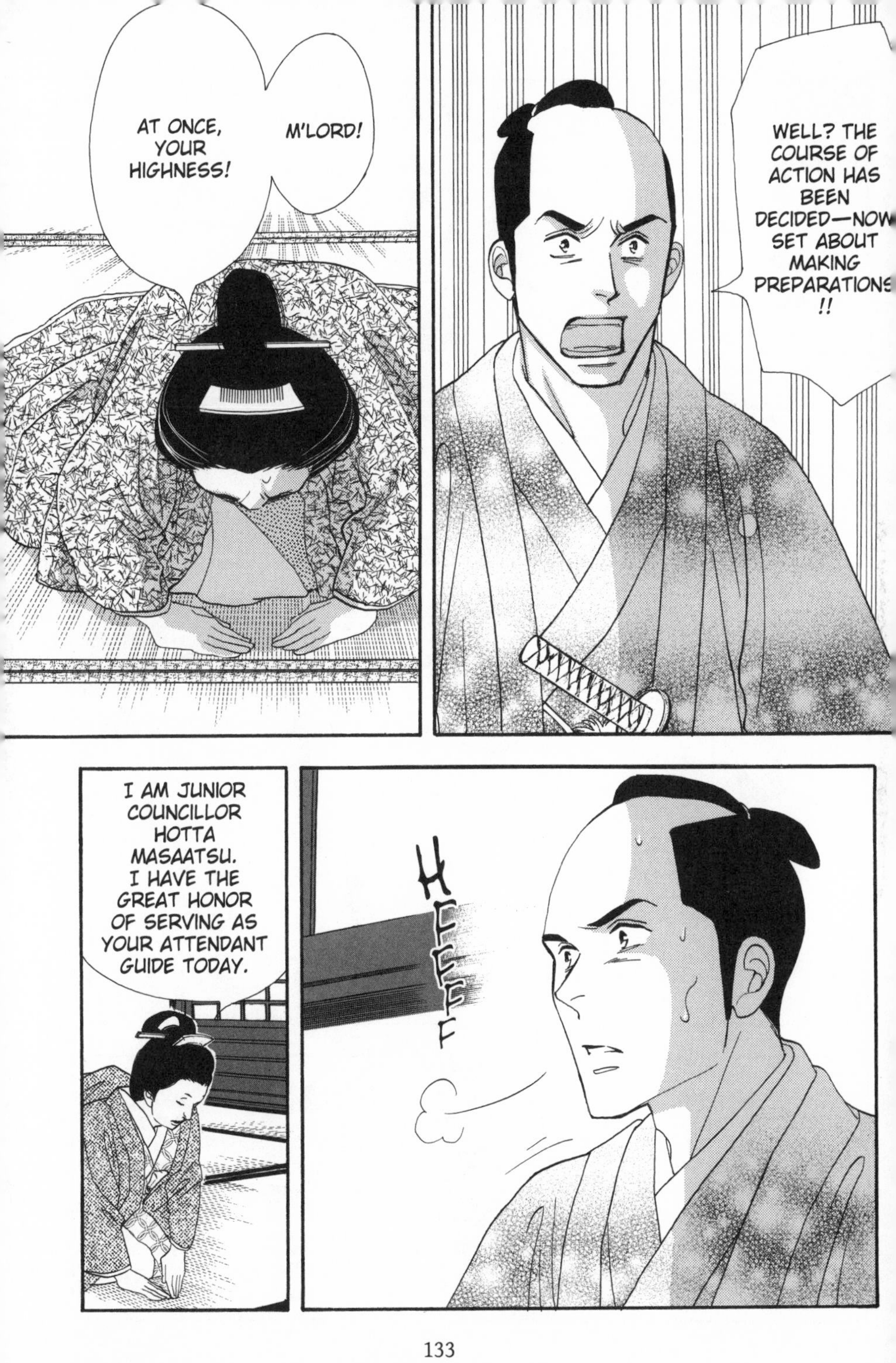
WELL? THE COURSE OF ACTION HAS BEEN DECIDED—NOW SET ABOUT MAKING PREPARATIONS!!
M'LORD!
AT ONCE, YOUR HIGHNESS!
HFFFF
I AM JUNIOR COUNCILLOR HOTTA MASAATSU. I HAVE THE GREAT HONOR OF SERVING AS YOUR ATTENDANT GUIDE TODAY.

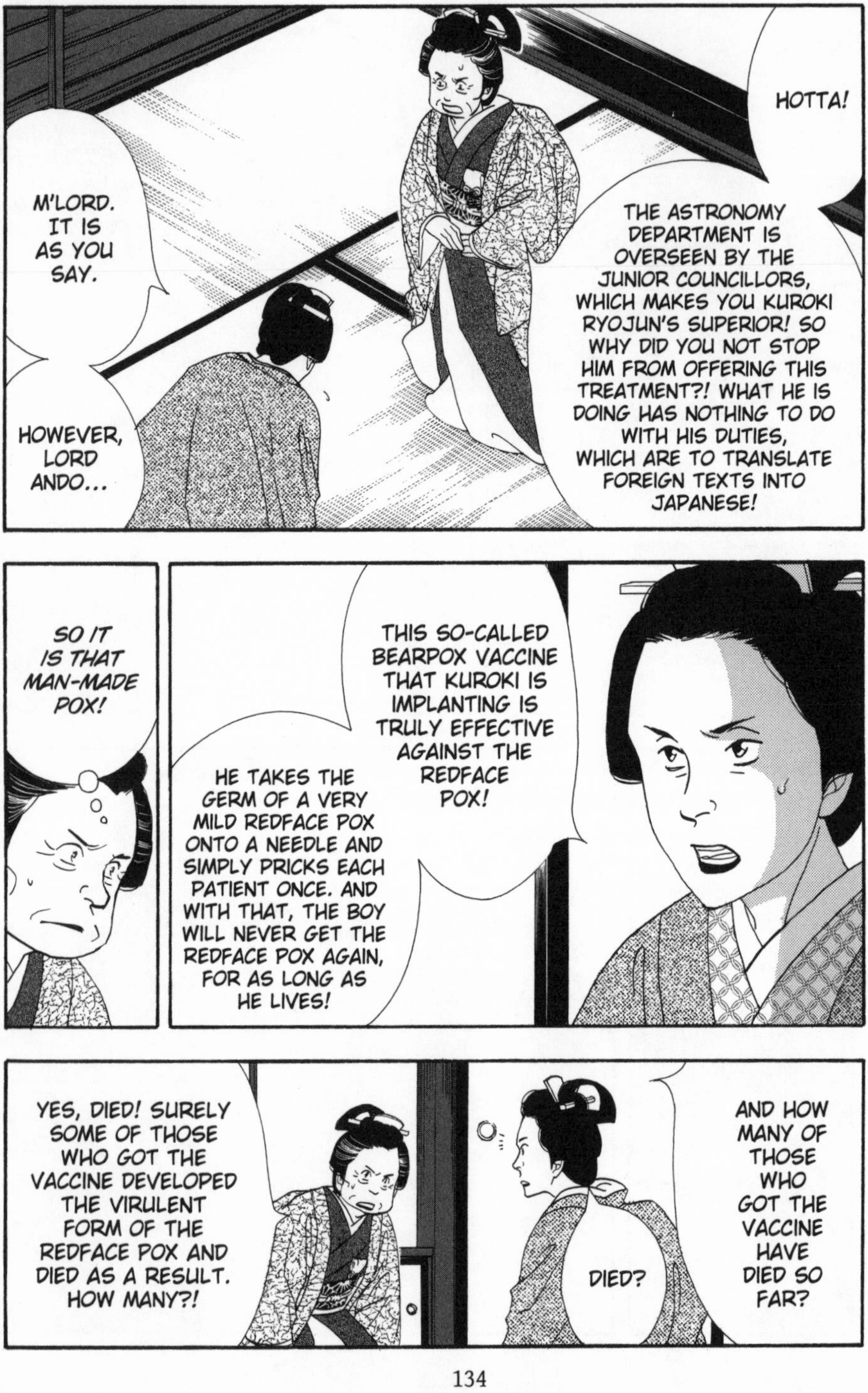
HOTTA!
THE ASTRONOMY DEPARTMENT IS OVERSEEN BY THE JUNIOR COUNCILLORS, WHICH MAKES YOU KUROKI RYOJUN'S SUPERIOR! SO WHY DID YOU NOT STOP HIM FROM OFFERING THIS TREATMENT?! WHAT HE IS DOING HAS NOTHING TO DO WITH HIS DUTIES, WHICH ARE TO TRANSLATE FOREIGN TEXTS INTO JAPANESE!
M'LORD. IT IS AS YOU SAY.
HOWEVER, LORD ANDO...
THIS SO-CALLED BEARPOX VACCINE THAT KUROKI IS IMPLANTING IS TRULY EFFECTIVE AGAINST THE REDFACE POX!
HE TAKES THE GERM OF A VERY MILD REDFACE POX ONTO A NEEDLE AND SIMPLY PRICKS EACH PATIENT ONCE. AND WITH THAT, THE BOY WILL NEVER GET THE REDFACE POX AGAIN, FOR AS LONG AS HE LIVES!
SO IT IS THAT MAN-MADE POX!
AND HOW MANY OF THOSE WHO GOT THE VACCINE HAVE DIED SO FAR?
DIED?
YES, DIED! SURELY SOME OF THOSE WHO GOT THE VACCINE DEVELOPED THE VIRULENT FORM OF THE REDFACE POX AND DIED AS A RESULT. HOW MANY?!

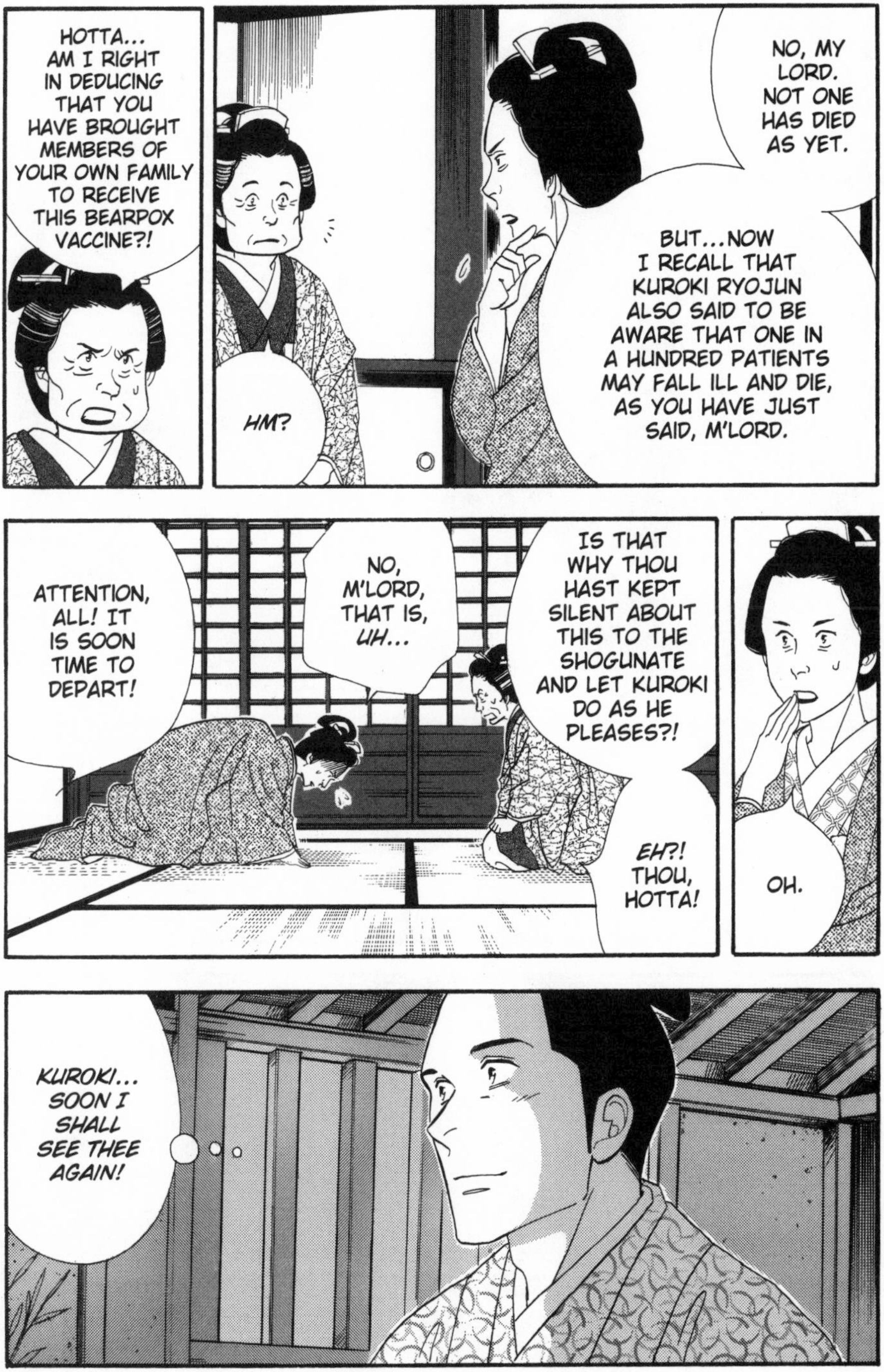
NO, MY LORD. NOT ONE HAS DIED AS YET.
BUT...NOW I RECALL THAT KUROKI RYOJUN ALSO SAID TO BE AWARE THAT ONE IN A HUNDRED PATIENTS MAY FALL ILL AND DIE, AS YOU HAVE JUST SAID, M'LORD.
HM?
HOTTA... AM I RIGHT IN DEDUCING THAT YOU HAVE BROUGHT MEMBERS OF YOUR OWN FAMILY TO RECEIVE THIS BEARPOX VACCINE?!
OH.
IS THAT WHY THOU HAST KEPT SILENT ABOUT THIS TO THE SHOGUNATE AND LET KUROKI DO AS HE PLEASES?!
EH?! THOU, HOTTA!
NO, M'LORD, THAT IS, UH...
ATTENTION, ALL! IT IS SOON TIME TO DEPART!
KUROKI... SOON I SHALL SEE THEE AGAIN!

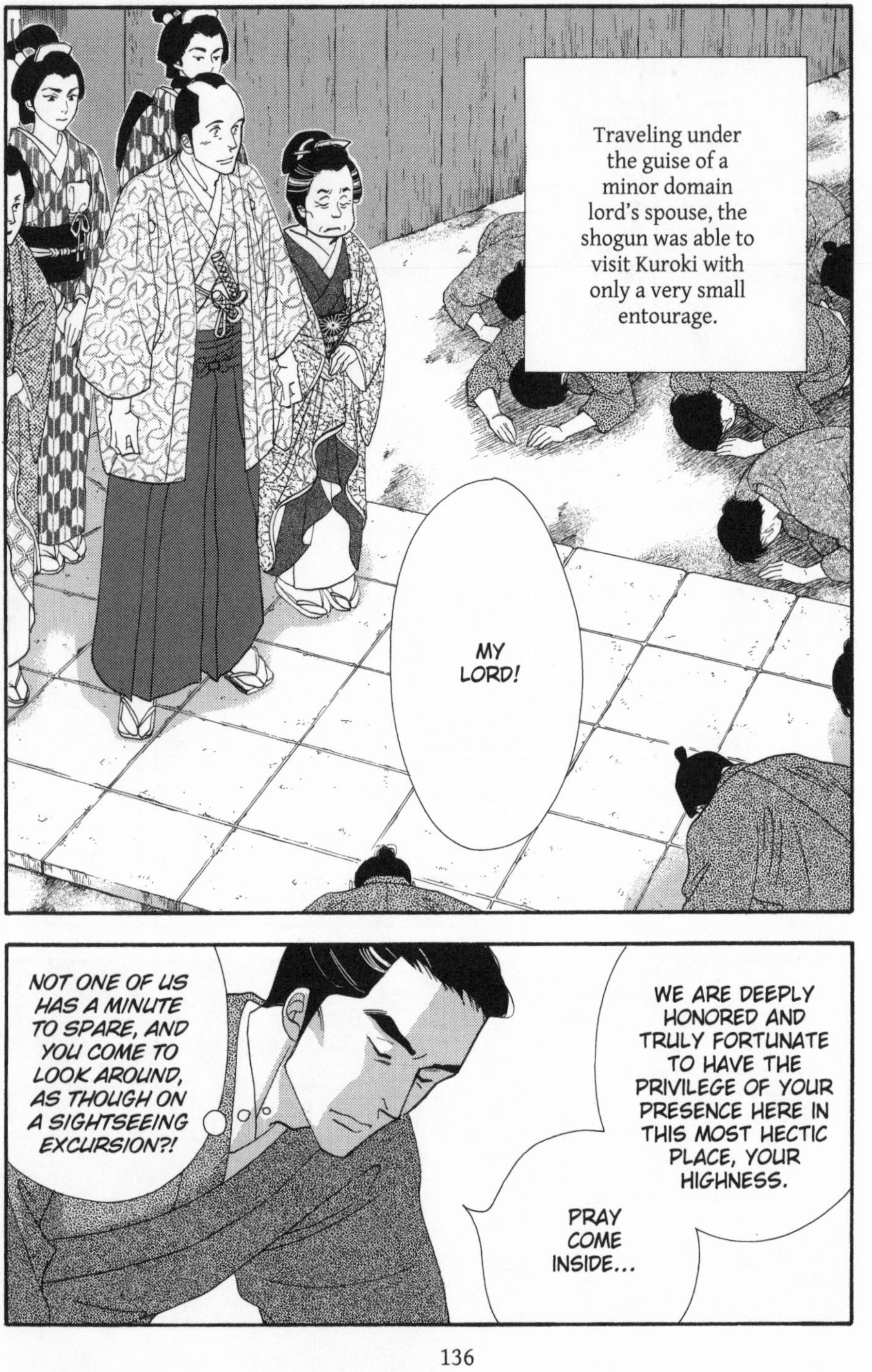
Traveling under the guise of a minor domain lord's spouse, the shogun was able to visit Kuroki with only a very small entourage.
MY LORD!
WE ARE DEEPLY HONORED AND TRULY FORTUNATE TO HAVE THE PRIVILEGE OF YOUR PRESENCE HERE IN THIS MOST HECTIC PLACE, YOUR HIGHNESS.
PRAY COME INSIDE...
NOT ONE OF US HAS A MINUTE TO SPARE, AND YOU COME TO LOOK AROUND, AS THOUGH ON A SIGHTSEEING EXCURSION?!

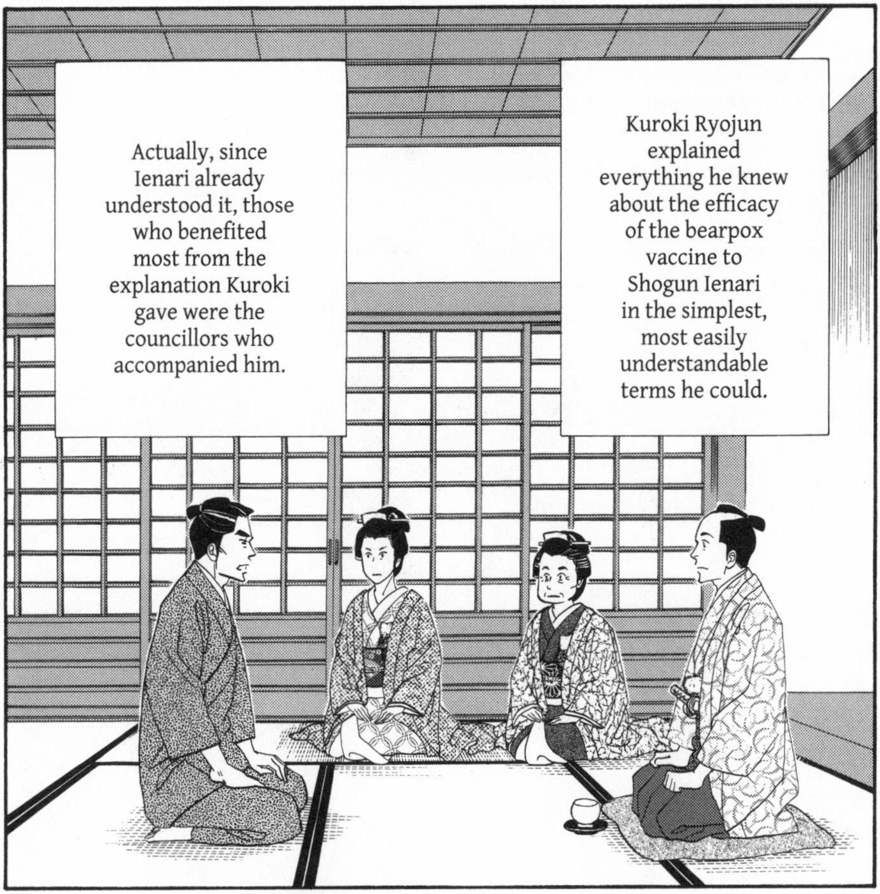
Kuroki Ryojun explained everything he knew about the efficacy of the bearpox vaccine to Shogun Ienari in the simplest, most easily understandable terms he could.
Actually, since Ienari already understood it, those who benefited most from the explanation Kuroki gave were the councillors who accompanied him.

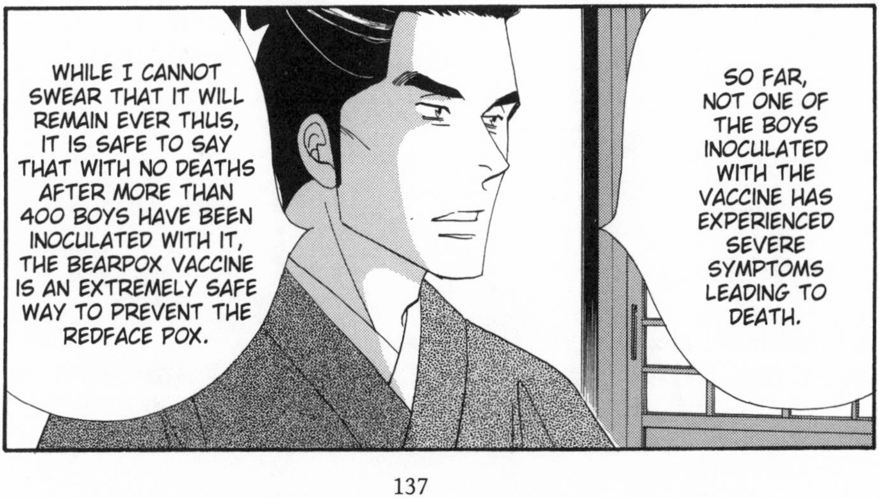
SO FAR, NOT ONE OF THE BOYS INOCULATED WITH THE VACCINE HAS EXPERIENCED SEVERE SYMPTOMS LEADING TO DEATH.
WHILE I CANNOT SWEAR THAT IT WILL REMAIN EVER THUS, IT IS SAFE TO SAY THAT WITH NO DEATHS AFTER MORE THAN 400 BOYS HAVE BEEN INOCULATED WITH IT, THE BEARPOX VACCINE IS AN EXTREMELY SAFE WAY TO PREVENT THE REDFACE POX.

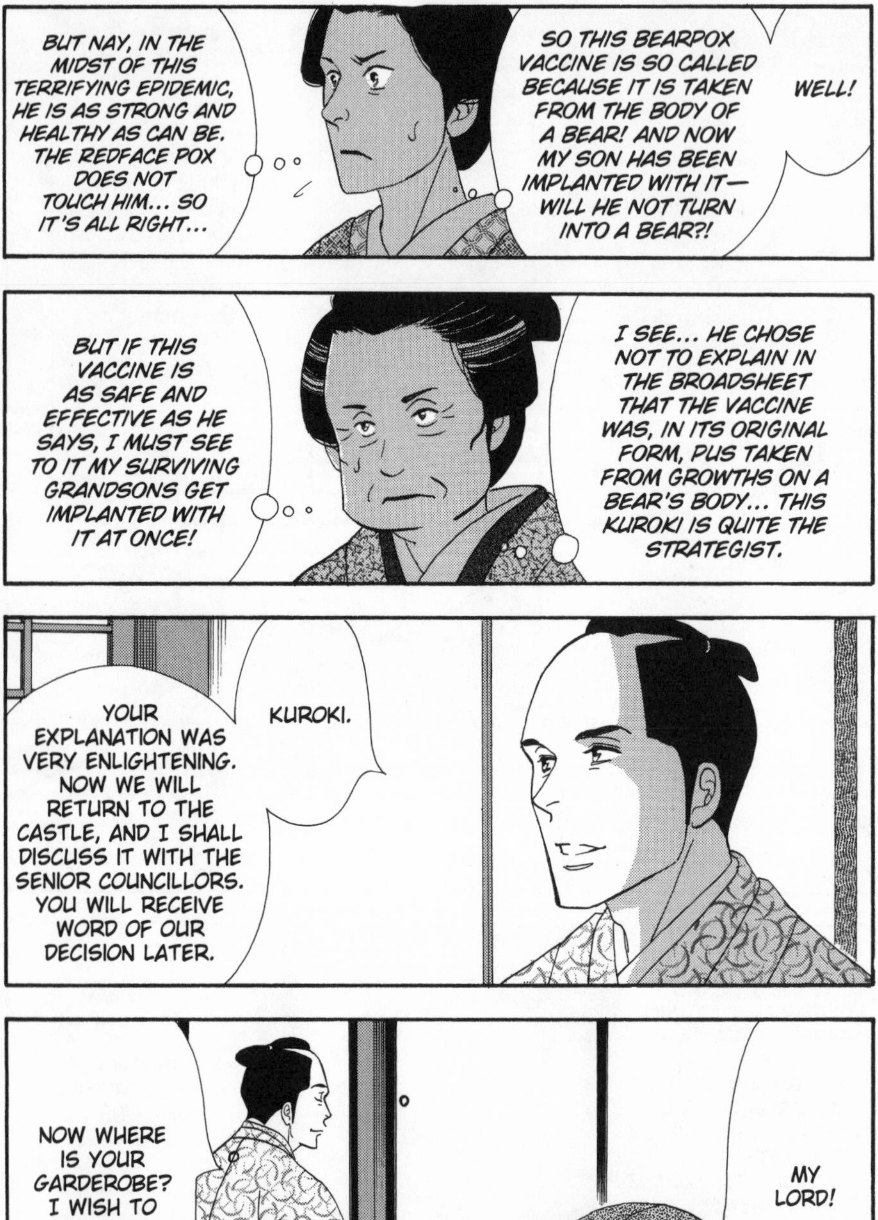
WELL!
SO THIS BEARPOX VACCINE IS SO CALLED BECAUSE IT IS TAKEN FROM THE BODY OF A BEAR! AND NOW MY SON HAS BEEN IMPLANTED WITH IT— WILL HE NOT TURN INTO A BEAR?!
BUT NAY, IN THE MIDST OF THIS TERRIFYING EPIDEMIC, HE IS AS STRONG AND HEALTHY AS CAN BE. THE REDFACE POX DOES NOT TOUCH HIM... SO IT'S ALL RIGHT...
I SEE... HE CHOSE NOT TO EXPLAIN IN THE BROADSHEET THAT THE VACCINE WAS, IN ITS ORIGINAL FORM, PUS TAKEN FROM GROWTHS ON A BEAR'S BODY... THIS KUROKI IS QUITE THE STRATEGIST.
BUT IF THIS VACCINE IS AS SAFE AND EFFECTIVE AS HE SAYS, I MUST SEE TO IT MY SURVIVING GRANDSONS GET IMPLANTED WITH IT AT ONCE!
KUROKI.
YOUR EXPLANATION WAS VERY ENLIGHTENING. NOW WE WILL RETURN TO THE CASTLE, AND I SHALL DISCUSS IT WITH THE SENIOR COUNCILLORS. YOU WILL RECEIVE WORD OF OUR DECISION LATER.
MY LORD!
NOW WHERE IS YOUR GARDEROBE? I WISH TO RELIEVE MYSELF.

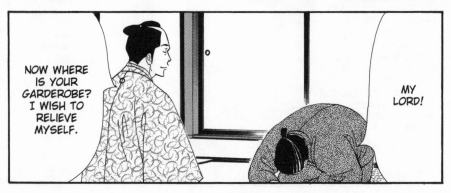

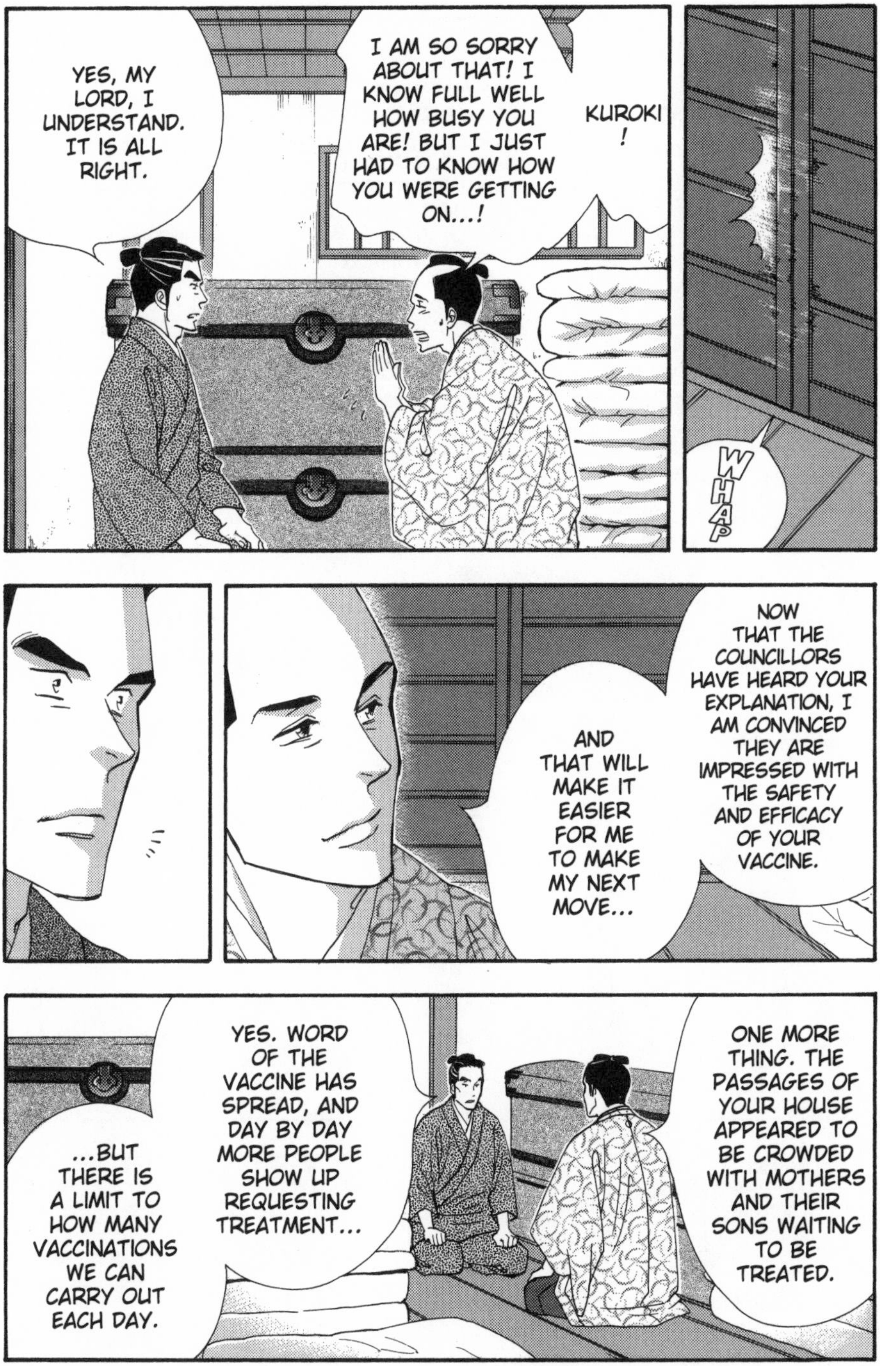
WHAP
KUROKI!
I AM SO SORRY ABOUT THAT! I KNOW FULL WELL HOW BUSY YOU ARE! BUT I JUST HAD TO KNOW HOW YOU WERE GETTING ON...!
YES, MY LORD, I UNDERSTAND. IT IS ALL RIGHT.
NOW THAT THE COUNCILLORS HAVE HEARD YOUR EXPLANATION, I AM CONVINCED THEY ARE IMPRESSED WITH THE SAFETY AND EFFICACY OF YOUR VACCINE.
AND THAT WILL MAKE IT EASIER FOR ME TO MAKE MY NEXT MOVE...
ONE MORE THING. THE PASSAGES OF YOUR HOUSE APPEARED TO BE CROWDED WITH MOTHERS AND THEIR SONS WAITING TO BE TREATED.
YES. WORD OF THE VACCINE HAS SPREAD, AND DAY BY DAY MORE PEOPLE SHOW UP REQUESTING TREATMENT...
...BUT THERE IS A LIMIT TO HOW MANY VACCINATIONS WE CAN CARRY OUT EACH DAY.

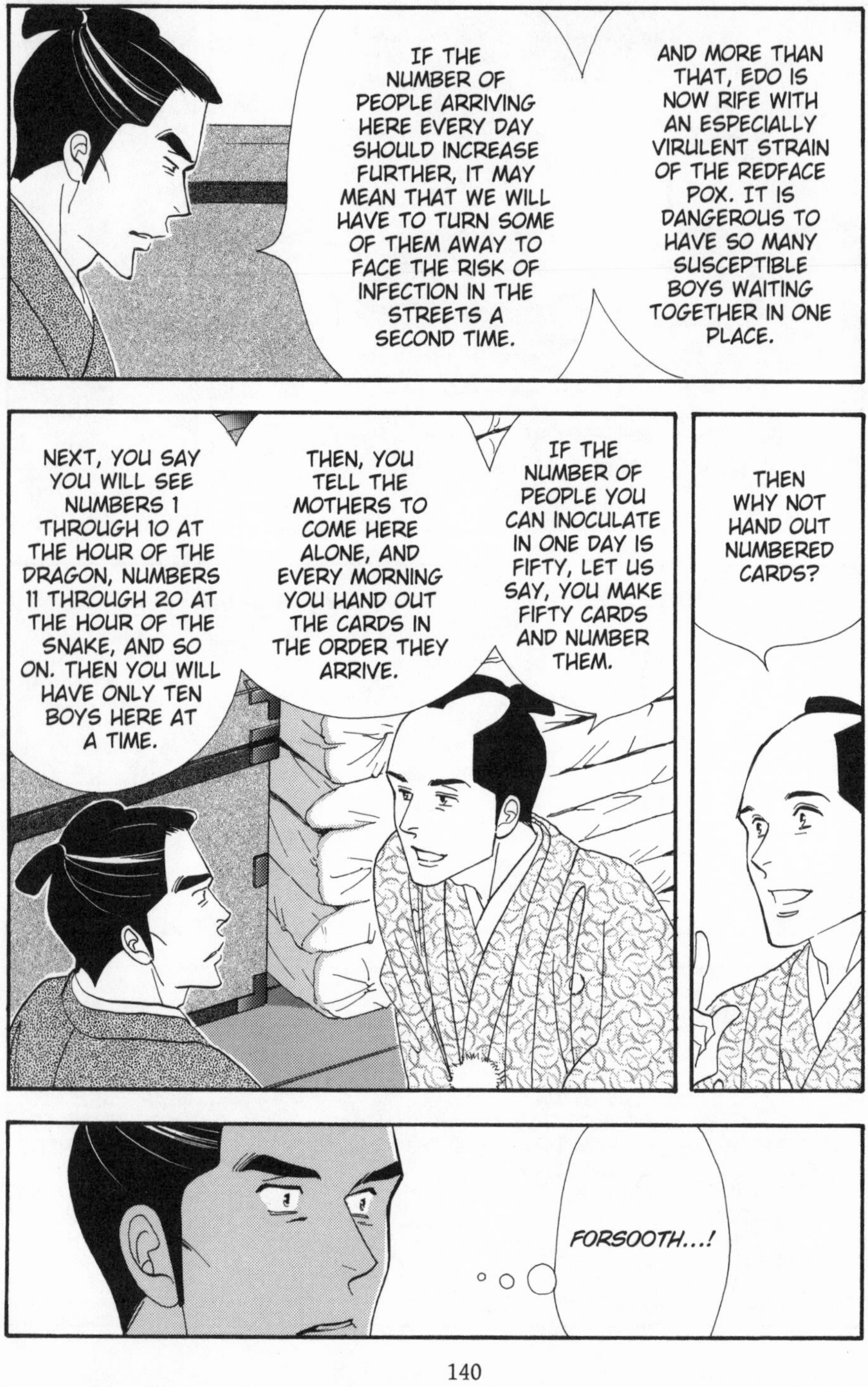
IF THE NUMBER OF PEOPLE ARRIVING HERE EVERY DAY SHOULD INCREASE FURTHER, IT MAY MEAN THAT WE WILL HAVE TO TURN SOME OF THEM AWAY TO FACE THE RISK OF INFECTION IN THE STREETS A SECOND TIME.
AND MORE THAN THAT, EDO IS NOW RIFE WITH AN ESPECIALLY VIRULENT STRAIN OF THE REDFACE POX. IT IS DANGEROUS TO HAVE SO MANY SUSCEPTIBLE BOYS WAITING TOGETHER IN ONE PLACE.
THEN WHY NOT HAND OUT NUMBERED CARDS?
IF THE NUMBER OF PEOPLE YOU CAN INOCULATE IN ONE DAY IS FIFTY, LET US SAY, YOU MAKE FIFTY CARDS AND NUMBER THEM.
THEN, YOU TELL THE MOTHERS TO COME HERE ALONE, AND EVERY MORNING YOU HAND OUT THE CARDS IN THE ORDER THEY ARRIVE.
NEXT, YOU SAY YOU WILL SEE NUMBERS 1 THROUGH 10 AT THE HOUR OF THE DRAGON, NUMBERS 11 THROUGH 20 AT THE HOUR OF THE SNAKE, AND SO ON. THEN YOU WILL HAVE ONLY TEN BOYS HERE AT A TIME.
FORSOOTH...!

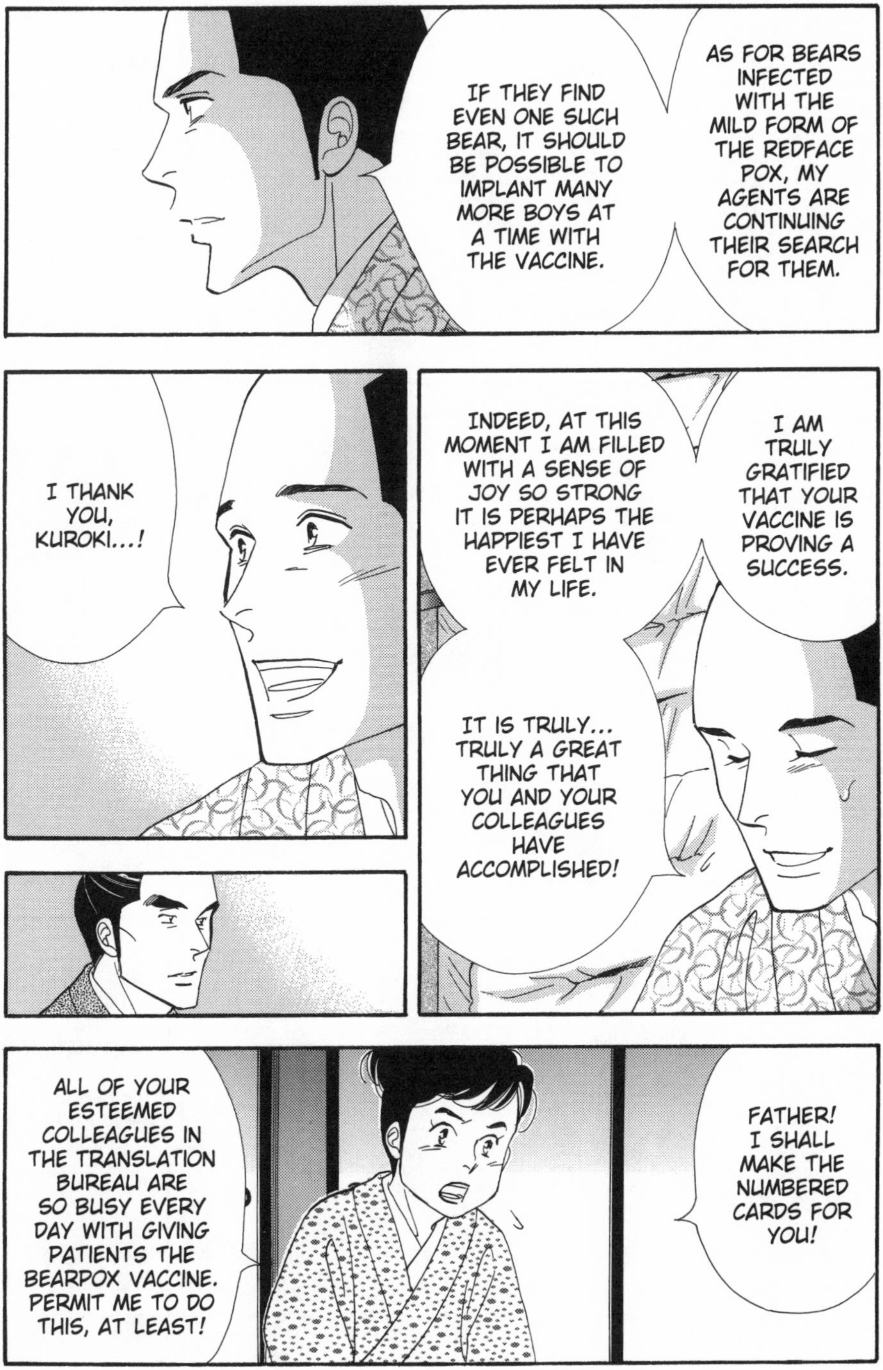

AS FOR BEARS INFECTED WITH THE MILD FORM OF THE REDFACE POX, MY AGENTS ARE CONTINUING THEIR SEARCH FOR THEM.
IF THEY FIND EVEN ONE SUCH BEAR, IT SHOULD BE POSSIBLE TO IMPLANT MANY MORE BOYS AT A TIME WITH THE VACCINE.
I AM TRULY GRATIFIED THAT YOUR VACCINE IS PROVING A SUCCESS.
INDEED, AT THIS MOMENT I AM FILLED WITH A SENSE OF JOY SO STRONG IT IS PERHAPS THE HAPPIEST I HAVE EVER FELT IN MY LIFE.
IT IS TRULY... TRULY A GREAT THING THAT YOU AND YOUR COLLEAGUES HAVE ACCOMPLISHED!
I THANK YOU, KUROKI...!
FATHER! I SHALL MAKE THE NUMBERED CARDS FOR YOU!
ALL OF YOUR ESTEEMED COLLEAGUES IN THE TRANSLATION BUREAU ARE SO BUSY EVERY DAY WITH GIVING PATIENTS THE BEARPOX VACCINE. PERMIT ME TO DO THIS, AT LEAST!

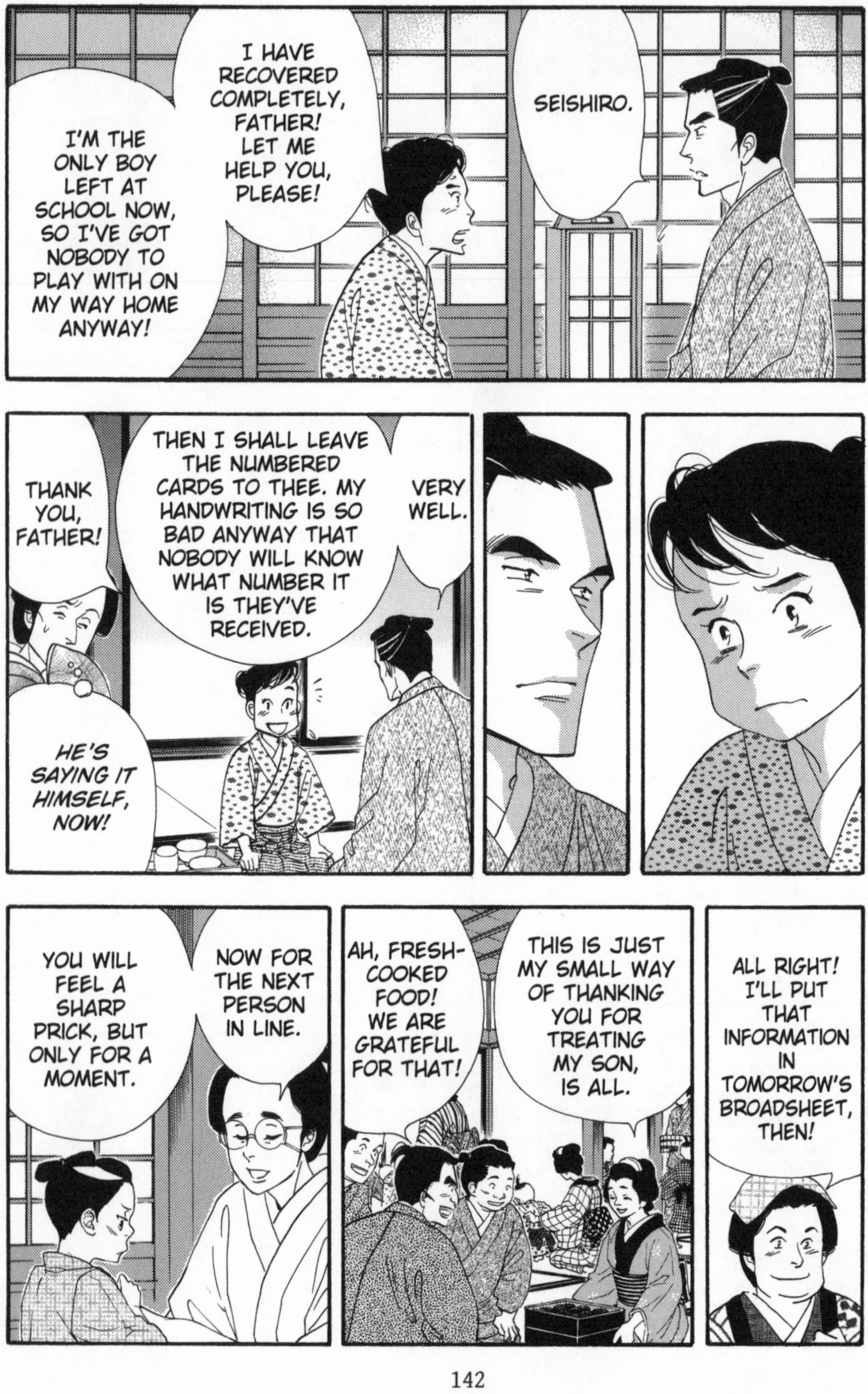
SEISHIRO.
I HAVE RECOVERED COMPLETELY, FATHER! LET ME HELP YOU, PLEASE!
I'M THE ONLY BOY LEFT AT SCHOOL NOW, SO I'VE GOT NOBODY TO PLAY WITH ON MY WAY HOME ANYWAY!
VERY WELL.
THEN I SHALL LEAVE THE NUMBERED CARDS TO THEE. MY HANDWRITING IS SO BAD ANYWAY THAT NOBODY WILL KNOW WHAT NUMBER IT IS THEY'VE RECEIVED.
THANK YOU, FATHER!
HE'S SAYING IT HIMSELF, NOW!
ALL RIGHT! I'LL PUT THAT INFORMATION IN TOMORROW'S BROADSHEET, THEN!
THIS IS JUST MY SMALL WAY OF THANKING YOU FOR TREATING MY SON, IS ALL.
AH, FRESH-COOKED FOOD! WE ARE GRATEFUL FOR THAT!
NOW FOR THE NEXT PERSON IN LINE.
YOU WILL FEEL A SHARP PRICK, BUT ONLY FOR A MOMENT.

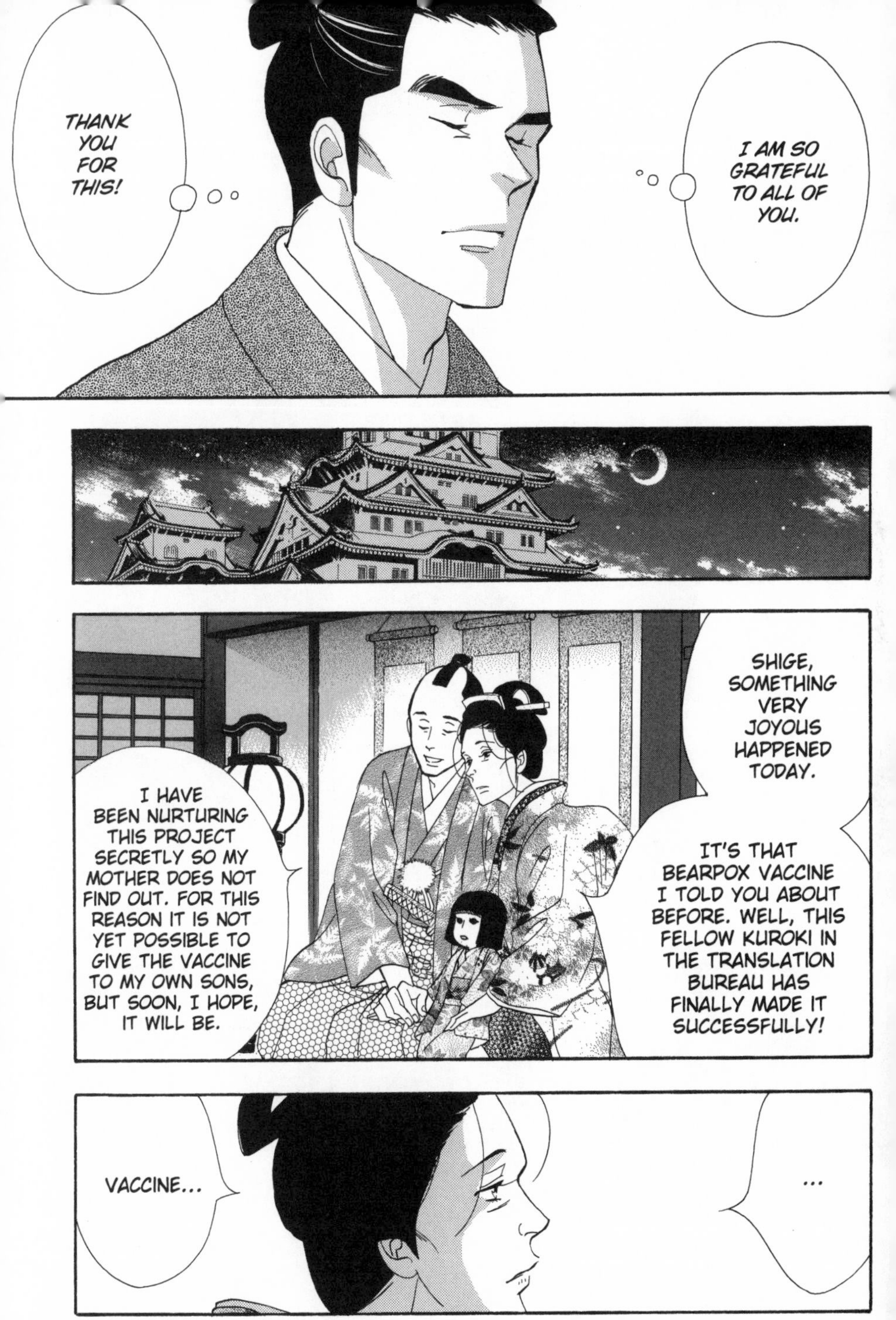
I AM SO GRATEFUL TO ALL OF YOU.
THANK YOU FOR THIS!
SHIGE, SOMETHING VERY JOYOUS HAPPENED TODAY.
IT'S THAT BEARPOX VACCINE I TOLD YOU ABOUT BEFORE. WELL, THIS FELLOW KUROKI IN THE TRANSLATION BUREAU HAS FINALLY MADE IT SUCCESSFULLY!
I HAVE BEEN NURTURING THIS PROJECT SECRETLY SO MY MOTHER DOES NOT FIND OUT. FOR THIS REASON IT IS NOT YET POSSIBLE TO GIVE THE VACCINE TO MY OWN SONS, BUT SOON, I HOPE, IT WILL BE.
...
VACCINE...

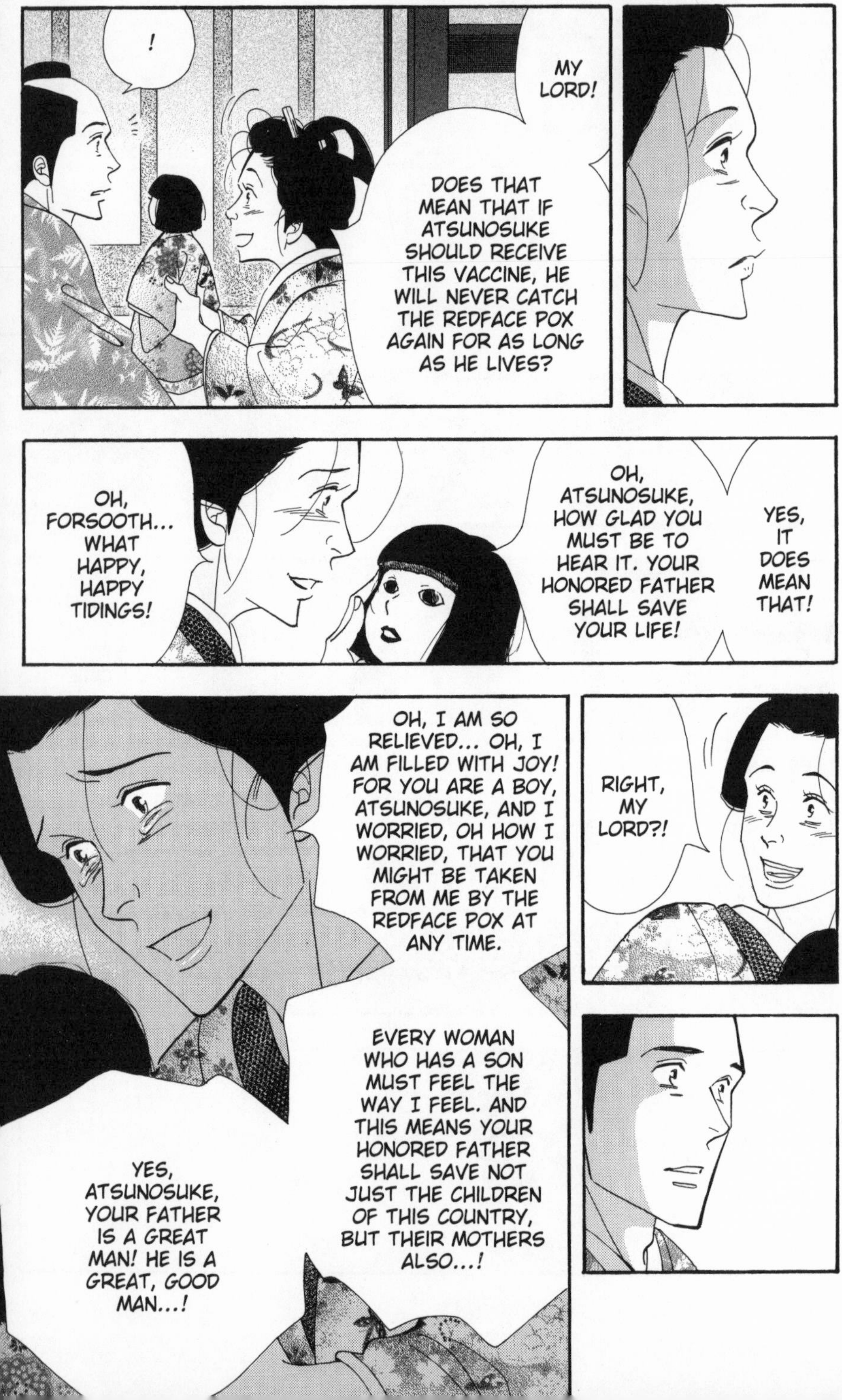
MY LORD!
DOES THAT MEAN THAT IF ATSUNOSUKE SHOULD RECEIVE THIS VACCINE, HE WILL NEVER CATCH THE REDFACE POX AGAIN FOR AS LONG AS HE LIVES?
!
YES, IT DOES MEAN THAT!
OH, ATSUNOSUKE, HOW GLAD YOU MUST BE TO HEAR IT. YOUR HONORED FATHER SHALL SAVE YOUR LIFE!
OH, FORSOOTH... WHAT HAPPY, HAPPY TIDINGS!
RIGHT, MY LORD?!
OH, I AM SO RELIEVED... OH, I AM FILLED WITH JOY! FOR YOU ARE A BOY, ATSUNOSUKE, AND I WORRIED, OH HOW I WORRIED, THAT YOU MIGHT BE TAKEN FROM ME BY THE REDFACE POX AT ANY TIME.
EVERY WOMAN WHO HAS A SON MUST FEEL THE WAY I FEEL. AND THIS MEANS YOUR HONORED FATHER SHALL SAVE NOT JUST THE CHILDREN OF THIS COUNTRY, BUT THEIR MOTHERS ALSO...!
YES, ATSUNOSUKE, YOUR FATHER IS A GREAT MAN! HE IS A GREAT, GOOD MAN...!

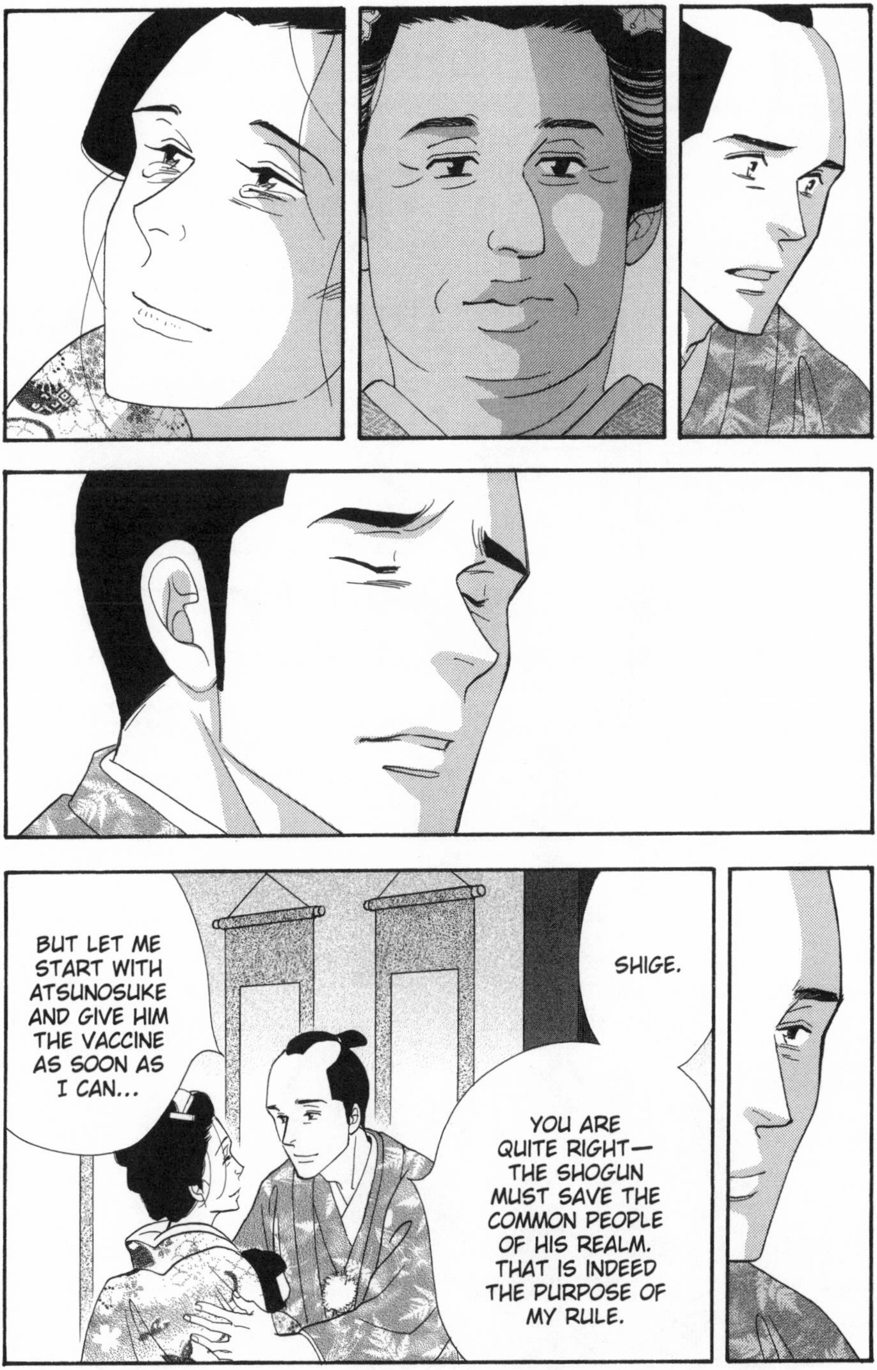
BUT LET ME START WITH ATSUNOSUKE AND GIVE HIM THE VACCINE AS SOON AS I CAN...
SHIGE.
YOU ARE QUITE RIGHT— THE SHOGUN MUST SAVE THE COMMON PEOPLE OF HIS REALM. THAT IS INDEED THE PURPOSE OF MY RULE.

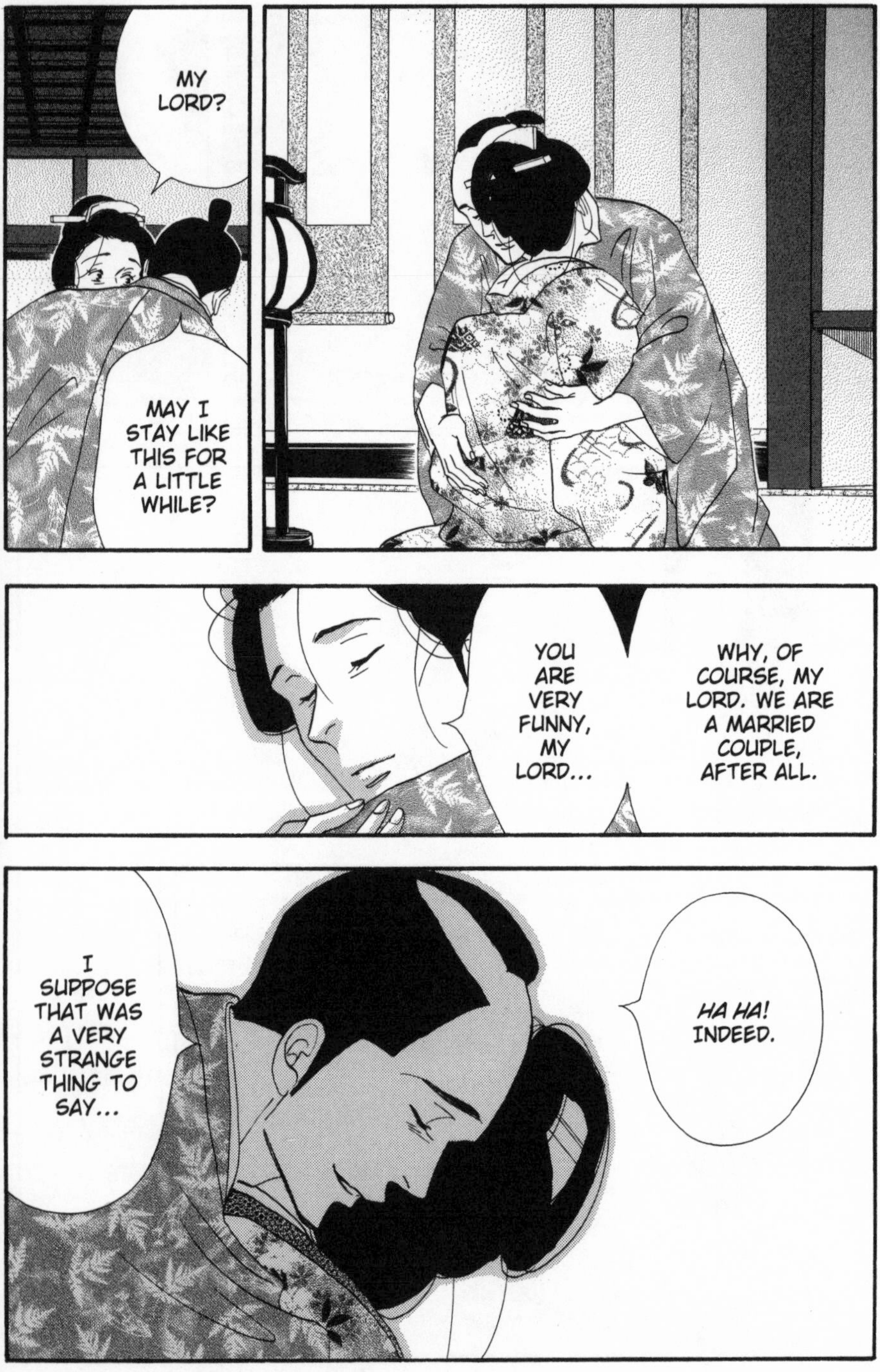
MY LORD?
MAY I STAY LIKE THIS FOR A LITTLE WHILE?
WHY, OF COURSE, MY LORD. WE ARE A MARRIED COUPLE, AFTER ALL.
YOU ARE VERY FUNNY, MY LORD...
HA HA! INDEED.
I SUPPOSE THAT WAS A VERY STRANGE THING TO SAY...

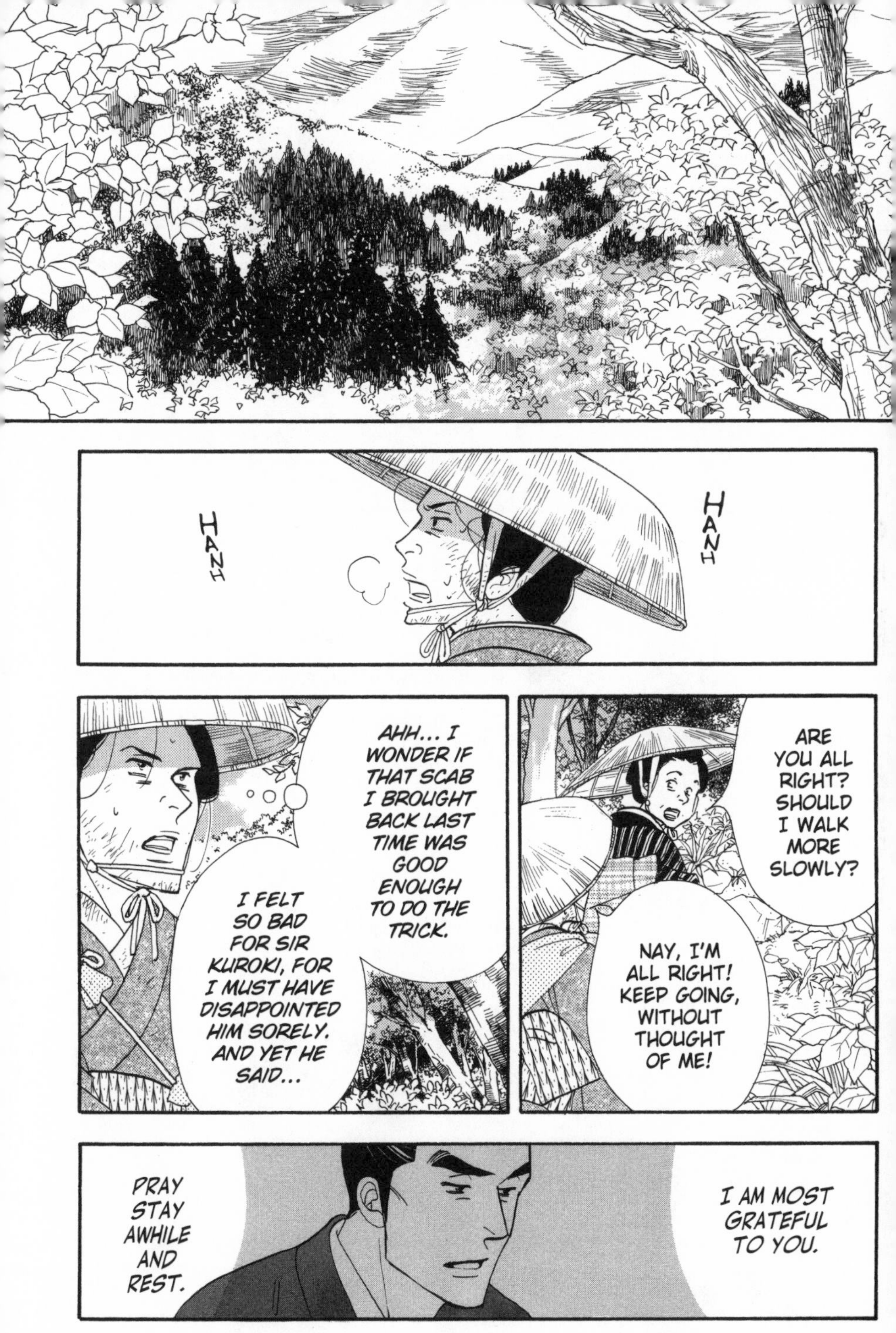
HANH
HANH
ARE YOU ALL RIGHT? SHOULD I WALK MORE SLOWLY?
NAY, I'M ALL RIGHT! KEEP GOING, WITHOUT THOUGHT OF ME!
AHH... I WONDER IF THAT SCAB I BROUGHT BACK LAST TIME WAS GOOD ENOUGH TO DO THE TRICK.
I FELT SO BAD FOR SIR KUROKI, FOR I MUST HAVE DISAPPOINTED HIM SORELY. AND YET HE SAID...
I AM MOST GRATEFUL TO YOU.
PRAY STAY AWHILE AND REST.

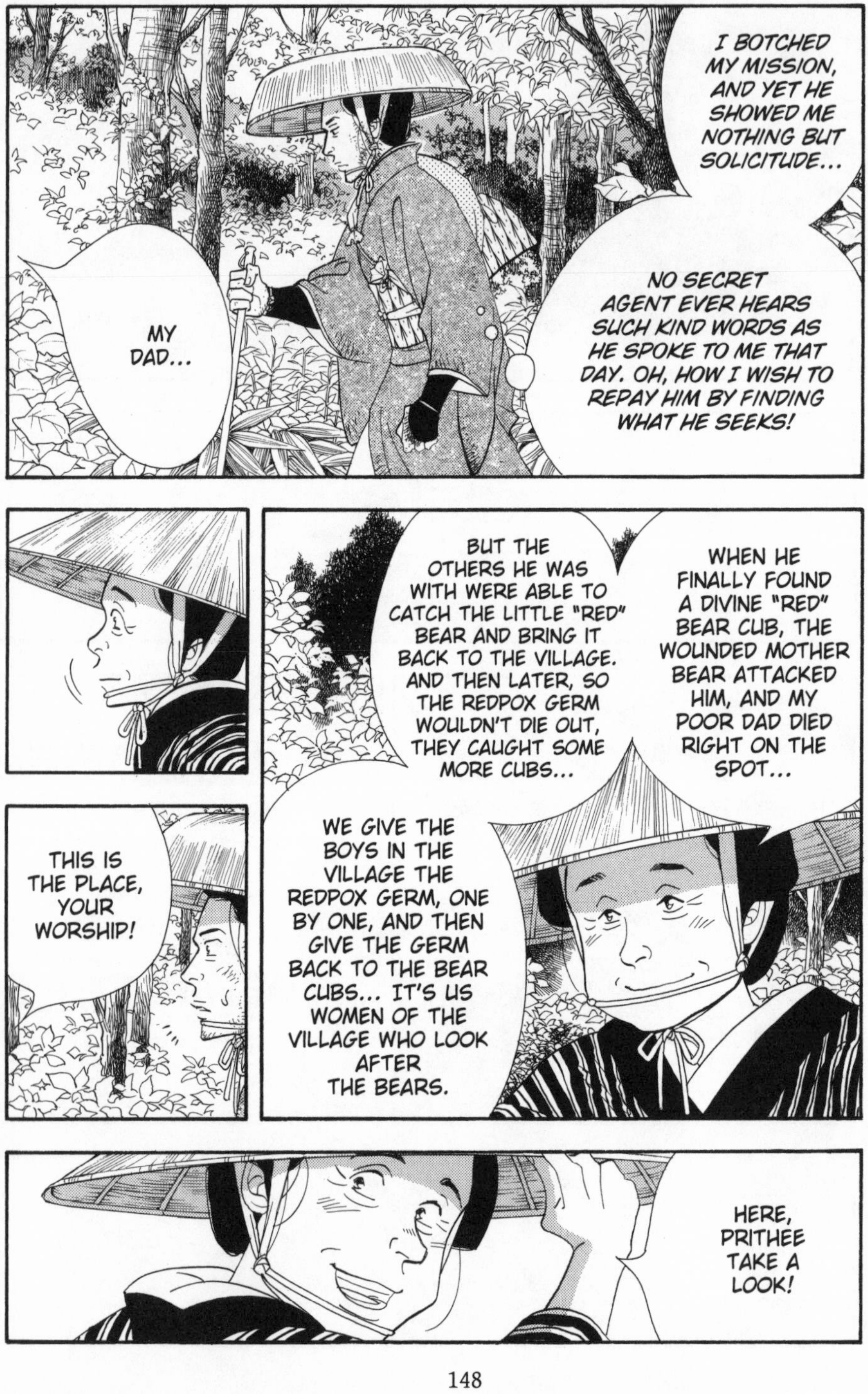

I BOTCHED MY MISSION, AND YET HE SHOWED ME NOTHING BUT SOLICITUDE...
NO SECRET AGENT EVER HEARS SUCH KIND WORDS AS HE SPOKE TO ME THAT DAY. OH, HOW I WISH TO REPAY HIM BY FINDING WHAT HE SEEKS!
MY DAD...
WHEN HE FINALLY FOUND A DIVINE "RED" BEAR CUB, THE WOUNDED MOTHER BEAR ATTACKED HIM, AND MY POOR DAD DIED RIGHT ON THE SPOT...
BUT THE OTHERS HE WAS WITH WERE ABLE TO CATCH THE LITTLE "RED" BEAR AND BRING IT BACK TO THE VILLAGE. AND THEN LATER, SO THE REDPOX GERM WOULDN'T DIE OUT, THEY CAUGHT SOME MORE CUBS...
WE GIVE THE BOYS IN THE VILLAGE THE REDPOX GERM, ONE BY ONE, AND THEN GIVE THE GERM BACK TO THE BEAR CUBS... IT'S US WOMEN OF THE VILLAGE WHO LOOK AFTER THE BEARS.
THIS IS THE PLACE, YOUR WORSHIP!
HERE, PRITHEE TAKE A LOOK!

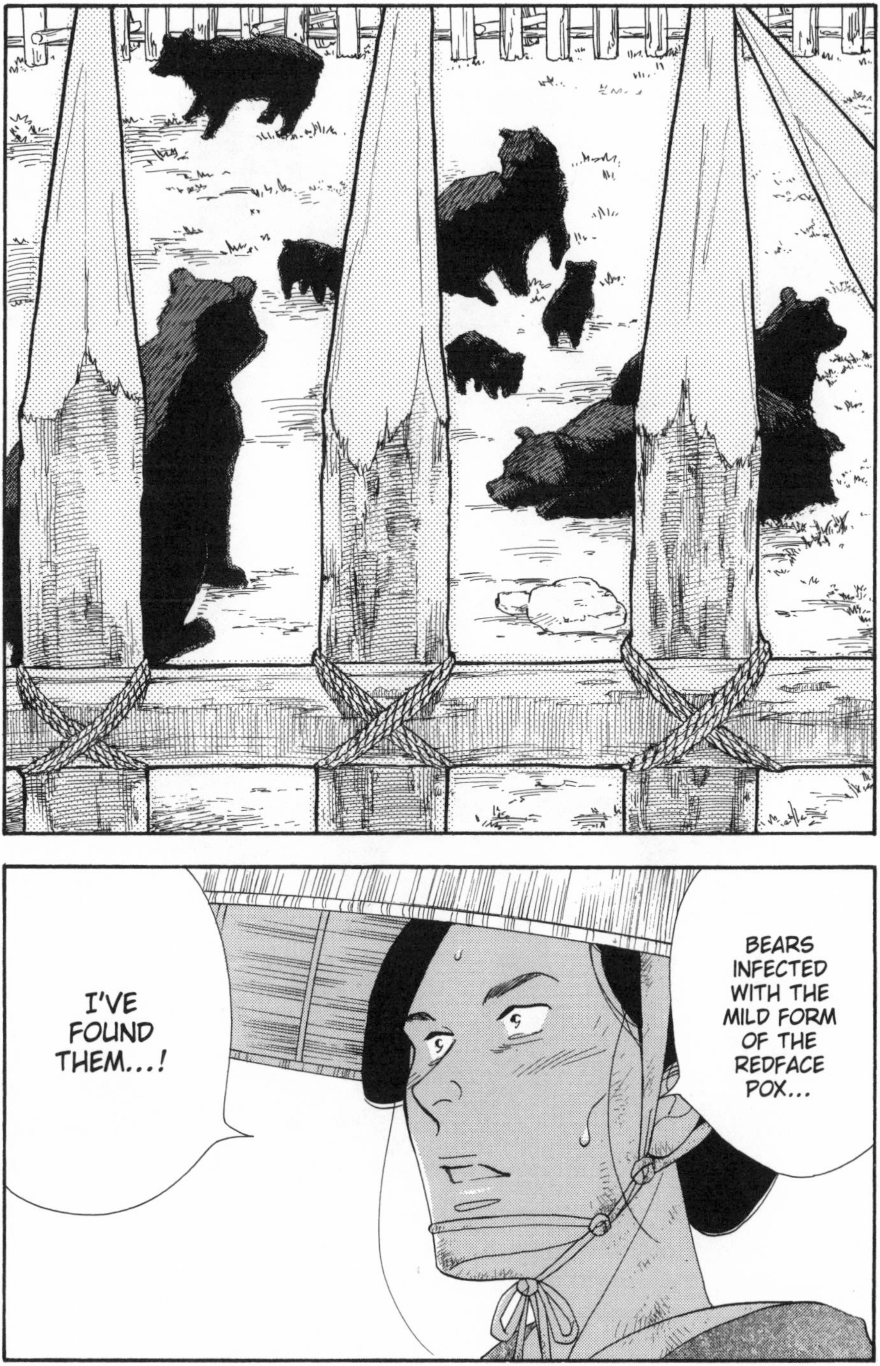
BEARS INFECTED WITH THE MILD FORM OF THE REDFACE POX...
I'VE FOUND THEM...!

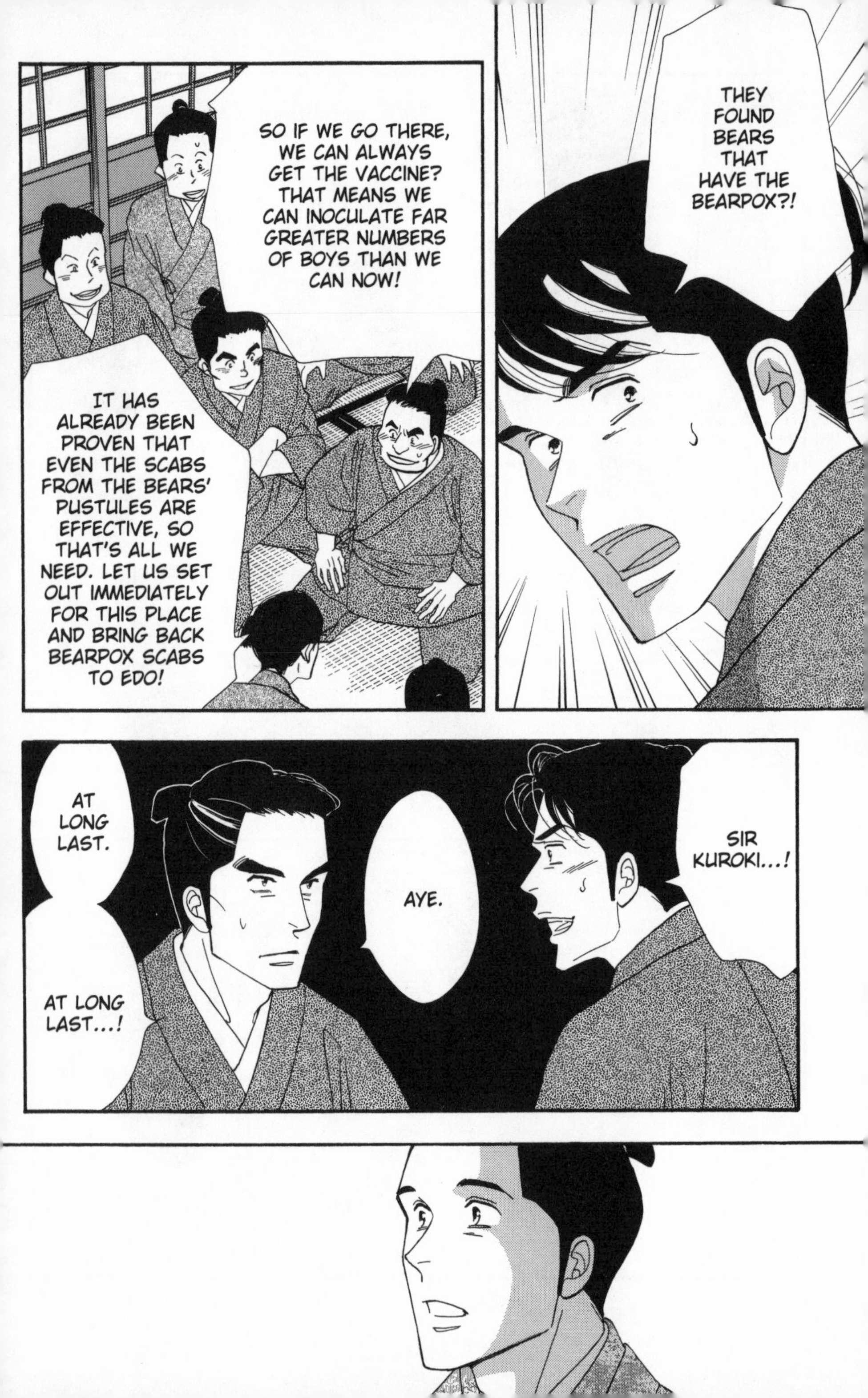
THEY FOUND BEARS THAT HAVE THE BEARPOX?!
SO IF WE GO THERE, WE CAN ALWAYS GET THE VACCINE? THAT MEANS WE CAN INOCULATE FAR GREATER NUMBERS OF BOYS THAN WE CAN NOW!
IT HAS ALREADY BEEN PROVEN THAT EVEN THE SCABS FROM THE BEARS' PUSTULES ARE EFFECTIVE, SO THAT'S ALL WE NEED. LET US SET OUT IMMEDIATELY FOR THIS PLACE AND BRING BACK BEARPOX SCABS TO EDO!
SIR KUROKI...!
AYE.
AT LONG LAST.
AT LONG LAST...!

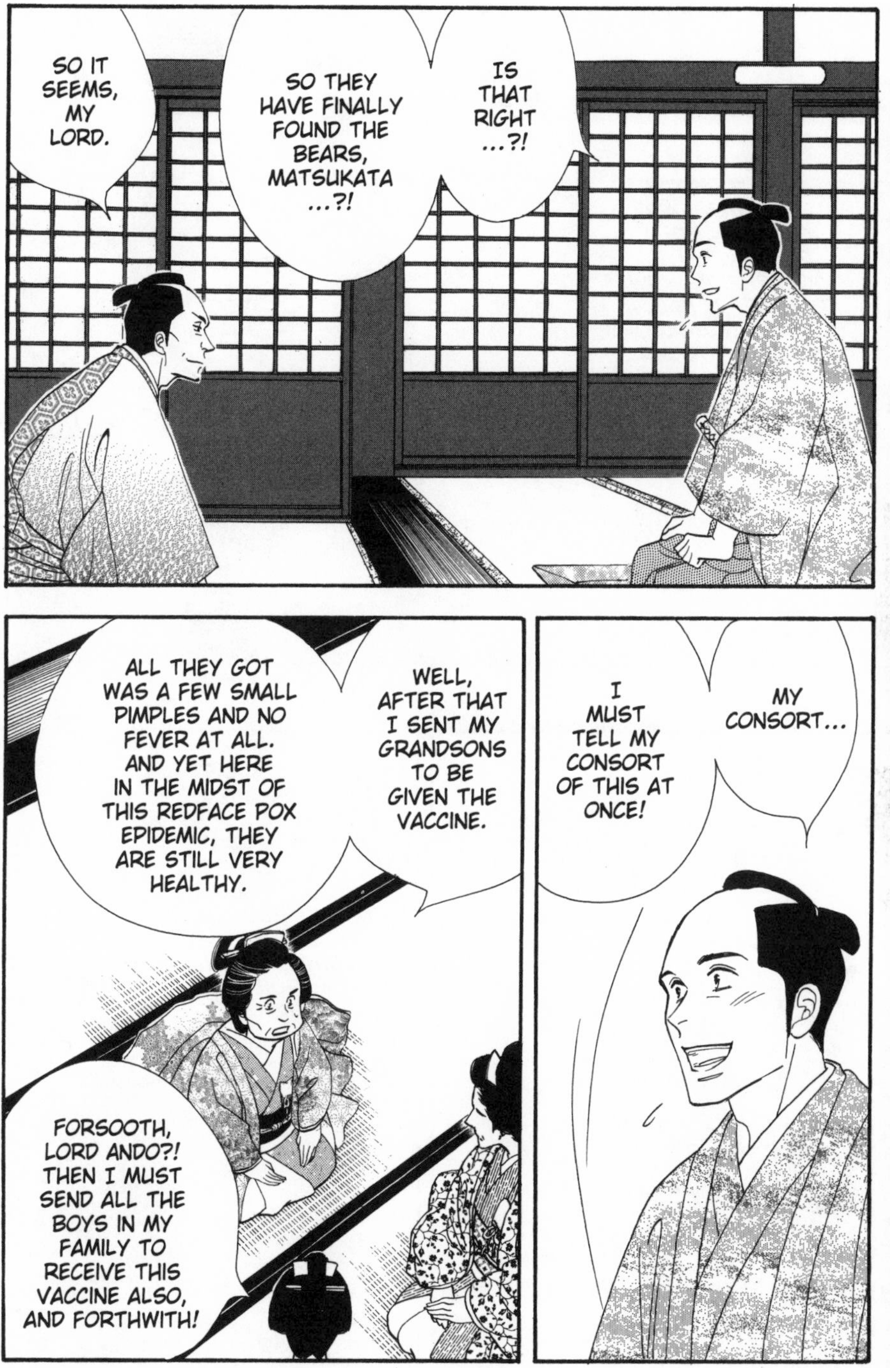
IS THAT RIGHT ...?!
SO THEY HAVE FINALLY FOUND THE BEARS, MATSUKATA ...?!
SO IT SEEMS, MY LORD.
MY CONSORT...
I MUST TELL MY CONSORT OF THIS AT ONCE!
WELL, AFTER THAT I SENT MY GRANDSONS TO BE GIVEN THE VACCINE.
ALL THEY GOT WAS A FEW SMALL PIMPLES AND NO FEVER AT ALL. AND YET HERE IN THE MIDST OF THIS REDFACE POX EPIDEMIC, THEY ARE STILL VERY HEALTHY.
FORSOOTH, LORD ANDO?! THEN I MUST SEND ALL THE BOYS IN MY FAMILY TO RECEIVE THIS VACCINE ALSO, AND FORTHWITH!

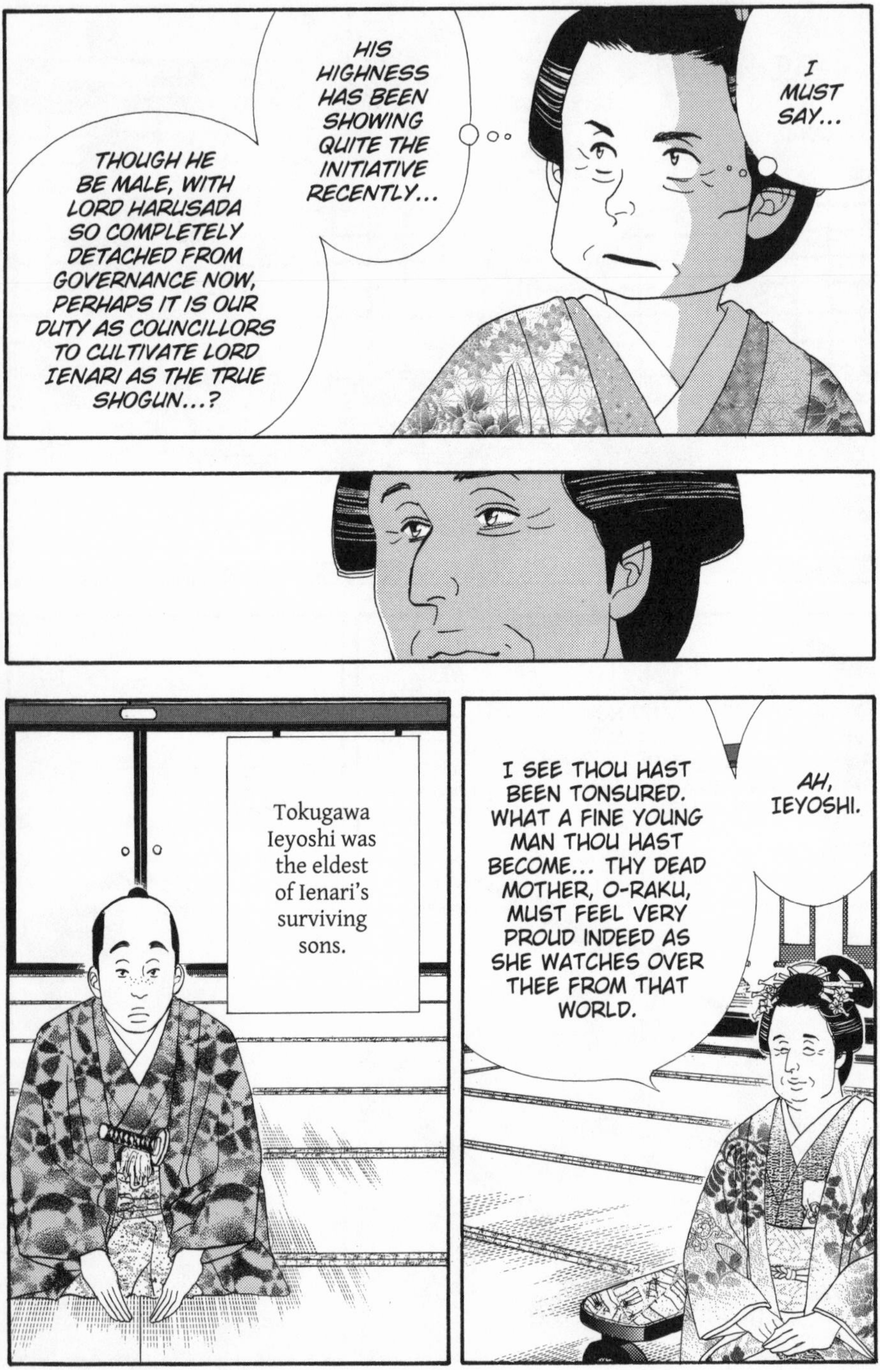
I MUST SAY...
HIS HIGHNESS HAS BEEN SHOWING QUITE THE INITIATIVE RECENTLY...
THOUGH HE BE MALE, WITH LORD HARUSADA SO COMPLETELY DETACHED FROM GOVERNANCE NOW, PERHAPS IT IS OUR DUTY AS COUNCILLORS TO CULTIVATE LORD IENARI AS THE TRUE SHOGUN...?
AH, IEYOSHI.
I SEE THOU HAST BEEN TONSURED. WHAT A FINE YOUNG MAN THOU HAST BECOME... THY DEAD MOTHER, O-RAKU, MUST FEEL VERY PROUD INDEED AS SHE WATCHES OVER THEE FROM THAT WORLD.
Tokugawa Ieyoshi was the eldest of Ienari's surviving sons.

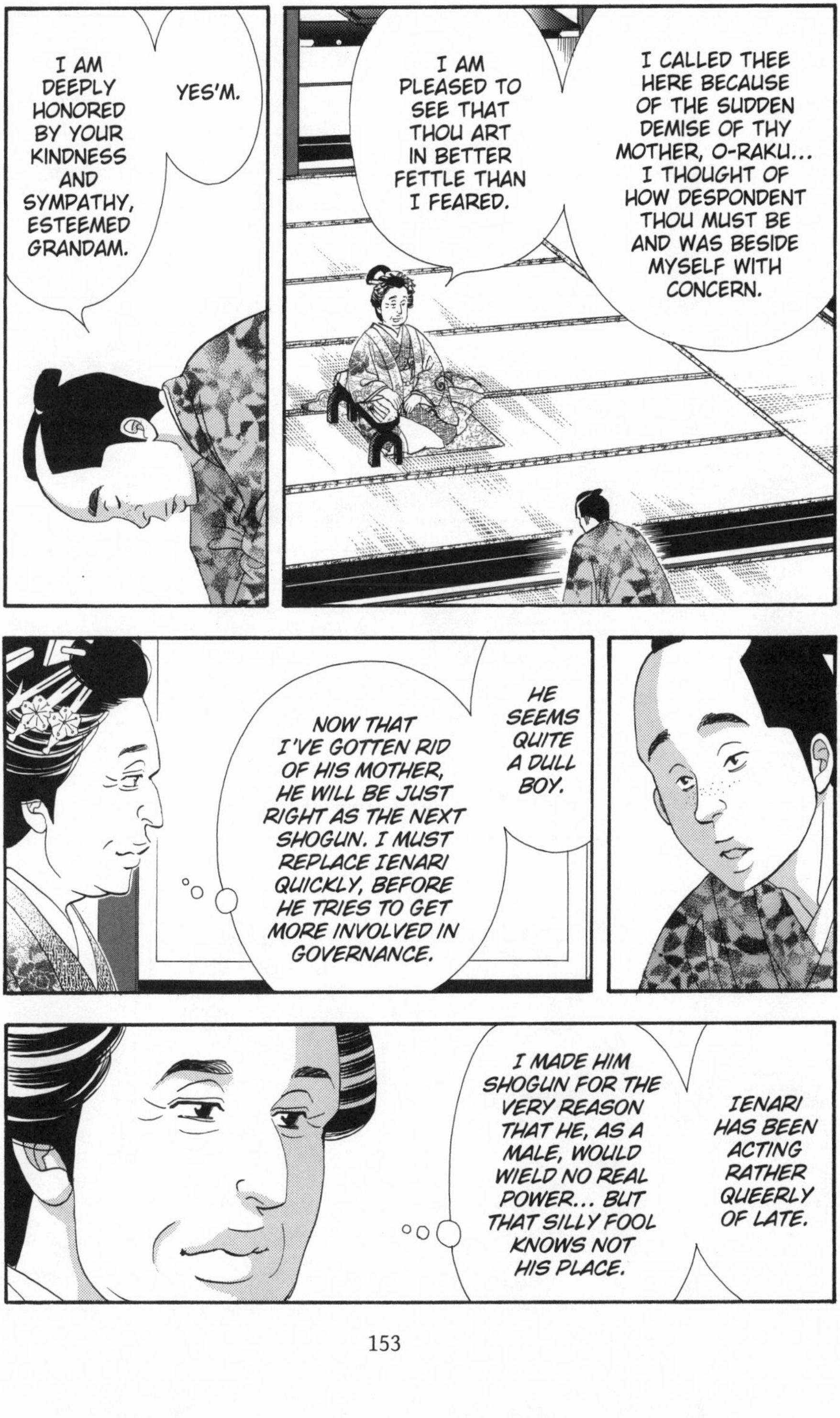
I CALLED THEE HERE BECAUSE OF THE SUDDEN DEMISE OF THY MOTHER, O-RAKU... I THOUGHT OF HOW DESPONDENT THOU MUST BE AND WAS BESIDE MYSELF WITH CONCERN.
I AM PLEASED TO SEE THAT THOU ART IN BETTER FETTLE THAN I FEARED.
YES'M.
I AM DEEPLY HONORED BY YOUR KINDNESS AND SYMPATHY, ESTEEMED GRANDAM.
HE SEEMS QUITE A DULL BOY.
NOW THAT I'VE GOTTEN RID OF HIS MOTHER, HE WILL BE JUST RIGHT AS THE NEXT SHOGUN. I MUST REPLACE IENARI QUICKLY, BEFORE HE TRIES TO GET MORE INVOLVED IN GOVERNANCE.
IENARI HAS BEEN ACTING RATHER QUEERLY OF LATE.
I MADE HIM SHOGUN FOR THE VERY REASON THAT HE, AS A MALE, WOULD WIELD NO REAL POWER... BUT THAT SILLY FOOL KNOWS NOT HIS PLACE.

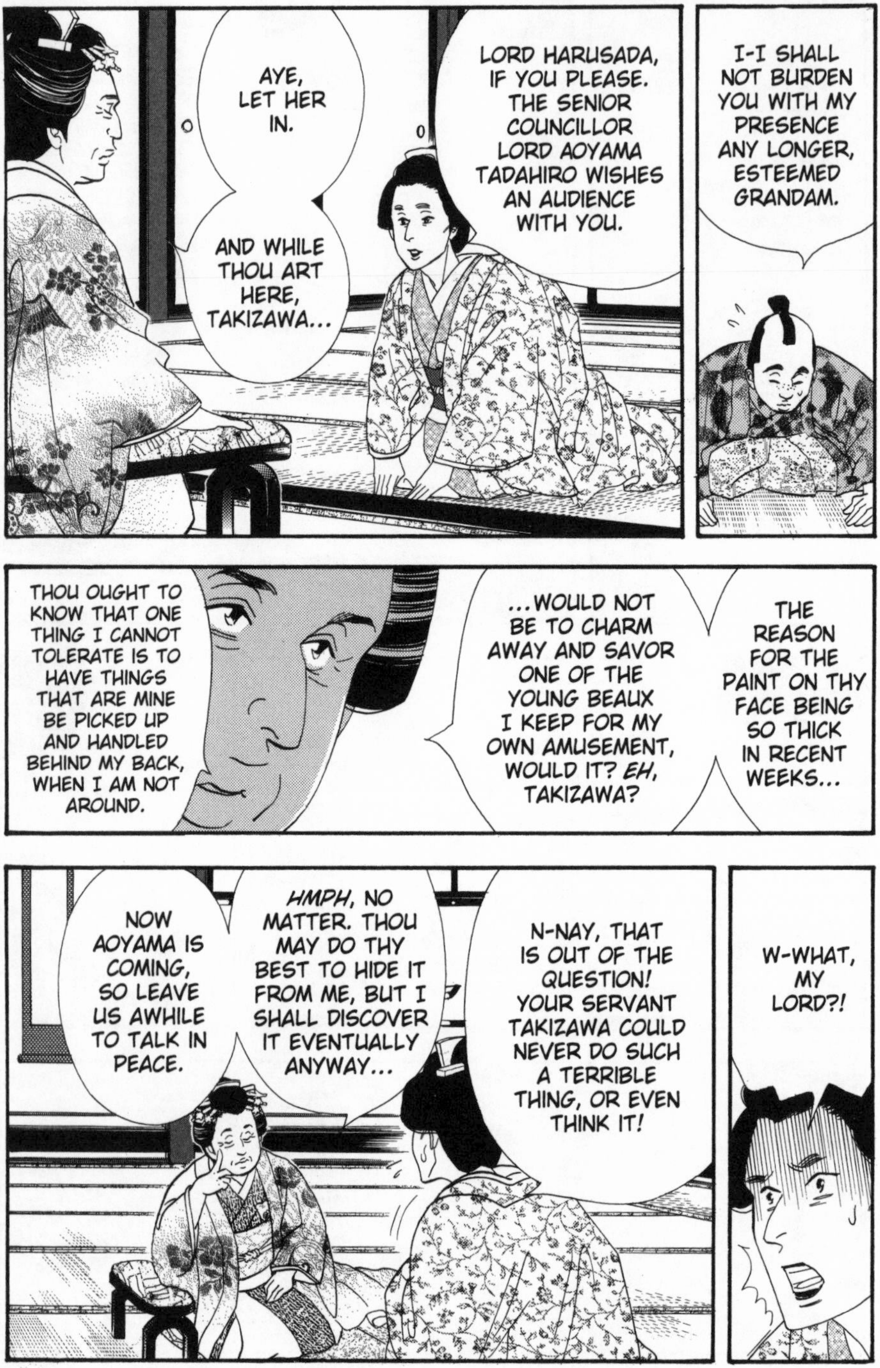
I-I SHALL NOT BURDEN YOU WITH MY PRESENCE ANY LONGER, ESTEEMED GRANDAM.
LORD HARUSADA, IF YOU PLEASE. THE SENIOR COUNCILLOR LORD AOYAMA TADAHIRO WISHES AN AUDIENCE WITH YOU.
AYE, LET HER IN.
AND WHILE THOU ART HERE, TAKIZAWA...
THE REASON FOR THE PAINT ON THY FACE BEING SO THICK IN RECENT WEEKS...
...WOULD NOT BE TO CHARM AWAY AND SAVOR ONE OF THE YOUNG BEAUX I KEEP FOR MY OWN AMUSEMENT, WOULD IT? *EH*, TAKIZAWA?
THOU OUGHT TO KNOW THAT ONE THING I CANNOT TOLERATE IS TO HAVE THINGS THAT ARE MINE BE PICKED UP AND HANDLED BEHIND MY BACK, WHEN I AM NOT AROUND.
W-WHAT, MY LORD?!
N-NAY, THAT IS OUT OF THE QUESTION! YOUR SERVANT TAKIZAWA COULD NEVER DO SUCH A TERRIBLE THING, OR EVEN THINK IT!
HMPH, NO MATTER. THOU MAY DO THY BEST TO HIDE IT FROM ME, BUT I SHALL DISCOVER IT EVENTUALLY ANYWAY...
NOW AOYAMA IS COMING, SO LEAVE US AWHILE TO TALK IN PEACE.

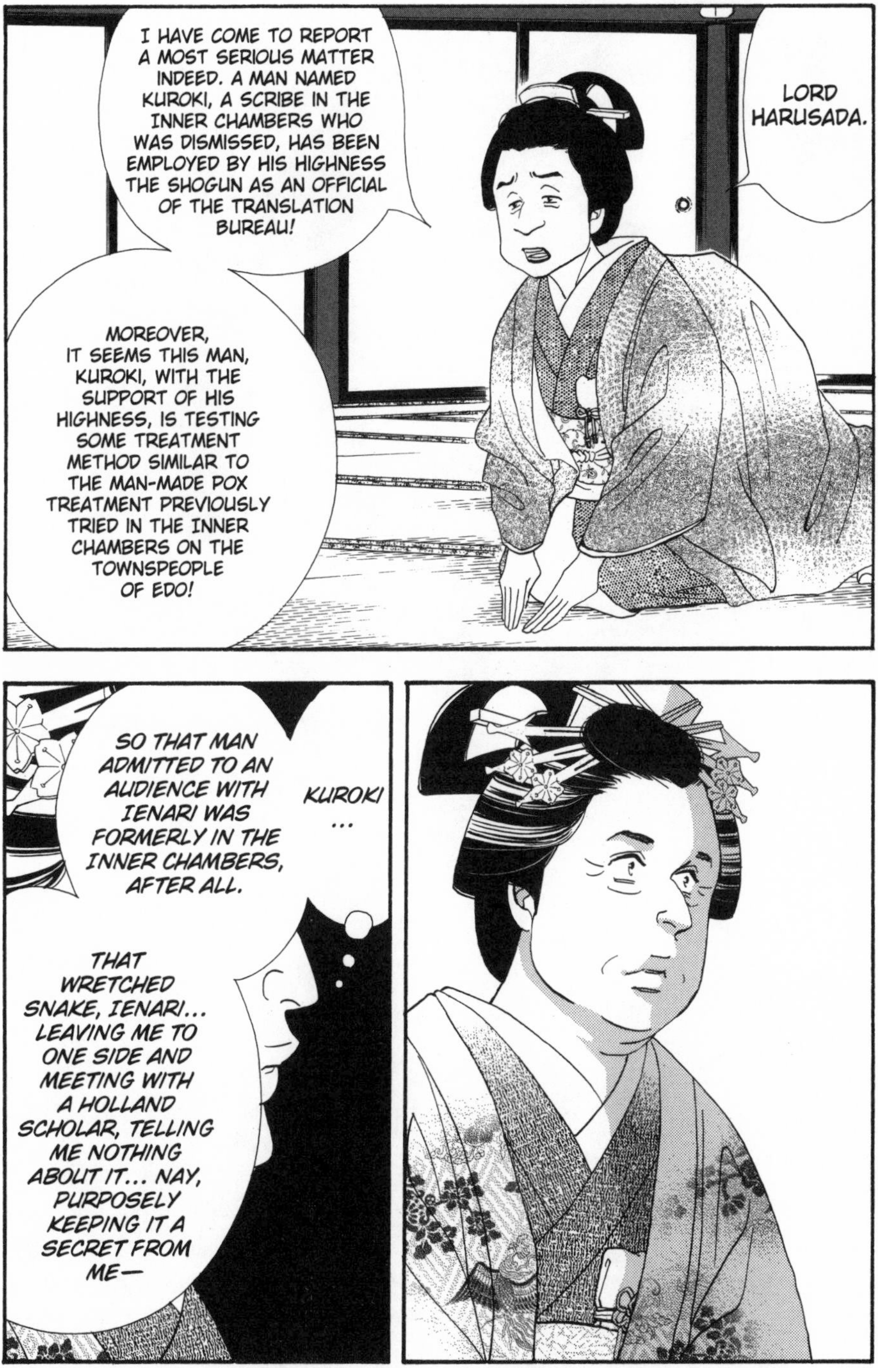
LORD HARUSADA.
I HAVE COME TO REPORT A MOST SERIOUS MATTER INDEED. A MAN NAMED KUROKI, A SCRIBE IN THE INNER CHAMBERS WHO WAS DISMISSED, HAS BEEN EMPLOYED BY HIS HIGHNESS THE SHOGUN AS AN OFFICIAL OF THE TRANSLATION BUREAU!
MOREOVER, IT SEEMS THIS MAN, KUROKI, WITH THE SUPPORT OF HIS HIGHNESS, IS TESTING SOME TREATMENT METHOD SIMILAR TO THE MAN-MADE POX TREATMENT PREVIOUSLY TRIED IN THE INNER CHAMBERS ON THE TOWNSPEOPLE OF EDO!
KUROKI ...
SO THAT MAN ADMITTED TO AN AUDIENCE WITH IENARI WAS FORMERLY IN THE INNER CHAMBERS, AFTER ALL.
THAT WRETCHED SNAKE, IENARI... LEAVING ME TO ONE SIDE AND MEETING WITH A HOLLAND SCHOLAR, TELLING ME NOTHING ABOUT IT... NAY, PURPOSELY KEEPING IT A SECRET FROM ME—

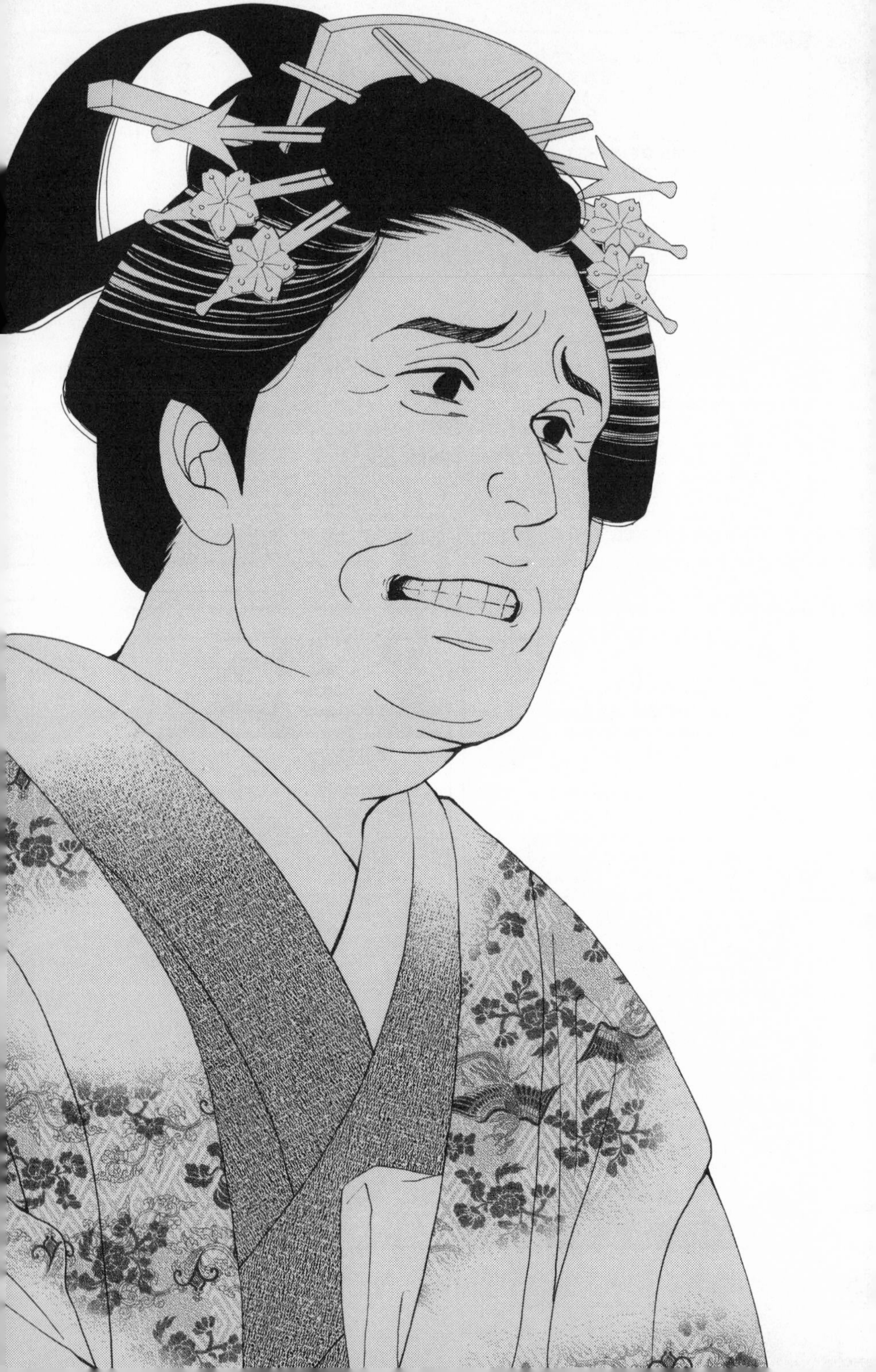

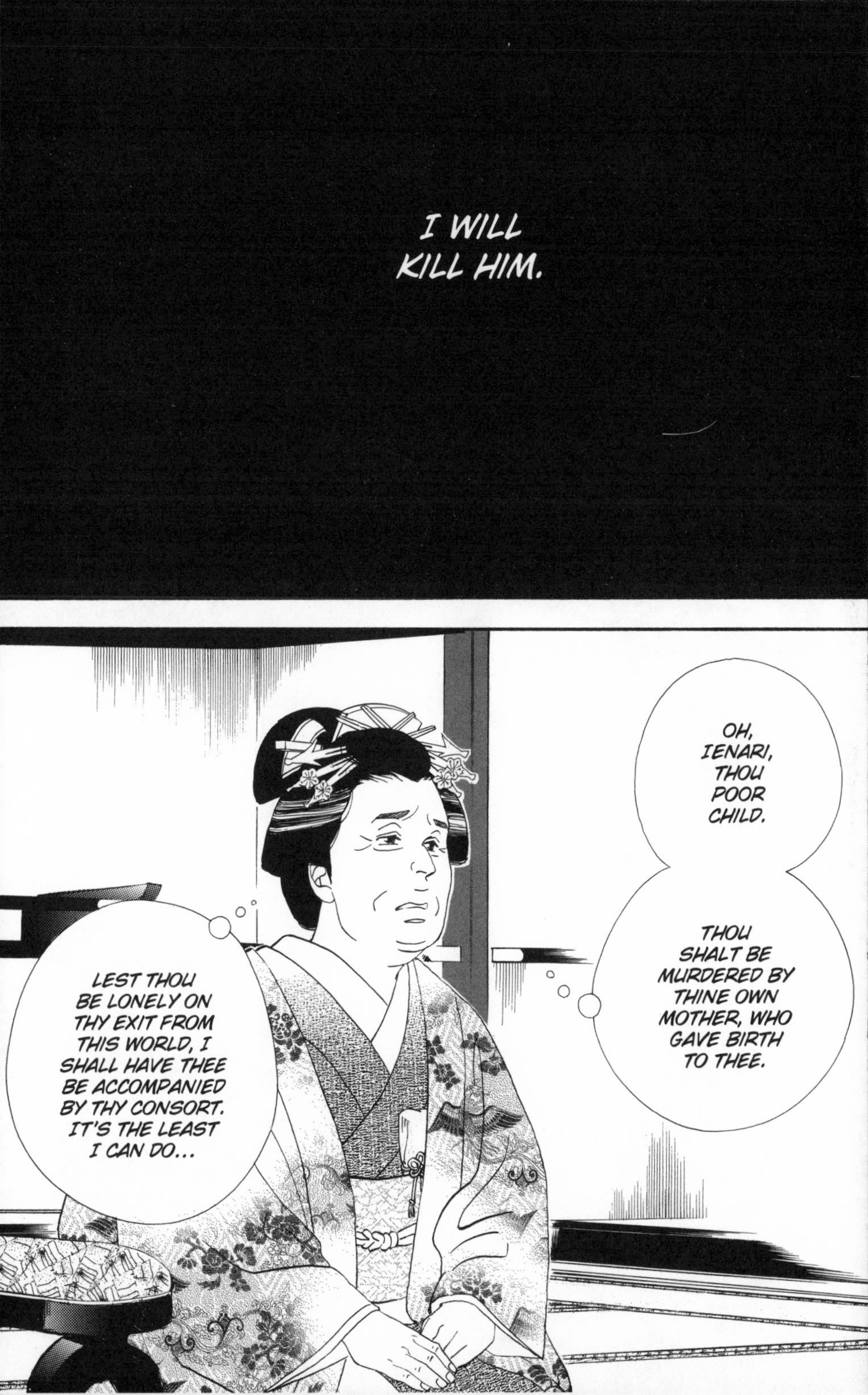
I WILL KILL HIM.
OH, IENARI, THOU POOR CHILD.
THOU SHALT BE MURDERED BY THINE OWN MOTHER, WHO GAVE BIRTH TO THEE.
LEST THOU BE LONELY ON THY EXIT FROM THIS WORLD, I SHALL HAVE THEE BE ACCOMPANIED BY THY CONSORT. IT'S THE LEAST I CAN DO...

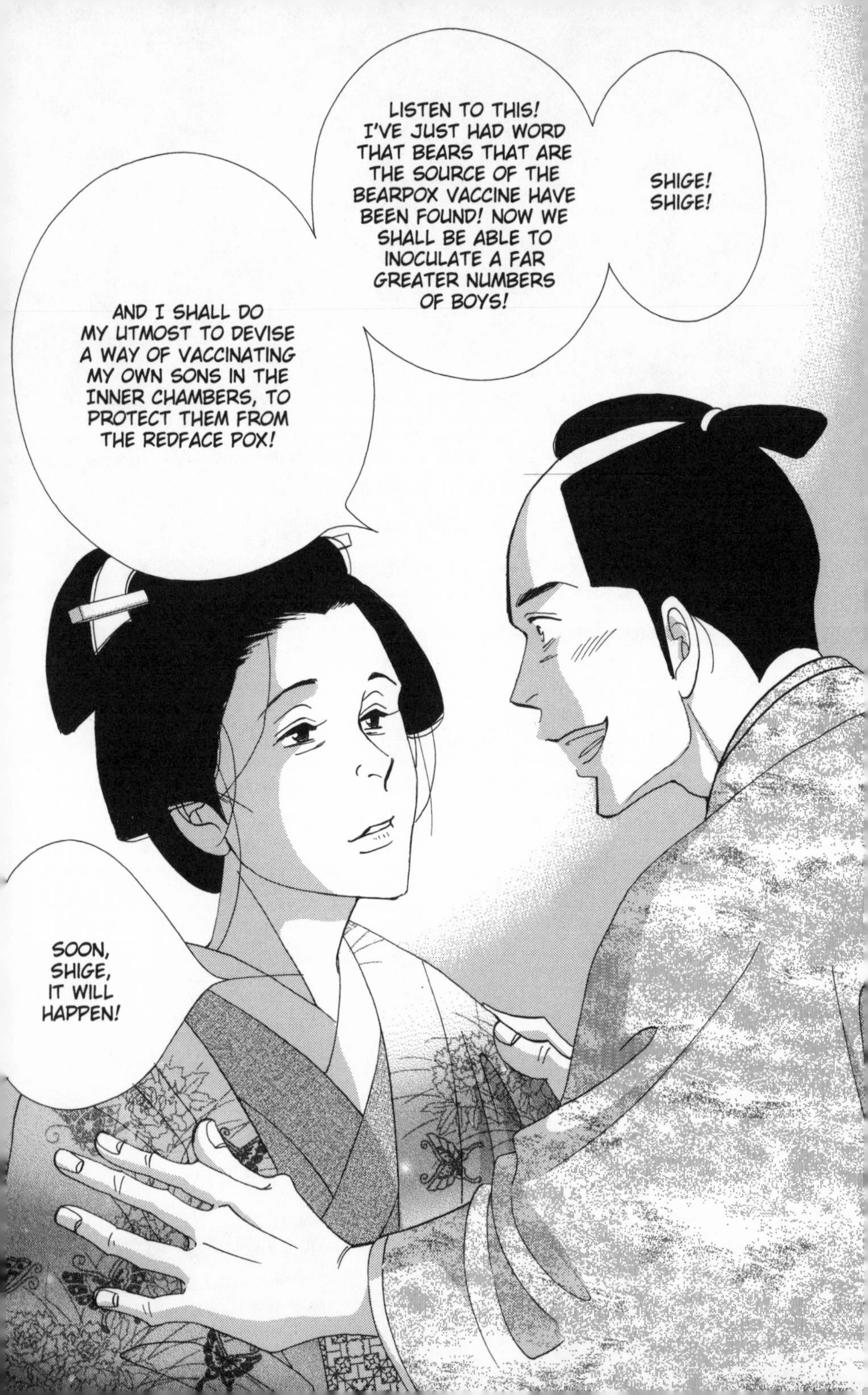
SHIGE! SHIGE!
LISTEN TO THIS! I'VE JUST HAD WORD THAT BEARS THAT ARE THE SOURCE OF THE BEARPOX VACCINE HAVE BEEN FOUND! NOW WE SHALL BE ABLE TO INOCULATE A FAR GREATER NUMBERS OF BOYS!
AND I SHALL DO MY UTMOST TO DEVISE A WAY OF VACCINATING MY OWN SONS IN THE INNER CHAMBERS, TO PROTECT THEM FROM THE REDFACE POX!
SOON, SHIGE, IT WILL HAPPEN!

Ôoku

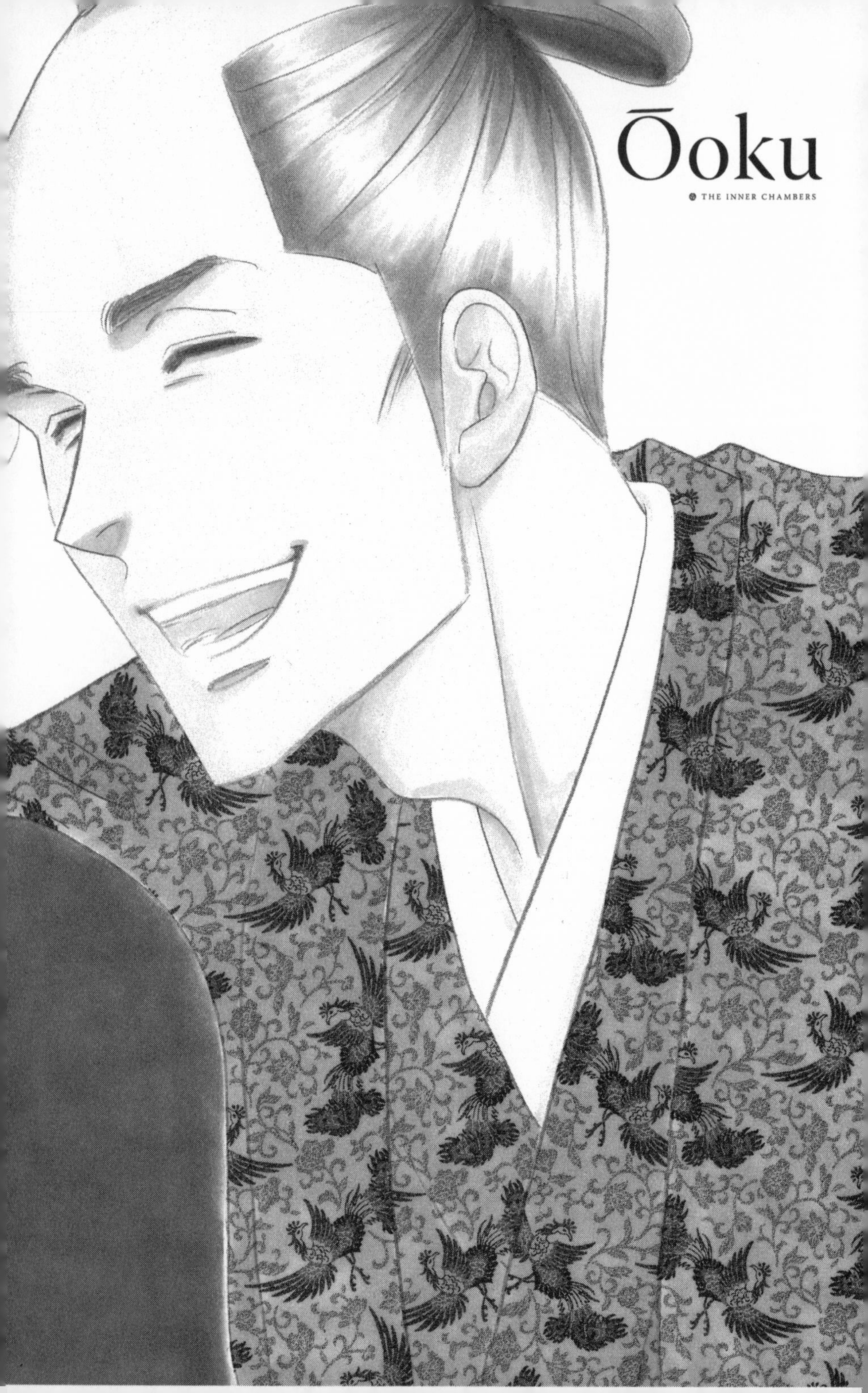
Ōoku
THE INNER CHAMBERS

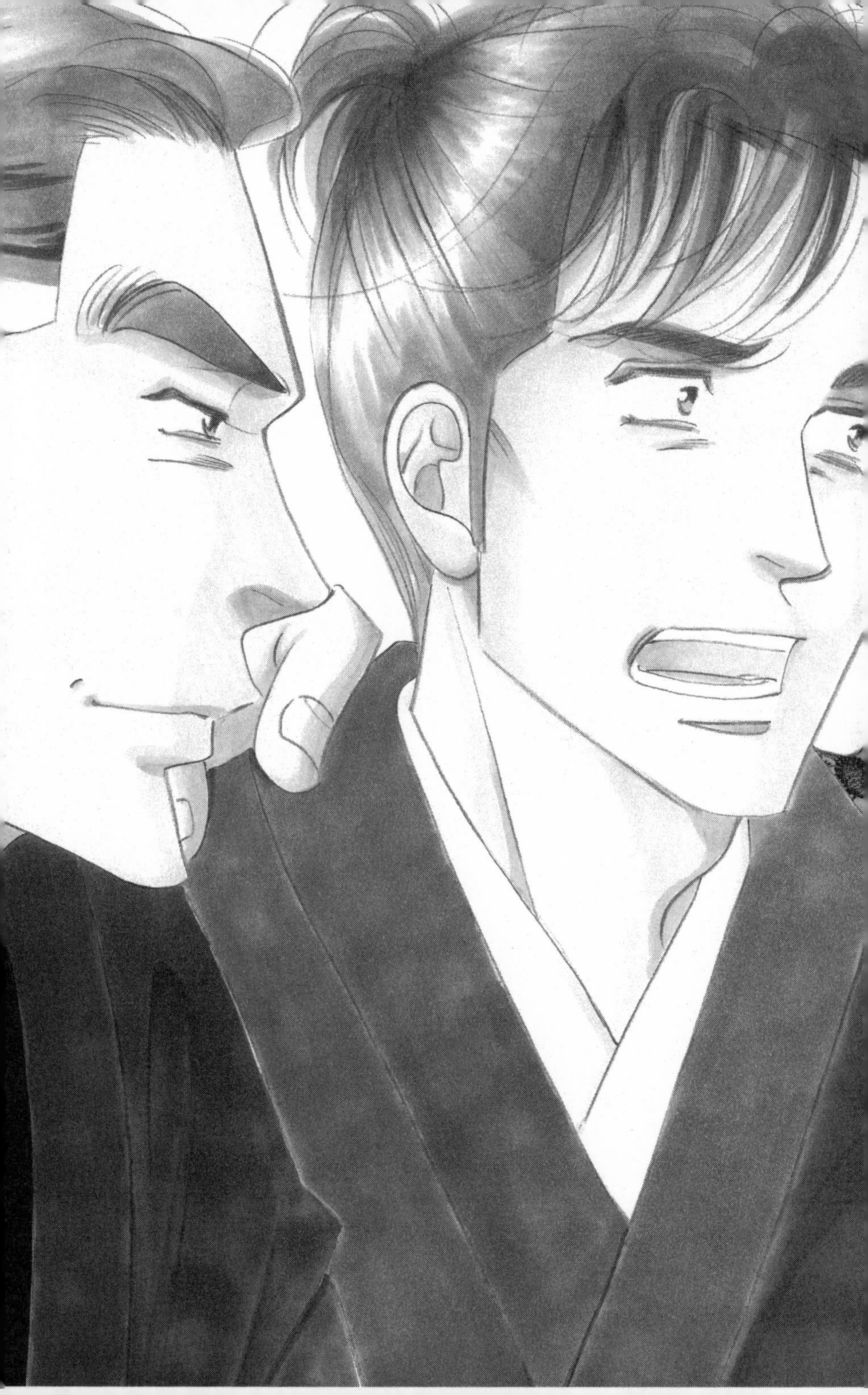

Ōoku

THE INNER CHAMBERS

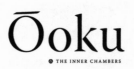

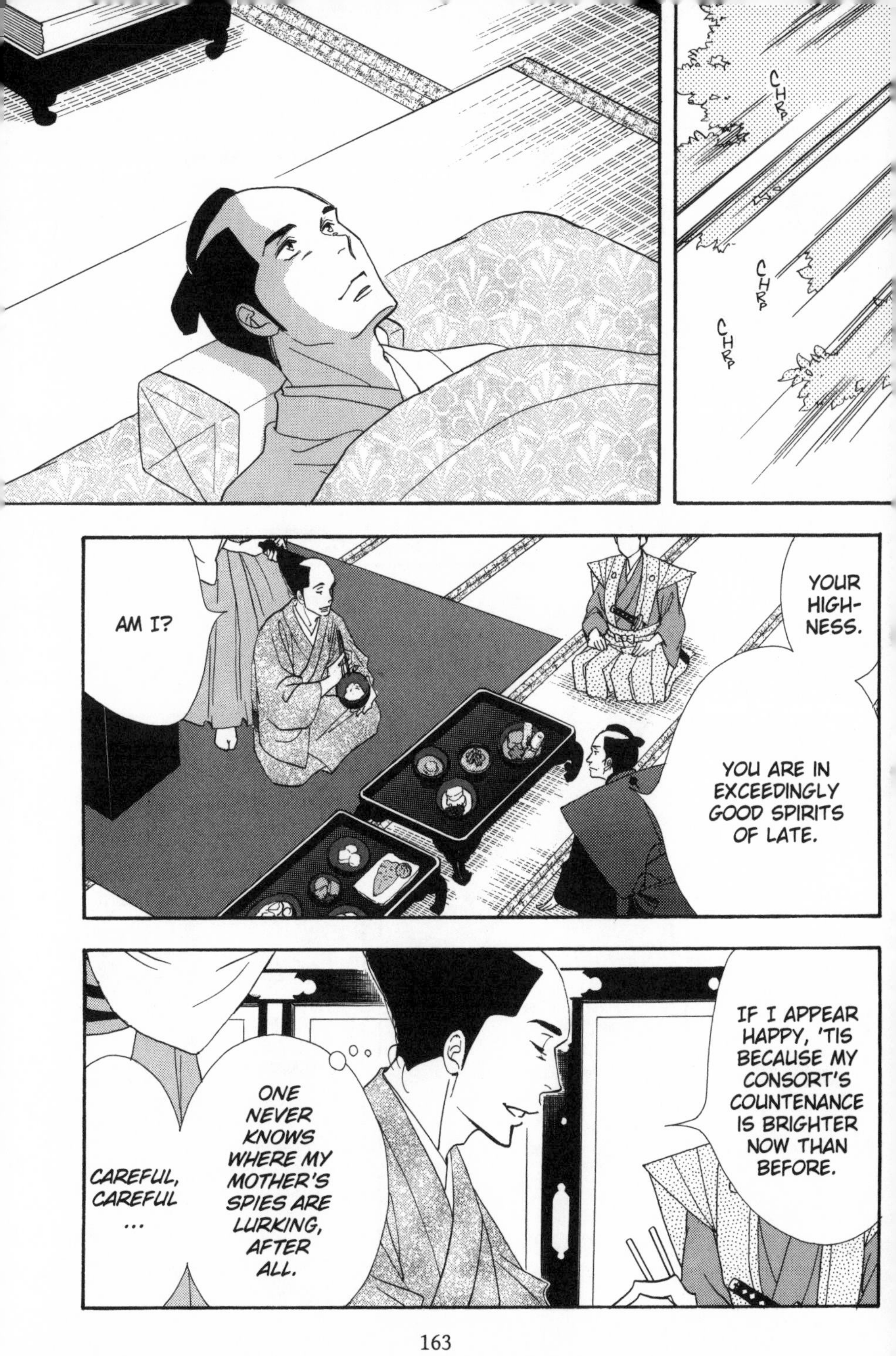
CHRP
CHRP
CHRP
YOUR HIGHNESS.
YOU ARE IN EXCEEDINGLY GOOD SPIRITS OF LATE.
AM I?
IF I APPEAR HAPPY, 'TIS BECAUSE MY CONSORT'S COUNTENANCE IS BRIGHTER NOW THAN BEFORE.
ONE NEVER KNOWS WHERE MY MOTHER'S SPIES ARE LURKING, AFTER ALL.
CAREFUL, CAREFUL ...

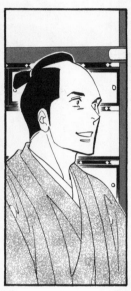

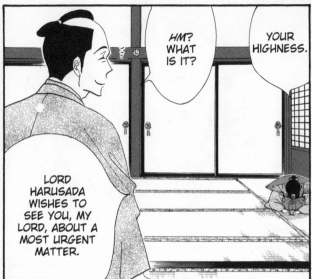

YOUR HIGHNESS.
HM? WHAT IS IT?
LORD HARUSADA WISHES TO SEE YOU, MY LORD, ABOUT A MOST URGENT MATTER.
I HAVE NOT SEEN YOU IN QUITE A WHILE, IENARI.
N-NAY, M'LORD!
I AM MOST GRATIFIED TO SEE YOU IN GOOD HEALTH AND—
ULP!

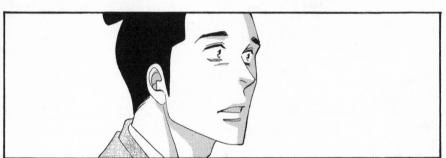

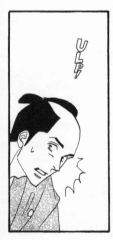

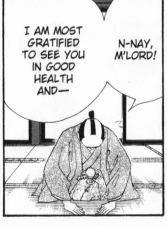

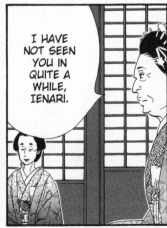

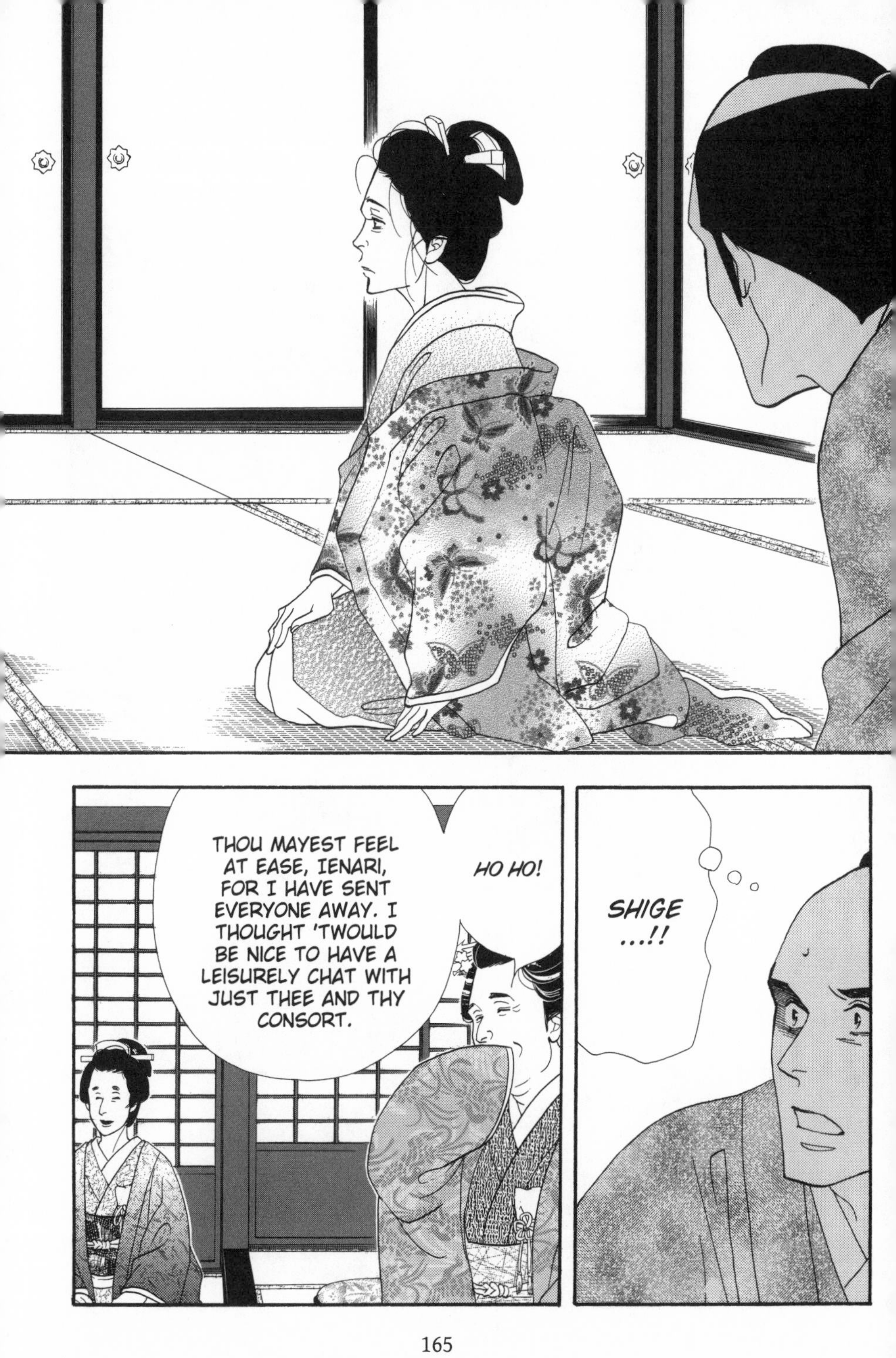
SHIGE ...!!
THOU MAYEST FEEL AT EASE, IENARI, FOR I HAVE SENT EVERYONE AWAY. I THOUGHT 'TWOULD BE NICE TO HAVE A LEISURELY CHAT WITH JUST THEE AND THY CONSORT.
HO HO!

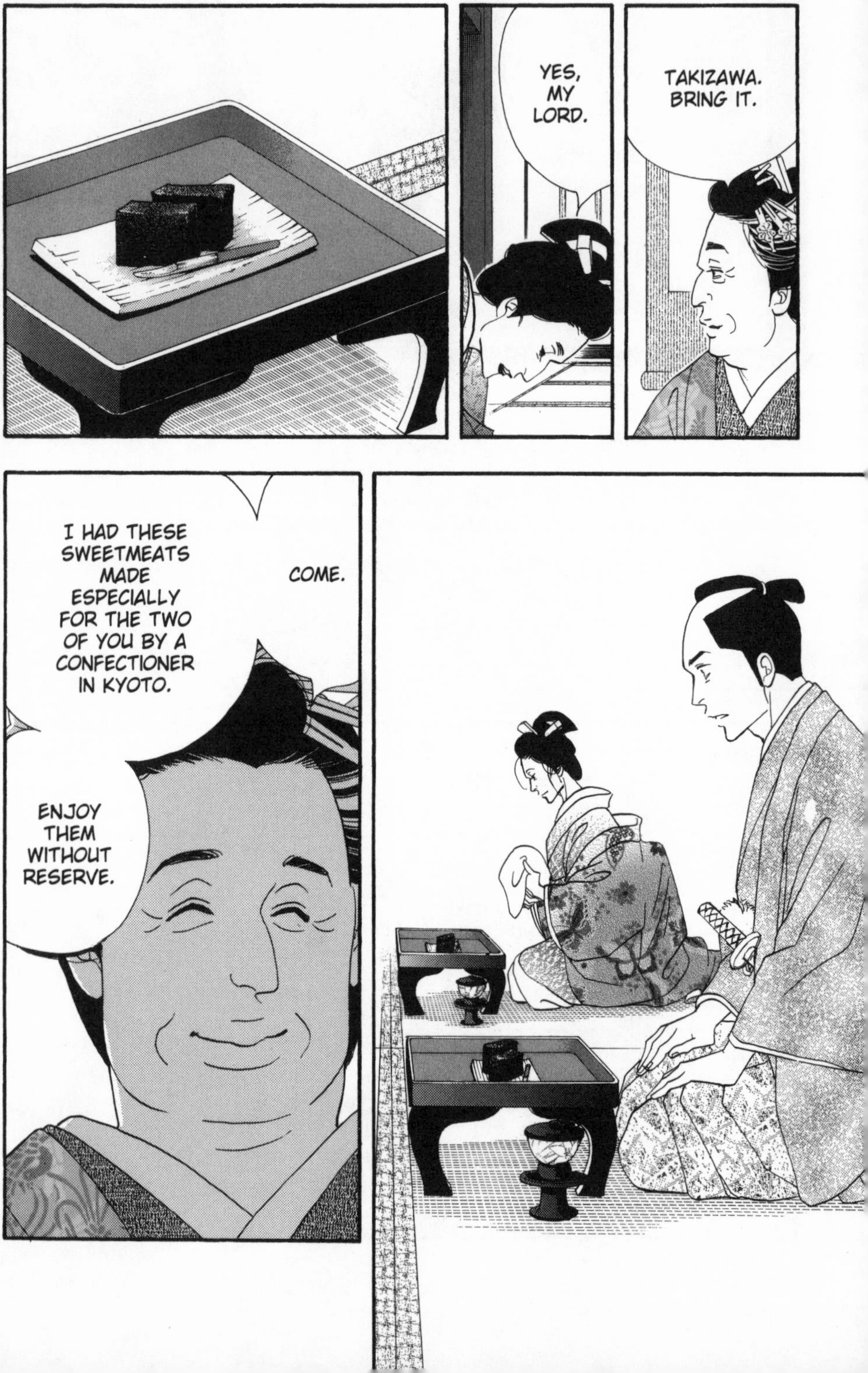
TAKIZAWA. BRING IT.
YES, MY LORD.
COME.
I HAD THESE SWEETMEATS MADE ESPECIALLY FOR THE TWO OF YOU BY A CONFECTIONER IN KYOTO.
ENJOY THEM WITHOUT RESERVE.

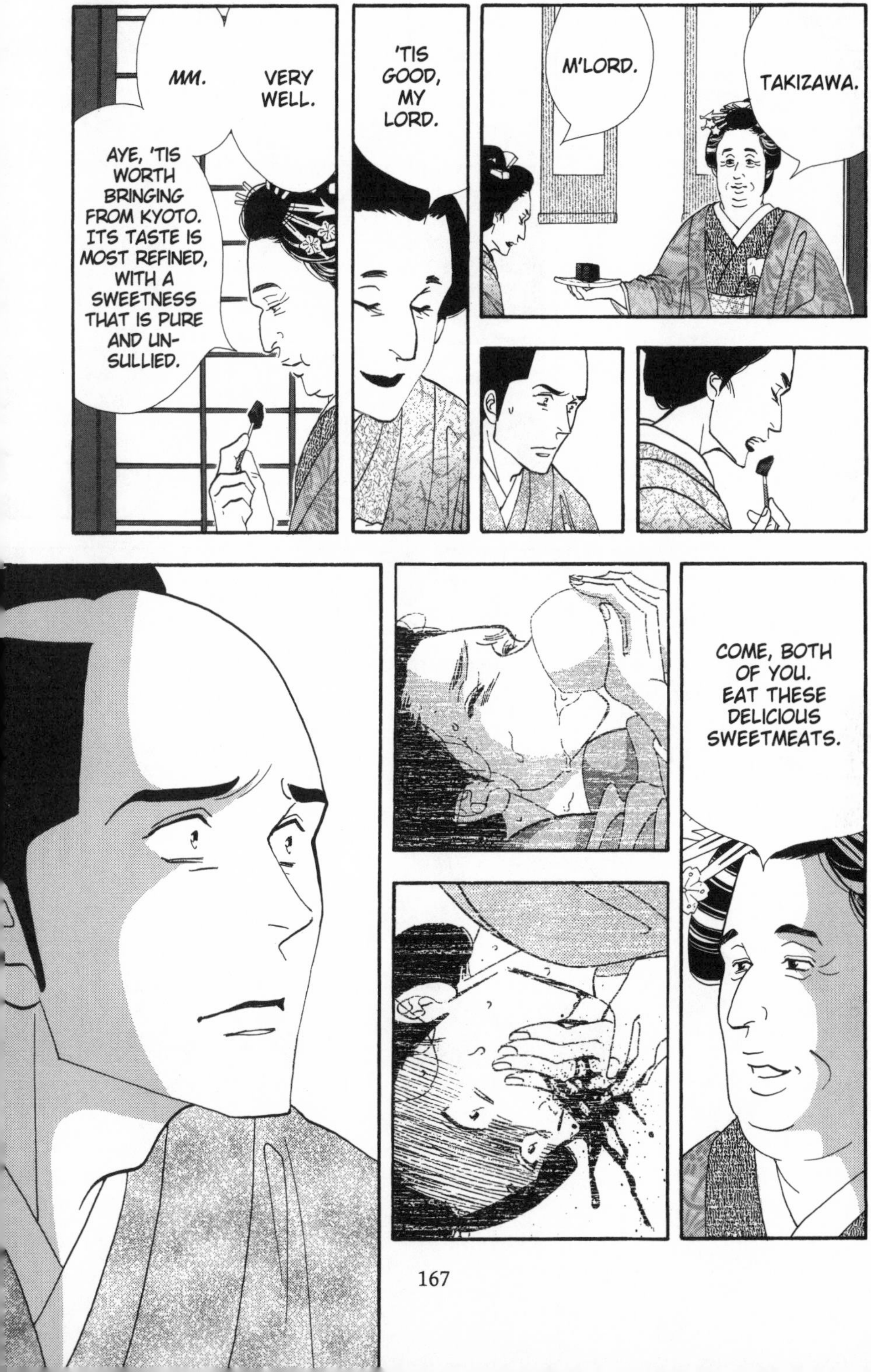
TAKIZAWA.
M'LORD.
'TIS GOOD, MY LORD.
MM. VERY WELL.
AYE, 'TIS WORTH BRINGING FROM KYOTO. ITS TASTE IS MOST REFINED, WITH A SWEETNESS THAT IS PURE AND UN-SULLIED.
COME, BOTH OF YOU. EAT THESE DELICIOUS SWEETMEATS.

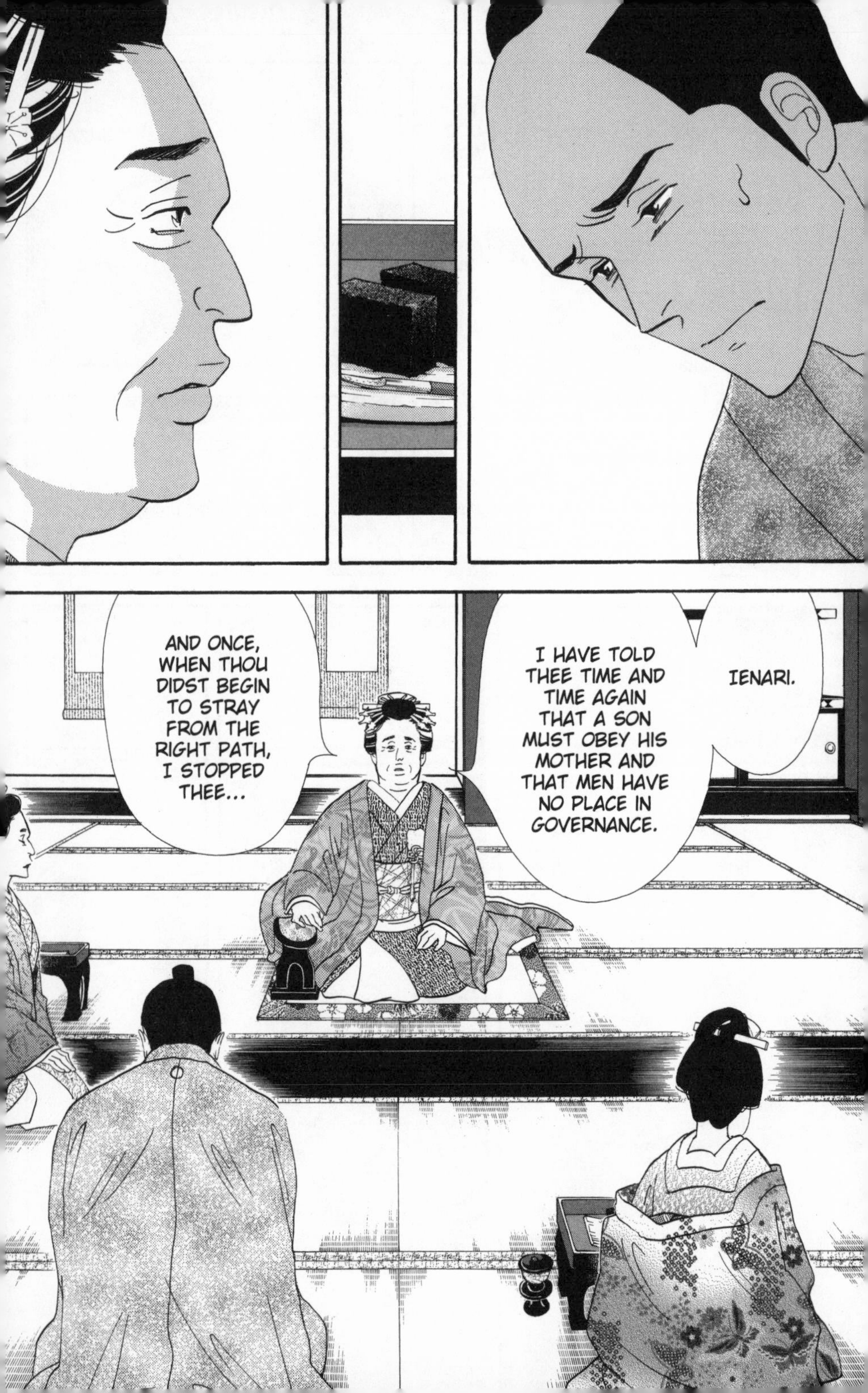
IENARI.
I HAVE TOLD THEE TIME AND TIME AGAIN THAT A SON MUST OBEY HIS MOTHER AND THAT MEN HAVE NO PLACE IN GOVERNANCE.
AND ONCE, WHEN THOU DIDST BEGIN TO STRAY FROM THE RIGHT PATH, I STOPPED THEE...

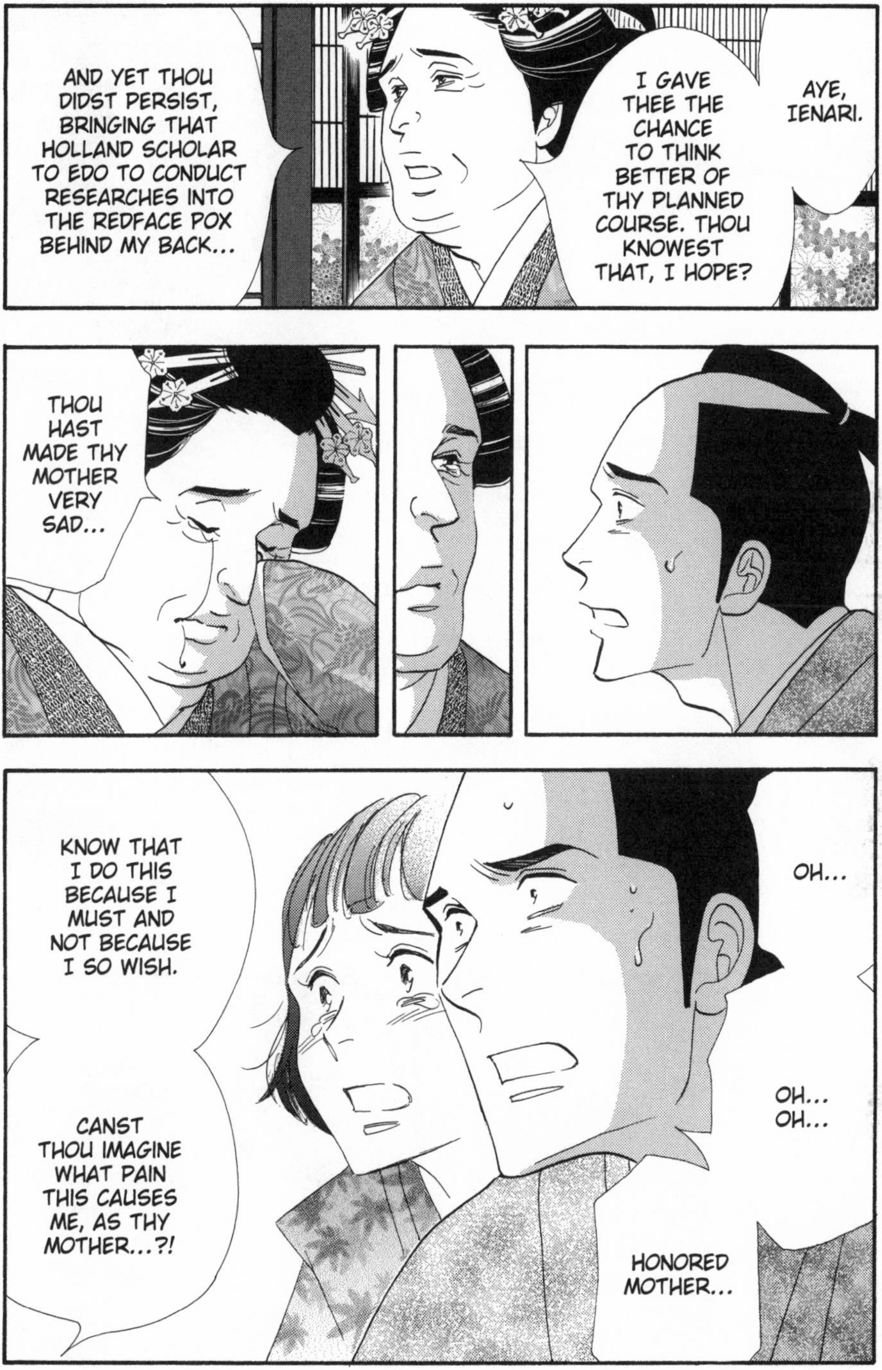
AYE, IENARI.
I GAVE THEE THE CHANCE TO THINK BETTER OF THY PLANNED COURSE. THOU KNOWEST THAT, I HOPE?
AND YET THOU DIDST PERSIST, BRINGING THAT HOLLAND SCHOLAR TO EDO TO CONDUCT RESEARCHES INTO THE REDFACE POX BEHIND MY BACK...
THOU HAST MADE THY MOTHER VERY SAD...
OH...
KNOW THAT I DO THIS BECAUSE I MUST AND NOT BECAUSE I SO WISH.
OH... OH...
CANST THOU IMAGINE WHAT PAIN THIS CAUSES ME, AS THY MOTHER...?!
HONORED MOTHER...

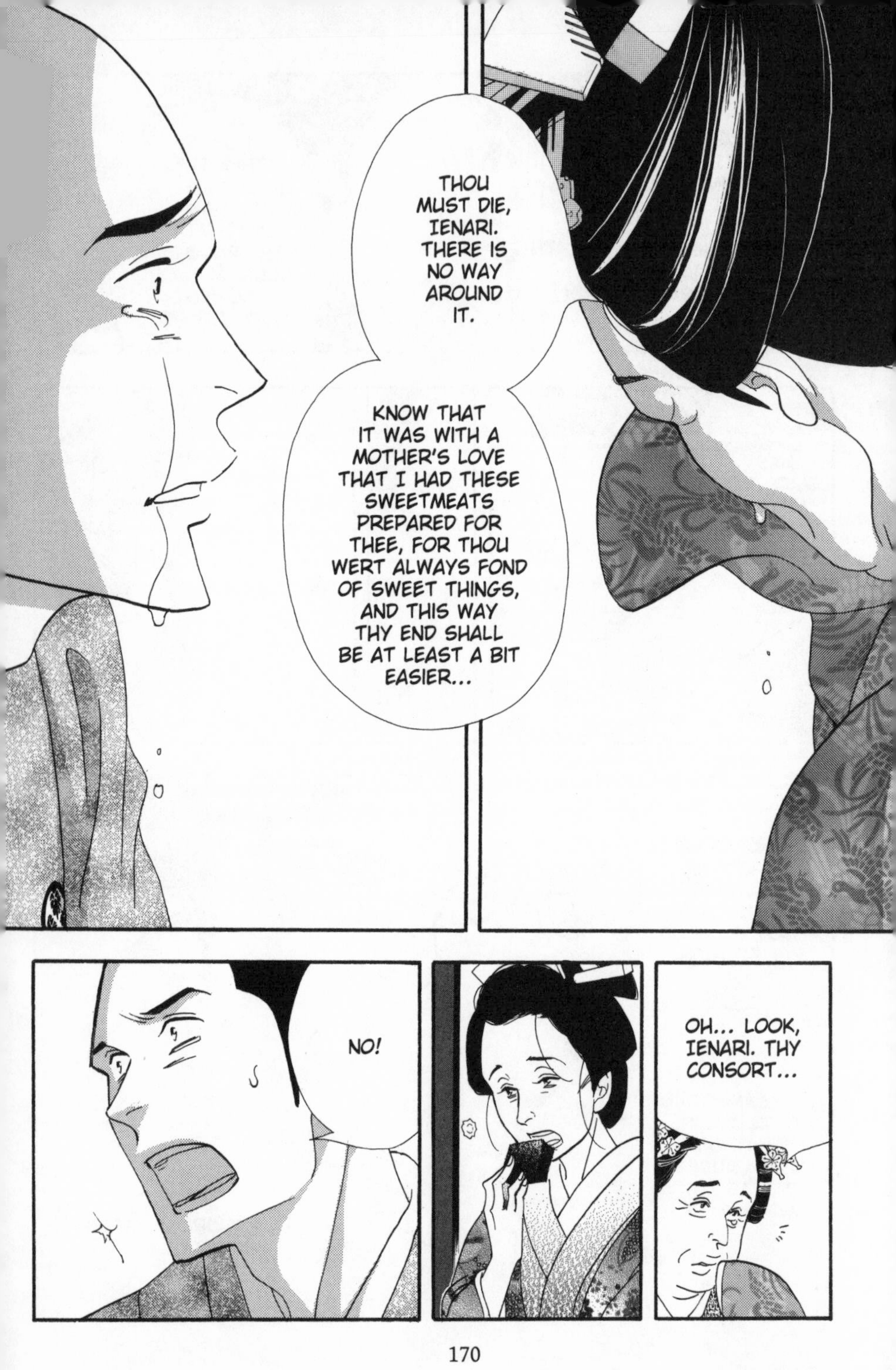
THOU MUST DIE, IENARI. THERE IS NO WAY AROUND IT.
KNOW THAT IT WAS WITH A MOTHER'S LOVE THAT I HAD THESE SWEETMEATS PREPARED FOR THEE, FOR THOU WERT ALWAYS FOND OF SWEET THINGS, AND THIS WAY THY END SHALL BE AT LEAST A BIT EASIER...
OH... LOOK, IENARI. THY CONSORT...
NO!

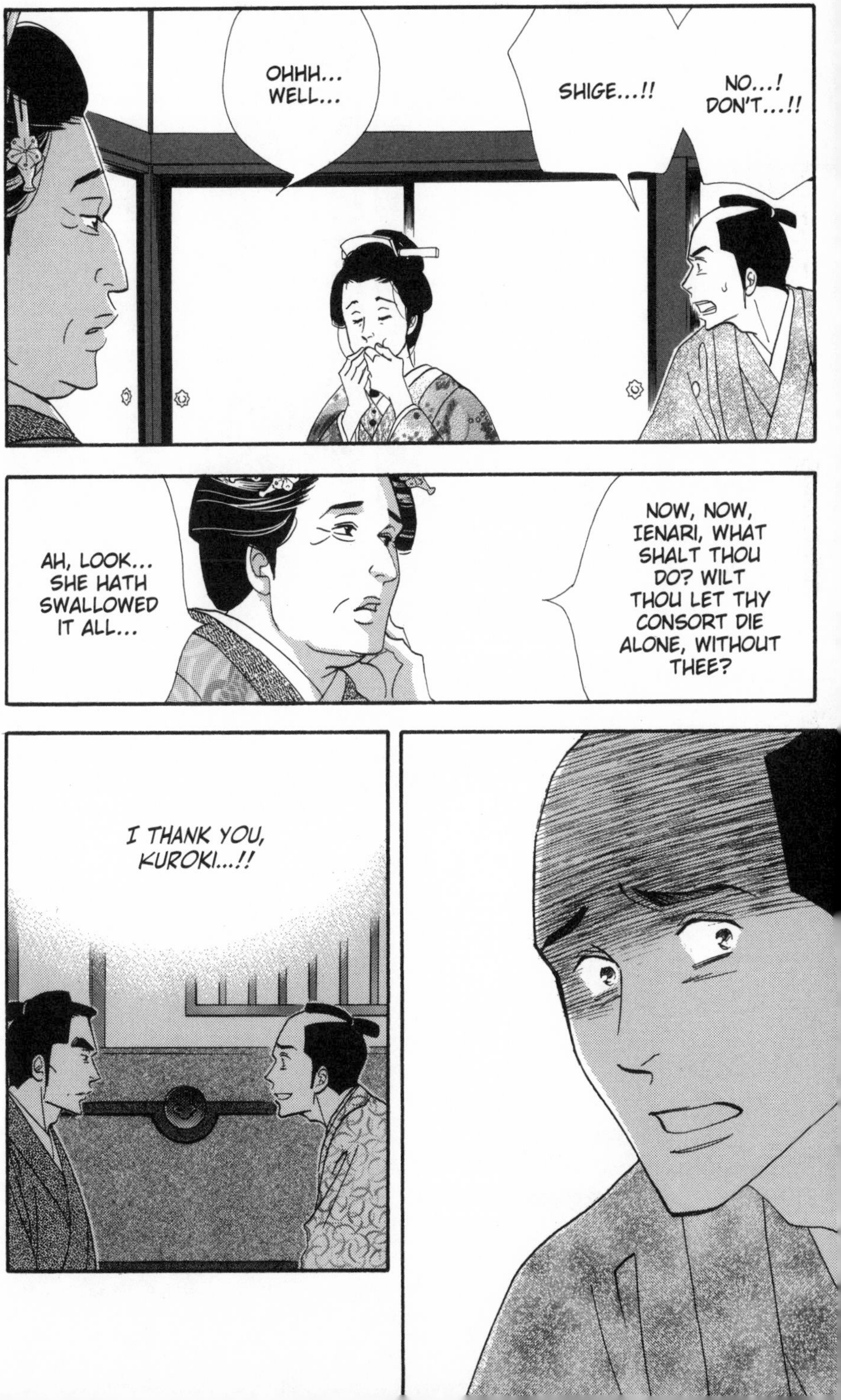
NO...! DON'T...!!
SHIGE...!!
OHHH... WELL...
NOW, NOW, IENARI, WHAT SHALT THOU DO? WILT THOU LET THY CONSORT DIE ALONE, WITHOUT THEE?
AH, LOOK... SHE HATH SWALLOWED IT ALL...
I THANK YOU, KUROKI...!!

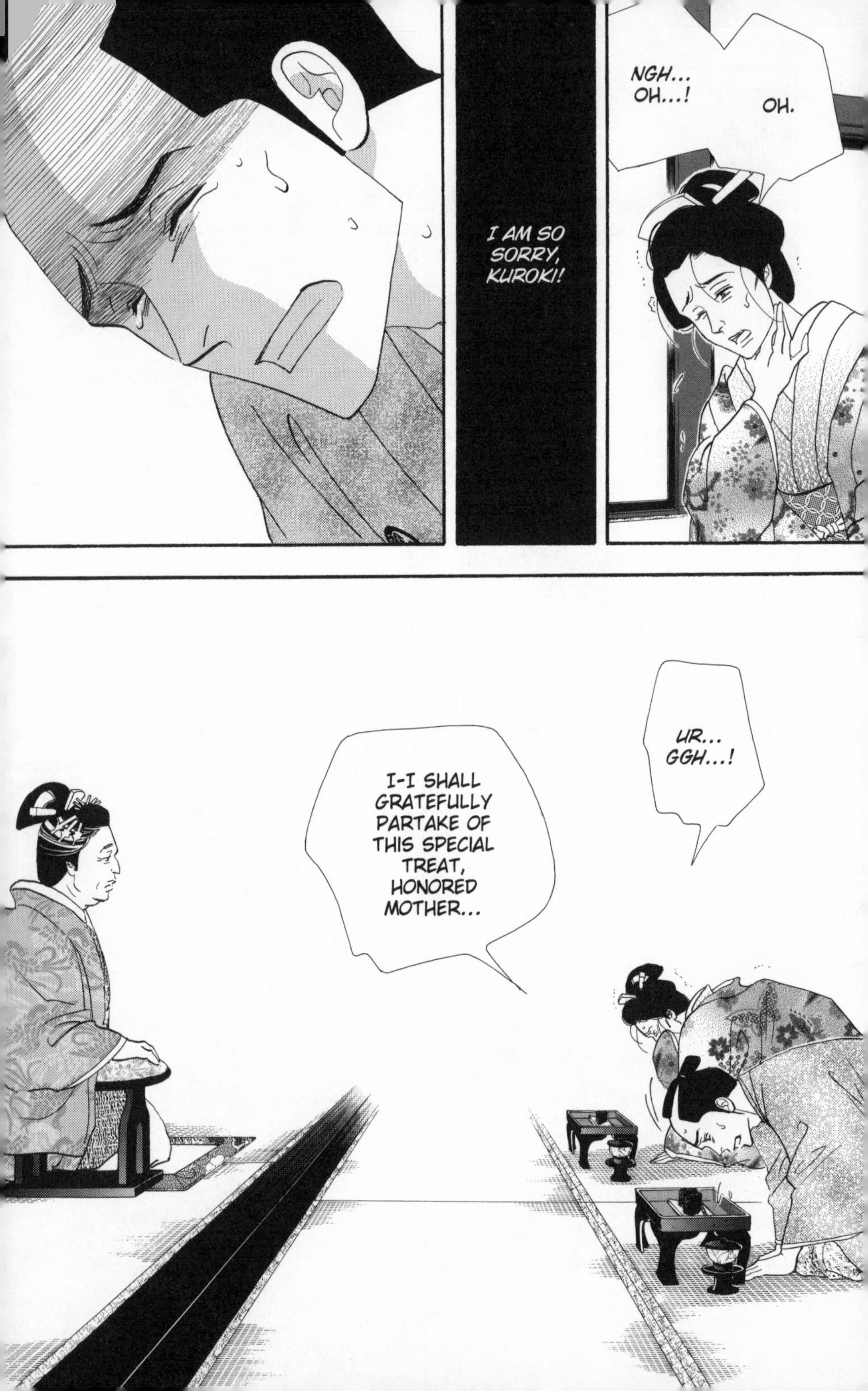
NGH... OH...!
OH.
I AM SO SORRY, KUROKI!
UR... GGH...!
I-I SHALL GRATEFULLY PARTAKE OF THIS SPECIAL TREAT, HONORED MOTHER...

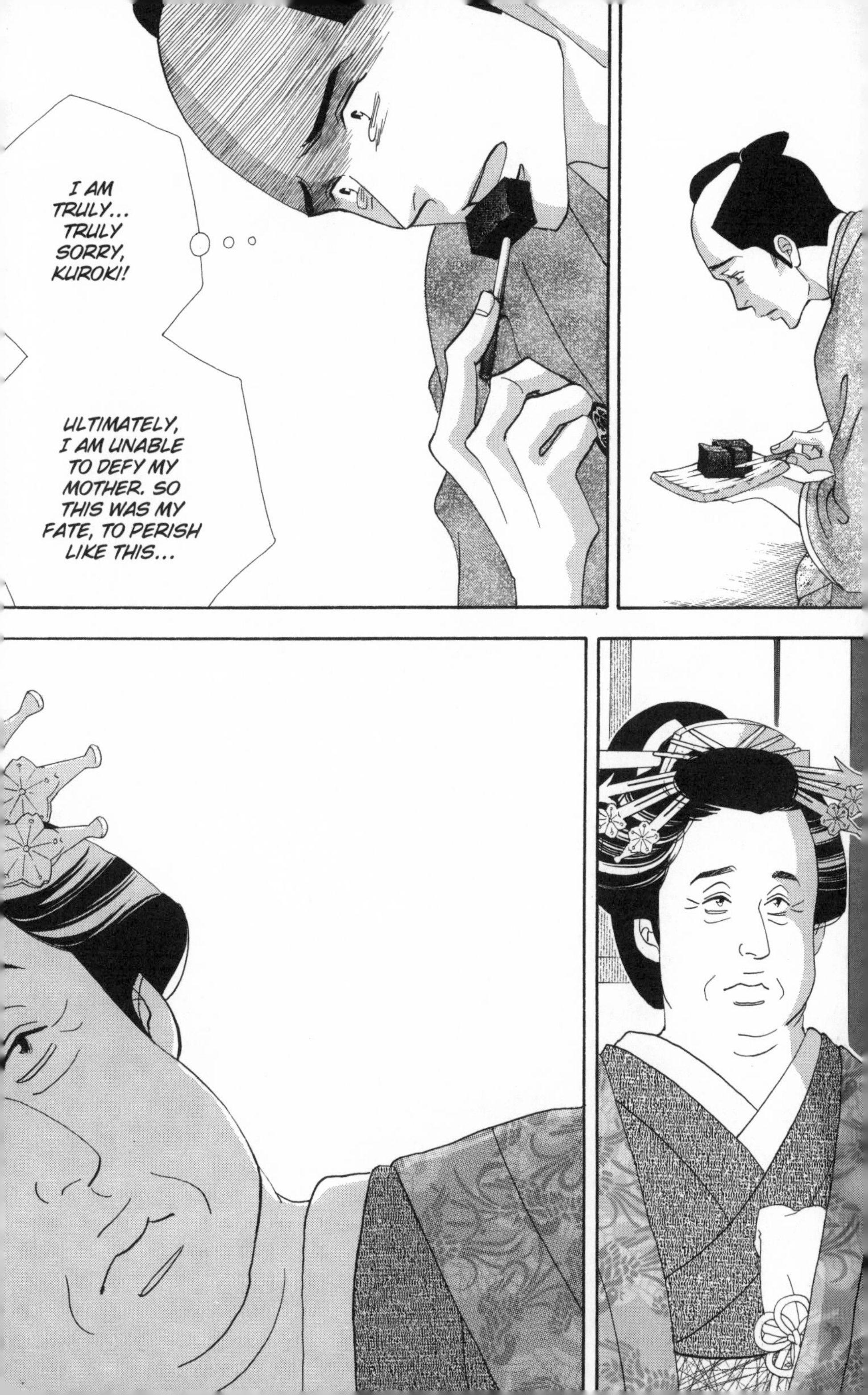
I AM TRULY... TRULY SORRY, KUROKI!
ULTIMATELY, I AM UNABLE TO DEFY MY MOTHER. SO THIS WAS MY FATE, TO PERISH LIKE THIS...

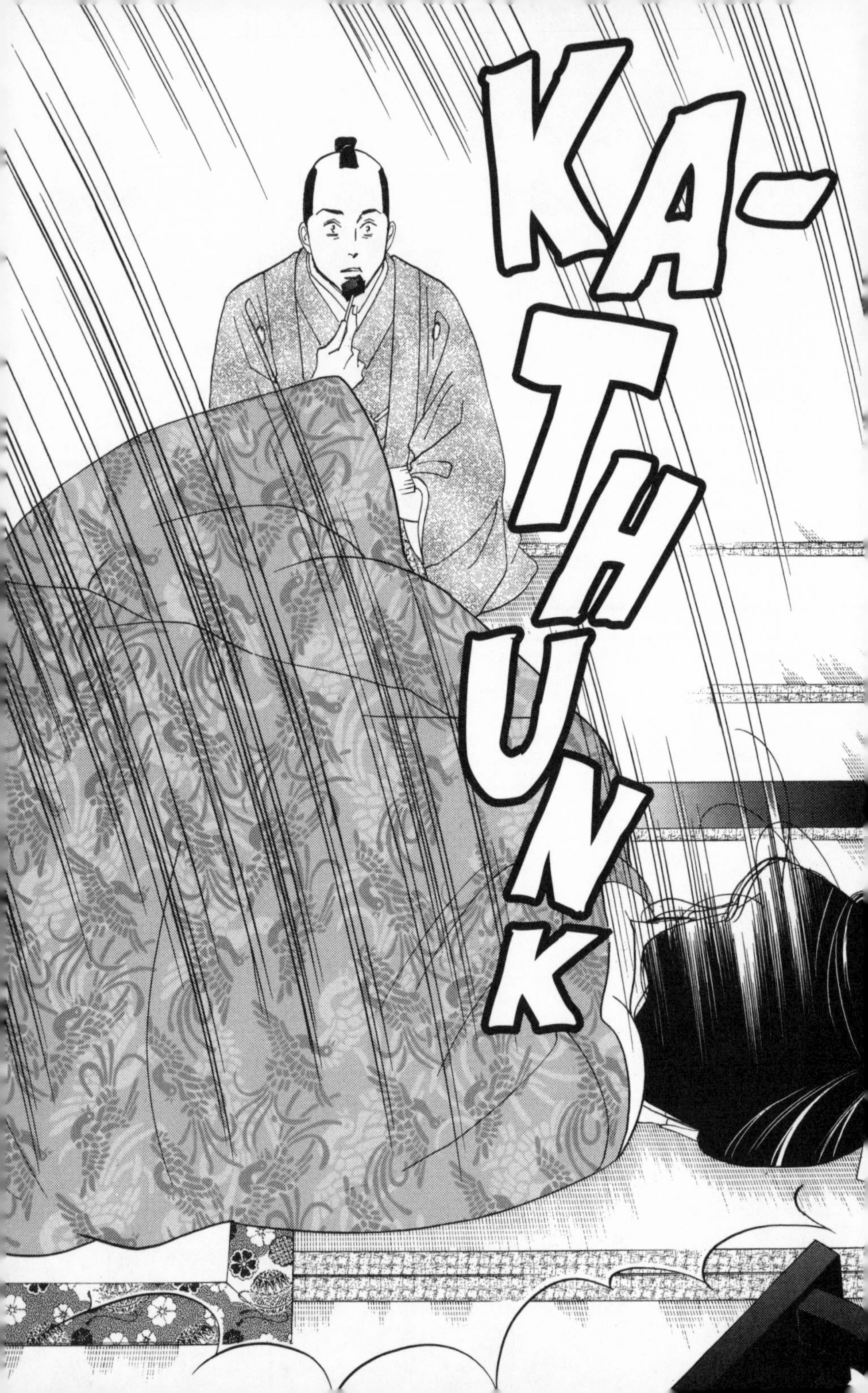
KA-THUNK

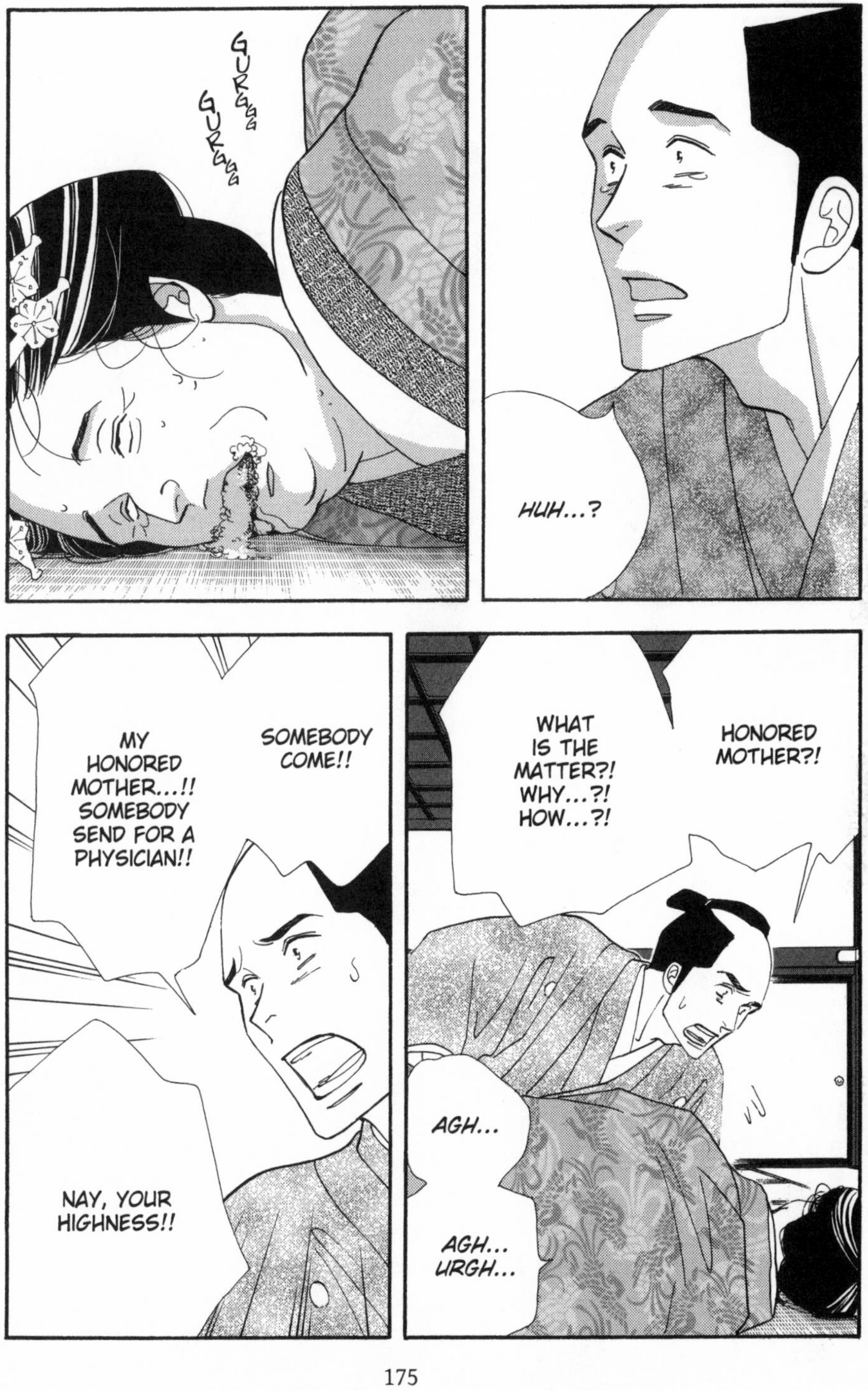
HUH...?
GURGGG
GURGGG
HONORED MOTHER?!
WHAT IS THE MATTER?! WHY...?! HOW...?!
AGH...
AGH... URGH...
SOMEBODY COME!!
MY HONORED MOTHER...!! SOMEBODY SEND FOR A PHYSICIAN!!
NAY, YOUR HIGHNESS!!

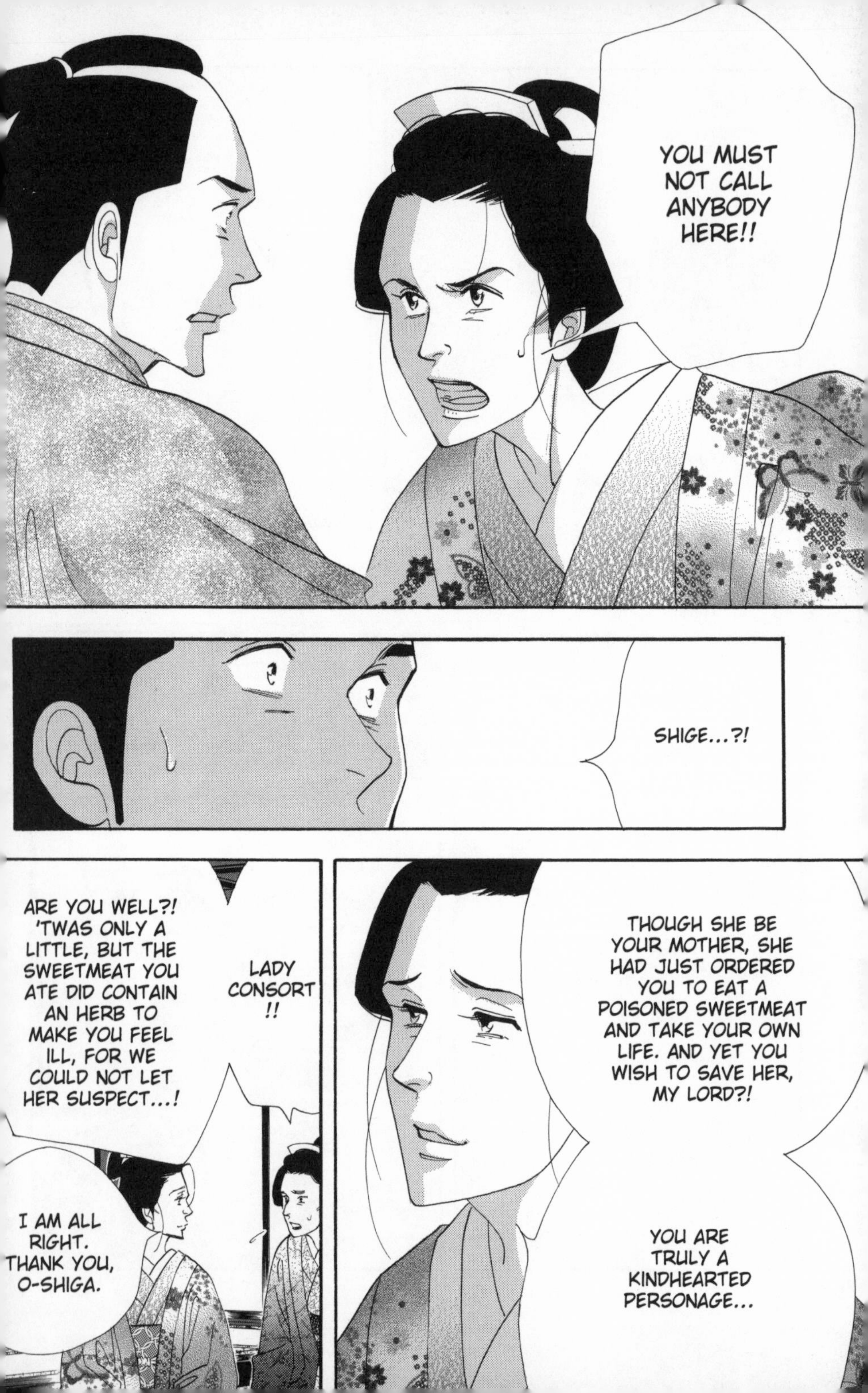
YOU MUST NOT CALL ANYBODY HERE!!
SHIGE...?!
THOUGH SHE BE YOUR MOTHER, SHE HAD JUST ORDERED YOU TO EAT A POISONED SWEETMEAT AND TAKE YOUR OWN LIFE. AND YET YOU WISH TO SAVE HER, MY LORD?!
YOU ARE TRULY A KINDHEARTED PERSONAGE...
LADY CONSORT!!
ARE YOU WELL?! 'TWAS ONLY A LITTLE, BUT THE SWEETMEAT YOU ATE DID CONTAIN AN HERB TO MAKE YOU FEEL ILL, FOR WE COULD NOT LET HER SUSPECT...!
I AM ALL RIGHT. THANK YOU, O-SHIGA.

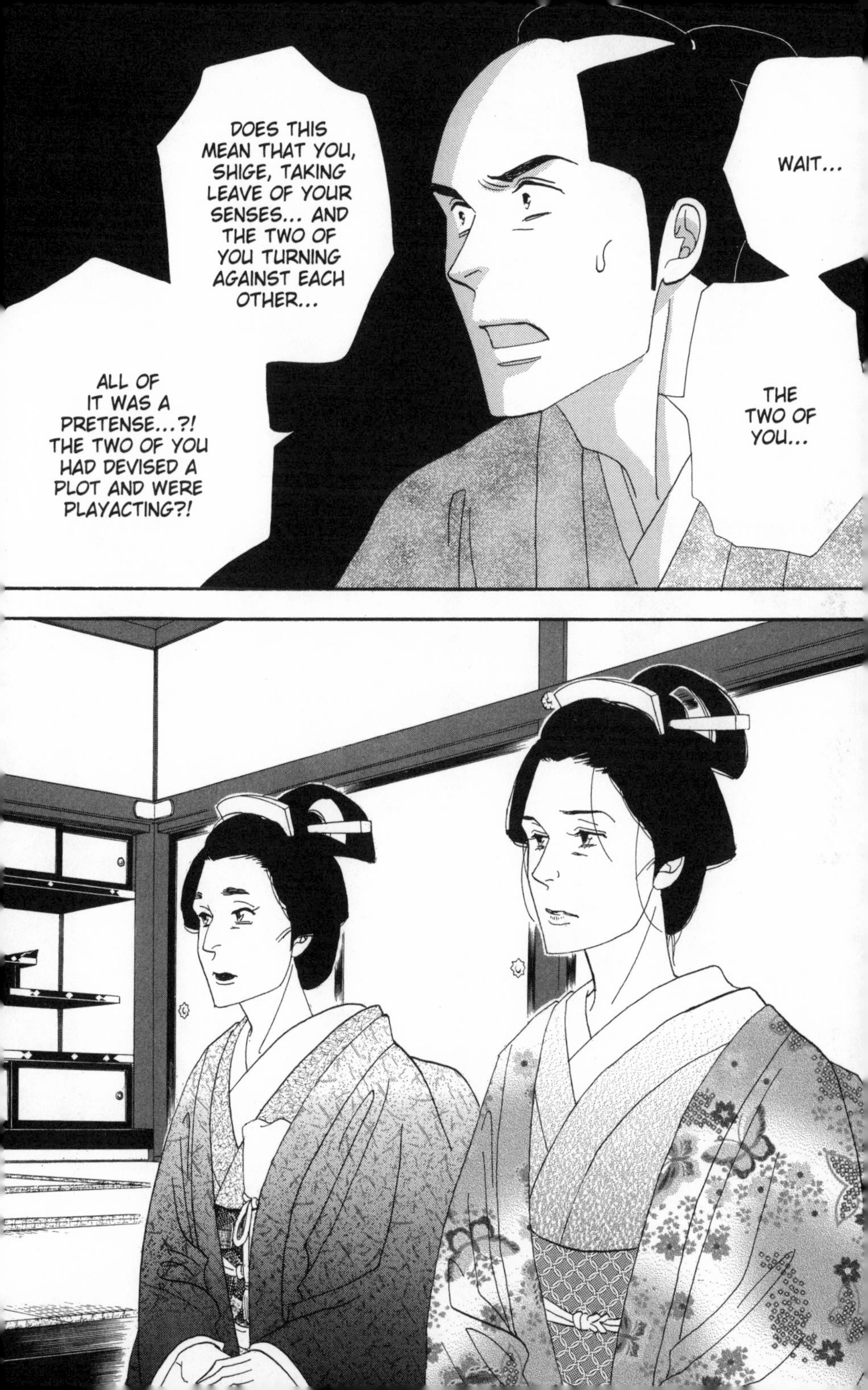
WAIT...
THE TWO OF YOU...
DOES THIS MEAN THAT YOU, SHIGE, TAKING LEAVE OF YOUR SENSES... AND THE TWO OF YOU TURNING AGAINST EACH OTHER...
ALL OF IT WAS A PRETENSE...?! THE TWO OF YOU HAD DEVISED A PLOT AND WERE PLAYACTING?!

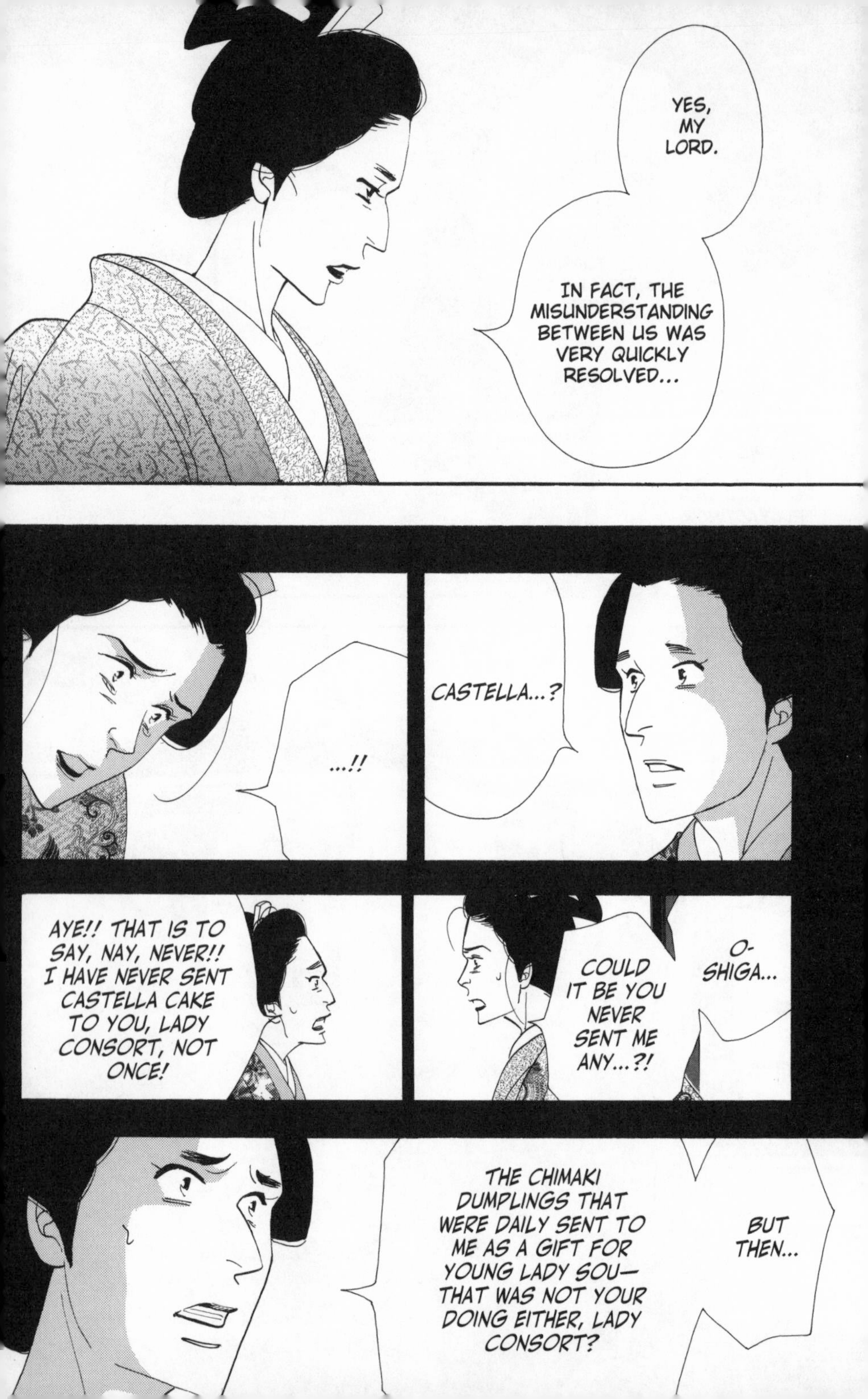
YES, MY LORD.
IN FACT, THE MISUNDERSTANDING BETWEEN US WAS VERY QUICKLY RESOLVED...
CASTELLA...?
...!!
O-SHIGA...
COULD IT BE YOU NEVER SENT ME ANY...?!
AYE!! THAT IS TO SAY, NAY, NEVER!! I HAVE NEVER SENT CASTELLA CAKE TO YOU, LADY CONSORT, NOT ONCE!
BUT THEN...
THE CHIMAKI DUMPLINGS THAT WERE DAILY SENT TO ME AS A GIFT FOR YOUNG LADY SOU—THAT WAS NOT YOUR DOING EITHER, LADY CONSORT?

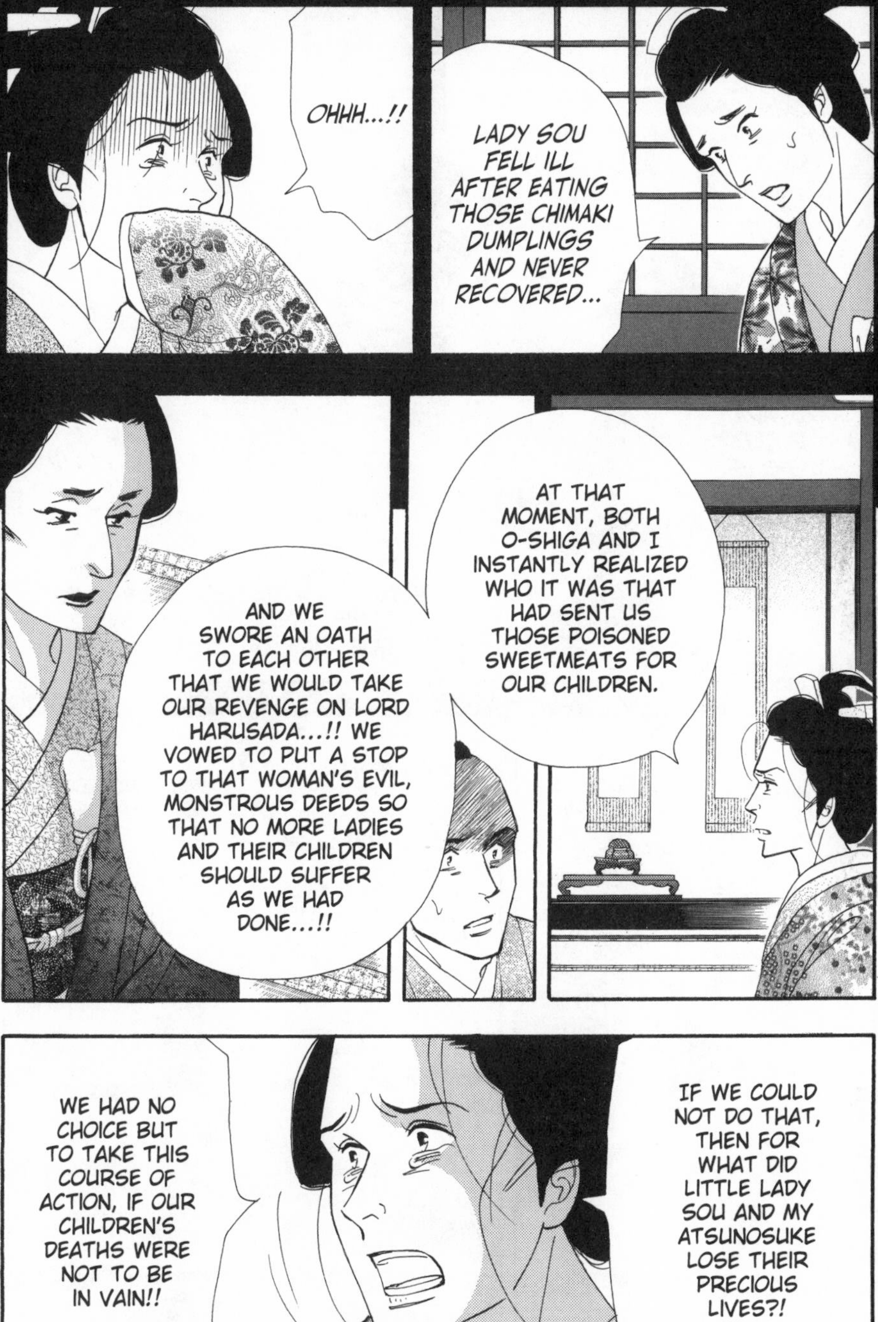
LADY SOU FELL ILL AFTER EATING THOSE CHIMAKI DUMPLINGS AND NEVER RECOVERED...
OHHH...!!
AT THAT MOMENT, BOTH O-SHIGA AND I INSTANTLY REALIZED WHO IT WAS THAT HAD SENT US THOSE POISONED SWEETMEATS FOR OUR CHILDREN.
AND WE SWORE AN OATH TO EACH OTHER THAT WE WOULD TAKE OUR REVENGE ON LORD HARUSADA...!! WE VOWED TO PUT A STOP TO THAT WOMAN'S EVIL, MONSTROUS DEEDS SO THAT NO MORE LADIES AND THEIR CHILDREN SHOULD SUFFER AS WE HAD DONE...!!
IF WE COULD NOT DO THAT, THEN FOR WHAT DID LITTLE LADY SOU AND MY ATSUNOSUKE LOSE THEIR PRECIOUS LIVES?!
WE HAD NO CHOICE BUT TO TAKE THIS COURSE OF ACTION, IF OUR CHILDREN'S DEATHS WERE NOT TO BE IN VAIN!!

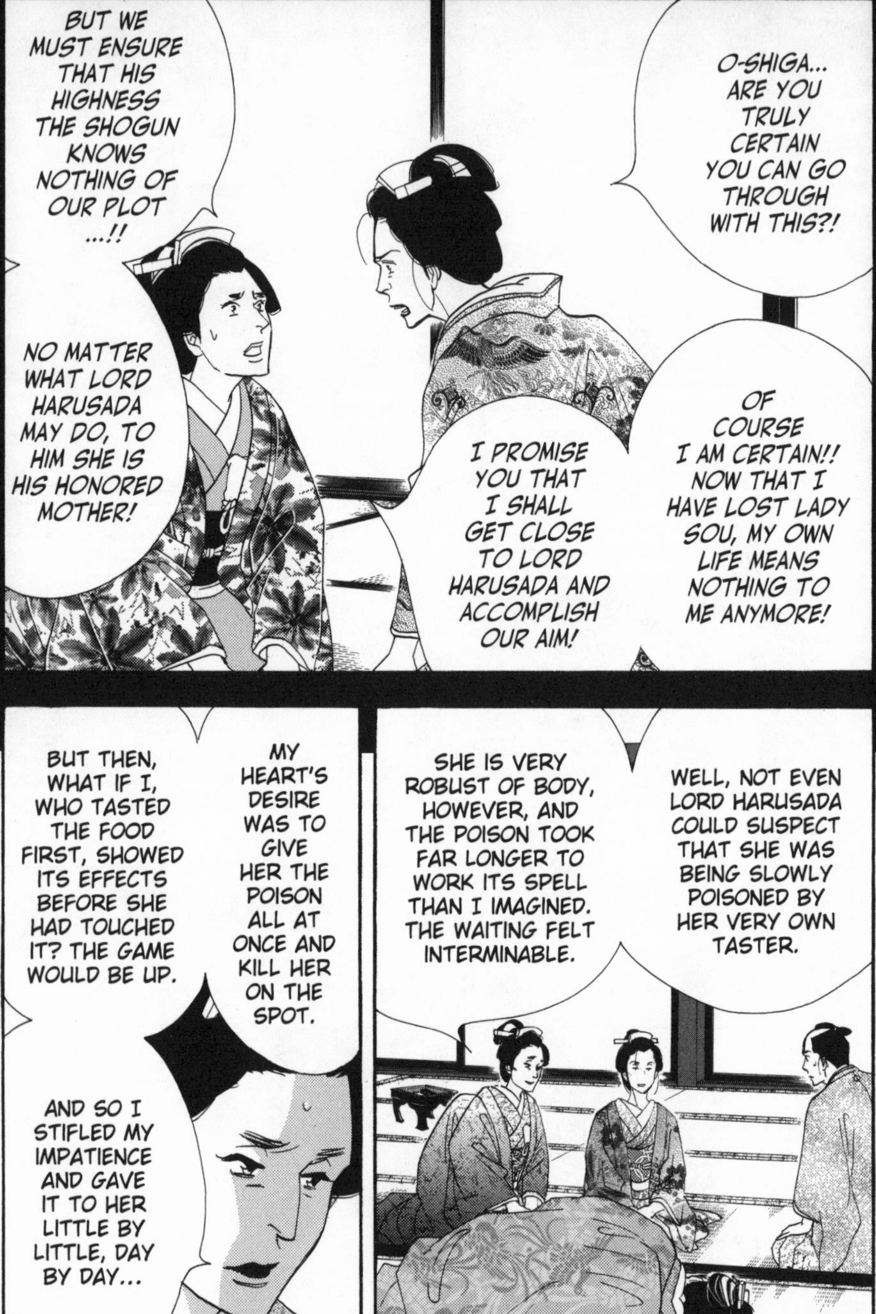
O-SHIGA... ARE YOU TRULY CERTAIN YOU CAN GO THROUGH WITH THIS?!
OF COURSE I AM CERTAIN!! NOW THAT I HAVE LOST LADY SOU, MY OWN LIFE MEANS NOTHING TO ME ANYMORE!
I PROMISE YOU THAT I SHALL GET CLOSE TO LORD HARUSADA AND ACCOMPLISH OUR AIM!
NO MATTER WHAT LORD HARUSADA MAY DO, TO HIM SHE IS HIS HONORED MOTHER!
BUT WE MUST ENSURE THAT HIS HIGHNESS THE SHOGUN KNOWS NOTHING OF OUR PLOT ...!!
WELL, NOT EVEN LORD HARUSADA COULD SUSPECT THAT SHE WAS BEING SLOWLY POISONED BY HER VERY OWN TASTER.
SHE IS VERY ROBUST OF BODY, HOWEVER, AND THE POISON TOOK FAR LONGER TO WORK ITS SPELL THAN I IMAGINED. THE WAITING FELT INTERMINABLE.
MY HEART'S DESIRE WAS TO GIVE HER THE POISON ALL AT ONCE AND KILL HER ON THE SPOT.
BUT THEN, WHAT IF I, WHO TASTED THE FOOD FIRST, SHOWED ITS EFFECTS BEFORE SHE HAD TOUCHED IT? THE GAME WOULD BE UP.
AND SO I STIFLED MY IMPATIENCE AND GAVE IT TO HER LITTLE BY LITTLE, DAY BY DAY...

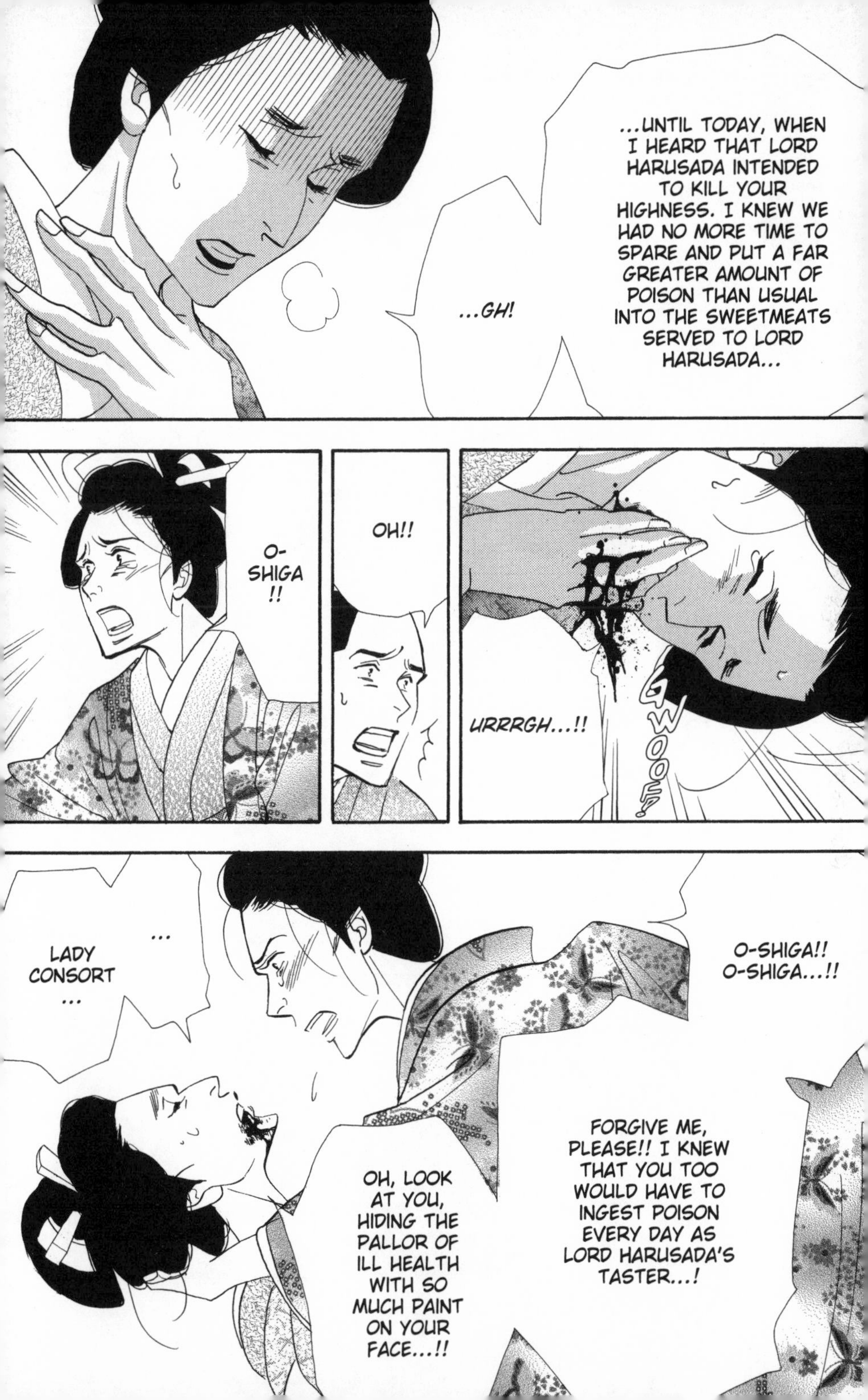
...UNTIL TODAY, WHEN I HEARD THAT LORD HARUSADA INTENDED TO KILL YOUR HIGHNESS. I KNEW WE HAD NO MORE TIME TO SPARE AND PUT A FAR GREATER AMOUNT OF POISON THAN USUAL INTO THE SWEETMEATS SERVED TO LORD HARUSADA...
...GH!
URRRGH...!!
GWOOF!
OH!!
O-SHIGA!!
O-SHIGA!! O-SHIGA...!!
...
LADY CONSORT ...
FORGIVE ME, PLEASE!! I KNEW THAT YOU TOO WOULD HAVE TO INGEST POISON EVERY DAY AS LORD HARUSADA'S TASTER...!
OH, LOOK AT YOU, HIDING THE PALLOR OF ILL HEALTH WITH SO MUCH PAINT ON YOUR FACE...!!

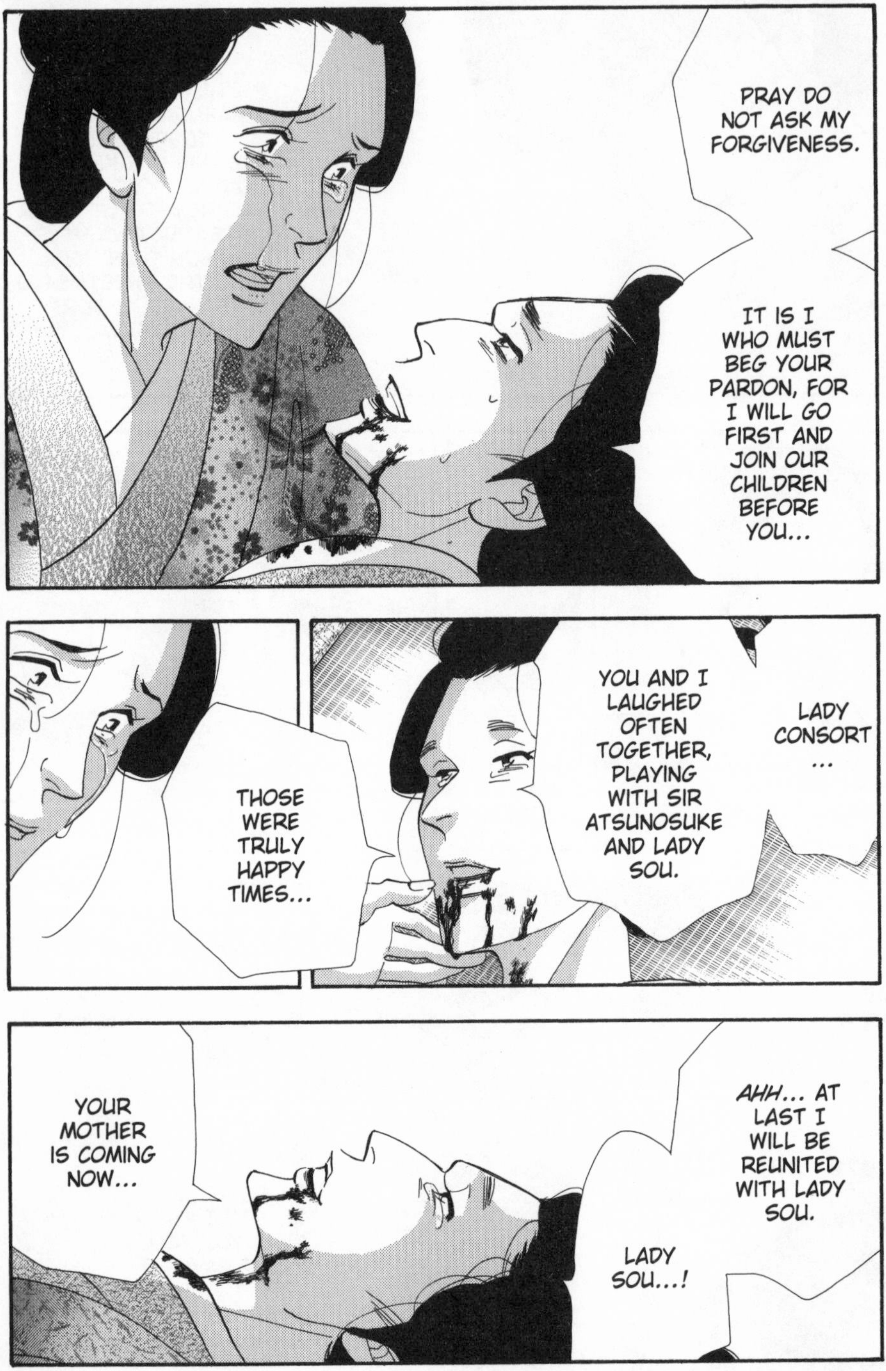
PRAY DO NOT ASK MY FORGIVENESS.
IT IS I WHO MUST BEG YOUR PARDON, FOR I WILL GO FIRST AND JOIN OUR CHILDREN BEFORE YOU...
LADY CONSORT ...
YOU AND I LAUGHED OFTEN TOGETHER, PLAYING WITH SIR ATSUNOSUKE AND LADY SOU.
THOSE WERE TRULY HAPPY TIMES...
AHH... AT LAST I WILL BE REUNITED WITH LADY SOU.
LADY SOU...!
YOUR MOTHER IS COMING NOW...

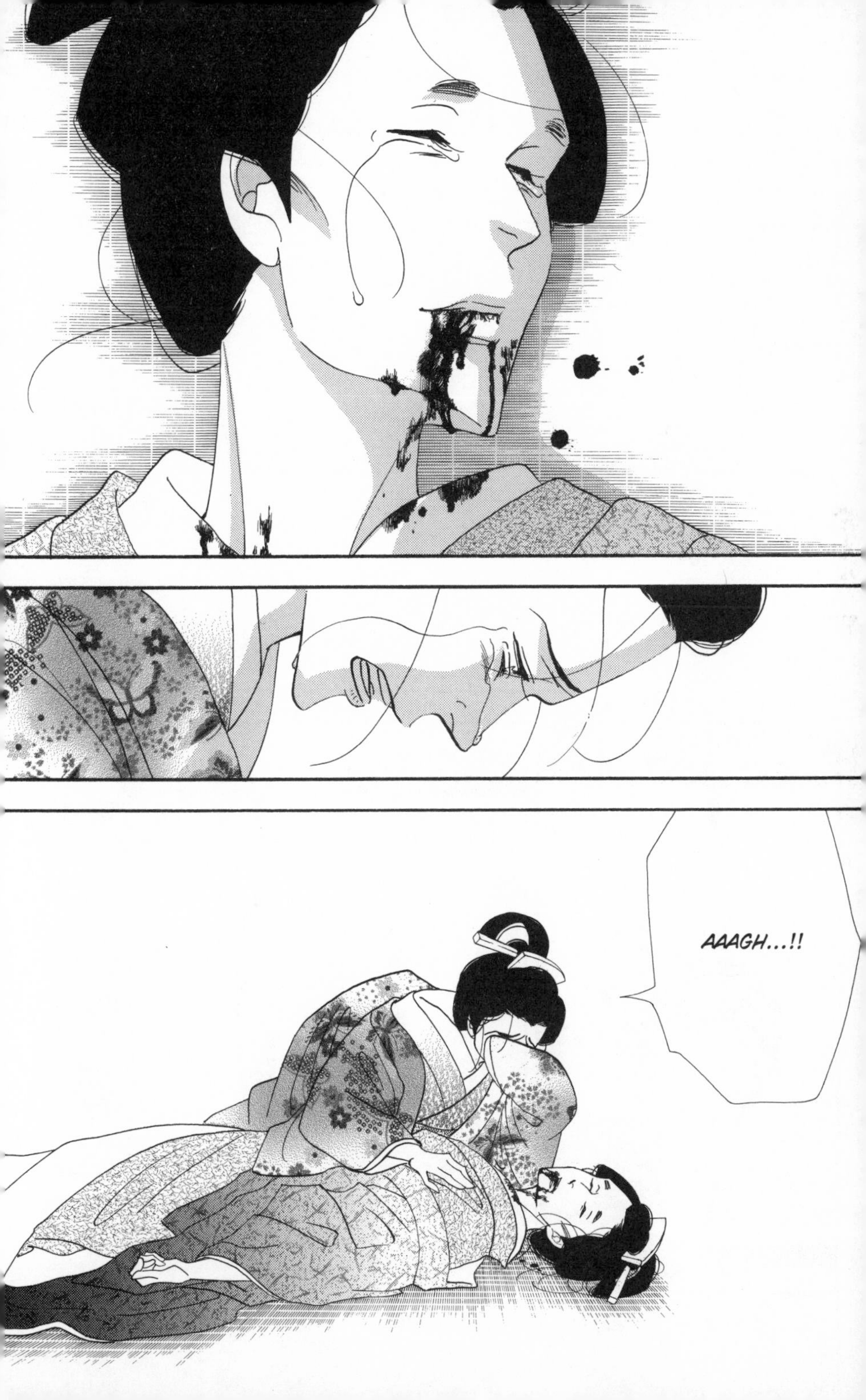
AAAGH...!!

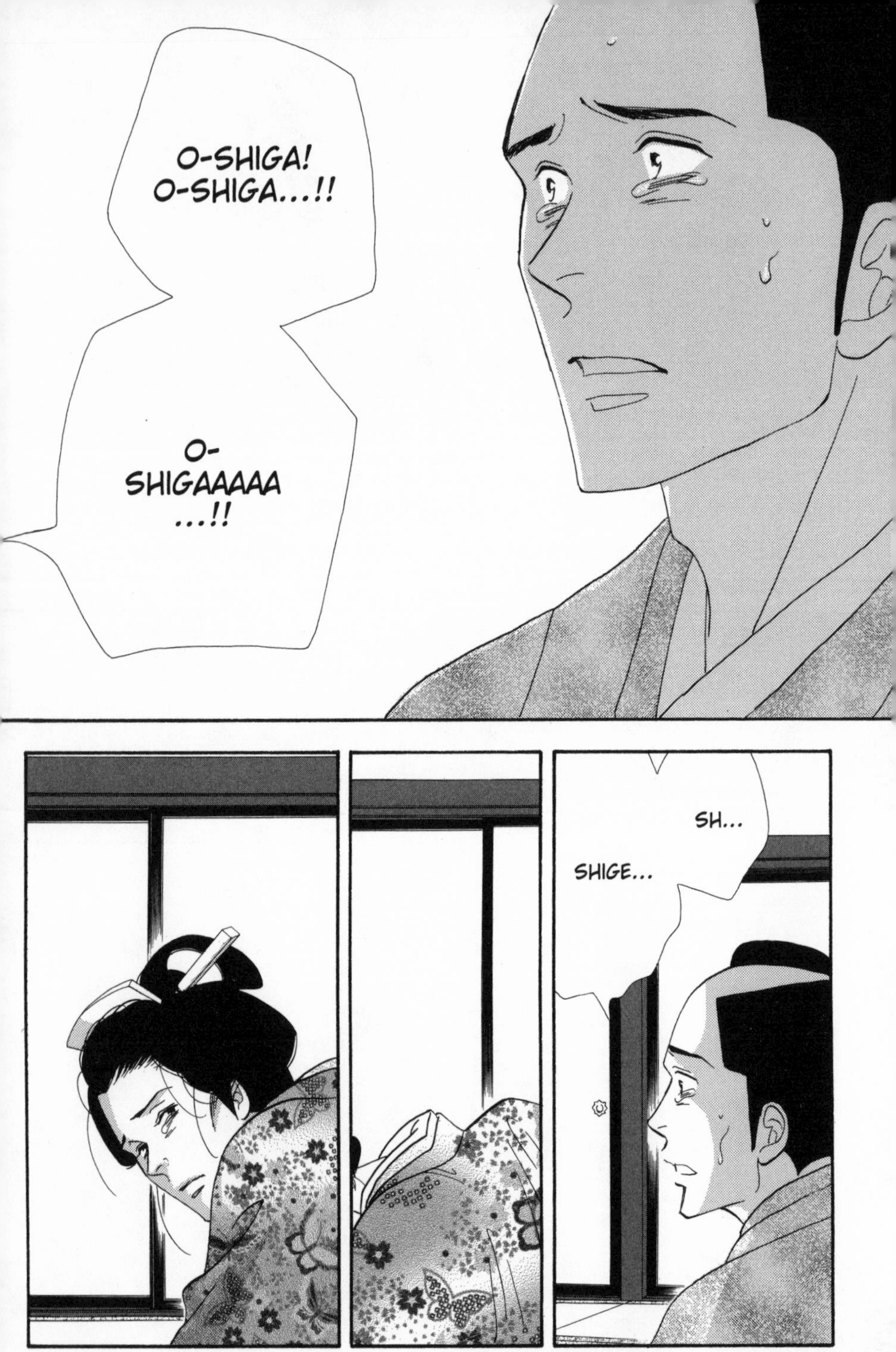
O-SHIGA! O-SHIGA...!!
O-SHIGAAAAA...!!
SH...
SHIGE...

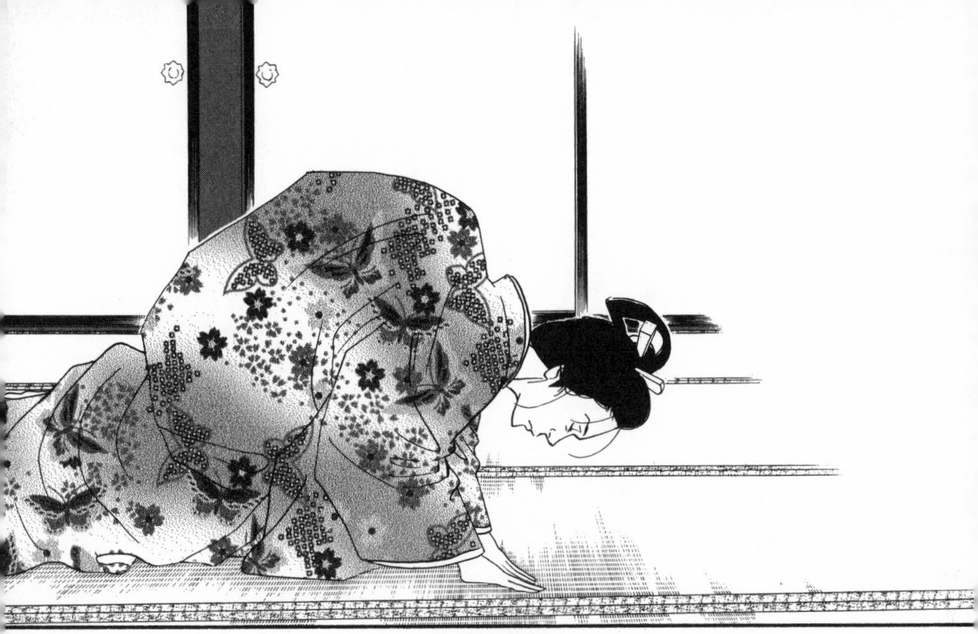

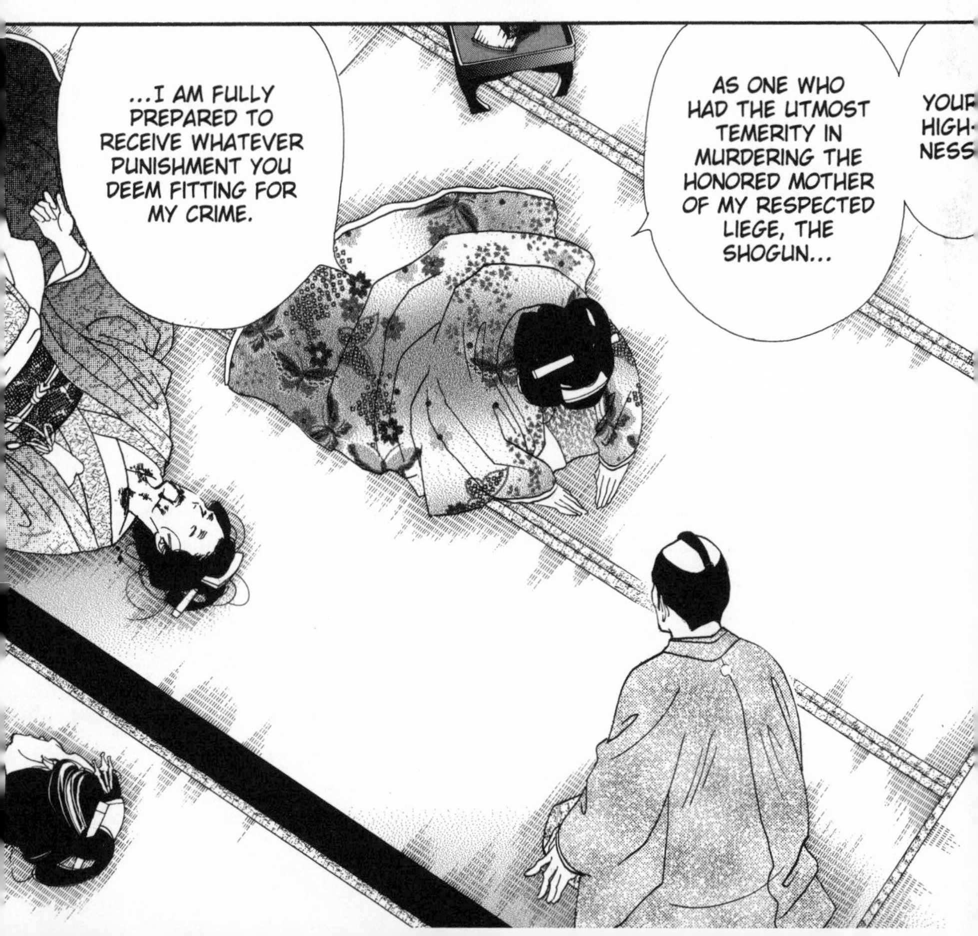
YOUR HIGH-NESS
AS ONE WHO HAD THE UTMOST TEMERITY IN MURDERING THE HONORED MOTHER OF MY RESPECTED LIEGE, THE SHOGUN...
...I AM FULLY PREPARED TO RECEIVE WHATEVER PUNISHMENT YOU DEEM FITTING FOR MY CRIME.

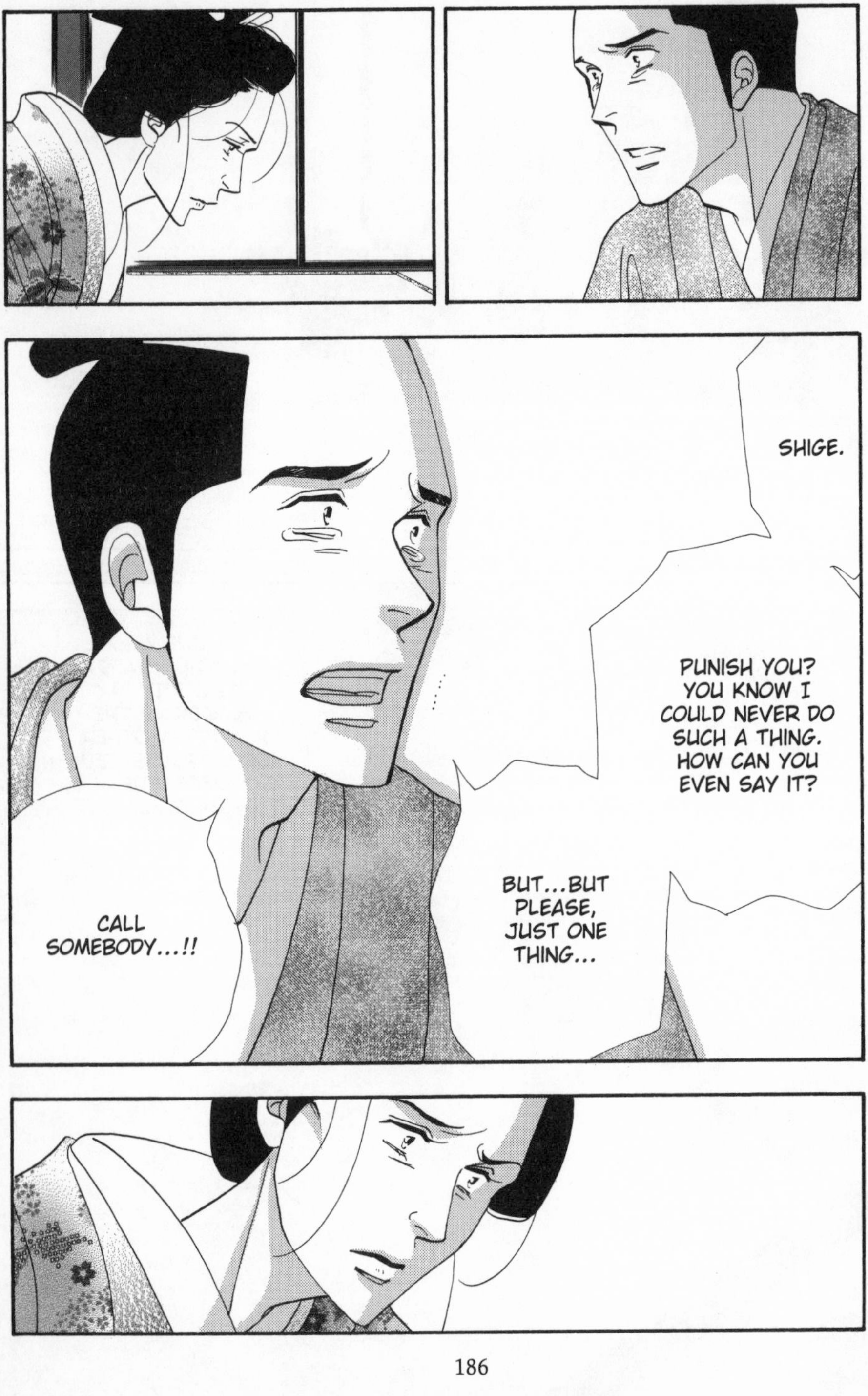
SHIGE.
PUNISH YOU? YOU KNOW I COULD NEVER DO SUCH A THING. HOW CAN YOU EVEN SAY IT?
BUT...BUT PLEASE, JUST ONE THING...
CALL SOMEBODY...!!

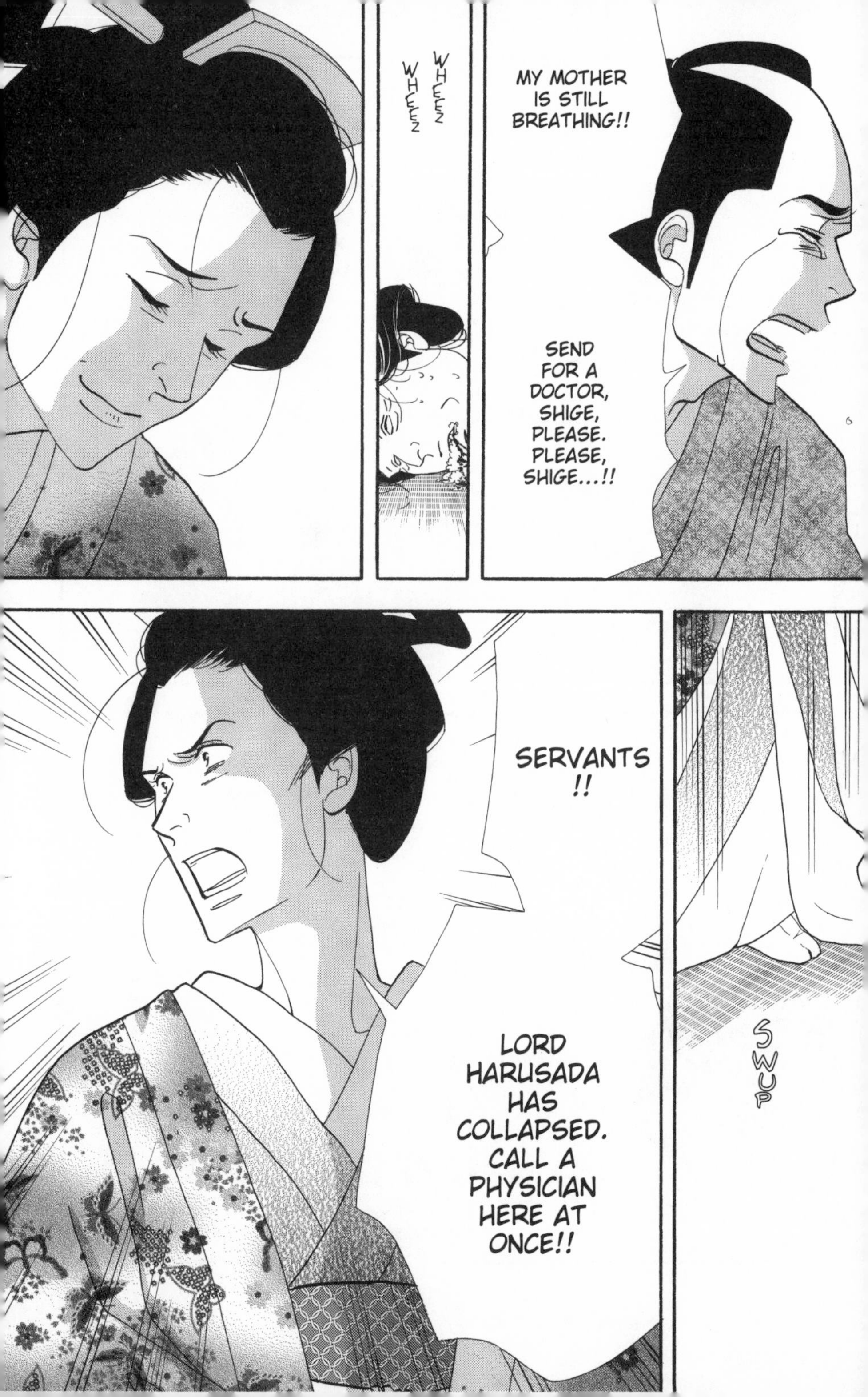
MY MOTHER IS STILL BREATHING!!
SEND FOR A DOCTOR, SHIGE, PLEASE. PLEASE, SHIGE...!!
WHEEZ WHEEZ
SWUP
SERVANTS!!
LORD HARUSADA HAS COLLAPSED. CALL A PHYSICIAN HERE AT ONCE!!

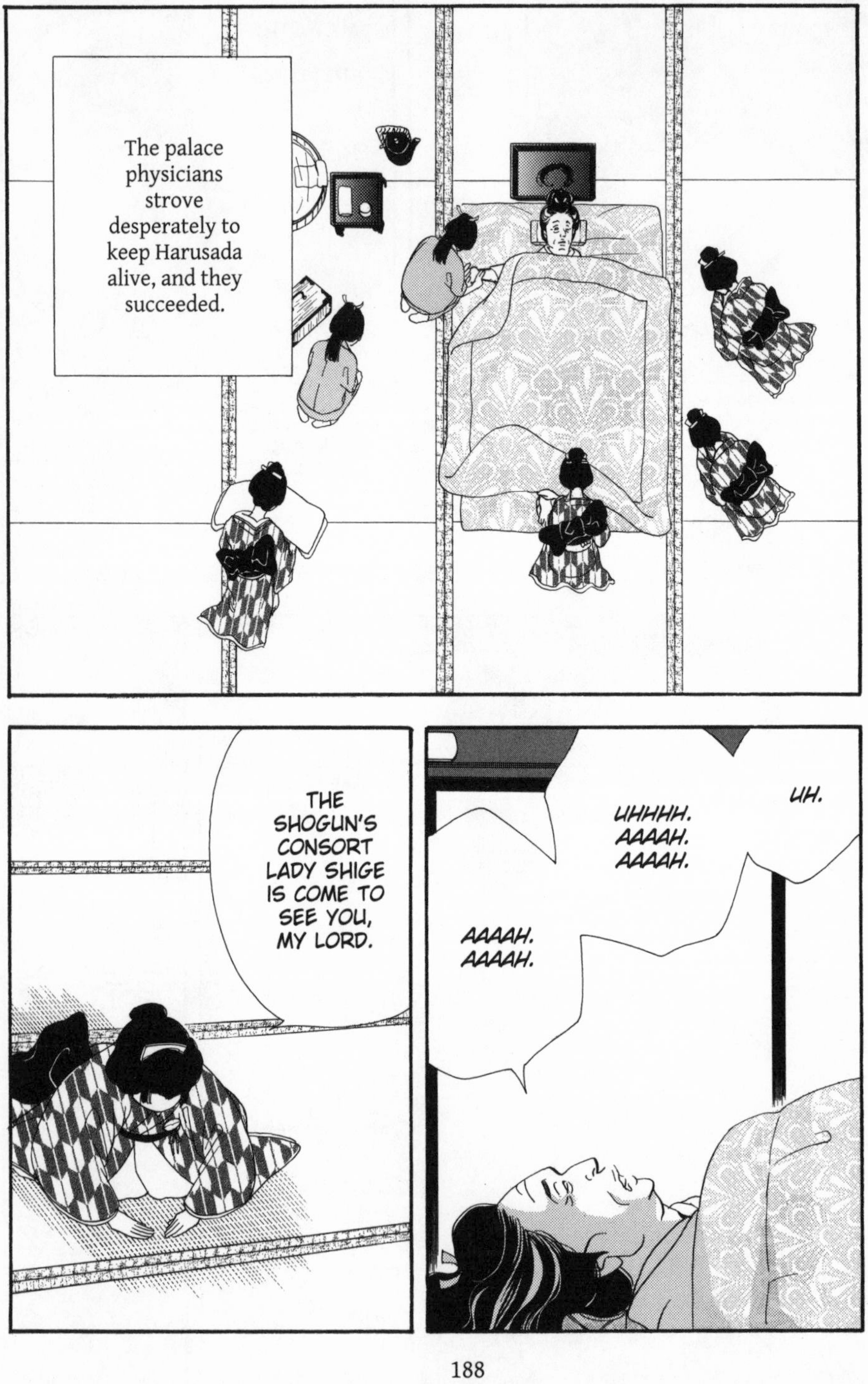
The palace physicians strove desperately to keep Harusada alive, and they succeeded.
UH.
UHHHH. AAAAH. AAAAH.
AAAAH. AAAAH.
THE SHOGUN'S CONSORT LADY SHIGE IS COME TO SEE YOU, MY LORD.

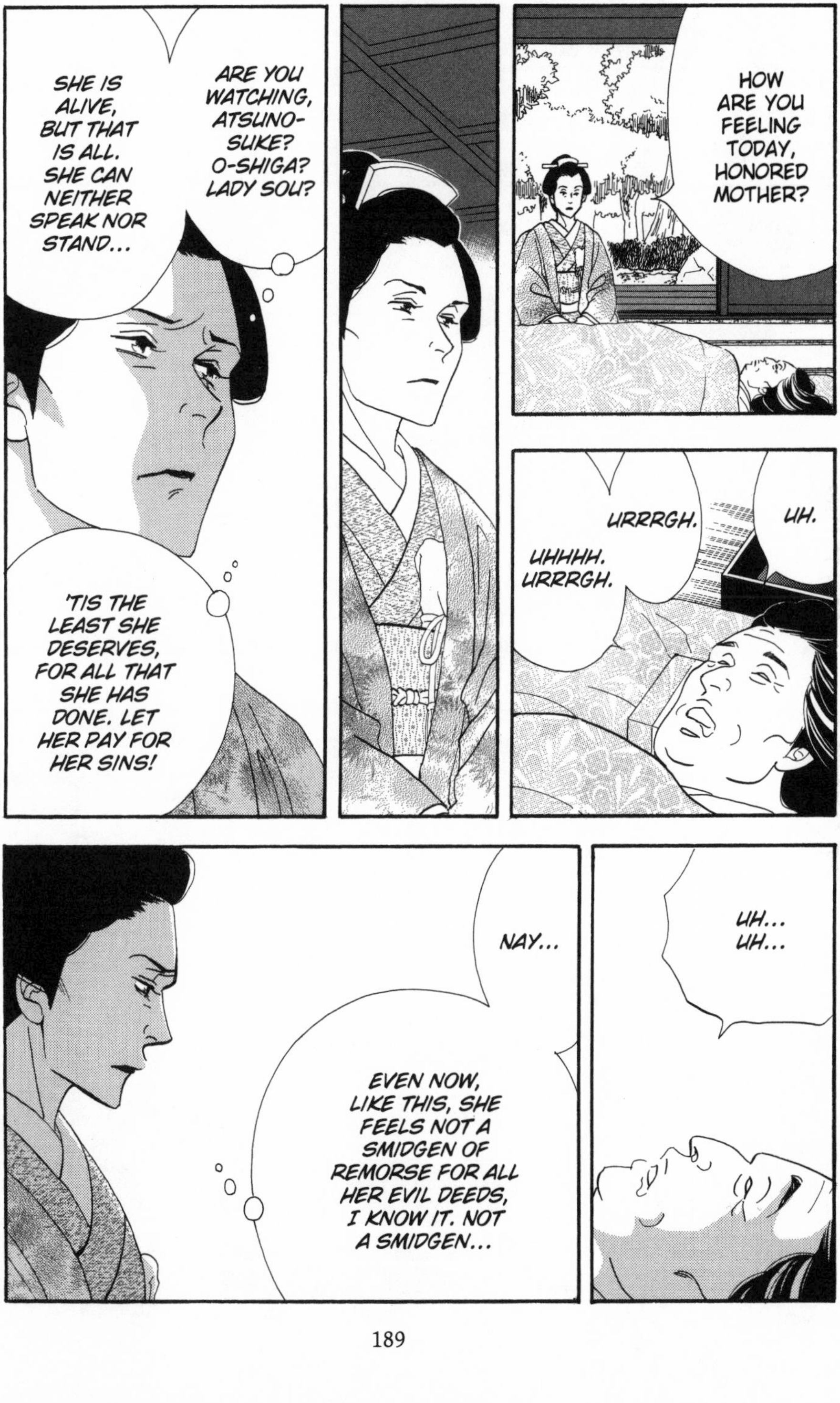
HOW ARE YOU FEELING TODAY, HONORED MOTHER?
UH.
URRRGH.
UHHHH. URRRGH.
ARE YOU WATCHING, ATSUNO-SUKE? O-SHIGA? LADY SOU?
SHE IS ALIVE, BUT THAT IS ALL. SHE CAN NEITHER SPEAK NOR STAND...
'TIS THE LEAST SHE DESERVES, FOR ALL THAT SHE HAS DONE. LET HER PAY FOR HER SINS!
UH... UH...
NAY...
EVEN NOW, LIKE THIS, SHE FEELS NOT A SMIDGEN OF REMORSE FOR ALL HER EVIL DEEDS, I KNOW IT. NOT A SMIDGEN...

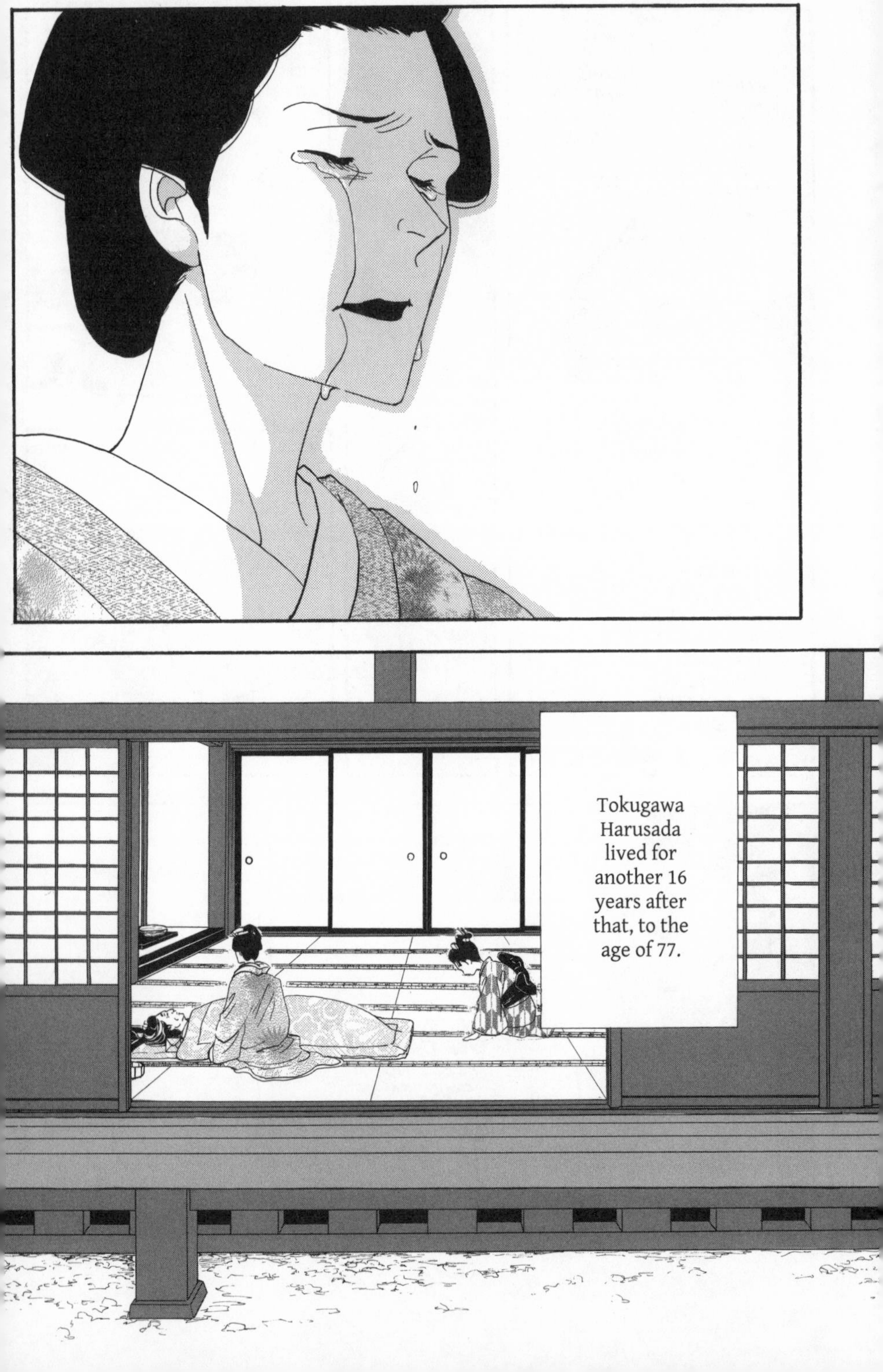
Tokugawa Harusada lived for another 16 years after that, to the age of 77.

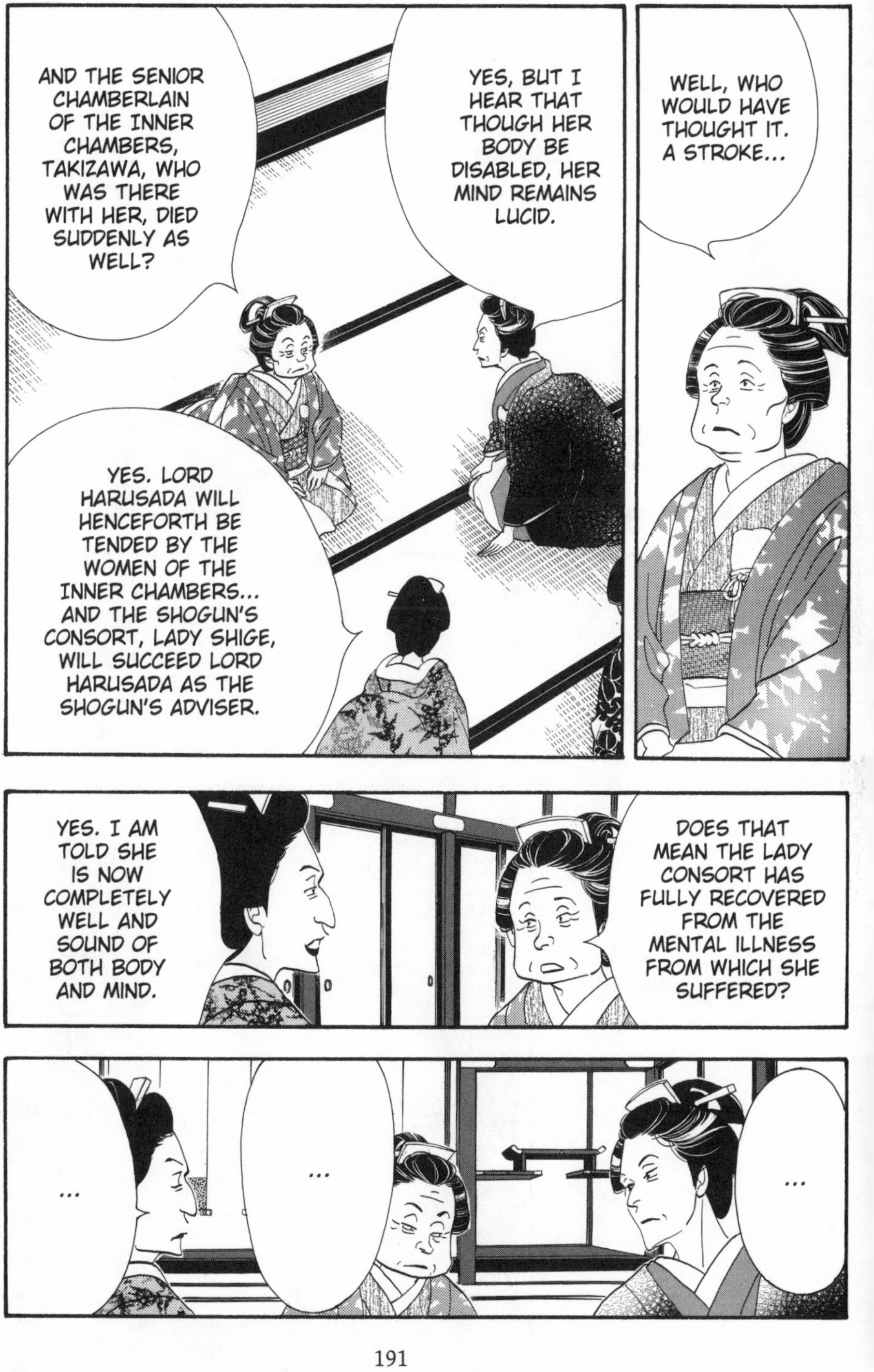
WELL, WHO WOULD HAVE THOUGHT IT. A STROKE...
YES, BUT I HEAR THAT THOUGH HER BODY BE DISABLED, HER MIND REMAINS LUCID.
AND THE SENIOR CHAMBERLAIN OF THE INNER CHAMBERS, TAKIZAWA, WHO WAS THERE WITH HER, DIED SUDDENLY AS WELL?
YES. LORD HARUSADA WILL HENCEFORTH BE TENDED BY THE WOMEN OF THE INNER CHAMBERS... AND THE SHOGUN'S CONSORT, LADY SHIGE, WILL SUCCEED LORD HARUSADA AS THE SHOGUN'S ADVISER.
DOES THAT MEAN THE LADY CONSORT HAS FULLY RECOVERED FROM THE MENTAL ILLNESS FROM WHICH SHE SUFFERED?
YES. I AM TOLD SHE IS NOW COMPLETELY WELL AND SOUND OF BOTH BODY AND MIND.
...
...
...

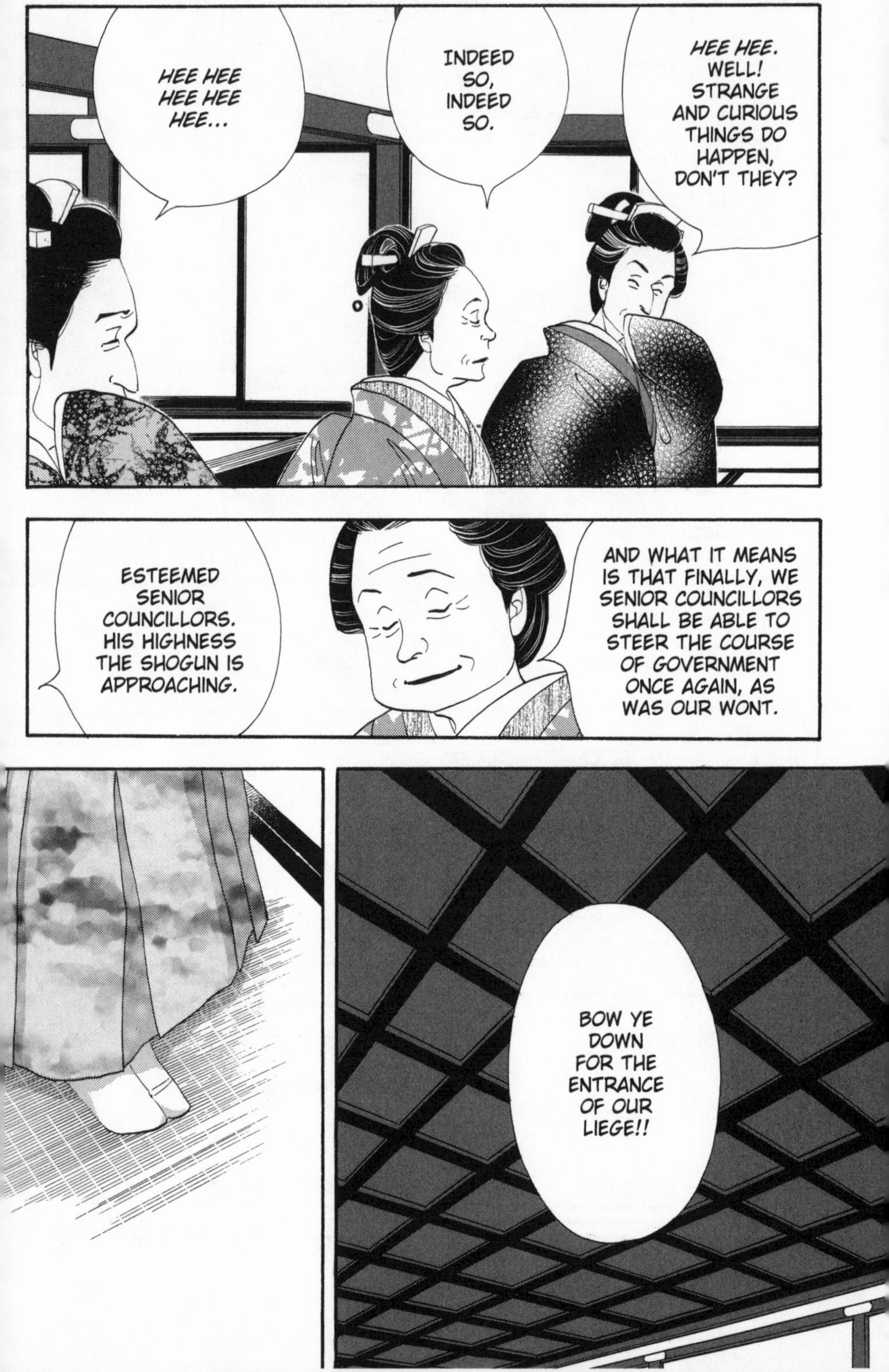
HEE HEE. WELL! STRANGE AND CURIOUS THINGS DO HAPPEN, DON'T THEY?
INDEED SO, INDEED SO.
HEE HEE HEE HEE HEE...
AND WHAT IT MEANS IS THAT FINALLY, WE SENIOR COUNCILLORS SHALL BE ABLE TO STEER THE COURSE OF GOVERNMENT ONCE AGAIN, AS WAS OUR WONT.
ESTEEMED SENIOR COUNCILLORS. HIS HIGHNESS THE SHOGUN IS APPROACHING.
BOW YE DOWN FOR THE ENTRANCE OF OUR LIEGE!!

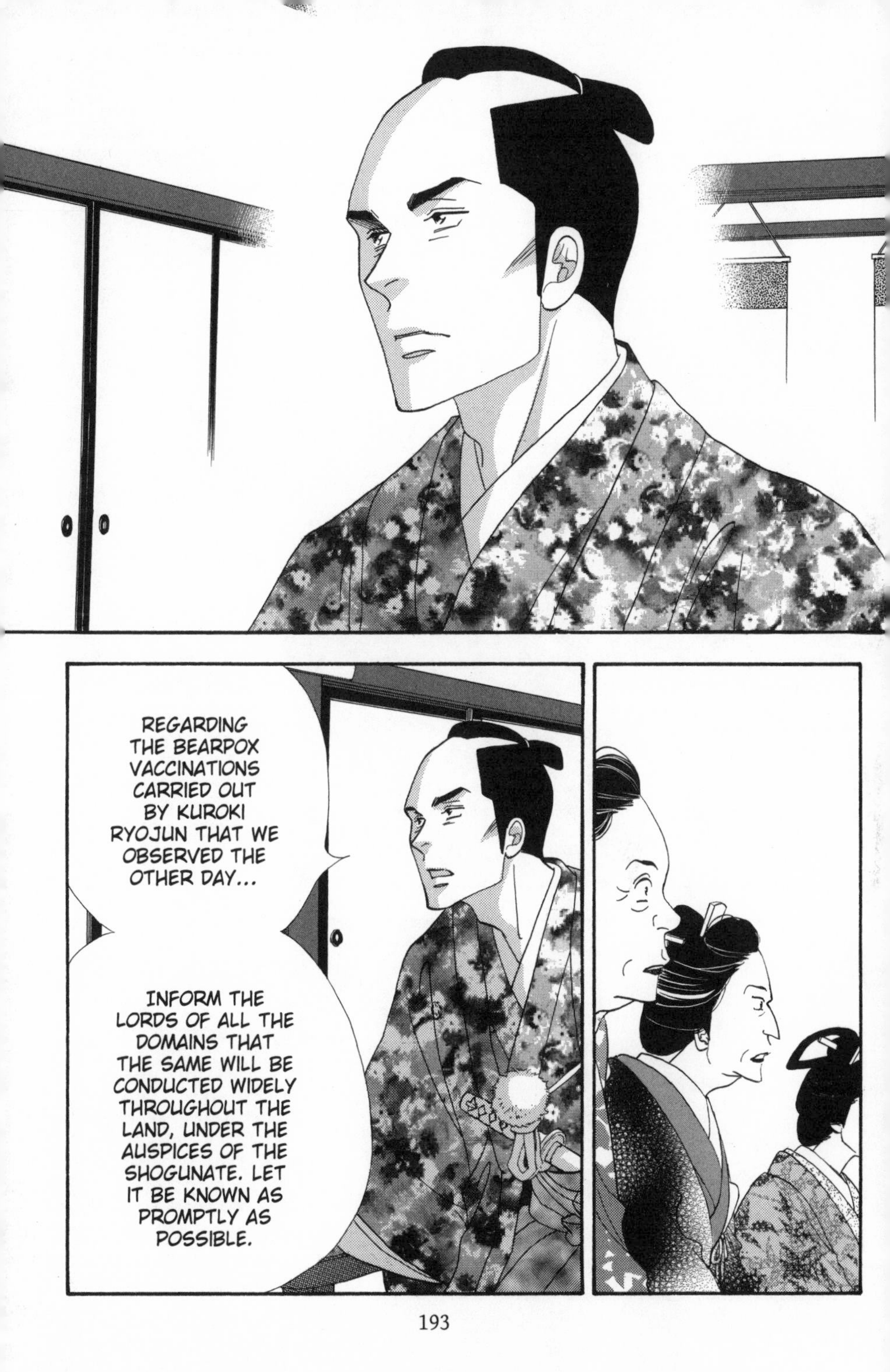
REGARDING THE BEARPOX VACCINATIONS CARRIED OUT BY KUROKI RYOJUN THAT WE OBSERVED THE OTHER DAY...
INFORM THE LORDS OF ALL THE DOMAINS THAT THE SAME WILL BE CONDUCTED WIDELY THROUGHOUT THE LAND, UNDER THE AUSPICES OF THE SHOGUNATE. LET IT BE KNOWN AS PROMPTLY AS POSSIBLE.

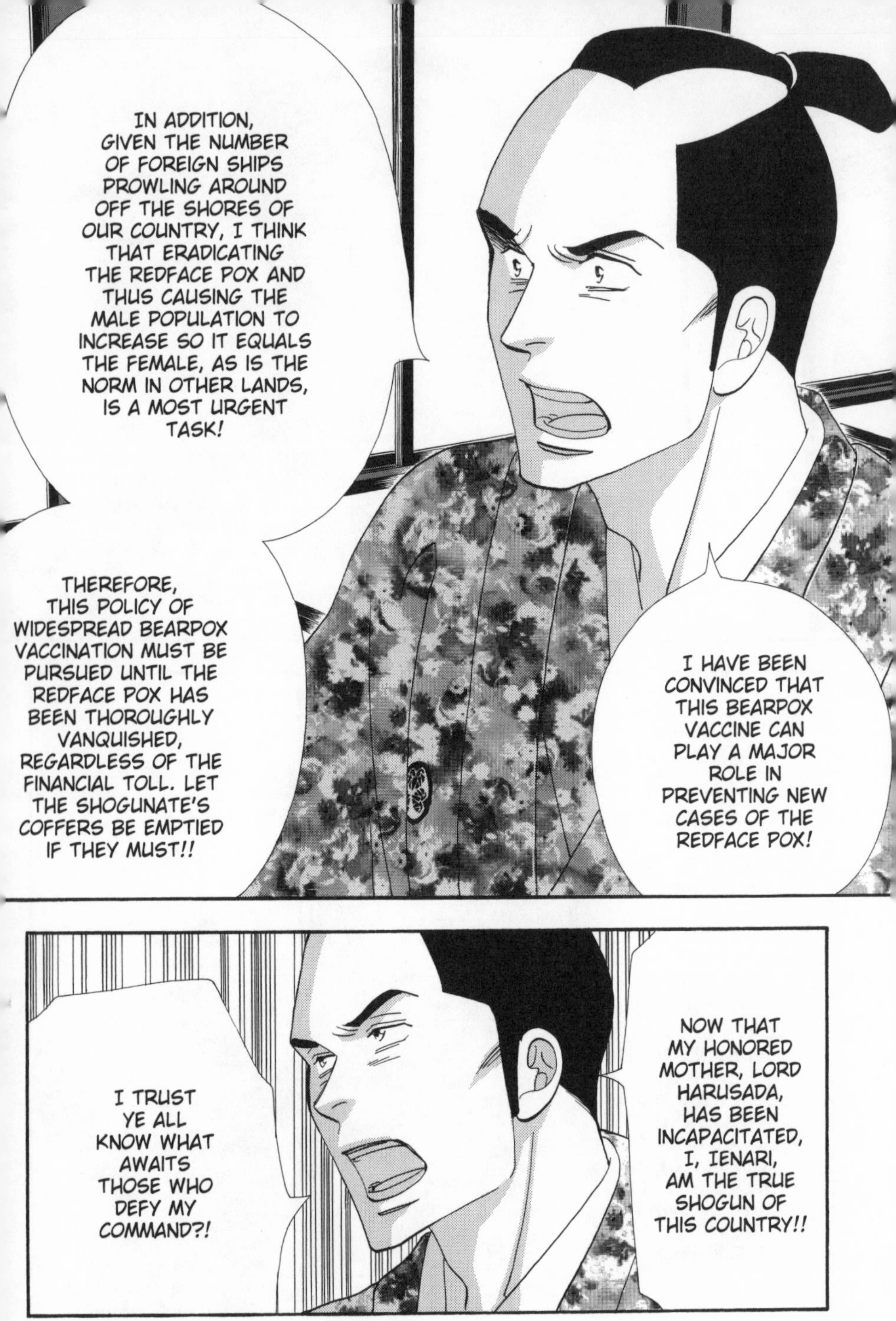

I HAVE BEEN CONVINCED THAT THIS BEARPOX VACCINE CAN PLAY A MAJOR ROLE IN PREVENTING NEW CASES OF THE REDFACE POX!
IN ADDITION, GIVEN THE NUMBER OF FOREIGN SHIPS PROWLING AROUND OFF THE SHORES OF OUR COUNTRY, I THINK THAT ERADICATING THE REDFACE POX AND THUS CAUSING THE MALE POPULATION TO INCREASE SO IT EQUALS THE FEMALE, AS IS THE NORM IN OTHER LANDS, IS A MOST URGENT TASK!
THEREFORE, THIS POLICY OF WIDESPREAD BEARPOX VACCINATION MUST BE PURSUED UNTIL THE REDFACE POX HAS BEEN THOROUGHLY VANQUISHED, REGARDLESS OF THE FINANCIAL TOLL. LET THE SHOGUNATE'S COFFERS BE EMPTIED IF THEY MUST!!
NOW THAT MY HONORED MOTHER, LORD HARUSADA, HAS BEEN INCAPACITATED, I, IENARI, AM THE TRUE SHOGUN OF THIS COUNTRY!!
I TRUST YE ALL KNOW WHAT AWAITS THOSE WHO DEFY MY COMMAND?!

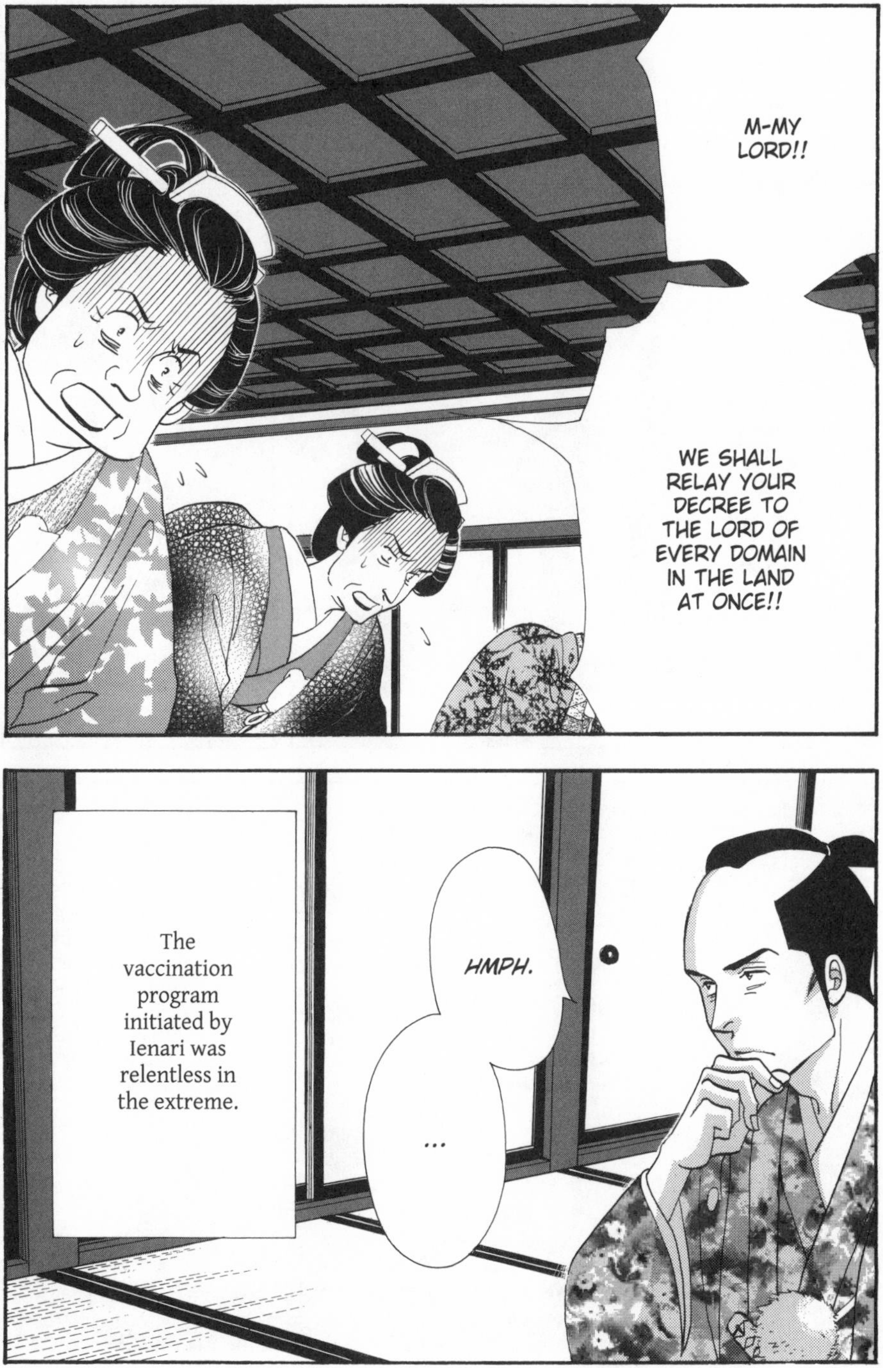
M-MY LORD!!
WE SHALL RELAY YOUR DECREE TO THE LORD OF EVERY DOMAIN IN THE LAND AT ONCE!!
HMPH.
...
The vaccination program initiated by Ienari was relentless in the extreme.

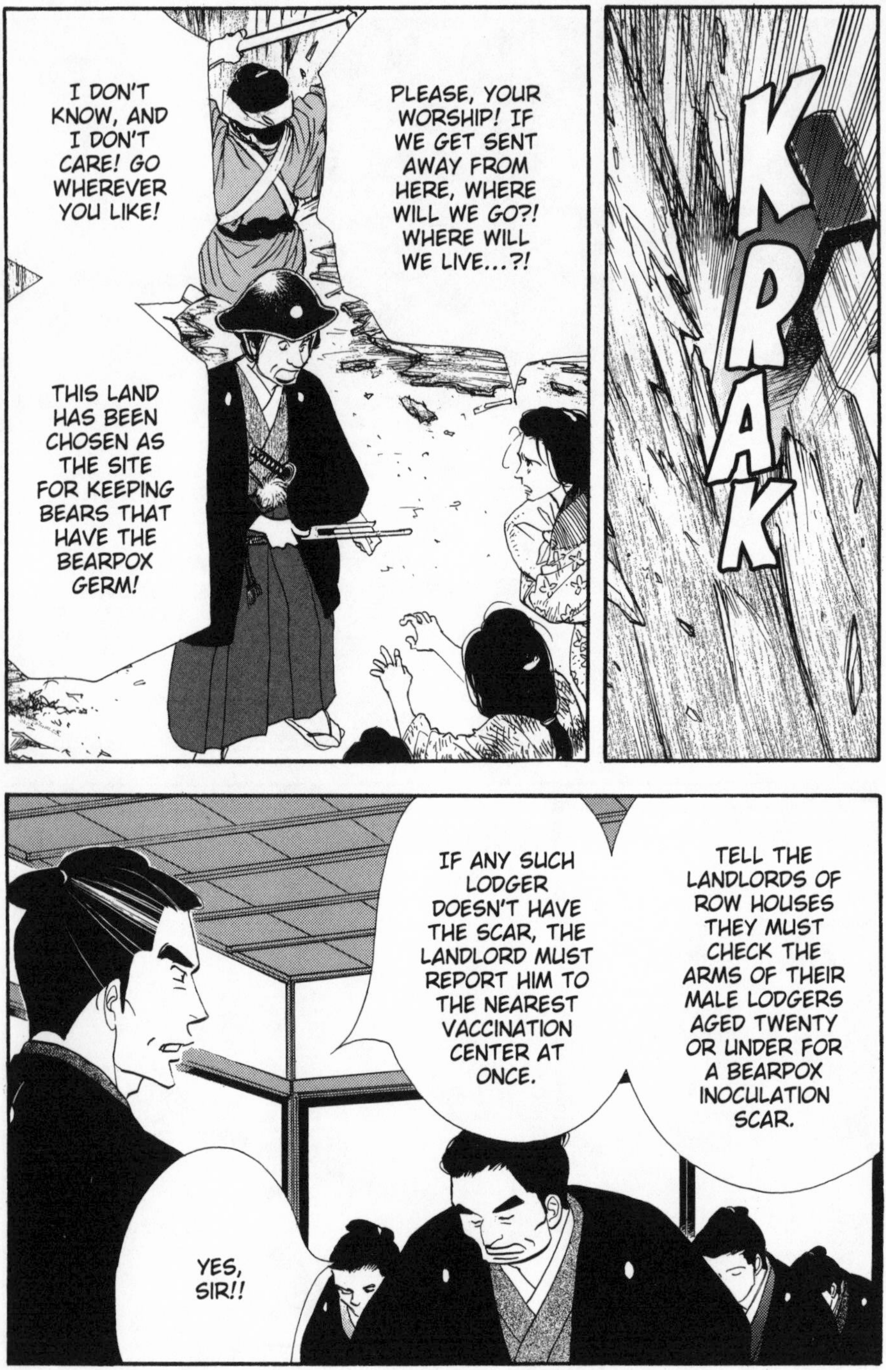
KRAK
PLEASE, YOUR WORSHIP! IF WE GET SENT AWAY FROM HERE, WHERE WILL WE GO?! WHERE WILL WE LIVE...?!
I DON'T KNOW, AND I DON'T CARE! GO WHEREVER YOU LIKE!
THIS LAND HAS BEEN CHOSEN AS THE SITE FOR KEEPING BEARS THAT HAVE THE BEARPOX GERM!
TELL THE LANDLORDS OF ROW HOUSES THEY MUST CHECK THE ARMS OF THEIR MALE LODGERS AGED TWENTY OR UNDER FOR A BEARPOX INOCULATION SCAR.
IF ANY SUCH LODGER DOESN'T HAVE THE SCAR, THE LANDLORD MUST REPORT HIM TO THE NEAREST VACCINATION CENTER AT ONCE.
YES, SIR!!

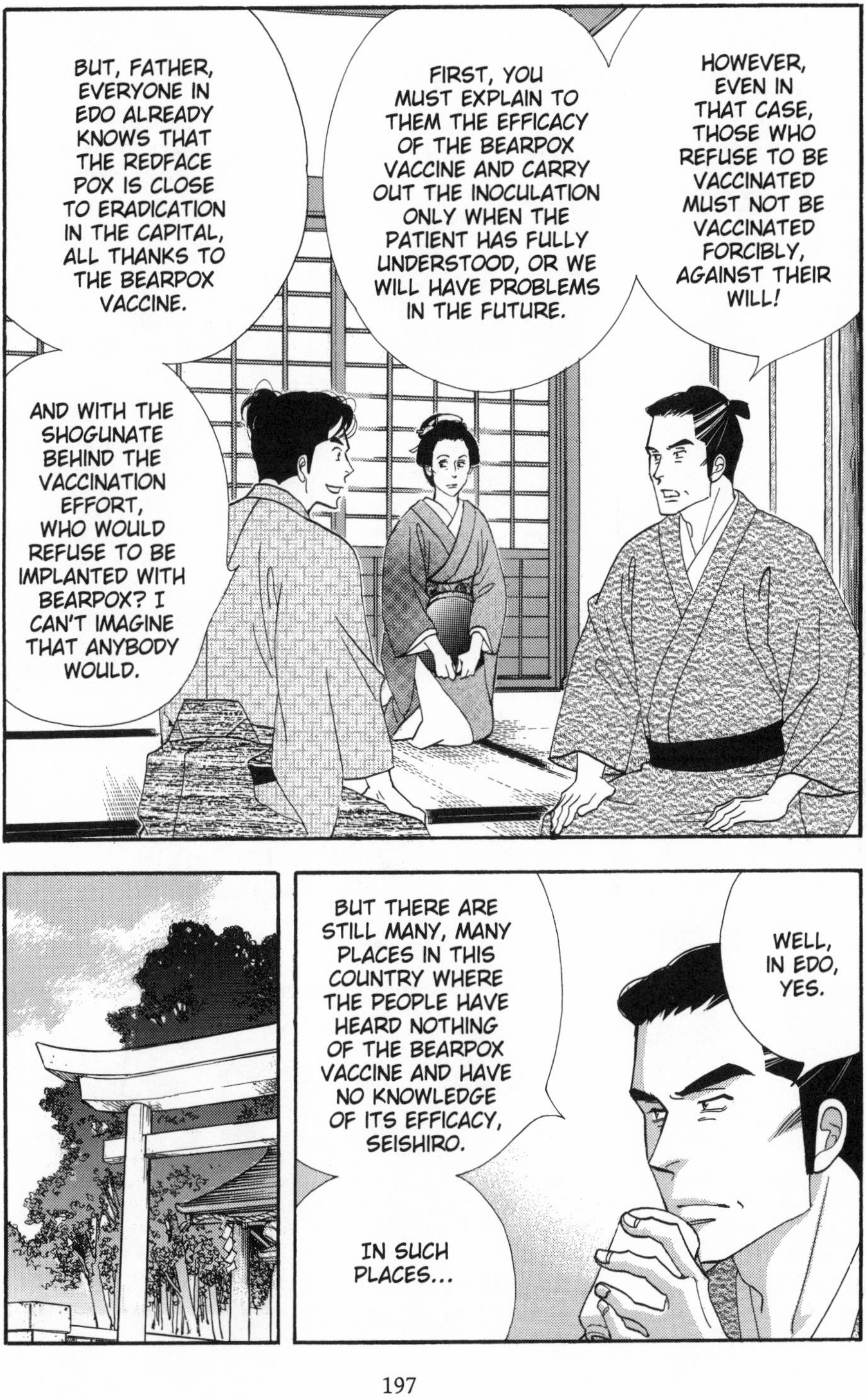
HOWEVER, EVEN IN THAT CASE, THOSE WHO REFUSE TO BE VACCINATED MUST NOT BE VACCINATED FORCIBLY, AGAINST THEIR WILL!
FIRST, YOU MUST EXPLAIN TO THEM THE EFFICACY OF THE BEARPOX VACCINE AND CARRY OUT THE INOCULATION ONLY WHEN THE PATIENT HAS FULLY UNDERSTOOD, OR WE WILL HAVE PROBLEMS IN THE FUTURE.
BUT, FATHER, EVERYONE IN EDO ALREADY KNOWS THAT THE REDFACE POX IS CLOSE TO ERADICATION IN THE CAPITAL, ALL THANKS TO THE BEARPOX VACCINE.
AND WITH THE SHOGUNATE BEHIND THE VACCINATION EFFORT, WHO WOULD REFUSE TO BE IMPLANTED WITH BEARPOX? I CAN'T IMAGINE THAT ANYBODY WOULD.
WELL, IN EDO, YES.
BUT THERE ARE STILL MANY, MANY PLACES IN THIS COUNTRY WHERE THE PEOPLE HAVE HEARD NOTHING OF THE BEARPOX VACCINE AND HAVE NO KNOWLEDGE OF ITS EFFICACY, SEISHIRO.
IN SUCH PLACES...

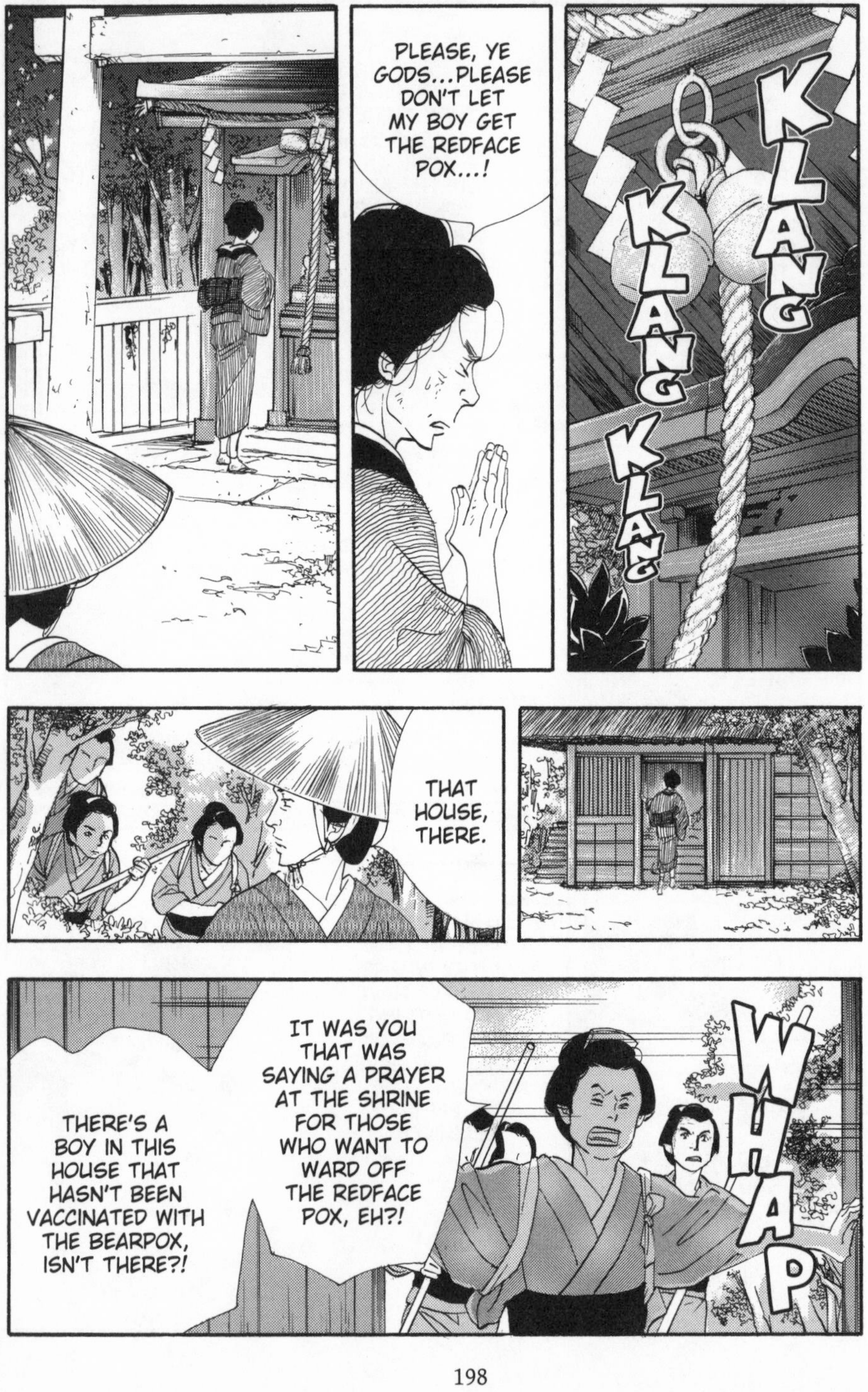
KLANG
KLANG
KLANG
KLANG
PLEASE, YE GODS...PLEASE DON'T LET MY BOY GET THE REDFACE POX...!
THAT HOUSE, THERE.
WHAP
IT WAS YOU THAT WAS SAYING A PRAYER AT THE SHRINE FOR THOSE WHO WANT TO WARD OFF THE REDFACE POX, EH?!
THERE'S A BOY IN THIS HOUSE THAT HASN'T BEEN VACCINATED WITH THE BEARPOX, ISN'T THERE?!

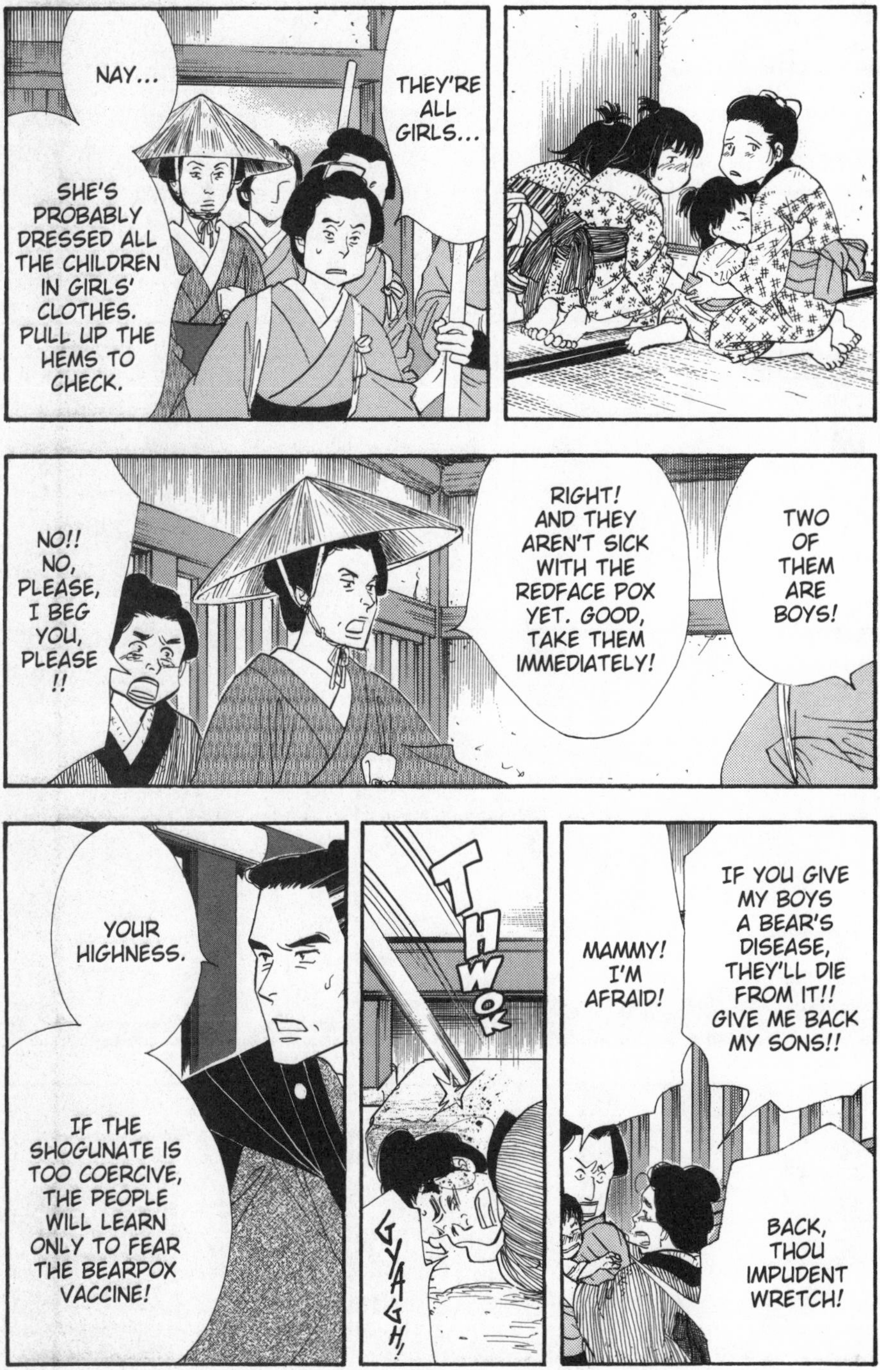
THEY'RE ALL GIRLS...
NAY...
SHE'S PROBABLY DRESSED ALL THE CHILDREN IN GIRLS' CLOTHES. PULL UP THE HEMS TO CHECK.
TWO OF THEM ARE BOYS!
RIGHT! AND THEY AREN'T SICK WITH THE REDFACE POX YET. GOOD, TAKE THEM IMMEDIATELY!
NO!! NO, PLEASE, I BEG YOU, PLEASE!!
IF YOU GIVE MY BOYS A BEAR'S DISEASE, THEY'LL DIE FROM IT!! GIVE ME BACK MY SONS!!
MAMMY! I'M AFRAID!
BACK, THOU IMPUDENT WRETCH!
THWOK
GYAGH!
YOUR HIGHNESS.
IF THE SHOGUNATE IS TOO COERCIVE, THE PEOPLE WILL LEARN ONLY TO FEAR THE BEARPOX VACCINE!

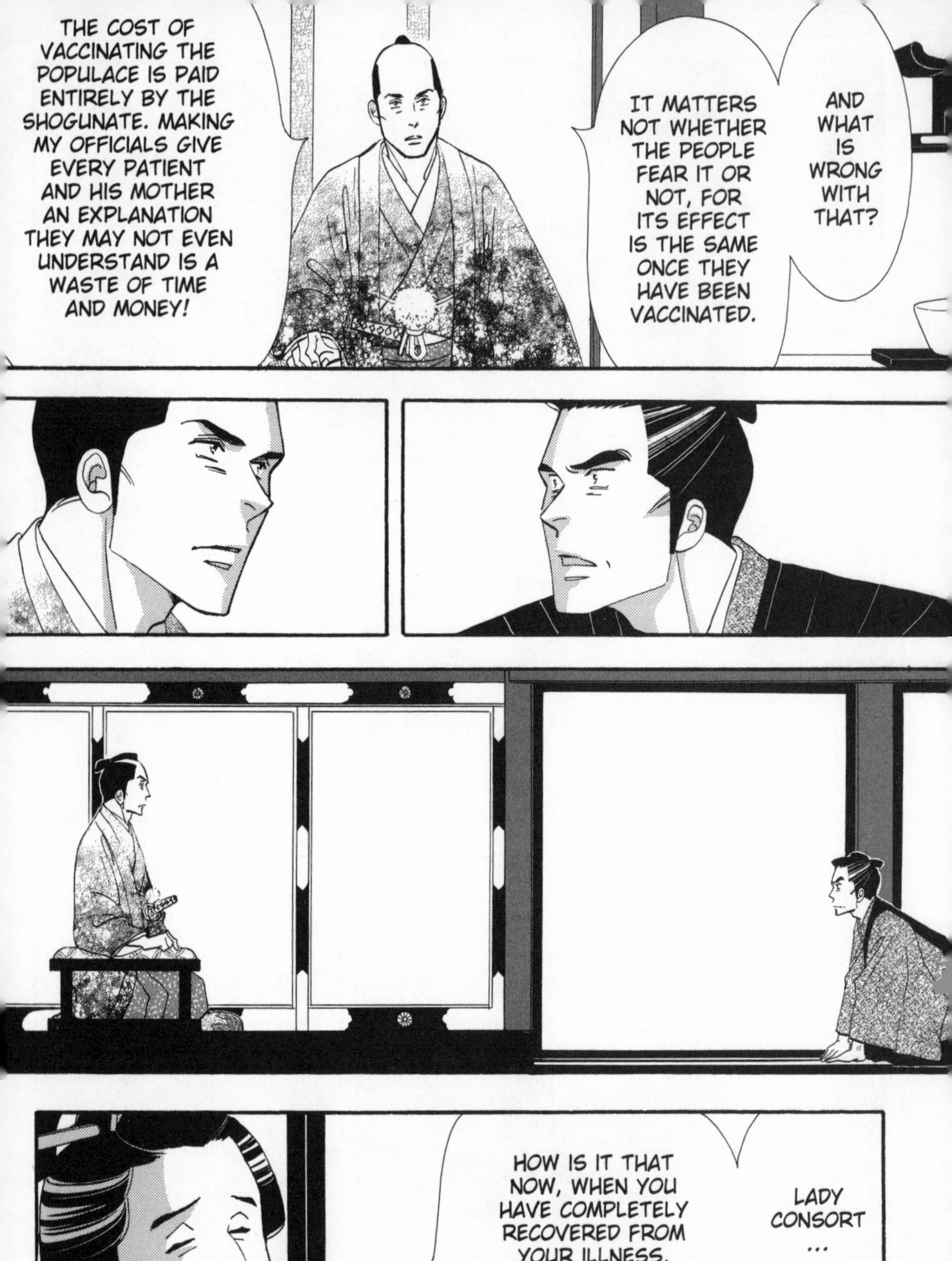
AND WHAT IS WRONG WITH THAT?
IT MATTERS NOT WHETHER THE PEOPLE FEAR IT OR NOT, FOR ITS EFFECT IS THE SAME ONCE THEY HAVE BEEN VACCINATED.
THE COST OF VACCINATING THE POPULACE IS PAID ENTIRELY BY THE SHOGUNATE. MAKING MY OFFICIALS GIVE EVERY PATIENT AND HIS MOTHER AN EXPLANATION THEY MAY NOT EVEN UNDERSTAND IS A WASTE OF TIME AND MONEY!
LADY CONSORT ...
HOW IS IT THAT NOW, WHEN YOU HAVE COMPLETELY RECOVERED FROM YOUR ILLNESS, HIS HIGHNESS THE SHOGUN DOTH NO LONGER PAY YOU ANY VISITS?

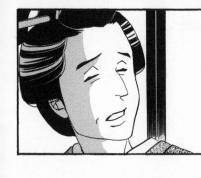

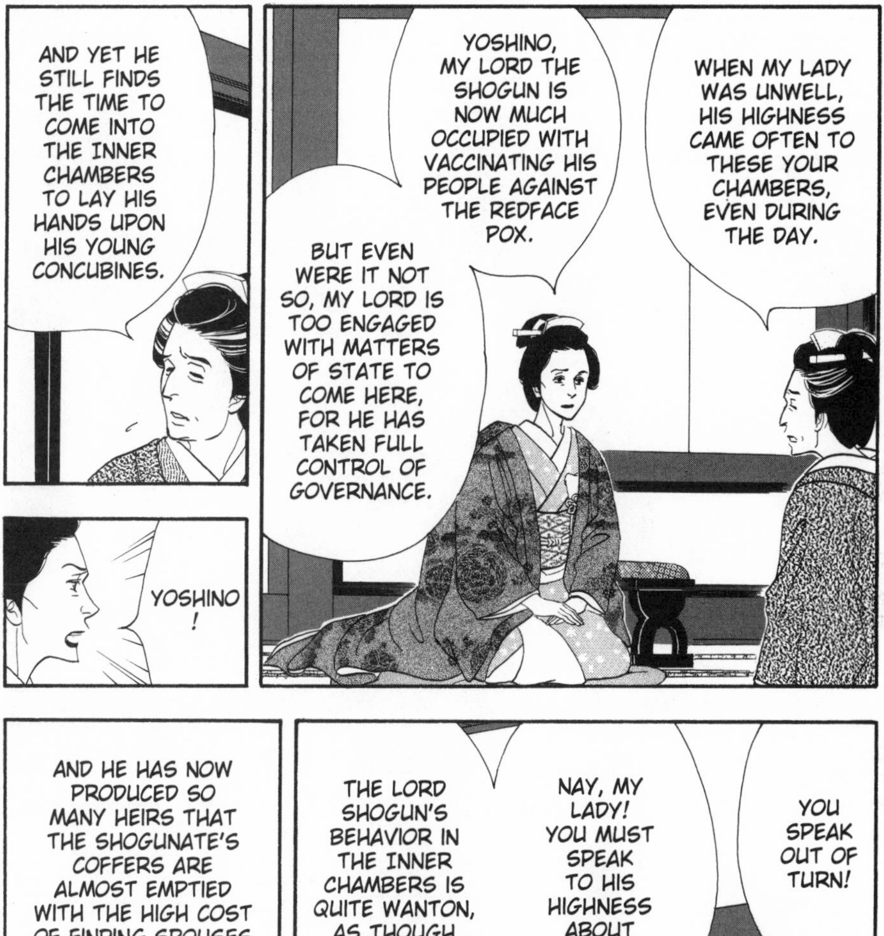
WHEN MY LADY WAS UNWELL, HIS HIGHNESS CAME OFTEN TO THESE YOUR CHAMBERS, EVEN DURING THE DAY.
YOSHINO, MY LORD THE SHOGUN IS NOW MUCH OCCUPIED WITH VACCINATING HIS PEOPLE AGAINST THE REDFACE POX.
BUT EVEN WERE IT NOT SO, MY LORD IS TOO ENGAGED WITH MATTERS OF STATE TO COME HERE, FOR HE HAS TAKEN FULL CONTROL OF GOVERNANCE.
AND YET HE STILL FINDS THE TIME TO COME INTO THE INNER CHAMBERS TO LAY HIS HANDS UPON HIS YOUNG CONCUBINES.
YOSHINO!
YOU SPEAK OUT OF TURN!
NAY, MY LADY! YOU MUST SPEAK TO HIS HIGHNESS ABOUT THIS!
THE LORD SHOGUN'S BEHAVIOR IN THE INNER CHAMBERS IS QUITE WANTON, AS THOUGH ANY WOMAN WOULD DO!
AND HE HAS NOW PRODUCED SO MANY HEIRS THAT THE SHOGUNATE'S COFFERS ARE ALMOST EMPTIED WITH THE HIGH COST OF FINDING SPOUSES FOR THE YOUNG LORDS AND LADIES.
JUST THIS YEAR ALONE, THREE MORE BABIES HAVE ALREADY BEEN BORN...

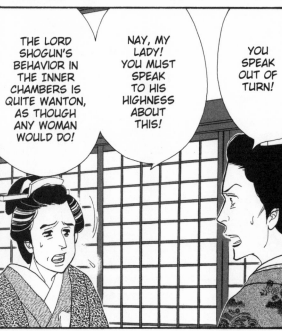

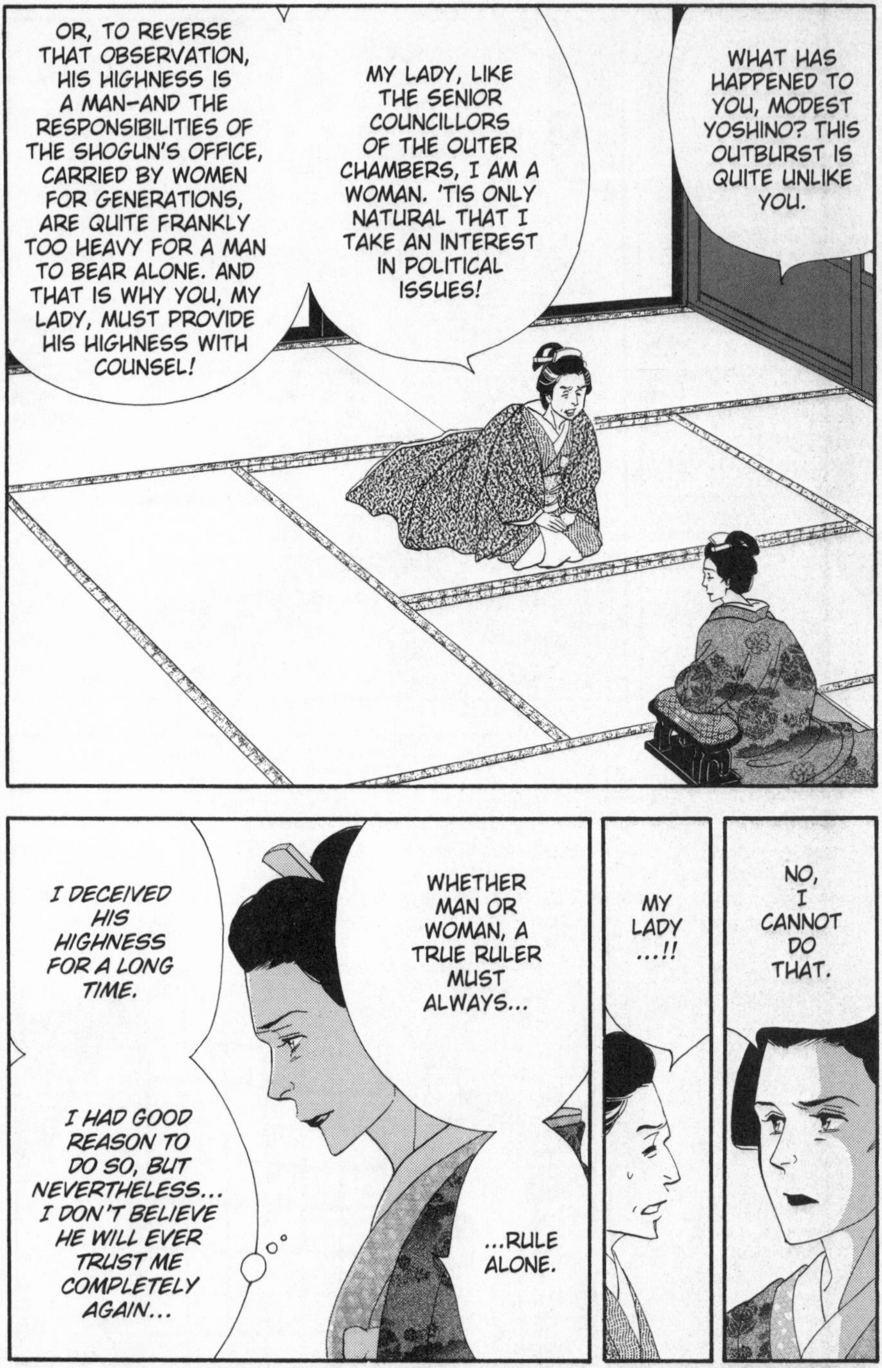
WHAT HAS HAPPENED TO YOU, MODEST YOSHINO? THIS OUTBURST IS QUITE UNLIKE YOU.
MY LADY, LIKE THE SENIOR COUNCILLORS OF THE OUTER CHAMBERS, I AM A WOMAN. 'TIS ONLY NATURAL THAT I TAKE AN INTEREST IN POLITICAL ISSUES!
OR, TO REVERSE THAT OBSERVATION, HIS HIGHNESS IS A MAN–AND THE RESPONSIBILITIES OF THE SHOGUN'S OFFICE, CARRIED BY WOMEN FOR GENERATIONS, ARE QUITE FRANKLY TOO HEAVY FOR A MAN TO BEAR ALONE. AND THAT IS WHY YOU, MY LADY, MUST PROVIDE HIS HIGHNESS WITH COUNSEL!
NO, I CANNOT DO THAT.
MY LADY ...!!
WHETHER MAN OR WOMAN, A TRUE RULER MUST ALWAYS...
I DECEIVED HIS HIGHNESS FOR A LONG TIME.
...RULE ALONE.
I HAD GOOD REASON TO DO SO, BUT NEVERTHELESS... I DON'T BELIEVE HE WILL EVER TRUST ME COMPLETELY AGAIN...

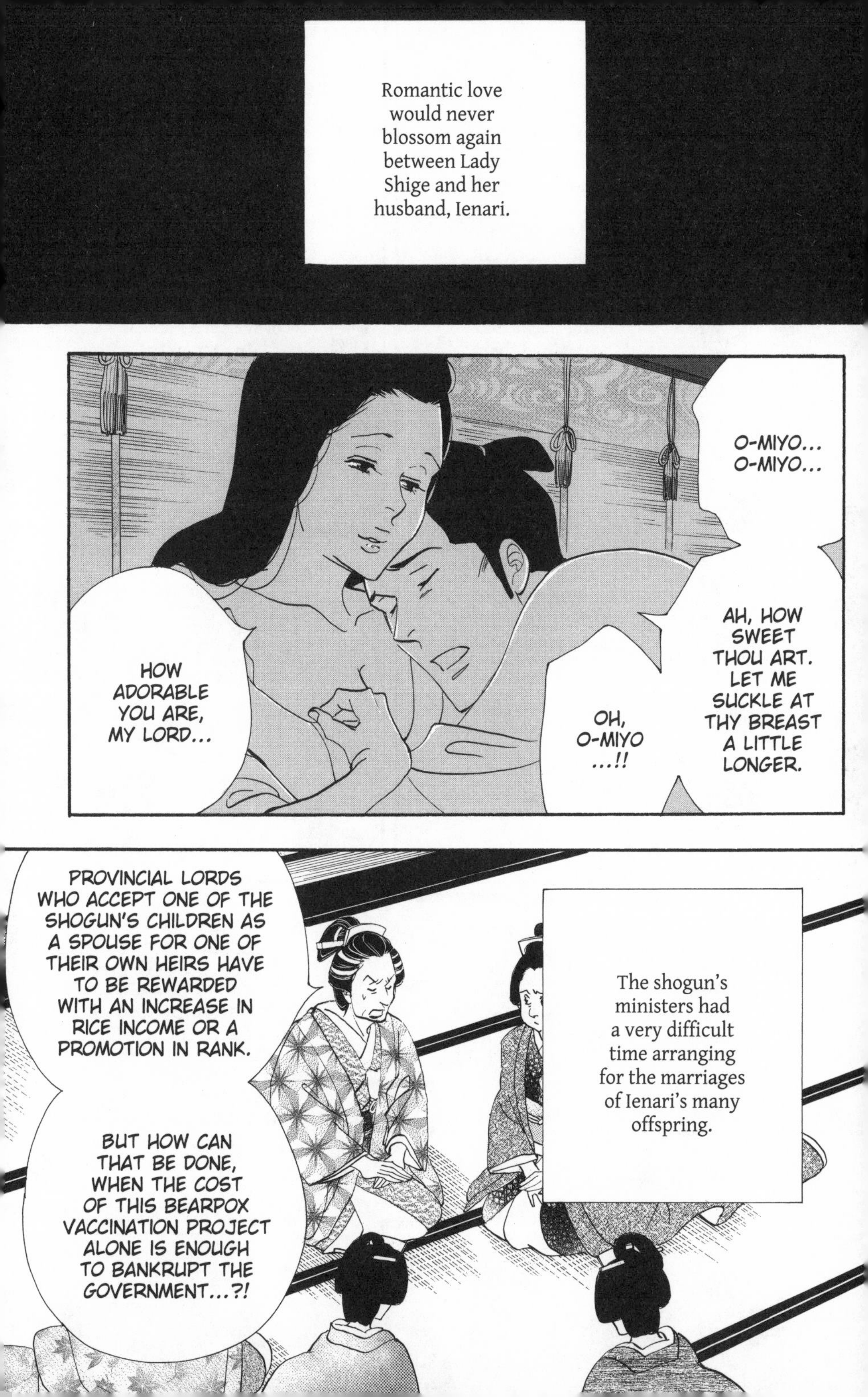
Romantic love would never blossom again between Lady Shige and her husband, Ienari.
O-MIYO... O-MIYO...
AH, HOW SWEET THOU ART. LET ME SUCKLE AT THY BREAST A LITTLE LONGER.
OH, O-MIYO ...!!
HOW ADORABLE YOU ARE, MY LORD...
The shogun's ministers had a very difficult time arranging for the marriages of Ienari's many offspring.
PROVINCIAL LORDS WHO ACCEPT ONE OF THE SHOGUN'S CHILDREN AS A SPOUSE FOR ONE OF THEIR OWN HEIRS HAVE TO BE REWARDED WITH AN INCREASE IN RICE INCOME OR A PROMOTION IN RANK.
BUT HOW CAN THAT BE DONE, WHEN THE COST OF THIS BEARPOX VACCINATION PROJECT ALONE IS ENOUGH TO BANKRUPT THE GOVERNMENT...?!

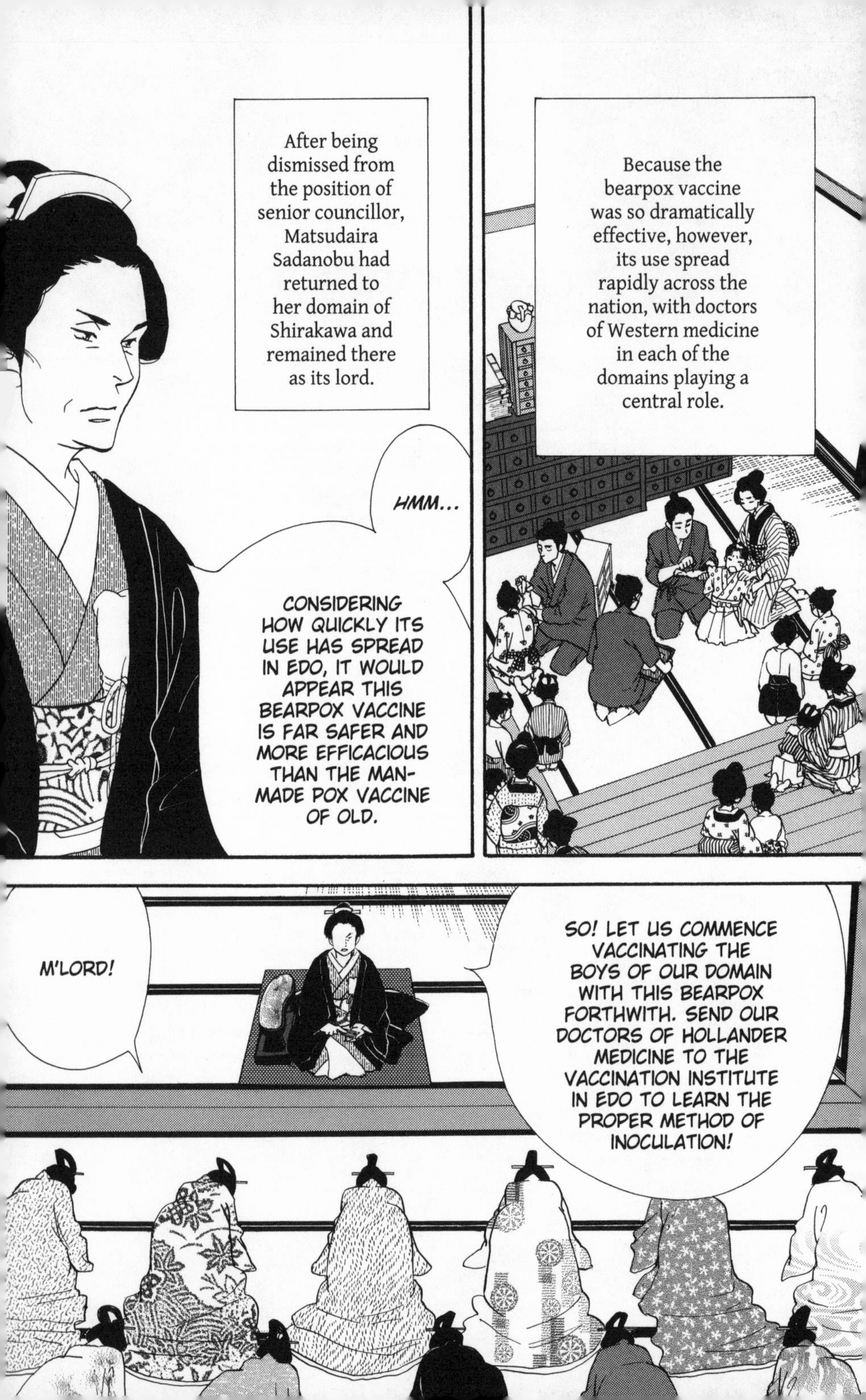
Because the bearpox vaccine was so dramatically effective, however, its use spread rapidly across the nation, with doctors of Western medicine in each of the domains playing a central role.
After being dismissed from the position of senior councillor, Matsudaira Sadanobu had returned to her domain of Shirakawa and remained there as its lord.
HMM...
CONSIDERING HOW QUICKLY ITS USE HAS SPREAD IN EDO, IT WOULD APPEAR THIS BEARPOX VACCINE IS FAR SAFER AND MORE EFFICACIOUS THAN THE MAN-MADE POX VACCINE OF OLD.
SO! LET US COMMENCE VACCINATING THE BOYS OF OUR DOMAIN WITH THIS BEARPOX FORTHWITH. SEND OUR DOCTORS OF HOLLANDER MEDICINE TO THE VACCINATION INSTITUTE IN EDO TO LEARN THE PROPER METHOD OF INOCULATION!
M'LORD!

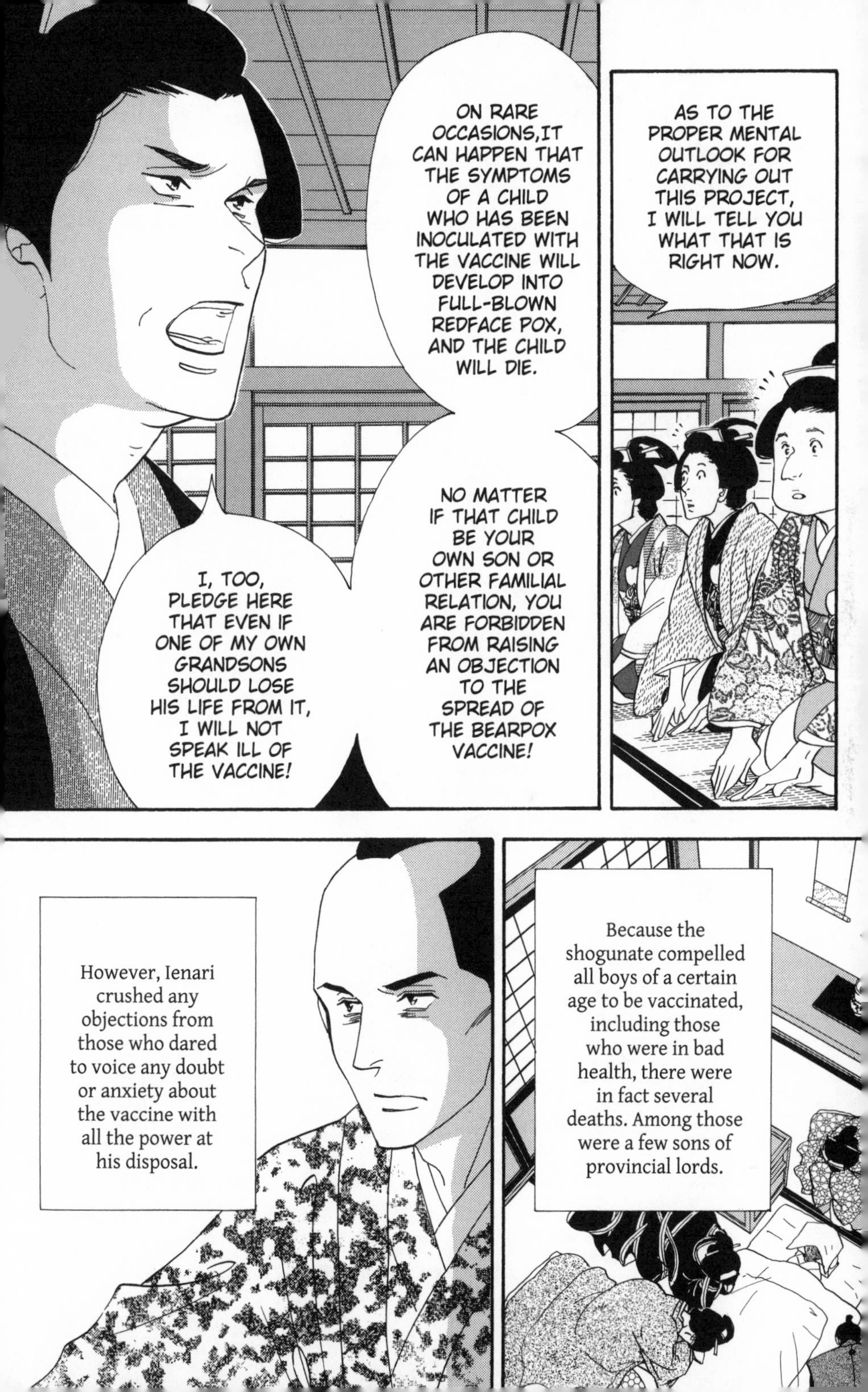
AS TO THE PROPER MENTAL OUTLOOK FOR CARRYING OUT THIS PROJECT, I WILL TELL YOU WHAT THAT IS RIGHT NOW.
ON RARE OCCASIONS,IT CAN HAPPEN THAT THE SYMPTOMS OF A CHILD WHO HAS BEEN INOCULATED WITH THE VACCINE WILL DEVELOP INTO FULL-BLOWN REDFACE POX, AND THE CHILD WILL DIE.
NO MATTER IF THAT CHILD BE YOUR OWN SON OR OTHER FAMILIAL RELATION, YOU ARE FORBIDDEN FROM RAISING AN OBJECTION TO THE SPREAD OF THE BEARPOX VACCINE!
I, TOO, PLEDGE HERE THAT EVEN IF ONE OF MY OWN GRANDSONS SHOULD LOSE HIS LIFE FROM IT, I WILL NOT SPEAK ILL OF THE VACCINE!
Because the shogunate compelled all boys of a certain age to be vaccinated, including those who were in bad health, there were in fact several deaths. Among those were a few sons of provincial lords.
However, Ienari crushed any objections from those who dared to voice any doubt or anxiety about the vaccine with all the power at his disposal.

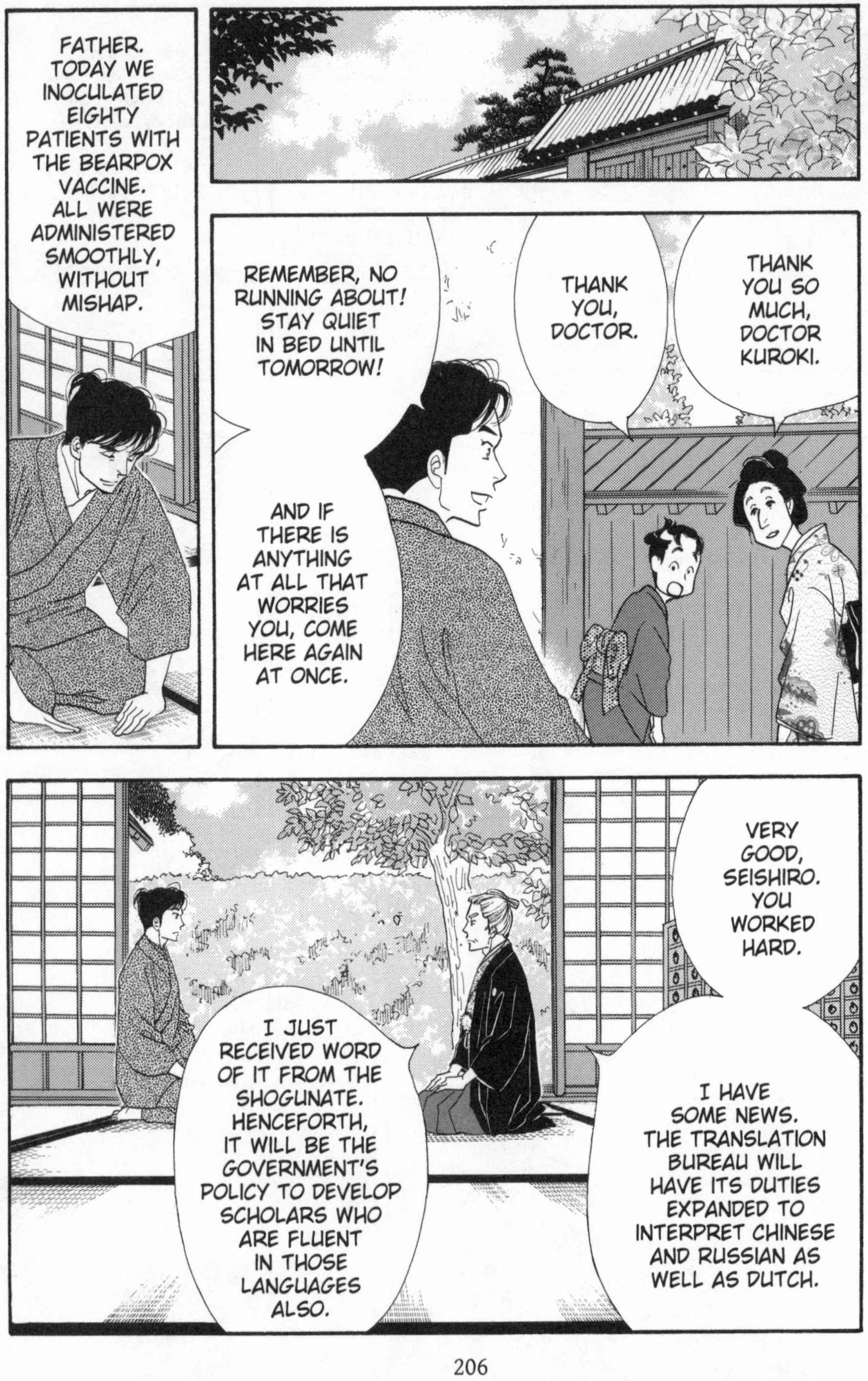
THANK YOU SO MUCH, DOCTOR KUROKI.
THANK YOU, DOCTOR.
REMEMBER, NO RUNNING ABOUT! STAY QUIET IN BED UNTIL TOMORROW!
AND IF THERE IS ANYTHING AT ALL THAT WORRIES YOU, COME HERE AGAIN AT ONCE.
FATHER. TODAY WE INOCULATED EIGHTY PATIENTS WITH THE BEARPOX VACCINE. ALL WERE ADMINISTERED SMOOTHLY, WITHOUT MISHAP.
VERY GOOD, SEISHIRO. YOU WORKED HARD.
I HAVE SOME NEWS. THE TRANSLATION BUREAU WILL HAVE ITS DUTIES EXPANDED TO INTERPRET CHINESE AND RUSSIAN AS WELL AS DUTCH.
I JUST RECEIVED WORD OF IT FROM THE SHOGUNATE. HENCEFORTH, IT WILL BE THE GOVERNMENT'S POLICY TO DEVELOP SCHOLARS WHO ARE FLUENT IN THOSE LANGUAGES ALSO.

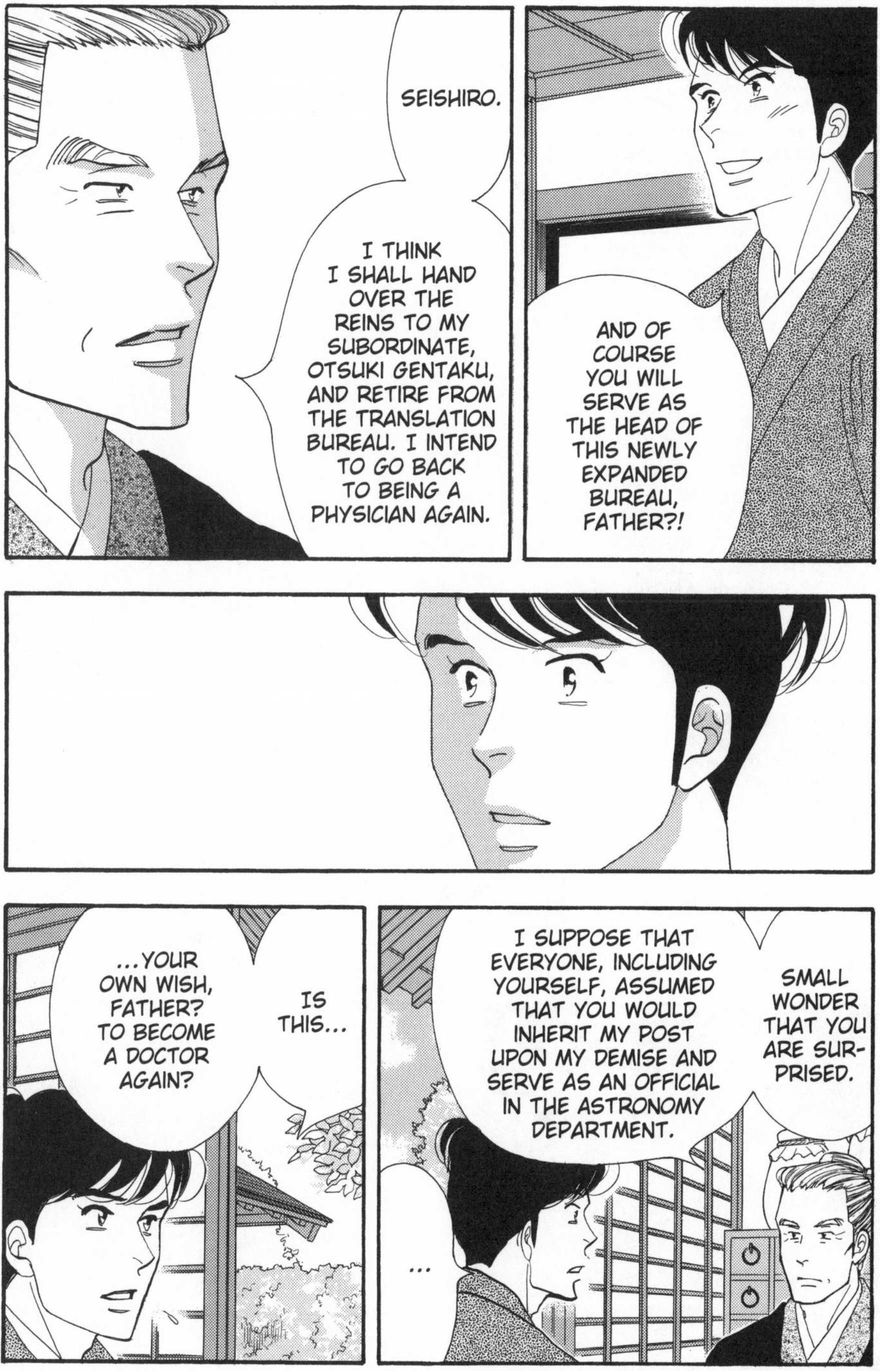
AND OF COURSE YOU WILL SERVE AS THE HEAD OF THIS NEWLY EXPANDED BUREAU, FATHER?!
SEISHIRO.
I THINK I SHALL HAND OVER THE REINS TO MY SUBORDINATE, OTSUKI GENTAKU, AND RETIRE FROM THE TRANSLATION BUREAU. I INTEND TO GO BACK TO BEING A PHYSICIAN AGAIN.
SMALL WONDER THAT YOU ARE SURPRISED.
I SUPPOSE THAT EVERYONE, INCLUDING YOURSELF, ASSUMED THAT YOU WOULD INHERIT MY POST UPON MY DEMISE AND SERVE AS AN OFFICIAL IN THE ASTRONOMY DEPARTMENT.
...
IS THIS...
...YOUR OWN WISH, FATHER? TO BECOME A DOCTOR AGAIN?

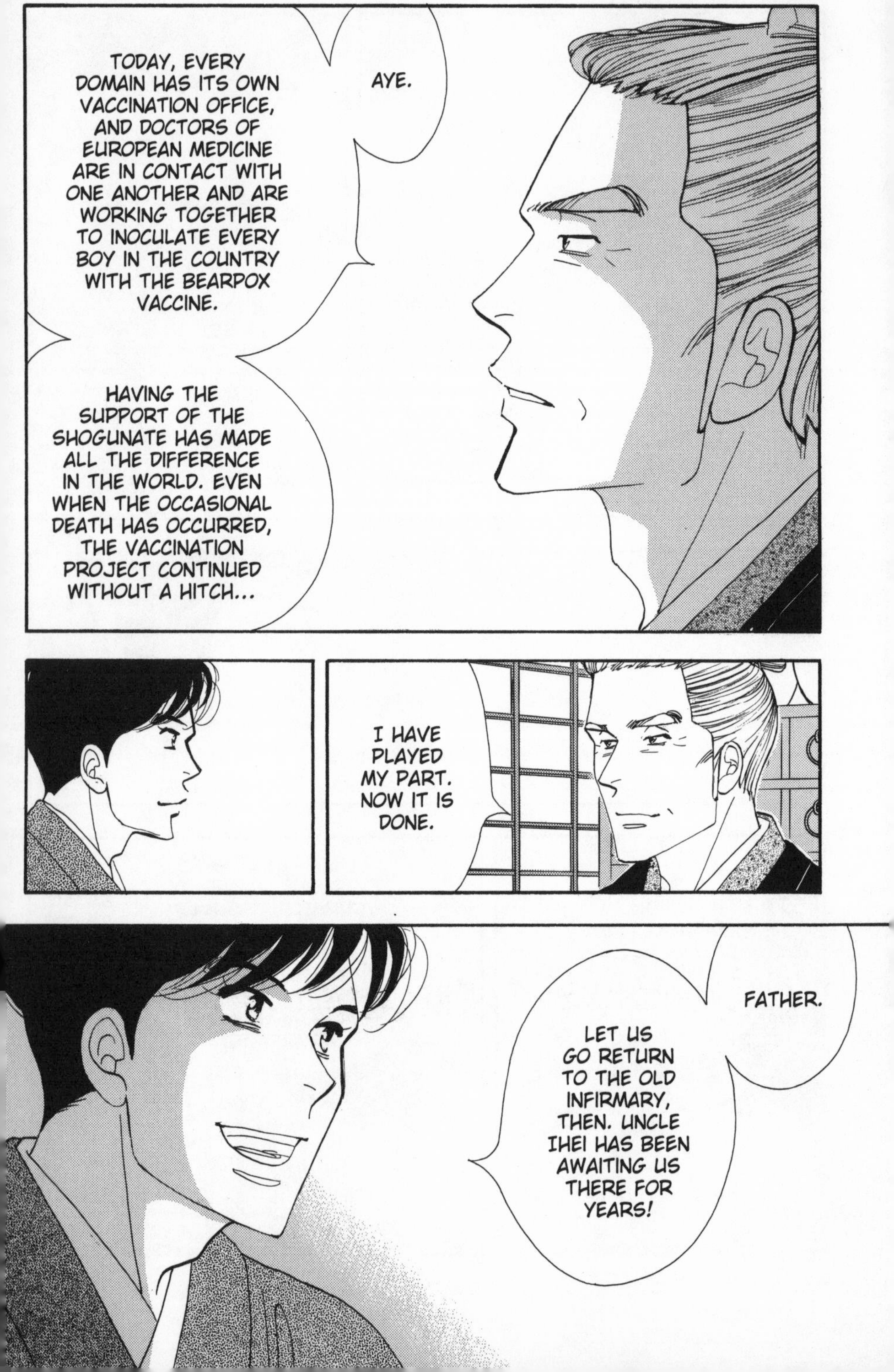
AYE.
TODAY, EVERY DOMAIN HAS ITS OWN VACCINATION OFFICE, AND DOCTORS OF EUROPEAN MEDICINE ARE IN CONTACT WITH ONE ANOTHER AND ARE WORKING TOGETHER TO INOCULATE EVERY BOY IN THE COUNTRY WITH THE BEARPOX VACCINE.
HAVING THE SUPPORT OF THE SHOGUNATE HAS MADE ALL THE DIFFERENCE IN THE WORLD. EVEN WHEN THE OCCASIONAL DEATH HAS OCCURRED, THE VACCINATION PROJECT CONTINUED WITHOUT A HITCH...
I HAVE PLAYED MY PART. NOW IT IS DONE.
FATHER.
LET US GO RETURN TO THE OLD INFIRMARY, THEN. UNCLE IHEI HAS BEEN AWAITING US THERE FOR YEARS!

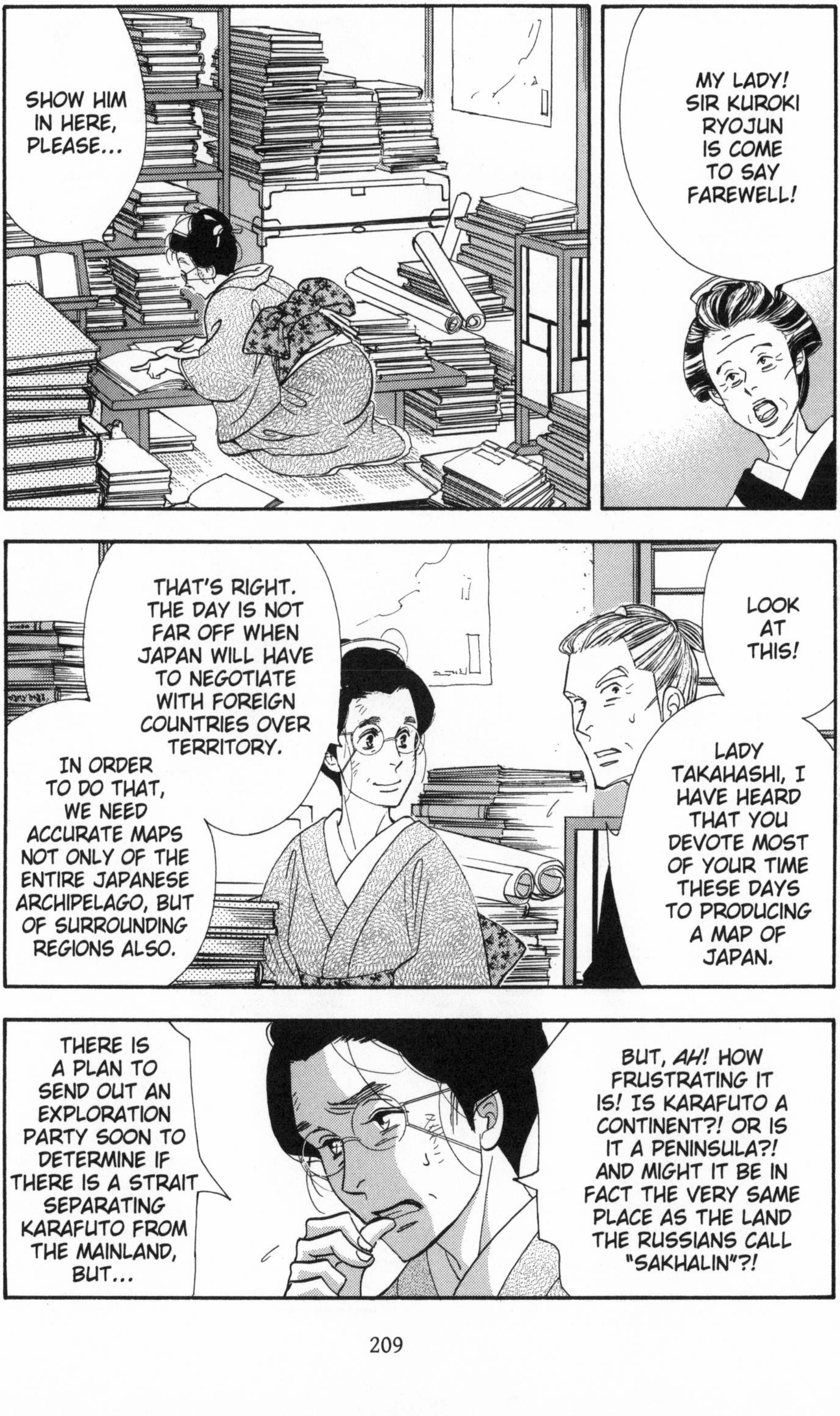
MY LADY! SIR KUROKI RYOJUN IS COME TO SAY FAREWELL!
SHOW HIM IN HERE, PLEASE...
LOOK AT THIS!
LADY TAKAHASHI, I HAVE HEARD THAT YOU DEVOTE MOST OF YOUR TIME THESE DAYS TO PRODUCING A MAP OF JAPAN.
THAT'S RIGHT. THE DAY IS NOT FAR OFF WHEN JAPAN WILL HAVE TO NEGOTIATE WITH FOREIGN COUNTRIES OVER TERRITORY.
IN ORDER TO DO THAT, WE NEED ACCURATE MAPS NOT ONLY OF THE ENTIRE JAPANESE ARCHIPELAGO, BUT OF SURROUNDING REGIONS ALSO.
BUT, *AH!* HOW FRUSTRATING IT IS! IS KARAFUTO A CONTINENT?! OR IS IT A PENINSULA?! AND MIGHT IT BE IN FACT THE VERY SAME PLACE AS THE LAND THE RUSSIANS CALL "SAKHALIN"?!
THERE IS A PLAN TO SEND OUT AN EXPLORATION PARTY SOON TO DETERMINE IF THERE IS A STRAIT SEPARATING KARAFUTO FROM THE MAINLAND, BUT...

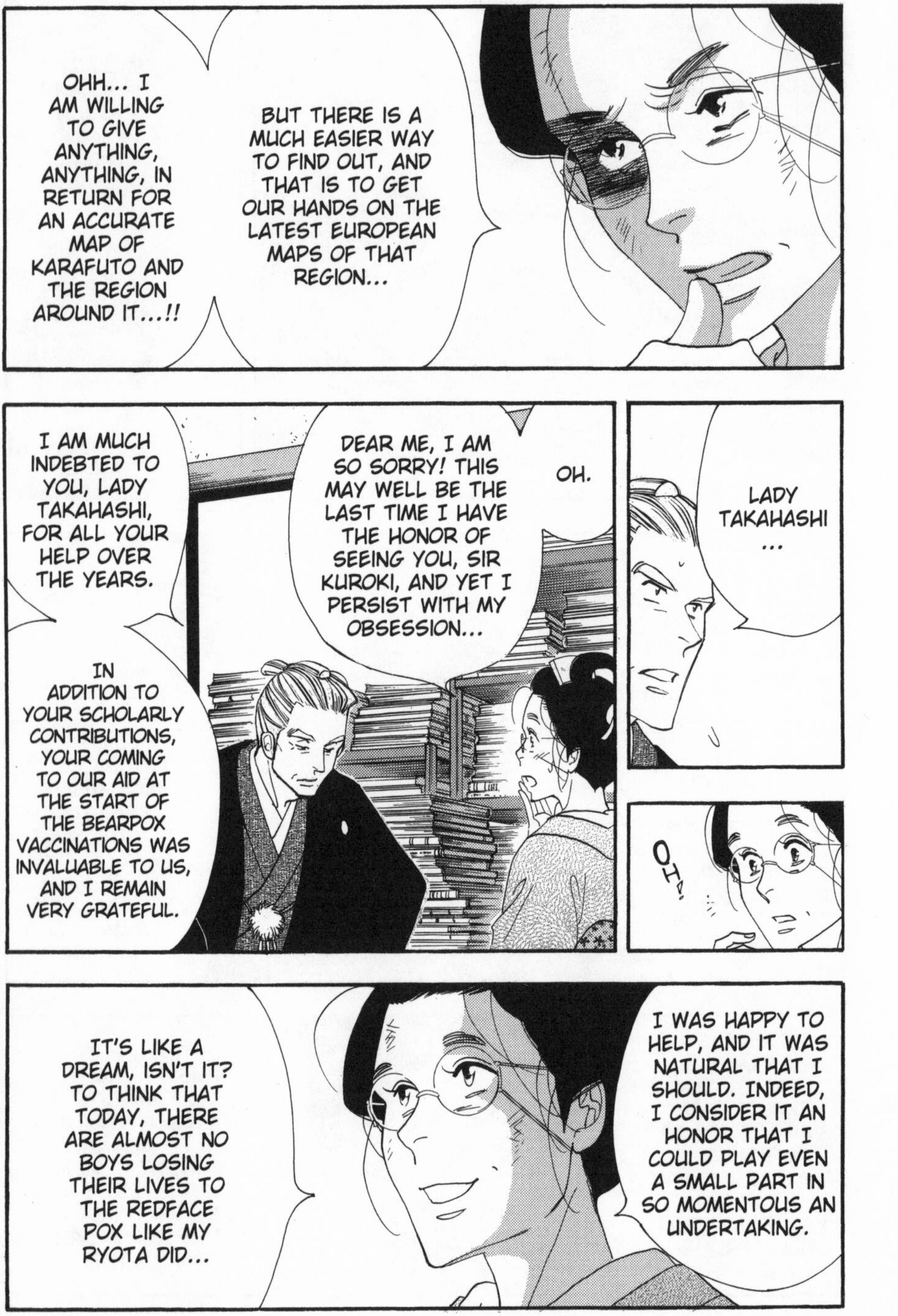
BUT THERE IS A MUCH EASIER WAY TO FIND OUT, AND THAT IS TO GET OUR HANDS ON THE LATEST EUROPEAN MAPS OF THAT REGION...
OHH... I AM WILLING TO GIVE ANYTHING, ANYTHING, IN RETURN FOR AN ACCURATE MAP OF KARAFUTO AND THE REGION AROUND IT...!!
LADY TAKAHASHI ...
OH!
OH.
DEAR ME, I AM SO SORRY! THIS MAY WELL BE THE LAST TIME I HAVE THE HONOR OF SEEING YOU, SIR KUROKI, AND YET I PERSIST WITH MY OBSESSION...
I AM MUCH INDEBTED TO YOU, LADY TAKAHASHI, FOR ALL YOUR HELP OVER THE YEARS.
IN ADDITION TO YOUR SCHOLARLY CONTRIBUTIONS, YOUR COMING TO OUR AID AT THE START OF THE BEARPOX VACCINATIONS WAS INVALUABLE TO US, AND I REMAIN VERY GRATEFUL.
I WAS HAPPY TO HELP, AND IT WAS NATURAL THAT I SHOULD. INDEED, I CONSIDER IT AN HONOR THAT I COULD PLAY EVEN A SMALL PART IN SO MOMENTOUS AN UNDERTAKING.
IT'S LIKE A DREAM, ISN'T IT? TO THINK THAT TODAY, THERE ARE ALMOST NO BOYS LOSING THEIR LIVES TO THE REDFACE POX LIKE MY RYOTA DID...

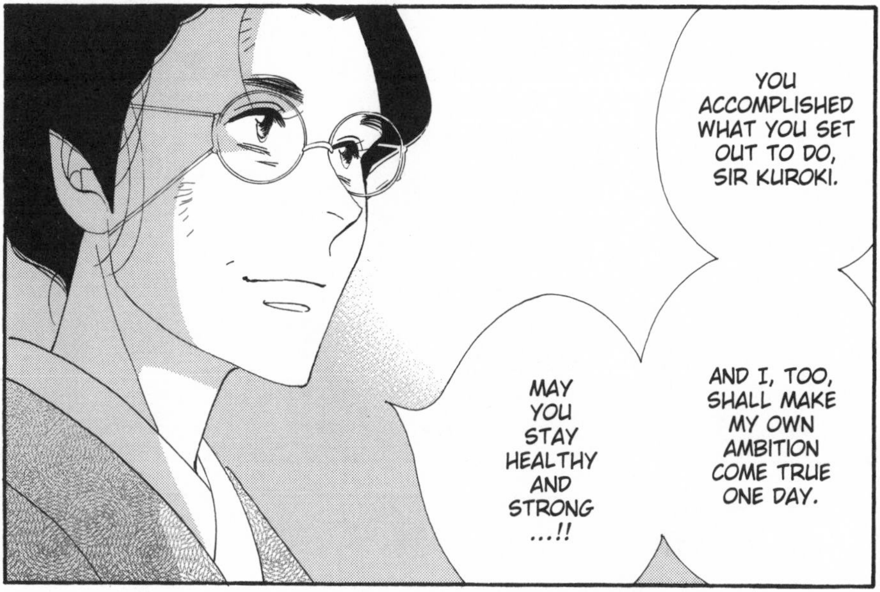
YOU ACCOMPLISHED WHAT YOU SET OUT TO DO, SIR KUROKI.
AND I, TOO, SHALL MAKE MY OWN AMBITION COME TRUE ONE DAY.
MAY YOU STAY HEALTHY AND STRONG ...!!

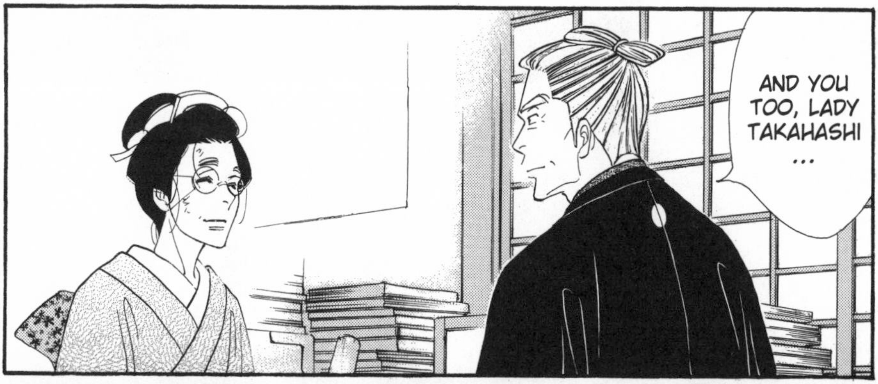
AND YOU TOO, LADY TAKAHASHI ...

Some time later, Takahashi Kageyasu gave Philipp Franz von Siebold a map of Japan that she herself had produced, in exchange for a European map of the region around Sakhalin (Karafuto). She was sentenced to death for this and died in prison.

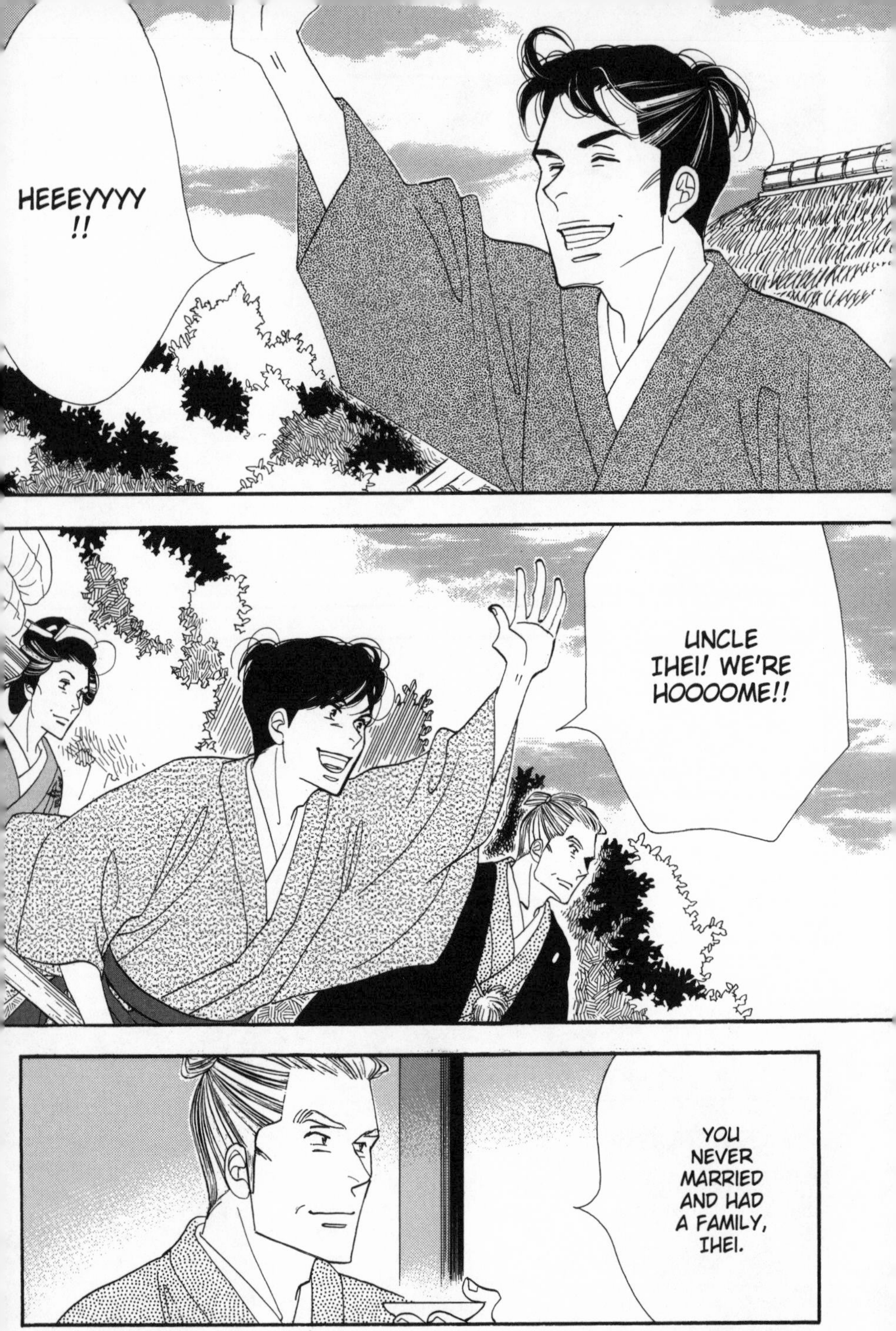
HEEEYYYY !!
UNCLE IHEI! WE'RE HOOOOME!!
YOU NEVER MARRIED AND HAD A FAMILY, IHEI.

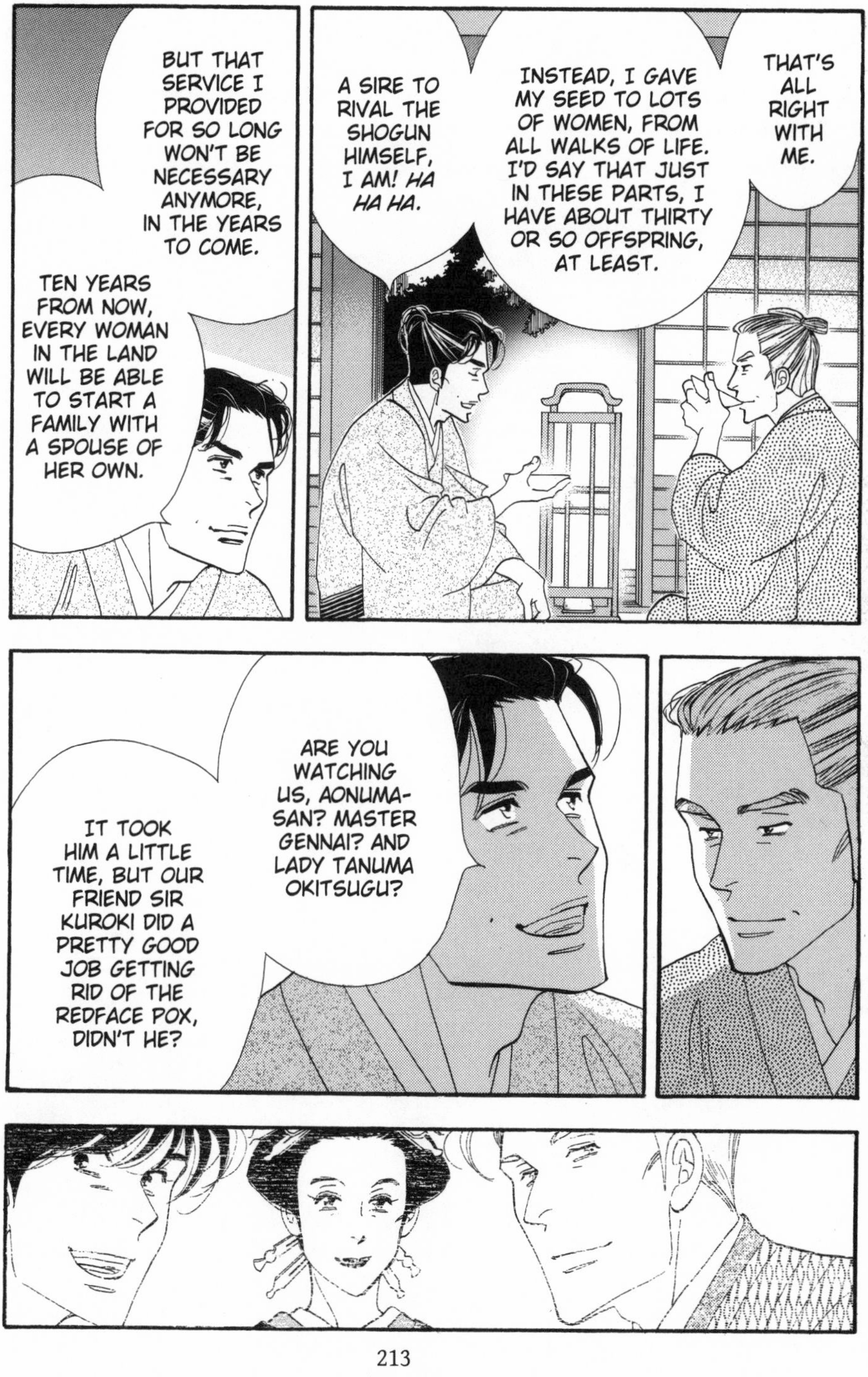
THAT'S ALL RIGHT WITH ME.
INSTEAD, I GAVE MY SEED TO LOTS OF WOMEN, FROM ALL WALKS OF LIFE. I'D SAY THAT JUST IN THESE PARTS, I HAVE ABOUT THIRTY OR SO OFFSPRING, AT LEAST.
A SIRE TO RIVAL THE SHOGUN HIMSELF, I AM! *HA HA HA.*
BUT THAT SERVICE I PROVIDED FOR SO LONG WON'T BE NECESSARY ANYMORE, IN THE YEARS TO COME.
TEN YEARS FROM NOW, EVERY WOMAN IN THE LAND WILL BE ABLE TO START A FAMILY WITH A SPOUSE OF HER OWN.
ARE YOU WATCHING US, AONUMA-SAN? MASTER GENNAI? AND LADY TANUMA OKITSUGU?
IT TOOK HIM A LITTLE TIME, BUT OUR FRIEND SIR KUROKI DID A PRETTY GOOD JOB GETTING RID OF THE REDFACE POX, DIDN'T HE?

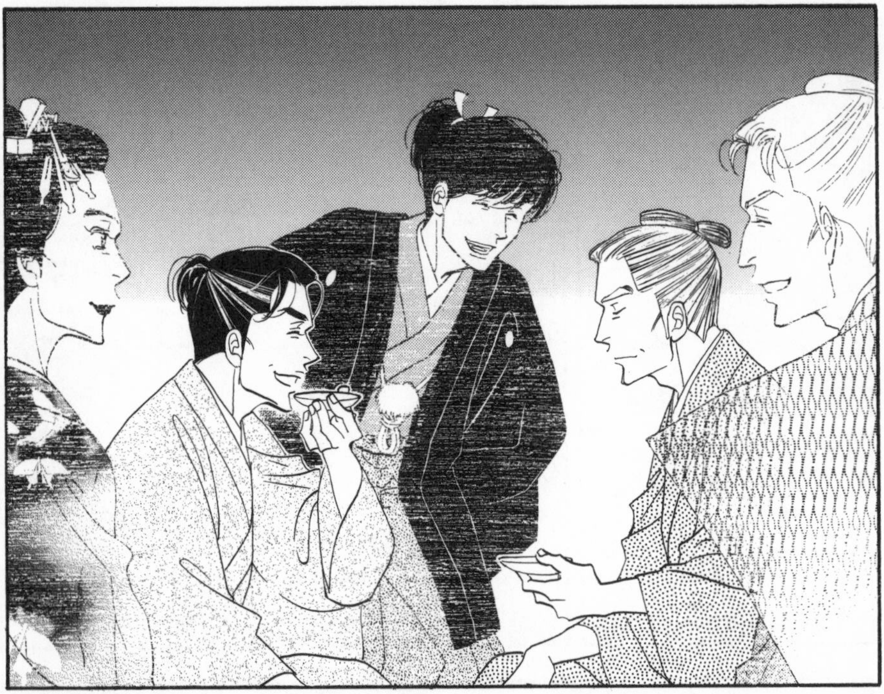

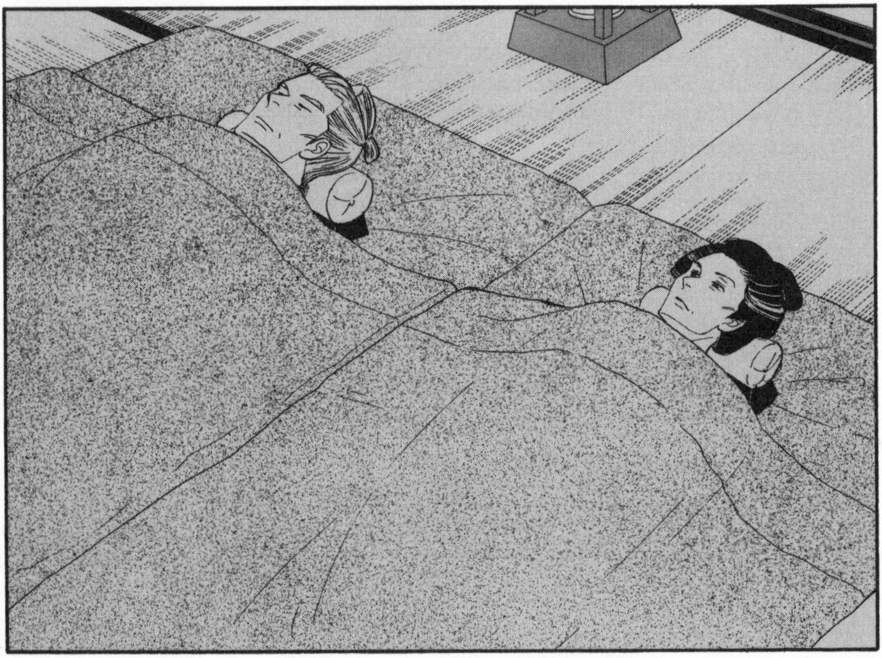

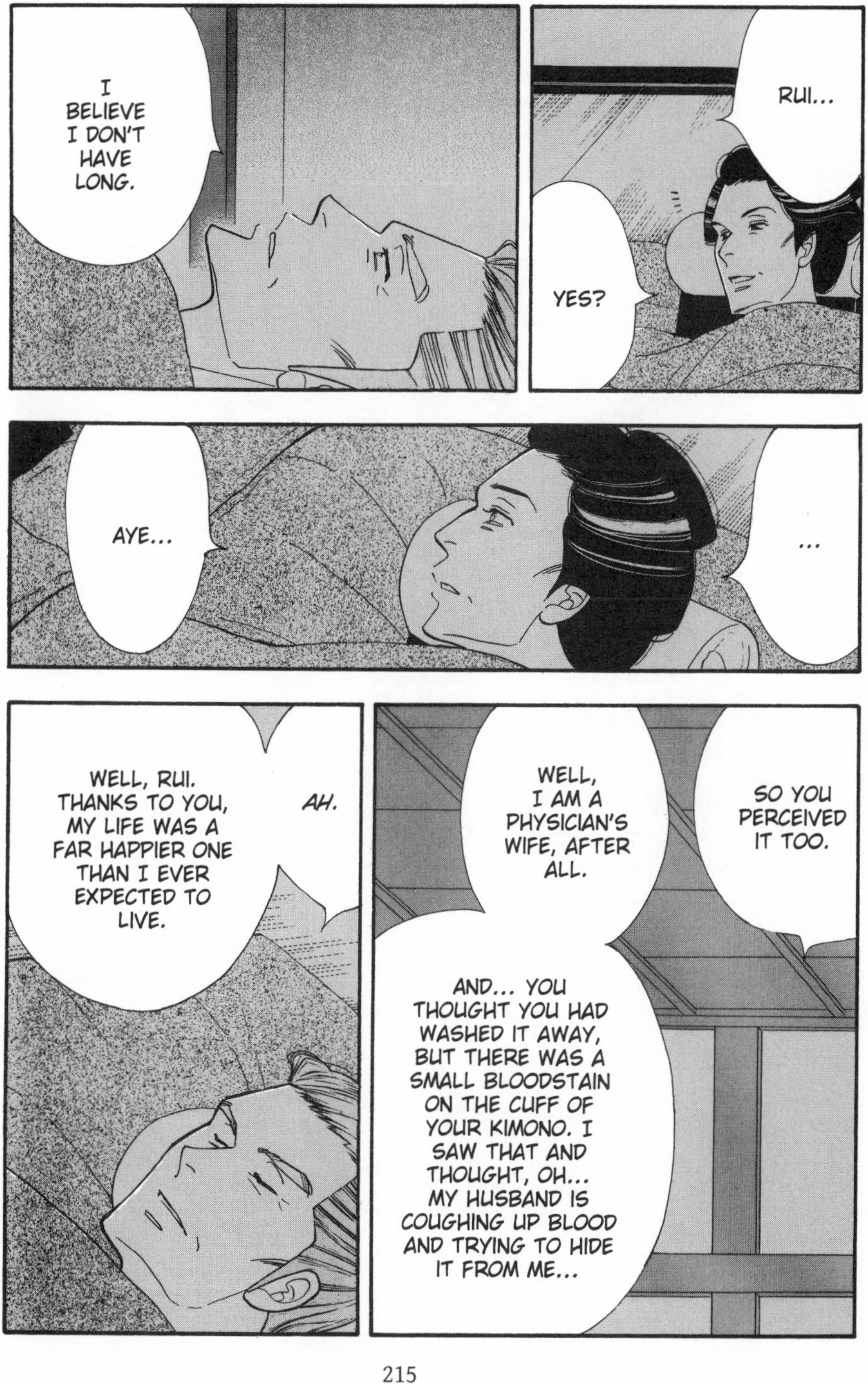
RUI...
YES?
I BELIEVE I DON'T HAVE LONG.
...
AYE...
SO YOU PERCEIVED IT TOO.
WELL, I AM A PHYSICIAN'S WIFE, AFTER ALL.
AND... YOU THOUGHT YOU HAD WASHED IT AWAY, BUT THERE WAS A SMALL BLOODSTAIN ON THE CUFF OF YOUR KIMONO. I SAW THAT AND THOUGHT, OH... MY HUSBAND IS COUGHING UP BLOOD AND TRYING TO HIDE IT FROM ME...
AH.
WELL, RUI. THANKS TO YOU, MY LIFE WAS A FAR HAPPIER ONE THAN I EVER EXPECTED TO LIVE.

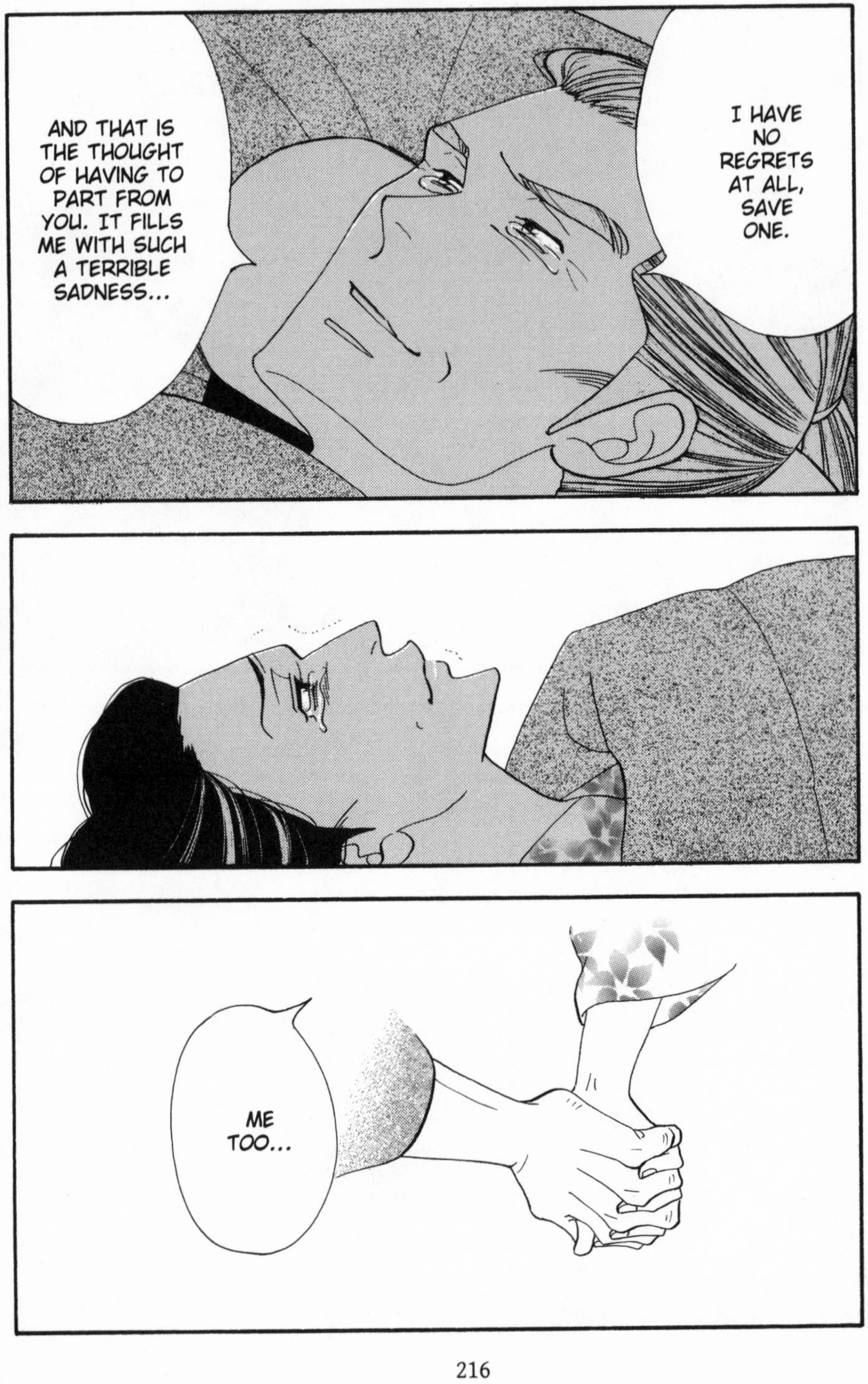
I HAVE NO REGRETS AT ALL, SAVE ONE.
AND THAT IS THE THOUGHT OF HAVING TO PART FROM YOU. IT FILLS ME WITH SUCH A TERRIBLE SADNESS...
ME TOO...

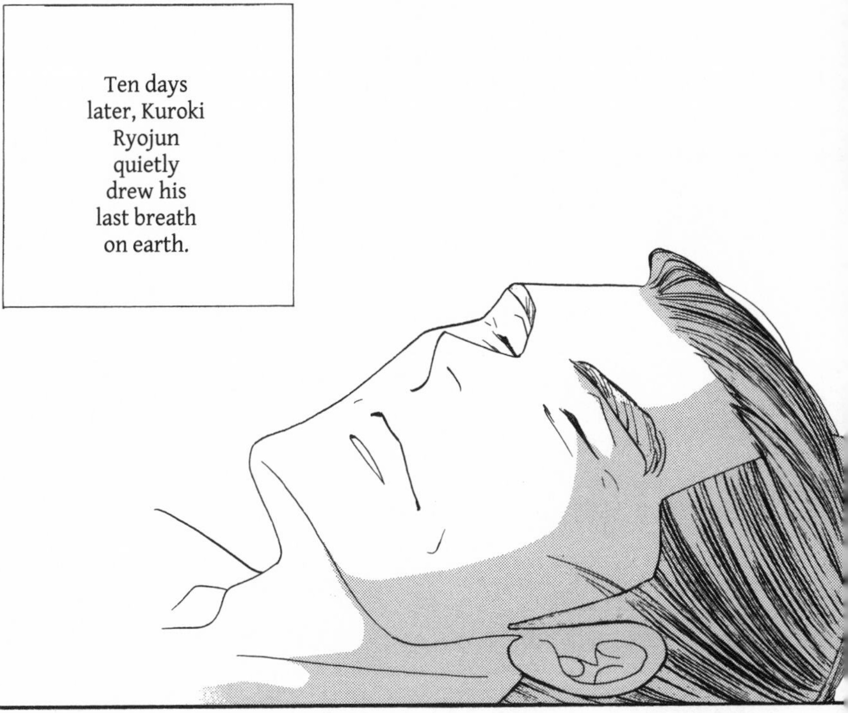
Ten days later, Kuroki Ryojun quietly drew his last breath on earth.

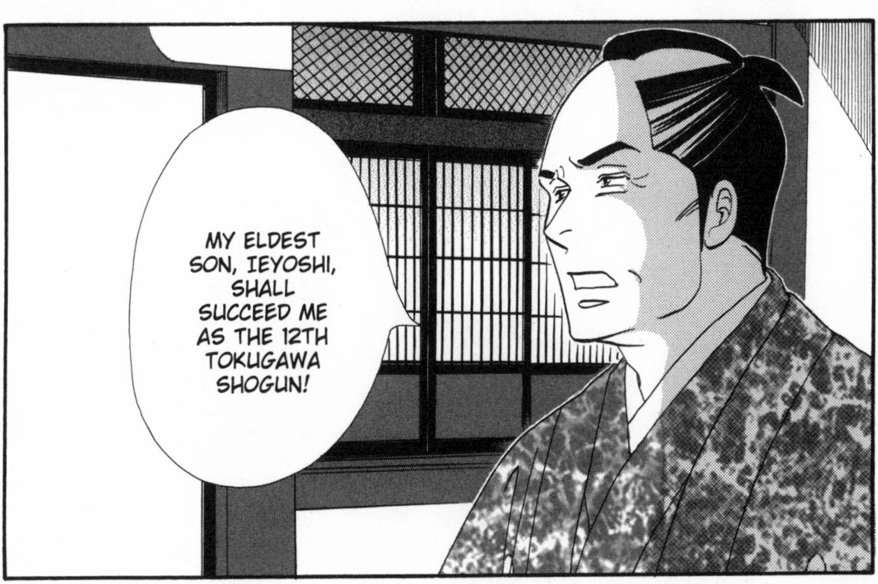
MY ELDEST SON, IEYOSHI, SHALL SUCCEED ME AS THE 12TH TOKUGAWA SHOGUN!

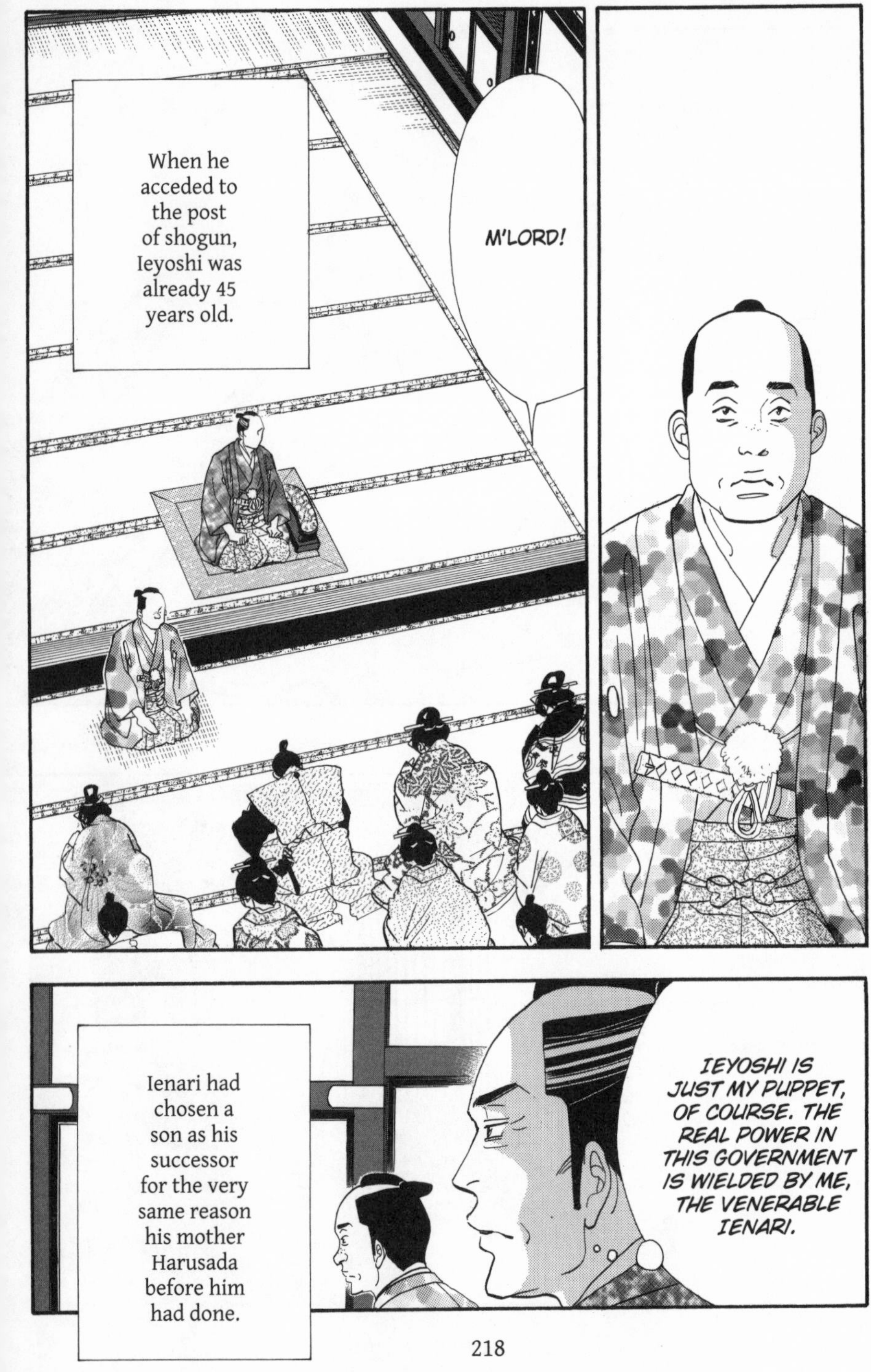
M'LORD!
When he acceded to the post of shogun, Ieyoshi was already 45 years old.
IEYOSHI IS JUST MY PUPPET, OF COURSE. THE REAL POWER IN THIS GOVERNMENT IS WIELDED BY ME, THE VENERABLE IENARI.
Ienari had chosen a son as his successor for the very same reason his mother Harusada before him had done.

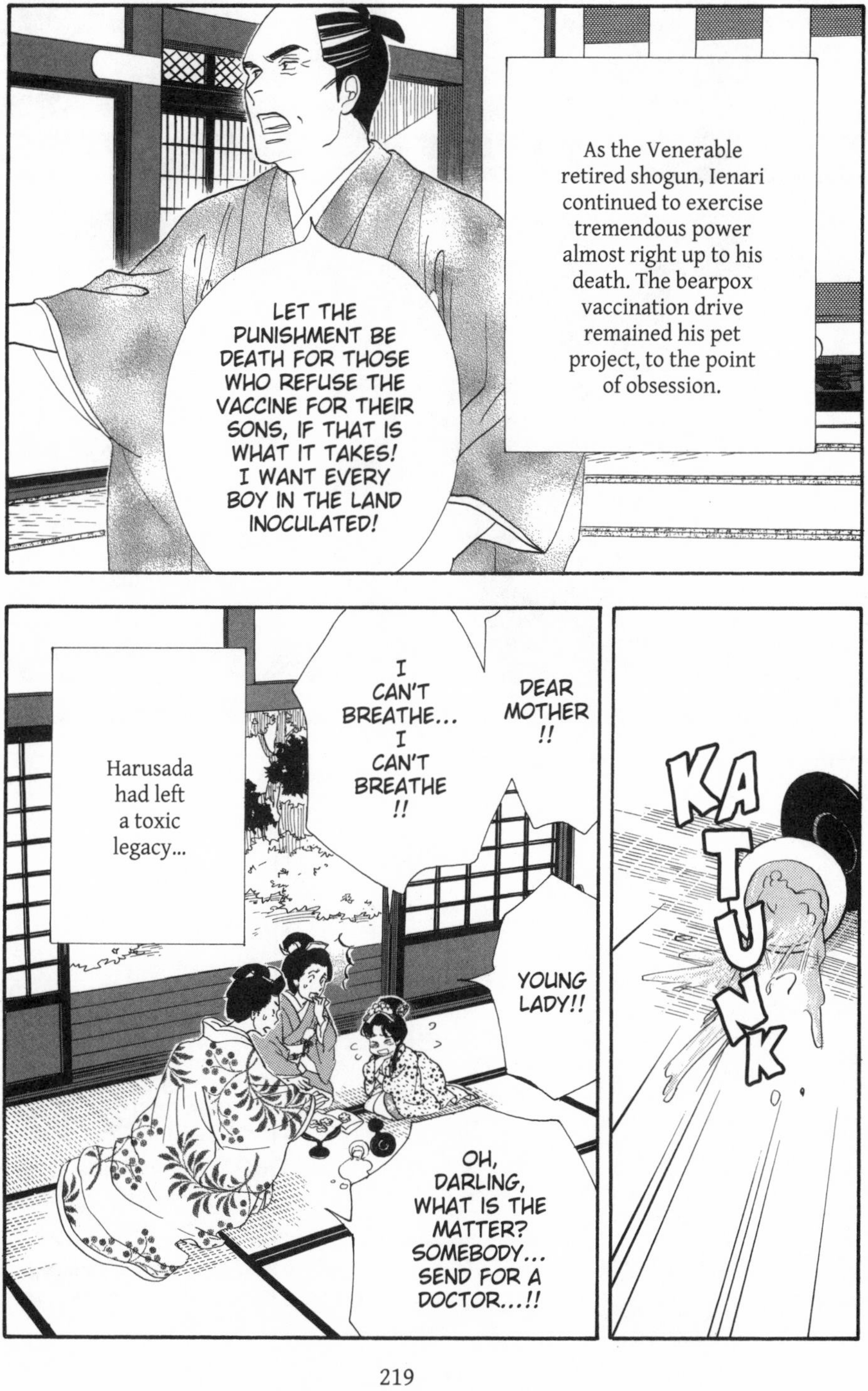
As the Venerable retired shogun, Ienari continued to exercise tremendous power almost right up to his death. The bearpox vaccination drive remained his pet project, to the point of obsession.
LET THE PUNISHMENT BE DEATH FOR THOSE WHO REFUSE THE VACCINE FOR THEIR SONS, IF THAT IS WHAT IT TAKES! I WANT EVERY BOY IN THE LAND INOCULATED!
KATUNK
DEAR MOTHER!!
I CAN'T BREATHE... I CAN'T BREATHE!!
Harusada had left a toxic legacy...
YOUNG LADY!!
OH, DARLING, WHAT IS THE MATTER? SOMEBODY... SEND FOR A DOCTOR...!!

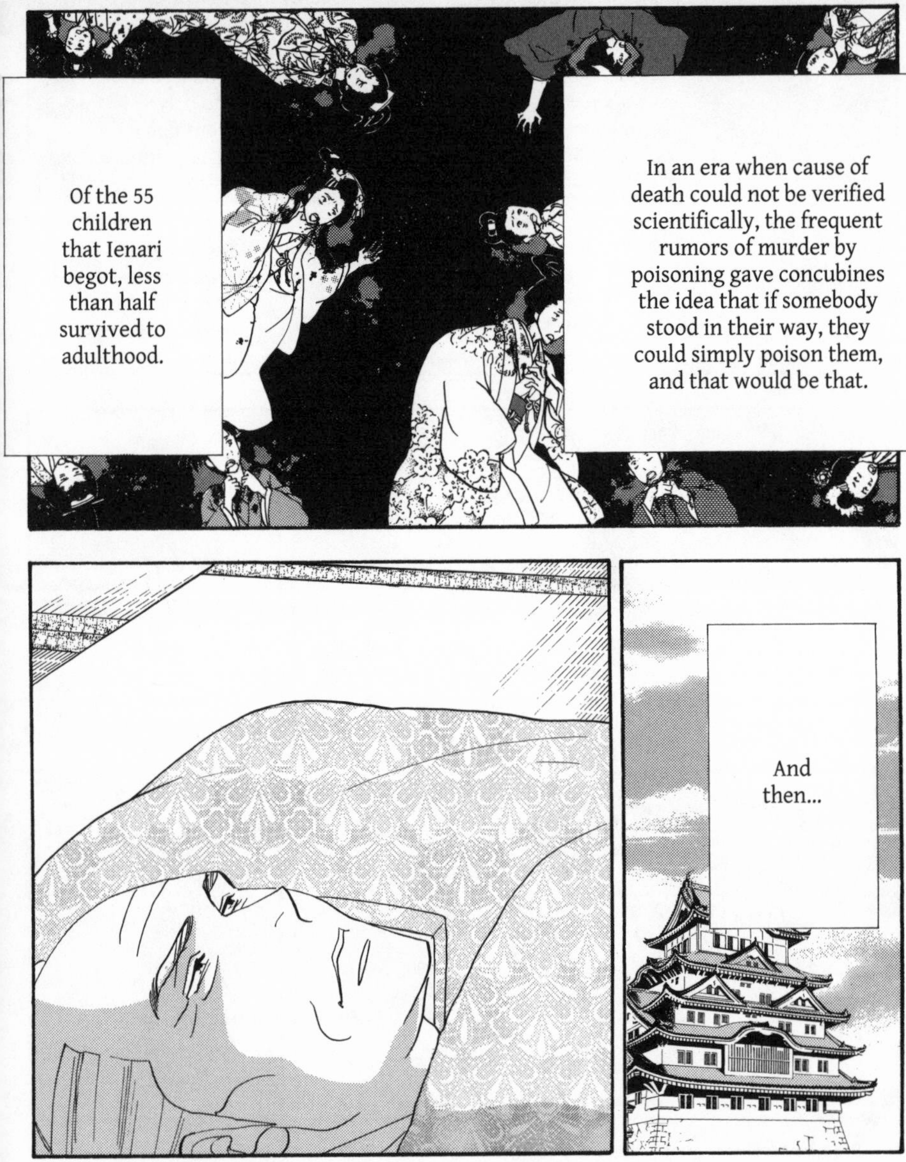
In an era when cause of death could not be verified scientifically, the frequent rumors of murder by poisoning gave concubines the idea that if somebody stood in their way, they could simply poison them, and that would be that.
Of the 55 children that Ienari begot, less than half survived to adulthood.
And then...

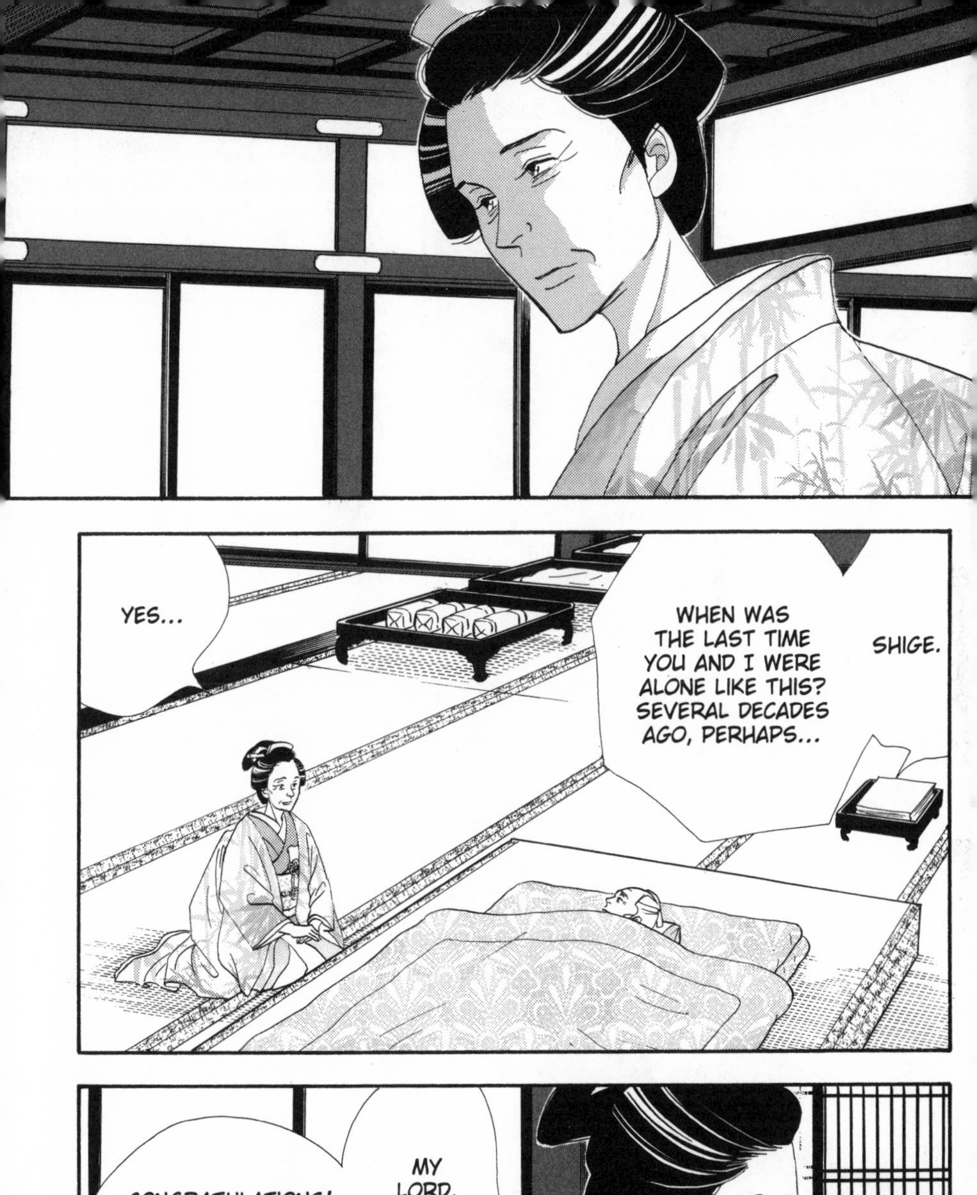
SHIGE.
WHEN WAS THE LAST TIME YOU AND I WERE ALONE LIKE THIS? SEVERAL DECADES AGO, PERHAPS...
YES...
MY LORD.
CONGRATULATIONS! IN THIS COUNTRY TODAY, THERE IS NOT ONE BOY WHO MUST FEAR CATCHING THE REDFACE POX, FOR EVERY LAST ONE IS NOW PROTECTED AGAINST IT.

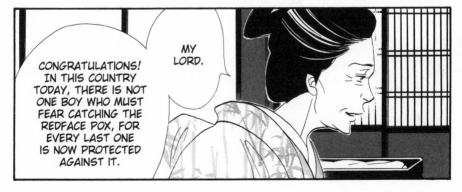

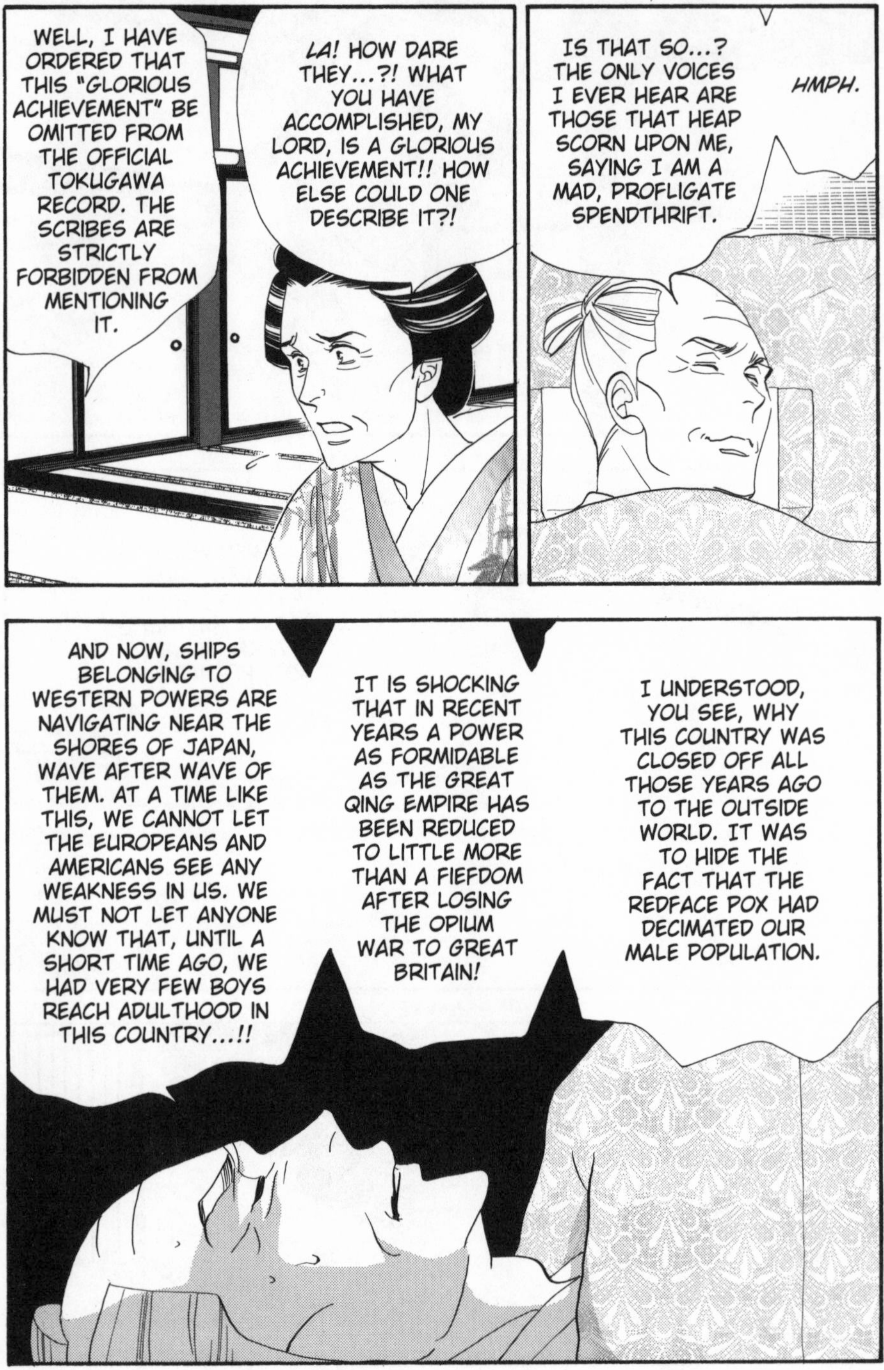
HMPH.
IS THAT SO...? THE ONLY VOICES I EVER HEAR ARE THOSE THAT HEAP SCORN UPON ME, SAYING I AM A MAD, PROFLIGATE SPENDTHRIFT.
LA! HOW DARE THEY...?! WHAT YOU HAVE ACCOMPLISHED, MY LORD, IS A GLORIOUS ACHIEVEMENT!! HOW ELSE COULD ONE DESCRIBE IT?!
WELL, I HAVE ORDERED THAT THIS "GLORIOUS ACHIEVEMENT" BE OMITTED FROM THE OFFICIAL TOKUGAWA RECORD. THE SCRIBES ARE STRICTLY FORBIDDEN FROM MENTIONING IT.
I UNDERSTOOD, YOU SEE, WHY THIS COUNTRY WAS CLOSED OFF ALL THOSE YEARS AGO TO THE OUTSIDE WORLD. IT WAS TO HIDE THE FACT THAT THE REDFACE POX HAD DECIMATED OUR MALE POPULATION.
IT IS SHOCKING THAT IN RECENT YEARS A POWER AS FORMIDABLE AS THE GREAT QING EMPIRE HAS BEEN REDUCED TO LITTLE MORE THAN A FIEFDOM AFTER LOSING THE OPIUM WAR TO GREAT BRITAIN!
AND NOW, SHIPS BELONGING TO WESTERN POWERS ARE NAVIGATING NEAR THE SHORES OF JAPAN, WAVE AFTER WAVE OF THEM. AT A TIME LIKE THIS, WE CANNOT LET THE EUROPEANS AND AMERICANS SEE ANY WEAKNESS IN US. WE MUST NOT LET ANYONE KNOW THAT, UNTIL A SHORT TIME AGO, WE HAD VERY FEW BOYS REACH ADULTHOOD IN THIS COUNTRY...!!

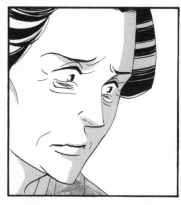

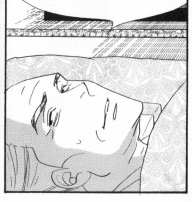

THEREFORE, THE HISTORICAL RECORD WILL CONTAIN NOT A WORD ABOUT THE REDFACE POX. I WILL ENTER POSTERITY AS A LUSTFUL, PHILANDERING RAKE WHO DEPLETED THE GOVERNMENT COFFERS—A THOROUGHLY USELESS SHOGUN FROM FIRST TO LAST.
AND THAT IS ALL RIGHT.
MY LORD.
DO YOU REMEMBER WHAT I SAID TO YOU ONCE, A LONG, LONG TIME AGO?
I SAID IT WAS GOOD FORTUNE THAT YOU HAD BECOME THE LORD SHOGUN, FOR I WAS SURE YOU WOULD BE A VERY GOOD RULER.
WELL, MY LORD? I WAS RIGHT. IT TURNED OUT JUST AS I SAID...

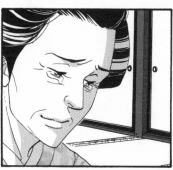

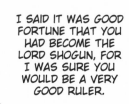

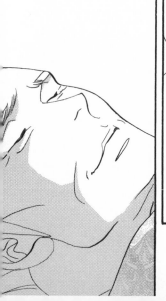

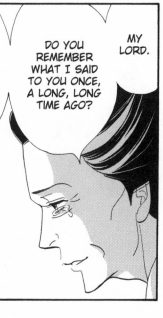

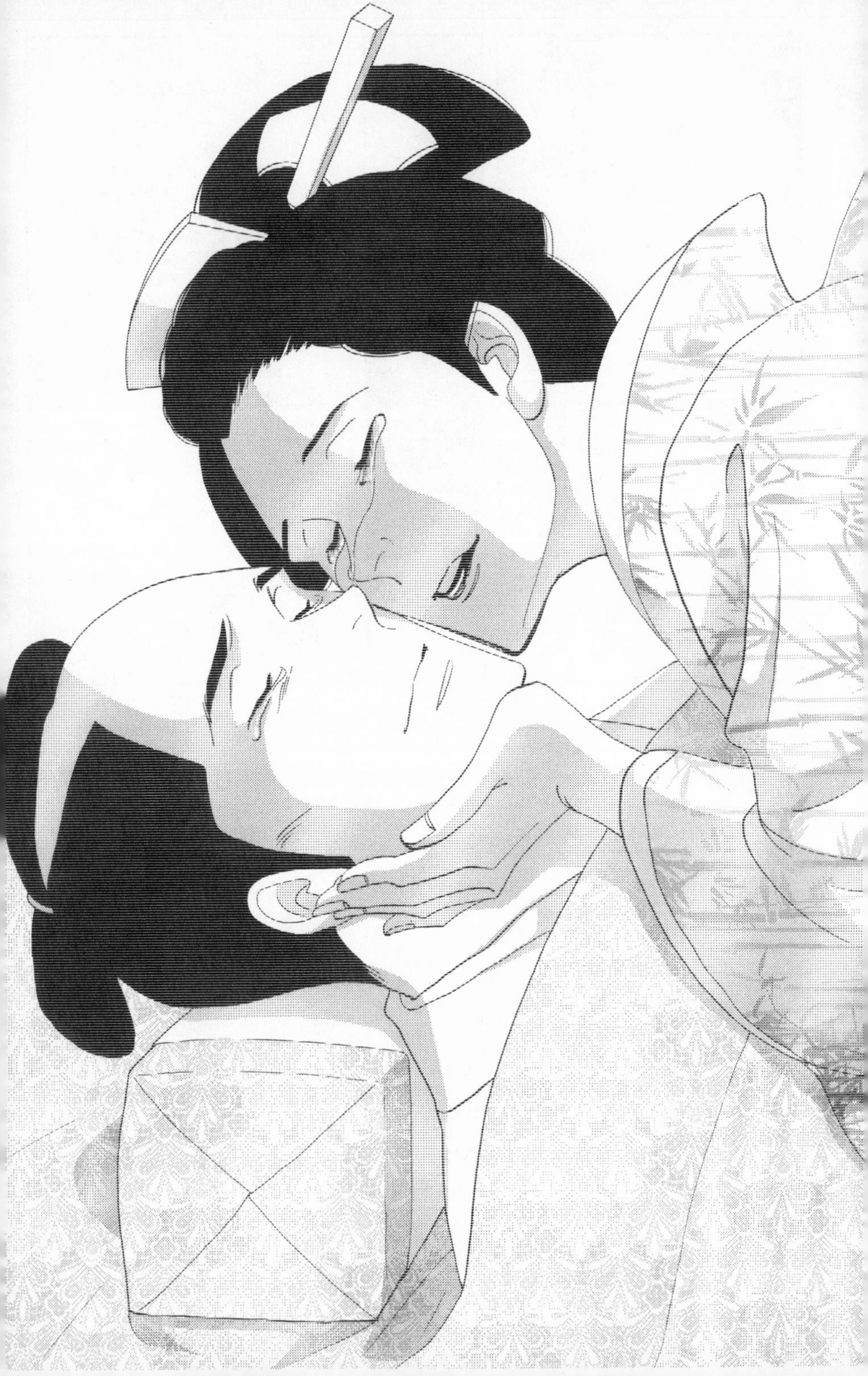

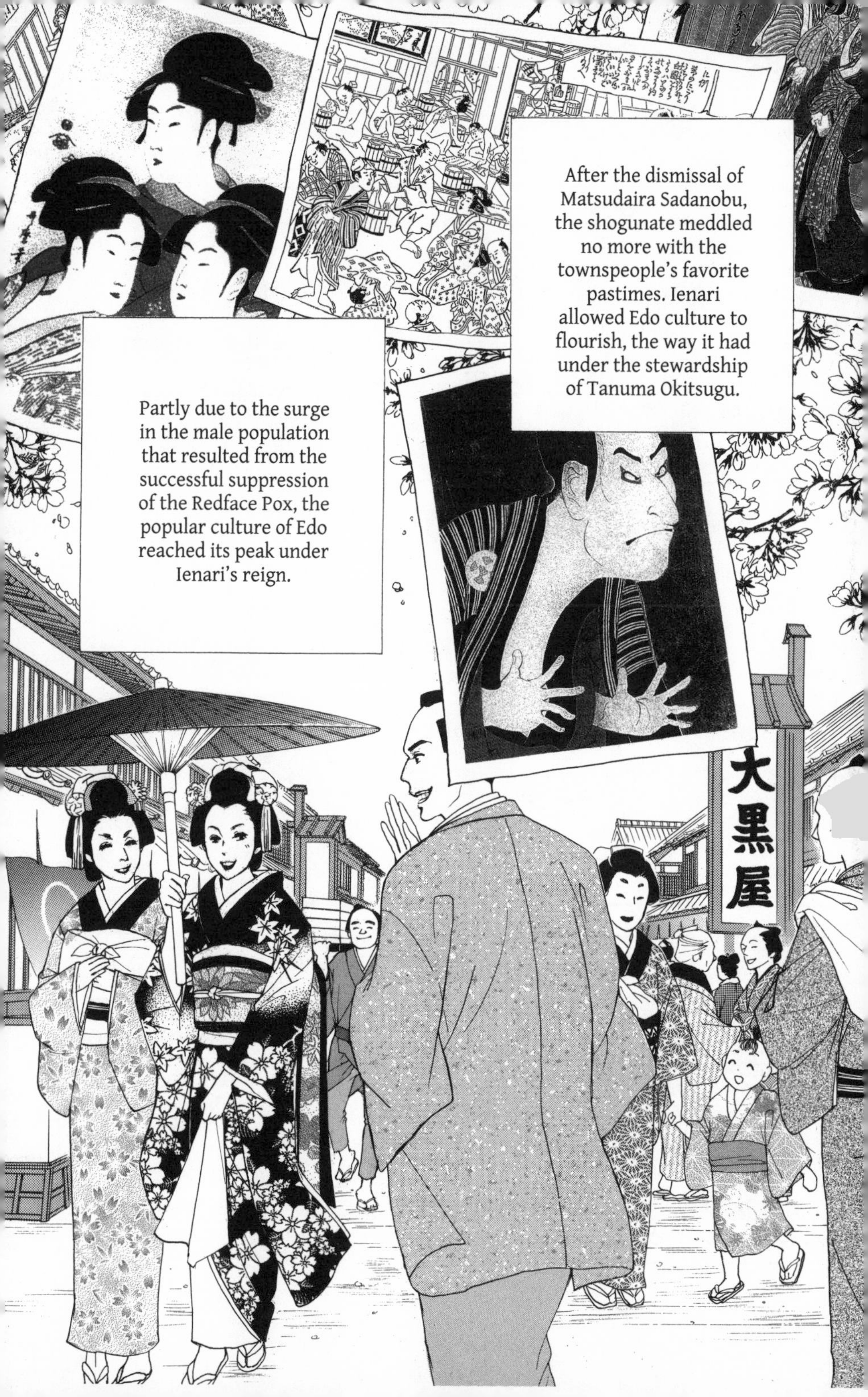
After the dismissal of Matsudaira Sadanobu, the shogunate meddled no more with the townspeople's favorite pastimes. Ienari allowed Edo culture to flourish, the way it had under the stewardship of Tanuma Okitsugu.
Partly due to the surge in the male population that resulted from the successful suppression of the Redface Pox, the popular culture of Edo reached its peak under Ienari's reign.
大黒屋

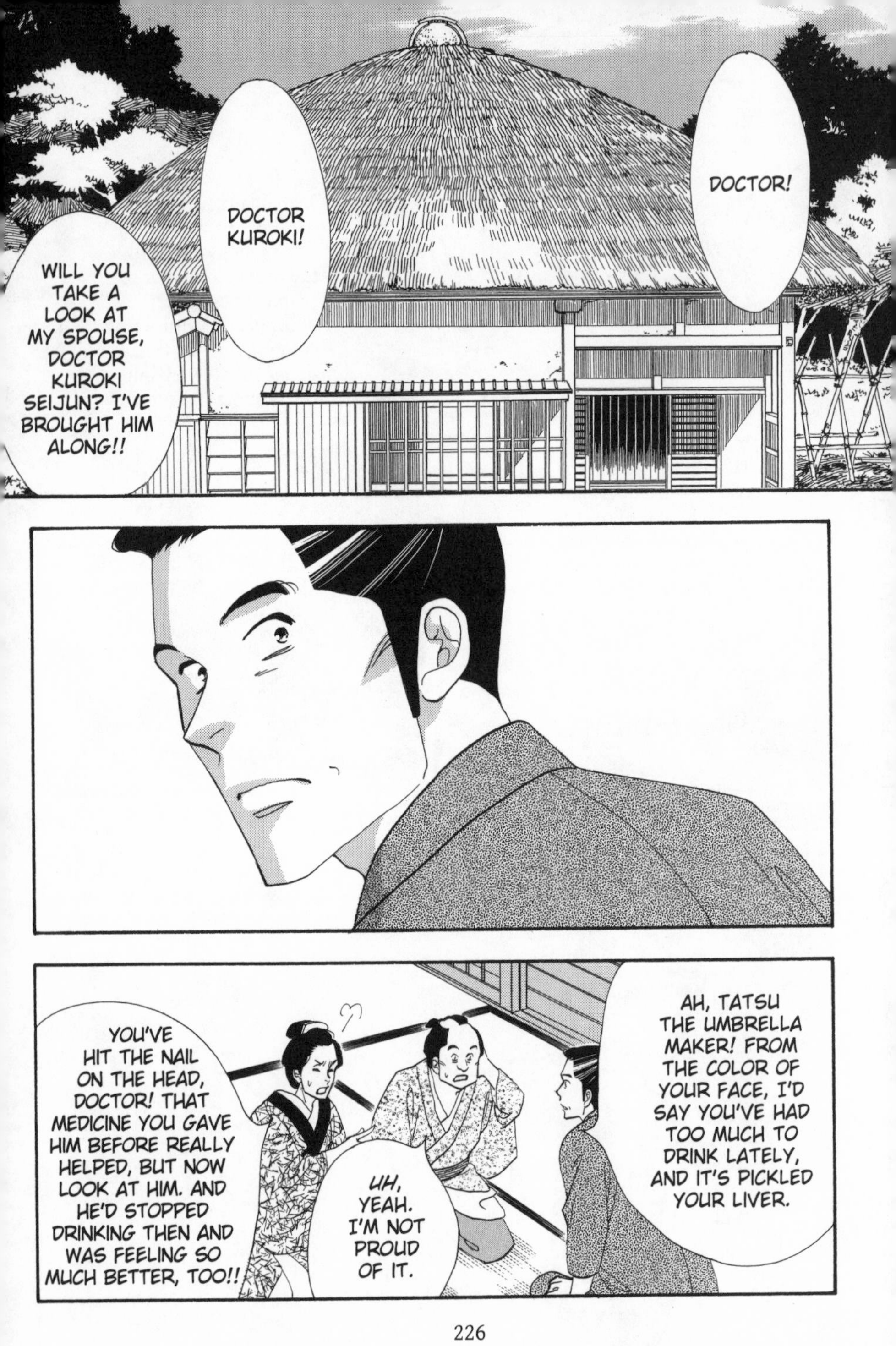
DOCTOR!
DOCTOR KUROKI!
WILL YOU TAKE A LOOK AT MY SPOUSE, DOCTOR KUROKI SEIJUN? I'VE BROUGHT HIM ALONG!!
AH, TATSU THE UMBRELLA MAKER! FROM THE COLOR OF YOUR FACE, I'D SAY YOU'VE HAD TOO MUCH TO DRINK LATELY, AND IT'S PICKLED YOUR LIVER.
YOU'VE HIT THE NAIL ON THE HEAD, DOCTOR! THAT MEDICINE YOU GAVE HIM BEFORE REALLY HELPED, BUT NOW LOOK AT HIM. AND HE'D STOPPED DRINKING THEN AND WAS FEELING SO MUCH BETTER, TOO!!
UH, YEAH. I'M NOT PROUD OF IT.

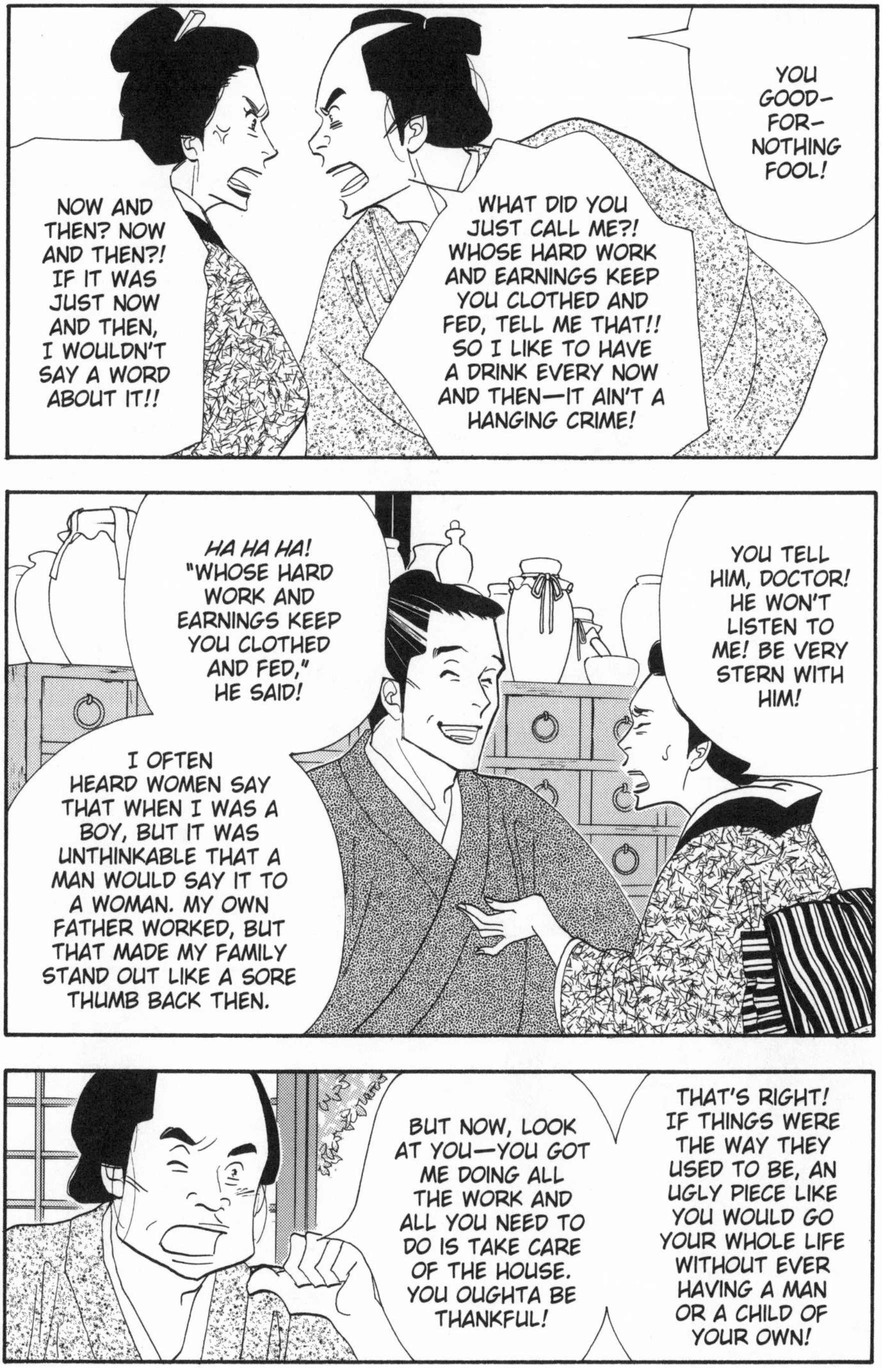
YOU GOOD-FOR-NOTHING FOOL!
WHAT DID YOU JUST CALL ME?! WHOSE HARD WORK AND EARNINGS KEEP YOU CLOTHED AND FED, TELL ME THAT!! SO I LIKE TO HAVE A DRINK EVERY NOW AND THEN—IT AIN'T A HANGING CRIME!
NOW AND THEN? NOW AND THEN?! IF IT WAS JUST NOW AND THEN, I WOULDN'T SAY A WORD ABOUT IT!!
YOU TELL HIM, DOCTOR! HE WON'T LISTEN TO ME! BE VERY STERN WITH HIM!
HA HA HA! "WHOSE HARD WORK AND EARNINGS KEEP YOU CLOTHED AND FED," HE SAID!
I OFTEN HEARD WOMEN SAY THAT WHEN I WAS A BOY, BUT IT WAS UNTHINKABLE THAT A MAN WOULD SAY IT TO A WOMAN. MY OWN FATHER WORKED, BUT THAT MADE MY FAMILY STAND OUT LIKE A SORE THUMB BACK THEN.
THAT'S RIGHT! IF THINGS WERE THE WAY THEY USED TO BE, AN UGLY PIECE LIKE YOU WOULD GO YOUR WHOLE LIFE WITHOUT EVER HAVING A MAN OR A CHILD OF YOUR OWN!
BUT NOW, LOOK AT YOU—YOU GOT ME DOING ALL THE WORK AND ALL YOU NEED TO DO IS TAKE CARE OF THE HOUSE. YOU OUGHTA BE THANKFUL!

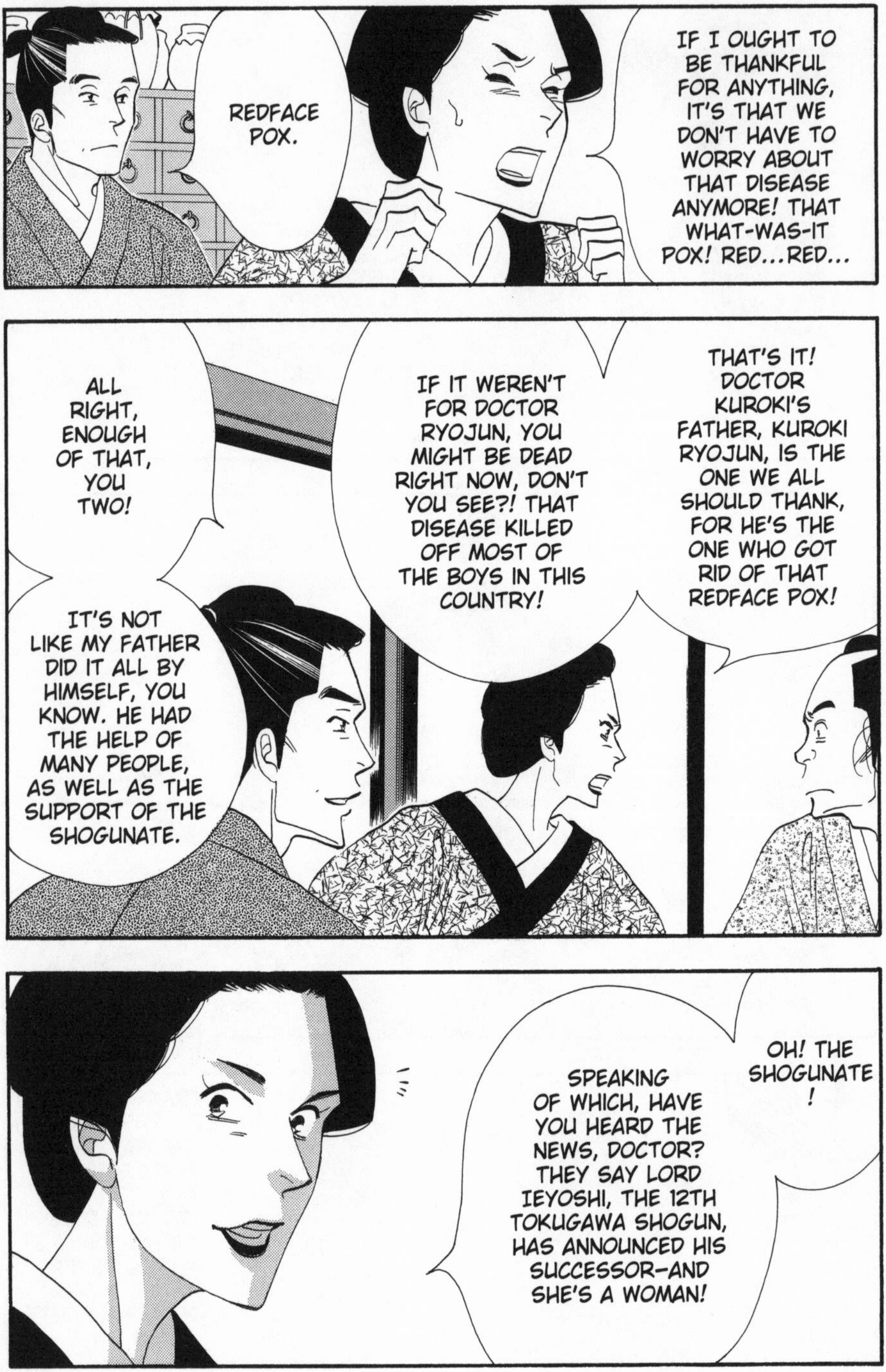
IF I OUGHT TO BE THANKFUL FOR ANYTHING, IT'S THAT WE DON'T HAVE TO WORRY ABOUT THAT DISEASE ANYMORE! THAT WHAT-WAS-IT POX! RED...RED...
REDFACE POX.
THAT'S IT! DOCTOR KUROKI'S FATHER, KUROKI RYOJUN, IS THE ONE WE ALL SHOULD THANK, FOR HE'S THE ONE WHO GOT RID OF THAT REDFACE POX!
IF IT WEREN'T FOR DOCTOR RYOJUN, YOU MIGHT BE DEAD RIGHT NOW, DON'T YOU SEE?! THAT DISEASE KILLED OFF MOST OF THE BOYS IN THIS COUNTRY!
ALL RIGHT, ENOUGH OF THAT, YOU TWO!
IT'S NOT LIKE MY FATHER DID IT ALL BY HIMSELF, YOU KNOW. HE HAD THE HELP OF MANY PEOPLE, AS WELL AS THE SUPPORT OF THE SHOGUNATE.
OH! THE SHOGUNATE!
SPEAKING OF WHICH, HAVE YOU HEARD THE NEWS, DOCTOR? THEY SAY LORD IEYOSHI, THE 12TH TOKUGAWA SHOGUN, HAS ANNOUNCED HIS SUCCESSOR—AND SHE'S A WOMAN!

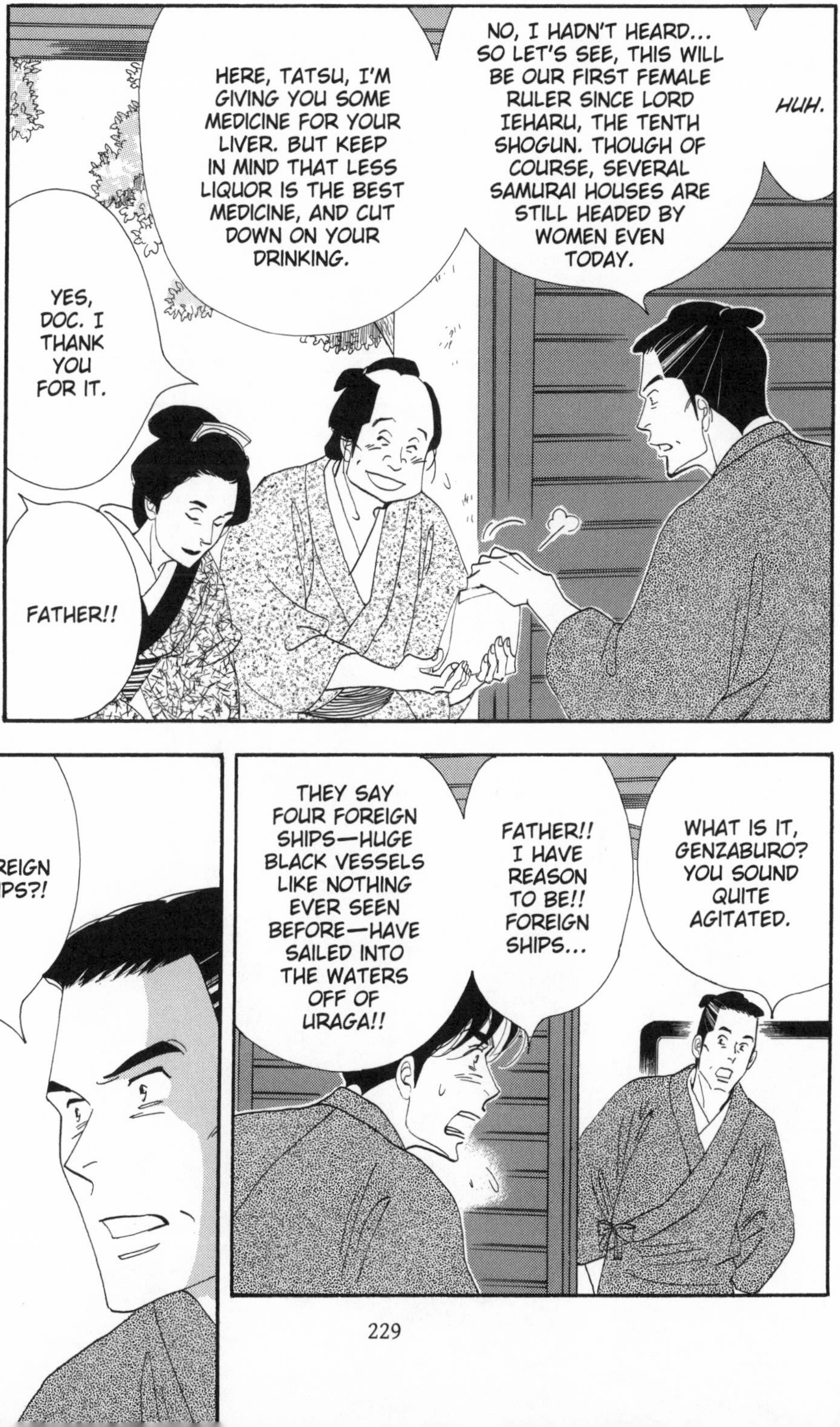
HUH.
NO, I HADN'T HEARD... SO LET'S SEE, THIS WILL BE OUR FIRST FEMALE RULER SINCE LORD IEHARU, THE TENTH SHOGUN. THOUGH OF COURSE, SEVERAL SAMURAI HOUSES ARE STILL HEADED BY WOMEN EVEN TODAY.
HERE, TATSU, I'M GIVING YOU SOME MEDICINE FOR YOUR LIVER. BUT KEEP IN MIND THAT LESS LIQUOR IS THE BEST MEDICINE, AND CUT DOWN ON YOUR DRINKING.
YES, DOC. I THANK YOU FOR IT.
FATHER!!
WHAT IS IT, GENZABURO? YOU SOUND QUITE AGITATED.
FATHER!! I HAVE REASON TO BE!! FOREIGN SHIPS...
THEY SAY FOUR FOREIGN SHIPS—HUGE BLACK VESSELS LIKE NOTHING EVER SEEN BEFORE—HAVE SAILED INTO THE WATERS OFF OF URAGA!!
FOREIGN SHIPS?!

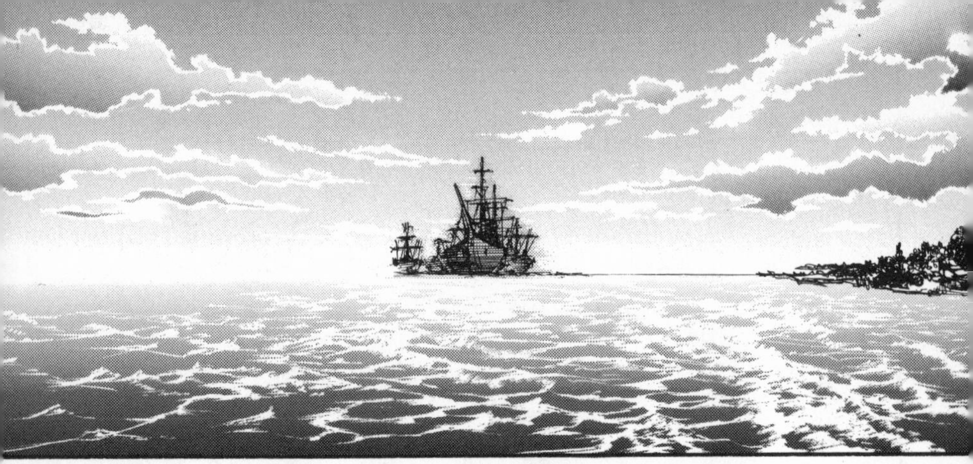

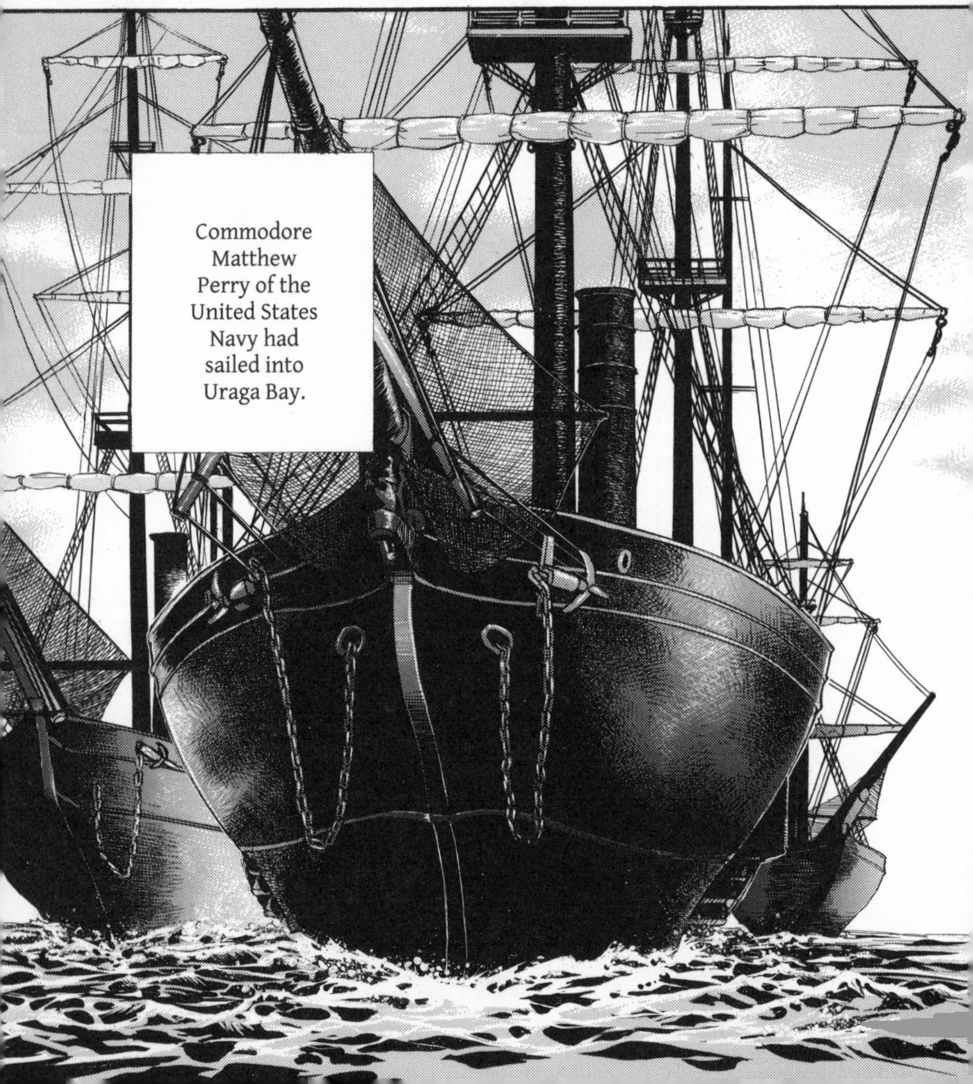
Commodore Matthew Perry of the United States Navy had sailed into Uraga Bay.

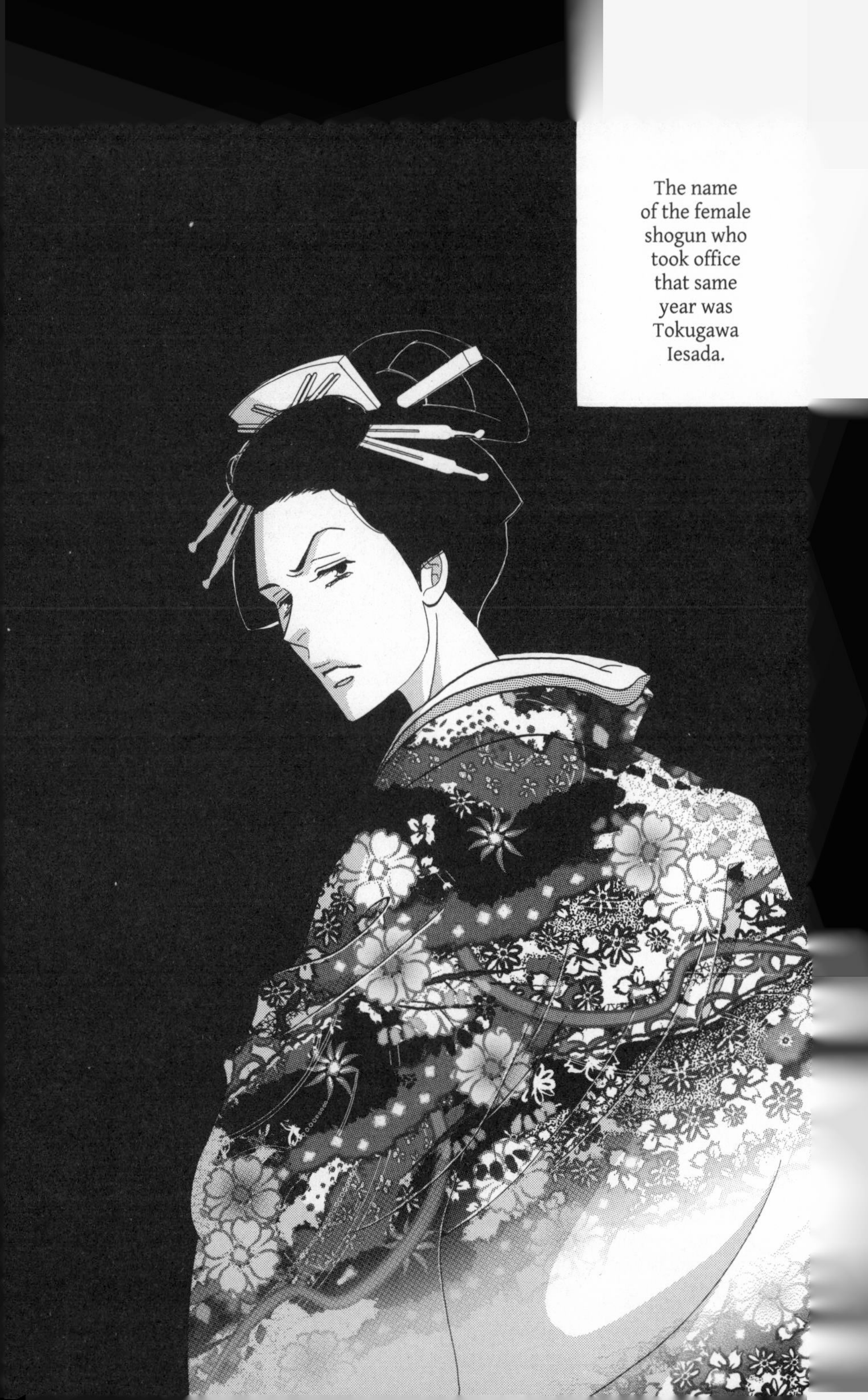
The name of the female shogun who took office that same year was Tokugawa Iesada.

Ōoku.

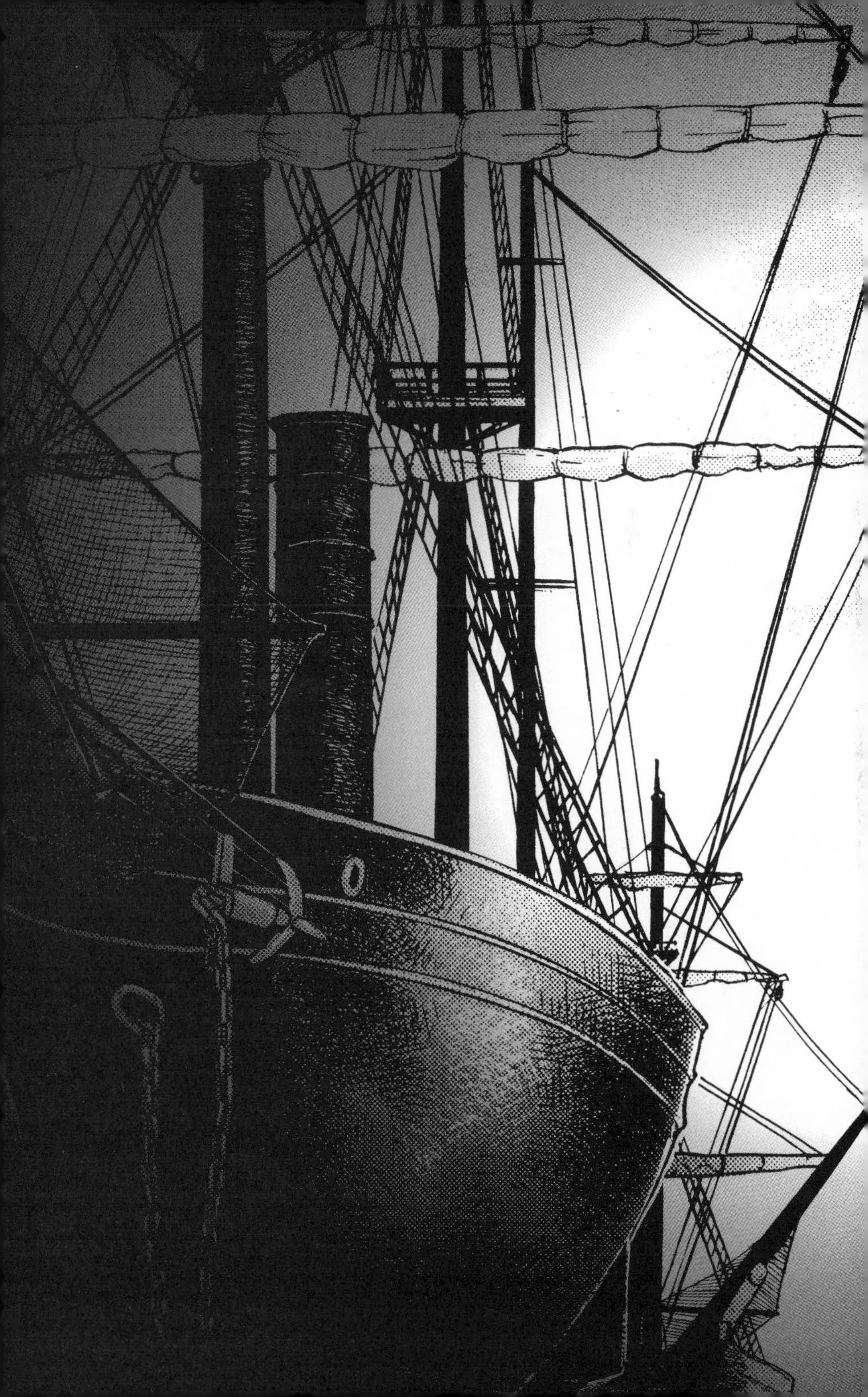

Ōoku: The Inner Chambers

VOLUME 12 · END NOTES

by Akemi Wegmüller

Page 54, panel 2 · HYO
A *hyo* is the same as a *tawara*, which is a cylindrical straw sack holding about 60 kg of rice.

Page 56, panel 1 · DUTCH-JAPANESE DICTIONARY
This dictionary is the 13-volume *Halma Wa-ge*, which was the first Dutch-Japanese dictionary ever published (1798–1799). It was created by taking a Dutch-to-French dictionary compiled by the Frenchman François Halma in 1729 and simply substituting Japanese definitions for the French.

Page 75, panel 1 · ISE, KARASUMI, KATSUO, TANBA
Ise is a city on the eastern coast of Honshu island.
Karasumi is bottarga, or salted, cured fish roe.
Katsuo is bonito, or fish like tuna and mackerel.
Tanba Province was located in what is now Kyoto Prefecture and Hyogo Prefecture on the Japanese mainland.

Page 89, panel 1 · HOUR OF THE SHEEP
The animal clock is an ancient way to tell time based on the Chinese zodiac. The Hour of the Sheep is the period between 1 p.m. and 3 p.m.

Page 92, panel 1 · KOSHU
Another name for the province of Kai, which is roughly the same area as Yamanashi Prefecture today.

Page 178, panel 6 · CASTELLA CAKE, CHIMAKI DUMPLINGS
Castella is a sponge cake of Portuguese origin, originally brought into Japan through Nagasaki.
Chimaki dumplings are wrapped in bamboo or other types of leaves and steamed. They can be filled with sweet or savory ingredients.

Page 225, panel 1 · POPULAR CULTURE OF EDO
Also called Kasei Culture, which is derived from the second syllables of the two eras during which it occurred—Bunka and Bunsei.

CREATOR BIOGRAPHY
FUMI YOSHINAGA

Fumi Yoshinaga is a Tokyo-born manga creator who debuted in 1994 with *Tsuki to Sandaru* (*The Moon and the Sandals*). Yoshinaga has won numerous awards, including the 2009 Osamu Tezuka Cultural Prize for *Ōoku*, the 2002 Kodansha Manga Award for her series *Antique Bakery* and the 2006 Japan Media Arts Festival Excellence Award for *Ōoku*. She was also nominated for the 2008 Eisner Award for Best Writer/Artist.

Ōoku

 THE INNER CHAMBERS

Ōoku: The Inner Chambers
Vol. 12

VIZ Signature Edition

Story and Art by Fumi Yoshinaga

Translation & Adaptation/Akemi Wegmüller
Touch-up Art & Lettering/Monalisa De Asis
Design/Fawn Lau
Editor/Pancha Diaz

Ōoku by Fumi Yoshinaga © Fumi Yoshinaga 2015
All rights reserved. First published in Japan in 2015 by
HAKUSENSHA, Inc., Tokyo. English language translation
rights arranged with HAKUSENSHA, Inc., Tokyo.

Printed in the U.S.A.

Published by VIZ Media, LLC
P.O. Box 77010
San Francisco, CA 94107

10 9 8 7 6 5 4 3 2 1
First printing, November 2016

www.viz.com

VIZ SIGNATURE
www.vizsignature.com

PARENTAL ADVISORY
ŌOKU: THE INNER CHAMBERS is rated
M for Mature and is recommended for
ages 18 and up. Contains violence and
sexual situations.
ratings.viz.com

THIS IS THE LAST PAGE.

Ōoku: The Inner Chambers has been printed in the original Japanese format in order to preserve the orientation of the original artwork.